Civilizations of the World

The Human Adventure

Third Edition

Volume A: To 1500

Richard L. Greaves
Florida State University

Robert Zaller
Drexel University

Philip V. Cannistraro
Queens College, CUNY

Rhoads Murphey
University of Michigan

An imprint of Addison Wesley Longman, Inc.

New York • Reading, Massachusetts • Menlo Park, California • Harlow, England
Don Mills, Ontario • Sydney • Mexico City • Madrid • Amsterdam

Executive Editor: Bruce Borland
Director of Development: Betty Slack
Developmental Editor: Judith M. Anderson
Supplements Editor: Jessica Bayne
Project Editor: Dora Rizzuto
Design Manager and Text Designer: Wendy Ann Fredericks
Color Insert Designer: Paul Agresti
Cover Designer: Paul Lacy
Cover Photo: Aztec mask, Museo di Antropologia, Florence, Italy. (Scala/Art Resource, New York)
Art Studio: Mapping Specialists Limited
Photo Researcher: Joanne de Simone
Electronic Production Manager: Valerie A. Sawyer
Desktop Administrator: Jim Sullivan
Manufacturing Manager: Helene G. Landers
Electronic Page Makeup: BookMasters, Inc.
Printer and Binder: RR Donnelley & Sons Company
Cover Printer: The Lehigh Press, Inc.
Insert Printer: RR Donnelley & Sons Company

Library of Congress Cataloging-in-Publication Data

Civilizations of the world : the human adventure / Richard L. Greaves . . . [et al.]. — 3rd. ed.

p. cm.

Includes bibliographical references and index.

ISBN 0-673-98310-2 (SVE free copy). — ISBN 0-673-98000-6 (single v. ed.). — ISBN 0-673-98001-4 (v. 1). — ISBN 0-673-98002-2 (v. 2). — ISBN 0-673-98003-0 (v. A). — ISBN 0-673-98004-9 (v. B). — ISBN 0-673-98005-7 (v. C)

1. Civilization—History. I. Greaves, Richard L.

CB69.C576 1997

909—dc20 96-15134 CIP

ISBN 0-673-98000-6 (single volume)
ISBN 0-673-98310-2 (instructor's edition)
ISBN 0-673-98001-4 (volume one)
ISBN 0-673-98002-2 (volume two)
ISBN 0-673-98003-0 (volume A)
ISBN 0-673-98004-9 (volume B)
ISBN 0-673-98005-7 (volume C)

12345678910–DOW–99989796

Brief Contents

Detailed Contents

Chapter 9
The Civilizations of Early Africa 227

Chapter 10
The Americas to 1500 249

Chapter 11
Medieval India and Southeast Asia 273

Chapter 12
A Golden Age in East Asia 295

Chronologies and Genealogies

Maps and Graphs

Preface

The demise of the Soviet empire and the subsequent restructuring of international relations underscore the premise of this book: Our ability to relate to other cultures and peoples demands some understanding of their history and values, and without this understanding there can be no responsible citizenship, no informed judgment, and no effective commitment to seek peace and dignity for all. Americans do not live in isolation from people in Asia, Africa, Europe, Latin America, and the Middle East. Our ability to understand and respect one another necessitates an awareness of our historical roots.

Civilizations of the World was from its beginning a *world* history—a conscious effort to broaden the Western cultural background of most students by giving substantial coverage to all the major civilizations and by trying to place historical events, customs, and cultures in a global context. The enthusiastic reception of the first and second editions of *Civilizations of the World: The Human Adventure* has shown the extent to which many of our professional colleagues and their students find this approach meaningful.

Biographical Portraits

World histories sometimes fail to give students a sense of personal intimacy with the subject. Migratory movements, famines and plagues, trading patterns, and imperial conquests are all important in history, but the individual also matters. Scholars used to write about the past in terms of its "great men" (rarely its women). The great figures still appear in our text, of course, as in any broad historical study. But to give a true sense of the diversity of the human achievement, we have included in most chapters biographical portraits of significant personalities from each epoch and region of the globe, not all famous in their own time but each an important reflection of it. Among them are cultural figures, such as the Greek poet Sappho, the Japanese artist Hokusai, and the American dancer Josephine Baker. Others are religious leaders, such as Gautama Buddha; the accomplished musician Hildegard of Bingen; and the Quaker pamphleteer Margaret Fell. Some were prominent in the political world: the rebel Chinese emperor Hung-wu; the South American liberator Simón Bolívar; India's Indira Gandhi; and David Ben-Gurion, a founding father of Israel. Others, such as England's Mary Wollstonecraft and the Soviet feminist Alexandra Kollontai, were especially concerned with women's rights; some, like Isabella Katz, testified to the endurance of the human spirit. All offer special insights into the times of which they were a part. Biographical portraits are marked in the text with this symbol .

Urban Portraits

Civilization begins with the city, and modern society is increasingly urban. We have therefore provided accounts of how cities around the world have developed. Some of the cities—Italy's Pompeii and Mexico's Teotihuacán, for example—are now in ruins, while others—Shanghai, Baghdad, Moscow—are thriving. Jerusalem, Paris, Tokyo (Edo), and Rome are revisited at different periods to give a sense of how they changed over time. Like the biographical portraits, the urban portraits are fully integrated into the narrative and provide instructors with excellent topics for discussion, essay questions, and unusual lecture themes. Students will find them intriguing subjects for term papers. In the text, this symbol identifies urban portraits.

Women and Minorities

This text continues to focus particularly on women and minorities. The contributions of women to both Western and non-Western societies—whether as rulers, artists and writers, revolutionaries, workers, or wives and mothers—are systematically considered. The biographical portraits are the most obvious illustrations of the attention given to women, but discussions of their contributions are also interwoven throughout the text's narrative. Special consideration is also given to the role of minorities. Four African or African-American figures are highlighted in the portraits: the dancer and social activist Josephine Baker, the African monarch Mansa Musa, Jomo Kenyatta of modern Kenya, and Dr. Martin Luther King, Jr. As one of the founders of Western civilization and a significant force throughout their history, the Jews are covered more fully in this text than in any comparable work. They are followed from their settlement in ancient Palestine to their persecution and exile under the Romans and from their medieval migrations to their return to Palestine and the founding of modern Israel. By recounting the histories of these groups, we hope to make students aware of their achievements.

Social and Cultural Coverage

Recent scholarship has placed considerable emphasis on social and cultural history. That scholarship is reflected throughout this text, but perhaps most clearly in two chapters that are unique among survey texts. Chapter 7, "The Ancient World Religions," offers a comparative overview of the great religions and philosophies of the ancient world, with a discussion of Islam immediately following, in Chapter 8. Chapter 23, "The Societies of the Early Modern World," provides a broad overview of such key aspects of the world's societies in the sixteenth and seventeenth centuries as marriage, the family, sexual customs, education, poverty, and crime. Moreover, at eight different points throughout the text we pause to consider four significant sociocultural themes: writing and communication, the human image, mapping, and the human experience of death. Here again are special opportunities for distinctive lectures, discussions, essay topics, and research papers.

Map Atlas and Full-Color Art Inserts

Two types of special color inserts are featured in the book. The first, included in the front matter, is an eight-page full-color atlas showing the physical characteristics of major areas of the globe. This section is intended as a reference that students can use to improve their knowledge of geography. More than 100 maps appear in the text itself.

In addition to the atlas, the combined volume includes eight full-color inserts titled "The Visual Experience," each insert featuring about eight illustrations—of painting, sculpture, architecture, and *objets d'art*—that are related in a meaningful way to the text's presentation of history. In the split volumes, selected color inserts are included. The text illustrations consist of a separate program of nearly 400 engravings, photographs, and other images chosen for their historical relevance.

Primary Source Documents

To enhance the usefulness of this text, we have provided not only a generous complement of maps and illustrations but also a comprehensive selection of primary sources. By studying these documents—usually four or five per chapter—students can sample the kinds of materials with which historians work. More important, they can engage the sources directly and so participate in the process of historical understanding. To emphasize the sense of history as a living discipline, we survey changing historiographic interpretations of the Renaissance, the French Revolution, imperialism, and fascism.

Reading Lists

The discipline of history goes far beyond merely amassing raw data such as names, places, and dates. Historical study demands analysis, synthesis, and a critical sense of the worth of each source. As a guide to students who wish to hone their historical understanding and analytical skills, an up-to-date reading list is provided at the end of each chapter.

Major Changes in the Third Edition

The most significant change in the third edition is the addition of a chapter on Africa, 1400–1800. Inclusion of this new chapter (Chapter 21) gives added depth to this period of African history; the chapter is enriched with new documents and maps. The discussion of modern Africa in Chapter 42 has also been substantially rewritten, and recent developments in Africa and Latin America are discussed. New biographical portraits featuring Hildegard of Bingen and Christine de Pizan appear in Chapters 14 and 16, respectively. Chapter 39 has been extensively revised to emphasize and consolidate the events occurring during the Cold War. The final chapter, "The Contemporary Age" (Chapter 43), has been updated to reflect the many changes which have occurred as a result of the collapse of the Soviet Union and the emerging republics. New sections on music have been added to Chapters 14 and 16. Other changes appear throughout the text, reflecting both new scholarship and suggestions from readers, and a number of new primary source readings have been added.

In revising this book the authors have benefited from the research of many others, all of whom share our belief in the importance of historical study. To the extent that we have succeeded in introducing students to the rich and varied heritage of the past, we owe that success in a very special way to our fellow historians and to the discipline to which we as colleagues have dedicated our careers.

Richard L. Greaves
Robert Zaller
Philip V. Cannistraro
Rhoads Murphey

Supplements

The following supplements are available for use in conjunction with this book.

For Instructors

- *Instructor's Resource Manual* by Richard L. Greaves and Robert Zaller. Prepared by authors of the text, this instructor's manual includes lecture themes, special lecture topics, topics for class discussion and essays, an extensive film list, identification and map items, and term paper topics. Also included is *Mapping the Human Adventure: A Guide to Historical Geography* by Glee Wilson, Kent State University. This special addition provides over 30 reproducible maps and exercises covering the full scope of world history.
- *Discovering World History Through Maps and Views,* Second Edition, by Gerald Danzer, University of Illinois, Chicago, winner of the AHA's James Harvey Robinson Award for his work in the development of map transparencies. The second edition of this set of 100 four-color transparencies is completely updated and revised to include the newest reference maps and the most useful source materials. The collection includes source and reference maps, views and photos, urban plans, building diagrams, and works of art.
- *Test Bank* by Edward D. Wynot, Florida State University. Approximately 50 multiple-choice and 10 essay questions per chapter. Multiple-choice items are referenced by text page number and type (factual or interpretive).
- *TestMaster Computerized Testing System.* This flexible, easy-to-master test bank includes all of the test items in the printed *Test Bank.* The TestMaster software allows you to edit existing questions and add your own items. Tests can be printed in several different formats and can include figures such as graphs and tables. Available for DOS and Macintosh computers.
- *Text Map Transparencies.* A set of all the maps in the text bound in a three-ring binder with teaching tips.

For Students

- *Study Guide* by Richard L. Greaves and Robert Zaller. Prepared by authors of the text, each chapter contains a chapter overview; map exercises; study questions; a chronology; and identification, completion, short answer, and document exercises, along with a list of term paper topics.
- *SuperShell Computerized Tutorial* by David Mock of Tallahassee Community College. This interactive program for DOS computers helps students learn major facts and concepts through drill and practice exercises and diagnostic feedback. SuperShell provides immediate correct answers and the text page number on which the material is discussed. Missed questions appear with greater frequency; a running score of the student's performance is maintained on the screen throughout the session.
- *World History Map Workbook* in two volumes. Volume I (to 1600) and Volume II (from 1600) by Glee Wilson of Kent State University. Each volume includes over 40 maps accompanied by more than 120 pages of exercises. Each volume is designed to teach the location of various countries and their relationship to one another. There are numerous exercises aimed at enhancing the student's critical thinking abilities.
- *World History Atlas.* This four-color atlas contains a variety of historical maps. Current scholarship and global coverage is reflected in this up-to-date atlas. It is available shrink-wrapped with *Civilizations of the World* at a low cost.
- *TimeLink Computer Atlas of World History* by William Hamblin, Brigham Young University. This HyperCard Macintosh program presents three views of the world—Europe/Africa, Asia, and the Americas—on a simulated globe. Students can spin the globe, select a time period, and see a map of the world at that time, including the names of major political units. Special topics such as the conquests of Alexander the Great are shown through animated sequences that depict the dynamic changes in geopolitical history. A comprehensive index and quizzes are also included.

Acknowledgments

The authors are grateful to Bruce Borland, history editor; Judith Anderson, developmental editor; and Dora Rizzuto, project editor. This book could not have been completed without the invaluable assistance of Judith Dieker Greaves, editorial assistant to the authors. The authors wish additionally to thank the following persons for their assistance and support: Lili Bita Zaller, Philip Rethis, Kimon Rethis, Robert B. Radin, Stanley Burnshaw, Julia Southard, Robert S. Browning, Sherry E. Greaves, Stephany L. Greaves, and Professors Eric D. Brose, Peter Garretson, Roger Hackett, Victor Lieberman, Winston Lo, Bawa S. Singh, Donald F. Stevens, Thomas Trautmann, Ralph V. Turner, and Edward D. Wynot, Jr.

The following scholars read the manuscript in whole or in part and offered numerous helpful suggestions:

J. Chris Arndt
James Madison University

James S. Austin, Jr.
Hawaii Pacific University

Roger B. Beck
Eastern Illinois University

Martin Berger
Youngstown State University

Donna Bohanan
Auburn University

Allen Cronenberg
Auburn University

Cecil B. Egerton
Chaffey College

Thomas C. Fiddick
University of Evansville

Mary B. Hagerty
Iona College

Kennell Jackson
Stanford University

Mario D. Mazzarella
Christopher Newport University

Barbara Mitchell
Chaffey College

Dennis J. Mitchell
Jackson State University

David E. Rison
Charleston Southern University

David R. Smith
California State Polytechnic University, Pomona

William A. Sumruld
College of the Southwest

Arlene F. Wolinski
Mesa College

We are also indebted to the reviewers of the first and second editions:

Dorothy Abrahamse
California State University, Long Beach

Winthrop Lindsay Adams
University of Utah

George M. Addy
Brigham Young University

Jay Pascal Anglin
University of Southern Mississippi

Karl Barbir
Siena College

Charmarie J. Blaisdell
Northeastern University

Robert F. Brinson
Santa Fe Community College

William A. Bultmann
Western Washington University

Thomas Callahan, Jr.
Rider College

Miriam Usher Chrisman
University of Massachusetts, Amherst

Jill N. Claster
New York University

Cynthia Schwenk Clemons
Georgia State University

Allen T. Cronenberg
Auburn University

John Dahmus
Stephen F. Austin State University

Elton L. Daniel
University of Hawaii at Manoa

Leslie Derfler
Florida Atlantic University

Joseph M. Dixon
Weber State College

John Patrick Donnelly
Marquette University

Mark U. Edwards, Jr.
Harvard University

Charles A. Endress
Angelo State University

Stephen Englehart
California State Polytechnic University, Pomona

William Wayne Farvis
University of Tennessee

Jonathan Goldstein
West Georgia College

Edwin N. Gorsuch
Georgia State University

Joseph M. Gowaski
Rider College

Tony Grafton
Princeton University

Coburn V. Graves
Kent State University

Janelle Greenberg
University of Pittsburgh

Christopher E. Guthrie
Tarleton State University

Craig Harline
University of Idaho

Udo Heyn
California State University, Los Angeles

Clive Holmes
Cornell University

Leonard A. Humphreys
University of the Pacific

Donald G. Jones
University of Central Arkansas

William R. Jones
University of New Hampshire

Thomas Kaiser
University of Arkansas at Little Rock

Thomas L. Kennedy
Washington State University

Frank Kidner
San Francisco State University

Winston L. Kinsey
Appalachian State University

Thomas Kuehn
Clemson University

George J. Lankevich
Bronx Community College

Richard D. Lewis
Saint Cloud State University

David C. Lukowitz
Hamline University

Thomas J. McPartland
Bellevue Community College

Elizabeth Malloy
Salem State College

John A. Mears
Southern Methodist University

V. Dixon Morris
University of Hawaii at Manoa

Marian Purrier Nelson
University of Nebraska at Omaha

William D. Newell
Laramie County Community College

James Odom
East Tennessee State University

William G. Palmer
Marshall University

William D. Phillips, Jr.
San Diego State University

Paul B. Pixton
Brigham Young University

Ronald R. Rader
University of Georgia

Dennis Reinhartz
University of Texas at Arlington

Leland Sather
Weber State College

Irvin D. Solomon
Edison Community College

Gerald Sorin
State University of New York, New Paltz

Kerry E. Spiers
University of Louisville

Paul Stewart
Southern Connecticut State University

Richard G. Stone
Western Kentucky University

Alexander Sydorenko
Arkansas State University

Teddy Uldricks
University of North Carolina at Asheville

Raymond Van Dam
University of Michigan, Ann Arbor

John Weakland
Ball State University

David L. White
Appalachian State University

Richard S. Williams
Washington State University

Glee E. Wilson
Kent State University

John E. Wood
James Madison University

Edward D. Wynot, Jr.
Florida State University

Martin Yanuck
Spelman College

Donald L. Zelman
Tarleton State University

About the Authors

Philip V. Cannistraro. A native of New York City, Philip V. Cannistraro is an authority on modern Italian history and culture as well as on the Italian American experience. He received the Ph.D. degree from New York University in 1971. Cannistraro is Distinguished Professor of Italian-American Studies at Queens College and at the Graduate School, City University of New York. He has also taught at Drexel University, where he served twice as head of the Department of History and Politics, and at Florida State University. Cannistraro has lectured widely in Italy and in the United States and is American editor of the Italian historical quarterly *Storia Contemporanea.* His professional service includes membership on the editorial board of *The Journal of Modern Italian Studies* and several other scholarly reviews. The recipient of two Fulbright-Hays fellowships, Cannistraro is an active member of the Society for Italian Historical Studies and the American Italian Historical Association. His numerous publications include *La Fabbrica del Consenso: Fascismo e Mass Media* (1975), *Poland and the Coming of the Second World War* (with E. Wynot and T. Kovaleff, 1976), *Italian Fascist Activities in the United States* (1976), *Fascismo, Chiesa e Emigrazione* (with G. Rosoli, 1979), *Historical Dictionary of Fascist Italy* (1981), *Italian Americans: The Search for a Usable Past* (with R. Juliani, 1989), and *Il Duce's Other Woman,* a biography of Margherita Sarfatti (with B. Sullivan, 1993). Cannistraro is currently writing a biography of Italian American businessman and publisher Generoso Pope.

Richard L. Greaves. Born in Glendale, California, Richard L. Greaves, a specialist in Reformation and British political, social, and religious history, earned his Ph.D. degree at the University of London in 1964. After teaching at Michigan State University, he moved in 1972 to Florida State University, where he is now Robert O. Lawton Distinguished Professor of History and chairman of the Department of History. A Fellow of the Royal Historical Society, Greaves has received fellowships from the National Endowment for the Humanities, the American Council of Learned Societies, the Andrew Mellon Foundation, the Huntington Library, and the American Philosophical Society. The 22 books he has written or edited include *John Bunyan* (1969), *Theology and Revolution in the Scottish Reformation: Studies in the Thought of John Knox* (1980), *Saints and Rebels: Seven Nonconformists in Stuart England* (1985), *Deliver Us from Evil: The Radical Underground in Britain, 1660–1663* (1986), *Enemies Under His Feet: Radicals and Nonconformists in Britain, 1664–1677* (1990), *Secrets of the Kingdom: British Radicals from the Popish Plot to the Revolution of 1688–1689* (1992), and *John Bunyan and English Nonconformity* (1992). The Conference on British Studies awarded Greaves the Walter D. Love Memorial Prize for *The Puritan Revolution and Educational Thought: Background for Reform* (1969), and his *Society and Religion in Elizabethan England* (1981) was a finalist for the Robert Livingston Schuyler Prize of the American Historical Association. The American Society of Church History awarded him the Albert C. Outler Prize for his forthcoming book, *God's Other Children: Protestant Nonconformists and the Emergence of Denominational Churches in Ireland, 1660–1700* (1997). He was president of the American Society of Church History in 1991 and president of the International John Bunyan Society from 1993 to 1995.

Rhoads Murphey. Born in Philadelphia, Rhoads Murphey, a specialist in Chinese history and in geography, received the Ph.D. degree from Harvard University in 1950. Before joining the faculty of the University of Michigan in 1964, he taught at the University of Washington; he has also been a visiting professor at Taiwan University and Tokyo University. From 1954 to 1956 he was the director of the Conference of Diplomats in Asia. The University of Michigan granted him a Distinguished Service Award in 1974. A former president of the Association for Asian Studies, Murphey has served as editor of the *Journal of Asian Studies, Michigan Papers in Chinese Studies,* and *A.A.S. Monographs in Asian Studies.* The Social Science Research Council, the Ford Foundation, the Guggenheim Foundation, the National Endowment for the Humanities, and the American Council of Learned Societies have awarded him fellowships. A prolific author, Murphey's books include *Shanghai: Key to Modern China* (1953), *An Introduction to Geography* (4th ed., 1978), *A New China Policy* (with others, 1965), *Approaches to Modern Chinese History* (with others, 1967), *The Scope of Geography* (3rd ed., 1982), *The Treaty Ports and China's Modernization* (1970), *China Meets the West: The Treaty Ports* (1975), *The Fading of the Maoist Vision* (1980), and *A History of Asia* (1992). *The Outsiders: Westerners in India and China* (1977) won the Best Book of the Year award from the University of Michigan Press.

Robert Zaller. Robert Zaller was born in New York City and received a Ph.D. degree from Washington University in 1968. An authority on British constitutional history and modern American literature, he has written, edited, translated, and contributed to some 25 books of history, criticism, and belles-lettres. He has taught at Queens College, City University of New York; the University of California, Santa Barbara; the University of Miami; and Drexel University, where he is currently Professor of History. He has been a Guggenheim Fellow, has served on the advisory board of the Yale Center for Parliamentary History, and is a Fellow of the Royal Historical Society. His *The Parliament of 1621: A Study in Constitutional Conflict* (1971) received the Phi Alpha Theta prize, and his *The Cliffs of Solitude: A Reading of Robinson Jeffers* (1983) was the inaugural volume of the Cambridge Studies in American Literature and Culture series. With Richard L. Greaves, he has coedited the *Biographical Dictionary of British Radicals in the Seventeenth Century* (1982–1984) and is coauthor of *Civilizations of the West: The Human Adventure* (2nd ed., 1997). He is president of the Robinson Jeffers Association.

A Note on the Spelling of Asian Names and Words

Nearly all Asian languages are written with symbols different from our Western alphabet. Chinese, Japanese, and Korean are written with ideographic characters, plus a phonetic syllabary for Japanese and Korean. Most other Asian languages have their own scripts, symbols, diacritical marks, and alphabets, which differ from ours. There can thus be no single "correct spelling" in Western symbols for Asian words or names, including personal names and place names—only established conventions. Unfortunately, conventions in this respect differ widely and in many cases reflect preferences or forms related to different Western languages. The Western spellings used in this book, including its maps, are to some extent a compromise, in an effort to follow the main English-language conventions but also to make pronunciation for English speakers as easy as possible.

Chinese presents the biggest problem since there are a great many different conventions in use and since well-known place names, such as Peking or Canton, are commonly spelled as they are here in most Western writings, even though this spelling is inconsistent with all of the romanization systems in current use and does not accurately represent the Chinese sounds. Most American newspapers and some journals now use the romanization system called *pinyin,* approved by the Chinese government, which renders these two city names, with greater phonetic accuracy, as Beijing and Kwangzhou. However, pinyin presents other problems for most Western readers, and the words are commonly mispronounced.

The usage in this book follows the most commonly used convention for scholarly publication when romanizing Chinese names, the Wade-Giles system, but gives the pinyin equivalents for modern names (if they differ) in parentheses after the first use of a name. Readers will encounter both spellings, plus others, in other books, papers, and journals, and some familiarity with both conventions is thus necessary.

In general, readers should realize and remember that English spellings of names from other languages (such as Munich for München, Vienna for Wien, and Rome for Roma), especially in Asia, can be only approximations and may differ confusingly from one Western source or map to another.

Beginnings of Civilization

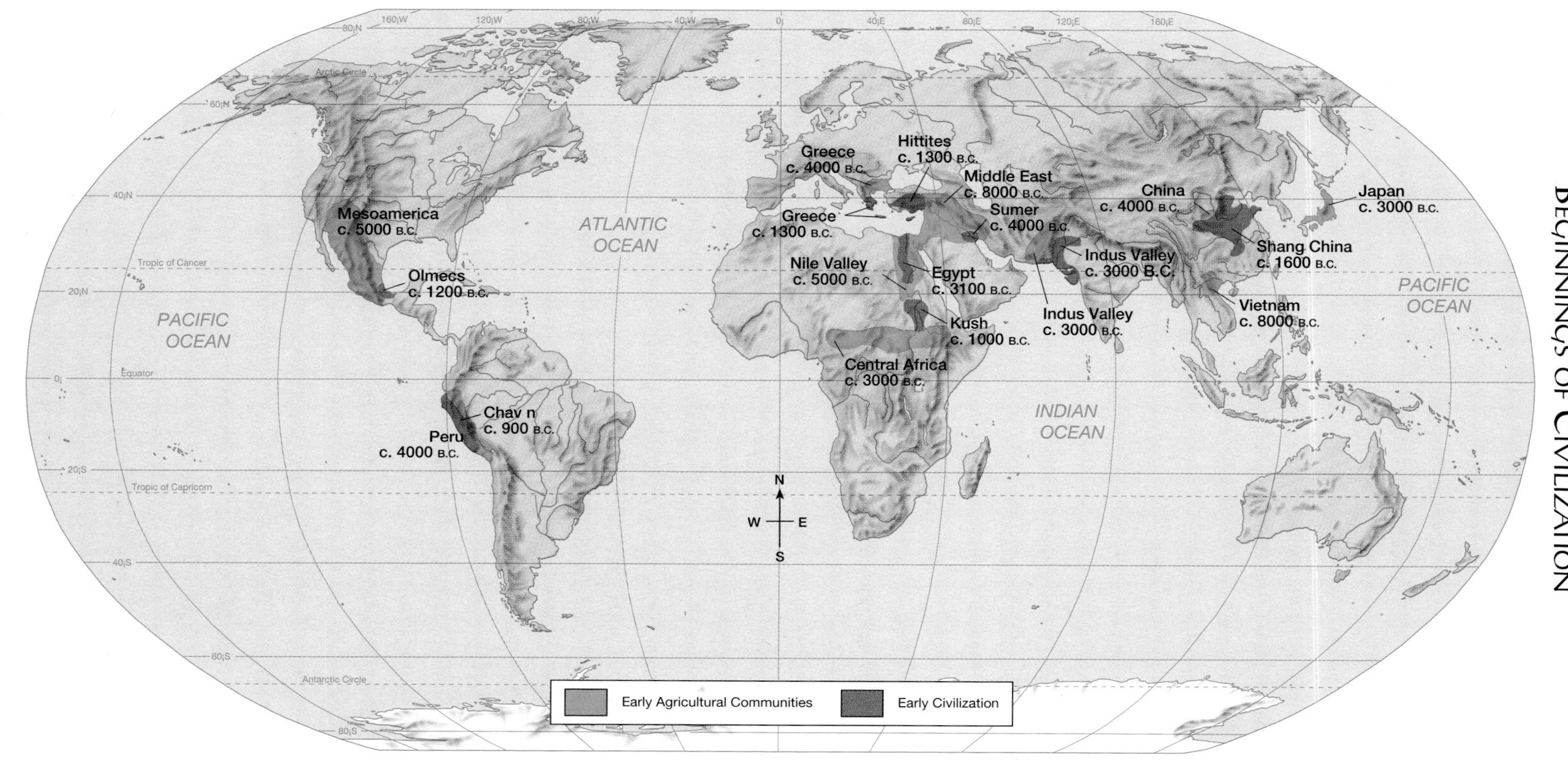

Africa

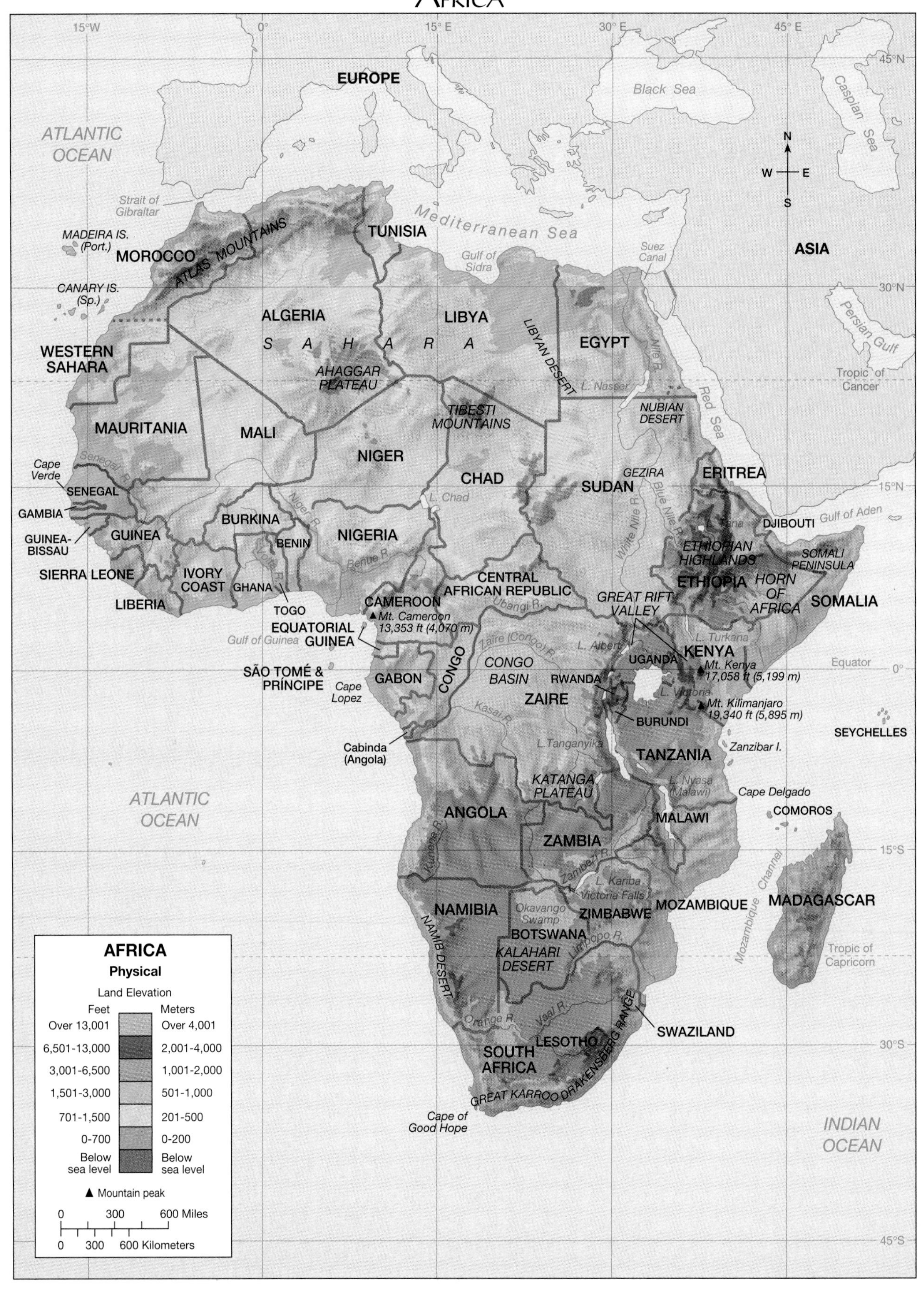

15°W
0°
15° E
30° E
45° E
45°N
30°N
15°N
0°
15°S
30°S
45°S
EUROPE
Black Sea
Caspian Sea
ATLANTIC OCEAN
N
W
E
S
Strait of Gibraltar
Mediterranean Sea
MADEIRA IS. (Port.)
MOROCCO
ATLAS MOUNTAINS
TUNISIA
Gulf of Sidra
Suez Canal
ASIA
CANARY IS. (Sp.)
ALGERIA
LIBYA
LIBYAN DESERT
EGYPT
Persian Gulf
S A H A R A
WESTERN SAHARA
AHAGGAR PLATEAU
Nile R.
Tropic of Cancer
L. Nasser
Red Sea
NUBIAN DESERT
TIBESTI MOUNTAINS
MAURITANIA
MALI
NIGER
Senegal R.
Cape Verde
CHAD
GEZIRA
ERITREA
SENEGAL
SUDAN
L. Chad
GAMBIA
Blue Nile R.
White Nile R.
Niger R.
BURKINA
DJIBOUTI
Gulf of Aden
Tana
GUINEA
GUINEA-BISSAU
BENIN
NIGERIA
ETHIOPIAN HIGHLANDS
SOMALI PENINSULA
Benue R.
Volta R.
SIERRA LEONE
IVORY COAST
CENTRAL AFRICAN REPUBLIC
ETHIOPIA
HORN OF AFRICA
GHANA
GREAT RIFT VALLEY
SOMALIA
LIBERIA
TOGO
CAMEROON
Ubangi R.
Mt. Cameroon 13,353 ft (4,070 m)
EQUATORIAL GUINEA
L. Turkana
Gulf of Guinea
Zaire (Congo) R.
L. Albert
KENYA
UGANDA
CONGO
CONGO BASIN
Mt. Kenya 17,058 ft (5,199 m)
Equator
SÃO TOMÉ & PRÍNCIPE
GABON
RWANDA
Cape Lopez
ZAIRE
L. Victoria
Mt. Kilimanjaro 19,340 ft (5,895 m)
Kasai R.
BURUNDI
SEYCHELLES
Cabinda (Angola)
L.Tanganyika
Zanzibar I.
TANZANIA
KATANGA PLATEAU
L. Nyasa (Malawi)
Cape Delgado
ATLANTIC OCEAN
COMOROS
ANGOLA
MALAWI
ZAMBIA
Kunene R.
Zambezi R.
L. Kariba
Mozambique Channel
Victoria Falls
NAMIBIA
Okavango Swamp
ZIMBABWE
MOZAMBIQUE
MADAGASCAR
BOTSWANA
Limpopo R.
NAMIB DESERT
KALAHARI DESERT
Tropic of Capricorn
AFRICA
Physical
Land Elevation
Feet
Meters
Over 13,001
Over 4,001
6,501-13,000
2,001-4,000
3,001-6,500
1,001-2,000
1,501-3,000
501-1,000
701-1,500
201-500
0-700
0-200
Below sea level
Below sea level
▲ Mountain peak
0 300 600 Miles
0 300 600 Kilometers
Orange R.
Vaal R.
DRAKENSBERG RANGE
SWAZILAND
LESOTHO
SOUTH AFRICA
GREAT KARROO
Cape of Good Hope
INDIAN OCEAN

ASIA

ASIA
Physical

Land Elevation

Feet	Meters
Over 13,001	Over 4,001
6,501-13,000	2,001-4,000
3,001-6,500	1,001-2,000
1,501-3,000	501-1,000
701-1,500	201-500
0-700	0-200
Below sea level	Below sea level

▲ Mountain peak

0 400 800 Miles
0 400 800 Kilometers

North Pole
ARCTIC OCEAN
FRANZ JOSEF LAND
SEVERNAYA ZEMLYA
NEW SIBERIAN IS.
EAST SIBERIAN SEA
LAPTEV SEA
KARA SEA
BARENTS SEA
Novaya Zemlya
BERING SEA
KAMCHATKA PENINSULA
SEA OF OKHOTSK
SAKHALIN
KURIL IS.
HOKKAIDO
HONSHU
JAPAN
SEA OF JAPAN
SHIKOKU
KYUSHU
RYUKYU IS.
PACIFIC OCEAN
Tropic of Cancer
Arctic Circle
Equator 0°
EUROPE
RUSSIA
SIBERIA
URAL MOUNTAINS
N. Dvina R.
Ob R.
Yenisey R.
Lena R.
Don R.
Volga R.
Ural R.
Irtysh R.
L. Baikal
Amur R.
SAYAN MTS.
ALTAI MTS.
MONGOLIA
MONGOLIAN PLATEAU
GOBI
DA HINGGAN MTS.
NORTH KOREA
KOREAN PEN.
SOUTH KOREA
YELLOW SEA
EAST CHINA SEA
Huang He (Yellow R.)
KAZAKSTAN
Aral Sea
L. Balqash
KYRGYZSTAN
JUNGGAR BASIN
TIAN SHAN
UZBEKISTAN
TURKMENISTAN
TAJIKISTAN
PAMIR MTS.
TAKLIMAKAN (DESERT)
KUNLUN MTS.
KARAKORAM RANGE
HINDU KUSH
AFGHANISTAN
PLATEAU OF TIBET
TIBET
HIMALAYAS
Mt. Everest
NEPAL
BHUTAN
CHINA
SICHUAN BASIN
Chang Jiang (Yangtze R.)
Xi Jiang (West R.)
WUYI MTS.
TAIWAN
Luzon Strait
PHILIPPINE SEA
LUZON
PHILIPPINES
VISAYANS
MINDANAO
HAINAN
SOUTH CHINA SEA
LAOS
VIETNAM
THAILAND
CAMBODIA
INDOCHINA PENINSULA
Gulf of Thailand
Mekong R.
Brahmaputra R.
Ganges R.
Indus R.
MYANMAR (BURMA)
BANGLADESH
INDIA
DECCAN PLATEAU
WESTERN GHATS
EASTERN GHATS
THAR DESERT
PAKISTAN
BAY OF BENGAL
ANDAMAN IS.
NICOBAR IS.
INDIAN PENINSULA
SRI LANKA
LACCADIVE IS.
MALDIVES
ARABIAN SEA
INDIAN OCEAN
Gulf of Oman
Strait of Malacca
MALAYSIA
MALAY PENINSULA
SUMATRA
BRUNEI
BORNEO
CELEBES
CELEBES SEA
MOLUCCAS
BANDA SEA
ARAFURA SEA
NEW GUINEA
INDONESIA
GREATER SUNDA ISLANDS
JAVA SEA
JAVA
LESSER SUNDA IS.
FLORES
TIMOR
AUSTRALIA
CASPIAN SEA
CAUCASUS MTS.
GEORGIA
ARMENIA
AZERBAIJAN
ELBURZ MTS.
ZAGROS MTS.
PLATEAU OF IRAN
IRAN
IRAQ
Tigris R.
Euphrates R.
BLACK SEA
ANATOLIAN PLATEAU
TURKEY
CYPRUS
LEBANON
ISRAEL
SYRIA
SYRIAN DESERT
JORDAN
EGYPT
SINAI PENINSULA
MEDITERRANEAN SEA
SAUDI ARABIA
KUWAIT
BAHRAIN
QATAR
Persian Gulf
UNITED ARAB EMIRATES
ARABIAN PENINSULA
OMAN
YEMEN
Gulf of Aden
RED SEA
AFRICA
N
W E
S
80°N
60°N
40°N
20°N
20°S
160°W
180°
160°E
140°E
120°E
100°E
80°E
60°E
40°E

Australia and Oceania

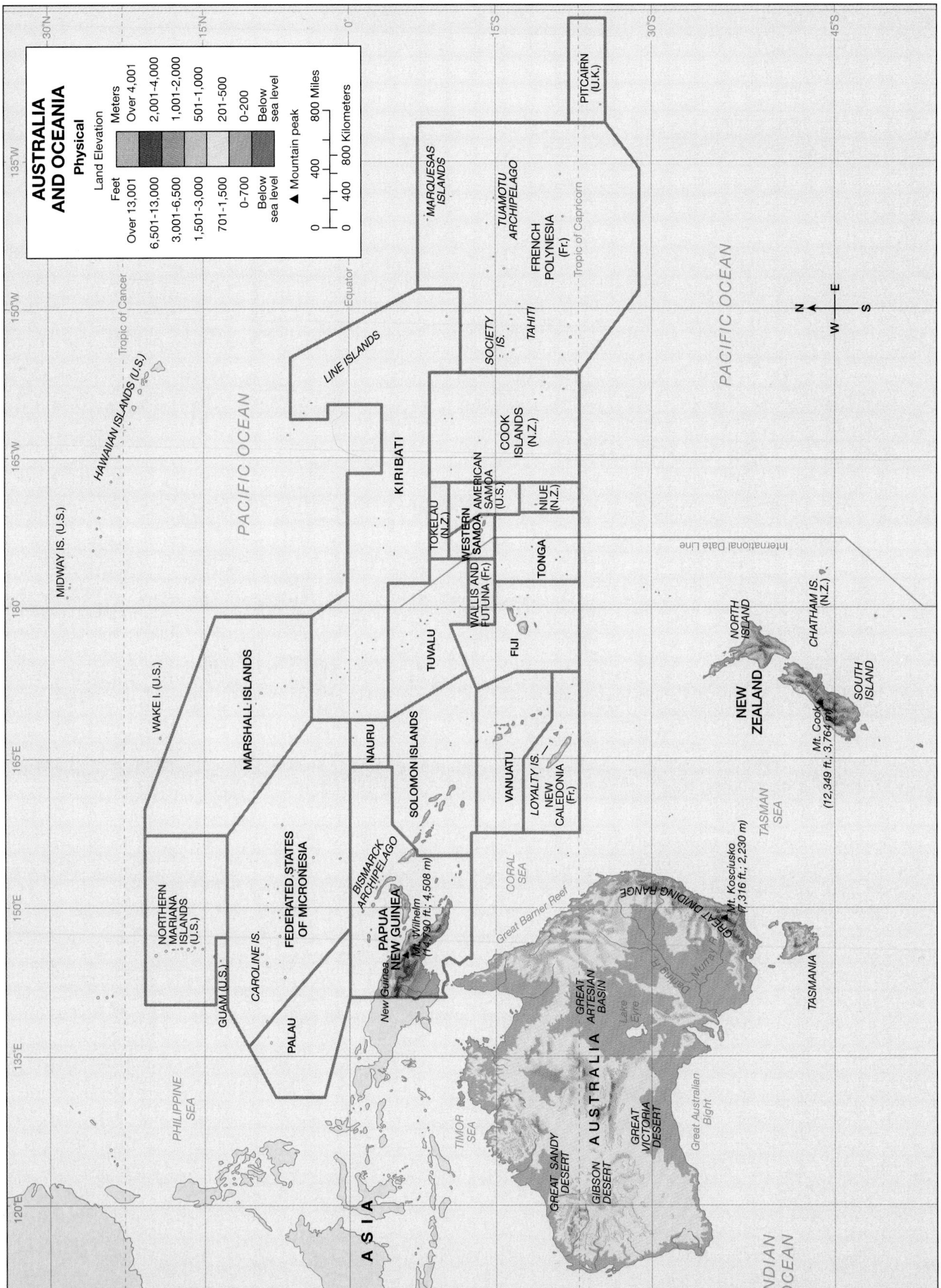

Europe

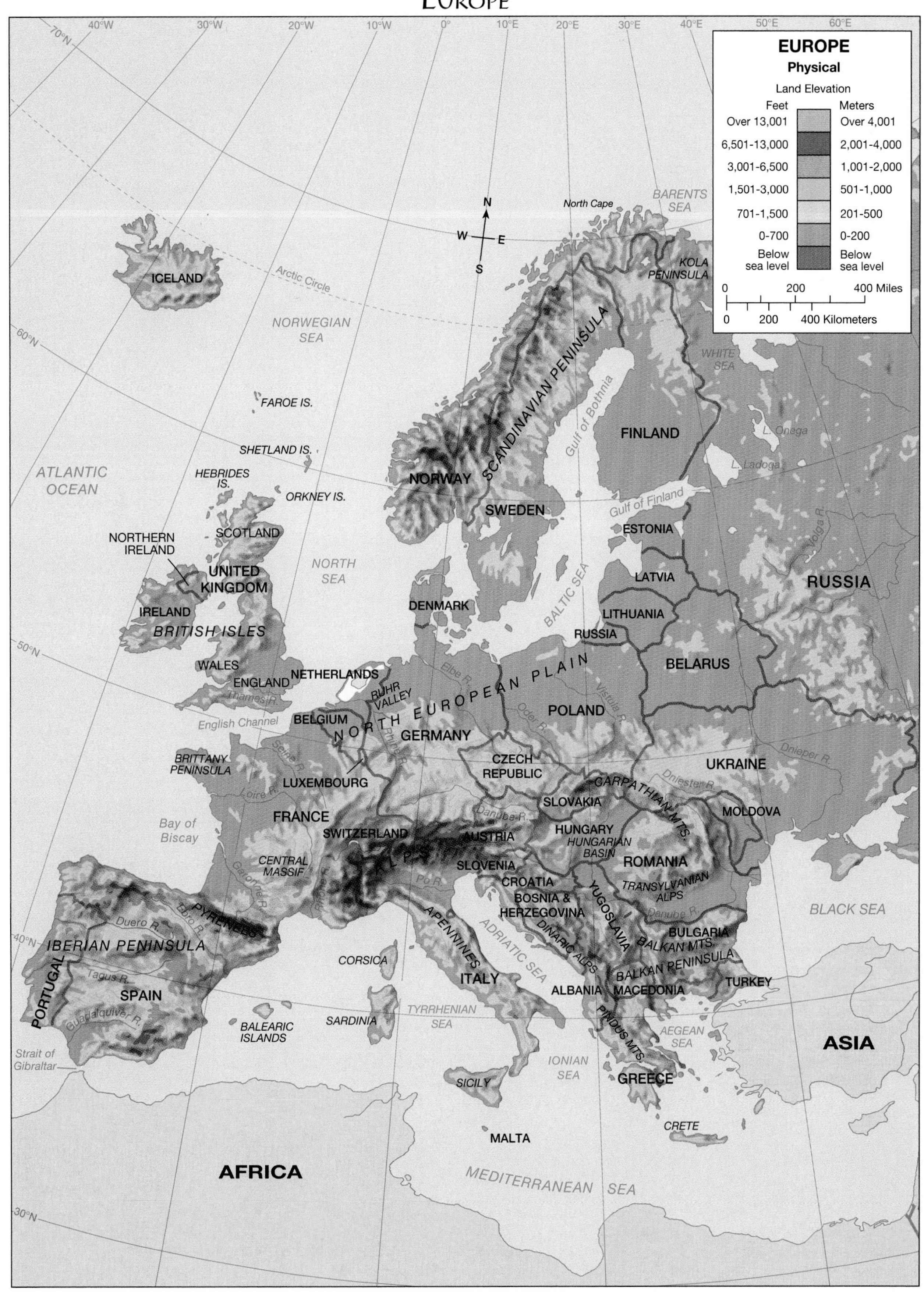

EUROPE
Physical
Land Elevation
Feet
Meters
Over 13,001
Over 4,001
6,501-13,000
2,001-4,000
3,001-6,500
1,001-2,000
1,501-3,000
501-1,000
701-1,500
201-500
0-700
0-200
Below sea level
Below sea level
0 200 400 Miles
0 200 400 Kilometers
40°W
30°W
20°W
10°W
0°
10°E
20°E
30°E
40°E
50°E
60°E
70°N
60°N
50°N
40°N
30°N
N
W
E
S
ICELAND
Arctic Circle
NORWEGIAN SEA
FAROE IS.
SHETLAND IS.
HEBRIDES IS.
ORKNEY IS.
ATLANTIC OCEAN
NORTH SEA
SCOTLAND
NORTHERN IRELAND
UNITED KINGDOM
IRELAND
BRITISH ISLES
WALES
ENGLAND
Thames R.
English Channel
NETHERLANDS
RUHR VALLEY
BELGIUM
LUXEMBOURG
GERMANY
NORTH EUROPEAN PLAIN
Elbe R.
Oder R.
Rhine R.
BRITTANY PENINSULA
Seine R.
Loire R.
Bay of Biscay
FRANCE
CENTRAL MASSIF
Garonne R.
Rhone R.
SWITZERLAND
ALPS
AUSTRIA
Danube R.
Po R.
PYRENEES
Ebro R.
Duero R.
IBERIAN PENINSULA
PORTUGAL
SPAIN
Tagus R.
Guadalquivir R.
Strait of Gibraltar
BALEARIC ISLANDS
CORSICA
SARDINIA
TYRRHENIAN SEA
APENNINES
ITALY
SICILY
MALTA
ADRIATIC SEA
IONIAN SEA
North Cape
BARENTS SEA
KOLA PENINSULA
WHITE SEA
SCANDINAVIAN PENINSULA
NORWAY
SWEDEN
FINLAND
Gulf of Bothnia
Gulf of Finland
L. Onega
L. Ladoga
Volga R.
DENMARK
BALTIC SEA
ESTONIA
LATVIA
LITHUANIA
RUSSIA
BELARUS
POLAND
Vistula R.
CZECH REPUBLIC
SLOVAKIA
CARPATHIAN MTS.
UKRAINE
Dnieper R.
Dniester R.
MOLDOVA
HUNGARY
HUNGARIAN BASIN
ROMANIA
TRANSYLVANIAN ALPS
SLOVENIA
CROATIA
BOSNIA & HERZEGOVINA
DINARIC ALPS
YUGOSLAVIA
Danube R.
BULGARIA
BALKAN MTS.
BALKAN PENINSULA
ALBANIA
MACEDONIA
TURKEY
PINDUS MTS.
GREECE
AEGEAN SEA
CRETE
BLACK SEA
ASIA
AFRICA
MEDITERRANEAN SEA

North America

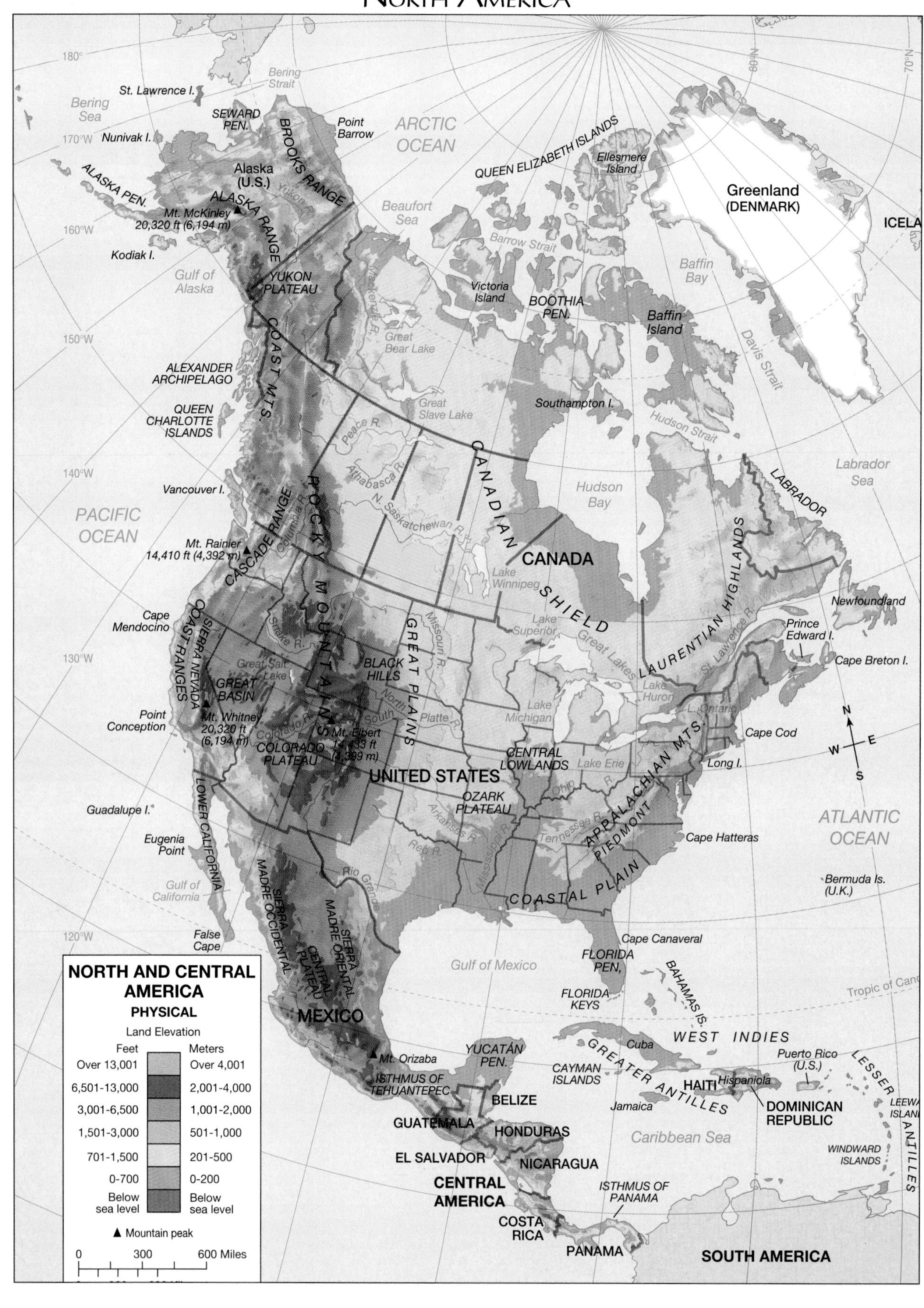

South America

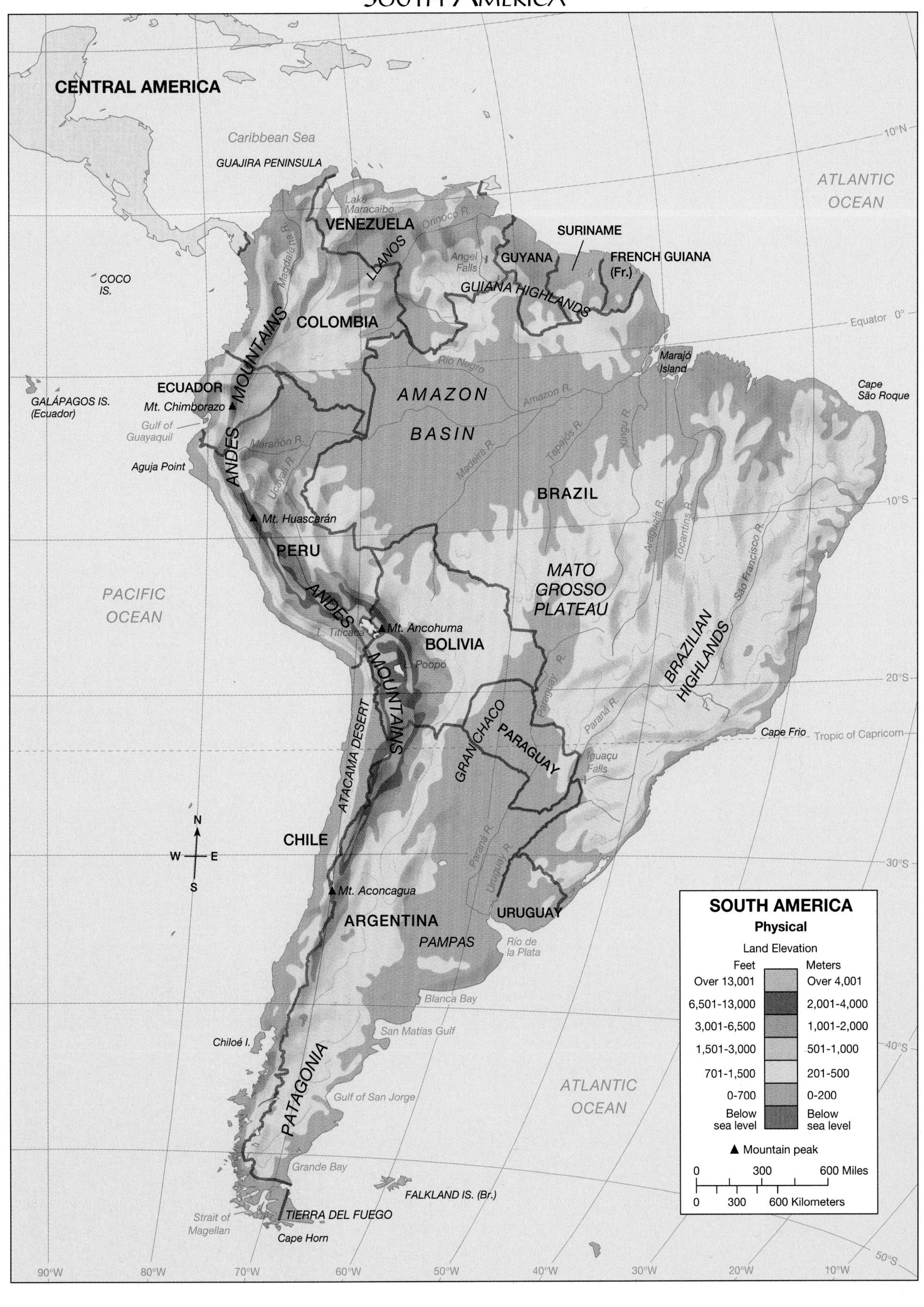

The Contemporary World

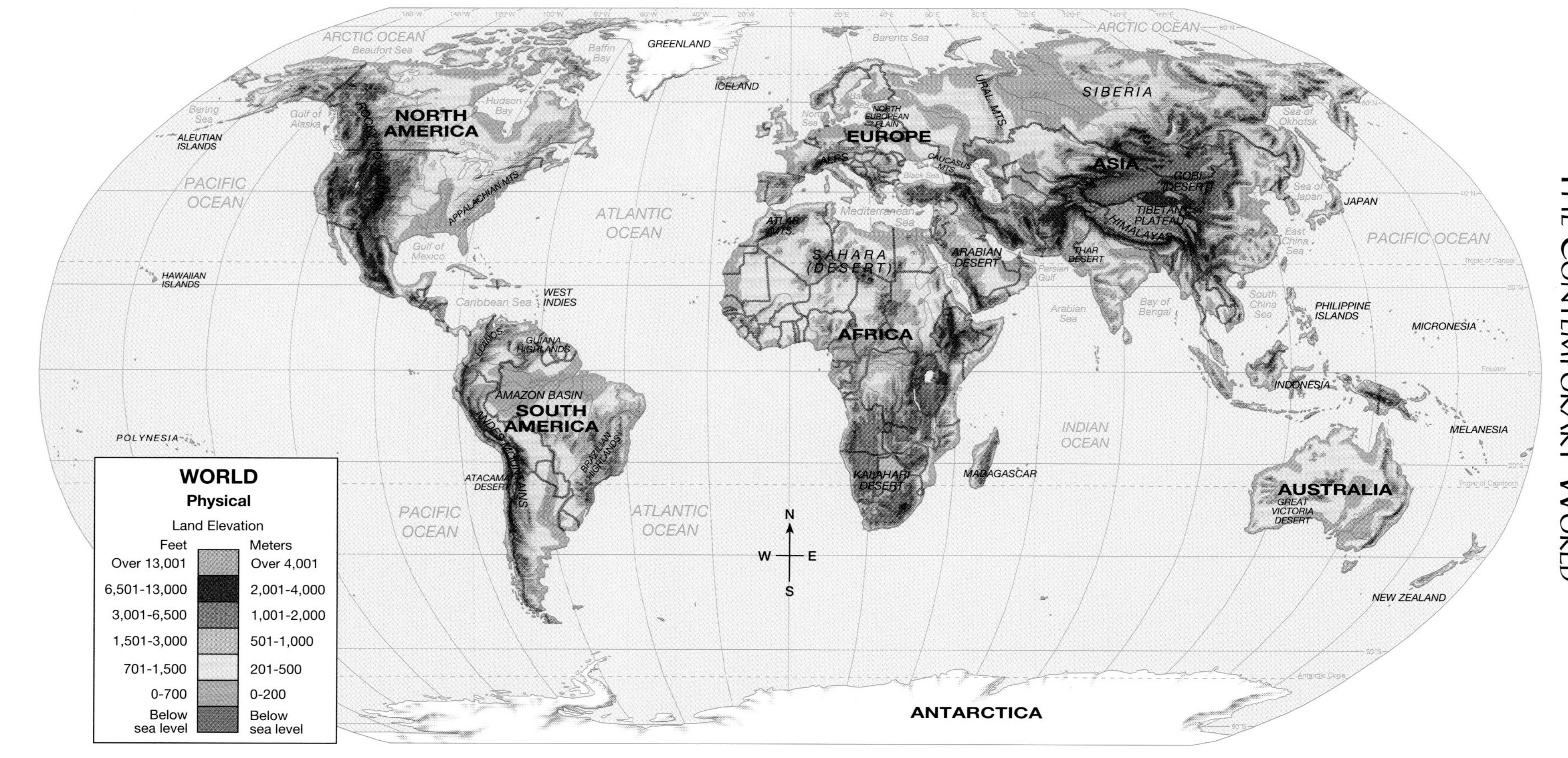

PROLOGUE

History and Human Beginnings

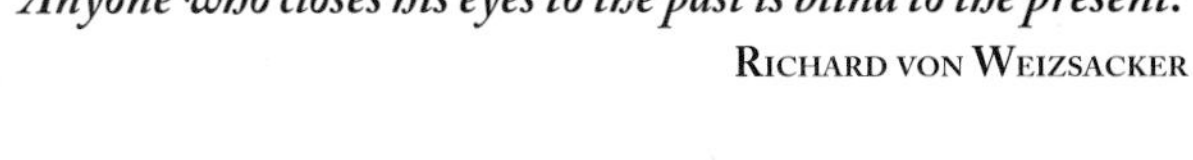

Anyone who closes his eyes to the past is blind to the present.

RICHARD VON WEIZSACKER

The study of history is the best way and, other than by bitter experience, perhaps the only way to be inoculated against the terrible simplifiers, those people who lead nations into trouble.

GEORGE WILL

The human genus has existed for several million years, and human cultures for tens and perhaps hundreds of thousands of years. Only within the past 10,000, however, have these cultures exhibited the form that we call *civilization,* a word derived from *civilis,* a Latin term meaning "relating to a citizen or a state." A civilization is a culture characterized by the building of cities, the development of a complex social and political structure through stratification, and the evolution of a formal economic structure through the division of labor. Civilization implies the willingness of familial groups to embrace outsiders, although clan and kinship patterns may remain important even in the most highly developed civilizations.

Civilization also came to entail the keeping of records and, for this purpose, the development of a system of writing. People kept the first records to levy taxes, take inventories, and chronicle business transactions. Records were also maintained for compiling royal genealogies, perpetuating sacred texts, describing military expeditions, and recording laws, poems, and stories hitherto transmitted orally. From these latter functions evolved the idea of keeping chronologies of major events,

Venus of Lespugue. The exaggerated sexual features indicate the significance of reproduction to early humans.

particularly those of political or religious significance, and, in time, the notion of binding these together as a narrative. Such narratives of past events came to be called *histories* by the early Greeks. History as a human activity thus grew out of the basic processes of civilization itself and, in its most developed form, is not only the record of civilization but also civilization's way of reflecting on itself.

History and the Historian

Historical study is a living process that involves the systematic interpretation of issues. It consists of far more than the simple chronicle of past events. The historian is not the mere conservator of the past but its active shaper. To study the past is to help mold the future by providing the basis for informed judgments. The historical consciousness of modern society, even when it results in an endeavor to return to past values, is inseparable from the attempt to consider options and to make decisions. Not surprisingly, historians often differ in the philosophical approach they bring to their material. The very act of writing history entails making critical judgments and selecting events; most historians strive for objectivity and cite the evidence on which they base their conclusions. Some historians, however, reflect a predetermined ideological position and write history with a view to proving or justifying it. All historians reflect their time and culture.

In seeking to make sense of the past, historians focus on key themes. Religion has often been a major factor in interpreting the past. The Christian and Islamic historians of the Middle Ages and the early modern era viewed the past through the lens of their faiths. Not all scholars have used religion as a basis for historical interpretation or civilized values; the secular, rationalistic outlook of the eighteenth-century British author Edward Gibbon led him to assess Christianity's historical role in largely negative terms. Other historians, such as the classical Greek Thucydides and the sixteenth-century Florentine Niccolò Machiavelli, explained earlier societies on the basis of theories of human behavior. Some, from Thucydides in classical times to the twentieth-century historian Arnold Toynbee, have searched for patterns and cycles of repetition in past events. In contrast to this has been the conviction that the study of history reveals a steady improvement in human life in accordance with a divine scheme for progress. Marxist historians have seen progress in secular terms, as a series of class conflicts that will ultimately lead to the emergence of a classless, egalitarian society. Other writers have seen history essentially in terms of a steady decline. Few historians would now deny the importance of social and economic elements in the historical process, just as few would seek to explain the past primarily in terms of the actions of great men and women. Most historians now recognize the impossibility of providing a compelling explanation of the past without giving due attention to ideological, social, economic, and political factors.

We should expect history neither to determine our future nor to impose neat patterns on the past. The aim should rather be to establish as clear an understanding as possible of past events and cultures and of the place of our own society in the historical context. This is no easy task. Rulers of all ages have manipulated the truth for their own ends, making it necessary for the historian to weigh the evidence meticulously. Furthermore, the lives of vast numbers of people—the slaves of ancient Egypt or nineteenth-century America, women in the ancient and medieval eras, peasants and proletarians everywhere—are often difficult to document apart from general characteristics.

The historical picture depends on sources that are inevitably biased, whether by deliberate attempts to distort the truth or by the chance survival of some records but not others. Better and more abundant evidence for recent times has increased the likelihood of a fuller, more accurate historical analysis of the modern world. The horrors of the forced-labor camps of Stalinist Russia and the Nazi extermination camps have been documented despite attempts to conceal or destroy the record. In assessing the history of the distant past, historians use new discoveries and sophisticated research techniques to refine the traditional picture. However, nearness or remoteness in time is not the sole criterion for historical accessibility. Much more is known about life in Athens during the fifth century B.C. than about life in Africa or North America in the fifteenth century A.D. The nature and the amount of evidence are crucial in the work of every historian.

Fields of History

Much modern historical writing has concentrated on political institutions and practices, diplomatic relations, and warfare—subjects that have formed the traditional core of historical study. Especially in the period after World War II, historians began looking to wider fields, often with the aid of new research techniques, many of them borrowed from the social sciences. Social historians are concerned with social organization and behavior in the past. Interaction between the sexes, the role of women, attitudes toward death, the rearing of children, class and kinship structure, patterns of mobility, the rules of inheritance and property, and the formation of elites are major concerns of the social historian. A special aspect of social organization is the study of urban life, one of the key distinguishing marks of civilization. Here, too, the material evidence is generally more plentiful, and shifting social patterns are easier to discern than in the more slowly changing life of the countryside. Most of the following chapters include portraits of individual cities and the lifestyles of their inhabitants. Cities have changed greatly in size and structure throughout the centuries, and yet over time they exhibit many common characteristics and functions.

Economic, demographic, and environmental history, too, are crucial to an understanding of the past. The movement of people, the flow of trade, the development of technology and its diffusion by contact and exchange, the fluctuations in population and in the rates of birth and death, and the changing patterns of climate all contribute to our perception of human dealings with the world, with each other, and with survival, creating and sustaining civilization.

The history of ideas, including religious beliefs and political ideologies, casts light on the general principles and assumptions of society, the transmission of elite norms, the interplay and conflict between cultural values, and the common threads that unite such diverse cultural products as religion, art, science, and law. Cultural historians concentrate on such subjects as art, architecture, music, and literature. Indeed, virtually every product of human endeavor sheds light on the period in which it was created.

Sources and Their Interpretation

In seeking to understand the past, historians draw on a wide range of materials. These sources fall into two categories: *primary sources,* which consist of materials produced in the period under examination, and *secondary sources,* which comprise accounts by writers of a later age. Primary sources include letters, diaries, tax rolls, treaties, statutes, birth and death registers, census returns, sermons, and court records. Historians work largely from primary sources, even as they keep abreast of findings by other scholars and incorporate those results in their own studies. Any evidence a historian uses must first be evaluated. In the words of the British historian Sir Geoffrey Elton:

> **Evaluation of all historical evidence must start from one basic question: how and with what end in mind did this come into existence? It matters whether a letter is written to a friend or an enemy; whether an account of income is prepared by a taxpayer or a tax collector; whether witnesses in a lawsuit are (as they were in the Roman-law system) called by the court or (as they were in the old [English] Common Law) supplied by the parties.[1]**

Myths constitute a special category of written evidence, though originally they were transmitted orally from generation to generation. Myths are tales that incorporate religious or supernatural notions to explain natural phenomena and social events or to express cultural values. The earliest civilizations used myths to account for such things as floods and drought, birth and death, and gender differences. In a prescientific era, myths functioned in lieu of scientific explanations. Among the most famous myths are those that sought to explain the creation of the universe and the origin of life. Most modern scholars regard the biblical accounts of creation in the Book of Genesis as part of the corpus of ancient myth; Jewish and Christian theologians who accept this conclusion believe that the myths nevertheless point to the underlying truth of a divinely ordered creation. For the historian, myths of every sort provide valuable clues to the human effort to understand the world and our place in it.

Primary sources include much more than written records. Tools, clothing, religious artifacts, and eating and cooking utensils, for instance, tell us much about the tastes, social structure, and values of earlier societies. Fecal remains, as well as foodstuffs preserved in graves and tombs, can teach us much about prehistoric and ancient diets.

Such objects can often be dated with reasonable accuracy by measuring organic deposits of carbon–14, a radioactive form of carbon that disintegrates over time. This form of dating has been usable only for objects less than 50,000 years old, although current research should increase this to 100,000 years. The accuracy of radiocarbon dating has been considerably enhanced by coupling it with dendrochronology, the study of annual growth rings in trees (particularly the bristlecone pines in California's White Mountains, which date back to the seventh millennium B.C.). When ring samples are subjected to radiocarbon analysis, they can be accurately calibrated. Specialists can also date items by their position in the successive strata of objects that have accumulated over centuries at a specific location. At the Koster site near St. Louis, archaeologists have identified 15 distinctive strata (called *horizons*) covering a period from approximately 6000 B.C. to A.D. 1200.

Dramatic scientific advances have resulted in other systems of dating that are especially useful in working with cores of sediment from ocean bottoms and with loess (windborne soil) and microfauna deposited between glacial cycles. Measuring potassium and argon enabled scientists to determine that human fossils found at the Olduvai Gorge in Tanzania were 1,786,000 years old. Specialists can date some objects by measuring the decay of uranium, changes in the earth's magnetic field, or thermoluminescence (for such things as burned artifacts, teeth, and rocks heated by a campfire). Approximate dates for human and animal remains can be determined by measuring the proportion of "left-handed" to "right-handed" amino acid molecules; at the time of death, the number of molecules oriented in a leftward direction begins to increase through the action of aspartic acid in a process known as *amino-acid racemization.*

The fine arts reveal much about earlier civilizations. Paintings, sculpture, music, and architecture reflect the values of the people who produced them, as well as the audience for whom they were intended and the patrons who made their creation possible. Art is a valuable source of evidence, especially for social and religious historians. In the words of the twentieth-century American composer Carlisle Floyd, "What more accurate, more immediate access do we have to the hearts and minds of men than through what they reveal of themselves and their age in art? For art, after all is said and done, is revelation."[2]

The historian of more recent times has a wide range of additional material in the form of films, recordings, and other products of the era of mass communication. Newspapers (which originated in the seventeenth century), magazines, film, photography, popular literature, and folk songs are valuable historical evidence. In the case of recent events, oral accounts can provide significant information. A special subfield now exists called *oral history;* its practitioners interview people who participated in or witnessed historical events, thereby preserving their accounts as data for future scholars.

Interpreting the evidence demands appropriate analytical skills. Most historians are trained in the methodology of at least one additional field. Social historians must be familiar with the techniques of sociology and demography; economic historians, with statistics and economists' models; church historians, with theology and philosophy; intellectual historians, with philosophy and textual criticism; and historians of science, with scientific theory and methodology. Legal historians have often acquired formal training in the law. The controversial field of psychohistory, which applies psychological theories and models to explain the behavior of historical personalities, requires training in psychology. Historians of the ancient world work closely with archaeologists, who find and analyze such remains as pottery, inscriptions, and ruins. Scholars use anthropological studies of tribal behavior in modern times to formulate hypotheses about prehistoric society. Historians work closely with specialists in virtually all fields to explain the past and its relationship to the present. The discipline of history is the core of the modern academic community; no other discipline is so closely affiliated with so many other fields of intellectual behavior.

Time

The ordering of time is basic to any study of the past. Events must be examined in relation to those that preceded and followed them. Yet even the simplest chronology often poses a challenge. The dating of events in ancient cultures is dependent on our knowledge of their calendar systems, which are often extremely complex, both numerically and symbolically. Such calendars are not mere units of convenience but semisacred codes that touch on the most basic questions of ordering human experience. Traces of this remain in our modern religious calendars and in such customs as observances of the equinox and Halloween.

All notions of time are relative. Our most common experience is the alternation of light and dark that we call a day, yet the periods in this alternation vary from one latitude to another, and at the poles the sun at times never sets. We mark the seasons by periods of recurrent temperature, rainfall, vegetation, and the progression of the stars, yet these too vary with geographic position.

All of these experiences have a circular character; that is, we periodically return to a point of observation from which we had moved away. At the same time, we are conscious of the linear aspect of time in the biological facts of birth, aging, and death. Our conception of time is thus a compound of circular and linear elements that combine into larger patterns of passage and recurrence. We must take account not only of things that appear to change little, if at all, such as the regular phases of the moon or the annual positions of the stars, but also of those that change rapidly and unpredictably, such as the forms of life.

A calendar is a compromise that combines both circular and linear patterns of our experience into a single system. It is based on the most immediate patterns of recurrence (days, months, seasons, years), but it imposes a linear progression on them by the device of numbering and counting. Our most general ideas about history, too, tend to be either circular or linear—or an attempt to combine the two. Circular theories of history tend to emphasize the theme of recurrently rising and falling civilizations, while linear theories stress the idea of progress, whether along an indefinite path or toward a final destination.

The Western world has used the birth of Jesus Christ and thus of Christianity as the principal dividing point in history; all historical dates are commonly expressed as B.C. (before Christ) or A.D. (*Anno Domini*, "in the year of our Lord"), or sometimes as B.C.E. (before the common era) and C.E. (common era). This linear system, so familiar to us (its invention dates from the sixth century), has far less cultural significance for much of the non-Western world, yet it is now universally understood and widely accepted. Nonetheless, it is by no means the only historical reference point in use today. Jewish and Muslim cultures, among others, have their own dates of origin and continue to keep their own calendars. We have adopted the Western convention in this work.

The Origins of Humanity

Although the earth itself is approximately 4.5 to 5 billion years old, the earliest humanlike ancestors appeared several million years ago. They were (with the great apes) members of the hominid family. Among the hominids were primates similar to modern humans, although with considerably smaller brain capacities. Hominids walked on two feet, used tools, and ate meat. About 1.7 million years ago some hominids evolved into *Homo ergaster* ("work human"), probably in temperate regions of Africa first, after which some migrated into western and southern Asia and Europe. Specialists believe *H. ergaster* was probably the earliest human to domesticate fire, a development that occurred about 1.4 million years ago. Around 1 million years ago, *Homo erectus* evolved from *H. ergaster.* Anthropologists once believed modern humans are descended from *H. erectus,* but the skull shape of modern humans is more similar to that of *H. ergaster,* suggesting that we descended directly from *H. ergaster* around 500,000 B.C. rather than from *H. erectus.* At about this time, *Homo heidelbergensis* ("Heidelberg human") evolved from *H. ergaster* in Europe; some anthropologists regard these people, who lived in caves and used stone implements, as the earliest form of *Homo sapiens* ("wise human"). Many anthropologists believe that *H. erectus,* with its enlarged brain (about two-thirds the size of a modern human's), evolved independently in Java, the Philippines, and China.

Because these early humans used stone tools, the earliest period in the human saga is known as the Paleolithic, or Old Stone Age. During this long period, which probably began 600,000 or more years ago, tools, which were originally only primitive chips of stone, gradually became more sophisticated. Paleolithic people developed the hand ax, which could chop, cut, scrape, and punch holes. They also fashioned tools for scraping from flint.

Paleolithic people ate grain, fruits, vegetables, berries, roots, nuts, and game hunted with spears. Hunting large animals, such as deer, horses, and bison, required organization and communication, thus encouraging the development of speech and rudimentary social groups. These people organized themselves into bands, typically numbering several dozen persons, for the purposes of protection, the provision of food, and probably simple religious rituals. The basic social unit of this hunter-gatherer society was the family. Because of their role as gatherers and their bearing and raising of children, women were presumably the social equals of men. Nevertheless, the gradual division of labor along sexual lines contributed to a distinction of occupational roles that has lasted into the twentieth century.

In geologic terms, the Paleolithic age was roughly coterminous with the Pleistocene epoch, which extended from 2 million to approximately 10,000 years ago. During this epoch, glaciers advanced and retreated at least four and possibly as many as six or seven times, causing substantial climatic and topographic changes that required humans to adapt. They were, in other words, forced to think and thus to develop their critical capacities. Evolution therefore continued, leading to the appearance of *Homo sapiens neanderthalensis* between about 200,000 and 150,000 years ago; Neanderthal man was so named because his remains were discovered in the Neander River valley in modern Germany.

Neanderthal people lived in both caves and open-air sites, hunted mammals, and warmed themselves at large stone fireplaces. More striking was their preparation of elaborate funeral rites to deal with the needs of those who had died and presumably lived in some afterlife. They interred bodies in graves filled with shells and ornaments made of ivory and bone, and they colored the skin or bones of the deceased with red ocher, apparently to commemorate life. The corpses themselves were buried in the fetal position, possibly to facilitate rebirth or to restrict the movements of the dead and thereby prevent them from returning to haunt the living. Thus, in the process of trying to explain death, Neanderthal people seem to have developed a conception of an afterlife.

About 125,000 to 120,000 years ago modern humans, known anthropologically as *Homo sapiens sapiens,* first appeared in Africa. As the name implies, many anthropologists group these people with the Neanderthals,

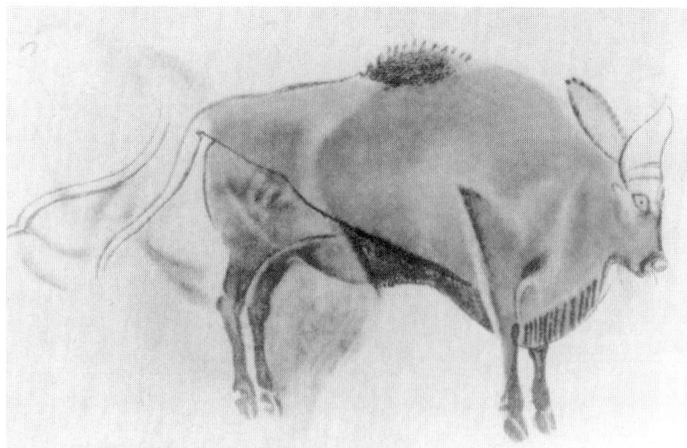

Drawing of bison, c. 15,000–10,000 B.C., *found in the Altamira cave in Spain.*

who coexisted with the new people for thousands of years. The earliest human culture of which we have much knowledge is that of the people who lived at Cro-Magnon in what is now southwestern France 25,000 to 30,000 years ago. Like the Neanderthals, Cro-Magnon people were hunter-gatherers; their prey included bison, deer, rhinoceros, and mammoth. The Cro-Magnon period was marked by changes in tools, some of which the people constructed of bone, ivory, and antler for the first time. They used needles made of antler or bone to sew clothing fashioned from animal skins. From flint they made microliths, such as arrow tips and barbs, and fashioned spears from yew wood. Engraving on some antlers and bones indicates that they may have been used as ornaments.

The earliest surviving paintings come from this period and exist deep inside more than 200 caves in southwestern Europe, particularly at Lascaux, Altamira, and Chauvet (near Avignon), the last discovered only in 1994. Most of the images depict animals, such as bulls, cows, horses, bison, rhinos, deer, and, rarely, lions, bears, and panthers. Because the drawings were in the inner recesses of the caves rather than in the inhabited areas or near the mouths, where natural illumination was available, they were probably associated with religious rites. Some paintings show arrows striking the animals, and others have sharp gouges in the animals' sides, as if hunters had thrown spears at them. Rarely do humans appear in these paintings, although one notable exception depicts a masked man—perhaps a priest or a hunter in disguise—wearing deer antlers, bear paws, a wolf's tail, and a lion skin.

Sculptures of humans from the same period typically depict women with enlarged breasts, thighs, and stomachs, emphasizing their reproductive role. The artists thus reflected women's crucial role as the source of life. Rarely do the statues show facial features, and some omit the head altogether; the emphasis was on fertility rather than the lifelike reproduction of physical features. Some scholars believe that these female figures reflect a primitive belief in a Mother Goddess.

Recent archaeological research suggests that some of the people of this age, although hunter-gatherers, were the first to settle in permanent communities, with facilities for the storage of food, patterns of trade that extended over long distances, and social and political hierarchies. The existence of such hierarchies is suggested by standardized beads and pendants made by western European foragers as long as 32,000 years ago. These people also knew how to fire clay to make ceramics. In central Russia archaeologists have found the remains of elaborate settlements constructed of mammoth bones; the people who lived here some 20,000 years ago traded for materials from the Black Sea region 500 miles away. Presumably they stored their food because their population was expanding, although this practice limited their mobility. As they settled into permanent communities, internal conflicts must have occurred, leading to the devel-

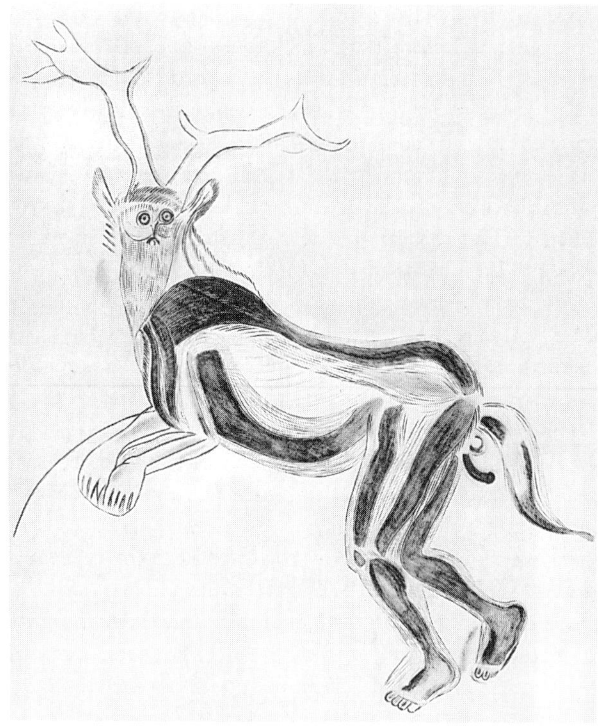

Drawing of a shaman or a disguised hunter wearing antlers, a bear's paws, a wolf's tail, a lion's skin, and a human beard, c. 13,000–11,000 B.C., *Ariège, France.*

opment of social and political organization to maintain order. Probably because of climatic changes, this society came to an end some 12,000 years ago, when the Europeans broke up into small bands and returned to a nomadic life.

By the end of the Paleolithic age some 10,000 years ago, the more advanced peoples customarily lived in shelters made of wood, hides, sod, or bones; dressed in clothing sewn from skins; used dogs to control, insofar as possible, herds of wild animals; traded with other regions; painted and sculpted; participated in primitive rituals; and buried their dead.

Paleolithic people in what is now Russia and Poland lived in huts built of the bones of mammoths.

Agricultural and Social Developments in the Neolithic Age

As long as people had an ample supply of animals to hunt and the population remained small, incentives to raise crops and domesticate animals were few. However, as the glaciers retreated and temperatures gradually warmed, large herbivores such as mammoth and bison began to disappear in many regions of human habitation. At the same time, the human population continued to increase rapidly. Specialists estimate that the population grew from 125,000 hominids 1 million years ago to 5,320,000 humans at the end of the Paleolithic age and to 133 million about 2,000 years ago. The need to expand the food supply by raising crops and grazing herds thus marked the end of the Paleolithic and the beginning of the Neolithic (New Stone Age).

Agriculture probably originated in the hill country and then was adapted to the valleys of the Tigris and Euphrates rivers in southwestern Asia and in eastern Asia Minor. Other peoples of the world, including those in Mesoamerica (Mexico and Central America), western Africa, southeastern Asia, China, and the Andes, developed agricultural techniques independently. The earliest farmers in western Asia grew wheat, barley, oats, and rye and grazed herds of sheep, goats, pigs, and cattle. People who lived near rivers or lakes could supplement their diet with fish. In time Neolithic people discovered how to brew beer from fermented grain and, in the Mediterranean region, how to make wine from grapes.

Agriculture based on tropical crops, especially root crops, appeared in Southeast Asia perhaps as early as 8000 B.C. The year-round warmth and moisture of most of the region gave it strong advantages for sustained cultivation. Rice was native to this area also. Although it was originally a swamp plant, farmers adapted it to upland fields or to irrigated paddies with relative ease. Pigs, chickens, and water buffalo were native to the region, and the former two soon spread among the late Neolithic cultures elsewhere in Eurasia.

Farming, in the view of some specialists, spread very slowly throughout Europe from western Asia. These experts, using carbon–14 dating, calculate that it took 1,500 years for agricultural techniques to expand from Asia Minor to central Italy and another 1,500 years to reach the central Iberian peninsula. In effect, each generation, they believe, extended the agricultural frontier an average of 11 miles, until farming populations existed throughout Europe by approximately 3800 B.C. More recently, some scholars have challenged this view on the basis of evidence that points to the development of European agriculture by indigenous peoples, not colonizers from western Asia. More sophisticated radiocarbon studies, for instance, have indicated that

> **the spread of farming in Europe was a stop-and-start process, a series of major expansions or explosions followed by substantial pauses, and not the gradual "wave of advance" inferred in the past from a few radiocarbon dates widely spaced across Europe.[3]**

The stops and starts correlated with major climatic changes and their impact on regional landscapes. Changes

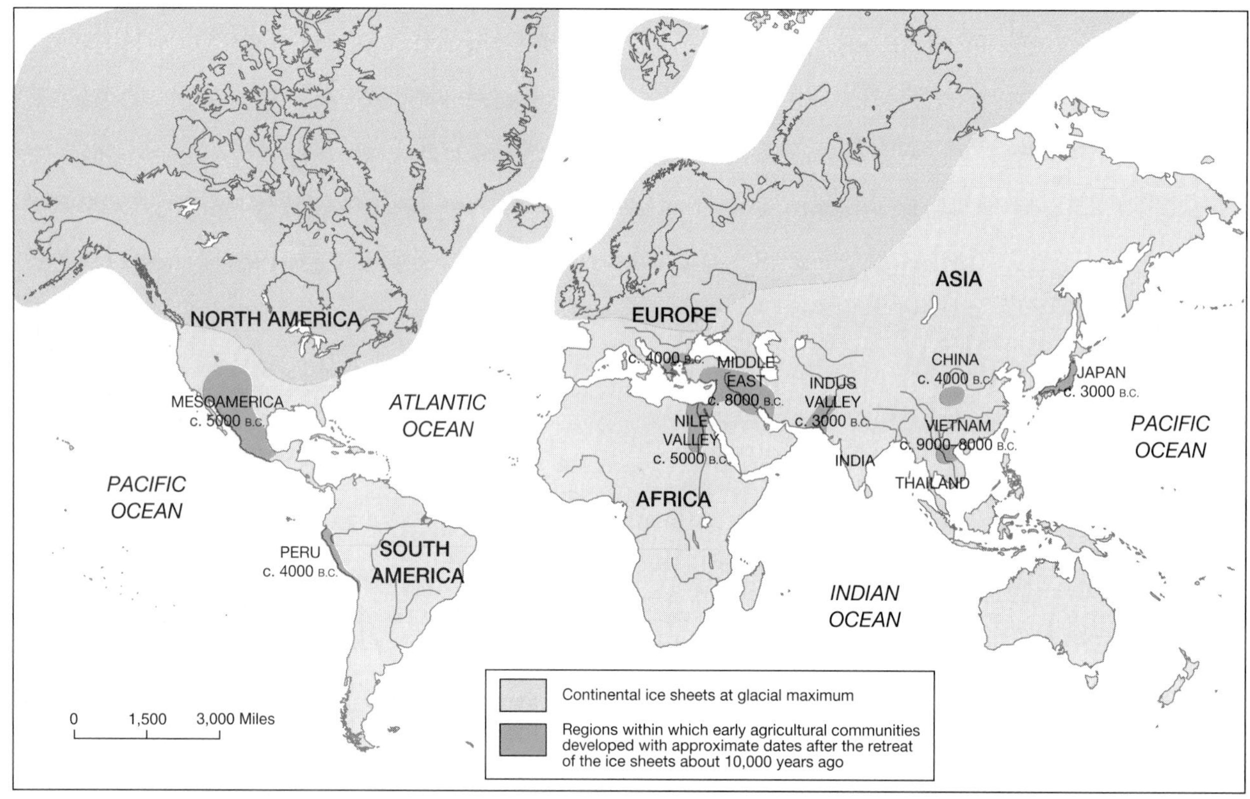

MAP P.1 THE DEVELOPMENT OF AGRICULTURE

in climate, in other words, played a major role in the expansion of farming.

Elsewhere, the earliest settlements in India were small farming villages in Baluchistan and lower Sind that date to the fourth millennium B.C. North Africa, physically close to western Asia, soon acquired the new techniques. Fully developed Neolithic culture existed in Egypt by 5000 B.C., and from there and from western Africa farming spread gradually throughout the African continent. In the Americas agricultural communities developed more slowly than in Asia and Europe, but by about 2000 B.C. sufficient amounts of food were being grown to make permanent settlements possible.

The change from a nomadic to a settled life made possible by agriculture had both advantages and disadvantages. A greater incentive now existed to build permanent homes, with improved shelter from the elements and with room to store manufactured products. Once the crops were in the ground, many Neolithic people had sufficient free time to hone skills for making tools, cooking utensils, and clothing, thus inaugurating a technological revolution. They learned to make better tools by grinding and polishing stone rather than by chipping, and they discovered how to make pottery, fire it in kilns, and glaze it to improve its capacity to hold liquids. The domestication of sheep provided supplies of wool and thus encouraged the invention of weaving. In time Neolithic people invented the plow and, by 3000 B.C., the wheel, improving both agricultural yield and the ability to transport their crops. Dependence on agriculture, however, rendered these people much more susceptible to climatic fluctuations, such as drought, floods, or unseasonable freezes. Settlements also increased the likelihood of illness through greater exposure to contaminated water, excrement, spoiled food, and decaying animal entrails.

In recent decades specialists have learned much about Neolithic trading patterns through chemical and physical analyses of raw materials, such as obsidian and flint. Obsidian, a volcanic glass used for grinding and flaking, spread throughout the western Mediterranean from sources in southern Italy and Sardinia; throughout the Aegean region, mostly from the island of Melos; throughout parts of Asia Minor and as far afield as Syria and Palestine from sites in central Turkey; and throughout the Carpathians from sources in Hungary's Bukk Mountains. Generally, quantities of a given item decrease as the distance from its source increases, but in several instances large amounts of a particular material have been found a considerable distance from the source site, indicating a redistribution center. Thus Neolithic communities were probably less self-sufficient than was once assumed, just as their trading patterns were more sophisticated than was once thought. Raw materials and manufactured items were presumably exchanged for food and perhaps hides. Neolithic potters in Cornwall, at the southwestern tip of England, traded their product to people who lived in western England, and axes made from the volcanic rock of northwestern England have been found in eastern England.

Like the Paleolithic hunter-gatherers who had established communities in central Russia, Neolithic settlers developed rudimentary forms of social and political organization. As in the Paleolithic age, the family continued to be of prime importance. Some scholars have argued that the basic unit was the extended family, embracing perhaps three generations or siblings and their spouses and children. The extended family could provide the labor necessary for wide-ranging agricultural tasks, such as clearing land or harvesting, and could ensure that the work was performed even if one or more persons became incapacitated. Against this assumption, however, is evidence that late Neolithic houses were normally too small to shelter more than the nuclear family (parents and children). Remains of larger buildings exist, but it is unclear whether they were the homes of extended families or dwellings that housed both nuclear families and their animals, a practice still followed among some Dutch farmers. Some Neolithic villages had a single large building, probably a community hall.

Scholars generally agree that within the community little emphasis was placed on the individual. Instead the people of the village worked together, essentially as equals, to build houses, clear forests, and plant crops. Each family had access to the community's resources as need required. The emphasis, in other words, was on mutual welfare, not, as in modern Western society, productivity for the sake of social differentiation and material accumulation. Archaeological excavation in Neolithic cemeteries tends to confirm this view of a largely egalitarian society, for little differentiation in goods usually exists from one grave to the next. We do not know whether all the deceased were interred in these cemeteries or whether Neolithic people buried only the elite.

Women played a key role in Neolithic society and may have enjoyed a higher status than men. Some scholars believe that women were largely responsible for the agricultural revolution in the Neolithic period. Mythology suggests confirmation of this: women are associated with raising crops, men with herding animals. The Neolithic village, however, could support a larger population than the hunter-gatherer tribe, intensifying the burden on women as bearers and raisers of children in addition to their expanded agricultural duties. Women's substantial contribution to the success of the agricultural revolution may, according to some scholars, have unwittingly sown the seeds for their subsequent subjugation by men. As mythology suggests, that repression may have begun with the introduction of the animal-drawn plow, which was widely used in western Asia by 3000 B.C.; early myths associated female deities with the hoe and their male counterparts with the plow. Yet the recurring competition between the sexes, so common to much of recorded history, may not have existed, or at least was less pronounced, in the long prehistoric era.

Archaeological discoveries have made it possible to reconstruct the outlines of Neolithic religious beliefs. Numerous figurines have been unearthed in prehistoric

The Laussel Venus, a stone relief carving from Les-Ezyies-de-Tarac, France.

The ruins of Jericho, perhaps the world's oldest city.

settlements and graves throughout eastern Europe. Most of these depict females, although others portray males and animals; many probably represented deities, especially an Earth Mother, responsible for both human and animal fertility and agricultural yields. Neolithic Europeans worshiped both the Great Goddess, who transformed death into life and was linked with moon crescents, and the Goddess of Vegetation, her intimate companion. Religious practice was thus concerned with nature and the cycle of the seasons, and occurred in both private houses and shrines or temples. Prehistoric models found in the Danube basin and in Russia indicate that some temples may have been large and even two-storied. Within these temples Neolithic people performed rituals, as suggested by the large number of surviving clay statuettes depicting masked and costumed men and women. "Myths and seasonal drama must have been enacted through the medium of the idol [the figurine], each with a different intention and with the invocation of appropriate divinities."[4] Worshipers sacrificed humans, animals, and assorted objects on altars, some of which were found in temples, others in open-air sanctuaries or caves. Archaeologists have discovered tens of thousands of miniature figurines, some of them inscribed with assorted designs, such as spirals, chevrons, zigzags, and parallel lines. The patterns may have had religious meaning. The extensive archaeological remains pertaining to religion underscore both the extent to which Neolithic people sought to explain and deal with their environment and the growing sense of community reflected in the widespread acceptance of ritual practices.

The Coming of Civilization

The Neolithic age, with its development of cereal cultivation and animal husbandry, permanent settlements, expanded trading patterns, and social groups, provided the roots from which civilization grew. Most Neolithic settlements were small: homesteads, with fewer than 10 people; hamlets, with populations of 10 to 50; and villages, ranging in size from 50 to several hundred inhabitants. Around 8000 B.C. the transition from village to city life began at Jericho in what was later called Palestine; 2,000 to 3,000 people lived at Jericho in multiroomed houses. They were sufficiently organized socially and politically to construct stone walls as much as 20 feet high and 6 feet thick at the base, beyond which was a ditch 25 feet wide and 6 feet deep. The extent of such fortifications suggests that warfare must have been commonplace, a thesis advanced by specialists on prehistoric Europe as well. Jericho's inhabitants raised grain, probably with the aid of an irrigation system that used spring waters, and traded sulfur and salt for precious stones from the Sinai and obsidian from Anatolia. Their artists created portrait busts by modeling plaster over human skulls.

Comparable protocities began developing at such places as Jarmo in what is now Iraq around 7000 B.C. and at Çatal Hüyük in Anatolia. The latter, founded approximately 6700 B.C. and excavated in the 1960s, was considerably larger than Jericho. Its inhabitants raised grains, nuts, peas, apples, grapes, and oil-producing seeds; grazed sheep; and hunted deer and wild boar. Residents made pottery, baskets, and wooden vessels; crafted fine weapons from flint; wove cloth; fashioned necklaces and bracelets; and applied cosmetics as they looked into polished obsidian mirrors. Like the people of Jericho, the Çatal Hüyükans traded widely for items that included shells from the Mediterranean and stones from southern Anatolia. They decorated the walls of their religious shrines with paintings of dancers, wild animals, vultures, and funeral rituals. Both females and males attended their chief deity, a female.

In addition to the emergence of cities, the development of metallurgy was important for the rise of civilization. In western Asia and the Balkans, late Neolithic people acquired the ability to smelt, hammer, and cast copper ores in the fifth millennium B.C. The earliest items fashioned of copper included personal ornaments, axes, daggers, awls, and hooks. Copper, however, is a relatively soft metal, and not until 3000 B.C. or shortly thereafter did metalworkers learn the technique of alloying it with tin to produce the more durable bronze. In the beginning, copper, like gold and silver, was rather scarce, and therefore objects made of it would have been prized. People fortunate enough to possess items made from gold, silver, copper, or precious stones thus distinguished themselves from other people on the basis of their wealth. Evidence for the rise of societies characterized by degrees of wealth has been found in late Neolithic graves in northern Europe, where prestigious goods such as copper daggers and beakers and fine flint battle-axes were buried in single rather than collective graves.

Social differentiation was undoubtedly encouraged as some people mastered metallurgical technology and more sophisticated techniques of pottery making and decorating. The British archaeologist Patricia Phillips has argued that

> **it seems likely that the larger populations of the Late Neolithic permitted more specialization, that their density forced more complexity of social structure, and these complexities fuelled the demand for high-value goods to indicate their status. These goods might acquire value because of their rarity, or because of the length of time they took in manufacture.[5]**

Essentially classless societies faded in the face of emerging distinctions based on wealth and technical skills.

A skill of a different kind involved the ability to write. Scholars may someday find that writing first appeared in southern and central Europe if it can be demonstrated that the engravings on the numerous Neolithic figurines found there are more than simple markings. For now, however, the earliest known writing system was devised by the people of Uruk (now Tal al-Warka), a principal city-state in ancient Sumer (modern Iraq). In the late Neolithic period, people kept records using small tokens in the shape of disks, spheres, cones, and other figures, some of which were marked with incisions. Usually kept in clay containers, such tokens might be used, for instance, to represent animals in a palace herd.

Late in the fourth millennium B.C., as cities and large-scale trade developed, the use of tokens to maintain records became too cumbersome. The people of Mesopotamia substituted written images known as *ideographs* for the tokens. During the third millennium B.C., these ideographs evolved into a series of wedge-shaped marks that could be impressed on a clay tablet quickly and easily with a split reed. The Sumerians also wrote on stone and metal, but clay, which was plentiful in their land and was already used for building and pottery, was much easier to inscribe. Mistakes could easily be smoothed out,

A rock painting showing warriors, c. 8000–3000 B.C., found near Castellón, Spain.

A Neolithic carving of a masked man holding a sickle and wearing rings on his arms, c. 5000 B.C. Such sickles were made of copper.

and the record could be made permanent by leaving the clay to dry in the sun or baking it. In this form it was light and easy to carry as well. The system of wedge-shaped marks on clay is known as *cuneiform,* after the Latin word *cuneus,* which means "wedge." Cuneiform combined pictographic signs (representing objects) and phonetic signs (representing sounds), creating a total of some 350 characters. This method of writing was useful to keep track of financial and other transactions, including records of religious beliefs, political and military achievements, and laws.

At about the time the Sumerians evolved their system of writing, a transportation revolution provided further impetus to the emergence of civilization. Farmers and others hauled large quantities of goods on animal-drawn two- and four-wheeled carts. Bulky goods in particular could be moved more efficiently thanks to the invention of the sail in the fourth millennium B.C. The new means of transportation were crucial in handling the increasing amounts of agricultural produce made possible by the development of better plows (antlers replaced sticks beginning in the fourth millennium B.C.) and of the larger quantities of pottery produced after the introduction of the potter's wheel. The first peoples to combine all these developments lived in the river valleys of Mesopotamia, Egypt, and India. Civilizations developed somewhat later in China and Southeast Asia.

NOTES

1. R. W. Fogel and G. R. Elton, *Which Road to the Past? Two Views of History* (New Haven, Conn.: Yale University Press, 1983), p. 92.
2. C. Floyd, "Society and the Artist," 1964 Distinguished Professor Lecture, Florida State University.
3. G. Barker, *Prehistoric Farming in Europe* (Cambridge: Cambridge University Press, 1985), p. 253.
4. M. Gimbutas, *The Goddesses and Gods of Old Europe, 6500–3500* B.C.: *Myths and Cult Images,* 2nd ed. (Berkeley: University of California Press, 1982), p. 236.
5. P. Phillips, *The Prehistory of Europe* (Bloomington: Indiana University Press, 1980), p. 187.

SUGGESTIONS FOR FURTHER READING

Barker, G. *Prehistoric Farming in Europe.* Cambridge: Cambridge University Press, 1982.

Champion, T., Gamble, C., Shennan, S., and Whittle, A. *Prehistoric Europe.* London: Academic Press, 1984.

Elias, N. *Time: An Essay.* Oxford: Blackwell, 1992.

Foley, R. *Humans Before Humanity.* Oxford: Blackwell, 1995.

Gimbutas, M. *The Goddesses and Gods of Old Europe, 6500–3500 B.C.: Myths and Cult Images,* 2nd ed. Berkeley: University of California Press, 1982.

Harris, M. *Cannibals and Kings: The Origins of Cultures.* London: Collins, 1978.

Johanson, D. C., and O'Farrell, K. *Journey from the Dawn: Life with the World's First Family.* New York: Villard, 1990.

Jones, S., Martin, R. D., and Pilbeam, D. *The Cambridge Encyclopedia of Human Evolution.* New York: Cambridge University Press, 1992.

Leakey, R. E., and Lewin, R. *The Making of Mankind.* New York: Dutton, 1992.

———. *Origins Reconsidered.* New York: Doubleday, 1992.

Lerner, G. *The Creation of Patriarchy.* New York: Oxford University Press, 1986.

Nitecki, M. H., and Nitecki, D. V., eds. *Origins of Anatomically Modern Humans.* New York: Plenum, 1994.

Phillips, P. *The Prehistory of Europe.* Bloomington: Indiana University Press, 1980.

Tattersall, I. *The Human Odyssey.* New York: Prentice Hall, 1993.

PART ONE

The Peoples and Cultures of Antiquity

CHAPTER 1

The Societies of Western Asia and Egypt

The first civilizations developed in one of the birthplaces of the agricultural revolution, western Asia and ancient Egypt, the region now known as the Middle East. Village-level agriculture had appeared earlier, in the uplands west of Mesopotamia and in mainland Southeast Asia. But the peoples of ancient Egypt and Mesopotamia were the first who systematically organized the growing of food in large, permanent fields under irrigation; developed improved techniques of mining and metal processing; founded cities; and devised social, legal, and ethical systems, as well as institutions of government and religion.

The discovery and use of new materials greatly advanced such large-scale developments. Pottery was produced by at least 5000 B.C. in western and southeastern Asia, and soon afterward metal began to replace stone in the manufacture of tools and weapons. Copper was the earliest material employed, but these people discovered the technique of alloying copper with tin to produce bronze, probably around 3000 B.C. It was at the fortified settlements of this new Bronze Age in Egypt and Mesopotamia that civilization in the West began. In the centuries that followed, other western Asian peoples began to form their own distinctive cultures, the most important of which were those of the Hebrews, the Hittites, and the Persians.

Egypt and Mesopotamia are dominated by great rivers—Egypt by the Nile, which regularly floods each year, and Mesopotamia by the Tigris and the Euphrates. The annual flooding of the Nile was consistent and predictable in its timing and in the scope of the land that it inundated. As the floodwater receded, people planted seeds in the wet soil; the new surface of fertile silt retained enough moisture to bring the crop to harvest. The Tigris and Euphrates rivers were far more irregular in

Pharaoh Menkaure and his queen, c. 2250 B.C.

their flooding and often wreaked destruction. Protection for farmland was therefore essential, as were means to irrigate the fields. Owing in part to these differences, the cultures of Egypt and Mesopotamia developed in distinctive ways, each making a special contribution to the development of civilization.

Life Between the Rivers: The City Dwellers of Mesopotamia

The history of ancient Mesopotamia consists of a succession of peoples, each with a somewhat different but related culture. Other peoples played a part in Mesopotamian history, notably the Hittites to the northwest and the peoples of ancient Iran (Persia) to the east. The more powerful Mesopotamian states generally overshadowed the neighboring peoples until well into the first millennium B.C., when the Persians established their mighty empire. The lack of natural barriers opened Mesopotamia to invaders, who used surprise, superior leadership, and technology to establish dominion over the area. The region's political history reflects these cycles of invasion both in the rise and fall of the states and in the eclectic nature of Mesopotamian civilization. The foundations of this civilization rested firmly on the culture of Sumer.

Sumer

The first Sumerian settlements were farming communities that developed around 4000 B.C. in the region between the Tigris and Euphrates rivers. The land in this area is flat, and the inhabitants had to construct dikes and canals to limit erosion during the rainy months and to collect water for the arid season. To acquire the means for such large-scale building projects, the early settlers pooled their resources and worked together; thus villages began to merge and new towns were born.

The need to organize and administer complex projects of this kind led to centralized control. The same necessity prompted the Mesopotamians to develop a system of writing by using images of tokens that had hitherto been employed for record keeping (see the essay "Writing and Communication (I)" on pp. 222–226). Sumerians marked the images on soft clay tablets with a split reed and then baked the tablets. The reeds made the distinctive wedge-shaped marks of the Mesopotamian system, known as *cuneiform.* With the ability to write came possibilities for trade and administration on a broader scale. The economic development this permitted led to the growth of powerful cities such as Ur.

Urban Life in Sumer: Ur

Ur was the most southerly of the great Sumerian cities, lying just to the south of the Euphrates River and about 200 miles northwest of the Persian Gulf. From the early third millennium b.c. its citizen-traders used the river as a means of navigating to the outer world, and the wider markets they could reach helped account for the extraordinary wealth the city accumulated. In the third millennium b.c. a Sumerian city was more like a regional complex than a densely inhabited core. Ur consisted of the city itself, suburbs, and smaller, more distant villages that depended on the central administration. The whole was surrounded with agricultural lands, including barley and wheat fields, palm groves, and gardens. The exact size of Ur is not known, but Lagash, a city of comparable importance, is estimated to have had a population of 30,000 to 35,000.

For their principal building materials the Sumerians used what lay at hand. Because the valley of the two rivers has virtually no supplies of stone, the builders of Ur used sun-dried bricks made from clay and straw. The center of the community was the temple, the dwelling place of the god who protected the town. Sumerians typically built their temples on raised mounds to prevent damage from flooding. Protected by its own walls, the temple compound housed the residences and workplaces of priests, scribes, and skilled artisans. Surrounding the compound were temples to minor deities and flat-roofed, one-story houses, the largest of which were built around inner courtyards and contained shrines and family burial plots. Residents decorated their houses with colorful mosaics. Streets were little more than narrow, dirty lanes, and brick walls enclosed the city.

The greatest monument at Ur is the ziggurat, the present form of which dates to around 2100 B.C. The word *ziggurat* means "pinnacle" or "mountaintop," and these layered artificial mountains were built from early Sumerian times throughout the Tigris and Euphrates valleys. Ur's ziggurat consisted of a huge platform, measuring 190 by 130 feet, surmounted with terraces. Its great central staircase led to the upper terrace, which housed a temple. Presumably on this pinnacle Nanna, the moon god and patron deity of Ur, appeared to the ruler, who

Ziggurat at Ur, c. 2100–2000 B.C. The huge staircases led to a shrine at the top.

acted as the interpreter and conveyor of divine wishes to the citizens and as the principal servant of the gods. One of his chief duties was the building and maintenance of the temples. Several monuments show Sumerian and later Mesopotamian rulers carrying on their heads baskets filled with bricks to construct a new sanctuary.

In early Sumer the ruler and the chief priests shared responsibility for governing the city. But a gradual separation of palace from temple took place, and at times conflicts developed between them. The temple owned about a third of the land around Ur, part of which provided food for priests and temple employees. The priests allotted some temple property to farmers and leased some to tenants, who paid a portion of their harvest as dues, or *tithes.* Most land under secular control was probably the property of the ruler, but individuals owned their own houses, fields, and gardens. The disparity of ownership reflected social status. A high government official might possess estates of as much as 500 acres, while a simple builder owned perhaps 5 acres. Apart from slaves, Sumerians of all classes could buy, sell, exchange, or rent privately owned houses, property, and livestock.

Private citizens constructed and manufactured both for the state and for one another. From Ur's earliest days its citizens had exported their manufactured products both overland and by sea. The state organized most foreign trade, but occasionally private contractors received licenses to export goods. In turn, the Sumerians imported stone for temple construction, metals, tools, wood, incense, and jewels.

The population of a city such as Ur was diverse, consisting of nobles, their clients, commoners, and slaves. The king and his family, the high priests, and the chief officials in the court comprised the nobility. Below them were clients or vassals, whose service to the nobility was repaid by the right to farm small plots of land. Such services included working for the temples, on farms, and in workshops. Temples employed women to do their spinning and weaving. At Lagash approximately one-sixth of the farmland was in the hands of the priests, who rented half of it to peasants and hired workers to farm the rest. Commoners generally owned their own land, though large family groups controlled it.

In ancient societies slavery typically developed as a result of military conquest. Most slaves were therefore

Headdress of Queen Shub-ad of Sumeria modeled over a face reconstructed from a female skull. The hairstyle is patterned after later terracotta paintings. The headdress includes gold ribbons and a wreath.

prisoners of war or kidnapped foreigners, although some were people who had sold themselves or their children into slavery to repay debts. Owners could beat or brand their slaves, but slaves who worked hard might earn profits and in some cases purchase their freedom. They could marry free persons; the offspring of such marriages were free. Few slaves toiled in agriculture; most were artisans, domestic servants, or concubines. Temple slaves were often women whose responsibilities probably included spinning, weaving, and grinding flour. Mesopotamia was not economically dependent on slave labor.

Much social and economic activity involved women as well as men. Sumerian women could buy and sell property, but over the ensuing centuries the lot of women in Mesopotamia slowly declined as the patriarchal household became dominant. Within the household women continued to exercise authority over children and servants, but men were the masters, both of the household in general and the state. At the lower end of the scale, enslaved women served as textile workers, domestic servants, cooks, and concubines, while among the upper classes a retinue of elaborately attired court ladies surrounded the ruler and his wife. The ruler's wife played an important part in public life; in cities where the principal deity was a goddess, the queen often took charge of temple affairs.

Mesopotamian Religion

Religion permeated Sumerian civic life. Sumerians regarded heaven and earth, the sun and the moon, and natural phenomena such as lightning and storms as manifestations of deities. The principal holidays marked the change of the seasons. The chief annual event was the New Year, which occurred with the arrival of spring. The worship of the Great Mother, which evolved out of the Neolithic cult of the Great Goddess, celebrated the earth's abundance, and the sterility of the winter was attributed to the death of her partner, Dumuzi (Tammuz). Worshippers mourned his disappearance as the 11-day New Year festival began. At the festival's culmination, they celebrated his resurrection together with the sacred marriage of god and goddess, renewed each spring as a symbol of hope.

The Mesopotamians received little comfort from their religion. Life was harsh and posed a continuous struggle against the natural disasters of drought and flood. If inhabitants preferred it to the afterlife, it was because their religion offered only darkness and dust after death, even for kings. Mesopotamian religion advanced the notion that the gods, depicted in human form, were demanding and that people were servants to them. As in many religious traditions, failure to obey the gods' wishes was thought to bring punishment. In addition to the four creator gods—of the sky, the moving force of nature, earth, and water—were 50 "great gods" and innumerable lesser deities and demons. The appeal of Mesopotamian religion was in the possibility of obtaining the assistance of the gods, particularly Enlil, for help in the travails of this life.

The Sumerian poem *The Epic of Gilgamesh* illustrated the Mesopotamians' grim vision of life. Gilgamesh ruled the city of Uruk around 2600 B.C. Legends grew up around his name, and these oral traditions were eventually recorded to become the world's first epic poem. Written in Sumerian about 2000 B.C., it was inscribed afterward on clay tablets in their own languages by the Babylonians, the Hittites, and others in western Asia. Although the general vision of *The Epic of Gilgamesh* is harsh and pessimistic, the early scenes, which chronicle the exploits of Gilgamesh and his friend Enkidu, express hope. When Enkidu perishes, Gilgamesh sets out to find a way to avoid death. When his quest fails, he returns home to record his adventure on a stone and by that means finds immortality. With Gilgamesh's assistance, Enkidu provides an account of the underworld, affirming the Mesopotamian belief in a shadowy, unappealing life after death. The existence of similar tales among other peoples, including the Hebrews and the inhabitants of Asia Minor and the Pacific islands, underscores the common human interest in questions of divine punishment, death, and immortality.

The story of the flood recounted in the epic has similarities with the later version in the biblical Book of Genesis, although the tone of the scriptural account differs. Moral disapproval motivates the God of the Hebrews, whereas the Sumerian gods apparently send the flood to punish mortals for making too much noise and keeping the gods awake. Nevertheless, like Noah in the Hebrew account, Utnapishtim, one of the epic's heroes, escaped drowning by sailing the waters of death in an ark and later recounted his adventure to Gilgamesh. An earlier Mesopotamian epic titled *When the Gods Were Men,* from which the author of the *Epic of Gilgamesh* may have borrowed, recounted a similar story. The recurrence of such myths illustrates the cultural continuity that characterized Mesopotamian civilization.

Akkadian and Babylonian Culture

Between approximately 2370 and 2130 B.C. Mesopotamia fell under the rule of King Sargon I and his descendants; his capital city of Akkad (or Agade) gives the period its name. The Akkadians had originally come from the fringes of the Arabian desert. Their new home base was to the north of the principal Sumerian cities, and their conquest and unification of Mesopotamia had a lasting effect on its political and cultural life. They introduced a new language, of the Semitic family, which includes Hebrew, Arabic, and Aramaic. At the same time, the Akkadians preserved some aspects of Sumerian culture, including cuneiform.

Whereas Sumerian monarchs had ruled large parts of Mesopotamia, Sargon was the first to create a unified kingdom throughout the region. This he accomplished by the judicious combination of military force and the establishment of a central administration. Semitic officials from Akkad served as governors throughout the kingdom, their authority reinforced by military garrisons in the subject cities. Sargon extended his rule westward into northern Syria and the Lebanon mountains (important as a source of cedar), making him the first western imperialist.

Either Sargon or his successor destroyed the Syrian city-state of Ebla, first rediscovered by archaeologists in 1964. The people of Ebla had been heavily influenced by Mesopotamian culture, as reflected in the large number of cuneiform-inscribed tablets unearthed there. Ebla's economy was primarily agricultural, with the emphasis on flax (for linen), barley, olive trees (for oil), vineyards, and sheepherding. Unlike southern Mesopotamia, where irrigation farming prevailed, adequate rainfall in northern Syria made it possible to dry-farm, relying on conservation of moisture in the soil without the use of irrigation. Ebla lay astride the trade routes between Anatolia and the lowland plains of Syria, enabling it to amass impressive quantities of gold, silver, and bronze. Gold and silver, in fact, served as means of exchange, much as coinage later would. Ebla's contact with Mesopotamia was not entirely peaceful, for it engaged in a bitter economic and political rivalry with the Babylonian city-state of Mari on the banks of the Euphrates.

In the reign of Sargon's grandson, Naram-Sin (c. 2250 B.C.), rulers of individual cities were called "slaves of the king," who himself assumed the title of King of the Four Quarters of the Universe. To reinforce his authority Naram-Sin, one of the great temple builders in Mesopotamian history, demanded that he be worshiped as a god. His empire extended from Armenia south to the Persian Gulf and the Red Sea and as far west as the Mediterranean coast. Traditionally, Akkadian rule ended

A Mesopotamian Account of Creation

The Sumerian poem The Epic of Gilgamesh *circulated widely in Mesopotamia in a variety of versions and languages. This is how it begins:*

O Gilgamesh, lord of Kullab, great is thy praise. This was the man to whom all things were known; this was the king who knew the countries of the world. He was wise, he saw mysteries and knew secret things, he brought us a tale of the days before the flood. He went on a long journey, was weary, worn-out with labor, and returning engraved on a stone the whole story.

When the gods created Gilgamesh they gave him a perfect body. Shamash the glorious sun endowed him with beauty, Adad the god of the storm endowed him with courage, the great gods made his beauty perfect, surpassing all others. Two-thirds they made him god and one-third man.

In Uruk he built walls, a great rampart, and the temple of blessed Eanna for the god of the firmament Anu, and for Ishtar the goddess of love. Look at it still today: the outer wall where the cornice runs, it shines with the brilliance of copper; and the inner wall, it has no equal. Touch the threshold, it is ancient. Approach Eanna the dwelling of Ishtar, our lady of love and war, the like of which no latter-day king, no man alive can equal. Climb upon the wall of Uruk; walk along it, I say; regard the foundation terrace and examine the masonry: is it not burnt brick and good? The seven sages laid the foundations.

Source: The Epic of Gilgamesh, trans. N. K. Sanders (Harmondsworth, England: Penguin Books, 1960), p. 59.

violently at the hands of the Guti, nomadic invaders from Iran, around 2130, but a more significant reason for the Akkadians' fall may have been a drought that lasted three centuries, according to recent archaeological studies of soil from this period.

Hammurabi, "King of Justice"

In the early eighteenth century B.C. Mesopotamia was once again unified, this time under another Semitic group, the Amorites. Their famous king, Hammurabi (c. 1792–1750 B.C.), having defeated the Assyrians and their allies, was determined to unify his Sumerian and Semitic subjects, in part by codifying the legal decisions rendered during his reign. Law was important to all peoples of western Asia and Egypt, who saw it as a means of bringing order out of chaos; as such, it was basic to religion as well as government. Hammurabi's achievement, though not a true code but rather a collection of case laws, has nevertheless received acclaim as one of the earliest attempts to formulate a legal code; the first examples date from around 2100 B.C. Hammurabi, who formally pronounced the code, had copies inscribed on stone slabs set up in temples to attest to the gods' approval. The code regulated the rights and obligations of the three Amorite classes—free people, state dependents, and slaves. The penalties, which differed according to social status, included fines, corporal punishment, mutilation, and execution; imprisonment and forced labor were not specified.

This portrait of an Akkadian king is thought to be of Sargon himself.

Unlike some earlier Mesopotamian laws, Hammurabi's code did not recognize the blood feud or private vengeance, but as in most early legal systems, its provisions were harsh. A surgeon whose patient died during a major operation had a hand cut off, and architects whose faulty work caused a building to collapse and kill a client were executed. The operative principle was normally "an eye for an eye," or the close equivalence between a crime and its punishment. Female adulterers faced capital punishment, though a husband had the power to pardon his wife. Incest could be punished by death or exile. A son who struck his father could have his hand amputated (the Old Testament later incorporated a similar law). Perjurers in capital cases, rapists, many thieves, adulterators of beer, and people who avoided mandatory state service also faced death, as did extravagant wives.

The code spelled out the rights of husbands and wives, of parents and children, and of masters and workers. Men were not only allowed to practice polygamy but were also permitted to have mistresses, and they had the power to sell their wives and children into slavery. A husband could divorce his wife at will, provided that he returned the dowry and paid child support if she had fulfilled her spousal responsibilities; if not, she received nothing. A wife could obtain a divorce only by demonstrating cruelty or neglect; if she sued and lost, she faced capital punishment. Women did, however, retain the right to own property and enter into contracts.

Fathers had absolute control over their children until the latter married. Parents arranged marriages and sealed them by a contract, sometimes while the betrothed children were very young; in such cases, the marriage took place but the couple lived in the home of the groom's or

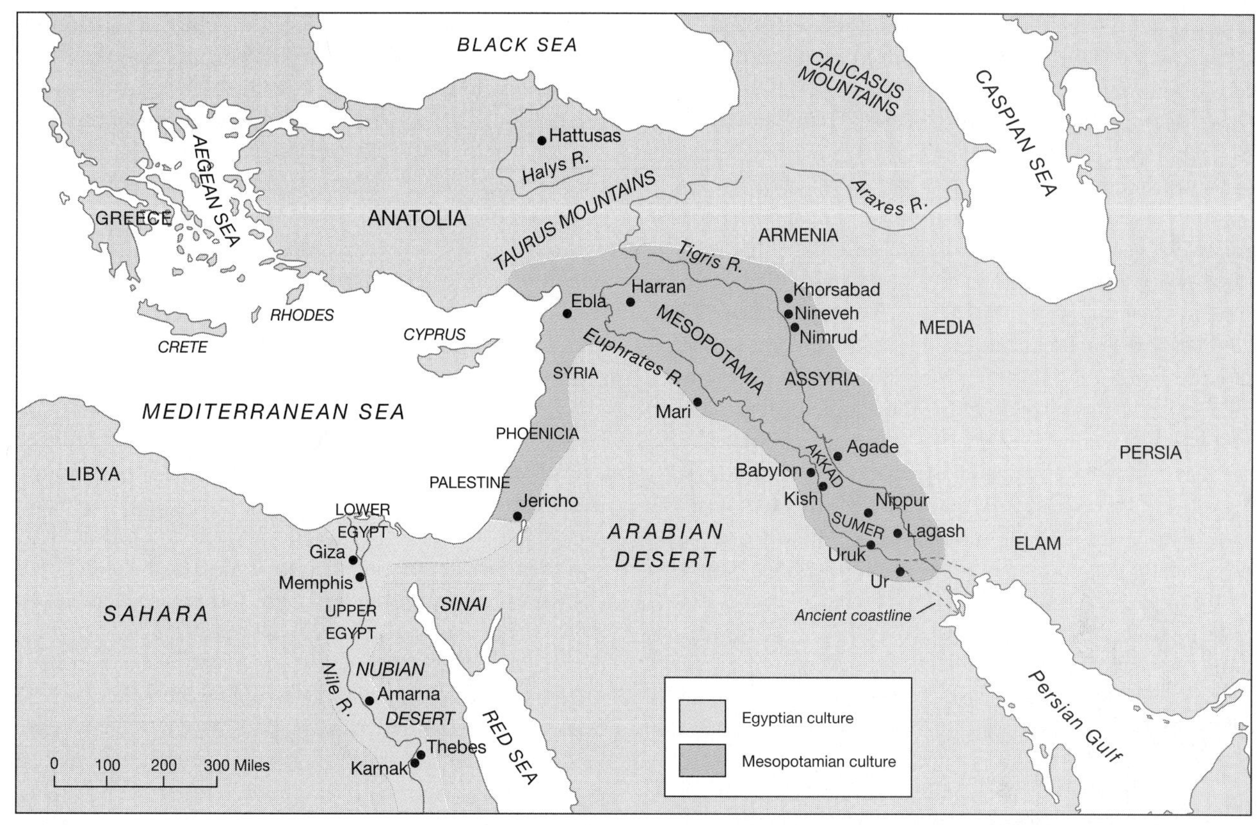

MAP 1.1 WESTERN ASIA AND EGYPT

the bride's parents until they were old enough to live on their own. Fathers could compel their daughters to become priestesses or concubines. The importance of property was underscored by a provision that prohibited a father from disinheriting his son unless the latter had twice committed major offenses.

The code also dealt with slavery. Slaves could own property, including other slaves, and run businesses for their masters. Branding distinguished slaves; removing the mark was an offense. Masters had the right to select spouses for their slaves. The spouses could be free persons, and children of half-free, half-slave marriages were born free. Slaves could purchase their freedom by accumulating or borrowing the manumission fee; the temples loaned sums for this purpose.

The code's legal procedures reveal a concern for justice, however harsh the penalties may have been. Because the state did not initiate prosecutions, private parties had to file complaints against alleged aggressors. The judge's verdict was final, and not even he could alter it without being fined and removed from the bench. A judge who had difficulty deciding a case could resort to trial by ordeal, according to which the accused was thrown into a body of water: a guilty person was presumed to float; an innocent one would sink. In addition to the code's concern for meting out justice, it was intended as a deterrent to offensive acts. By making these principles public, Hammurabi hoped to win repute as the "king of justice." Among those influenced by his code were the Hebrews, who embodied their legal principles in the Bible.

The Beginnings of Egyptian Civilization

Egypt is a desert country, most of which can support only a pastoral economy. That it served as a breadbasket for the ancient world is owing to the 4,000-mile-long Nile River, which flows north from central Africa and provides a fertile delta. Ancient Egypt was divided into two parts. Lower or northern Egypt occupied approximately 150 miles of broad, flat land in the Nile delta, from which the rest of the Mediterranean region was easily accessible. Lower Egypt had twice as much land as

Upper Egypt, which, upriver, was more remote from the outside world. Upper Egypt comprised a narrow band of fertile soil that ran between high cliffs and desert on either side of the Nile for approximately 525 miles.

The sparseness of rain in both regions meant that agriculture was possible only through extensive irrigation systems and by taking advantage of the annual flooding of the river. Here, as in Mesopotamia, it was possible to produce an agricultural surplus on river alluvium (silt) continually deposited by annual floods. Water from the Nile could supply arid areas throughout the year, and the Nile, like the Tigris and the Euphrates, also served as a vital avenue of transport, especially for the supply of food, fuel, and building materials. Deserts separated the Nile valley from other states, so outside aggressors seldom menaced Egypt. This allowed it to develop a homogeneous civilization of its own. Geographic factors profoundly affected political and economic life in Egypt, as in Mesopotamia.

Some rock carvings on the cliffs of the Nile valley date back to around 6000 B.C. Their depictions of hunters and animals, weapons, and traps illustrate the conditions of life before the development of civilization. As Neolithic culture began, drawings of cattle and boats appeared, but at this early period the small village communities were subject to damage caused by the floodwaters of the Nile. Starting around 4000 B.C., the Egyptians built larger villages on higher ground out of reach of the flooding. The cooperative efforts of neighboring communities in constructing canals and dikes to channel the waters seem to have been the original stimulus for the growth of organized districts.

As the villages joined together, the regions began to unite into two main kingdoms, Upper and Lower Egypt, the "Two Lands," and shortly before 3000 B.C. they united under a single ruler. An Egyptian priest, Manetho, the author of a history of Egypt (c. 280 B.C.), divided the vast span of Egyptian history into 31 dynasties, or periods of rule by members of a royal family. Today scholars group that history into five periods, each of roughly 500 years' duration: the Early Dynastic Period (c. 2925–c. 2575 B.C.), the Old Kingdom (c. 2575–c. 2130 B.C.), the Middle Kingdom (1938–1600 B.C.), the New Kingdom (c. 1540–1075 B.C.), and the Late Period (1075–525 B.C.), after which the Persian Empire absorbed Egypt. Times of instability separated these dynastic periods.

Unification: The Age of the Pyramids

The Old Kingdom was an age of prosperity and innovation. The Egyptians employed new technical skills to construct the massive religious and funerary monuments for which their culture is renowned. The central authority of the divine ruler, or pharaoh, maintained the unity of the state while providing a religious focus and the development of a large bureaucracy of priests and officials. Egyptians of the Old Kingdom undoubtedly had trading contacts with the Syrians and other peoples of western Asia, but these appear to have had little effect on their culture; scant evidence exists of contacts with Mesopotamia, except for an early resemblance between the Mesopotamian ziggurat and the Egyptian pyramid.

Throughout the Old Kingdom a strong pharaoh was both the symbol of and the principal reason for national unity; some of Egypt's earliest pharaohs had pyramids constructed to serve as their tombs and as sites of worship and devotion. The pharaoh Zoser commissioned the architect Imhotep to build the first pyramid during the Third Dynasty (before 2575 B.C.) as Zoser's tomb and memorial. Imhotep himself is the first architect known to history and in later ages was regarded as a god. Zoser's successors continued the tradition of building pyramids for their tombs. The great pyramid of Khufu at Giza (c. 2530 B.C.), which rises to a height of nearly 500 feet, was constructed of more than 2 million limestone blocks weighing as much as 30,000 pounds apiece. To get such stones into place the Egyptians constructed massive ramps, the height of which had to be raised as the builders progressed; the ramps were constructed of quarry debris or mud brick. Workers, who were not slaves but free Egyptians toiling for the gods, pulled blocks of stone up the ramps on sledges that rolled over timber. When a pyramid was completed, they removed the ramps, leaving viewers to marvel at the structure rising majestically from the desert floor. To transport large blocks of basalt for monuments at Giza and Saqqara, the Egyptians constructed the world's oldest paved road, which extended 8 miles from the quarry to the Nile.

Gods and Priests: Traditional Egyptian Religion

The pharaoh's person was regarded as divine, his authority as equal to that of any other deity. The priests who served the pharaoh regarded themselves as the preservers of traditional religious doctrines, the most fundamental of which was the concept of divine kingship. By the time of the New Kingdom, the priests, whose office was hereditary, would become a separate caste. Each temple had a priestly hierarchy responsible for undertaking a wide variety of tasks, ranging from menial chores to religious rites. Priestesses, however, were not professionals but wives of the nobility who assisted in some of the rituals. Some priests wore special clothing that reflected their status. Religion was woven into the very fabric of Egyp-

The Great Pyramids at Giza were constructed between 2650 and 2530 B.C.

tian political and social life, and society reflected the Egyptian view of creation. Just as the sun god, Amon, had created the universe by bringing order to the primeval chaos, so the pharaoh ruled the physical world.

Traditional Egyptian religious beliefs involved a host of deities, whose priests jealously guarded their rights and privileges. At the time of Egypt's unification, local guardian-deities were merged into Re (or Ra), the sun god, who sailed the skies in his boat by day and combated the forces of darkness in the underworld by night. Because of the political importance of Thebes (the capital beginning about 1938 B.C.), this god absorbed the Theban deity Amon, associated with the state's welfare, and became known as Amon-Re.

The worship of Osiris, god of the Nile, came to offer the hope of immortality to the masses. The cult of the afterlife involved elaborate funeral rituals at which the dead would be judged and move on to the next life. Each person, it was thought, would be judged by Osiris, who would assess the good and evil that had been done in life and then determine whether the person deserved punishment or admittance to the realm of bliss. Texts were written in hieroglyphics (pictorial symbols) on writing material made from the papyrus plant and placed in the

WESTERN ASIA AND EGYPT

Mesopotamia	Egypt	Other lands
Early Sumerians (c. 4000–c. 2370 B.C.)	Early Dynastic Period (c. 2925–2575 B.C.)	
• Gilgamesh (c. 2600 B.C.)	Old Kingdom (c. 2575–2130 B.C.)	
Akkadians (c. 2370–c. 1950 B.C.)	• Age of the pyramids	Hittites settle in Anatolia (c. 2000 B.C.)
Babylonians (Amorites, c. 1950–c. 1600 B.C.)	Middle Kingdom (1938–c. 1600 B.C.)	
• Hammurabi (c. 1792–1750 B.C.)		Semites settle in Palestine (2000–1700 B.C.)
	Hyksos invasion (early 1600s B.C.)	
	New Kingdom (c. 1540–1075 B.C.)	
	• Hatshepsut (c. 1503–1482 B.C.)	
	• Akhenaton (1353-c. 1332 B.C.)	
Assyrians (c. 1300–612 B.C.)	• Ramses II (1279–1213 B.C.)	Exodus of Hebrews from Egypt (before 1200 B.C.)
	Invasion of the Sea Peoples (1100s B.C.)	Collapse of Hittite empire (c. 1190 B.C.)
	Late Period (1075–525 B.C.)	
		David rules Palestine (c. 1000–970 B.C.)
		Assyrians conquer Israel (722 B.C.)
Chaldeans (612–539 B.C.)		
• Nebuchadnezzar (604–562 B.C.)		Fall of Judah (586 B.C.)
Cyrus the Great conquers Babylon (539 B.C.)	Persians conquer Egypt (525 B.C.)	Cyrus the Great (559–529 B.C.) rules Persia

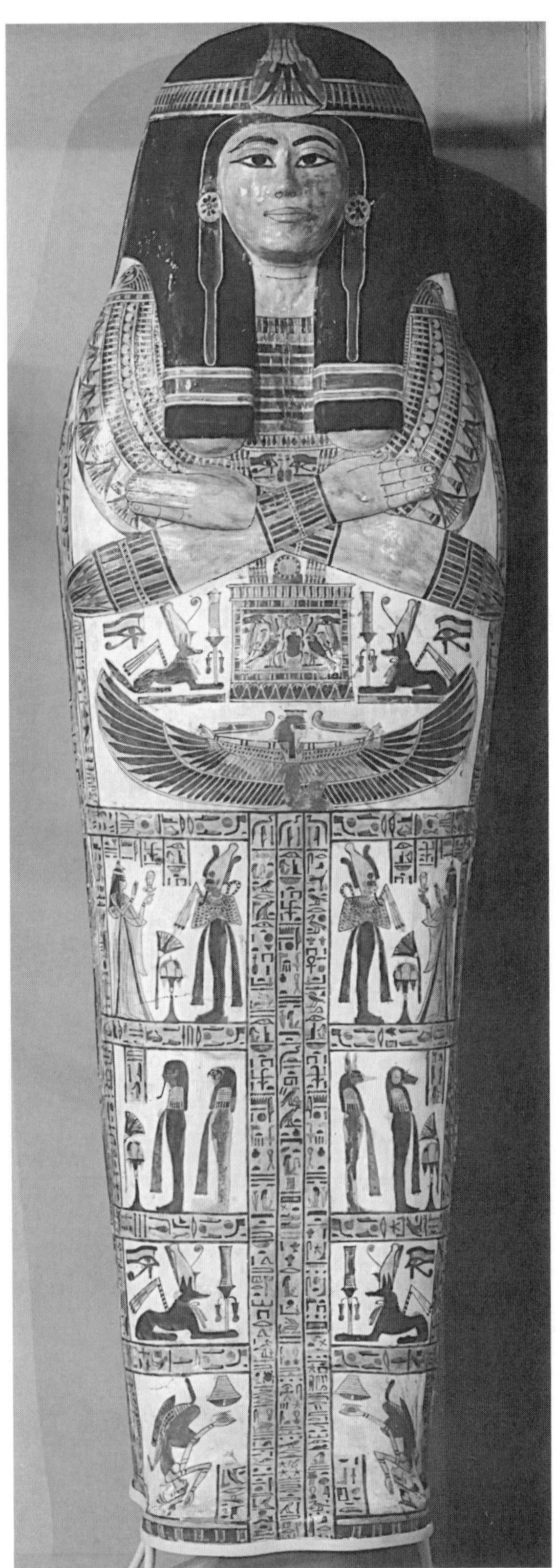

Outer coffin of Henettawy, Thebes.

graves to assist the deceased in the examinations that marked their entrance into the afterlife; collectively these are known as *The Book of the Dead.* The following excerpt suggests the standards of ethical and social behavior to which Egyptians were supposed to aspire:

> **I have not done evil to mankind. I have not oppressed the members of my family, I have not wrought evil in the place of right and truth. . . . I have not brought forward my name for exaltation to honors. I have not ill-treated servants. . . . I have not defrauded the oppressed one of his property. . . . I have made no man to suffer hunger. . . . I have done no murder. . . . I have not committed fornication. . . . I have not encroached upon the fields of others. . . . I have not caught fish with [bait made of] fish of their kind. . . . I am pure.[1]**

Osiris, the god who presided over funeral rituals, was the symbol of death and rebirth. The worship of Osiris; his wife Isis, goddess of the fertile earth; and their son Horus came to symbolize a sense of the afterlife beyond simple material survival. It represents the closest that Egyptian religion came to the notion of a true spiritual state. According to one common belief, Osiris was killed by his evil brother, Seth, who cut the corpse into pieces; Isis gathered them up, wrapped them in linen, and brought Osiris back to life. A different Horus, the sky god, eventually defeated Seth. This Horus was typically depicted as a hawk, the form in which pharaohs were believed to ascend to heaven after they died. The Egyptians worshiped many other divinities and spirits of nature, who were responsible for all aspects of existence. The mythology and ritual they inspired affected the lives of all Egyptians on a daily basis. Several animals, such as the jackal and the cat, had religious importance; their mummified remains have been found at a number of sanctuaries.

The differences in burial rites between the various classes reflected their social status. Even a minor royal official would spend much of his life and income preparing an elaborate tomb for himself in which he would be buried with treasures, and the burials of the ruling family became legendary for their sumptuousness. Corpses were mummified because Egyptians believed that the *ka,* the spirit of life in each person, periodically returned to the body. Yet the corpse of a poor Egyptian was typically wrapped in a piece of linen and left in a cave or a pit or even on the open sand of the desert, with only a staff and a pair of sandals for the journey to the next world. Beginning in the Middle Kingdom, some members of the lower classes had their corpses mummified. The concept of a future life was the only shared experience that united nobles, peasants, and slaves, since the Egyptian obsession with immortality offered the hope of a good life after death to all Egyptians, regardless of status.

Egypt in the Middle Kingdom: Consolidation, Expansion, and Decline

The ordered world of the Old Kingdom ended around 2130 B.C. as a result of several factors, notably rivalries among the provincial nobility, who now claimed offices by hereditary right, and economic strain caused by the pharaoh's exorbitant building projects and by crop failures. By challenging the unique status of the pharaohs, the courtiers provoked conflicts that led to the collapse of the monarchy. In the absence of a central authority, provincial governors attempted to seize power and maintain their regional independence, and not until 1938 B.C., when Mentuhotep conquered Lower Egypt and reunited the country, did peace return. The new royal capital was situated at Thebes.

The principal rulers of the Twelfth Dynasty maintained Theban domination of Egypt by brute force. Their domestic achievements included a massive drainage project that reclaimed 27,000 acres of arable land south of Memphis. They also developed an aggressive foreign policy. Egyptians occupied part of gold-rich

The Technique of Mummification

Because Egyptian literature provides little information about the technique of mummification, we have to rely on ancient travelers' accounts. The following one is by the Greek historian Herodotus, who visited Egypt around 450 B.C. Modern research has confirmed the accuracy of his information.

There are a set of men in Egypt who practice the art of embalming, and make it their proper business. These persons, when a body is brought to them, show the bearers various models of corpses, made in wood, and painted so as to resemble nature. The most perfect is said to be after the manner of him whom I do not think it religious to name in connection with such a matter; the second sort is inferior to the first, and less costly; the third is the cheapest of all. All this the embalmers explain, and then ask in which way it is wished that the corpse should be prepared. The bearers tell them, and having concluded their bargain, take their departure, while the embalmers, left to themselves, proceed to their task. The mode of embalming, according to the most perfect process, is the following: they take first a crooked piece of iron, and with it draw out the brain through the nostrils, thus getting rid of a portion, while the skull is cleared of the rest by rinsing with drugs; next they make a cut along the flank with a sharp Ethiopian stone, and take out the whole contents of the abdomen, which they then cleanse, washing it thoroughly with palm wine, and again frequently with an infusion of pounded aromatics. After this they fill the cavity with the purest bruised myrrh, with cassia, and every other sort of spicery except frankincense, and sew up the opening. Then the body is placed in natron for seventy days, and covered entirely over. After the expiration of that space of time, which must not be exceeded, the body is washed, and wrapped round, from head to foot, with bandages of fine linen cloth, smeared over with gum, which is used generally by the Egyptians in the place of glue, and in this state it is given back to the relations, who enclose it in a wooden case which they have had made for the purpose, shaped into the figure of a man. Then fastening the case, they place it in a sepulchral chamber, upright against the wall. Such is the most costly way of embalming the dead.

Source: Herodotus, *The Histories,* vol. 2, trans. G. Rawlinson (New York: Library of Living Classics, 1928), pp. 85–86.

The Sphinx at Giza was commissioned by the pharaoh Chefren to guard his tomb.

Nubia, south of Egypt, and the pharaoh Sesostris III led a military expedition into Palestine, opening a fresh sphere of influence and new commercial frontiers. Trade links were probably established at this time with the Minoans of Crete, and evidence appears of renewed contact with Mesopotamia, perhaps through Syrian mediation. Although Egyptian art and culture remained relatively untouched by foreign influence, the Egyptians were eager to appropriate the wealth of their neighbors by trade or conquest. By the late nineteenth century B.C., Egypt was at a peak of prosperity that made it the envy of its neighbors and lured Nubian and Semitic immigrants.

The successes of the Middle Kingdom pharaohs were followed by a sharp decline in royal authority occasioned by a series of short reigns and weak rulers. Nubia threw off Egyptian rule, but a worse catastrophe occurred after 1700 B.C., when the Hyksos, a nomadic or pastoral people from western Asia with horses and war chariots, invaded the country. Fortunately for the Egyptians, the Hyksos were impressed by their civilization and adopted Egyptian religious beliefs and customs. Our knowledge of the period of the Hyksos' invasion and occupation is sketchy, partly because the invaders left little written evidence and partly because the Egyptians of the New Kingdom were reluctant or unable to document life under occupation by foreigners.

For most of the seventeenth century B.C. the Hyksos apparently controlled Palestine and Syria as well as Egypt. In contrast to the Egyptians, with their desire to maintain a closed society, the Hyksos seem to have encouraged immigration. It was possibly under Hyksos rule that Hebrew immigrants, preceded by Joseph, arrived in Egypt and prospered there. Not until the sixteenth century B.C. were the Hyksos driven out of Egypt and back to Palestine by the king of Thebes and his brother Ahmose, founder of the Eighteenth Dynasty.

The New Kingdom: Imperial Conquest and Religious Reform

The early pharaohs of the New Kingdom, which began with the Eighteenth Dynasty around 1540 B.C., involved Egypt internationally for the first time on a broad scale. Among the most remarkable of them was Queen Hatshepsut (c. 1503–1482 B.C.), who initially wielded power as regent to her stepson, the future Thutmose III, and then proclaimed herself pharaoh with the support of the priests of Amon. Although in general Egyptian society was male-oriented, it was by no means unusual for a pharaoh's mother to take charge of government during his minority or while he was away at war. Indeed, the custom whereby the pharaoh generally married his sister or half sister strengthened such family connections, and Egyptian religion, with its many gods and goddesses, meant that Egyptians were accustomed to respect female figures. Women were sometimes active in government at the local level too.

Hatshepsut was an unusual case. Taking the title of king, she ruled for over 20 years and left as her principal legacy a massive temple. A funerary monument for herself and her father, Thutmose I, the temple at Deir el-Bahri was designed by one of the greatest figures in Egyptian art, the architect Sen-Mut. It combined opulence with attention to detail; decorating its facade were colossal statues of Hatshepsut, which her stepson Thutmose III, who loathed her, destroyed when he became pharaoh.

An aggressive ruler, Thutmose III led campaigns in western Asia and Nubia. By the end of his reign Palestine and Syria as far as the Euphrates were under Egyptian control, and a huge temple complex had been constructed in Nubia near Napata. Egyptian garrisons controlled the conquered territories, and inspectors supervised the shipping of raw materials and manufactured objects back to Egypt.

The effects of expansion on the economy were considerable. During the Old and Middle Kingdoms, manufacturing and foreign trade had played a relatively small part in social development. In part, this had resulted from the lack of a large commercial class whose activity might have threatened the hereditary nobility. The Egyptians' agricultural self-sufficiency, too, eliminated the need to look elsewhere for basic provisions. With their new possessions throughout western Asia, however, they operated on a wider economic scale. The New Kingdom's elite, with its opulent lifestyle, purchased the foreign luxury goods that were traded for Egyptian products, including stone vessels, pottery, colored glass, and fine linens. Egyptian artisans were especially noted for their production of luxury items, including jewelry, carved ivory, enamel work, pearl inlay, perfumed oils, ointments, and cosmetics, such as hair dyes, rouge, and eye shadow.

The pharaoh Amenhotep IV (1353–c. 1332 B.C.), concerned with the reform of political and religious institutions, broke the pattern of consolidation and expansion. In place of the innumerable traditional deities, he encouraged the worship of a single one, the sun god Aton. In the words of the *Hymn to Aton:*

> ***O sole god, like whom there is no other!***
> ***Thou didst create the world according to thy desire,***
> ***Whilst thou wert alone.***

Amenhotep took the name of Akhenaton, "servant of Aton." To implement his revolutionary changes and reduce the power of the priests at the royal court of Thebes, he transferred the capital to Amarna, which he called Akhetaton. Akhenaton's attempt to encourage belief in a single deity (without necessarily denying the existence of other, lesser gods) is reflected in the culture of the Amarna period. The monumentality and idealized features of traditional art were replaced by a new lightness, in which for the first time detailed physical features were shown. The stone reliefs depicting Akhenaton, his wife Nefertiti, and their children are remarkably different from the formalized style of previous eras.

Nefertiti, "Lady of the Two Lands"

Few women of antiquity were more intriguing, influential, and ultimately mysterious than Nefertiti. Egyptologists have discovered almost nothing about her background other than that she was of nonroyal birth. Her parents were probably members of the court circle, and she may have been a cousin of Amenhotep IV, whose principal wife she became. During the early years of the reign, when the capital was still at Thebes, court artists depicted her twice as often as her husband, a remarkable tribute that indicated unusual political prominence. Amenhotep thought highly of her, calling her "sweet of love" and "possessed of charm." She was a woman of striking physical beauty, as attested to by her portraits and by her husband's official recognition of her as the "exquisite beauty of the sun-disk." Indeed, her name itself means "a beautiful woman has come."

Much of what we know about Nefertiti is derived from paintings, sculpture, and inscriptions. She was already very powerful before the royal court established its new capital at Amarna, and she may have been the inspiration behind the religious revolution for which Akhenaton is remembered. Yet despite her undoubted political influence, she is never mentioned in the diplomatic correspondence of the reign.

The move to Amarna signaled not only a new religion but also a higher status for Nefertiti. During the Theban years she had often been portrayed alone, but even then her rising fortunes were reflected in the colossal statues of her and Amenhotep, unique in Egyptian art apart from reigning female pharaohs such as Hatshepsut. At Amarna the court artists habitually depicted her as the constant companion and virtual equal of Akhenaton. Each is shown wearing a royal crown, implying that Nefertiti was virtually a coruler. Indeed, Akhenaton seems to have made a special point of having artists emphasize her regal status. On one occasion she is shown in the stance of a warrior-king, astride a fallen foe, ready to slay him with a single blow. Most remarkably, in one temple painting the name of Aton is written back to front in her presence, symbolically underscoring her eminence.

Aton, the One God

This extract from the Hymn to Aton *composed by Akhenaton illustrates the pharaoh's belief in a single divine force.*

Thou appearest beautifully on the horizon of heaven,
Thou living Aton, the beginning of life!
When thou art arisen on the eastern horizon,
Thou has filled every land with thy beauty.
Thou art gracious, great, glistening, and high over every land;
Thy rays encompass the lands to the limit of all that thou hast made;
If thou art Re, thou reachest to the end of them;
Thou subduest them for thy beloved son.
Though thou art in their faces, no one knows thy going.
When thou settest in the western horizon,
The land is in darkness, in the manner of death.
They sleep in a room, with heads wrapped up,
Nor sees one eye the other.
All their goods which are under their heads might be stolen,
But they would not perceive it.
Every lion is come forth from his den;
All creeping things, they sting.
Darkness is a shroud, and the earth is in stillness,
For he who made them rests in his horizon.
At daybreak, when thou arisest on the horizon,
When thou shinest as the Aton by day,
Thou drivest away the darkness and givest thy rays.
The Two Lands are in festivity every day,
Awake and standing upon their feet,
For thou hast raised them up.
Washing their bodies, taking their clothing.
Their arms are raised in praise at thy appearance.
All the world, they do their work. . . .

Source: J. B. Pritchard, ed., *Ancient New Eastern Texts Relating to the Old Testament,* trans. J. Wilson (Princeton, N.J.: Princeton University Press, 1969), p. 370.

At Amarna, Nefertiti played a major role in the worship of Aton, as reflected by her adoption of the additional name of Nefernefruaton, "beautiful are the beauties of Aton." She refused to limit herself to the traditional role of women in an Egyptian temple—ringing the sistrum, a metal rattle—but instead performed the same rites as her husband; in most respects their priestly roles were interchangeable. Courtiers responded by invoking her name with those of Aton and Akhenaton in their prayers. Although she apparently never held the office of "God's wife," she wore the costume associated with it (a clinging robe tied with a red sash) and carried out its duties, namely, the supervision of the Mansion of the Ben-Ben, a college of choristers and instrumentalists who provided music for religious services. She also had a priestly duty to maintain Aton "in a state of perpetual arousal"; since Aton was abstract, she could do this only by alluring his son (and her husband), Akhenaton, by her erotic attire, which often consisted of open coat dresses made of transparent fabric.[2]

Apart from her religious functions, we have only tantalizing glimpses of Nefertiti's activities. She drove a chariot, probably to transport herself between royal palaces, and she dispensed gold collars to worthy persons, making them "People of Gold." Late in their reign, she and Akhenaton presided over an international pageant at which dazzling tribute was presented to the royal couple: ivory, gold, monkeys, leopards, and shields from Nubia and the Sudan; chariots, horses, weapons, and an antelope from Syria; ostrich eggs and feathers from Libya; incense, sandalwood, and spices from the Hittites. This was the last occasion on which artists depicted Nefertiti, Akhenaton, and their six daughters together; at least one and possibly three of the children died in the next two years, perhaps victims of a plague.

This bust of Nefertiti was rendered by an artist at Amarna when she was in her mid-twenties.

Nefertiti's last years are shrouded in mystery. Not even the date of her death is known. Based on fragmentary evidence, three principal versions of Nefertiti's final days have been suggested. One of these has her adopting the names and customs of a male pharaoh and ruling as a coregent with her husband. An alternative theory posits that after 1335 B.C. she took her son, Tutankhaton (the future pharaoh Tutankhamen), and established a virtual government in exile until she died some three years after her husband. More credible is the view that Nefertiti's influence waned after 1337, in part because of Akhenaton's favoritism toward another wife, Kiya, and in part because of the rising influence of Nefertiti's own daughter, Meritaton, whose husband, Smenkhkare, was appointed coregent with Akhenaton at the age of 14. If Nefertiti outlived Akhenaton, her influence over Tutankhaton probably delayed the return to the traditional religion until after her death.

The Waning Empire

Clearly, so revolutionary a change in culture and religion as that implemented by Akhenaton and Nefertiti posed a serious threat to the priests, whose interests lay in the preservation of traditional ways. After Akhenaton's death, they condemned him as a heretic, and his name was removed from the monuments of his era. His son-in-law and successor, Tutankhamen, is perhaps the most famous of all Egyptian rulers, although for reasons that have nothing to do with his religion or politics. His unopened tomb, excavated in 1922, contained the richest hoard of Egyptian artifacts ever recovered. Tutankhamen's restoration of the old religion was recorded in the temple at Karnak:

> **Then his majesty made monuments for the gods, fashioning their cult-statues of genuine fine gold from the**

highlands, building their sanctuaries anew as monuments for the ages of eternity, established with possessions forever, setting for them divine offerings as a regular daily observance, and provisioning their food-offerings upon earth. He surpassed what had been previously. . . . He inducted priests and prophets from the children of the nobles.[3]

Akhenaton's lack of interest in foreign policy had weakened Egypt's control of conquered territories. The Hittites, another imperial power in western Asia, fomented revolts in Egyptian possessions in Syria and Palestine. From approximately 1300 B.C. to the end of the New Kingdom in 1075 B.C., pharaohs involved Egypt in constant wars in which they tried, unsuccessfully, to maintain control of their imperial possessions. Ramses II (1279–1213 B.C.), perhaps best remembered for completing the magnificent temple at Karnak with its 70-foot columns, failed to conquer the Hittites, though he concluded a defensive treaty with them that left southern Syria in Egyptian hands. The splendors of Ramses' building projects notwithstanding, Egyptian might was on the wane. Shortly after 1200 B.C. a new wave of migrants, known to us only as the Peoples of the Sea, threatened Egypt. Ramses III (1187–1156 B.C.) repelled them, but only at great cost, and Egyptian imperial power continued to decline. The ever-larger building projects of the later New Kingdom seem as much attempts at restoring self-confidence as triumphal monuments.

In the last centuries of independent Egyptian history a succession of invaders attacked and occupied various parts of the country, from the Assyrians in the seventh century B.C. to Alexander the Great (331 B.C.). With its conquest by Alexander, Egypt at last became absorbed into the larger Mediterranean world.

Egyptian Society

The ruling elite in Egypt, the apex of which was the pharaoh, included the hereditary nobility and the high priests, guardians of Egypt's religious traditions. The pharaoh's power was theoretically absolute; the advisers, scribes, and others who made up the growing bureaucracy of governing officials carried out his commands. At the head of the bureaucracy was the vizier, who served as the intermediary between the pharaoh and local officials, tried important cases, appointed magistrates, entertained foreign envoys, and supervised agriculture, road and building maintenance, record keeping, the army and internal security, and tax assessment and collection. The pharaoh's family formed the center of a royal court attended by the nobility. He could demand taxes ranging up to 20 percent of annual income, which were typically paid in kind, for example, in grain.

The upper middle class consisted of scribes, priests, and other court servants. The importance of scribes, who underwent a lengthy period of education, was evident by the fact that they, unlike even the priests, were not subject to forced labor or military service. The upper middle class expanded during the New Kingdom by the addition of professional soldiers, though the officers enjoyed a status roughly equivalent to that of the nobility. Merchants, artisans, and farmers of substance comprised the lower middle class. In the early centuries the artisans worked primarily for the pharaoh and the nobility, but they also produced pottery, textiles, and glassware for the people. Because most trade was in the hands of the priesthood, the number of merchants was never great, and foreign trade in particular was a royal monopoly.

Apart from slaves, the lowest level in the social order was occupied by the agricultural laborers and the miners who extracted turquoise and copper in the Sinai. A few laborers were independent and self-supporting, but the vast majority were essentially serfs, bound for all practical purposes to the land. The government could force them to work on state building projects, though it recruited much of this labor by persuading the people of the real or imagined benefits that would accrue from pyramids, temples, irrigation canals, and the like.

The institution of slavery in Egypt began in the Middle Kingdom, when wealthy households sometimes owned as many as 50 slaves to run their estates. The use of slaves became widespread only in the New Kingdom. Most toiled on temple estates and in the mines, though some had positions in the military or in royal service. Relatively few engaged in domestic service. Their ranks were filled by prisoners of war.

Although Egyptian society was stratified, some upward mobility was possible, especially in the Middle and New Kingdoms. This was especially so for talented people whose services were required by the state. Immigrants, including dark-skinned Nubians, had ample opportunity to enhance their social status. The best-known example of social mobility is the story of Joseph, an Israelite whom his brothers sold into slavery; in Egypt, his managerial skills and ability to interpret dreams attracted the attention of the pharaoh, who made him overseer of the kingdom's food supplies.

The lot of Egyptian women was mixed. Although a handful ruled as pharaohs, women were generally excluded from the bureaucracy, and few became scribes.

Virtually all other occupations, including business, were open to them. Women had the right to own property, even to the point that wives retained control over whatever possessions had been theirs before marriage. They could engage in financial transactions, own slaves, purchase land, and witness documents, and they had to pay taxes. Polygamy was legal, but most marriages were monogamous, and wives had the same right to a divorce as their husbands. The priesthood was open to women as well as men, and Egyptian death rituals treated both sexes equally. Egyptian women enjoyed a status greater than that of their western Asian contemporaries.

In general, the state supervised the production and distribution of agricultural and manufactured products. Control of the food supply was one of the government's most important functions. It had enormous granaries and warehouses and was normally able to provide for the people when harvests were bad. From Nubia and along the Red Sea coast the Egyptians traded for ivory, incense, dwarfs, and exotic animals, and they obtained cedar from the Phoenicians. In return for such goods they exported such items as wheat, gold, and linen.

The Legacy of Egyptian Culture

The earliest Egyptian writing was in the form of hieroglyphics, or pictorial symbols, which represented individual objects or actions. As early as the Old Kingdom, the Egyptians had a system of characters for the 24 consonants, although they had no way to indicate vowels. The Frenchman Jean-François Champollion finally deciphered the Egyptian hieroglyphic script by means of a trilingual inscription, the Rosetta Stone, found in the Nile delta in the early nineteenth century. Champollion compared the three languages on the stone—hieroglyphic, the demotic script of the common Egyptian people, and ancient Greek. The Rosetta Stone is, among other things, a monument to the passing of ancient Egyptian culture. The Egyptians had ceased to use the demotic script, whereas the Greek that was largely replacing it has never fallen out of use from ancient times to the present. Similarly, the beliefs that sustained the ancient Egyptians for millennia had begun to disappear along with their language.

Living in or with easy access to the rocky upper valley of the Nile, Egyptian artists used stone to produce everything from vast temple complexes to tiny figurines. Their skill at rendering the human form influenced the Greek colonizers who moved to Egypt shortly after 700 B.C. Comparison proves instructive: When the Greeks went to Egypt, they found the Egyptians producing statues not very different from those of 2,000 years earlier. The Greeks borrowed their style and in just over 100 years adapted it to their own purposes. The Egyptians' art was primarily conditioned by the character and requirements of their religion. In addition to the images of deities, artists provided temples and shrines for religious ceremonies. Even the buildings or sculptures that commemorated the images, names, or deeds of real people generally served religious purposes. The largely undeviating style that resulted from the joint control of state and religion seems to have appealed to the Egyptians' cultural conservatism. In troubled times during the Middle Kingdom or the Late Period, with its foreign invaders, artists tended to turn back to Old Kingdom art. As late as the Roman period, architects in the Nubian city of Meroë were still building pyramids as funerary monuments.

Although the Egyptians maintained their social and political structure substantially unchanged over thousands of years, they were not immune to outside influences. Among them was the idea of writing, probably borrowed from the Sumerians; the adoption of the chariot, the horse, and long-range bows from the Hyksos; and the use of luxury items imported from Asia and Europe. Nevertheless, apart from the widespread use of slaves, the economic expansion of the New Kingdom had little social effect on one of the most static and rigidly stratified societies that has ever existed.

The Hebrews

The history of the Hebrews is intertwined with that of the other peoples of ancient Egypt and western Asia, including the Canaanites and the Phoenicians, both of whom had settled in Palestine from very early times. Much Canaanite culture reflects Mesopotamian influence. Ugarit, the leading Canaanite city, was founded before 3500 B.C. and thrived until its destruction by the Sea Peoples around 1200 B.C. A major commercial center, Ugarit traded with Mesopotamia, Anatolia, Egypt, and eventually Greece. The people of Ugarit pioneered the development of an alphabet comprised of 30 wedge-shaped signs, each of which denoted a letter rather than a word or syllable.

By 1000 B.C. the Semitic-speaking Phoenicians, who were descended from the Canaanites, were concentrated in the area now known as Lebanon. Taking advantage of their access to the sea, the Phoenicians constructed ships capable of ranging throughout the Mediterranean. The heart of their export trade consisted of magnificent cedar and textiles dyed with a rich purple derived from a shellfish found along their coast. The Phoenicians established colonies as far away as Carthage in North Africa and Cadiz in the Iberian peninsula, where they traded for silver and tin. From the Hittites the Phoenicians learned how to smelt iron, a technology they later introduced to the Greeks and the North Africans. Another major Phoenician contribution was the development of an alphabet consisting of 22 characters, each of which represented a distinct sound; unlike the Ugaritic cuneiform alphabet, the Phoenician alphabet showed no trace of a pictographic origin. Both the Hebrews and the Greeks, in turn, adopted versions of this alphabet.

Like the Phoenicians, the Hebrews had early links with Mesopotamia. The family of Abraham, the traditional founder of the state of Israel, came from Ur, and we have already met its descendants in Egypt at the time of the Hyksos. The study of the early history of the Hebrews differs significantly from that of the other peoples of western Asia and Egypt. A crucial difference is the role played by written as well as archaeological evidence. Our picture of ancient Egypt and Mesopotamia is reconstituted from material remains, supplemented and at times amplified by inscriptions and surviving documents. Our principal source for the early history of the Hebrews, by contrast, is the first five books of the Old Testament, known as the Pentateuch. According to tradition, the author of the Pentateuch was Moses, a participant in the later stages of the story it tells, though the consensus of scholars is that the text we have was completed in the fifth century B.C. from oral and written traditions and laws. In places, archaeological discoveries have confirmed or filled out the biblical account; elsewhere they provide information that is missing from the Bible.

From the time of Abraham, the covenant between God and the Hebrews was the dominant theme of their history. Abraham believed he had made a covenant or agreement with God that placed the Jews in a special relationship with the Creator as a "chosen people." The biblical Book of Exodus records that Moses reconfirmed this covenant and on Mount Sinai received the tablets of the Law from God.* Abraham's family settled in northern Mesopotamia; his descendants moved south, living as pastoral nomads. Taking their flocks with them, they crossed the desert from one water source to the next, in general avoiding the major urban centers, always following what they perceived to be divine instructions.

*The following account focuses on Hebrew history; Judaism as a religion is discussed in Chapter 7.

After 1700 B.C. these wandering nomads, driven perhaps by hunger, settled in the Nile delta. Egyptian texts fail to record the presence of the Hebrews, and biblical accounts make no reference to a specific Egyptian ruler or time period. It is generally agreed, however, that the age of Hebrew prosperity in Egypt described in the story of Joseph is related to the period of Hyksos rule in the century or so following 1700 B.C. The Hyksos, themselves foreigners, were more likely to look with favor on an immigrant community. Furthermore, the Hebrews' connection with the Hyksos would help explain the Egyptian silence, both on the period itself and on the events that led to the Hebrew exodus described in the Bible, which was undertaken primarily to escape enslavement.

The exodus from Egypt, under the leadership of Moses, probably occurred during the reign of Ramses II (1279–1213 B.C.). Paintings of the period show "Asiatics" toiling as slaves in brickmaking and other building labors, and archaeological evidence indicates migration into Palestine around 1200 B.C. For the Hebrews, and for subsequent Jewish tradition, the exodus became the basis for the foundation of Israel. It demonstrated the intervention of their God, Yahweh, and was the occasion for the renewal of the covenant under Moses' leadership.

The Kingdom of Israel

Following Moses, the migrants traveled northeast toward their "promised land," although the final crossing of the Jordan River and the conquest of Palestine were accomplished only after Moses' death, under the leadership of Joshua. The details of the foundation and growth of the kingdom of Israel are far from clear. The biblical account is incomplete, and archaeological excavations have generally complicated matters. The picture is of almost two centuries of struggle between the Hebrews and other migrant peoples, particularly the Philistines, before the establishment of a Hebrew monarchy. Even then the new kingdom of Israel was far from secure. Saul, its first king, died in battle, and only with the accession of David, his successor (c. 1000–c. 970 B.C.), was stability established.

David was first proclaimed king by the Hebrews who lived in Judah, an arid frontier region in southern Palestine that Saul had never effectively governed. It took some seven years before David could take advantage of internal dissension in the north to unite all of Israel. Displaying considerable talent as a political and military leader, he conquered Jerusalem from a local tribe known as the Jebusites and defeated the Philistines. Jerusalem, in a nearly impregnable geographic position, became his new capital and eventually the historic center of the nation of Israel.

David expanded his state until it extended from the Euphrates to the Gulf of Aqaba at the head of the Red Sea; Hebrew troops even occupied Damascus. In a symbolic attempt to unify the disparate peoples of his empire, David married wives from the various groups; ultimately this contributed to dissension within his own family and to the rebellion and death of his son Absalom. To solidify his authority, David interpreted kingship in distinctly religious terms. At his command, the ark, a symbol of the covenant between the Hebrews and their God, was enshrined in Jerusalem. There it signified the renewal of the covenant through David, "the anointed (messiah) of the Lord," and established Jerusalem as the religious as well as the political capital of Israel.

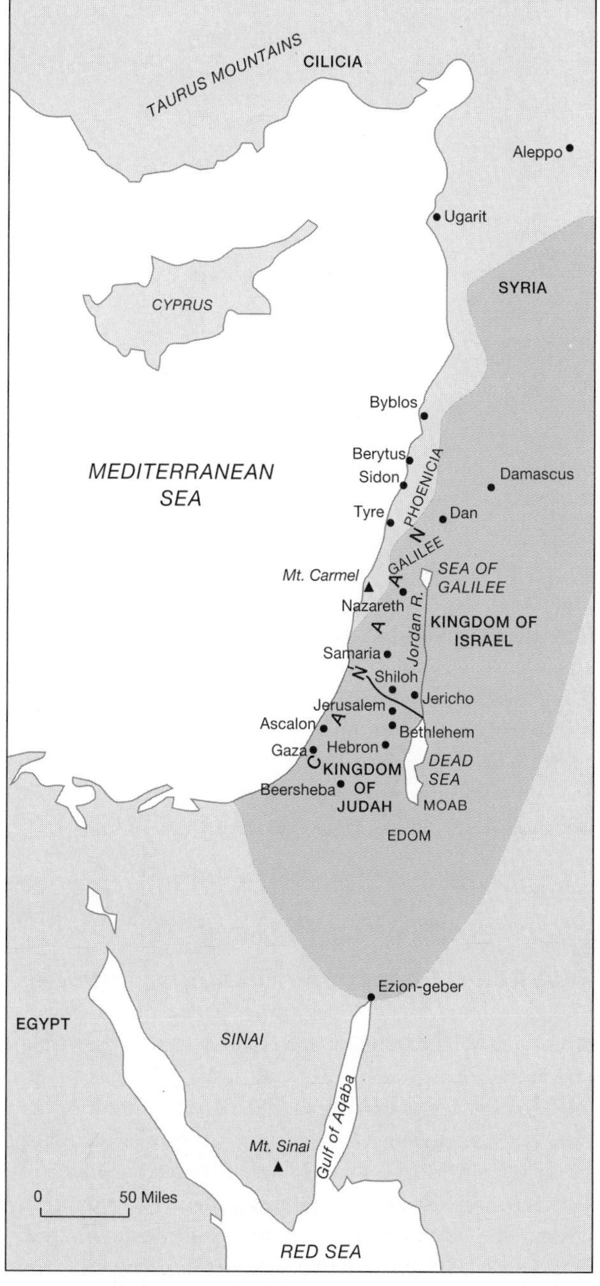

MAP 1.2 ANCIENT PALESTINE

Under David's successor, his son Solomon, who reigned from around 970 to 930 B.C., Israel reached its greatest prosperity. This was in part the result of an absence of competing powers in western Asia at this time. Egyptian power was on the wane, and the Assyrians had yet to embark on their foreign conquests. That Solomon was aware of the necessity of coming to terms with his neighbors is suggested by the fact that one of his many wives was an Egyptian, daughter of the reigning pharaoh.

Solomon sought to consolidate and extend the power of his kingdom. He expanded foreign trade by building a large merchant fleet, manned by Phoenician sailors, that imported gold from Arabia and Ethiopia. Excavations at the port of Ezion-geber on the Gulf of Aqaba suggest the existence of a large-scale metal industry. The Hebrews traded objects manufactured there for foreign products and raw materials, including the cedars of Lebanon used in the construction of Solomon's temple, a majestic building that housed the Great Sanhedrin (the supreme rabbinic court) and served as the center of national worship. Solomon also strengthened his army by the use of iron, which was introduced throughout the Mediterranean shortly after 1000 B.C. His building projects in Jerusalem and elsewhere in the kingdom reflect his ambitious intentions; the fortified city of Megiddo, with stables for almost 500 horses, is just one of the cities he rebuilt.

The Society of Ancient Israel

Jerusalem became a major international capital, its population swollen by the workers involved in Solomon's building projects; more than 200,000 reportedly constructed the temple. Camels replaced asses as the principal means of transporting goods such as spices from Arabia; Sardinia, with its copper refineries, and Spain, a source of mineral wealth, were accessible by sea. The introduction of iron, perhaps borrowed from the Philistines, helped Hebrew farmers and artisans in their work. The iron-tipped plough, probably introduced during Solomon's reign, made possible increased food production, and iron sickles speeded harvesting. Carpenters replaced their bronze saws and axes with sharp, efficient iron ones. The ensuing improvements in production served both the needs of an expanding Jerusalem and the increasing export trade.

Throughout their wanderings, the Hebrews had been under strict injunction from the Law of Moses to preserve rigorous standards of hygiene. Almost every pri-

Reconstruction of the temple in Jerusalem as it appeared in A.D. 41–44.

vate house built at Jerusalem from the mid-tenth century B.C. had a cistern to collect rainwater in the winter and keep it cool and clean throughout the summer. Unlike many of their contemporaries, who collected water at the nearest spring and who were accustomed to pouring refuse into open street drains, Israelite women could count on a fresh water supply, and the city had underground drains. The houses themselves had two stories, a ground floor for storage and an upper level for living.

The status of Hebrew women declined as the worship of Yahweh, a male deity, replaced other gods, including Canaanite fertility deities. Before the establishment of the monarchy under Saul, women had served as prophetesses, the most famous of whom was the "judge" (or tribal leader) Deborah. The role of women decreased under the monarchy, both politically and religiously. They could not enter the inner temple at Jerusalem, and they were barred from synagogues, which developed in the sixth century B.C., in periods of ritual uncleanliness following childbirth and during menstruation. Moreover, in a society concerned about propagation, men were permitted to be polygamous. Parents usually arranged marriages, with the prospective groom or his family required to compensate the bride's family; the latter did not pay a dowry. If the marriage proved unworkable, only the husband had the right to seek a divorce, and only the wife faced execution if she committed adultery. A widow who had not borne a son had to marry her brother-in-law if her husband died. Even the creation account in Genesis 2:18–25 (unlike that in Genesis 1:27–29) placed woman in a subordinate position by proclaiming that she was created after Adam.

The Kingdom Divided

Toward the end of Solomon's life he began to succumb to foreign influences, and the extravagance of his greatest monuments, the temple and the palace in Jerusalem, proved fatal to the kingdom's survival. A bitter civil war followed his death, leading to the division of the kingdom into two parts, Israel to the north, with its capital at Samaria, and Judah, with its capital at Jerusalem, to the south. Fatally divided, the Hebrew states were tempting prizes. The Assyrians invaded, and by 722 B.C. ruined the kingdom of Israel and deported its leaders to Mesopotamia. Judah lasted until 586 B.C., when the Babylonians destroyed Jerusalem and herded the Hebrews into captivity in Babylon. Some 40 years later they were permitted to return to Palestine by the intervention of the Persians, who incorporated Palestine into their empire. During these trying centuries the Hebrew prophets, including Isaiah and Jeremiah, explored the religious implications of Israel's trials in terms of divine punishment and the promise that a remnant of the Hebrew nation would be preserved. Although the pharaoh Akhenaton professed a belief in a single creator-god, the Hebrew prophets first fully enunciated ethical monotheism.

The Hittites

Unlike the Hebrews and the other Semitic-speaking peoples of western Asia, the Hittites were Indo-Europeans, members of a large group of peoples who spoke a language related to Greek, Persian, Sanskrit, and Latin. The Hittites first migrated into Anatolia, probably from central Europe or the steppes of central Asia, no later than 2700 B.C., bringing with them horses and wheeled carts. There they intermingled with earlier inhabitants. By the middle of the second millennium B.C. the Hittite kings of Asia Minor were among the most powerful rulers in western Asia, equals of the monarchs of Babylon and Assyria or the Egyptian pharaohs. Yet with the fall of their empire around 1190 B.C., the Hittites virtually disappeared from history until they were rediscovered at the end of the nineteenth century.

The principal Hittite territory was located in what is now modern Turkey. Its capital was at Hattusas (modern Bogazkoy). From there, beginning around 1650 B.C., the Hittite kings embarked on aggressive military campaigns, pushing south across the Taurus Mountains into the more fertile territory of their southern and eastern neighbors. Sometime after 1600 B.C. they sacked Babylon with their ally, the Kassites.

Internal feuding eroded these initial successes, and the apparent obscurity of the following century may imply that the Hittites were more concerned with defending their territory against invaders than with empire building. The powerful military leader Suppiluliumas (c. 1375–c. 1335 B.C.) put Hittite armies once again on the attack. They conquered Syria, and even the Egyptians made peace overtures. The widow of the pharaoh (probably Tutankhamen, who had just died at the age of 18) sent a letter to Suppiluliumas begging him to send one of his sons to provide her with a new husband. Such an attractive alliance could hardly be turned down, and a Hittite prince was duly dispatched, only to be murdered en route to the Egyptian court. Suppiluliumas thus lost the opportunity to place his son on the Egyptian throne, which would have firmly linked the two empires. The career of King Hattusilis III (c. 1275–c. 1250 B.C.) and his queen, the priestess Puduhepa, provides a vivid picture of power and politics in the ancient world. He was an experienced military commander in his late forties when he deposed the reigning king, his nephew, in a coup. A powerful and ruthless leader, he engaged in incessant fighting to protect the kingdom's northern frontiers and negotiated with Egypt to retain control of Syria. Royal decrees were issued jointly in the names of Hattusilis and Puduhepa, and she corresponded independently with the Egyptian queen.

Hittite Society and Religion

The Hittite kingdom was basically agricultural. Many documents from the royal archives consist of land deeds, together with laws governing farming mishaps—the escape of a pig or an accidental fire in an orchard, for example. Unlike the Mesopotamians, the Hittites cultivated the vine, and wine, olive oil, and grain figure prominently in their records. In the fourteenth century B.C. the Hittites were one of the first peoples to discover the technique of iron smelting, but iron remained a precious metal, in short supply until about 1000 B.C. Hittite trading was widespread throughout western Asia, and much of the royal correspondence dealt with trade concessions and the protection of merchants traveling abroad. Egypt and Syria provided the principal markets, although the Hittites also traded with the Babylonians and were probably in commercial contact with the Mycenaeans, the chief Bronze Age people of the Greek mainland. Hittite objects sold or traded included bronze and iron vessels as well as gold and silver, and among the commodities Hittite merchants tried to buy was lapis lazuli, a precious blue stone mined in northeastern Afghanistan.

Like the Babylonians and other ancient peoples, the Hittites developed legal codes to organize their society. They made detailed provisions concerning homicide, theft, and arson, as well as regulations governing employment, property holding, and the treatment of slaves. Many provisions reflect the agricultural nature of Hittite society: rulings on crimes related to vineyards and orchards, offenses related to cattle, and accidents at river crossings.

Hittite society was patriarchal, but unlike the Semitic-speaking peoples, the Hittites did not practice polygamy. Fathers "gave away" their daughters, and the Hittites

Hittite Laws

Hittite laws were designed for reparation rather than retribution, as these examples demonstrate.

If anyone breaks a freeman's arm or leg, he pays him twenty shekels of silver and he [the plaintiff] lets him go home.

If anyone breaks the arm or leg of a male or female slave he pays ten shekels of silver and he [the plaintiff] lets him go home.

If anyone steals a plough-ox, formerly he used to give fifteen oxen, but now he gives ten oxen; he gives three oxen two years old, three yearling oxen, and four sucklings(?) and he [the plaintiff] lets him go home.

If a freeman kills a serpent and speaks the name of another [a form of sorcery], he shall give one pound of silver; if a slave does it, he shall die.

If a man puts filth into a pot or a tank, formerly he paid six shekels of silver; he who put the filth in paid three shekels of silver [to the owner?], and into the palace they used to take three shekels of silver. But now the king has remitted the share of the palace; the one who put the filth in pays three shekels of silver only and he [the plaintiff] lets him go home.

If a freeman sets a house on fire, he shall rebuild the house; but whatever perishes inside the house, be it a man, an ox, or a sheep, for these he shall not compensate.

Source: O. R. Gurney, *The Hittites* (Harmondsworth, England: Penguin Books, 1954), p. 96.

regarded marriage primarily as a financial contract. Nevertheless, young Hittite women seem to have enjoyed a little more independence than their Babylonian counterparts. The initial betrothal was accompanied by a present from the future bridegroom, but if the young woman decided to marry someone else, she could do so, with or without her parents' consent, provided that she returned the engagement present. Other regulations governed the treatment of widows and children; they included a provision that if a man died childless, it was the responsibility of his brother, father, or other male relative to marry and take care of his widow. Any children born of such a marriage took the name of the dead man and thus perpetuated his line. Although Babylonian law did not make this provision, a similar law existed in the ancient Jewish tradition, so that the dead man's name would not be "blotted out of Israel."[4]

As might be expected among an agricultural people, the principal Hittite deity was a weather god called Teshub. In contrast to the predictability of the Mesopotamian cycle of seasons, the weather in the Taurus Mountains in southern Asia Minor is stormy and uncertain. The son of the weather god, Telipinu, an agricultural deity, who may have become the center of a cult similar to that of Osiris in Egypt, symbolized death and rebirth. As Hittite society developed, a complicated interweaving of deities, local and statewide, came into being, but the weather god remained the dominant figure, and Hittite kings claimed to rule as his deputy. The language of a treaty guaranteeing security throughout western Asia during Hattusilis III's reign describes the agreement as being between "the Sun God of Egypt and the Weather God of Hatti."

The End of the Hittite Empire

The treaty with Egypt may have secured the Hittites' eastern frontiers, but trouble soon developed in the west. Local governors there had revolted, and when the mass migrations of the Peoples of the Sea, who were repelled with such difficulty by Ramses III, swept across western Asia, the Hittites were unable to repulse the invaders. With the collapse of their capital at Hattusas around 1190 B.C., the population scattered. Drought, famine, and volcanic eruptions may also have contributed to the Hittite decline. Hittite culture continued in a few cities in the extreme south, in what is now Syria, but the Assyrians soon annexed them. The heirs of the Hittites in Asia Minor were the Phrygians, whose worship of Cybele, the Great Mother, became widespread in the Roman world, and the Lydians, who were probably the inventors of coinage. Hittite influence also extended, perhaps indirectly, to the Greeks and the Romans, whose conception of the pantheon of gods apparently owed much to Hittite mythology. The historical importance of the Hittites stems from their role in transmitting Mesopotamian culture to peoples of the Mediterranean.

The Assyrians and the Urartians

The Hittites' sometime ally, the Kassites, briefly dominated Mesopotamia. Formerly nomadic, they occupied Babylon sometime after 1700 B.C., only to fall, in turn, under the rule of the Assyrians, a Semitic people who evolved the last great culture of Mesopotamia. The peak of Assyrian power was between 900 and 612 B.C. The three centuries of Assyrian domination were marked by powerful, aggressive rulers whose armies were frequently on the march throughout western Asia.

The Assyrians' militancy stemmed from the recurring need to defend themselves from the aggressive inhabitants of the mountains to the north. Throughout the ninth century B.C. the Assyrians carried out raids against their neighbors, including the Hittites, Phoenicians, Syrians, and Israelites. The architect of Assyrian imperialism was Tiglath-Pileser III (c. 745–727 B.C.), whose army overran Babylonia, northern Syria, and Israel. Iron weapons, siege equipment (towers, rams, and mines), and troops capable of rapid deployment made his troops highly effective. So too did their discipline. But Assyrian rule provoked repeated uprisings by some of the subject peoples, who resented the payment of tribute and subjection to forced labor. By the late seventh century B.C. Assyria had extended its control over Egypt, making the empire the largest in the world to that point in history.

Although impressive in its size, the empire lasted little more than a century. The Assyrian monarchs ruled in splendor with the aid of a vast court and bureaucracy. The very title of the sovereign reflects the sense of grandeur: "the great king, the legitimate king, the king of the world, king of Assyria, king of all the four rims of the earth, king of kings, prince without rival." Yet the

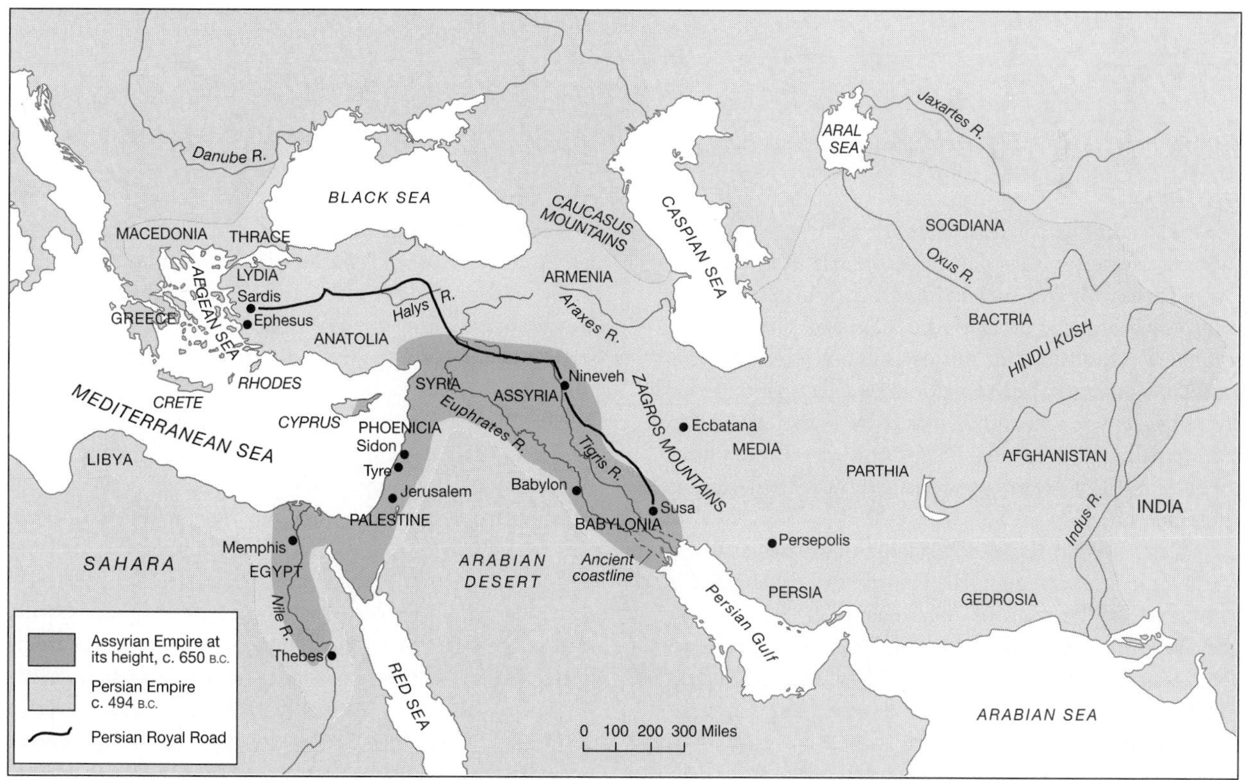

MAP 1.3 THE EMPIRES OF ASSYRIA AND PERSIA

Colossal human-headed lions such as this guarded the entrances to Assyrian palaces.

monarchs were not absolute, for councils of elders governed Assyrian cities under the terms of urban charters, and powerful lords oversaw the affairs of rural districts and were responsible for raising military forces. Beyond the Assyrian homeland some of the subject peoples were ruled by Assyrian deputies, others by local leaders who were obedient to their Assyrian overlords; some, known to be loyal to Assyria, were virtually left to determine their own affairs.

The Assyrian monarchs ruled from a succession of royal capitals, each of which required extensive building programs. In the reign of Ashurnasirpal (884–859 B.C.) the Assyrians constructed a huge palace at Calah (modern Nimrud) and decorated it with elaborately carved reliefs. Under Sargon II (722–705 B.C.) the Assyrians built a walled city at Khorsabad, which covered almost a square mile. The gates had guard posts that could serve for defense in time of war and as customs and police posts in peacetime. Both the outer gates and the entrance doors into the palace featured huge statues of the Assyrians' most powerful demons, the Lamassu, splendidly depicted as winged human-headed bulls that represent Assyrian power. The palace itself was built around a large open court, with separate quarters for officers and servants, a number of temples, and the king's residential apartments. Most impressive were the state rooms, where the king received foreign ambassadors. The approach to the throne room was through an open courtyard lined with greater-than-life-size statues of the king and his courtiers. Around its entrance was a collection of demonic figures, again of vast size. The Assyrian kings hoped to intimidate their neighbors, discouraging them from attacking and their subjects from rebelling. The ambassadors or petitioners who had made their way through the ceremonial halls and into the throne room faced the carved base of the king's throne, which showed Sargon standing in his war chariot over heaps of dead bodies while his soldiers piled severed heads in front of him.

Assyrian brutality toward their conquered enemies has obscured their accomplishments. Like the later Romans, they built roads, promoted urban development, and maintained order in a turbulent region. They forced Egypt and Babylon to open their borders to foreign trade and used units of silver virtually as coinage. Although they practiced slavery, slaves could operate their own businesses and win their freedom by faithful service. Like the Hittites, the Assyrians played an important role in the transmission of Mesopotamian culture.

Nineveh, which had become the Assyrian capital after Sargon's death, fell in 612 B.C., and with it the Assyrian empire. Western Asia Minor came under the control of the Medes (from Media, the ancient name for northwestern Iran) and then the Persians (from Persis, in southern Iran), while the Chaldeans of southern Babylonia dominated Palestine, Syria, and the whole of Mesopotamia. Yet even at this point the cultural fertility of Mesopotamia was not exhausted. The ancient kingdom of Babylon came under the rule of a dynasty of monarchs of whom the best known is Nebuchadnezzar and for 70 years or so underwent a remarkable cultural revival. This period, which lasted from 612 to 539 B.C., is generally called the Neo-Babylonian period, and its culture harks back to that of Babylon 1,000 years earlier. The greatest building project of the age was Nebuchadnezzar's palace at Babylon, little of which has survived. The Ishtar Gate, the principal entry into Babylon, was decorated with painted and glazed bricks, giving an impression of splendor, and Nebuchadnezzar's hanging

The Ishtar Gate of the city of Babylon has been reconstructed in the National Museum in Berlin.

gardens and 300-foot-high ziggurat made Babylon perhaps the most impressive city in the world.

To the north of Assyria, in what is now eastern Turkey, the Urartians established a powerful state that was virtually contemporaneous with the Assyrian empire. The history of the kingdom of Urartu (which appears in the Bible as Ararat) extended from the ninth to the late seventh century B.C. Geographically this was a region blessed with forests; rich in such minerals as iron, silver, and copper; and endowed with grazing lands that helped the Urartians achieve fame as horse breeders. Unlike some other peoples of western Asia, they produced substantial quantities of wine. To ensure adequate water supplies for their crops, horses, and more than 750 towns and villages, the Urartians constructed aqueducts, reservoirs, and vast irrigation canals. Originally the capital was at Arzashkun (near Manizert), but the Urartians later moved it to Van (Tushpa), where they built a citadel nearly 1 mile long and 200 yards wide using limestone blocks, some of which weighed more than 30 tons.

In many respects Urartian culture reflected Assyrian influence, as for instance in their adoption of Assyrian cuneiform to write their own language. The Urartians also demonstrated some independence, particularly in architecture, where they used stone rather than brick, as in Assyria. Throughout their history they periodically engaged in warfare with the Assyrians, which helps to explain why they constructed so many terraced fortresses throughout their domain. Near the end of the eighth century B.C. the Assyrians inflicted a major defeat on Urartu, seized—and cataloged—333,500 items from the royal palace, and hauled hundreds of tons of spoils to Assyria. But the size, natural wealth, and relative inaccessibility of Urartu were so great that the kingdom recovered in the early seventh century B.C. Late in that century, however, the Scythians and Medes exerted pressure in the north. After the Armenians moved in, the Urartians seem to have intermarried with them and eventually lost their identity. They left behind some of the finest bronze work in antiquity, pieces of which were found as far away as the Etruscan towns of Italy.

The Rise of Persia

The land of the Persians had been inhabited for millennia, perhaps from as early as 15,000 B.C. Persia itself, or Iran ("land of the Aryans"), as it is now called, lies at a crossroads between the rugged lands of western Asia, the plains of central Asia, the great steppes to the northeast, and Afghanistan and the Indus valley to the east. At the heart of Persia is a high central plateau surrounded by mountains, which separate the plains of the interior from the Caspian Sea to the north and the Persian Gulf to the south. Two extensive deserts, virtually impassable in the summer, lie in the center of the immense plateau; from time immemorial they have diverted nomads from central Asia into India to the east or the Tigris-Euphrates valley to the west. The lowlands beyond the mountains receive most of the region's precipitation and thus contrast sharply with the dry interior. The land is rich in minerals, particularly iron, copper, and brilliant blue lapis lazuli. Early in its history western Iran, known then as Elam, fell under Sumerian influence. Persia as a whole, however, was only sparsely settled by prehistoric peoples throughout the centuries of Sumerian and Babylonian rule.

Around 1000 B.C., as we have seen, conditions in western Asia were generally unstable. The Egyptians had begun their decline, the Assyrians had not yet established firm rule, and the mass movements of the Peoples of the Sea had created havoc, destroying the Hittites in the process. About the same time, tribes of nomadic horse-riding warriors migrated from central Asia into Iran, bringing their flocks and herds. Without horses, the prehistoric inhabitants were no match for them. Among the invading tribes were the Indo-European Medes and Persians, both of whom were related to the Aryans who settled India. The Medes and Persians were soon joined by the warlike Scythians, who had in turn been driven from the far eastern steppe, where the Huns, a people from central Asia, were at war with the Chinese.

The Medes and Persians established a number of small kingdoms, each of which was ruled by a king who was little more than a warlord supported by a band of warriors. Below this elite group, early Iranian society was comprised of free farmers, skilled artisans, peasants who owed labor to the king, and slaves. The Medes and Persians traded with other peoples in the region, particularly the Assyrians to the west, who were attracted by Iranian horses and minerals. The Medes, who had settled in northern Iran, united in the late eighth century B.C., after which they imposed their rule on the Persians in the south.

An alliance of Medes and Scythians, together with the help of other nomadic tribes, sacked Nineveh in 612 B.C., ending the Assyrian empire. Throughout these tumultuous events the Persians retained their tribal identity and through a process of intermarriage and aggression established their rule over most of Iran. In 550 B.C. the Medes, weakened by their struggles to the west, were resoundingly defeated by Cyrus (559–530 B.C.), chief of the Persian tribes. The land of the Medes became Cyrus' first province, or satrapy.

Approximately 546 B.C. Cyrus conquered prosperous Lydia and the Greek cities on the Anatolian coast, in what is now western Turkey. This gave him possession of the ports that marked the western terminus of the trade routes extending from the Aegean Sea deep into Asia. After securing his eastern frontiers by fighting that extended as far as Afghanistan and western India, he turned to the southwest and in 539 B.C. captured Babylon. That city, which had recently witnessed the splendid reign of Nebuchadnezzar, became an important symbol of Persian success. Cyrus included the title "king of Babylon" in his inscriptions and spent considerable time there. As a conqueror he distinguished himself by his appreciation of the cultures of his new subjects; local customs and religious beliefs were not suppressed.

Cyrus' son and successor, Cambyses (530–522 B.C.), conquered Egypt in 525 B.C. and tried to reach Carthage (modern Tunis), but he failed to persuade his Phoenician allies to attack their Carthaginian kinsmen. His plan to conquer Ethiopia also remained largely unfulfilled because of inadequate supplies. Cambyses was said to have been mentally unbalanced, and he was cruel enough to kill his own brother.

The accession of Darius I (522–486 B.C.) returned stability to the Persian Empire and inaugurated nearly two centuries of peaceful Persian rule. Among his accomplishments were the introduction of a uniform system of gold and silver coinage, standard weights and measures, a postal service, an imperial law code based on Mesopotamian principles, and a common calendar derived from the Egyptians'. Darius' reign saw further attempts to extend the empire. Around 513 or 512 B.C. he sent expeditions into southeastern Europe, reaching as far as the river Danube, and into India, the northwestern portion of which became the satrapy of Hindush. Darius wanted to improve communications and trade, and to that end supported an expedition that sailed from the Indus River to the northern end of the Red Sea. Darius also became embroiled with the people to the far west, the Greeks, against whom he and his successor, Xerxes, launched three unsuccessful expeditions. Despite his failure to conquer the Greeks, Darius' empire enjoyed trade relations with people as far away as India to the east and Phoenicia on the Mediterranean. The Persians planned to construct a canal from the Nile to the Red Sea; had they succeeded, Alexander the Great, with better supply lines at his disposal, might have conquered India, and fifteenth-century explorers might not have sought a passage across the Atlantic Ocean to East Asia as an alternative to sailing around the African continent.

Life and Government in the Persian Empire

At its height the Persian Empire was prosperous and cosmopolitan. Foreign artisans worked with materials that came from Greece, Lebanon, and India to decorate the royal palaces. The Persians traded widely, using their gold coin, the daric, and maintained contacts throughout western Asia. Many of the people under their control did not speak their language, and the monuments on the Royal Road, the principal highway to cross part of the empire, featured inscriptions in Babylonian and Elamite as well as Persian. Some 1,600 miles long (the distance from New York to Dallas), the Royal Road extended from Susa in western Persia to Sardis, near the port of Ephesus, a Greek city on the Aegean. It took caravans three months to travel this road, although royal couriers, using fresh horses provided at the 111 post stations along the route, could make the trip in a week.

For all the power of their ruler, the "king of kings," the Persians' view of their monarchy differed from that of the Assyrians. The king was not an object of fear but a righteous leader, elected by the gods. The empire was in general ruled with efficiency, justice, and tolerance. It was so large that it had to be divided into some 20 satrapies or provinces, each of which was administered by a governor (or satrap), aided by a military force under a separate commander. The presence of military officials, royal agents, and spies prevented the governors, who were Mede or Persian nobles, from exercising excessive power. The king was interested primarily in receiving from the satraps appropriate tribute and recruits for the military; if those demands were fulfilled, the governors enjoyed substantial autonomy.

Persian Capitals: Susa and Persepolis

The principal centers of the empire were at Susa, eastern terminus of the Royal Road; Ecbatana, the former Mede capital; and ancient Babylon. Susa, which had been inhabited since Neolithic times, was situated at the foot of the Zagros Mountains, near the bank of the river Karkheh. Beginning in 521 b.c. Darius made it his principal capital for most of the year, leaving only in the summer to escape the intense heat. He ordered the construction of a citadel and a sumptuous palace, as well as walls and a moat for protection. He imported workers from many lands: stonecutters from Greece and Asia Minor, goldsmiths from Egypt, brickmakers from Babylon. Their materials included cedar from Lebanon, gold from Bactria, and ivory from Ethiopia. Susa became a cosmopolitan center; the biblical Book of Esther is set there.

In 518 B.C. Darius began the construction of a new capital at Persepolis, a remote site in an alpine region southeast of Susa. The style of architecture and sculpture that developed at Persepolis, like that at Susa, was highly eclectic. Lacking their own architectural traditions, the Persians drew on those of others. Like the Sumerians, they employed mud brick and constructed their palaces on terraces, although they used the kind of glazed decoration found on Nebuchadnezzar's palace at Babylon. Assyrian human-headed bulls, Egyptian doorways, and Greek columns can be found at Persepolis; visiting Greek and Egyptian artists almost certainly produced some of the decorative sculpture.

The site of Persepolis was topped by a citadel. The lower slopes of the mountain on which it stands were leveled to allow construction on a terrace ranging from 14 to 41 feet above the ground. The terrace was reached by a stairway broad enough to be used by groups of riders. Upon it were monumental public buildings, each intended to reinforce the impression of splendor. The approach to the vast audience hall of the royal palace built by Darius and Xerxes between 520 and 460 B.C. was by an elaborate staircase lined with sculptural decoration. The reliefs showed a procession of officials, soldiers, and representatives of the peoples of the empire bringing tribute to the king. The great hall was 60 feet high and contained three dozen 40-foot columns. On a retaining wall, Darius inscribed a prayer for his subjects: "God protect this country from foe, famine, and falsehood."

Darius' successors maintained the Persian Empire until Alexander the Great conquered it between 334 and 326 B.C. The arrival of Alexander and his troops thrust

The audience hall of Darius and Xerxes at Persepolis, with the palace of Darius in the background.

Europe and Asia into the long period of mutual influence that has lasted, despite interruptions, to our own time.

SUMMARY

The peoples of western Asia and Egypt achieved some of the greatest artistic and cultural innovations in history. The invention of metalworking and writing and the development of architectural techniques and drainage and irrigation systems are only the most obvious of the many technological advances of the period. These made possible the development of cities, and with them came the growth of legal systems and complex urban relationships that remain, in one form or another, the basis of our daily lives.

Growing economic prosperity, coupled with technological developments such as wheeled vehicles and seagoing ships that simplified long-distance travel, encouraged the expansion of trade. This in turn led, on the one hand, to stimulating contact with foreign ideas as well as goods and, on the other hand, to conflict, since what could be bought peacefully could also be taken in war. It is no accident that much of the new technology was devoted to making better weapons and stronger fortifications. Internal and external expansion required professional planners and administrators, giving rise to the new profession of bureaucrat.

The same drive that laid the foundations of civilized life in western Asia and Egypt was responsible for the art that helps us interpret the character and world view of each of the peoples who produced them. Some monuments are more familiar than others. The pyramids of Egypt, for example, were known to Roman soldiers and to Napoleon, whereas the Hittites, the Urartians, and the people of Ebla have been rediscovered only within the past century. Time after time, works of art that were created in a world remote from our own succeed in communicating to us with vividness and power. The fascination they continue to exert confirms the underlying unity of human experience.

NOTES

1. *The Book of the Dead According to the Theban Recension,* trans. E. A. Wallis Budge, in *Egyptian Literature,* ed. E. Wilson (London: Colonial Press, 1901).
2. C. Aldred, *Akhenaten: King of Egypt* (London: Thames & Hudson, 1988), p. 224.
3. J. B. Pritchard, ed., *Ancient Near Eastern Texts Relating to the Old Testament,* trans. J. Wilson (Princeton, N.J.: Princeton University Press, 1969), pp. 251–252.
4. Deut. 25:6.

SUGGESTIONS FOR FURTHER READING

Aldred, C. *Akhenaten: King of Egypt.* London: Thames & Hudson, 1988.

Aubet, M. E. *The Phoenicians and the West,* trans. M. Turton. New York: Cambridge University Press, 1993.

Bright, J. *A History of Israel,* 3rd ed. Philadelphia: Westminster Press, 1981.

Cameron, A., and Kuhrt, A., eds. *Images of Women in Antiquity.* Detroit: Wayne State University Press, 1983.

Cook, J. M. *The Persian Empire.* New York: Schocken Books, 1983.

Dandamaev, M. A. *A Political History of the Achaemenid Empire.* New York: Brill, 1989.

———, and Lukonin, V. G. *The Cultural and Social Institutions of Ancient Iran.* New York: Cambridge University Press, 1989.

Davies, W. D., and Finkelstein, L., eds. *The Cambridge History of Judaism.* Vol. I: *The Persian Period.* Cambridge: Cambridge University Press, 1984. Vol. 2: *The Hellenistic Age.* Cambridge: Cambridge University Press, 1987.

Grimal, N. *A History of Ancient Egypt.* Oxford: Blackwell, 1992.

Jacobsen, T. *The Treasures of Darkness: A History of Mesopotamian Religion.* New Haven, Conn.: Yale University Press, 1976.

James, T. G. H. *Pharaoh's People: Scenes from Life in Imperial Egypt.* London: Bodley Head, 1984.

Knapp, A. B. *The History and Culture of Ancient Western Asia and Egypt.* Homewood, Ill.: Dorsey Press, 1988.

Kramer, S. N. *History Begins at Sumer,* 3rd ed. Philadelphia: University of Pennsylvania Press, 1981.

Lloyd, S. *Ancient Turkey.* London: British Museum Publications, 1989.

Macqueen, J. G. *The Hittites and Their Contemporaries in Asia Minor,* rev. ed. London: Thames & Hudson, 1986.

Manniche, L. *City of the Dead: Thebes in Egypt.* Chicago: University of Chicago Press, 1987.

———. *Sexual Life in Ancient Egypt.* London: KPI, 1987.

Oates, J. *Babylon,* rev. ed. London: Thames & Hudson, 1986.

Oppenheim, A. L. *Ancient Mesopotamia,* rev. ed. Chicago: University of Chicago Press, 1977.

Pettinato, G. *Ebla: A New Look at History.* Baltimore: Johns Hopkins University Press, 1991.

Redford, D. B. *Egypt, Canaan, and Israel in Ancient Times.* Princeton, N.J.: Princeton University Press, 1992.

Rice, M. *Egypt's Making: The Origins of Ancient Egypt, 5000–2000 B.C.* London: Routledge & Kegan Paul, 1990.

Robins, G. *Women in Ancient Egypt.* London: British Museum Press, 1993.

Saggs, H. W. F. *The Greatness That Was Babylon,* rev. ed. London: Sidgwick & Jackson, 1988.

——— *Civilization Before Greece and Rome.* London: Batsford, 1989.

Samson, J. *Nefertiti and Cleopatra: Queen-Monarchs of Ancient Egypt.* London: Rubicon, 1985.

Sandars, N. K. *The Sea Peoples,* rev. ed. London: Thames & Hudson, 1985.

Silver, M. *Prophets and Markets: The Political Economy of Ancient Israel.* Boston: Kluwer-Nijhoff, 1983.

———. *Economic Structures of the Ancient Near East.* Totowa, N.J.: Barnes & Noble Books, 1987.

CHAPTER 2

Ancient India

India's civilization is the oldest in continuous existence. If one defines civilization as involving a writing system, metalworking, and some concentration of settlement in cities where most of the inhabitants are not farmers, the earliest such developments seem to have occurred in Mesopotamia by about 4000 B.C. and at about the same time in Egypt. By about 3000 B.C. civilization in these terms had emerged in the Indus valley of India and by about 2000 B.C. in China. Mesopotamian and Egyptian civilizations came to an end by Roman times and were later superseded by the Arab conquest. The present cultures of these areas have little or no connection with ancient Sumer or the time of the pharaohs, leaving India as the oldest survivor. The Indus civilization is the clearly traceable direct ancestor of subsequent Indian civilization, and the continuities are strong.

The *Indian subcontinent,* as it is called, from the mountain borders of Afghanistan to the Bay of Bengal on the east and from the towering Himalayas to the southern tip of the peninsula, is about the size of all of Europe (excluding Russia) and is even more varied physically, linguistically, and culturally. This huge, diverse area has only briefly during its long history been united under a single ruler, and then only partly so. It is now composed of the separate states of Pakistan, India, Nepal, Bangladesh, and Sri Lanka, but within each of these political divisions remain major regional differences. For every period of Indian history it is thus difficult to generalize about this vast and varied part of the world, containing about a fifth of the world's people. Nevertheless, an

The genius of Indian sculpture was well established by Harappan times but was developed further in subsequent centuries. This sandstone pillar showing Yakshis, the goddess of the life-giving waters, was carved in the second century A.D. as a love figure; the bird cage she holds signifies "I've caught him!"—as can be deduced from her sweet smile as well.

underlying culture shared by inhabitants of the subcontinent, periodically enriched by new infusions, gave and still gives Indian civilization its basic identity.

Although a literate urban culture was in existence in India by around 3000 B.C. and lasted for about 1,000 years, we know relatively little about it. We cannot yet decipher the marks its people inscribed on clay tablets and seals, and the evidence we have is mainly the partly excavated ruins of the very large cities they built. After the collapse of the Indus civilization, northern India was invaded, over many centuries, by a central Asian people who called themselves Aryans. They gradually became the dominant group in the north, although they intermarried with the indigenous people. By the time Alexander the Great invaded India in 326 B.C., many regional kingdoms had arisen. These were welded together into an empire by the Maurya dynasty (c. 322–c. 180 B.C.) after Alexander withdrew, which unified most of the north. A new group of invaders reunified the north under the Kushan dynasty from 100 B.C. to about A.D. 200. In the following century the indigenous Gupta dynasty restored most of the Mauryan accomplishments in the north from 320 to 550, while the south remained divided among flourishing rival kingdoms. Gupta rule collapsed around 550, as did the short-lived northern empire of Harsha by 648. Once more, India became a complex pattern of separate states. But in most of its basic elements, Indian civilization has remained continuous from the third millennium B.C. to the present.

Origins of Civilization in India

Agriculture had evolved much earlier than civilization, probably independently in a number of places including tropical Southeast Asia, western Asia (what is now eastern Turkey, Syria, and northern Iraq), Africa, and, by about 2000 B.C., Central and South America. Agriculture in permanent fields, as opposed to a food-gathering culture, requires permanent settlement. Villages or even small towns of this sort inhabited by farmers began to emerge soon after 10,000 B.C. in southwestern Asia.

It was not far from Sumer to India, and the way was relatively easy: by ship along the sheltered coasts of the Persian Gulf and thence, still following the coast, to the mouth of the Indus River. The route by land across Iran and Baluchistan ran through a desert with few oases, but it was used too. Neolithic developments in agriculture and the beginnings of large villages or towns were taking place at several locations along this land route and in the upland Baluchistan borderlands west of the Indus during the fifth millennium B.C. These developments were probably independent of Sumer but may have benefited indirectly from early Sumerian achievements. Agriculture had also appeared on the Indus floodplain by the fifth millennium B.C. and may thus have developed independently there. By 3000 B.C. or so, true cities had arisen in the Indus plain and in tributary river valleys, much as early agriculture in the highlands around Mesopotamia later spread onto the riverine lowlands. As in Mesopotamia,

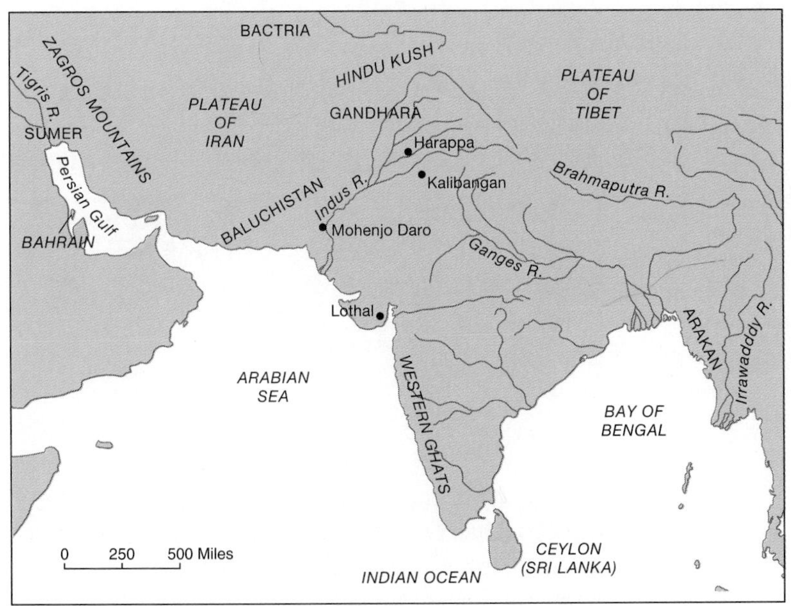

MAP 2.1 SOUTH ASIA

the floodplain presented new challenges to early agriculturists: how to control river flooding, manipulate irrigation, and drain swampy land. The long experience with an evolving set of agricultural techniques ultimately made it possible to exploit the potentially rich agricultural resources of the lowlands. Consistent agricultural surpluses provided the basis for real cities, as opposed to towns; the cities were literate, metal-using, food-surplus-storing centers with a division of labor and great sophistication in the arts, in building, and in planning.

The Indus Civilization

The chief urban centers so far discovered are Kalibangan in modern Rajasthan (probably the oldest city site yet found in India), Harappa in what is now the Pakistani part of Punjab, and Mohenjo Daro on the lower course of the Indus. All three, as well as nearly 200 smaller town or village sites from the same period scattered over an immense area from the Indus valley east to the upper Ganges and south to near modern Bombay, show similar forms of settlements, pottery, seals (for marking pieces of property), and artwork. This vast complex, extending over by far the largest area of any ancient culture, is called the Indus civilization. It clearly had a close relationship to the river and its tributaries, a situation very similar to that in Sumer and in Egypt. Like the Nile and the Tigris and Euphrates, the Indus is an "exotic" river, that is, one that originates in a well-watered area. Rising with its tributaries in the Himalayas, the source of snowmelt and heavy summer monsoonal rains, it flows across lowland Punjab and arid Rajasthan into the desert of Sind to reach the sea near modern Karachi. All of this lowland area is dry, and the lower half of the Indus valley is virtually desert, as in Sumer and Egypt, so that agriculture is dependent on irrigation. Annual river floods provided both water and highly fertile, easily worked alluvium, or silt. Combined with a long growing season of high temperatures and unbroken sunshine, this was the same set of agricultural advantages that helped explain the early prominence of Egypt and Sumer after the management and use of floodwater had been mastered. The river also offered cheap, easy transport for bulky goods such as grain or building materials and, together with the treeless and level plain, created the access for transport that is essential for exchange and hence for the division of labor.

Relations with Sumer

We know much less about the Indus civilization and its cities than about Sumer or ancient Egypt, in part because the Indus script has not yet been deciphered. The texts we have are incised on clay tablets and seals, as in Sumer, and contain over 300 different symbols. They may help provide some clue to who the writers were. It is plausible to assume that they were part ancestors of the present inhabitants of South India, for which there is some linguistic evidence. But the Indus script has no resemblance to cuneiform, which by at least 3200 B.C. had replaced pictographic writing in Sumer, almost certainly before the beginnings of city-based civilization in India. The clear superiority of cuneiform ensured its rapid spread. If the Indus civilization had been an outgrowth of Sumer, it would surely have used cuneiform or at least shown some connection with earlier Sumerian writing systems.

The art of the Indus people and their remarkable city planning are also completely distinctive and show no relation to Sumerian equivalents. The seals that they used are very similar to those of earlier and contemporary Mesopotamia, and we know that from at least 2500 B.C. there was trade between them. Objects from India at this period have been found in Sumer and Sumerian objects in India. It seems likely that since seals were probably used primarily to mark property or goods, they were adopted by the Indus people in the course of their trade with Sumer. But in all other respects, their civilization was distinctively their own.

Seal from Mohenjo Daro. The bovine figure at top right suggests the early veneration of cattle.

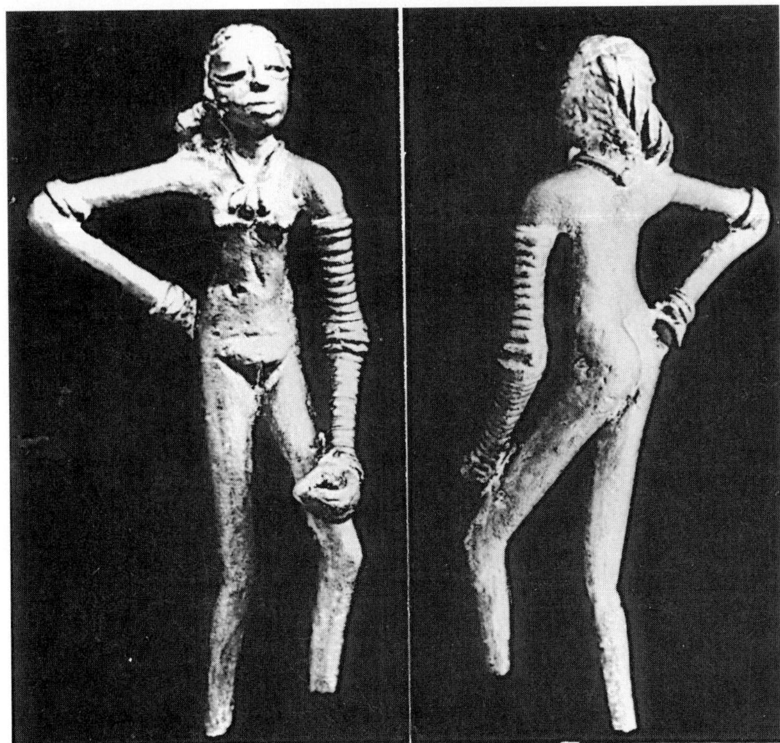

Dancing girl in bronze, from Mohenjo Daro, c. 2500 B.C. The figure is stylized, even abstract, but powerfully conveys the spirit and movement of the dance.

When the Indus civilization emerged is difficult to determine exactly, but it was probably around 3000 B.C. The city sites, including the three major ones at Kalibangan, Harappa, and Mohenjo Daro, were necessarily close to the Indus or its tributaries. Water levels and stream courses have changed since these cities were built some 5,000 years ago. Flooding and silt deposition have carried away, buried, or drowned most of the earliest archaeological evidence. As in the case of the Nile delta and for similar reasons, we can no longer see beginnings that may be considerably earlier than we can now prove. The earliest objects dated so far cluster around 2500 B.C., but they come necessarily from upper site levels and from a period when the urban culture was already well advanced. Especially in the emerging phase of civilization, development is relatively slow. One must assume that it began many centuries before 2500, during which it evolved, built the first city levels, and acquired the form and quality evident by 2500.

We do not know what the builders of these cities called themselves or their settlements. The place names we use for them are modern—Mohenjo Daro means "place of the dead." The Greeks called the land they encountered in Alexander's time "India." This name was derived from the Sanskrit *Sindhu,* the Aryan name for the river and, by association, the river's valley and the land beyond it. From *Sindhu* comes the Persian and modern Indian name for the country, *Hind,* and its derivatives, *Indus, Hindu,* and *Hindustan* (*stan* means "country").*

Trade with Sumer took place both overland and through the port of Lothal on the coast near the mouth of the Indus, where the remains of large stone docks and warehouses have been found. These were associated with a city that was clearly part of Harappan culture (a convenient shorter label for the Indus civilization). Goods from Sumer have been found there and elsewhere in Harappan India, and Harappan goods in Sumer. A site along the route between them, on Bahrain Island, has yielded both sorts of objects and seems to have supported a major trade center where many routes to and from Sumer met. Sumerian texts speak of a place called Dilmun, which was probably Bahrain, a number of days' sail south from the mouth of their river, where were found goods from a place they called Meluha, to the east: ivory, peacocks, monkeys, precious stones, incense, and spices, the "apes, ivory, and peacocks" of the Bible. Meluha

**India* is the label commonly used for the entire subcontinent, including the present states of Pakistan, India, and Nepal, which date in this form only from 1947, and Bangladesh, which was founded in 1971.

must have been India, but it is not clear whether people from Sumer went there or whether the Indus people, or some intermediary, carried their cargoes to Dilmun.

The Cities of the Indus

Perhaps the most remarkable thing about this civilization was the planned layout of its cities, including wells, a piped water supply, bathrooms, and wastepipes or drains in nearly every house. There is no parallel for such planning anywhere in the ancient world, and indeed one must leap to the late nineteenth century in western Europe and North America to find such achievements on a similar scale. The rivers that nourished these cities were the source of their water supply, led by gravity from upstream, a technique later used by the Mughal emperors for their palaces in Delhi and Agra. The importance attached by the Indus people to personal use of water already suggests the distinctively Indian emphasis on both bathing or washing and ritual purity. Religious remains are varied, but they include many figures that suggest an early representation of the Indian god Shiva, Creator and Destroyer, god of the harvest, of the cycle of birth, life, death, and rebirth, and also the primal yogi,* represented even then seated with arms folded and gaze fixed on eternity. Figures of a mother goddess, phallic images, and the worship of cattle are other elements that provide a link with classical and modern Indian civilization. Some scholars have suggested that the distinctively Indian ideas of reincarnation and the endless wheel of life were Harappan beliefs. Indeed, the roots of most of traditional and modern Indian culture can be found or guessed at in what we can piece together from the Indus culture.

The houses in these cities were remarkably uniform, suggesting an absence of great divisions in the society, arranged along regular streets in a semigrid pattern. There were a few larger buildings, including in most of the cities a large public bath and others that were probably municipal granaries or storehouses. The art these still unknown people have left behind is strikingly varied and of high quality. Its variety may suggest that it was produced over a very long time, during which styles changed, as anywhere else in the world over 1,000 years: abstract, realistic, idealized, and so on. One of the most appealing forms is the enormous number of clay and wooden children's toys, including tiny carts pulled by tiny oxen or little monkeys that could be made to climb a string. This suggests a relatively prosperous society that could afford such nonessential production—a tribute to the productivity of its irrigated agriculture—and one whose values seem admirable. Complementing the picture, very few weapons or other indications of warfare have been found at these sites. The Indus civilization seems to have been notably peaceful and humane as well as organized and sophisticated. Cotton, indigenous to India, was woven into cloth earlier here than anywhere else. The animal sculpture and bas-relief, including the figures on many of the seals, were superbly done and include very large numbers of bovines, mainly the familiar humpbacked cattle, which suggests the importance attached to cattle and their veneration ever since in India. This and other evidence indicates that the reverence for life and the quest for nonviolent solutions that mark the consistent Indian stress on the great chain of being and the oneness of creation had emerged by Harappan times.

The chief Indus food crop was wheat, probably derived originally from areas to the west, augmented by barley, peas, beans, oil seeds, fruits, and vegetables and by dairy products from domesticated cattle and sheep. Tools were made of bronze, stone, and wood, but in later centuries iron began to appear and was used, for example, in axle pins for wheeled carts. Rice appeared as a minor crop only toward the end of the Indus period, imported from its Southeast Asian origins as a crop plant via contact with the Ganges valley, to which it had spread earlier. Sugarcane is native to India and was first used there, especially in the well-watered Ganges valley. Riverine location was essential for irrigation but also made for recurrent problems from irregular and occasionally disastrous flooding. The remains of successive dikes speak of efforts to protect the cities themselves against floods and major course changes, not always successfully. There was no building stone in this flat, semiarid or desert region, and the cities were built of brick, as in Sumer, some of it sun-baked and some kiln-fired, using fuel from riverside stands of trees (which must soon have been exhausted) or brought down the rivers from forested hills and mountains upstream. The ruins of Harappa were first investigated in the 1850s by a British military engineer whose sharp eye noticed the strange dimensions of the bricks and other fragments brought to him by Indian contractors for railway ballast and the equally strange markings on some of them, samples of the Indus script, which he traced back to the site of Harappa and realized were the remains of a civilization earlier than any in India then known.

*One who practices yoga, the Hindu philosophy that entails a strict spiritual and physical discipline in order to attain unity with the Universal Spirit.

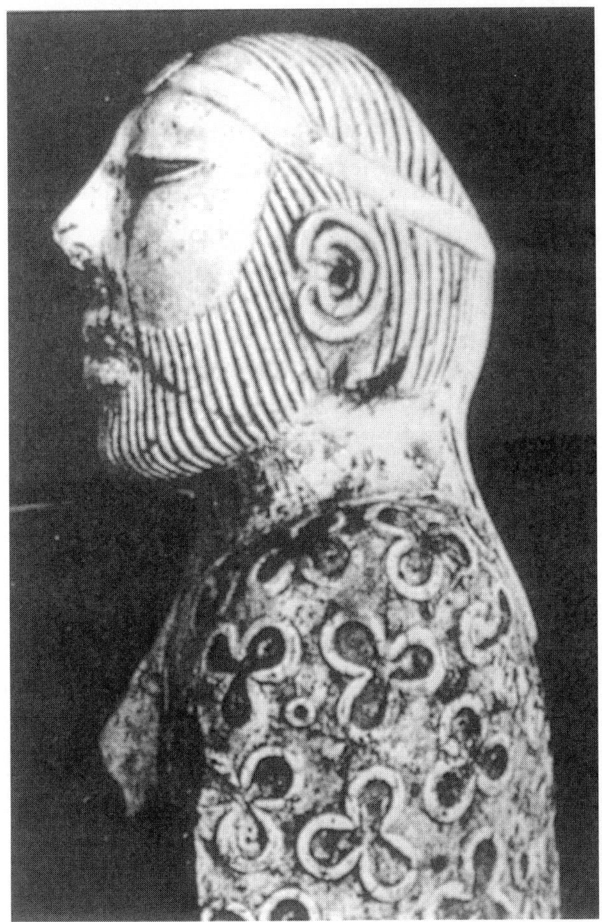

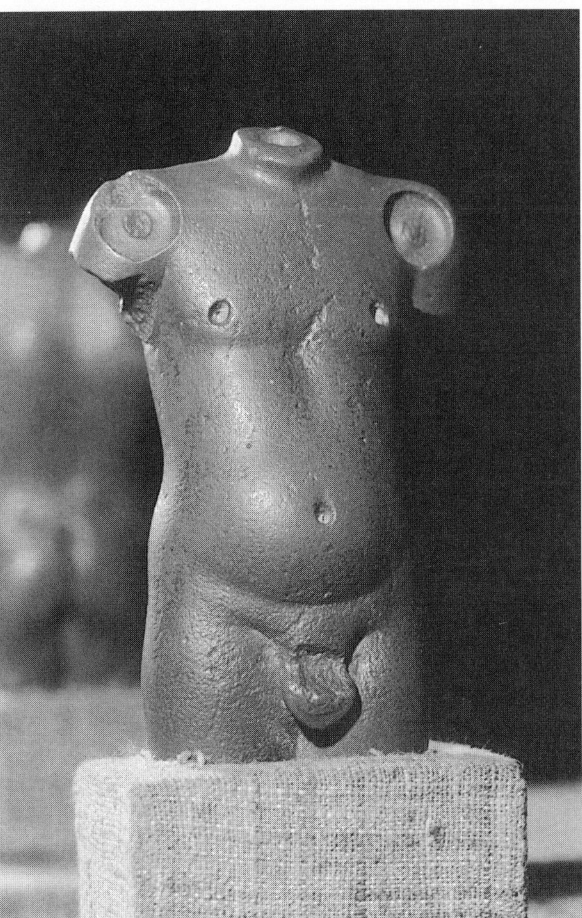

Two strikingly different objects from the Indus civilization: a priestlike figure from Mohenjo Daro and a torso from Harappa. The highly stylized priest suggests Minoan (Cretan) art; the torso, classical Greek sculpture. That both come from the Indus civilization may suggest that they were produced at different periods and reflect stylistic changes over time.

Decline and Fall

Toward the end of the third millennium B.C. the Indus civilization began to decay. We can only guess at the reasons, but there is clear evidence of progressive shrinking of the area under cultivation or irrigation and of the urban area occupied. The port of Lothal was abandoned by about 1900 B.C., and the other major centers probably supported only a fraction of their earlier populations, huddled in a small part of the decaying city. There is also evidence of violence at some of these sites: ashes and unburied or headless corpses, victims perhaps of bandit raids against largely defenseless cities. The Indus people encountered some specific problems resulting from their desert or semiarid environment, problems that may quickly have become overwhelming. Continued irrigation of any arid area leads to the progressive buildup of salts and alkalies left behind by the evaporating water and not washed away adequately by rainfall. Irrigation also raises the water table, which may drown crop roots. When accumulated salts and alkalies reach levels toxic to plants or when the root zone is flooded, agriculture may rather suddenly come to an end. We have modern experience with both problems in many arid irrigated areas, including the drier parts of the United States.

In the Indus valley large parts of the areas cultivated in ancient times appear to have been abandoned for these reasons, as the telltale white deposits on the ancient surface indicate. In addition, recurrent flooding and course changes not only menaced the cities directly but also indirectly undermined their agricultural base by destroying or choking with silt the irrigation channels that fed the fields. Course changes could also deprive a city or an irrigated area of its water. All of this is characteristic of the behavior of exotic rivers, rising in the mountains and then flowing across a treeless desert. There is no evidence that the climate changed, as has often been asserted despite clear evidence to the contrary, but plenty to suggest that the agricultural surpluses that had built the cities and nourished their culture shrank and then disappeared, leaving only a remnant population living on a relatively primitive level in the ruins of the once great cities on what they could still wring from the remaining but far less productive fields, in addition to hunting and gathering. In this reduced state, they were less and less able to defend themselves against raiders. The Aryan invaders, arriving later, could never have seen the Indus civilization in its prime and are thus unlikely causes for its decline. The people who built it, or their descendants, probably dispersed eastward into the Ganges valley and southward into peninsular India, taking their culture and technology with them.

The Aryans

Aryan is, strictly speaking, a linguistic term, but it has been used (and widely misused) to mean a people or, even more inappropriately, a race. In the centuries after about 2000 B.C. a series of migration waves moved out from south-central Asia, including what is now Iran, to richer areas both eastward and westward. One such group was probably the seaborne invaders of Greece soon after 1100 B.C., another the Kassites who invaded and conquered Sumer, and another the Hittites who occupied northern Anatolia, while still another group moved eastward through passes in the Hindu Kush range into India sometime after about 1800 B.C. and called themselves Aryans. They spoke an early form of Sanskrit but were still preliterate, preurban, seminomadic tenders of cattle, sheep, and goats who also lived in part from hunting, plough agriculture of wheat and barley, and raiding more highly developed agricultural settlements and trade centers or routes. What little we know about them comes from their ritual hymns, the Vedas, and from the later epic poems of heroic deeds and warfare, the *Mahabharata* and the *Ramayana,* which were written down many centuries later in Sanskrit, the classical language of India. By that time the Aryans had acquired literacy, as well as the arts of agriculture, city building, and other aspects of civilization, presumably from contact and intermarriage with the more highly developed people already in India.

Vedic period culture (c. 1000–c. 500 B.C.) was, like its people, a combination of originally Aryan, Harappan, and other indigenous Indian strains. Sanskrit is the oldest written language among the ancestors of modern European languages, and it is also the direct ancestor of the languages of modern North India.* The connection was not realized until the pioneering research of a British judge in Bengal in the late eighteenth century, Sir William Jones, established the clear link among the Indo-European tongues—Greek, Latin, Celtic, Persian, and Sanskrit, as well as their modern derivatives—all of which had originally stemmed from the great migration of linguistically related peoples from south-central Asia beginning around 2000 B.C. Later research has shown that the common ancestor of the Indo-European languages was probably spoken in western Asia around 4000 B.C. and that the derived languages diverged from it as groups migrated east and, later, west.

Aryan Domination

The Aryans had a telling advantage, despite their more primitive culture: By the time they reached India, they had acquired not only metal-tipped weapons but also a light, fast war chariot with spoked wheels drawn by two or more horses, equivalent to the Greek war chariots of Homer's time, with a driver and an archer or spear thrower. Their culture glorified war, and they made a disproportionate military impact on a more peaceful Indian population. The Kassites, Hittites, Hyksos, and Mycenaeans, all possibly coming originally out of central Asia, made a similar impact with the same tactics. The horse had been known to the Indus people but was not used in fighting. The Vedas and the epics tell the story of Aryan victories over "alien" peoples, whose cities they besieged and conquered, led often by their warrior god Indra, riding in his chariot with his great war bow. Like most history written by the victors, the Vedas and the epics portray the Aryans as godlike heroes and the conquered as "irreligious," inferior people. The archaeological record of the Indus civilization abundantly disproves such propaganda, but the Aryan language triumphed, presumably because, though a minority numerically, the Aryans became the ruling class of ancient India. *Arya* means "noble" or "pure" in Sanskrit; the same root word appears in the Greek *arios* ("good quality") and in the names of Iran and Eire (Ireland), illustrating the Indo-European connection.

We do not know exactly when the institution of caste, the division of Indian society into ranked status groups that could marry or eat only within the group, first

*Sanskrit *nava,* "ship"; *deva,* "god"; *dua,* "two"—these and many other Sanskrit words are easily recognizable as the roots of Latin and related English words (*naval, divine, dual,* for example).

appeared. One possibility is that it evolved later out of distinctions made in Vedic times between a conquering group of Aryans, insecure because of their numeric weakness, and a conquered people, although such distinctions must in time have been submerged by intermarriage and by cultural hybridization. In any case, caste distinctions and rules, including bans on intermarriage, seem not to have been widely observed until much later, perhaps as late as the fifth century A.D. The Aryan immigrants brought with them their male warlike gods and their male-dominated culture, which slowly blended with the female goddesses and matriarchal culture of early India.

By around 1000 B.C. these Aryan-speaking groups had conquered or absorbed most of India north of the Vindhya range, which divides and protects the peninsular south and the Deccan plateau from the Ganges and Indus valleys of the north. Their language never prevailed in the south, whose people still speak mainly four non-Indo-European languages collectively known as Dravidian, each with its own extensive and ancient literature. The south has also tended to resist what it still refers to as "Aryan" pressures or influences, but in fact interactions with the "Aryan" north have been a heavily traveled two-way street for thousands of years in religion, art, literature, philosophy, and many other aspects of culture. There is a clear north-south distinction in Indian culture, but Indian civilization is a generic whole. We can only guess at what the south was like in Vedic times. The great epics, the *Ramayana* and the *Mahabharata,* speak of the south and Ceylon (Sri Lanka) as inhabited by savages and demons with whom the Vedic heroes were at war, in keeping with their pejorative descriptions of the people they conquered in the north. But although there were probably battles and raids, the south remained beyond Aryan control except where coastal plains at the western and eastern ends of the Vindhyas allowed easier access. Ceylon was, however, invaded by sea and settled by an Aryan-speaking group in the sixth century B.C. and at about the same time by Dravidians from South India.

Vedic Culture

The basis of traditional Indian culture and most of its details evolved in the Vedic period. We know little of that process or of worldly events. The Vedas and the epics are concerned with romantic adventure involving gods and demons or with philosophical and religious matters rather than with accounts of actual events or daily life. We know only that these centuries saw the maturation of a highly sophisticated culture, no longer simply Aryan or Aryan-dominated but Indian, which we can see in worldly terms for the first time in any detail through the eyes of Greek observers after 326 B.C., following Alexander's invasion of northwestern India. They show us a culture remarkable for its absorption in philosophy and metaphysics but also for its achievements in more mundane respects. The later classical West, like the Chinese, acknowledged India as the home of the most advanced knowledge and practice of medicine; of mathematics, including the numbering system we still use, miscalled "Arabic" (the Arabs got it from India); and of working iron and steel. Indian steel was later to be transmitted to the West, also through the Arabs, as "Damascus" or "Toledo," though the steel itself was Indian. The Indian practice of medicine, known as *Ayurveda,* enriched both Greek and Chinese knowledge and was widely disseminated, although it also benefited from Greek and Chinese medical practices.

These and other elements of Indian science had something to do with Vedic period assumptions about the universe and the physical world. Like some of the Greek philosophers, but even more consistently, Vedic India thought in terms of universal laws affecting all things—a supreme principle or indwelling essence, an order of nature that they called *Rta.* This order, unlike the Greek conception, was thought to exist above and before even the gods and to determine all observable and nonobservable phenomena. Modern science and technology are not conceivable without such an assumption of universal physical laws. The Greeks were on the right track in those terms, but the Indians anticipated the Greeks and probably influenced them.

The Rise of Empire: Mauryan India

By about 500 B.C. kingdoms had emerged in the Ganges valley, already established as India's primary center of population, productivity, and commerce. This was the area traditionally known as Hindustan, which stretched from Delhi in the upper valley to Bengal near the river's mouth. Population had multiplied many times since the fall of the Indus civilization, and agriculture had spread from the Indus valley into the Ganges, a potentially more productive area watered far more plentifully by monsoonal rains and with the advantage of rich alluvial soils and a long growing season. In Harappan times the Ganges valley was still heavily forested and probably only thinly settled by hunter-gatherers. With the increasing use of iron tools after about 1000 B.C. and the rise in population, the forest was progressively cleared and most of Hindustan settled and cultivated. Growing population and surplus production provided the basis for the emergence of territorial states with revenue bases, officials, cities, roads, and armies.

Alexander the Great and the Greek Impact on India

When Alexander, fresh from his conquest of the Persian Empire and eager to add what the Persians had earlier controlled in northwestern India, burst through the northwestern passes in 326 B.C. (providing thereby the first certain date in Indian history), India was composed of many rival states covering both the north and the south. Alexander encountered and defeated some of them in the Indus valley and Punjab and heard accounts of others. His campaign against Porus, king of West Punjab, with his large army and his battalions of war elephants, was the most difficult of his career. When the proud but wounded and defeated Porus was brought before him, Alexander asked how he wished to be treated. Though barely able to stand, Porus boldly replied: "As befits me—like a king!" Alexander was so impressed that he gave him back his kingdom as an ally, a pact that Porus kept to his death. Alexander's invasion was undertaken with a strong sense of mission, to unite East and West and to create a cosmopolitan fusion of cultures, a plan he had already begun to carry out by merging Greek, Persian, and Medean elements and by taking a wife and a male companion from Persia. He encouraged his 10,000 Greek and Macedonian soldiers to take Persian and Indian wives, in keeping with his larger vision, although, like most soldiers far from home, his men probably needed little urging.

The Greek impact is symbolic of the continuous link between India and the West, not only in common linguistic roots but in physical and cultural terms too. Hellenic-style art continued to be produced by the post-Alexandrian Greek kingdoms in the northwest, such as Bactria and Gandhara, and influenced the evolution of Buddhist art in India. Indian philosophical ideas circulated more widely in the West as a result of the link that Alexander's invasion strengthened. He was himself a widely curious person. Realizing the Indian penchant for philosophy, he summoned Indian scholars to instruct and debate with him and recorded much of what he learned and observed for his own teacher, Aristotle. One Indian sage whom he summoned refused at first to come, saying that Alexander's evident preoccupation with conquest and empire could leave little place for philosophy. Alexander had him brought in, and the two men apparently impressed each other enough that they became friends and companions until Alexander's untimely death in 323 B.C. Before his homesick and rebellious troops obliged him to turn back, far short of his goal of descending the Ganges to the Bay of Bengal, he made several alliances (as with Porus), set up several Hellenic kingdoms in the northwest, and received a number of Indian princes, among them the young Chandragupta

Standing Buddha from Gandhara, a Greek-ruled kingdom in northwestern India that flourished in the second and first centuries B.C. Notice the close similarity in style to Hellenistic sculpture, including the conventional representation of the folds of the garment and the generally realistic portrayal.

Advice to Indian Princes

The Arthashastra, *in addition to its advice to princes on how to seize and hold power and to outwit rivals by often unscrupulous means, stressed the responsibility of the king to take care of his people.*

The king's pious vow is readiness in action,
his sacrifice the discharge of his duty. . . .
In the happiness of his subjects, his welfare.
The king's good is not that which pleases him,
but that which pleases his subjects.
Therefore the king should be ever active,
and should strive for prosperity,
for prosperity depends on effort,
and failure on the reverse. . . .
A single wheel cannot turn,
and so government is possible only with assistance.
Therefore a king should appoint councillors
and listen to their advice.

Source: A. L. Basham, *The Wonder That Was India,* 3rd ed. (New York: Grove Press, 1959), pp. 89, 98.

Maurya, who was to found the first Indian empire and the Maurya dynasty.

The Mauryan Conquest

By 322 B.C. Chandragupta had emerged as head of an empire that included the whole of Hindustan and most of the northwest, with its capital on the Ganges at Pataliputra, near modern Patna in what is now the state of Bihar. The age of heroic chivalry, as recorded in the Vedas and the epics, was long past, and the time of ruthless power politics had arrived. We may also guess this from the book attributed to Chandragupta's prime minister, Kautilya, the *Arthashastra.* This is one of the earliest samples we have of what was to become a genre, a handbook for rulers with advice on how to seize, hold, and manipulate power, of which the most famous in the West is *The Prince* by Niccolò Machiavelli. The *Arthashastra* also deals with the wise and humane administration of justice, but the text we have was composed by many hands over several centuries after Kautilya's time, although he may well have been the author of a now lost original. In any case, empire building is a rough game everywhere, and the writing of such a manual fits the circumstances of the time. It is paralleled very closely by a similar text, the Book of Lord Shang, and the doctrines of Li Ssu, prime minister to China's first imperial unifier, Ch'in Shih Huang Ti, about a century later as warring states were welded into an empire by conquest.

In both India and China in the sixth century B.C., warfare and political rivalries had begun to break up the institutions and values of an earlier age. This period saw the emergence of new philosophical and religious efforts to restore the social order (Confucianism in China) or to provide an escape from worldly strife through contemplation, mysticism, and otherworldly salvation (Taoism in China, Buddhism and the Hindu revival in India). These religious and philosophical developments are dealt with in Chapter 7. We know very little about actual political forms or events in India during these centuries before the rise of the Mauryan Empire. The documents we have are, as indicated earlier, concerned almost exclusively with heroic deeds or with metaphysical and religious matters. Politics and the rise and fall of kingdoms, by their nature transitory, were perhaps considered not important enough to record by comparison with the eternal quest for the mysteries of humankind and the universe, the consistent emphasis of Indian thinkers. We know the names of some of the states immediately preceding the Mauryan conquest, including the kingdom of Magadha in the central Ganges valley, which seems to have been Chandragupta's original base. But even for Mauryan India we are dependent for actual descriptions largely on Greek sources, including surviving fragments of the Book of Megasthenes, who was posted by Alexander's successor, Seleucus Nicator, to Chandragupta's court at Pataliputra. The book itself is lost, but later Greek and Latin writers drew on it extensively. It is the earliest description we have of India by an outsider.

Pataliputra and the Glory of Mauryan India

In Megasthenes' time and for some two centuries or more after, Pataliputra was probably the largest and most sophisticated city and center of culture in the world, rivaled in its later days perhaps only by the Han dynasty capital at Ch'ang An and larger than anything in the West, as the Greek accounts state. It was the seat of a famous university and library, to which scholars came, reputedly, from all over the civilized world, a city of magnificent palaces, temples, gardens, and parks. Megasthenes describes a highly organized bureaucratic system that controlled the economic and social as well as political life of Mauryan India, complete with a secret service to spy on potential dissidents, suspected criminals, and corrupt or ineffective officials. But he clearly admired Chandragupta for his conscientious administration of justice and for his imperial style. The emperor presided personally over regular sessions at court, where cases were heard and petitions presented, and ruled on disputes in similar fashion on his travels around the empire. His enormous palace at Pataliputra was a splendid complex, and visitors were awed by its magnificence and by the throngs of courtiers, councillors, and guests at state receptions.

Pataliputra was surrounded by a huge wall with 570 towers and 64 gates. All mines and forests were owned and managed by the state, and there were large state farms and state granaries, shipyards, and factories for spinning and weaving cotton cloth, all supervised by appropriate government departments. To guard against corruption and favoritism, departments were supposed to be headed by more than one chief, and officials were to be transferred often. Even prostitution was controlled by the state. Megasthenes describes Mauryan India as a place of great wealth and prosperity and remarks on the bustling trade and rich merchants. By this time, if not before, there was already an extensive seaborne trade as well, perhaps extending to Southeast Asia, and a large seaport city in Bengal, Tamralipiti, close to the mouth of the Ganges not far from modern Calcutta. Roads were essential to hold the empire together, and by Mauryan times the main trunk road of India had been built from Tamralipiti along the Ganges valley to Pataliputra, Banaras, and Delhi, through Punjab, and on to the borders of Afghanistan. Other routes branched southward, to the mouth of the Indus, linking together all the chief cities of Hindustan. The road system was apparently well maintained, marked with milestones, provided with wells and rest houses at regular intervals, and planted with trees to provide shade. Megasthenes says that famine was unknown, although it seems more likely merely that he did not hear of it during his years there. Famine was endemic everywhere in the world, and northern India especially was prone to drought, given the fickleness of the monsoon rains.

The Emperor Ashoka, "Beloved of the Gods"

Chandragupta died about 297 B.C.; we do not know the exact year, and one legend has it that he wearied of affairs of state and became a wandering ascetic, in the Indian tradition, for the last few years of his life. The empire was further expanded and consolidated by his son Bindusara, who maintained the Greek connection and exchanged gifts with Antiochus I, the Seleucid king of Syria. But the greatest Mauryan ruler was Chandragupta's grandson Ashoka, one of the great kings of world history. Here, however, is another reminder of the traditional Indian lack of interest in political history. Ashoka was perhaps the greatest Indian ruler ever, yet he

Ashoka's Goals

Ashoka had edicts inscribed on rocks and pillars at widely scattered locations all over India, stating official policy and giving instructions and advice. In one he recounts his conversion and outlines his new goals.

When the king, of gracious mien and Beloved of the Gods, had been consecrated eight years, Kalinga was conquered. 150,000 people were taken captive, 100,000 were killed, and many more died. Just after the taking of Kalinga, the Beloved of the Gods began to follow righteousness, to love righteousness, to give instruction in righteousness. When an unconquered country is conquered, people are killed. . . . That the Beloved of the Gods finds very pitiful and grievous. . . . If anyone does him wrong it will be forgiven as far as it can be forgiven. The Beloved of the Gods even reasons with the forest tribes in his empire and seeks to reform them. . . . The Beloved of the Gods considers that the greatest of all victories is the victory of righteousness.

Source: A. L. Basham, *The Wonder That Was India,* 3rd ed. (New York: Grove Press, 1959), pp. 53–54.

was all but forgotten until his rediscovery by British antiquarians and archaeologists in the late nineteenth century, thanks to Ashoka's habit of inscribing his name and imperial edicts on rocks and pillars, which he set up all over his immense empire. He came to the throne about 269 B.C. and spent the first several years of his rule in military campaigns to round out the empire by incorporating the south. According to his own rock-cut inscriptions, Ashoka saw and was grieved by the carnage that his lust for power had brought about. His campaign against the Kalingas of Orissa and northern Andhra in the northern Deccan plateau was apparently a turning point. After the campaign he foreswore further territorial aggression in favor of what he called "the conquest of righteousness." Ashoka was converted to the teachings of the Buddha, who had died four centuries earlier, and vowed to spend the rest of his life, and his great imperial power and prestige, in spreading the Buddhist message.

The beautifully carved stones and pillars that presumably marked Ashoka's empire extend far into the south, well beyond Andhra, and may suggest that he added to his military conquests those of the spirit. We do not know to what extent the south was ruled from Pataliputra during his time, although we know that a Mauryan governor was appointed for the southern provinces. Ashoka clearly felt a sense of mission, not only to spread Buddhism but also to set an example of righteousness in government that could persuade others elsewhere to follow it. He declared that all people everywhere were his children, and he softened the harsher aspects of Chandragupta's police state methods of control. He advocated the ancient Indian ideal of nonviolence (adopted also by the Buddha), urged pilgrimages as a substitute for hunting, and encouraged the spread of vegetarianism. But he kept his army, law courts, and systems of punishment, including execution for major crimes, and remained an emperor in every sense, with his feet firmly in the world of politics. Nevertheless, his reign was remarkable for its humanity and its vision. The modern Republic of India appropriately adopted for its state seal the sculptured lions from the capital of one of Ashoka's pillars. Ashoka also sent explicitly Buddhist missions to Ceylon, and missionaries later went to Burma and Java. They converted the first two countries almost entirely to that faith, which they still hold, while establishing Buddhism as a new religion in much of the rest of Southeast Asia. Indian traders and adventurers, as well as priests and scholars, also carried Indian high culture in art, literature, written language, and statecraft to Southeast Asia. This cultural diffusion from India marked the beginning of literate civilization, in the Indian mode, in much of that extensive region, an origin still evident in many respects.

Kushans and Greeks

Soon after Ashoka's death around 232 B.C., the Mauryan empire seems to have disintegrated into civil war among provincial governors, although the Mauryan name continued through several successive rulers at Pataliputra. By 180 B.C. or so, India had returned to its more traditional pattern of separate regional kingdoms. The northwest was again invaded by Greeks, descendants of groups left behind by Alexander. Northern India was subsequently invaded by new groups of outsiders, the Sakas (Scythians) from west-central Asia, and by other originally nomadic peoples from east-central Asia who were driven from their pasturelands by the ancestors of the Mongols and by the rise of the first Chinese empire, the Ch'in, in the late third century B.C. One such group around 100 B.C. crossed the passes into Kashmir and down onto the Indian plain, where they defeated the Greek, Saka, and Indian kingdoms and welded most of the north into a new empire, the Kushan dynasty. The Kushans restored much of the former Mauryan grandeur, ruling also from Pataliputra, but they too declined after some three centuries, and by A.D. 200 the north was once again, like the south, a regional patchwork. The Kushans adopted and promoted Buddhism and disseminated it to their former homelands in central Asia, from which it later reached China. In other respects, like nearly all invaders or conquerors of India, they became thoroughly Indianized, including not only their adoption of the other aspects of Indian culture and language but also widespread intermarriage, adding still further to the hybrid character of the population. The most obvious and enduring legacy of the Kushans is probably the magnificent Buddhist sculpture produced under their rule and patronage. It is interesting also for the clear traces of Hellenistic artistic influence, still important in India in the time of the Kushans, deriving both from the remaining Greek-style kingdoms in the northwest and from direct contact with the Hellenic world by sea.

Throughout the centuries after Alexander, Greek traders and travelers visited India on a regular basis. Greek ships carried Indian goods to the Mediterranean: spices, precious stones, incense, brasswork, fine cotton textiles, ivory, peacocks, monkeys, and even larger wild animals. Indian philosophers visited Mediterranean and Levantine cities, perhaps making some contribution to the Western intellectual heritage. In return, there seems little reason to doubt the claim of Indian Christians that their early church was begun by Thomas the Apostle, who probably reached India and founded there what may well be the world's oldest Christian community. The trip from Suez—or from Alexandria, where we know the apostles preached—was routine in the first century A.D. India was connected to the Greco-Roman world, and one of the apostles probably preached there in carrying out the command recorded in Mark 16:15: "Go ye into

Perhaps the best-known samples of Mauryan art are the pillars erected by the emperor Ashoka, usually bearing Buddhist edicts and surmounted by sculptured figures. This triad of royal lions in stone, still used as an official symbol of India, formed the capital of one of Ashoka's columns and effectively captures the splendor of Mauryan India.

all the world and preach the gospel to every creature." To this day, a large proportion of Indian Christians, clustered in the southwest near the ports the Greeks and Romans used, carry the surname Thomas.

Our most important source for this period of Indian history is a Greek handbook for traders and travelers to India called the *Periplus of the Erythrean Sea,* dated about A.D. 80, which gives sailing directions, information on prices and sources for Indian goods, and brief descriptions of Indian culture. Large hoards of Roman coins, to pay for India's exports, and Roman pottery have been found at many ports along the west coast, from Mannar in Ceylon through Cochin and Calicut to the Bombay area and now abandoned ports south of the Indus mouth.

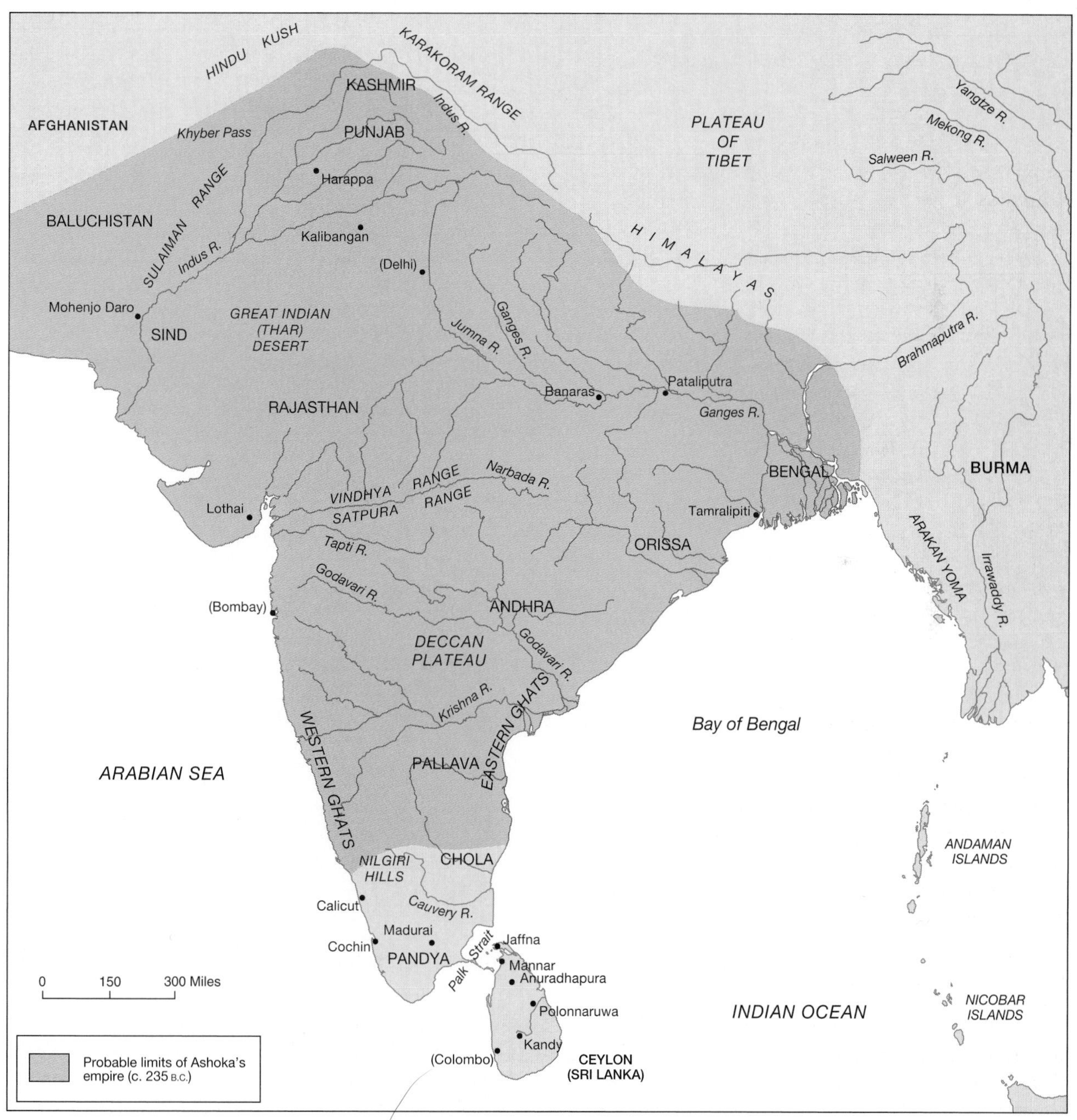

MAP 2.2 ANCIENT INDIA

Southern India

The south was protected against pressures from successive states or empires in the north by the uplifted plateau of the Deccan and its fringing mountains, the Vindhya and Satpura ranges, punctuated by the Narbada and Tapti rivers as further barriers. There was also fierce southern resistance to the repeated attempts at conquest from the north. We know very little about the lower half of India before about the time of Ashoka. By then it is clear that southern cultures and states, though divided into often rival groups, were fully as rich and sophisticated as those of the Aryan-influenced north. They shared what was by the third or second century B.C. a common Indian civilization, including Hinduism, philosophy, values, art forms, and material culture. The three largest political states of the south were Chola, Pandya, and Pallava, which vied with each other for regional dominance but were never able to unite the whole area under the control of any one of them. Each maintained extensive trade relations by sea, mainly with Southeast Asia, and the cultural, economic, religious, and political life of each centered in their respective capitals, which were dominated by temple complexes.

The City of Madurai

Probably the largest and best-preserved temple complex is the former Pandya capital of Madurai. The fullest and most detailed account of any ancient Indian city is included in an early Tamil poem of the third century A.D. called *The Garland of Madurai,* which may be summarized in part as follows:

> **The poet enters the city by its great gate, the posts of which are carved with the images of the goddess Lakshmi. It is a festival day, and the city is gay with flags; some, presented by the king to commemorate brave deeds, fly over the houses of captains; others wave over the shops which sell toddy [a fermented drink made from the blossom of the palm tree]. The streets are broad rivers of people of every race, buying and selling in the market place or singing to the music of wandering minstrels.**
>
> **The drum beats and a royal procession passes down the street, with elephants leading and the sound of conchs [shell trumpets]. An unruly elephant breaks his chain and tosses like a ship in an angry sea until he is brought under control. Chariots follow, with prancing horses and fierce footmen. Stall keepers ply their trade, selling sweet cakes, garlands of flowers, scented powder, and rolls of betel nut [to chew]. Old women go from house to house selling nosegays and trinkets. Noblemen drive through the streets in their chariots, their gold-sheathed swords flashing, wearing brightly dyed garments and wreaths of flowers. The jewels of the perfumed women watching from balconies and turrets flash in the sun.**
>
> **People flock to the temples to worship to the sound of music, laying flowers before the images. Craftsmen work in their shops, bangle-makers, goldsmiths, cloth weavers, coppersmiths, flower sellers, wood carvers, and painters. Foodshops are busily selling mangoes, sugar candy, cooked rice, and chunks of cooked meat. [At this period, only the more pious Hindus were strict vegetarians.] In the evening, the city's prostitutes entertain their patrons with dancing and singing to the accompaniment of the lute. The streets are filled with music. Drunken villagers, in town for the festival, reel about in the streets. Respectable women visit the temples in the evening with their children and friends, carrying lighted lamps as offerings. They dance in the temple courts, which resound with their singing and chatter.**
>
> **At last the city sleeps . . . all but the ghosts and goblins who haunt the dark and the housebreakers, armed with rope ladders, swords, and chisels. But the watchmen are also vigilant, and the city passes the night in peace. Morning comes with the sounds of brahmins intoning their sacred verses. The wandering bands renew their singing, and the shopkeepers open their booths. The toddy-sellers ply their trade for thirsty early morning travelers. The drunkards stagger to their feet. All over the city the sound is heard of doors opening. Women sweep the faded flowers of the festival from their courtyards. The busy everyday life of the city is resumed.[1]**

This gives a vivid picture of what urban life must really have been like; with few adjustments, it could serve as a description of a festival day in a small Indian city even today.

Ceylon

The island of Ceylon (called Sri Lanka since 1975, reviving an ancient name for the country) lies within view of the tip of South India, only some 20 miles across the shallow Palk Strait via a disconnected chain of islands. Nevertheless, the two countries have always been separate politically, and Ceylon developed a distinctive culture and sense of separate identity even though it remained, understandably, a part of greater Indian culture. Sometime in the sixth century B.C. a Sanskrit- or Aryan-speaking prince named Vijaya came to Ceylon by sea from northwestern India with a large band of followers and established a kingdom. It is likely that Indian merchants had visited Ceylon earlier and perhaps settled there, but we have no record of such earlier contact. The followers of Vijaya called themselves Sinhala ("lion people") and became the dominant inhabitants of Ceylon as the Sinhalese (Singhalese). This is also the name of their Indo-European language, which is related to those of North India. The Sinhalese brought with them not only the literacy, writing forms, and religion of late Vedic North India but also much of the rest of its culture and technology, including the knowledge of irrigation and the cultivation of rice. They were probably joined shortly by a second wave of settlement from Bengal, which merged with them. The Sinhalese soon displaced the earlier and far less technically developed Neolithic inhabitants of the island, the Vaddas, a few survivors of whom still live in the remoter jungles, although in the earlier centuries there was considerable intermarriage.

Beginning no later than the first century B.C. the Sinhalese constructed an extensive system of irrigated rice agriculture, centered in the northern half of the island with its capital at Anuradhapura and a secondary urban center at Polonnaruwa. This area was part of the so-called Dry Zone of Ceylon, where permanent field agriculture is impossible without irrigation but where fertile soils, level land, and an unbroken growing season of strong sun and high temperatures can produce high crop yields if water is available. Considerable rain falls there in a brief period of three months during the northeast monsoon of winter, leaving the rest of the year mainly dry. The Sinhalese kingdom constructed large reservoirs to catch the winter rain and stream runoff and then to distribute it to rice fields through an intricate system of canals. Dams also diverted water from the few year-round streams that flowed through the area. The population of the Dry Zone grew substantially, and Anuradhapura at its height in about the tenth century A.D. may have contained 100,000 people or more, while Ceylon as a whole may have had as many as 3 or 4 million. Only with such a large population, controlled by the state through corvée (conscript labor), could the massive irrigation works be built and maintained and the many large palaces and temples at Anuradhapura constructed. Nowhere else in the premodern world was there such a dense concentration of irrigation facilities at such a high technical level, but it was dependent on maintaining state control over mass labor.

Ceylon was the first area beyond India to which Buddhism spread. The pious legend is that Ananda, a disciple of the Buddha, brought the message himself in the Buddha's own lifetime, but Buddhism probably did not extend beyond North India, and almost certainly not to Ceylon, until Ashoka's time in the third century B.C., when missionaries were specifically dispatched to Ceylon and Burma. The Sinhalese rapidly accepted and have retained Buddhism. They produced beautiful works of sculpture and architecture in the Buddhist-Indian tradition, including the world's largest mound temples or stupas and colossal statues of the Buddha and his disciples. The great stupa at Anuradhapura is bigger than all but one of the pyramids of ancient Egypt and is surrounded for miles by others nearly as big, as well as by a host of beautiful, monumental stone buildings and large baths. All of this gorgeous display suggests large, consistent surpluses from the agricultural system to pay for the costs of construction and art and an economy that could spare labor for such purposes. The classical Sinhalese chronicles, compiled and preserved by Buddhist monks, deal mainly with the pious acts of successive kings, especially their building or endowing of temples, but indirectly they reflect a prosperous and generally controlled society.

Given the short and easy journey from southern India to Ceylon, continuous interaction probably began before the sixth century B.C. By or before the Christian era, the northern tip of Ceylon had been settled by people from the Dravidian Tamil-speaking area of South India, who practiced their own form of irrigated agriculture based mainly on wells. They became the dominant inhabitants of the Jaffna peninsula and the immediately adjacent parts of the north but retained their cultural ties with South India as well as their Hinduism. Immigration from South India continued for several centuries, and there was some intermarriage with the Sinhalese. These two groups of Indian immigrants, Sinhalese and Tamils, coexisted for most of Ceylon's history, until their differences exploded into a violent political issue in the 1950s (described in Chapter 41).

The Sinhala kingdom based at Anuradhapura periodically controlled the Tamil areas of the north but had to protect itself against intermittent raiding from the far larger Tamil kingdoms in South India. These raids often stimulated or increased internal dissension when rival Sinhalese claimants to the throne made common cause with the invaders, especially after about the sixth century A.D. The Chola empire, which arose in the early centuries of the Christian era in South India, launched a particularly destructive invasion of Ceylon in the eleventh century that sacked Anuradhapura in 1017. The Sinhalese capital was moved to Polonnaruwa, from which the local forces finally drove the Cholas out of the country by 1070. In the following century King Parakrama Bahu (1153–1186) unified the whole of Ceylon from his capital at Polonnaruwa, invaded South India and Burma, and constructed huge new irrigation works and public buildings that made his capital almost as impressive as Anuradhapura had been. But his death was followed by civil war and by new and especially destructive invasions from South India, which led by the thirteenth century to the virtual abandonment of the Dry Zone, whose vital irrigation works could no longer be maintained. The much reduced population clustered from then on in the protection of the hills and mountains of southeastern Ceylon, centered on the medieval capital of Kandy, and later in the lowlands around the port of Colombo.

The Guptas and the Empire of Harsha

An imperial revival of the Mauryan model in India, the Gupta dynasty, ruled the north from about A.D. 320 to about 550. Pataliputra was again the imperial capital and seems once more to have played the role of cultural center for surrounding areas. Contact with the West appears to have diminished or ceased by this time, as the eastern Roman Empire was largely cut off from India by the rise of the Sassanid dynasty in Persia. Trade and cultural exchange, however, was still extensive with Southeast Asia, although most of it probably took place from the South Indian kingdoms of Chola, Pandya, and Pallava and from ports on the southeast coast, beyond Guptan imperial control. For much of what we know about the Gupta period, as for earlier periods, we are dependent on foreign observers. The chief source is the diary of Fa Hsien, a Chinese Buddhist monk who made the long and arduous journey to India via central Asia and the Himalayas to seek true copies of the Buddhist sutras (scriptures) and who lived and traveled there for six years in the early 400s. A typical literate Chinese, he carefully recorded what he observed, at Pataliputra and elsewhere, and gives a picture of a rich and sophisticated society and of its culturally brilliant capital in the early fifth century, when it was probably at its height.

Life and Culture in the Guptan Period

Fa Hsien noted the peacefulness of Guptan India and the mildness of its government. His journal remarks that crime was rare and that one could travel from one end of the empire to another without harm and with no need for travel documents. He made special note of the free hospitals for treatment of the sick, supported by private donations. He also says that all "respectable" people (by which he probably means those of high caste) were vegetarians, a trend that seemed to have picked up momentum from the time of Ashoka, but that the lower orders ate meat and hence were regarded as sources of "pollution," an aspect of caste that he was the first outsider to describe. Buddhism he describes as still flourishing, but apparently in the process of being reabsorbed into the Hinduism from which it had originally sprung. In general, Fa Hsien's account shows us a prosperous, tranquil, and smoothly operating society, which probably contrasted with the turbulent China of his time.

The Gupta period was the golden age of Sanskrit literature and of classical Indian sculpture and monumental building, although unfortunately only fragments have survived. This cultural flowering was equally vigorous in the south, beyond Gupta control, and in both south and north seems to have taken the form of a renaissance of Mauryan grandeur. Kalidasa, widely acclaimed as India's greatest poet and playwright, lived and worked in the late fourth and early fifth centuries, near the peak of Gupta vigor. Many of his works have survived, as have fragments of some others. They still make fresh and enchanting reading, as well as moving commentaries on the foibles of human existence.

The Collapse of Gupta Rule

By 550 or so the Gupta power was destroyed by new invaders, the so-called White Huns (probably Iranians or Turks from central Asia), one more group in the long succession of ethnically and culturally different outsiders drawn to India by its wealth and sophistication and then woven into the hybrid Indian fabric. Like earlier and later invaders, they came from the west, through the only easy entrance into the subcontinent, the passes that punctuate the northwest frontier. As the linguistic tie still reminds us, India's relations were and remained overwhelmingly with the West since at least Harappan times and, except for the sea connection with Southeast Asia, hardly at all with the East and with China, the other major cultural center of Asia. Buddhism did move from India, first into central Asia and then into China by Han times, but it seems to have carried very little of Indian culture with it except for some art forms, and almost nothing of Chinese culture seems to have penetrated into India. Cotton, native to India and first woven into cloth there, spread to China only some 3,000 years later. Trade between the two societies, the other common vehicle of cultural exchange, was minimal and indirect. The reason is clear from a glance at the map: The world's highest mountains lie between India and China, and behind them the desert or alpine wastelands of Sinkiang and Tibet. It is in fact a very long and exceptionally difficult way between the centers of Indian and Chinese civilization, from the plains of Hindustan to the lower Yellow and

The Port of Puhar

A graphic passage in the Tamil epic the Silappatikaram, *of uncertain date but probably fourth or fifth century A.D., describes the port city of Puhar, not far from modern Madras, in this period a great center of foreign trade.*

The riches of Puhar shipowners made the kings of faraway lands envious. The most costly merchandise, the rarest foreign produce reached the city. . . . The sunshine lighted up the open terraces, the harbor docks, the towers with their loopholes like the eyes of deer. In various quarters of the city the homes of wealthy Greeks were seen. Near the harbor seamen from far-off lands appeared at home. In the streets hawkers were selling unguents, bath powders, cooling oils, flowers, perfume, and incense. . . . Each trade had its own street in the workers' quarter of the city. At the center of the city were the wide royal street, the street of temple cars, the bazaar, and the main street where rich merchants had their mansions . . . with warehouses of merchandise from overseas. . . . Near the sea, flags raised high toward the sky seemed to be saying: "On these stretches of white sand can be found the goods that foreign merchants, leaving their own countries to stay among us, have brought here in great ships." . . . All night lamps were burning, the lamps of foreigners who talk strange tongues, and of the guards who watch over precious cargoes near the docks.

Source: A. Danielou, trans., in M. Singer, "Beyond Tradition and Modernity in Madras," *Comparative Studies in Society and History* 13 (1971): 169–170.

Yangtze river valleys. The shorter route from eastern India through Burma and into mountainous southwest China (still a long way from the Chinese center) has proved even more difficult, with its combination of mountains, deep gorges, and rain forest, and has never carried more than a trickle of indirect trade.

With the collapse of the Gupta empire, India reverted once more to its regional structures. The new invaders from central Asia did not succeed in building their own empire, and for a time there was political chaos, but the first half of the seventh century saw a final indigenous effort at unification. This was the reign of Harsha (606–648), who in a series of campaigns joined the separate kingdoms of the north together and presided over a notable reflowering of Sanskrit literature and art. Harsha also encouraged Buddhism, and the Chinese Buddhist monk Hsuan Tsang visited his court, leaving a valuable account of it and of the contemporary India through which he traveled. His journal gives an admiring picture of Harsha as a charismatic, energetic, and able administrator and an impressive emperor of his domains, through which he made repeated tours to supervise its government. Like earlier and later Indian emperors, he held court wherever he went, to hear complaints and dispense justice. Like them, he lived in luxury and pomp but loved literature and philosophy and was a generous patron; he even found time to write plays himself. By this time Hsuan Tsang's account shows Buddhism declining and Hinduism again dominant, but, perhaps because of the brevity and idiosyncrasy of Harsha's rule, law and order were not as well kept as in Guptan times. Hsuan Tsang reports banditry and was himself robbed twice on

INDIA TO A.D. 648

c. 3000–c. 1900 B.C.	Indus civilization
After 2000 B.C.	Arrival of the Aryans
c. 1000–c. 500 B.C.	Vedic culture
326 B.C.	Invasion by Alexander the Great
c. 322–c. 297 B.C.	Reign of Chandragupta
c. 269–c. 232 B.C.	Reign of Ashoka
c. 180 B.C.	New Greek invasions begin
c. 100 B.C.	Kushan invasion
c. A.D. 320–c. 550	Gupta dynasty
A.D. 606–648	Reign of Harsha

his travels. Harsha's empire was so much his own creation that when he died in 648, leaving no heirs, it disintegrated into factional fighting.

Women in Ancient India

Medieval and early modern India tended to fit the popular stereotype applied to most traditional Asian societies: heavy male dominance and female subservience or even servitude. That situation has been changing fast in twentieth-century Asia and was, like most stereotypes, not totally accurate even for the past. In particular, it overlooks the major part nearly all women played in the basic Asian institution of the family, a private as opposed to public role but often critically important, and it also overlooks the many women writers and performers of other public roles, including political ones. However, ancient India was substantially different from the later period of Indian history in this respect. There is much evidence to show that pre-Mauryan Indian society, especially in the south, was matriarchal; women held important economic power, property, and status, and family names often descended through the female line. This ancient pattern survives in parts of South India today. The Aryan north was from Vedic times more clearly patriarchal, and women were conventionally seen as subject to their parents, husbands, and male relatives. But they had some control over personal property, and a number of women even owned businesses. Women could not serve as priests but were free to become nuns, several of whom were notable poets and scholars. The *Upanishads,* treatises dating from about the seventh century B.C., tell the story of an exceptionally learned woman, Gargi Vacaknavi, who took an active part in discussions with the sage Yajnavalkya and outdistanced all her male counterparts. Other women attended lectures by sages and mastered the Vedas. Goddesses were as important as gods in Vedic religion, and a goddess's name was commonly recited before that of a god, a practice that still persists.

By the Mauryan era, however, the scope for women in religious and intellectual pursuits seems to have been reduced. Convention shifted to an emphasis on marriage and care of the family as the proper female role, although many upper-class women continued to be taught privately or to educate themselves, and several wrote poetry and drama that was widely read. Others learned music (both performance and composition), dancing, and painting. In early Vedic times (we know too little about society in Harappan times to speculate about it), unmarried men and women seem to have mixed freely. By the time of the *Arthashastra* (third century B.C.), upper-class women were more circumscribed by convention, although widows were still free to marry. By late Gupta times (sixth century A.D.), restrictions on women had increased, and widows could no longer remarry. Women were to be cherished but protected—and restricted—a trend that had apparently begun under Mauryan rule, at least in the north. In the south, women remained freer and less submissive.

The freest women in ancient India were probably the courtesans (high-class prostitutes). In many traditional societies, including India, they were usually well educated and well versed in the classics, the arts of music, dance, poetry and its composition, flower arranging, the composition of riddles and other mental puzzles, and even fencing. There were lower grades of prostitutes, but the standard was generally high. Such women were often praised for their learning and quick verbal wit, sometimes even more than for their beauty, as in China and Japan. Even the Buddha is said to have chosen to dine with a famous courtesan rather than with the city fathers, no doubt duller company. Many of the courtesans were celebrated poets, but most of them were considered especially sensitive and as having "great souls."

Another group of women were hereditary dancers in the service of temples; most of them also served as prostitutes, but in any case they never married, having dedicated themselves to the god, like the temple priestesses and vestal virgins of classical Greece and Rome. Dance was a particularly important religious ritual in India, as well as a beautiful art form. The god Shiva was thought to have created the world through his cosmic dance and to dance on the harvest floor as the spirit of life and of creation. From at least the Gupta period, classical Indian dance came to be associated with the temple dancers, servants of the god and a special class of women, some of whom were also prostitutes. They were honored and admired for their art but socially discriminated against. Other women were discouraged from dancing because of this association until recent years, when the classical dance forms have seen a national revival and have once again become respectable.

The custom of *sati* (suttee), wives burning themselves to death on their husbands' funeral pyres, does not seem to have extended to most widows at any period in Indian history. Although it was known in ancient India, Sumer, and China, it was uncommon. When it was practiced, it was mainly as part of the custom of burning or burying all the followers, retainers, horses, and prized possessions of a dead ruler or aristocrat with him. *Sati* was relatively rare until late Gupta times, when widow remarriage had begun to be strongly discouraged or prohibited, as it had not been before. It became more com-

Art of Ancient India and China

Bronze mirror inlaid with gold and silver from the late Chou dynasty. Mirrors like this, highly polished to give a good reflection, were made in great quantities, especially in the Chou and Han dynasties, and were often beautifully decorated. The pierced knob in the center was to permit hanging by a cord.

The terra-cotta army of the first emperor. Ch'in Shih Huang Ti was buried in a huge underground tomb near modern Sian with an army of life-size clay figures to guard the approaches. Excavations in the 1970s brought them to light again after more than two thousand years. Each figure is a faithful representation of a real individual.

Tomb figure from northwestern China, fourth century A.D. The artistic creativity of ancient cultures was manifested in their music. From paintings and sculpture, such as this pottery figure of a woman playing bamboo pipes, musicologists can learn much about ancient music.

In this painting, attributed to Ku K'ai-chih (344–406), an instructress is writing down directions for her pupils, ladies of the court. In China, as elsewhere, court ladies were expected to be literate and accomplished in several arts.

The temple complex at Madurai in South India is one of the classic buildings saved from the Muslim onslaught that swept northern India starting in the twelfth century A.D.

The art of ancient Ceylon: divine nymph dropping flowers on the earth, from a mural of the fifth century A.D. painted on the rock face of the fortress of Sigiriya in the southern Dry Zone, preserved better than most Indian painting of this period, which it closely resembles.

This figure of a tree goddess from the second century A.D. is a fine example of the grace and voluptuousness that Indian sculptors were able to capture in stone.

Virtues of an Indian Wife

A passage in the Mahabharata *extolls the virtues of a wife.*

The wife is half the man, the best of friends,
the root of the three ends of life,
and of all that will help him in the other world.
With a wife a man does mighty deeds,
with a wife a man finds courage.
A wife is the safest refuge;
a man aflame with sorrow in his soul or sick with disease
finds comfort in his wife as a man parched with heat finds relief in water.
Even a man in the grip of rage will not be harsh to a woman,
remembering that on her depend the joys of life, happiness, and virtue.
For a woman is the everlasting field
in which the self is born.

Some centuries later the Laws of Manu, *written about the second century A.D., reflected the growing emphasis on the domesticity and dependency of women.*

She should always be cheerful, and skillful in her domestic duties with her household vessels well cleaned and her hand tight on the purse-strings. In season and out of season her lord, who wed her with sacred rites, ever gives happiness to his wife, both here and in the other world. Though he be uncouth and prone to pleasure, though he have no good points at all, the virtuous wife should ever worship her lord as a god.

Source: A. L. Basham, *The Wonder That Was India,* 3rd ed. (New York: Grove Press, 1959), pp. 180–182.

mon thereafter, although it was supposed to be voluntary, as a mark of exceptional fidelity. Social and family pressure, as well as the emptiness and often the material hardship of a young widow's life, doubtless added other incentives. *Sati* horrified early Western observers, and the British tried to suppress it in the nineteenth century. Many ancient and even medieval Indian writers and poets condemned it, and in the end the Hindu renaissance and reform movement of the late nineteenth century turned educated Indian opinion against it. There is some evidence that *sati* is occasionally practiced even now.

The Indian Heritage

The building and maintaining of empires exacts a heavy human cost everywhere. India's return to its more normal regionalism after the collapse of the Gupta empire and the death of Harsha was hardly a tragedy. But it leaves the historian, whose data are only fragmentary, to try to deal with a confused tapestry woven, like India's history and culture as a whole, of many threads. The revival of regional kingdoms did, however, encourage the continued development of the rich regional cultures that make up the Indian fabric.

Given India's size and diversity, it is not surprising that the subcontinent has only very briefly been united into a single empire, and even under Ashoka and the later rule of the British some areas remained outside imperial control. We are accustomed to thinking of Europe as properly composed of a large number of separate states and cultures, despite the heritage of common Roman rule over much of it for some four centuries and despite its common membership in the Greek, Roman, and Christian traditions. India too has long shared common traditions, including the universal spread of Hinduism, and like Europe has experienced successive efforts at unification by conquest. But the strength of separate regional cultures and states remained at least as great as in Europe, reinforced by different languages, literatures, and political rivalries. India's more recent success in building a modern state—or rather the three states of Pakistan, India, and Bangladesh—contrasts with the continued political division of Europe but still encompasses regional differences, each with its own proud tradition reaching back before Ashoka. In these terms, there is nothing improper or backward about regional separatism for India, Europe, or any other area of the size and variety of the subcontinent. India, like Europe, would be the poorer without its array of different cultural and regional traditions. Their separate contributions in literature, philosophy, and the arts in the centuries of political disunity after the death of Harsha continued to enrich the varied tapestry of Indian civilization. But our political picture of those centuries is confusing, frequently changing, and plagued by a severe shortage of information.

Ancient and classical India as a whole had a deep respect for learning and for education, beginning with literacy and mathematics and continuing to philosophy and the study of the Vedas. But education was a privilege enjoyed only by the upper classes, and after the Vedic age for the most part only by males, as in nearly all premodern societies. The several Greek and Chinese travelers to classical India who have left accounts describe the rural scene as productive and prosperous and compare it and the lot of villagers favorably with their own homelands. India during these centuries may have been less burdened by mass poverty or communal tensions than it is now, but we have no way to measure that. Contemporary accounts from that period could, of course, make judgments only in terms of what they knew of conditions elsewhere. Our modern perspectives are different. But the classical accounts we have nearly all stress the relatively high level of material well-being, the orderliness of the society, and its impressive achievements in science, technology, philosophy, and the arts. It is a tradition of which modern Indians are justly proud.

From the modern perspective, classical India seems especially noteworthy for its scientific accomplishments. Mathematics had by Gupta times been brought to a high level of sophistication, including a rudimentary algebra and a numeration system using nine digits and a zero, far more efficient than the cumbersome Roman numerals. The Arabs, who transmitted it to the West, called mathematics the "Indian art" (*Hindisat*). Later European science would have been impossible without it. Medieval Indian mathematicians after Harsha's time developed the concepts of negative and positive quantities, worked out square and cube roots, solved quadratic and other equations, understood the mathematical implications of zero and infinity, worked out the value of pi to nine decimal places, and took important steps in trigonometry, sine functions, spherical geometry, and calculus. Earlier Indian scientists anticipated the classical Greeks in developing an atomic theory of elements, basic to twentieth-century Western science, by the sixth century B.C. Traditional Indian medicine had a very extensive pharmacopoeia and used a variety of herbal remedies and drugs discovered and used only much later in the West. Physicians appear to have understood the function of the spinal cord and the nervous system, and successful surgery included cesarean section, complicated bone setting, plastic surgery, and the repair of damaged limbs. Vaccination against smallpox was first used in Guptan India well over 1,000 years before it was tried in the West. Doctors were highly respected, and the textbook of the famous physician Caraka in the late first century A.D. includes a passage reminiscent of Hippocrates, the classical Greek physician:

> **If you want success in your practice . . . you must pray every day on rising and going to bed for the welfare of all beings . . . and strive with all your soul for the health of the sick. You must not betray your patients, even at the cost of your own life. . . . You must be pleasant of speech . . . and thoughtful, always striving to improve your knowledge.**
>
> **When you go to the home of a patient you should direct your words, mind, intellect, and senses nowhere but to your patient and his treatment. . . . Nothing that happens in the house of the sick man must be told outside, nor must the patient's condition be told to anyone who might do harm by that knowledge.[2]**

SUMMARY

For the Indians it was not particularly important to record the details of empires, kingdoms, rivalries, and political changes. We do have enough evidence to show us a sophisticated civilization, a remarkably humane set of values, and enough glimpses of the life of the common people to establish ancient and classical India as a great tradition, one of the major achievements of the human experience.

The Indus civilization, with major urban centers at Kalibangan, Harappa, and Mohenjo Daro, arose, flourished, and declined between 3000 and 2000 B.C. The migration of Aryan-speaking peoples from central Asia into North India after about 1800 B.C. produced Vedic culture, which became dominant in most of the north. Regional kingdoms had emerged by 500 B.C., some of which Alexander encountered when he invaded the northwest in 326 B.C. *By 322 the Mauryan empire had emerged under Chandragupta Maurya and unified most of the north from the imperial capital at Pataliputra in the central Ganges valley. Chandragupta's grandson Ashoka ruled as emperor from around 269 to 232* B.C. *and extended the empire southward. Troubled by the slaughter occasioned by his conquests, he converted to the non-violent faith of Buddhism and devoted the rest of his reign to spreading its message. The Mauryan power faded after his death, and both North and South India reverted to regional rule. New Greek and Scythian invaders in the north yielded to another dynasty of conquest, the Kushans, from around 100* B.C. *to* A.D. *200, while the south and Ceylon supported separate flourishing kingdoms and built impressive architectural monuments. The Gupta dynasty restored much of the Mauryan grandeur in the north from about 320 to 550, based again at Pataliputra, and Harsha from 606 to 648 re-united the Guptan empire. After his death India resumed its more typical political pattern of separate regional kingdoms, where art, learning, philosophy, and commerce continued to thrive.*

NOTES

1. A. L. Basham, *The Wonder That Was India,* 3rd ed. (New York: Grove Press, 1959), pp. 203–204.
2. Ibid., p. 500.

SUGGESTIONS FOR FURTHER READING

Allchin, B., and Allchin, R. *The Rise of Civilization in India and Pakistan.* Cambridge: Cambridge University Press, 1982.

Auboyer, J. *Daily Life in Ancient India.* London: Weidenfeld and Nicolson, 1965.

Basham, A. L. *The Wonder That Was India,* 3rd ed. New York: Grove Press, 1959.

Begley, V., and Puma, R. D., eds. *Rome and India.* Madison: University of Wisconsin Press, 1992.

Buck, W. *Ramayana.* Berkeley: University of California Press, 1976.

Dutt, A. K., and Selb, M. *Atlas of South Asia.* Boulder, Colo.: Westview, 1987.

Gokhale, B. G. *Asoka Maurya.* New York: Twayne, 1966.

Kalidasa. *The Cloud Messenger,* trans. F. Edgerton and E. Edgerton. Ann Arbor: University of Michigan Press, 1964.

Kautilya. *The Arthasastra,* trans. R. Shamasastry. Mysore, India: Raghuveer Printing Press, 1951.

Kosambi, D. D. *Ancient India: A History of Its Culture and Civilization.* New York: Pantheon, 1966.

Liu, X. *Ancient China and Ancient India: Trade and Religious Exchange.* New York: Oxford University Press, 1988.

McCrindle, J. W., trans. *Ancient India as Described in Classical Literature.* New Delhi: Today and Tomorrow Press, 1972.

Miller, B. S., ed. and trans. *Theater of Memory: The Plays of Kalidasa.* New York: Columbia University Press, 1984.

———, trans. *The Bhagavadgita.* New York: Columbia University Press, 1986.

Murphey, R. "The Ruin of Ancient Ceylon," *Journal of Asian Studies* 16 (1957): 181–200.

Nilakana, S. *A History of South India,* 4th ed. Madras: Oxford University Press, 1976.

Piggott, S. *Prehistoric India to 1000 b.c.* London: Cassel, 1962.

Possehl, G. L., ed. *Ancient Cities of the Indus.* Durham, N.C.: Carolina Academic Press, 1979.

Singhal, D. P. *A History of the Indian People.* London: Methuen, 1983.

Smith, B. *Classifying the Universe: The Ancient Indian Varna System and the Origins of Caste.* New York: Oxford University Press, 1993.

Tarn, W. W. *The Greeks in Bactria and India.* Cambridge: Cambridge University Press, 1951.

Thapar, R. *Asoka and the Decline of the Mauryas.* London: Oxford University Press, 1961.

———. *A History of India,* vol. 1. Baltimore: Penguin Books, 1966.

Van Buitenen, J. A. B., trans. *The Bhagavadgita and the Mahabharata.* Chicago: University of Chicago Press, 1981.

Wolpert, S. *A New History of India,* 4th ed. New York: Oxford University Press, 1993.

Woodcock, G. *The Greeks in India.* London: Faber, 1966.

CHAPTER 3

The Formation of China

Chinese civilization arose largely independent of contact with or influence from other areas and early developed its own distinctive form and style. China was effectively isolated by high mountains and deserts along its northwestern, western, and southwestern borders and by the distance across the great breadth of arid central Asia. Northward lay the desert and steppe of Mongolia and the subarctic lands of Siberia and northern Manchuria. In part because of its isolation until recent centuries, the Chinese civilized tradition was more continuous, coherent, and slow to change over a longer period than any other in history.

Interaction was much easier with areas to the east, and the model of Chinese civilization later spread to Korea, Vietnam, and Japan, where it still forms a basic part of the literate cultures of those areas. East Asia as a whole is accordingly sometimes called the *Sinic* world (from the Latin word for China).

The area also inherited most of the tradition of Chinese agriculture, as well as systems of writing, philosophy, literature, political and social institutions, and art forms. This diffusion took place, however, 2,000 years or more after Chinese civilization first began and after the establishment of the first empire in the third century B.C. This empire discarded some elements developed in earlier centuries and added others to create the model of imperial Chinese culture that subsequently spread to the rest of East Asia. But long before the beginning of the Christian era in the West, China had already produced one of the world's major civilized traditions, and the model of the Han dynasty (202 B.C.–A.D. 220) was to be reaffirmed by successive Chinese dynasties for the next 2,000 years.

An extraordinarily lifelike pottery figure from a Han dynasty tomb in Szechuan shows a groom whistling for his horse.

The Origins of China

We cannot fix a precise date for the emergence of a city-based, literate, metal-using civilization in China. As everywhere else, it happened over a long period of transition out of Neolithic beginnings. By about 2000 B.C., however, the late Neolithic culture we call Lung Shan, or Black Pottery, had begun to build walled settlements larger than villages, to make bronze tools, weapons, and ornaments, and to use a pictographic and ideographic script clearly recognizable as the ancestor of written Chinese. The towns and cities included large groups of non-farmers: scribes, metallurgists, artisans, and perhaps officials, and already the Lung Shan people had learned the art of silk making, long an exclusive Chinese skill and trademark. Approximately four centuries later, around 1600 B.C., the first authenticated Chinese dynasty, the Shang, was established in the area at or near the great bend of the Yellow River where the major Lung Shan settlements had also clustered, on the North China plain. The Shang probably consolidated or arose from a combination of the previously distinct Lung Shan and Yang Shao (Painted Pottery) cultures, but they and other late Neolithic cultures may well have begun to merge considerably earlier, perhaps to form the dynasty of Hsia (Xia), which was recorded as such by traditional Chinese texts but has not yet been confirmed by archaeological finds.

Whether the Hsia was a real state and dynasty or not, the name was certainly used, and a culture of the Shang's complexity could not have appeared without a predecessor. The existence of the Shang was also discounted by modern historians, despite its mention in the traditional texts giving the names of kings, until archaeological discoveries in the 1920s began to reveal its capitals and inscriptions that listed Shang kings exactly as the traditional texts had. *Hsia* may still be a convenient label for late Lung Shan–Yang Shao culture in the last stages of its evolution. By about 2000 B.C. Lung Shan towns were large and were surrounded by pounded-earth walls with heavy gates, clearly no longer farmers' villages and possibly organized into one or more kingdoms. What may have been a capital from this period 35 miles west of modern Chengchou (Zhengzhou), perhaps of the Hsia, had a rammed-earth wall 20 feet high and 1 mile square, with two bronze foundries outside the walls.

Lung Shan settlements with a similar material culture extended eastward to the sea and southward into the Yangtze valley and the south coast. The traditional Chinese texts give the names of five pre-Hsia "emperors" who are recognizable as mythological culture heroes, credited with the "invention" of fire, agriculture, animal domestication, calendrics, writing, and flood control. The last of these, the great Yü, is said to have founded the Hsia dynasty, which may tentatively be dated 2000–1600

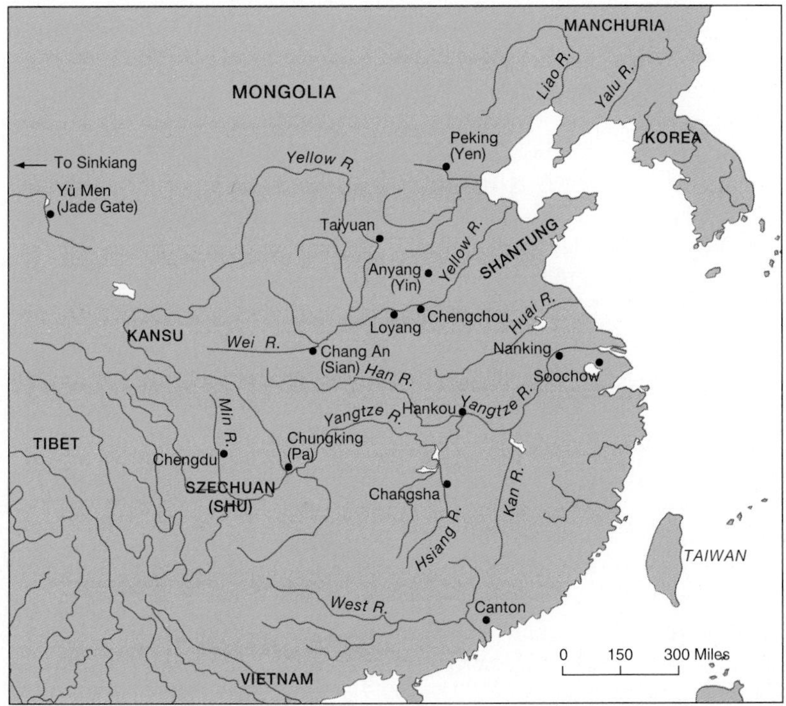

MAP 3.1 EAST ASIA

B.C., but we know almost nothing more about it. The earliest texts we have were written many centuries later.

By Shang times, in any case, many of the elements of a distinctively Chinese culture were present. How much Shang or its Chinese predecessors owed to earlier achievements farther west has long been debated. There seems no question that wheat and later donkeys, alfalfa, grapes, and some elements of mathematics were carried to China from western Asia, but well after 2000 B.C. (The chief crop of Shang China was millet, probably an indigenous grain.) The light spoke-wheeled chariot, an important Shang weapon of war, seems also to have come in by about 1500 B.C., perhaps in some way connected with the Aryan invasions of India. Rice, water buffalo, chickens, and pigs, also not native to northern China, came considerably earlier, but from Southeast Asia via southern China. Indeed, China owed far more to diffusion from the south than from the west, especially if we consider the basic place in its economy later occupied by these originally southern imports.

In Neolithic times South China was culturally and linguistically closer to adjacent Southeast Asia than to dry, cold North China. Recent archaeological finds in the lower Yangtze (Yangzi) valley and south of the great river suggest that civilization may have emerged there as early as or even earlier than in the better-surveyed and better-preserved north. The first East Asian bronzes and the first evidence of rice cultivation so far discovered come from what is now northern Thailand and Vietnam and presumably spread from there relatively easily into neighboring South China, probably long before Shang times. By the early Shang period, there already seems to have been a good deal of cultural mixing between North and South China, although the people were ethnically and linguistically distinct.

No aspect of Shang culture suggests any connection with Mesopotamia or India, including Shang art and two further basic and conclusive elements, writing and bronze technology. Both were developed earlier in Sumer and then in India, but the earliest Chinese writing resembles neither. It is highly unlikely that the Chinese, like the Indians, would have failed to adopt or adapt cuneiform instead of developing far more cumbersome ideographic characters if they had been in contact with Mesopotamia or had imported ideas or techniques from there. And Shang China stands alone in the technical perfection, beauty, and style of its bronze work, the result of a long history of experimental progress using varying proportions of copper, tin, lead, and zinc to achieve the optimum mix. The farther one goes from the Shang centers, the cruder the bronze artifacts become; no trail leads from Sumer or Harappa.

For these and other reasons it seems clear that Chinese civilization, like Indian, was an independent innovation, already well formed before it came into effective contact with other or older centers of equal sophistication. This is also consistent with the Paleolithic and early Neolithic records, where the stone tools of China remained distinct from those produced in the area from India westward through central Asia to Europe. Chinese civilization evolved largely on its own.

The Shang Dynasty

The Shang ruled from several successive capitals, first near modern Loyang (Luoyang), then near modern Chengchou (both close to the Yellow River), and finally, for about the last two centuries, at Anyang, which they called Yin. We do not know the extent of the Shang political domains, but cultural remains suggest that they were limited to the central Yellow River floodplain, although the Shang had or claimed vassals to the west, the east, the northeast, and possibly the south who shared much of Shang material culture. By this time wheat was beginning to share prominence with millet, and rice was also grown, though mainly in the Yangtze valley and the south. Hunting remained a subsidiary source of food in addition to domesticated cattle, pigs, and poultry. The Shang kept slaves, mainly war captives from less highly developed or subjugated groups on their borders. Slaves may have been an important part of the agricultural work force; they were also used extensively to build the cities and palaces and perhaps as troops.

Especially at Anyang, monumental building was impressive, and the city at its peak may have covered as much as 10 square miles, with nearly a dozen elaborate royal tombs complete with a variety of grave furniture. The tombs provide evidence of surplus production that could support extravagant display, including richly decorated chariots with bronze fittings and caparisoned horses to draw them; the horses had been harnessed, backed down a ramp into the underground tombs, and killed. Royal or aristocratic dead were accompanied in their burials not only by objects of use and value but also by tens or even hundreds of followers, buried as human sacrifices to serve in the afterlife and probably also as a mark of the dead person's status. Bronze vessels and weapons of great beauty and technical perfection attest to the high quality of Shang technology.

The only Shang texts we have are inscriptions used for divination, most of them incised on the flat shoulder bones of cattle or on tortoiseshells. First, the bones or shells were heated until cracks appeared; then questions, or perhaps requests, were inscribed. The cracks somehow provided answers. Other so-called oracle bone inscriptions, like the divination texts using characters so close to classical Chinese that most can still be read, provide lists of the Shang kings and brief accounts of royal activities.

Altogether this inscriptional material gives a picture of a hereditary aristocratic society in which warfare against surrounding groups was chronic, archers used a powerful compound bow, there were ranks of spearmen, and nobles rode in light, fast war chariots similar to those of the Indo-Europeans. The royal hunt remained important and was usually a very large affair in which hundreds took part and thousands of animals perished. The inscriptions make it clear that the spirits of royal and perhaps all aristocratic ancestors demanded respectful service from the living and could intercede for them with a supreme deity—the roots of traditional Chinese "ancestor worship." Slaves were not thought to have souls or spirits and thus could safely be killed; the Shang aristocrats seem not to have thought about what might happen if they became war captives themselves. Although those at the top lived in great luxury, the houses of the common people seem to have been quite crude, often simple pit dwellings, certainly not in a class with those of the Indus civilization. Many of the divination questions ask about the weather and suggest that the North China climate then, as now, was semiarid and prone to both drought and river flooding, but there is little evidence of any large-scale irrigation, apart from what one may assume was the possible use of floodwater. North China was not as dry as the Indus valley, and the agriculture there seems to have been primarily rain-fed, except perhaps in small areas adjacent to the river or on a small scale from local wells in long dry spells. Millet is highly drought-tolerant and can produce good yields when other crops might fail. The great agricultural advantage of North China was its loess (wind-laid alluvium), a highly fertile soil that is easily worked, and the level expanse of the largely treeless plain, which allows easy transport and exchange.

The Chou Dynasty

Relations between the Shang and their vassals were uneasy, and chronic warfare with other groups on the margins strained Shang resources. So too did the extravagant demands of royal building and display, much of it extorted from slave laborers. The last Shang king is said to have been a physical giant and a monster of depravity who, among other cruelties, made drinking cups of the skulls of his vanquished enemies. The dynasty ended in a great slave revolt, which was joined by one of the Shang vassals, the Chou (Zhou, pronounced like *Joe*), who guarded the western frontier in the Wei valley with their capital near modern Sian (Xian). The Chou were probably an original barbarian group taken over by the Shang, tough frontiersmen who seem to have been awaiting their chance to take over the whole kingdom. About 1050 B.C. they succeeded, together with the slave rebels, defeating the last Shang king and sacking Anyang (where the king died in the flames of his own palace). By that time the Chou had absorbed most of Shang culture and technology. The victorious Chou, now fully literate, gave their own account of the excesses and oppression of the Shang as justification for their conquest and first voiced what was to become a standard Chinese justification for change: "The iniquity of Shang is full; Heaven commands me to destroy it." The Shang had lost what they called the "mandate [approval] of Heaven" by their misgovernment, and it was the duty of responsible people to overthrow them.

The Chou set up their new capital in the Wei valley, their old base. They continued and extended the Shang system of dependent vassals whereby surrounding groups and areas, soon to begin emerging as states, were linked to the Chou king by oaths of fealty that acknowledged him as sovereign. The parallel with medieval European feudalism is not exact in details, but the basic system and the reasons for it were the same: a central kingdom with ambitions to control or administer a large area beyond its own immediate territory, which it thus arranged for by contracting with local chieftains. In addition, there were needs for joint defense against surrounding enemies or raiders. The Chou appear to have subdued by means of this system a much larger area than they inherited from the Shang, from the Wei valley to the sea, north into southern Manchuria, and south into the Yangtze valley. Mutual interest among evolving kingdoms, or *dukedoms*, as the Chou called them, may also have led them to join together in the defense of the "civilized" area against the outer barbarians and to keep order internally.

For a time this system seems to have worked reasonably well, based also on what appears to have been an institution like serfdom by which most land was cultivated under the ownership of hereditary lords, perhaps with some irrigation from shallow wells in a center plot. As in parts of medieval Europe, serfs were bound to the land and could not leave, becoming virtually the property of their lords. At both the royal Chou court and increasingly at the courts of other dependent states there was an unbroken evolution of technological and artistic development. Bronze remained the chief metal, and magnificent ritual vessels, often of great size, increasingly bore long texts recording events or decrees.

Although most writing was by now done with brush and ink on silk or on strips of bamboo, none of these perishable texts has survived, and we are dependent on much later and perhaps substantially altered copies. It is generally assumed that the central body of the Chinese classics originated in the early Chou, including the Book of Changes (*I-ching,* a cryptic handbook for diviners), the Book of Songs, the Book of Rituals, and collections of historical documents. Among the collections were the texts that give the story of the five culture-hero emperors and the Hsia dynasty, as well as a now confirmed account of the Shang and of the Chou conquest. The Chinese were already writing history and attaching characteristic importance to the keeping of records.

But fundamental changes were at work that were gradually to disrupt and then destroy the Chou structure. Iron was becoming slowly cheaper and more plentiful as technology improved, and it began to be available for agricultural implements, including iron-tipped plows, which the Chinese developed more than 1,000 years before the West. Helped by better tools, irrigation was spreading, especially in the semiarid north of China, and more and more land was being brought under cultivation. Iron axes speeded the attack on the remaining forests in the hilly margins of the north and in the Yangtze valley. Spurred by rising agricultural output, the population began to grow much more rapidly, perhaps to 20 million by the mid-Chou period. Except for recurrent years of drought, the population did not apparently outrun its food supply, and surpluses were common, providing the basis for increasing trade.

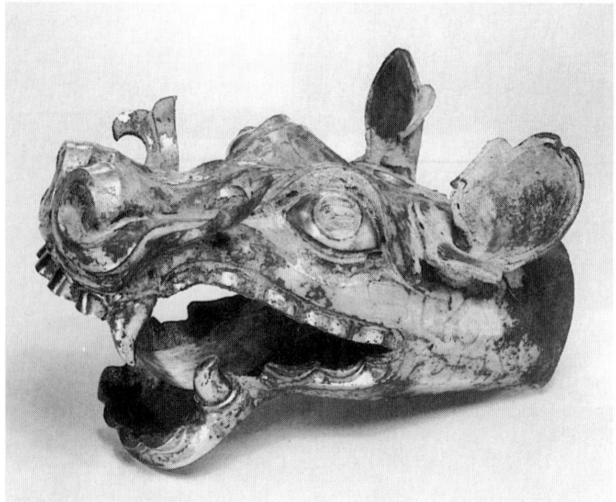

Early Chou bronzes show a trend away from abstraction and toward more lifelike representation, although the pieces remain highly ornamented.

New agricultural productivity freed increasing numbers of people from farm labor to serve as artisans, transport workers, soldiers, officials, scholars, and merchants. More and more towns, now more important as centers of trade than of royal or feudal control and dominated by merchants, began to dot the plain and the richer lands to the south in the Yangtze valley, where easier transport by water further stimulated the growth of trade and of urban centers. Fixed and hereditary serfdom and the domination of a landed aristocracy came to seem less and less suited to the changing conditions, a situation that may have been in some ways similar to that in the later periods of the medieval European feudal order. At the same time many of the original Chou vassals were evolving into separate states, each with a distinctive culture. After some four centuries of Chou rule, the political, social, and economic structure began to show strains, and eventually it disintegrated.

Warring States

In 771 B.C.* the royal capital in the Wei valley was sacked by a barbarian group from the north and the Chou king was killed. His son was installed as king the next year, but in a new and better-protected capital at Loyang, in the hope that a control point closer to the center of the royal domains would be more secure and more effective in holding the kingdom together. It was to be a vain hope. To guard the northwest borders, the old Chou base in the Wei valley was given as a fief to a loyal noble of the Ch'in (Qin) clan; five centuries later the Ch'in were to sweep away the crumbled remnants of Chou rule to found the first empire.

After 770 B.C. royal authority over the surrounding dependencies dwindled, and vassals became rival states: Ch'in to the west, Jin to the north, Yen to the northeast in the area around modern Peking (Beijing), Ch'i (Qi) to the east in Shantung (Shandong), Ch'u (Qu) to the south in the central Yangtze valley, and a number of smaller states including Shu in Szechuan (Sichuan) and

*From this time on, traditional Chinese dates, almost certainly inaccurate for earlier periods, are fully reliable. The earliest surviving books come from the ninth century B.C., and by the eighth century the Chou were recording eclipses of the sun, which we now know did in fact occur exactly when their records state.

Bronze vessels and weapons of great beauty and technical perfection attest to the high quality of Shang technology.

Lu in Shantung, where Confucius was born and served for a time as an adviser. It is still too early to speak of any of them, even of the Chou, as "China"; each was culturally and linguistically as well as politically and perhaps even racially distinct. China as we know it emerged only under the empire of Ch'in (Qin) in the third century B.C. The Ch'in empire put its own overpowering stamp on what was to become the dominant Chinese style in statecraft and social organization for the ensuing two millennia. Our name *China* comes, appropriately enough, from the Ch'in, as the creator of the first imperial Chinese identity.

Until then no one strand dominated the assortment of people, cultures, and states that occupied what is now China. They warred repeatedly among themselves and against the various groups around their edges, still well within the borders of modern China. Technology probably passed relatively easily and quickly from group to group, and by mid-Chou most seem to have shared achievements in metallurgy, agriculture, and irrigation, as well as other arts. But in spoken and written language, in many aspects of culture, and in political identity they were as different as, say, the evolving states of late medieval Europe.

Ch'u was one of the largest such states. Its location astride the central Yangtze valley made it probably the most productive of the rival states, since its agriculture benefited from the more adequate and reliable rainfall and the longer growing season of central China, as well as from the greater ease of irrigation. But it was different in character too, in particular in the size and importance of its merchant group and the role of waterborne trade and towns in its economy. Ch'u had evolved far beyond the earlier Shang pattern, where power had been held by a hereditary landowning nobility and virtually the sole source of wealth was agriculture worked by slaves or serfs. Ch'u was also a naval power, with fleets on the Yangtze and its tributaries and adjacent lakes, in contrast to the land armies of the north, and with even larger numbers of trading junks (riverboats). Ch'u was ultimately defeated by a coalition of northern states in a great battle in 632 B.C., and though it continued to exist, its power and further growth were greatly reduced while those of the other states rose. This may have been one of those battles that changed the course of history. A China that followed the Ch'u pattern would have been very different from what eventually emerged.

With increasing crop yields came changes in warfare. It was now possible to field large armies of men who could be spared from agriculture at least for parts of the year and could be fed on surpluses. Warfare became broader and more ruthless, and its character changed from that of earlier chivalric contests of honor between aristocrats to one of more wholesale conquest and fights for survival. The crossbow with a trigger mechanism greatly increased firepower, range, and accuracy, and by the fourth century B.C. foot soldiers were supported by armed cavalry. Such developments combined to undermine the earlier dominance of hereditary aristocrats, their chariots, and their personal retinues.

What was happening in China during this period paralleled the Indian pattern a century or so before, as described in Chapter 2, where a chivalric age gave way to power struggles between states and the emergence of the Mauryan empire, based on the spread of iron, improvements in agriculture, and a population boom. As in India, bronze and copper coins minted by the state became common in this period in China, trade and cities grew rapidly, roads were built, standing armies proliferated, and the bureaucratic apparatus of the state began to appear. All of this offered a range of new opportunities for able commoners. For many it was a positive and welcome change, but for others the passing of the old order and the great disruptions and sufferings of warfare engendered only chaos and moral confusion. Confucius, who lived at the beginning of the period of warring states, offered his prescriptions as an effort to reestablish order

MAP 3.2 CHINA IN THE SIXTH CENTURY B.C.

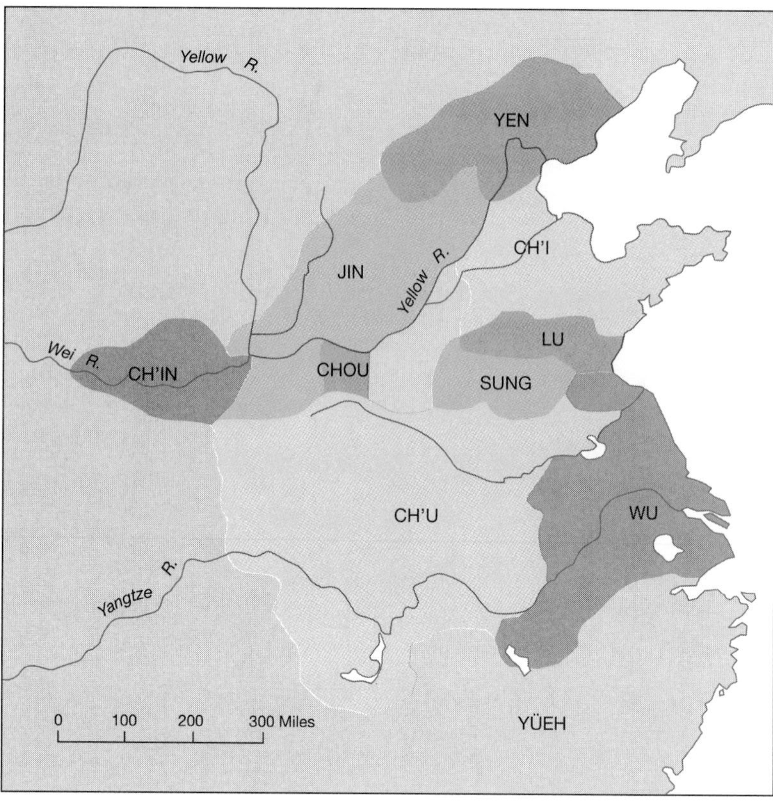

and what he referred to as "harmony," in an attempt to restore the values of an earlier "golden age."

Confucius the Sage

Confucius was born about 551 B.C. in one of the smaller states that arose out of the Chou domains in Shantung province and died about 479. He was a contemporary of the Buddha and died only a few years before the birth of Socrates. His family name was K'ung, and Chinese refer to him as K'ung Fu-tze (Kongfuzi, "Master K'ung"), which Europeans Latinized as Confucius. The K'ung family were low-ranking aristocrats in reduced circumstances, but they were able to arrange for their son's education. Confucius made a career out of teaching, periodically serving as consultant or counselor to various feudal lords. To his pupils he taught not only literacy and the classics but also his own philosophy of life and of government. Some of his pupils won high-level jobs in state administration, but Confucius himself was never very successful in such terms, and he apparently thought of himself as a failure. In reality, he was the founder of the most successful philosophical, moral, and ethical system in human history, measured by the number of people in China, Korea, Japan, and Vietnam who followed his precepts for more than 2,500 years and who are still profoundly influenced by them.

We have nothing that the sage himself wrote and not very much direct information about him or his teachings. All we know for certain comes from a collection of discourses, or sayings, known as the *Analects,* put together rather unsystematically after his death by his disciples and hence probably not wholly accurate. Later commentaries expanded on the meaning and application of his teachings.

The picture we derive from the *Analects,* though incomplete, is of a thoughtful but very human person. He complained that he could never seem to get the right kinds of students or the kinds of appointments he yearned for. In discussing his lack of success, he commented loftily: "I don't mind not being in office; I am more concerned about being qualified for it. I don't mind not having recognition; I strive to be worthy of recognition." Yet at the same time he complained about being treated "like a gourd fit only to be hung on the wall and never put to use." He seems to have been so eager for a post as adviser that he considered working even for rebel

Reflections on Social Reform

The philosopher Mo-tzu (Mozi), who was born in the fifth century B.C., while Confucius was still alive, was more interested in reforming society.

It is the sage's business to regulate the world; he must thus know whence disorder comes in order to be capable of regulating it. . . . The origin is the lack of mutual love. . . . All the disorders of the world have this cause and this alone. . . . If mutual love prevailed universally throughout the world, no state would attack another state; no family would trouble another family; thieves and brigands would not exist; princes and subjects, fathers and sons, would all be filial and good. Thus the world would be well governed. . . . Where do ills come from? They come from hatred of others, from violence toward others. . . . The love which makes distinctions among persons causes all the ills of the world. . . . This universal love is very advantageous, and far more easy to practice than you imagine. If it is not put into practice, that is because the rulers take no pleasure in it. If the rulers took pleasure in it, I believe that men would throw themselves into it. . . . Nothing on earth could stop them. . . . To kill a man is called an unjust thing; it is a crime deserving death. To kill ten men is ten times more unjust, to kill a hundred men a hundred times more unjust. Today every prince in the world knows that this must be punished; they declare it unjust. Yet the greatest of injustices, the making of war, they do not punish. On the contrary, they glorify it and declare it just! Truly they do not know how unjust they are.

Source: After H. Maspero, *La Chine antique* (Paris: Presses Universitaires de France, 1927), pp. 253–254.

groups, believing that, given any kind of opportunity, he could remake men and states in line with his philosophy—an attitude that Plato was to share a century later. But he also had a keen sense of the ridiculous and could even enjoy jokes on himself.

The basic message of all of Confucius' teachings is that people can be molded and elevated by education and by the virtuous example of superiors. "Civilized" people so formed will *want* to do what is morally right rather than what is merely expedient; hence they will preserve the harmony of society, which is what distinguishes humans from animals. Force and threats are ineffective controls, he asserts; only internalized values can produce correct behavior. Behavior should be modeled on that of people of superior status, beginning with the family and extending to the ruler, who thus must match power with responsibility and uprightness. For all relationships, he counsels in a variant of the Golden Rule, "Do not do unto others what you yourself would not like."

Confucianism is a prescription for benevolence in human affairs and in government, with an essentially conservative stress on order. Nevertheless, the focus on benevolence meant that bad government should rightly be rejected, despite the threat to civil order, a point that the *Analects* repeats in several contexts. The Confucian model is the upright man who unswervingly pursues the right moral course whatever the consequences, even at the expense of his own self-interest. Master K'ung's life seems to have conformed to the model he preached. Perhaps he was, like Socrates, too outspoken to win the favor of the powerful men of his day. But his teachings and his example have far outlived the petty politics of the age in which he lived.

The Ch'in Conquest

Ch'in, originally one of the poorest, smallest, and most remote of the Chou dependencies, seemed easily outclassed by the other contending states. Its succession of able rulers made a virtue of its relative poverty, its peasant base, and its frontier location by stressing the importance of hard work, frugality, and discipline and by emphasizing agriculture and peasant soldiery rather than trade or the development of an intellectual elite. The Ch'in rulers blended these elements to create a strong

The Path of the Sage

One of the most influential followers of Confucius was the philosopher Hsun-tzu (Xunzi, c. 300–c. 235 B.C.), who assembled his own teachings in a book that faithfully pursues the path of the sage, as the following sample indicates.

When his horse is uneasy harnessed to a carriage, a gentleman is not comfortable in it. When the common people are uneasy under a government, a gentleman is not comfortable in his post. When a horse is uneasy, nothing is as good as calming it. When the common people are uneasy under a government, nothing is as good as being kind to them. Recruit the worthy and respectable and appoint the sincere and humble. Support filial piety and human heartedness. . . . It is traditionally said that the ruler is like a boat and the common people are the water. Water supports the boat but may also upset it.

Source: After C. O. Hucker, *China's Imperial Past* (Stanford, Calif.: Stanford University Press, 1975), p. 101.

military power. Its tough armies defeated those of rival states in a long series of campaigns that were kept away from the mountain-ringed Ch'in home base in the Wei valley but often devastated the more fragile economies of its trade-dependent enemies. Opponents saw the menace of rising Ch'in power too late to unite against it and were picked off one by one. Ch'in generals and statesmen were masters of strategy and tactics who used diplomacy, propaganda, treachery, espionage, and various forms of psychological warfare adroitly.

A series of victorious campaigns during the 230s and 220s culminated in the final defeat of all the other states in 221 B.C. North China and the Yangtze valley were united politically for the first time, and the Ch'in ruler, who now took the title of emperor (Huang Ti) as Ch'in Shih Huang Ti (Di), applied to his entire empire the systems that had built Ch'in power. Further conquests after 221 began the long Chinese absorption of the south with the acquisition of the kingdom of Yüeh (Yue) centered in the Canton (Guangzhou) delta and the route to it southward from the Yangtze, together with Yüeh territory in what is now northern Vietnam. Throughout the new domains, as in the former state of Ch'in, primogeniture (the custom whereby the eldest son inherits all of the father's property and status) was abolished, as was slavery except for minor domestic servants. The former feudal and land tenure arrangements were dissolved. Land became privately owned and was freely bought and sold. The state levied a tax on all land in the form of a share of the crop. A new uniform law code was applied to all subjects without discrimination, ending many centuries of aristocratic privilege, a reform that clearly appealed to most people. Currency, weights, measures, and forms of writing, which had varied widely among what had been separate cultures as well as states, were also unified by imperial fiat to follow the Ch'in mode, a change essential for governing a large empire. An imperial system of roads and canals was begun, and a splendid new capital was built near modern Sian (Xian) in the Wei valley. Even axle lengths for carts were standardized, so that all carts would fit the same ruts.

Probably the most spectacular and best known of the new public works projects was the Great Wall, which Ch'in Shih Huang Ti ordered consolidated from a series of much earlier walls along the northern steppe border and reconstructed as a uniform barrier with regularly spaced watchtowers. It and subsequent reconstructions (the remains currently visible date from the Ming rebuilding in the fifteenth century A.D.) constitute probably the largest single works project in human history; the Great Wall is said to be the only human construction visible from the moon. A million men reportedly died in building the Ch'in Great Wall, working as conscript labor. Ironically, the wall was never very effective in its supposed purpose of preventing nomadic incursions; end runs around it and intrigues that opened the gates made it often quite permeable. But it did serve as a symbolic affirmation of empire and as a statement

The Great Wall was probably Ch'in Shih Huang Ti's most famous project. Here it is shown west of Peking, snaking along the mountain ridges separating northeastern China from Mongolia. The wall was built wide enough to allow two war chariots to pass abreast. The sections of it that remain standing date from its most recent major reconstruction under the Ming dynasty in the fifteenth century.

of territorial and sovereign limits. The new state control over mass labor tempted the emperor to plan more and more projects of monumental scope, including the road system, the new canals (useful for transporting troops and their supplies as well as for irrigation), and his own magnificent palace and tomb, in addition to fresh conquests.

Ch'in Authoritarianism

Agriculture was stressed as the basis of the economy and the state, with hardy peasants available in off seasons for conscript labor or for the army. Merchants were regarded as parasites and as potentially dangerous power rivals to the state. The removal of primogeniture also reduced the threat from hereditary landed power. But the chief target of the Ch'in system was the independence of intellectuals, people who ask questions, consider alternatives, or point out deficiencies. China already had a long tradition of scholars, philosophers, and moralists, of whom Confucius and his later disciple Mencius were honored examples. The Ch'in saw such people as potential troublemakers. It was an openly totalitarian state, and its sense of mission made it even more intolerant of any dissent.

Ch'in Shih Huang Ti persecuted intellectuals, buried several hundred scholars alive for questioning his policies, and ordered the burning of all books that could promote what he considered undesirable thoughts. In practice this meant most books other than trade manuals and the official Ch'in chronicles. The documents destroyed included valuable material accumulated from earlier periods. There was to be no admiration of the past, no criticism of the present, and no recommendations for the future except the state's. These policies were profoundly contrary to the Chinese reverence for the written word and the preservation of records. They earned the emperor the condemnation of all subsequent Chinese scholars. Certainly he was a cruel tyrant, inhumane and perhaps even depraved in his lust for absolute power. But his methods, harsh though they were, built an empire out of disunity and established most of the bases of the Chinese state all the way to the present.

The emperor's policies were actually in large measure the work of his prime minister, Li Ssu, whose career closely paralleled that of Kautilya in Mauryan India and who is credited with founding a new school of philosophy called Legalism, which embodied the Ch'in policies of strict state control through the application of harsh laws. This control was augmented by a greatly expanded state bureaucracy and by rigid supervision of all education. Only values that supported the state design were taught, and practical skills were stressed over critical inquiry. As in Mauryan India, there were a highly developed police system and a secret service to ferret out and punish dissidents. Travel, within the realm or abroad, was forbidden except by special permit.

China, once unified by the Ch'in, even by such ruthless means, was to cling to the idea of imperial unity ever thereafter. Each subsequent period of disunity following the fall of a dynasty was regarded as a time of failure, and each ended in the rebuilding of the empire. But one must also acknowledge the appeal of the new order that even the totalitarian methods of the Ch'in represented. By its time most people were clearly ready to break with their feudal past and to move toward a system based on achievement rather than birth. The Ch'in believed firmly that their new order was progress; they had a visionary conviction that they were creating a better society. The parallels with Communist China are striking, and indeed Ch'in Shih Huang Ti was praised as a model during the Cultural Revolution in the late 1960s. Sacrifice for an inspiring national goal has its own appeal; the end is seen to justify the means, including treachery, cruelty, and inhumanity toward the people, who are nevertheless seen as the supposed beneficiaries of the new order.

Lord Shang, an earlier Ch'in official and the true progenitor of the Legalist school, summarized state policy in classic totalitarian terms:

> **Punish heavily the light offenses. . . . If light offenses do not occur, serious ones have no chance of coming. This is said to be "ruling the people in a state of law and order." . . .**
>
> **A state where uniformity of purpose has been established for ten years will be strong for a hundred years; for a hundred years it will be strong for a thousand years . . . and will attain supremacy. . . .**
>
> **The things which people desire are innumerable, but that from which they benefit is one and the same. Unless the people are made one, there is no way to make them attain their desire. Therefore they are unified, and their strength is consolidated. . . .**
>
> **If you establish what people delight in, they will suffer from what they dislike, but if you establish what they dislike, they will be happy in what they enjoy.[1]**

In other words, in unity is strength, but the state knows best what is good for people. The major figure of the school of Legalism is the philosopher Han Fei (died 233 B.C.), who also stressed the need for severe laws and harsh punishments, the only means to establish order under the direction of the ruler. People, he taught, are naturally selfish, and they must be held mutually responsible for one another's actions.

Nevertheless, there was merit in the new equality under the law propounded by the Ch'in, new opportunities for advancement, and allure in its ambitious projects. The best illustration of the more constructive aspects of the Ch'in is the figure of Li Ping (Bing), provincial governor of the former state of Shu (Szechuan) and famed as a hydraulic engineer on many Ch'in projects, including the control works on the Yellow River. It was Li Ping who devised the best formula for minimizing the floods that had already made the Yellow River notorious: "Dig the bed deep, and keep the banks low." This helped prevent the buildup of silt in the river's bed, which over time had raised it above the level of the surrounding country and greatly worsened the destructive consequences of floods. Li Ping's sound advice was finally acted on effectively only under the Communist government after 1949.

Li Ping is credited with designing and constructing the famous irrigation works at Kuan Hsien (Guanxian) in western Szechuan (Sichuan), diverting the Min River where it emerges from the mountains and enters the wide plain around the capital city of Chengdu. These works, much visited by tourists, still stand, with Li Ping's statue overlooking them. They are reputed to have saved millions of people on the Chengdu plain from drought

The Perils of Mindless Traditionalism

Han Fei, a Legalist philosopher, was a contemporary and sometime colleague of Li Ssu, who ultimately poisoned Han Fei as a rival. Han Fei's writings, however, survived, including the following story illustrating the folly of mindlessly following old ways instead of adapting policies to fit new circumstances.

In a plowman's field was a tree stump. When a rabbit ran into the stump and broke its neck, the plowman left his plow and watched over the stump, hoping to pick up more rabbits. But he got no more and became the laughingstock of the whole kingdom. Wanting to apply the policies of former kings to govern people in these times belongs in the same class as watching over that stump.

Source: After C. O. Hucker, *China's Imperial Past* (Stanford, Calif.: Stanford University Press, 1975), p. 94.

and famine ever since. Like all big projects, they took enormous labor and hardship, mainly from conscript workers under iron discipline. According to the great Han dynasty historian Ssu Ma Ch'ien (Simaqian), Li Ping said toward the end of his life:

> **People can be depended on to enjoy the results, but they must not be consulted about the beginnings. Now the elder ones and their descendants dislike people like me, but hundreds of years later let them think what I have said and done.**

Li Ping's memory is still honored, while that of his emperor is reviled.

The Han Dynasty

Ch'in Shih Huang Ti died in 210 B.C., leaving the throne to his eldest son, but Li Ssu and other counselors suppressed the news of his death for fear of uprisings and then installed the second son as their puppet. But the harshness of Ch'in rule had left the country in turmoil, exhausted the people, drained the treasury, and alienated the educated upper classes. Without their cooperation, the regime was in trouble. Rebellion had already begun in several provinces. This was soon joined by the desertion of several army commanders. In 206 B.C. rebel armies occupied the capital and burned the emperor's splendid new palace. Rival forces contended for power in the ensuing struggle, in which large groups of soldiers, workers, and former officials roamed the country. Out of this chaos there emerged by 202 B.C. a new rebel leader, Liu Pang (Liu Bang), who founded a new dynasty, which he named the Han. Under Han rule China took the political, social, and territorial shape it was to retain until the present century. The Chinese still call themselves "People of Han," a label they carry with much pride as the heirs of a great tradition. Han imperial success, and that of later dynasties, depended, however, on retention of many of the techniques of control used by the Ch'in. The administration of an empire the size of Europe with a population of probably about 60 million could not have been managed otherwise.

Beginning with the Han, the harsher aspects of the Legalist approach of the Ch'in were softened by both common sense and the more humane morality of Confucianism. Liu Pang, who took the title Han Kao-tsu ("High Progenitor") as the first emperor, emphasized the Confucian precept that government exists to serve the people and that unjust rulers should forfeit both the mandate of Heaven and the support of the ruled. He abolished the hated controls on travel, education, and thought, lowered taxes, and encouraged learning so as to build a pool of educated men whose talents, in the Confucian mode, could be called on to serve the state. Conscription for the army and forced labor for public works such as road and canal building were retained, however, as was the administrative division of the empire into *hsien* (*xian,* counties), each under the control of an imperial magistrate. The imperial state superimposed its model on all things, including currency, weights, measures, script, and orthodox thought, on a vast and diverse area that had long been politically and culturally varied. Under beneficent rule, this system could be made to work successfully and could command general support. The early Han was a time of great prosperity and of enthusiasm for the new order.

Expansion Under Wu Ti

The new power of the Han empire, on Ch'in foundations and with the boost of economic and population growth, tempted successive emperors to further conquests and imperial glory. Liu Pang's son and grandson continued his frugal and benevolent model as rulers, but the bitter memories of Ch'in had faded by the time of the emperor Wu Ti (141–87 B.C.). He first tightened imperial control, removed the remaining power of the lords created by Liu Pang for faithful service, and imposed regulations on trade and merchants, new taxes, and new controls over salt, iron, and the supply of grain. The last measure, which created what came to be known as the *ever-normal granary system,* was intended to prevent famine by state collection of grain in good years or surplus areas, which could then be sold at low rather than inflated prices when lean years came. It was a good idea and was practiced with some success by subsequent dynasties, but, like Li Ping's projects, it was not always popular with the local producers or merchants.

Having put the imperial house in order and increased state revenues and power, Wu Ti began an ambitious program of new conquests in 111 B.C., beginning in the southeast against Yüeh in the Fukien and Canton areas, which had broken away after the fall of the Ch'in. The Yüeh kingdom had included the related people and culture of what is today northern Vietnam, and this too was now again added to the Chinese empire. Over the centuries the Vietnamese were to reassert their separate identity despite their adoption of much of Chinese culture. In Han times the people and culture of Yüeh were regarded as foreign and were very different from those of the north. More than traces of these differences remain even now, including the Cantonese language and cuisine, but the south has been an integral part of China for 2,000 years and has been largely remade in the greater Chinese image.

Turning northward after the successful southern campaign, in 109–108 B.C. Wu Ti's armies conquered Manchuria and northern Korea for the empire, while other campaigns established looser control over the still non-Chinese populations of Yunnan and Kweichou (Guizhou) in the southwest. Southern Manchuria was to remain solidly a part of the Chinese system, with large colonies, originally garrisons, planted there by Wu Ti. These became agricultural settlements in the fertile valley of the Liao River.

Similar garrisons were established in northern Korea, where there was heavy Chinese influence from Han times on. But the Koreans, like the Vietnamese, remained eager to reclaim their cultural identity and independence. Like Vietnam, Korea had already developed its own civilization and was linguistically and ethnically distinct from China despite Chinese cultural influence. After the Han collapse in A.D. 220, both areas broke away from Chinese control, Korea as a nominally tributary state, Vietnam to endure later Chinese reconquest under the T'ang and then successive wars of independence until modern times, which created a heavy legacy of mutual mistrust.

China's northern and northwestern frontiers had been and were to remain troublesome for other reasons. The Great Wall had been built as a barrier, but it could not prevent infiltrations by the horse-riding nomads who occupied the steppe border zone and who periodically harried Chinese agricultural areas and trade routes. The major route for international trade was the famous Silk Road through the Kansu (Gansu) Corridor and along the northern and southern edges of the Tarim Desert in Sinkiang (Xinjiang, Chinese Turkestan), where there are widely separated oases fed by streams from the surrounding mountains. The two routes met at Kashgar at the western end of the Tarim Desert and then crossed the Pamirs into central Asia, where the trade passed into other hands on its long way to

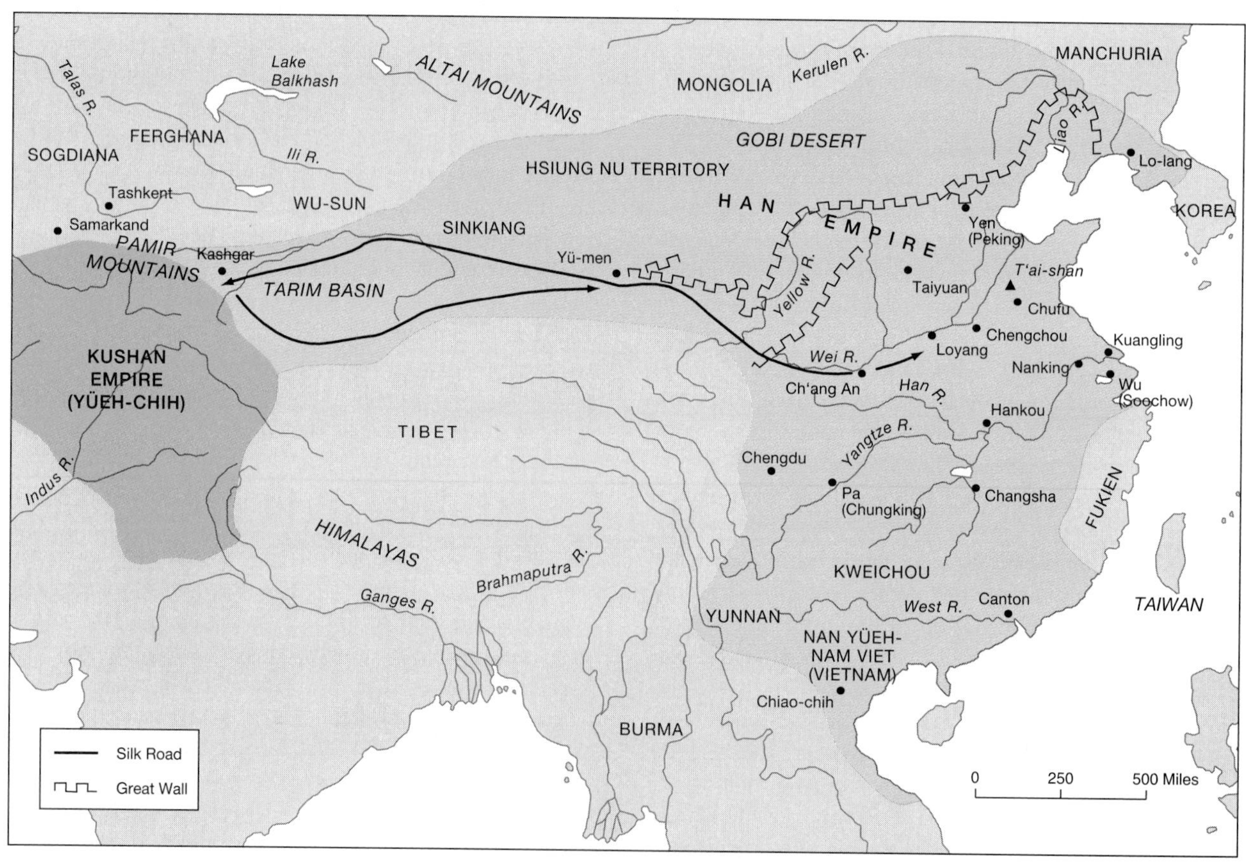

MAP 3.3 THE HAN EMPIRE

the Levant and eventually on to Rome. Silk was the main export, a Chinese monopoly since Lung Shan times and in great demand westward, especially in luxury-loving imperial Rome. The Romans were obliged to pay for it largely in gold, a drain that Pliny and other Roman historians felt weakened the economy and contributed to Rome's ultimate collapse in the West. It was profitable to China, and Wu Ti's pride in his new imperial power made him less willing to accept nomad interruptions of the trade and raids on Chinese territory.

The chief nomad group at this period was the Hsiung-nu (Xiong-nu), a Turkish people whose mounted mobility and cavalry tactics gave them the kind of military effectiveness later used by the Mongol leader Chinghis Khan. The Han generals complained that the Hsiung-nu "move on swift horses, and in their breasts beat the hearts of beasts. They shift from place to place like a flock of birds. Thus it is difficult to corner them and bring them under control." One can understand the frustration of the Han, but in a series of major campaigns Wu Ti defeated the Hsiung-nu, drove them for a time out of most of Inner Mongolia, Kansu, and Sinkiang, and planted colonies and garrisons in those areas and along the Silk Road, which is still marked by ruined Han watchtowers. Sinkiang and Inner Mongolia were to fall away from Chinese control in later periods whenever the central state was weak but were reclaimed by most subsequent strong dynasties as part of the empire. Non-Han groups such as the Hsiung-nu and the Mongols remained the major steppe inhabitants until the twentieth century, and another Turkish people, the Uighurs, remained the dominant oasis farmers in the desert region of Sinkiang. The Uighurs later embraced Islam and helped transmit it to China proper, where there are still a number of Chinese Muslims, concentrated in the northwest.

China and Rome

Wu Ti sent an ambassador westward in 139 B.C., a courtier named Chang Ch'ien (Zhangqian), to try to make an alliance with other nomads against the Hsiung-nu and to scout out the country more generally. He was captured instead by the Hsiung-nu but escaped after ten years. He returned to the Han capital at Ch'ang An (Qangan) in the Wei valley, where the Ch'in had ruled, in 126 B.C. with an account of central Asia that included bits of information about India and a great empire far to the west, where the silk went. This was China's first news of Rome, but it was never to learn much more. Travelers who said they had been to Rome turned up much later at the Han court in the second century A.D., as recorded in the Han annals. The Romans knew China only as the source of silk and called it, accordingly, *Seres,* the Latin word for silk.

Wu Ti was tempted by Chang Ch'ien's report to add central Asia to his conquests, partly out of vainglory and partly to secure supplies of the excellent horses to be found there, which he wanted for the imperial stables and his cavalry. If he or his successors had done so, the Chinese and Roman empires or their forward troops might have met and perhaps learned from each other. In the first century A.D., with the Han still in power and still occasionally probing westward, Rome was campaigning against the Parthian kingdom in Persia. If the Romans had conquered Parthia, they might have encountered at least Han patrols or might have followed the Silk Road, which they knew about, from central Asia to the borders of China. But both armies were very far from home. Moreover, the Parthians and other central Asian groups were formidable opponents and were eager to retain their profitable role as intermediaries in the silk trade rather than allow the two empires to meet. Han envoys reached the Parthians but were advised to return home, which they did.

Wu Ti's endless campaigns and his impositions on the people exhausted the country's patience and resources. One of his earlier reforms had been the establishment of imperial censors whose job it was to keep officials, even the emperor, faithful to their duty to serve the people. The censors finally convinced Wu Ti that he had neglected this basic precept and persuaded him to issue a famous penitential edict apologizing for his excesses and promising to be a better ruler, more deserving of the mandate of Heaven—and less likely to be overthrown by rebellion, which was already brewing. The institution of the censorate remained a regulatory feature of all subsequent dynasties.

Wu Ti's immediate successors, while largely abandoning further conquests, continued to press the Hsiung-nu as a defensive strategy and even sent an expeditionary force across the Pamirs into the Samarkand region in pursuit. There, in 42 B.C., on the banks of the Talas River near Tashkent in central Asia, they defeated a Hsiung-nu coalition that included mercenary troops who from the Chinese description may have been Roman auxiliaries; they had learned the Roman *testudo* formation with shields overlapping above their heads to ward off arrows and spears. The Han armies in central Asia, having marched across deserts and high mountains, were farther from their capital than regular Roman troops ever were from Rome. But this was the high point of Han power, and the empire that Wu Ti welded together was not to be significantly enlarged or altered in subsequent centuries, except for the much later incorporation of Tibet and the loss of Korea and Vietnam.

Wider Trade Patterns

Contacts across Eurasia had probably been important during and since the prehistoric period: Sumeria may have contributed to Indian civilization (and vice versa) and to the emergence of Chinese civilization. We have no adequate archaeological data to permit more than speculation about such interchanges. Given the multiplicity and often the mutual hostility of the various cultural groups and political alliances in central Asia during the ancient and medieval periods, the passage of goods and ideas through this area, in either direction, was necessarily slow and difficult. There was certainly trade linking China and India to western Asia, Greece, and Rome. From at least 600 B.C. there was also sea trade bringing Indian and Southeast Asian spices to the Mediterranean and Europe. But except for the visits of Greek and Roman traders to the Indian west coast, the travels of a few Indian philosophers to Greece and Rome, and Alexander's invasion of India, there was no direct contact between Eastern and Western civilizations from then until the time of Marco Polo in the thirteenth century. Arab ships traded by sea, and a chain of various central Asian peoples transmitted ideas as well as goods across Eurasia, but the transmission was incomplete, and understandably some of the ideas were garbled in the process.

The Chinese and Roman empires thus remained largely in ignorance of each other except for travelers' tales, although both were of comparable size, sophistication, power, and achievements. China might have developed a different and more open attitude to the rest of the world if it had had some experience with another culture, Roman or Indian, at its own level of sophistication. Like the Chinese, the Romans were builders of roads, walls, and planned cities, synthesizers of varied cultures under an expansionist and cosmopolitan system, and contenders with "barbarians" along the fringes of their empire. The Han empire was larger, and probably richer and more populous, than either the Roman or the Indian empire, but its level of cultural and technical sophistication was probably matched by the others.

Chinese merchants took the silk only as far as Sinkiang, handing it over there to a long series of central Asian traders who passed it along through the thousands of miles of central and western Asia to the shores of the Mediterranean, where Syrian, Greek, and Roman merchants picked it up for transport farther west. This trade continued after the fall of the Han dynasty and was later augmented by the export of porcelain and lacquer goods, all high-value commodities that could bear the very heavy costs of such long-distance transport. The camel caravans carrying them were also exposed to frequent raids from other central Asian groups along the route, risks that further increased the prices charged for Chinese exports when they finally reached their destinations. By the eleventh century much of the Chinese export trade was also being carried by ships westward to India (and later to Africa), while Indian exports westward—fine cotton textiles, spices, gems, and other goods—continued from the earliest period through the Middle Ages to move mainly by sea, from ports on the west coast. There must have been some return flow of trade by sea from India to China, but apart from the mention of what sound like Indian merchants in ports on the South China coast, we know very little about it.

Han Culture

The first two centuries of Han rule were a time of great cultural flowering in poetry, painting, music, philosophy, literature, and the writing of history. Confucianism was more firmly established as the official orthodoxy and state ideology, and the famous Chinese imperial civil service system recruited men of talent, schooled in classical Confucian learning, to hold office through competitive examination regardless of their birth. Liu Pang, the founder of the Han, had been born a peasant, and thus ability and education were stressed rather than inherited status. This approach was to remain a source of strength and effectiveness for the state for the next 2,000 years. Officeholding by the scholar-gentry, who were enriched in each generation by new blood rising from peasant or commoner ranks and entering the elite through the imperial examinations, became the most prestigious of all occupations. That, in turn, generally helped ensure that able people went into the administration and often preserved the political arena and government service from corruption, mediocrity, and ineffectiveness.

China was not free from the common problems of bureaucracy, but each new dynasty reestablished the system begun under the Han and on the whole probably managed the task of government better than many other states. Confucius, with his emphasis on duty, learning, "human-heartedness," and virtue, is to thank for this. Chinese society continued to choose that way and periodically reaffirmed the teachings of an obscure consultant to a small feudal lord in the sixth century B.C. who lived long before there was any thought of empire. Great landed-gentry

Han dynasty scientists in the second century A.D. *calculated the value of pi as 3.1622 and developed a highly accurate calendar, the wheelbarrow, and a bronze seismograph for recording earthquakes. The model shown here is based on a detailed description of the original. Eight dragons at major compass points along the outer edge of the vessel respond to tremors from the appropriate direction by spitting a pearl into the mouth of the frog below.*

families remained and periodically formed power cliques, together with court aristocrats, eunuchs, and ambitious generals—a pattern familiar from imperial Rome, Persia, and elsewhere. But the original Han ideal endured, through the rise and fall of successive dynasties, and with all its imperfections built a long and proud tradition of power combined with service that is still very much alive in China. The People's Republic is the conscious heir of an imperial past.

Han rule was briefly broken by the palace coup of the empress's nephew, Wang Mang, who made himself emperor from A.D. 9 to 23. As a model Confucian ruler, he tried to curb the resurgent power of merchants and landowning gentry. He also extended new state controls over the economy in an effort to reestablish the egalitarianism he claimed to derive from the sage's teaching. His reforms included the abolition of private estates, which had increasingly avoided paying taxes, and the nationalization of land. Such policies bitterly alienated the rich and powerful, and Wang Mang was murdered by a rebel group called the Red Eyebrows, with support from distressed peasants suffering from a drought-induced famine and from merchant and gentry groups.

Landowning and its abuses were, of course, problems for all ancient and medieval empires. Ownership of land usually meant power and was usually (except in post-Ch'in China) passed on within the family by inheritance. Even in China the abolition of primogeniture did not always prevent powerful families from accumulating large blocks of land. Large landowners built up wealth but also threatened the supremacy of the state by their growing political power. By manipulating their influence, they often managed to reduce or avoid paying state taxes on their lands and often also supported or even constituted in themselves powerful political factions. Their tenants, the peasants who farmed the land, were often cruelly exploited, paying far more in rent and services to the landowner than the latter paid to the state. As these practices were carried to extremes, rebellion brewed, and reformers in government periodically tried to check the abuses of the large landowners, as in Wang Mang's abortive reforms. Throughout the empires of the ancient and medieval world, similar problems and similar efforts at solution can be observed, as in the case of the revolt of the Gracchi in Rome (see Chapter 6) or the reforms of Wang An-Shih in Sung China.

In A.D. 25 the Han dynasty was reestablished, under new rulers and with a new capital at Loyang, following the earlier model of the Chou and for the same reasons. It is thus known as the Eastern or Later Han, while the Ch'ang An period from 202 B.C. to A.D. 9 is called the Western or Former Han. A succession of strong and conscientious emperors restored the power, prosperity, and cultural vigor of Wu Ti's time. Learning, philosophy, and the arts flourished once more, and elite society reached new levels of affluence, elegance, and sophistication. Peace was reestablished along all the imperial frontiers by reconquest. In 97 a Han army marched all the way to the Caspian Sea, and its advance scouts reached either the Persian Gulf or the Black Sea. In 89 a Han army invaded Mongolia and again defeated the Hsiung-nu, probably contributing to the start of the latter's subsequent migration westward and their ultimate role as invaders of Europe as the Huns. Sinkiang, northern Vietnam, northern Korea, southern Manchuria, and

Bronze casting continued its development under the Han. This magnificent bronze horse from the second century A.D. shows the sophistication of Han technology and art.

Inner Mongolia were all reincorporated into the empire, trade flourished, and China gloried in its confidently reasserted power and cultural leadership.

After the first century, landlords' power and oppression grew again; Wang Mang had been right to try to curb them. Imperial relatives and powerful families jockeyed for position or influence, peasant revolts were growing, and the elite, especially those at court surrounding weak emperors, indulged themselves in luxurious living, heedless of the problems around them—all echoes of the problems Rome was facing at the same time. Palace intrigues grew out of control, and eunuch groups* acquired more and more power. Generals in the provinces became rival warlords after suppressing peasant uprisings. The entire imperial structure was crumbling, and in 220 the last Han emperor abdicated. The loss of trade and revenue contributed to the fall of the dynasty, but the primary cause was self-destructive indulgence and factional fighting at court, in addition to local and provincial rivalries.

Chinese control over Sinkiang was lost with the fall of the Han, by which time nearly all Chinese originally settled there as garrison troops had withdrawn, although their watchtowers and fortified bases remained, to crumble away in succeeding centuries. With the reassertion of empire under the T'ang, Sinkiang was reclaimed as imperial territory, only to fall away again with the collapse of the T'ang order, a pattern repeated under the Ch'ing (Manchu) dynasty (1644–1911). Only with the advent of modern means of communication have large numbers of Chinese again settled in Sinkiang, but the dominant inhabitants remain Turkish and other central Asian peoples.

The Collapse of the Han Order

A new dynasty called Wei was proclaimed in 220, but it failed to hold the empire together, and rival dynasties soon emerged. In ensuing years the north was progressively overrun by barbarians, Hsiung-nu and other steppe nomadic groups, who sacked both Ch'ang An and Loyang by the early fourth century. The north disintegrated into a bewildering series of minor rival kingdoms under barbarian control, while the south was similarly divided into rival Chinese states.

The period from the fall of the Han in 220 to the ultimate reunification in 589 is sometimes rather misleadingly called the Six Dynasties (there were many more than six) but is better described as a long interval of disunity, invasion, disruption, intrigue, and warfare that shattered the imperial image and left most Chinese disheartened. Much of the former high culture survived, especially in the arts, and little of it was forgotten by educated Chinese, but the period was a time of troubles. Except among the elite, many of whom fled south, most people suffered. These centuries suggest comparison with what began only a little later in the breakup of the Roman Empire and the Germanic and Hun invasions of southern Europe. In China too the period was thought of as a Dark Age, and as in Europe confidence was lost. As Europe saw the spread of a new mass religion of otherworldly salvation, Christianity, so Buddhism took root in China. The Wei dynasty, founded by an originally barbarian group, was vigorous in promoting Buddhism and left behind a rich legacy of Buddhist art, even

CHINA TO A.D. 589

c. 2000 B.C.	Beginning of Lung Shan culture
c. 1600–c. 1050 B.C.	Shang dynasty
c. 1050–221 B.C.	Chou dynasty
c. 551–c. 479 B.C.	Confucius
c. 230–221 B.C.	Ch'in conquest
202 B.C.–A.D. 220	Han dynasty
A.D. 220–589	The Six Dynasties

*Eunuchs were men castrated as youths and hence without heirs. They were often used as courtiers (because they could not engage in intrigue on behalf of their sons) and as harem guards. However, they often formed cliques of their own and seldom used power responsibly.

The Fall of the Han

The popular Chinese novel Romance of the Three Kingdoms, *first written down in the fourteenth century A.D., tells of the fall of the Han and the civil war that ensued. The account begins as follows:*

Empires wax and wane; states cleave asunder and coalesce. When the rule of Chou weakened, seven contending principalities sprang up, warring one with another until they settled down as Ch'in, and when its destiny had been fulfilled there arose Ch'u and Han to contend for the mastery. And Han was the victor. . . . In a short time the whole empire was theirs, and their magnificent heritage was handed down in successive generations till the days of Kuang-wu, whose name stands in the middle of the long line of Han. . . . The dynasty had already passed its zenith. . . . The descent into misrule hastened in the reigns of the two emperors who sat on the dragon throne about the middle of the second century. They paid no heed to the good men of the court but gave their confidence to the palace eunuchs. . . . The two trusted advisers, disgusted with the abuses resulting from the meddling of the eunuchs in affairs of state, plotted their destruction. But the chief eunuch was not to be disposed of so easily. The plot leaked out and the two honest men fell, leaving the eunuchs stronger than before. . . . [Some years later] the earth quaked in Loyang, while along the coast a huge tidal wave rushed in, which, in its recoil, swept away all the dwellers by the sea. . . . Certain hens developed male characteristics, a miracle that could only refer to the effeminate eunuchs meddling in affairs of state. Away from the capital, a mountain fell in, leaving a great rift in its flank. . . . But the eunuchs grew bolder. Ten of them, rivals in wickedness, formed a powerful party. One of them became the emperor's most trusted adviser. The emperor even called him Daddy. So the government went from bad to worse, till the country was ripe for rebellion and buzzed with brigandage.

Source: After C. H. Brewitt-Taylor, trans., *Romance of the Three Kingdoms* (Tokyo: Tuttle, 1959), vol. 1, pp. 1–2.

though Wei control was limited to the north. But the imperial idea continued to appeal to Chinese pride, and in time it was to be reestablished in a new birth of unification, power, and glory: the T'ang.

Cities in Ancient China

The Shang capitals, and their immediate Lung Shan predecessors, were primarily ceremonial centers, symbols of royal authority. The late Lung Shan city on the site of modern Chengchou and the Shang capitals there, at Loyang, and at Anyang were massively walled and gated. The walls enclosed royal palaces and tombs, royal residences, quarters for priests, slaves, kept artisans, and military guards, but much of the enclosed area was not built on. Most nonroyal inhabitants and most of the workers lived in unplanned villagelike settlements outside the walls. By at least the late Shang period, the Chinese character and the spoken word for "city" were the same as those for "wall" and have remained so to the present. Cities, in other words, were designed as statements of authority; the wall was a symbol of state or, later, imperial power and thus distinguished cities from villages or market towns. Apart from the capitals, imperial and provincial, most cities first arose as county seats, the lowest rung of national administration and, from Han times, the base of an imperial magistrate.

Chinese cities were built predominantly of wood, which is why little evidence remains from this early period to show what they looked like. Some written documents surviving from Chou times describe the precise planning of all walled cities and their ritual or symbolic importance, including their exact north-south orientation, and the arrangement and dimensions of the royal or imperial buildings within the walls. Religious cults such as ancestor worship and the worship of what the Chinese called Heaven, or the Supreme Deity, were represented in every walled city by carefully placed temples.

By the time of the Han dynasty, China had nearly 2,000 years of urban experience; much of it was reflected in the Han capital at Ch'ang An. The site was carefully chosen by Liu Pang, the first Han emperor, but it was not until the reign of his successor, in 192 B.C., that the city walls were begun, of pounded earth 52 feet thick at the base, 27 feet high, and over 3 miles long on each of the four sides. The walls enclosed imperial palaces, tombs, and temples to the ancestors, among other temples. The government regulated and supervised market areas inside as well as outside the walls, and the city was divided into 160 wards. Straight, broad avenues led from each of the major gates at the main compass points, with an apparently less planned growth of lanes and alleys in the wards. The ideal city form was a square, which Ch'ang An approximated, with one major central gate and two lesser ones on each of the four sides.

The Han now ruled an immense territory, much of it newly conquered, especially in the south. The imperial stamp on these new lands was achieved primarily through the building of walled cities, county seats on the imperial model but on a far smaller scale. Once the original inhabitants had been subdued and the land cleared, settled, and farmed, garrison towns or fortresses gave way to such walled county seats from which the imperial magistrate could keep order, dispense justice, and supervise the collection of taxes and the exactions of forced labor and military conscription.

In the hilly south, such cities often had to accommodate to the terrain and sometimes altered the square shape somewhat. But the imperial model was apparent in all of them, including their official buildings, temples, military barracks, and regulated market areas inside and outside the walls. One can in fact chart the southward spread of Han occupation and the growth of Chinese-style agricultural settlement by noting the successive establishment of new walled county seats. They appeared first along the rivers leading south from the Yangtze and then progressively inland from the rivers. They were linked with each other and with the imperial and provincial capitals by the imperial road system begun under the Ch'in and greatly extended under the Han.

Pottery figure called the "Balladeer," part of the grave furniture from a Han dynasty tomb in Szechuan. The afterlife was clearly supposed to be a happy time, replete with worldly pleasures. This figure beautifully captures the human quality of Han folk culture.

The Han Legacy

China by Han times was highly developed technologically as well as culturally. Ch'ang An and Loyang were built of wood, and little has survived to tell us much about them, but what accounts we have suggest that they rivaled imperial Rome in size and splendor. It is symptomatic of this vast bureaucratic empire, whose culture also put a high value on education and learning, that paper was first made there, before A.D. 100 (more than 1,000 years passed before the knowledge of papermaking spread to Europe). Another Han innovation was an early form of porcelain, one more Chinese gift to the world known everywhere simply as "china." Waterpowered mills were invented in Han China, as was the basis of the modern horse breast strap and collar, which made it possible for draft animals to pull much heavier loads more efficiently and without being choked. Lacquer had made its appearance by Wu Ti's time, and samples of fine lacquer ware have been found in Han tombs. Han dynasty alchemists invented the technique of distillation, not discovered in Europe until the fourteenth century. Artisans of the Han period built ships with watertight compartments, multiple masts, and sternpost rudders, and mariners used a magnetic compass. The circulation of the blood was also discovered in Han China; Europeans first knew of it only in the seventeenth century. Metallurgy, already well advanced, was given a further boost by the invention of a double-acting piston-bellows, something not achieved in Europe until the seventeenth century. Suspension bridges became common under the Han; it was not until the eighteenth century that they were copied in Europe.

Probably the greatest literary achievement of the Han was in the writing of history. Many Chou records destroyed by Ch'in Shih Huang Ti were reconstructed by Han scholars from memory, and the texts we have date largely from this period. New pride in empire and tradition produced the man called China's Grand Historian, Ssu-ma Ch'ien (Simaqian, died c. 85 B.C.). His massive *Historical Records* put together materials from earlier texts in an effort to provide an accurate record of events dating back before the Shang. He added summary essays on geography, culture, the economy, and biographies of important people. A century later, Pan Ku (Bangu, died A.D. 92) compiled a similarly comprehensive *History of the Han Dynasty*, which became the model for the standard histories commissioned by each subsequent dynasty, another respect in which the Han set the pattern for later centuries.

Han writers set a high standard for historical scholarship that many scholars feel was not equaled until the eighteenth century in the West. Here is another point of comparison between Han China and imperial Rome, where the writing of history also reached a high degree of cultivation and reflected a similar pride in accomplishment and the tradition that had led to it. The Roman ideal remained appealing to the European mind and still underlies much of the modern West, while in China the state system, the imperial model, and most of the other institutions and forms first established under the Han endured to shape the course of the next 2,000 years.

SUMMARY

Civilization in China can be traced through the rise of the Shang, the first authenticated dynasty, about 1600 B.C., its conquest by the Chou about 1050 B.C., the warring-states period in the last centuries of nominal Chou rule, the Ch'in empire from 221 to 206 B.C., and the rise, flourishing, and decline of the Han empire from 202 B.C. to A.D. 220. The pattern of subsequent Chinese history was largely set by the achievement of the Han empire, much of it based, in turn, on the teachings of Confucius, who lived in the sixth century B.C. From local beginnings on the north China plain under the Shang, the Chinese state and empire had grown by the end of the Han period to incorporate most of the area within the borders of modern China. During the same centuries the traditional model of Chinese civilization was established, a model that was largely adhered to for the next 20 centuries.

NOTES

1. J. J. L. Duyvendak, trans., *The Book of Lord Shang* (London: Arthur Probsthain, 1928), pp. 193–229 passim.

SUGGESTIONS FOR FURTHER READING

Bodde, D. *China's First Unifier.* Hong Kong: Hong Kong University Press, 1967.

Chang, K. C. *The Archeology of Ancient China,* 4th ed. New Haven, Conn.: Yale University Press, 1987.

Creel, H. G. *The Origins of Statecraft in China.* Chicago: University of Chicago Press, 1970.

Dawson, R., ed. *The Legacy of China.* Oxford: Clarendon Press, 1964.

De Crespigny, R. *Northern Frontier Policies and Strategies of the Later Han Empire.* Canberra: Australian National University Press, 1985.

Gernet, J. *A History of Chinese Civilization,* trans. J. R. Foster. Cambridge: Cambridge University Press, 1995.

Hsu, C. Y. *Ancient China in Transition: An Analysis of Social Mobility.* Stanford, Calif.: Stanford University Press, 1965.

———, and Linduff, K. M. *Western Chou Civilization.* New Haven, Conn.: Yale University Press, 1988.

Li, C. *Anyang.* Seattle: University of Washington Press, 1976.

Liu, X. *Ancient China and Ancient India: Trade and Religious Exchange, a.d. 1–600.* New York: Oxford University Press, 1988.

Loewe, M. *Everyday Life in Early Imperial China.* New York: Putnam, 1968.

Needham, J. *Science in Traditional China.* Cambridge, Mass.: Harvard University Press, 1981.

Owen, S. *Remembrances: The Experience of the Past in Classical Chinese Literature.* Cambridge, Mass.: Harvard University Press, 1986.

Peerenborm, R. P. *Law and Morality in Ancient China.* Albany: State University of New York Press, 1993.

Rubin, V. A. Individual and State in Ancient China. New York: Columbia University Press, 1976.

Schwarz, B. I. *The World of Thought in Ancient China.* Cambridge, Mass.: Harvard University Press, 1985.

Sullivan, M. *The Arts of China.* Berkeley: University of California Press, 1977.

Twitchett, D., ed. *The Cambridge History of China.* Vol. 1: *Ch'in and Han.* Cambridge: Cambridge University Press, 1986.

Wang, Z. *Han Civilization.* New Haven, Conn.: Yale University Press, 1982.

Watson, W. *Ancient China: Discoveries of Post-Liberation Archeology.* London: British Broadcasting Corporation, 1974.

———. *Courtier and Commoner in Ancient China.* New York: Columbia University Press, 1977.

Yu, Y. S. *Trade and Expansion in Han China.* Berkeley: University of California Press, 1967.

CHAPTER 4

Early and Classical Greece

Immigrants from the east arrived in the Aegean Sea area approximately 6000 B.C., bringing with them the newly developed agricultural techniques of the Neolithic period. For some 3,000 years life continued on a simple, pastoral basis. Around 3000 B.C. a brilliant and sophisticated Bronze Age culture began to develop, first among the Minoans of Crete and then, about 1650 B.C., among the Mycenaeans who inhabited the Greek peninsula.

A major turning point in the Mediterranean region occurred around 1100 B.C. when the Bronze Age civilization collapsed, to be succeeded, after a period of disorder, by the Iron Age. Over the centuries that followed, a new culture emerged that was to provide in large part the matrix for subsequent Western civilization. By the fifth century B.C. Greek culture reached its zenith in the Classical Age.

Neolithic Greece

Crossing the Bosporus, people from Asia in search of new farmlands settled in northern Greece. From here some spread northwest into central Europe, while others moved south to central Greece and the rich plains of Thessaly. In time they built villages and manufactured fine pottery, often with painted decorations. These early settlers may have related the productivity of the earth to human fertility, for a number of little statues have been found, almost always of female nudes.

Other settlers from Asia Minor founded their own communities on the large island of Crete. In many cases they chose to live in caves rather than construct drafty huts. Their pottery was elaborate and stylistically

Porch of the Maidens, the Erechtheum, Athens. These female figures, serving as pillars for a small temple on the Acropolis of Athens, display superbly the classical Greek ideal of the human form.

different from that of the mainland. The animals they reared included pigs, cattle, and sheep. None of these previously existed on Crete, and the transport of the original herds by sea from Asia must have presented a considerable challenge for their owners. The largest Neolithic settlement on Crete was at Knossos, the future site of the grandest Bronze Age palaces.

The continuity of civilization at Knossos underlines the fact that the transition from stone to metal tools was gradual, producing no immediate revolution in ways of life. The Cretan Bronze Age began shortly after 2900 B.C. On the neighboring islands of the Cyclades bronze tools were in use by that date, and with them came other changes. The inhabitants of the Cycladic communities cut tombs in the rock or built them of stone, and they often buried weapons with the dead, a sign that the peace of the Neolithic farms was beginning to erode.

The people of the Cyclades also produced elegant sculpture, including marble statues that in many cases were also buried with the dead. These figurines, most of which represent women, vary in size from a few inches to 5 feet. The function of the statues is not clear. They may have been used as part of the funeral ceremony, and the fact that the overwhelming majority are female suggests that they too, like the earlier Neolithic figures, were forerunners of the cult of the Earth Mother.

Shortly after 2000 B.C. a new wave of invaders from the east moved into the Cyclades and eventually the Greek peninsula, to be followed by immigrants from the Balkans. The newcomers caused considerable disruption to the earlier settlers, and many of the mainland communities of this period constructed massive walls and towers to defend themselves. From the numerous warriors' graves it appears that life on the mainland was marked by frequent warfare waged between rival settlements. On Crete, however, the picture is different. Instead of retreating behind walled settlements, the population of the island, isolated from the troubles farther north, began to gather in urban centers. Here they developed the richest and most durable Bronze Age culture, that of the Minoans.

The Minoans

In the Classical Age of the fifth and fourth centuries B.C., Crete's fame rested on its mythic past. The legendary King Minos was said to have ruled there from his great palace at Knossos. In 1906, while excavating Knossos, the British archaeologist Arthur Evans discovered ancient remains. Five years later, after further excavations, he determined that the discoveries were those of a hitherto unknown Bronze Age civilization of extraordinary richness. The quantity and quality of the finds were overwhelming: ceramics, frescoes, inscriptions, and jewels. In one room Evans found a raised seat with a high back set against elaborate paintings, which he identified as the throne room of King Minos. The civilization that Evans had discovered was named Minoan after the legendary king.

The Early Minoan period (2900–2100 B.C.) was a time of slow expansion that laid the foundation for the brilliant culture of the Middle Minoan period (2100–1575 B.C.). During these later centuries the people of southern and eastern Crete constructed splendid palaces at such places as Knossos, Phaestus, and Mallia. The palaces, which included warehouses (mostly for grain, olive oil, and wine), workshops, and chapels, served as centers of government and production. The main structure of a Cretan palace was typically built around an open rectangular courtyard and contained religious shrines, public halls for banquets, and quarters for administrators. Other parts of the structure held royal living quarters and working areas for slaves and artisans. The palaces contained drainage systems and were designed to provide shade in the hot summer months and insulation against the winter cold. Surrounding the palace were the private houses of the aristocrats and chief religious leaders. Unlike royal palaces in western Asia, those on Crete were not surrounded by defensive walls. Archaeologists have unearthed no temples independent of the palace complexes.

Contacts with Egypt, Mesopotamia, and Asia Minor taught Cretan artisans to make pottery with a glasslike finish, stone vessels, and seals. Cretan pottery was soon in demand in Egypt, and Egyptian goldsmiths learned from their counterparts in Crete. The Cretans exported timber to Egypt in return for luxury items, especially ivory, precious stones, and gold. Cretan traders also maintained contacts with the Greek mainland, the islands of the Aegean, Cyprus, and probably Syria.

Around 1700 B.C. the palaces suffered severe damage, probably due to an earthquake, only to be reconstructed in an even grander manner. About a century later they were rebuilt again, probably for the same reason. These later palaces represent Minoan culture's highest achievement, and their wall paintings illustrate the elaborate court ceremonial. The Minoans left only a small amount of written material, some of it in pictographs and the rest in a syllabic script called *Linear A.* Although scholars cannot yet decipher more than a few words of Linear A, they believe it may have been derived from either a Semitic or an Anatolian script.

The rulers of these communities were male and apparently modeled their government on those of the kingdoms of western Asia. The principal Minoan deity, however, may have been a Mother Goddess. Like the Great Mother of the Mesopotamians, she may have been a fertility figure, taking on a variety of forms associated at times with animals, at times with vegetation. Legend had it that the Minotaur, a monster part man and part bull, lived within King Minos' palace, appeased only by the annual sacrifice of seven youths and seven maidens, probably a symbol of tribute paid to Crete from the mainland. The scenes of bull leaping depicted in Cretan art may reflect religious rites, which in all likelihood focused on the forces of nature; unlike the people of Çatal Hüyük, who venerated bulls, the Cretans sacrificed them. Minoan murals also suggest that men and women freely interacted in public life and that women danced publicly, perhaps in religious ceremonies or simply to entertain spectators.

Snake Goddess, from the Temple Repository at Knossos, c. 1600 B.C. The figure probably represents a priestess rather than the goddess herself; she is wearing the characteristic Minoan open bodice and an apron, symbol of her religious function.

At the beginning of the Late Minoan period (1575–1150 B.C.), Minoan artistic styles began to make an impact on the Greek mainland. The political and military power of the Minoans, however, was beginning to decline, and mainlanders seem to have occupied Knossos around 1460 B.C., not long after the city suffered a natural catastrophe (probably again an earthquake). In subsequent years Knossos, with a population of 50,000, subjected other palaces to its rule. Disaster—whether another natural catastrophe or an invasion is hotly debated—struck once more around 1400 B.C., after which time only small, impoverished mountainous settlements survived the remaining centuries of the Bronze Age.

The Mycenaeans

The Mycenaeans, dominant in mainland Greece during the Bronze Age, are so called because the greatest and richest of their settlements was named Mycenae. Other Mycenaean communities in central Greece included Athens and Thebes, but most of their settlements were in southern Greece, an area known as the Peloponnesus. The Mycenaeans, like the Minoans, had their fame preserved in legend long before the discovery of their palaces. Their principal claim to renown was the war they launched in the later thirteenth century B.C. against the fortress of Troy on the Hellespont, whose rulers exacted tolls from passing shippers and amassed quantities of iron. The Trojan War and its consequences were celebrated in subsequent Greek poems attributed to Homer.

The German Heinrich Schliemann (1822–1890) devoted much of his life to demonstrating that the Homeric legends were based on actual events. In 1870 he began work at the site of what he believed to be Troy, in modern Turkey. During the next three years he uncovered the town's walls and gate as well as gold, silver, and bronze jewelry and weapons. On the basis of these finds, Schliemann then set out to discover the Mycenaeans, who had been responsible for the Trojan War. In 1876 he excavated inside the walls of Mycenae, where he discovered the cemetery known as the Royal Grave Circle, consisting of impressive pits cut into the rock. The gold treasures found in the shafts date to 1550–1500 B.C., a time when Mycenaean power had begun to expand.

Mycenaean culture was influenced by the Minoans, particularly in its artistic style and possibly in its system of writing as well. The Minoans' Linear A script may have inspired the development of a Mycenaean script, Linear B, an early form of Greek. But unlike the Minoans, the Mycenaeans built their principal settlements, including Mycenae, Tiryns, and Pylos, on hills for defensive purposes. Their palaces were surrounded by walls, and even Mycenaean art emphasizes military motifs as well as hunting. Mycenaean kings amassed considerable wealth and governed with the aid of scribes who kept records of the taxes, property, and livestock of their subjects. As the principal power in the western Mediterranean world after the decline of the Minoans, the Mycenaeans traded not only with the peoples of the Italian peninsula and Sicily but also with those of Egypt and western Asia. They even established trading colonies in the eastern Mediterranean. Commercial rivalry or a quest for iron apparently prompted the Mycenaeans to attack Troy sometime between 1250 and 1200 B.C.

Shortly after the assault on Troy, some Mycenaean palaces, including Pylos and Mycenae, were destroyed by invaders. The sea raiders who attacked the Hittite empire, Syria, Palestine, and Egypt at about the same time may have been responsible. Possibly they were the Philistines, who settled in Palestine in the early twelfth century B.C. In any event, during the twelfth century the remaining Mycenaean palaces suffered extensive damage, partly at the hands of the invaders but possibly also because of fighting among themselves. When Mycenaean power crumbled, the population began to decline sharply, the number of settlements drastically decreased, and many of the survivors migrated to safer regions, such as the mountainous area in the northern Peloponnesus, the eastern coast of Attica, the coasts of Asia Minor, the Aegean islands, and Cyprus.

Mask of Agamemnon, c. 1550 B.C., the death mask of one of the earliest Mycenaean rulers. It was one of five death masks found in the Royal Grave Circle.

The Homeric Epics and the Dark Age

In most important areas the Greeks of the ensuing Dark Age (c. 1100–800 B.C.) had to develop afresh almost all the techniques of the visual arts, architecture, literature, and the ability to write. All but the simplest manufacturing disappeared. Much of this decline has traditionally been blamed on the migration of Dorian-speaking Greeks to the southern part of the peninsula, but the primary cause was the series of invasions that we have noted.

Although there are no written or artistic records from the Dark Age, we can reconstruct something about life in this period from the two great epic poems that emerged from it. The *Iliad* and the *Odyssey* are traditionally attributed to Homer, but modern scholars generally agree that they were composed by a number of poets over a long period of time and possibly compiled or put into definitive form by one of them. The first version was probably produced in the ninth century B.C., and the poems were apparently in more or less their present form by 700 B.C.

Both works have the Trojan War as their background. Throughout them are fitful glimpses of the world of the Bronze Age, and some of the tales may well have been passed down from that earlier period. For the most part, though, the Homeric world reflects life in Greece during the Dark Age. The poems, especially the *Iliad,* reflect such aristocratic values as heroic combat as well as the quest for booty, but they also explore human strengths and weaknesses. The Greek historian Herodotus would later comment that Homer and the seventh-century B.C. poet Hesiod gave the Greeks their gods; certainly they shaped the vision of later generations, who saw their deities at least in part as projections of themselves, human but for their immortality.

Like *The Epic of Gilgamesh* and the Vedas, the Homeric epics were shaped orally. In their early stages the poems were recited by itinerant professional bards who traveled throughout the Greek world. Their audiences consisted of the small groups of aristocrats who ruled each community in the Dark Age. Apart from assorted clues in the epics, our impression of the lives of

Homer's World

In describing the scenes decorating the shield Hephaistos made for Achilles, Homer paints a picture of his own early Iron Age world.

On it he wrought in all their beauty two cities of mortal men. And there were marriages in one, and festivals.

They were leading the brides along the city from their maiden chambers under the flaring of torches, and the loud bride song was arising.

The young men followed the circles of the dance, and among them the flutes and lyres kept up their clamor as in the meantime the women standing each at the door of her court admired them.

The people were assembled in the market place, where a quarrel had arisen, and two men were disputing over the blood price for a man who had been killed.

One man promised full restitution in a public statement, but the other refused and would accept nothing.

Both then made for an arbitrator, to have a decision; and people were speaking up on either side, to help both men.

But the heralds kept the people in hand, as meanwhile the elders were in session on benches of polished stone in the sacred circle and held in their hands the staves of the heralds who lift their voices.

The two men rushed before these, and took turns speaking their cases, and between them lay on the ground two talents of gold, to be given to that judge who in this case spoke the straightest opinion.

Source: Homer, *The Iliad,* trans. R. Lattimore (Chicago: University of Chicago Press, 1961), bk. 18, II. 490–508, p. 388.

these communities is limited, for the most part, to the objects buried with the dead. Certainly some of the graves of the ninth and eighth centuries B.C. in the Dipylon Cemetery at Athens suggest a considerable concentration of wealth and power in the hands of a few.

Greece and the Mediterranean

By 800 B.C. Greek civilization had entered a new phase. Literacy had been recovered, with an alphabet borrowed from the Phoenicians and adapted to the Greek tongue. Extensive trade resumed, and the pressures of a growing population produced both social conflict and colonization. Ambitious Greeks traveled overseas in search of wealth. A number of the colonies they founded, such as Syracuse in Sicily and Croton in southern Italy, grew richer and more powerful than their mother cities. Colonies were also founded in Egypt and around the Black Sea. It was perhaps inevitable that intercity rivalries accompanied the settlers, often creating tension in their relations with each other and with the communities of the Greek homeland.

Simultaneously, along the coast of Asia Minor the Greek settlements founded in the Dark Age established trade links with much of western Asia; these were to have important consequences for Greek culture. After several centuries of isolation, the Greeks came into contact with the developed cultures of western Asia and Egypt, which they rapidly assimilated.

As the Greeks continued to expand, they gradually shaped the characteristic sociopolitical institution that they called the *polis.* Each of the *poleis* was an independent political unit consisting of a town or village and the surrounding territory, the inhabitants of which were bound together in a community based on kinship relations. Geographic conditions in Greece played a crucial

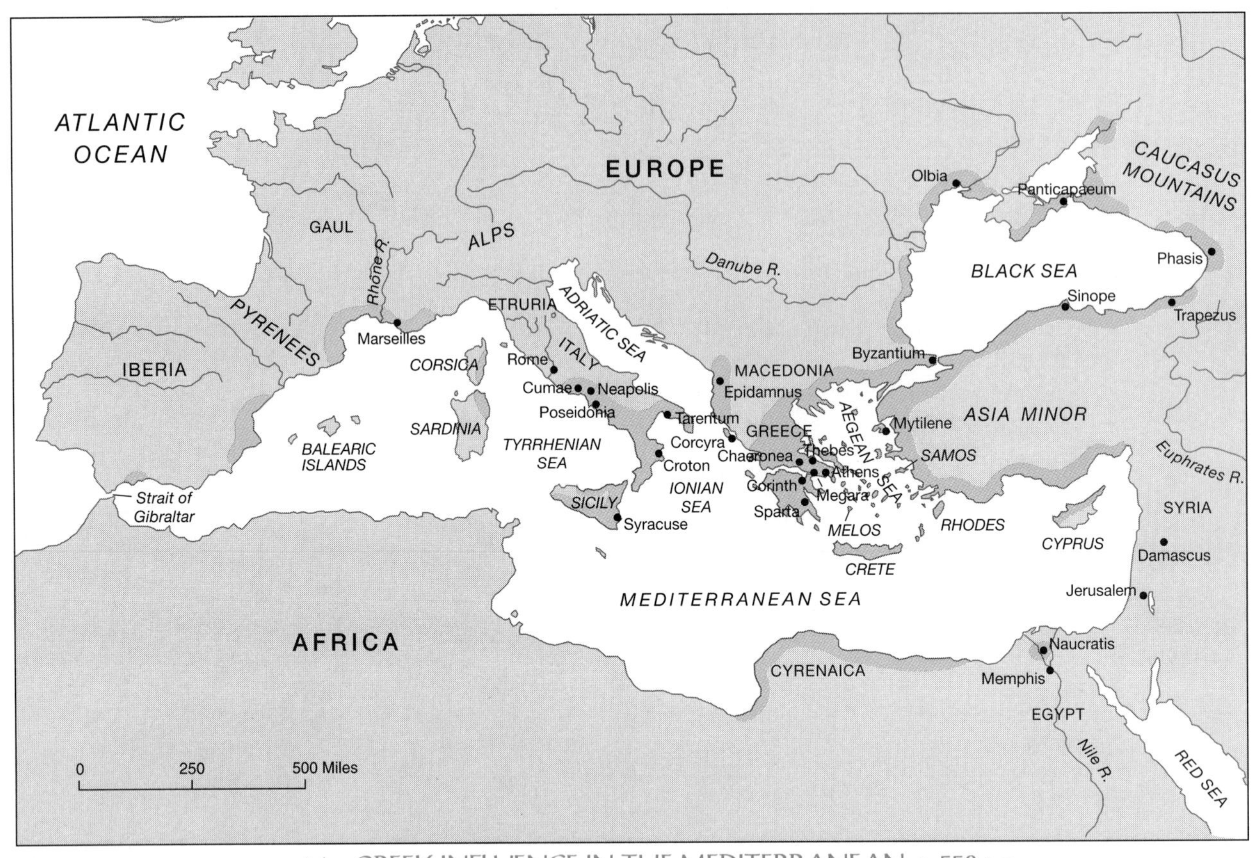

MAP 4.1 GREEK INFLUENCE IN THE MEDITERRANEAN, c. 550 B.C

role in shaping these small political units, for the mountainous terrain encouraged communities to develop in relative isolation. Communication was difficult; unlike Mesopotamia and Egypt, Greece has no major rivers, although many communities had ready access to the sea and to the myriad islands that dot the Aegean.

The polis provided the basis for social, political, religious, and cultural life. The loyalty of its citizens toward their city was far more powerful than any sense of fellowship with other Greeks, producing fierce intercommunal rivalries. The polis was thus both the most distinctive achievement of Greek civilization and its most destabilizing element.

Many poleis sent out colonizers as a way to release tensions and population pressures at home. The success of the colonizers often created new problems, however. The wealth made possible by colonial trade produced unsettled conditions both abroad and in the mother cities in Greece. The more prosperous the polis, the more likely was a political upheaval created by the newly powerful traders, manufacturers, and farmers, who challenged the traditional elites. In these unstable conditions, power in many of the poleis was seized by local leaders with popular support. The Greeks called these revolutionary leaders *tyrants.* The term was not derogatory; it meant simply those who attained office through insurrection or, sometimes, consensus. Indeed, many tyrants became famous for their public works and enlightened rule, although there was no shortage of those whose behavior explains the notoriety of the term in later times.

The experience of Corinth was typical of many poleis that willingly submitted to tyrants. Corinth was among the richest Greek cities in this period. Corinthian colonies were established in the west, and Corinthian vases, oil, and perfume were exported throughout the Mediterranean. This growth of the trading class undermined the old aristocracy, and around 655 B.C. Cypselus overthrew them and became tyrant of Corinth. Supposedly related to the ruling family he had overturned, he governed for 30 years. It was a mark of his popularity that he never had a bodyguard.

The success of Cypselus illustrates the basic conditions that made possible the phenomenon of the tyrants. On the one hand, tyranny was a form of monarchy. Not only did the tyrants wield power, but they passed it on to their descendants; Cypselus was succeeded by his son, Periander. On the other hand, the tyrants could continue to rule only if they maintained popular support. The citizen-militia that often gave them power in the first place could, and did, dislodge them if that proved necessary.

These citizen-armies were made possible by a new form of warfare that had developed in the late eighth century B.C. Previously, fighting had been undertaken by small troops of mounted horsemen and individual champions, who dueled with spears and swords. The new military style involved large numbers of armed infantrymen, called *hoplites,* who fought in a tightly organized block, or *phalanx.* Because the hoplite needed only a shield, a sword, a pike, a breastplate, and leg armor, it was economically feasible to organize citizen-armies, especially since each hoplite had to provide his own equipment. The absence of a standing professional army that could be used by an oppressive ruler against his people was the ultimate guarantee of popular control. Paradoxically, therefore, the concentration of power in the hands of one person, checked by the citizen-militia, made possible a general move toward wider community participation in the affairs of government.

The social and economic discontents that gave rise to the tyrants were not always resolved as in the case of Cypselus. At Miletus in Asia Minor, the center of the earliest school of Greek philosophy, the common people rose up against the aristocrats who ruled them and slaughtered their wives and children; when the aristocrats regained power, they roasted their opponents alive.

The scene painted on this Corinthian vase shows hoplites in close formation marching into battle.

The new merchant traders and the tyrants who ruled them were often patrons of artistic projects intended to perpetuate their memory and fame. The sculptures they commissioned were the first life-size stone figures in Western art. The earliest surviving figures, dating to the mid- and late seventh century B.C., are stiff and formalized, with flat planes and rigid stances. These figures, both male and female, showed Egyptian influence. Yet whereas Egyptian statuary emphasized the undulating surfaces of the skin, from the beginning Greek sculptors manifested their primary interest in rendering bone structure and anatomy. By the middle of the next century Greek sculptors had learned to produce works with individual character, and in doing so developed a new style in art that reached its fulfillment in the Classical Age. The intermediate period beginning around 600 B.C., during which the Greeks gradually eliminated Asian elements from their art and developed their own style, is known as the Archaic period. It was during this period as well that pottery and vase painting reached their highest development. Most subjects represented were mythological scenes, but many showed everyday activities and events, including games and revels, and some depicted erotic acts with considerable frankness.

In literature two new forms emerged. The heroic verse of Homer had served the ruling class of an aristocratic society, with the leisure to hear about the deeds of mighty leaders such as Achilles. The poets of the age of the tyrants were more interested in individual feelings and emotions, and the medium invented to express their feelings about life, death, and love was lyric poetry.

Hesiod, who lived in Boeotia in the seventh century B.C., is chiefly remembered for his *Works and Days,* an almanac in verse that praised peasants rather than aristocrats, frugality rather than ostentatiousness, and hard work rather than heroic adventures. Himself of humble birth, he demonstrated no comparable concern for slaves or women. Wives, in his view, were either obnoxious because of their nagging or contemptible because of their unthinking obedience. Hesiod's pessimism shaped his view of history, which he saw as a relentless decline from a golden age free of toil and pain to a future overwhelmed by labor, anguish, and death in which infants would be born with gray hair, decency would perish, might would take precedence over right, and family relationships would disintegrate. In another work, the *Theogony (Creation of the Gods),* he collected many of the religious myths that reflected Hellenic belief, giving shape and coherence to the scattered stories and conflicting chronologies that profoundly influenced future generations.

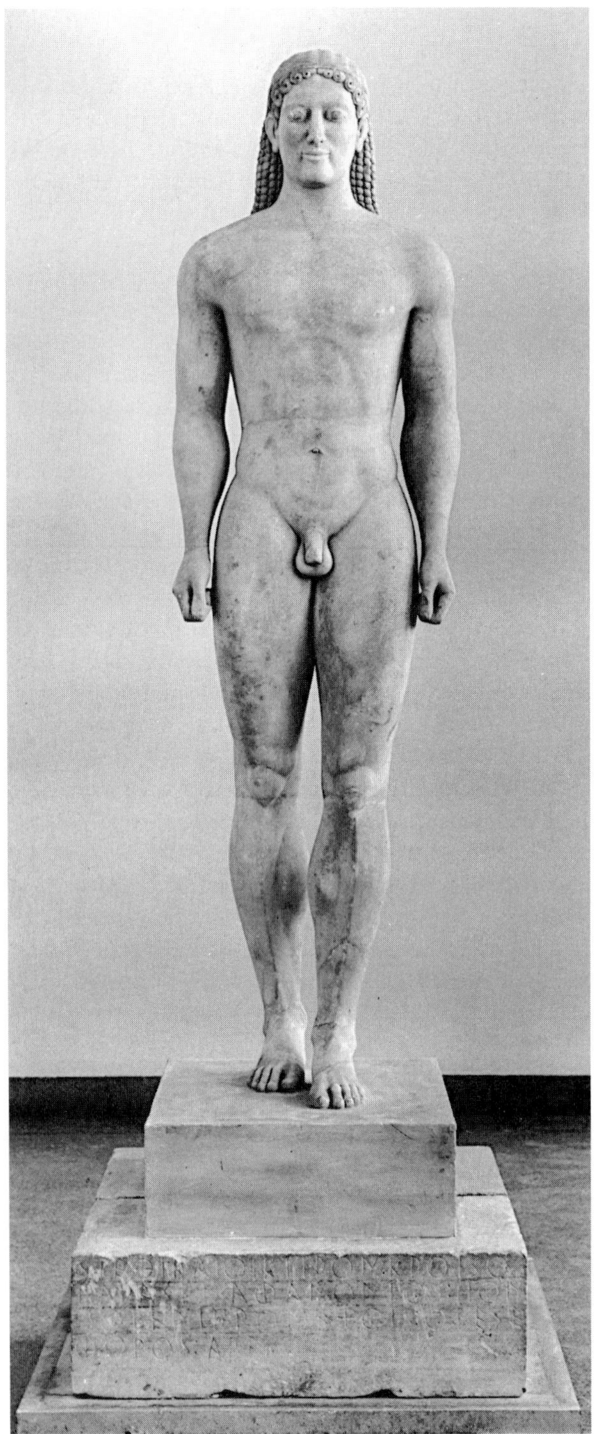

The base of this kouros, c. 530 B.C., bears an inscription saying that the statue represents a young man, Kroisos, who died heroically in battle. The hairstyle and rigid pose reflect Egyptian influence.

Sappho and the Poetry of Love

Although women played an important part in Greek mythology and religion, we have almost no account of their experience from their own hands. Virtually all of our knowledge is derived from sources written by men, and Sappho, the first Greek woman to enshrine her personal experiences in literary form, is therefore an important exception.

Sappho was born around 612 B.C. on the island of Lesbos, where she lived most of her life. She apparently combined the domestic functions of wife and mother with her writing and teaching. She earned considerable admiration as a poet during her own lifetime and taught younger women on Lesbos. The warm bond between Sappho and her students was deep, for it recurs as a constant theme in her poetry. Her appearance itself is uncertain: one ancient authority described her as a "beautiful day," while another said that "physically she was very ugly, being small and dark, like a nightingale with misshapen wings enfolding a tiny body." In the ancient world the women of Lesbos were notorious in the popular imagination for uninhibited sexual behavior. Sappho's poetry makes clear her sexual feeling for other women, but we have no evidence that her contemporaries thought this unseemly. Erotic friendship played an im-

Sappho, as depicted in a Spartan mosaic dating from around the fourth century A.D.

portant role in Greek society, both between women and between men.

The principal topic of Sappho's poetry is love; the only one of her poems to survive intact is a prayer to Aphrodite, the goddess of sexual love, expressing Sappho's fondness for an unnamed young woman about to be married. In other works Sappho expresses the conflicting emotions of isolation and of intense erotic involvement. Her tone is distinctive, but her theme, the celebration of sexual love, is quite common in Greek culture.

Sappho's writing shows a remarkably objective self-awareness, and she makes it clear that the agony her love often causes her is worth the price. Her most outstanding gift is her skill in describing the complexity of her emotional responses. In the same way as sixth-century B.C. sculptors and painters understood the workings of the human body by portraying it, Sappho revealed the process of her personal development. In so doing, she learned to temper her feelings, and much of her work expresses the kind of resignation that is the fruit of deep self-understanding. Throughout antiquity Sappho's work evoked the highest praise. Plato described her as the "tenth muse," and the Hellenistic poet Meleager said of her poems that they were "few but roses." In Roman times poets such as Catullus and Horace imitated her forms, and from there they were passed down into the long history of European lyric poetry.

Sappho's Poetry

This poem by Sappho exemplifies the directness and emotional intensity of her work.

Seizure

To me that man equals a god
as he sits before you and listens
closely to your sweet voice
and lovely laughter—which troubles
the heart in my ribs. For now
as I look at you my voice fails
my tongue is broken and thin fire
runs like a thief through my body.
My eyes are dead to light, my ears
pound, and sweat pours down over me.
I shudder, I am paler than grass,
and I am intimate with dying—but
I must suffer everything, being poor.

Source: Sappho, trans. W. Barnstone (New York: Doubleday/Anchor Books, 1965), p. 11.

The Growth of the Polis

The political ideal of the polis involved the devotion of the citizens to their city-state at the expense of any wider community. This had practical consequences wherever the Greeks settled. A polis that represented the collective image of its citizens needed to have impressive public buildings and, if possible, an organized town plan. In the case of the older cities of the Greek mainland, cluttered by the buildings of several centuries, planners and architects were constrained by the work of their predecessors. Where new sites were settled, however, as at Poseidonia in southern Italy (later known by its Roman name, Paestum), streets were laid in straight lines to form city blocks, intersected by other streets running at right angles. At a convenient flat space within the city was the main square, or *agora,* surrounded by the principal public buildings, where the citizens could meet both formally and informally. The inhabitants of Paestum embellished their city with impressive temples, constructed between 550 and 450 B.C.

If great buildings could give visible character to a city, so could coinage. The coins each city minted bore a figure or design that identified its origins. Corinthian coins, for example, showed Pegasus, the legendary winged horse, which, according to the myth, was born at the fountain in Corinth's main square. The citizens of Metapontum, the fertile plain of southeast Italy, chose an ear of grain as their symbol.

Coins and manufactured objects such as pottery and terra-cotta statues were used to pay for raw materials the Greeks lacked. One basic commodity, iron, was close at hand in central and northern Italy, and a thriving trade developed between the western Greek colonies and the Etruscans. The individual cities often established their own trade patterns. The citizens of Aegina in central Greece transported grain from their colonies on the Black Sea back to the mother city. In some cases cities were founded precisely to serve as exchange ports, as in the case of Naucratis in Egypt.

The culminating demonstration of Greek civic pride was provided by the athletic festivals at which the poleis

The agora *or marketplace of ancient Athens served not only as a center of commerce but as a meeting place for friends and a forum for debate; here Socrates often met with his students.*

came together to compete against one another. Olympia, Delphi, and Nemea were known as Panhellenic (all-Greek) shrines, and games were held at each of them. Victors, upon their return home, were given a civic welcome at public expense, and odes were composed to celebrate their triumphs.

In all these ways individual citizens were constantly reminded of the differences between themselves and their fellow Greeks. Certain shared characteristics were never lost. The Greek language and alphabet varied slightly from one part of the Greek world to another, but not enough to prevent communication. Furthermore, although there were regional variations in Greek religious practices and beliefs, there was enough common ground to sustain the great Panhellenic sanctuaries such as Delphi. Yet apart from these common events and observances and a shared artistic taste, even neighboring poleis failed to develop a sense of community until after the Macedonian conquest of the fourth century B.C. That conquest was a direct result of divisive civic pride and of a great fifth-century civil war that fatally weakened the polis.

However flawed in practice, the Greek civic ideal represents a distinctive concept in the development of civilization. From the earliest history of Egypt and Meso-

GREEK CIVILIZATION

Period	Important events	Cultural highlights
Bronze Age (3000–1100 B.C.)	• Minoan civilization • Mycenaean civilization	• Minoan frescoes and statuettes
Dark Age (1100–800 B.C.)	• Calamity and recovery • Development of the polis	• Homeric epics • Hesiod's poems
Age of Expansion (800–500 B.C.)	• Colonization of the Mediterranean • Rise of Athens, Sparta, and Corinth • Age of the tyrants	• Lyric poets • Ionian school of philosophers • Archaic sculpture
Classical Age (500–338 B.C.)	• Persian Wars • Growth of Athenian empire • Age of Pericles • Peloponnesian War • Spartan and Theban hegemonies • Philip of Macedon conquers Greece	• Herodotus • Thucydides • Aeschylus • Sophocles • Euripides • Parthenon • Myron • Plato • Aristotle

potamia, the city had represented the focus of political, economic, and technological development. For the Greeks, their poleis took on a moral significance that transcended any sense of nationhood. The polis represented a complete and self-contained way of life in which each adult male citizen had his civic and moral being. During the relatively brief period of its ascendancy as the dominant political body of the eastern Mediterranean, it nurtured a culture of astonishing fecundity, diversity, and brilliance.

Athens and the Birth of Democracy

The greatest of the poleis was Athens, situated strategically on the Attic peninsula, with easy access to the Aegean Sea. To later ages Athens symbolized the pinnacle of Greek civilization. Its beginnings, however, were modest. While other Greek poleis were founding colonies abroad and developing politically at home, Athenian society in the eighth and seventh centuries B.C. underwent no dramatic changes. There was little or no rise in population and virtually no overseas trade. The would-be tyrant Cylon attempted to overthrow the aristocratic government in 632 or 628 B.C. but failed for lack of popular support. However, the continuing power of the wealthy aristocracy combined with the increasing poverty of the peasantry was ominous. Growing numbers of poor Athenians were reduced to the state of pledging themselves and their families as security against their debts. When they were unable to pay, they were sold into slavery, often abroad, a fate that many avoided by fleeing into exile.

The Athenian solution to this social and economic problem was characteristically daring and farsighted. Around 594 B.C. the Areopagus, a council of wealthy citizens, gave the archon (magistrate) Solon special powers to head off a popular insurrection by introducing sweeping reforms. An aristocrat, a poet, and a man of wide cultural interests as well as a trader with extensive experience abroad, Solon gave shape to the development of an Athenian constitution that was to last for 200 years. He abolished all agrarian debts and restored freedom to all Athenians who had been sold into slavery. To enhance the city's commercial prosperity, he reformed the coinage and encouraged skilled artisans to immigrate to Athens in return for citizenship.

Under Solon's reforms, all citizens received the right to vote in the popular assembly, although only landowners could qualify as citizens. At the other end of the scale, high offices were no longer limited to males born within the old aristocracy but were opened to all wealthy men. With the exception of poor laborers, all male citizens qualified for membership in a new Council of Four Hundred, which comprised 100 members selected from each of the four Athenian tribes. The Council discussed proposed legislation before it was submitted to the assembly for final approval or rejection.

Although hindsight suggests that these reforms were essential to the stability of Athens, Solon was not uniformly popular. The aristocrats feared the erosion of their power, and the poorer citizens were at first disappointed and then enraged at the absence of any real redistribution of wealth or land. Ultimately disappointed by their complaints, Solon allegedly scorned his fellow Athenians as "individually foxes and collectively geese."

After Solon's death, competing factions jockeyed for power. Pisistratus, an aristocrat, twice attempted to seize control, but failed. Returning with a mercenary army and new financial resources acquired from his gold-mining operations in northern Greece, he finally attained power in 546 B.C. and ruled as tyrant until 527. Large sections of the population, especially the small farmers, supported him, not least because he helped them with loans to plant their crops. His encouragement of overseas trade also aided them by providing expanded markets for their olive oil and wine. But although Pisistratus enjoyed substantial popular support and left the democratic machinery of government intact, the traditional institutions exercised no independent power.

The tyranny of Pisistratus and his sons Hipparchus and Hippias, who ruled after him until 510 B.C., marked the first sustained period of peace and economic growth in Athenian history. The peaceful conditions enjoyed at this time encouraged cultural developments, and at Athens itself the period of Pisistratus' rule was one of great artistic development. Vase painters such as Exekias and Amasis produced works of exquisite refinement and skill that were increasingly sought abroad. In sculpture, artists continued to move toward more naturalistic styles, applying their techniques not only to freestanding figures but to relief carving as well. The expanding overseas trade encouraged the arts by increasing the demand for Attic pottery. To pay for an ambitious building program (including new temples), however, Pisistratus introduced a land tax that many Athenians found oppressive.

Pisistratus' pleasure-loving sons failed to maintain their father's legacy of civil peace. After a group of young Athenians assassinated Hipparchus in 514 B.C., Hippias employed severe repressive measures against his real and supposed enemies. In 510, however, he was driven into exile by a group of Athenian nobles led by Cleisthenes, a reformer who looked to the people for his political support. Cleisthenes' success was made possible by the

Solon on Injustice

In this fragment of verse, Solon, the reformer of Athenian political life, expresses his own perplexity at the injustices of the world.

In every activity there is danger, nor does anyone know, at an enterprise's start, where he will end up.

One man, striving to do what is right, but lacking foresight, falls headlong into great folly and great hardship, while to another who acts wrongly, God in all things gives pure good luck, redemption from his own thoughtlessness. . . .

The immortals bestow rich profits upon men, but folly often appears as the result, which when Zeus sends it to punish, strikes now this man, now that one.

Source: J. J. Pollitt, *Art and Experience in Classical Greece* (Cambridge: Cambridge University Press, 1972), p. 4.

assistance of Athens' archrival, Sparta, whose army, led by King Cleomenes, helped expel Hippias. Presumably Cleomenes hoped that Hippias would be replaced by a friendly government that would be more to the Spartans' aristocratic taste. Cleisthenes, however, proved to be democratic. The Spartans, together with the more conservative Athenian aristocrats, drove him out of Athens for a brief period. In the end, however, popular will triumphed, and in 508 Cleisthenes returned to Athens.

Like Solon, Cleisthenes set out to produce a more broadly based government. The citizens were given membership in *demes,* or local districts, that were then combined in such a way as to cut across the old borders of tribes and factions. The day-to-day business of running the state was entrusted to the *Boule,* or People's Council, consisting of 500 members. Fifty men were chosen by lot from each of the city's ten new tribes and served a term of one year. Each group of 50 supervised the magistrates one-tenth of the year. The Council supervised the routine work of running the state: control of expenditures, organization of religious festivals, and superintendence of buildings and other public works. The Council also assumed the responsibility of the now defunct Council of Four Hundred to act as a steering committee for the Popular Assembly by preparing legislation for its consideration.

Under Cleisthenes' new constitution, all adult male citizens continued to serve as members of the Popular Assembly. It met three or four times a month, and major business could not be transacted unless at least 6,000 members were present. The Assembly debated all proposals put before it by the Council before passing them into law or rejecting them, thus providing for a direct exercise of sovereignty by all citizens who chose to participate. By rotating membership and offices, Cleisthenes ensured that a large number of Athenian citizens would have practical experience in civic administration. The Areopagus and the magistrates retained their aristocratic character, but with diminished authority.

When Solon had been called to power around 594 B.C., Athens was a polis of relatively minor significance. By the end of that century the Athenians had become a major political force. With the prosperity acquired during the years of Pisistratus and their newly won political freedom, they were soon to become the most energetic and influential power in the Greek world. First, however, both they and their fellow Greeks had to face a threat from a source far beyond their borders: Persia.

The Persian Wars

In the seventh century B.C. the two principal powers to the east of Greece were Lydia and Persia. The Lydian kings were generally well disposed toward the Greeks, some of whom settled in colonies on the coast of Asia Minor, an area known as Ionia. The Greeks learned much from contacts with their eastern neighbor; coinage, probably invented in Lydia, had first been introduced into Europe around 625 B.C. Greek relations with the Persians were less friendly, although trade contacts apparently existed.

In 546 B.C. the kingdom of Lydia fell to Cyrus the Great of Persia, who added to his conquests the Greek colonies in Ionia and installed Persian governors. In 513 and 512 the Persian king, Darius (522–486 B.C.), led a great campaign to subdue southeastern Europe. The expedition was unsuccessful, however, and for the moment the Persians withdrew, preoccupied with problems in central Asia.

Discontented with their Persian governors and the taxes levied to support Persian interests, the Ionians took advantage of the temporary relaxation of imperial control. In 499 B.C. they launched a rebellion and called on their fellow Greeks to the west for help. Only the Athenians and their allies the Eretrians, inhabitants of a minor polis on the island of Euboea in the western Aegean, sent ships and men. Their support could not save the Ionians from defeat. By 494 the last city to hold out, Miletus, was sacked after a decisive naval battle off its shore.

Darius, displeased by the interference of Athens and Eretria, reportedly ordered a servant to say to him three times every day before dinner: "Sire, remember the Athenians." Revenge was not long in coming. In 490 the king's troops sailed across the Aegean and sacked Eretria.

MAP 4.2 CLASSICAL GREECE

Proceeding south toward Athens, they landed at Marathon Bay north of the city to face an outnumbered Athenian army. The Athenians had desperately sought support from other Greeks in their struggle against mighty Persia, particularly from Sparta. The Spartans declined, offering the convenient excuse that the celebration of a religious festival prevented them from leaving home.

The Persians, despite their greater number, were less flexible in their tactics than the Athenians. Under the brilliant generalship of Miltiades, the Athenian soldiers outflanked the Persians at Marathon and drove them back to their ships or into the marshy shore, where thousands were trampled to death.

The Persians had been stopped only temporarily. The Athenians, under the leadership of the archon Themistocles (527–460 B.C.), built new warships and fortifications and cultivated allies. When the Persians returned under Darius' son Xerxes in 480, they found a combined Greek army with some semblance of unity. The subsequent battles and the final Greek triumph represent one of the high points of Greek history. Having marched virtually unopposed through northern Greece, the Persians were blocked at the pass of Thermopylae by 300 Spartans, together with several thousand other Greek soldiers. Only treachery on the part of local Greeks enabled the Persians to encircle the Spartan defenders, who were reputedly massacred to a man. The Greek historian Herodotus, born shortly before the war began, describes the last stage of the battle:

> **The Greeks under Leonidas [the Spartan general], as they now went forth determined to die, advanced. . . . They . . . carried slaughter among the barbarians, who fell in heaps. Behind them the captains of the squadrons, armed with whips, urged their men forward with continual blows. Many were thrust into the sea, and there perished; a still greater number were trampled to death by their own soldiers; no one heeded the dying. . . . They defended themselves to the last, such as still had swords using them, and the others resisting with their hands and teeth; till the barbarians . . . overwhelmed and buried the remnant left beneath showers of missile weapons.[1]**

The Persians proceeded toward Athens, still the object of their vengeance. They found the city abandoned, occupied it, and destroyed many of its buildings. But the Athenians had brought away their fleet and treasury intact, and they engaged the Persians in the narrow straits between the Attic mainland and the island of Salamis, where Athenian experience proved decisive. A few months later, in 479 B.C., the remaining Persian land forces were defeated at Plataea.

The details of the Greeks' success were chronicled by Herodotus, often called "the father of history," whose account is the earliest surviving prose record of historical events. Herodotus' explanation of the Greek victory attributed the Persian defeat not only to Greek arms but also to the Persians' moral flaw—*hubris,* or excessive ambition. The Greek victory thus demonstrated the triumph of justice over brute force and proved that the gods, who had helped determine the war's outcome, were on the side of right. In Herodotus' mind, the war had been fought to preserve not only the independence of the Greek poleis but also the rule of law, which had been directly threatened by the invaders from the east. Thus the conflict was important not only for its immediate outcome but also as a source of future Greek perceptions about Asia. The war sharpened the Greeks' sense of their separate identity, and that notion of Western distinctiveness was subsequently inherited by the Romans.

Herodotus also saw the war as the beginning of three generations of trouble for the Greeks, caused at least in part by disputes among themselves. Nevertheless, the Greeks' victory had been made possible by the fact that they had managed to unite in the face of a common enemy. Their success marked the high point of Greek political cooperation, but this unity proved only temporary.

Athens in the Age of Pericles: Democracy and Imperialism

The Athenian leader during much of the late fifth century B.C. was Pericles, whose name now symbolizes the glories of Athens' Golden Age. Born to an aristocratic family around 495 B.C., Pericles entered politics and by 459 had become the unofficial leader of Athens, although he ran for public office every year like other magistrates. He devoted his efforts to glorifying Athens by constructing the majestic buildings on the Acropolis that still testify to the grandeur of his age.

Pericles did not rule Athens in the sense that a modern head of state does. The Athenians governed themselves by the participation of every adult male citizen in the Popular Assembly. Any member of this body could address it and try to convince it of his point of view. Frequently the Assembly followed Pericles' advice, but his authority was personal, not constitutional.

Few Athenians, presumably, would have disagreed with Pericles' conviction of the superiority of their city. He claimed, according to the historian Thucydides, that Athens was the "school of Greece," its natural political and cultural leader, and his plans were devoted to maintaining

Cresilas carved a bust of Pericles around 440 B.C. (this Roman marble copy was based on the original). An idealized image rather than a realistic portrait, the sculpture shows Pericles wearing a helmet, symbolic of his office as general.

and increasing its greatness. His patriotism inspired him and his fellow Athenians to combine political liberty at home for citizens with control of an empire abroad.

Life in Periclean Athens

By the mid-fifth century B.C. the male citizen population of Athens numbered about 40,000 to 45,000. Including women and children the total population was probably around 170,000, with perhaps the same number of slaves. In 451 B.C., however, a law was passed limiting citizenship to those whose parents were both Athenian. The new decree may have prevented a flood of immigration from Athens' allies, states that remained voluntarily or involuntarily bound to it after the Persian wars. It did little, however, to soothe the allies' resentment of Athens' military and political domination.

Each Athenian citizen could be called on to participate in the daily running of Athens as well as in the deliberations of the Assembly. Citizens had the duty to serve as magistrates. The traditional nine archons, who in Solon's time had been drawn from the aristocracy, were now chosen by lot. They had been supplemented as chief magistrates by ten generals, who were elected by the ten tribes. Pericles held the office of general for many years, and during his tenure the generals played as large a part in domestic affairs as in military operations. Except for generals and treasurers, however, virtually every magistrate was chosen by lot. As a consequence, even the obscurest citizen could find himself in a prominent administrative position.

Trials were held in the people's courts, or dikasteria, typically numbering 201, 401, or 501 jurors apiece. Altogether 6,000 jurors were selected by lot, and from them the various juries were formed. They sat in judgment on both private and public affairs, including the evaluation of magistrates at the conclusion of their term in office. Treason, however, was prosecuted before the Assembly, and homicide was tried by one of the few survivals from predemocratic days, the Areopagus. Even in criminal cases the prosecutors and defenders had to speak for themselves; there were neither judges nor professional lawyers.

Clearly, a government in which so many of its citizens could participate required very special conditions. The average Athenian was expected to have a detailed knowledge of current affairs and the workings of the law. Financial hardship was no obstacle to holding public office, for the state paid almost all public servants an allowance to compensate for their loss of regular earnings. Thus even the poorest citizen might serve as juror, member of the Council, or magistrate; only the elected officials—the generals and the treasurers—were not paid. Furthermore, all magistrates, even the generals, were fully accountable to the Council of Five Hundred for their conduct in office.

A system known as *ostracism* prevented the ambitious from acquiring too much power. Any political figure whose name was marked often enough on fragments of pottery (ostraka) used for anonymous denunciations could be exiled for ten years. Themistocles, the hero of the resistance to Persia, was one of those proscribed; he ended his days in the Persian camp.

Pericles on the Government of Athens

In a speech on the occasion of the public funeral of the Athenian war dead, delivered in the fall of 430 B.C., Pericles describes his view of the Athenian system of government.

Let me say that our system of government does not copy the institutions of our neighbors. It is more the case of our being a model to others, than of our imitating anyone else. Our constitution is called a democracy because power is in the hands not of a minority but of the whole people. When it is a question of settling private disputes, everyone is equal before the law; when it is a question of putting one person before another in positions of public responsibility, what counts is not membership in a particular class, but the actual ability which the man possesses. No one, so long as he has it in him to be of service to the state, is kept in political obscurity because of poverty. And, just as our political life is free and open, so is our day-to-day life in our relations with each other. We do not get into a state with our next-door neighbor if he enjoys himself in his own way, nor do we give him the kind of black looks which, though they do no real harm, still do hurt people's feelings. We are free and tolerant in our private lives; but in public affairs we keep to the law. This is because it commands our deep respect.

Source: Thucydides, *History of the Peloponnesian War,* trans. R. Warner (Harmondsworth, England: Penguin Books, 1954), p. 117.

Athenian democracy—the word literally means "rule by the people (*demos*)"—was a remarkable and unprecedented experiment. It coincided with Athens' political and economic hegemony in Greece and its great cultural flowering as well. It remains the wellspring of the Western democratic tradition, and although it had severe critics even in its own day, it has remained the ideal of a political community of free, equal, and self-governing persons. Never, however, did it eradicate poverty. Nor did it embrace the entire community, for it excluded two large groups that together made up the majority of the adult population: women and slaves.

Ostraka from the Athenian Agora, fifth century B.C. The potsherds record the names of persons whom the Popular Assembly sought to exile, among them Themistocles; his main opponent, Aristides; Pericles; and Kimon.

Roughly half of the Athenian population resided outside Athens and its nearby harbor town, Piraeus. Apart from participation in public affairs, for which approximately 50 percent of the adult citizens received state pay during at least part of the year, most Athenians worked the land. Some Athenians still owned large estates, though most were small freeholders who worked the land themselves or with the assistance of a few slaves. A third of the land was normally left fallow each year, and the Athenians had to import 75 percent of the grain needed to feed themselves. Landless Athenians depended for employment on state building projects, the craft industries, and retailing, though most of the manufacturing and commerce were controlled by resident aliens known as *metics.* The latter competed with Athenians for jobs: the stonecutters, carpenters, and unskilled laborers who built the temple known as the Erechtheum consisted of 24 Athenians, 40 metics, and 17 slaves. Wages were such that a married man with two or three children lived at the subsistence level. The state did not intervene to regulate wages or working conditions.

A Critical View of the Athenians

A conservative critique of Athenian life is expressed by an anonymous writer of the late fifth century B.C. *known simply as the "Old Oligarch."*

Another point is the extraordinary amount of license granted to slaves and resident aliens at Athens, where a blow is illegal, and a slave will not step aside to let you pass him in the street. I will explain the reason of this peculiar custom. Supposing it were legal for a slave to be beaten by a free citizen, or for a resident alien or freedman to be beaten by a citizen; it would frequently happen that an Athenian might be mistaken for a slave or an alien and receive a beating, since the Athenian people are not better clothed than the slave or alien, nor in personal appearance is there any superiority.

Or if the fact itself that slaves in Athens are allowed to indulge in luxury, and indeed in some cases to live magnificently, be found astonishing, this too, it can be shown, is done of set purpose. Where you have a naval power dependent upon wealth we must perforce be slaves to our slaves, in order that we may get in our slave-rents, and let the real slave go free.

For my part I pardon the people its own democracy, as, indeed, it is pardonable in any one to do good to himself. But the man who, not being himself one of the people, prefers to live in a state democratically governed rather than in an oligarchical state may be said to smooth his own path towards iniquity. He knows that a bad man has a better chance of slipping through the fingers of justice in a democratic than in an oligarchical state.

Source: C. Starr, *The Ancient Greeks* (London: Oxford University Press, 1971), pp. 199–201.

Free time could be spent in religious festivals or state-supported exercise grounds known as *gymnasiums,* but civic responsibilities were demanding for many.

Women in Classical Athens

The first literary and dramatic representations of women we have from the ancient Western world, apart from the Hebrew Bible, are those of classical Greece. The Greeks added what the Hebrews lacked: the visual representation of women in paint and stone. The great tragic figures of the Greek stage—the avenging queen, Clytemnestra; the betrayed wife, Medea; the martyred princess, Antigone; and many others—are still the prototypes of Western drama. The magnificent representations of the female figure, including the first life-size nudes in Western art (beginning with those of Praxiteles in the fourth century B.C.), remain the acknowledged ideal of feminine beauty in Western culture. In mythology, too, women played a crucial and often commanding role, and the very name of Athens was derived from its patron goddess, Athena, whose 40-foot-high statue sat enthroned in the temple of the Parthenon.

The actual position of women in classical Greek society fell far short of these idealized images. The philosopher Aristotle reflected the prevailing view when he described women as the natural inferiors of men, born to serve and obey; he even denied them a full share in the procreation of children (their chief function), arguing that the male seed alone contained the full germ of the child, with the womb serving only as its receptacle. The role and status of women were far closer to those of slaves than those of citizens. Women had no independent legal standing and could have legal rights exercised for them only through male guardians. Marriages were generally arranged by the bride's father, who was also responsible for the wedding celebration and, of course, the dowry. Husbands could divorce their wives at will, whereas women had to find magistrates to represent them. Husbands could even dispose of their wives in

A Roman copy of a fifth-century B.C. *statue of a woman, perhaps representing a goddess.*

their wills; the orator Demosthenes describes the case of a widow ordered to marry her husband's former slave. The double standard was also applied to adultery: tolerated for men, it was regarded as automatic grounds for divorce in the case of women.

Only inside the home did women exert any authority. Within her house a woman was responsible for domestic finances, duties such as spinning and weaving, and the supervision of slaves. Even here, however, the sexes were socially segregated, with women consigned to their own part of the house while men entertained their visitors (including prostitutes and concubines) elsewhere. The woman's part of the house, the *gynaeconitis,* varied in size and complexity with the scale of the home. In small residences it consisted of one or two rooms, divided from the main section by a door that could be locked, apparently to keep the male and female slaves apart. In larger houses the woman's quarters had a separate dining room, an open courtyard, and occasionally additional suites of rooms.

The sexual life of most citizen-class women was as restricted as their social life. The eroticism of Greek vase paintings is very misleading. Procreation rather than pleasure was the primary aim of marital sexuality. The Greco-Roman historian Plutarch cited a law of Solon's that required married couples to have intercourse at least three times a month "for the same reason that cities renew their treaties from time to time." Athens and most other Greek cities supported a large population of male and female prostitutes; Corinth is said to have had 1,000 of the latter. These included the famous *hetairai,* or courtesans, who had the reputation of being cultivated companions as well as women skilled in the art of pleasure. Because hetairai were usually of metic status and did not generally come from citizen families, Athenian men desiring to beget sons who would enjoy civic rights were limited in their choice of wives to the comparatively uneducated women of the citizen class. Predictably, they also established liaisons with the more cultured hetairai as well. The division of women in Athens into a cultivated courtesan class and an uneducated citizen class suitable for providing heirs created considerable tensions. It is the hetairai who are largely represented in the vase paintings, often performing acts that were frowned on in the marriage bed. They were also sometimes represented as being beaten, raped, or otherwise abused.

Domestic occupation was viewed as good for women, but any kind of work for pay was considered socially demeaning. Women of the lower classes hired out as weavers, spinners, and wet nurses; many worked as vendors in the public market. Athenian women seldom worked at agriculture, but in periods of duress they sometimes went into the field or picked grapes in the harvest. A very few served in temples. Most upper-class women simply stayed home. It is unclear whether women were even able to attend the theaters where the tragic heroines were portrayed, but we do know that they were prohibited from acting the parts, which were played by men and boys.

Slaves and Metics

At Athens alone the number of slaves in the late fifth century B.C. is estimated to have been between 100,000 and 200,000, or roughly half the population. Almost none of these were of Greek origin; many, either captured in war or bought at slave markets in Greece and western Asia, came from Asia Minor or southern Russia. They were owned by individual citizens, metics, or the state. Those who were skilled in a craft could produce work for sale, on condition that their masters received a share of the profit. Many worked in industries such as mining and quarrying or in farming. About half worked as domestic servants. Since the wealthier households had several slaves—a famous shield manufacturer, Cephalus, owned 120—many Athenian households of the poorer classes must have functioned without slave labor.

The daily life of a domestic slave differed little from that of the average Athenian housewife. It was not possible for an outsider to distinguish between slaves and free workers by their dress or their treatment. Slaves were generally considered members of the household. They were allowed to marry and produce children, who then became the property of their owners; they could save money for their old age; and when they died they were buried in the family tomb. Although no laws existed to protect them from abuse, they could seek refuge from cruel masters in legal sanctuaries. There are even cases where slaves received their freedom, went into business, and became Athenian citizens. The lot of agricultural or mine workers was far grimmer. The quarriers and miners were often worked to death, and farm laborers shared the generally uncertain and penurious conditions of their farmer masters.

In addition to citizens and slaves there was another class in Athens, the metics. These included immigrants from other parts of the Greek world and their descendants, freed slaves and their descendants, and, after 451 B.C., the children of marriages between citizens and noncitizens. Like the slaves and female relations of citizens, they could not vote in the Assembly or serve as jurors, nor could they own houses or land, though they fought in the Athenian army and paid taxes. Metics were in general socially accepted, had freedom of worship, and were able to follow their chosen trade or profession. Many of them, in fact, played an important part in Athenian business and industry, and some acquired considerable wealth, though most were poor. They could also own slaves. The interests of metics were represented by Athenian officials known as *polemarchs,* who were appointed by lot. The opening pages of Plato's *Republic* indicate the high social esteem enjoyed by some metic families. Indeed, the metic Cephalus, who had moved from Syracuse to Athens at Pericles' urging, was included in the circle of Plato's friends.

The Spartan Ideal

Sparta, Athens' principal rival in the Greek world, espoused different values. The champion of conservative forces in Greece, the Spartans had been warlike from the beginning of their history. Gradually they evolved a way of life based on the military ideal, to which they subordinated all other aspects of social, economic, and cultural life. Their ideals are vividly illustrated in a description of the city of Ephesus in Asia Minor when it was under Spartan control in the early fourth century B.C.:

> **You could see the gymnasia full of men exercising, the hippodrome full of horsemen riding, the javelin-throwers and the archers at target practice. . . . The market-place was full of armaments and horses for sale, while the bronzesmiths and carpenters, ironworkers, leatherworkers and painters were all preparing military equipment. As a result you would truly have thought the city a workshop of war.[2]**

The Spartans dominated the region around them, known as Laconia. Because all adult Spartan males were soldiers, the work of cultivation was done by the neighboring population, the *perioikoi,* and the large class of serfs, or *helots,* who were owned by the Spartans, bound to the soil, and kept under strict control. Together these groups gave the Spartans an abundant supply of forced or semifree labor. This system also surrounded them with a permanently hostile population. The perioikoi enjoyed personal freedom and a measure of local self-government, but they were subject to Spartan governors and to conscription in the Spartan army. They were probably the descendants of former allies who had been reduced to subservience. The helots, descended from conquered peoples, were restive and frequently rebellious. Unlike the Athenian slaves, who were in large part integrated into the families of citizens or worked beside them in the fields, the helots had little incentive to identify themselves with the harsh and exclusive rule of their masters.

Sparta's military ideal was thus both a cause and an effect of its pattern of conquest, which left the Spartans an elite minority among a disaffected mass of serfs and subjects. But if the Spartans were hard on the people they ruled, they were demanding of themselves as well. Spartan babies were inspected at birth, and those deemed unfit were exposed to die. Children were taken from their mothers at the age of 7 to be trained in martial arts and athletics. Their clothes were scanty, their beds were hard, and their food was monotonous and strictly rationed. The training they received was calculated to increase their powers of endurance and inspire them with patriotic fervor. Students were encouraged to steal, because foraging was a military virtue, and were punished not for the act but only for failing at it. At the age of 20 each male enlisted in the army and spent the next ten years living in barracks. For the rest of his life he remained a member of a small peer group, with whom he took his meals, even though he was expected to marry by the age of 30. Girls were given a similar, though less rigorous, military education. In contrast to Athenian women, those in Sparta had legal standing, could inherit property and represent themselves in court, and played a major role in managing the large estates of the Spartan aristocracy.

At the age of 30 Spartan males were divided into two classes, "equals" and "inferiors." The equals made up the Assembly, whose principal function was to elect the 30 members of the Council. These comprised two kings, who shared power and ruled jointly, and 28 elders. The chief magistrates were the five *ephors* (overseers), who had almost unlimited powers; they could arrest and prosecute any citizen, including the kings.

In embracing this social and political system, the Spartans of classical times believed they were following a code of laws introduced by Lycurgus, a shadowy and perhaps mythical figure in early Spartan history. Even the oracle at Delphi was uncertain whether to regard Lycur-

Spartan Bravery

In this extract from Herodotus' account of the Persian Wars, Xerxes hears high praise for the valor of the Spartans.

Having sailed from one end to the other of the line of anchored ships, Xerxes went ashore again and sent for Demaratus, the son of Ariston, who was accompanying him in the march to Greece. "Demaratus," he said, "it would give me pleasure at this point to put to you a few questions. You are a Greek, and a native, moreover, of by no means the meanest or weakest city in that country—as I learn not only from yourself but [also] from the other Greeks I have spoken with. Tell me, then—will the Greeks dare to lift a hand against me? My own belief is that all the Greeks and all the other Western peoples gathered together would be insufficient to withstand the attack of my army—and still more so if they are not united. But it is your opinion upon this subject that I should like to hear."

"My lord," Demaratus replied, "is it a true answer you would like, or merely an agreeable one?"

"Tell me the truth," said the king; "and I promise that you will not suffer by it." Encouraged by this Demaratus continued:

"My lord, you bid me speak nothing but the truth, to say nothing which might later be proved a lie. Very well then; this is my answer: poverty is my country's inheritance from of old, but valor she won for herself by wisdom and the strength of law. By her valor Greece now keeps both poverty and bondage at bay.

"I think highly of all Greeks of Dorian descent, but what I am about to say will apply not to all Dorians, but to the Spartans only. First then, they will not under any circumstances accept terms from you which would mean slavery for Greece; secondly, they will fight you even if the rest of Greece submits. Moreover, there is no use in asking if their numbers are adequate to enable them to do this; suppose a thousand of them take the field—then that thousand will fight you; and so will any number, greater than this or less."

Source: Herodotus, *The Histories,* trans. A. de Selincourt (Harmondsworth, England: Penguin Books, 1954), pp. 447–448.

gus as a man or a god, and it is probable that the Spartan system of government developed, like that at Athens, over a period of time.

The Spartans' concern with military affairs limited their contacts with the rest of Greece and left them in relative economic and cultural isolation. Their self-sufficiency was, of course, voluntary. Indeed, the profound differences between the Athenian and Spartan interpretations of civic ideals underscore the diversity of the polis as an institution. The Athenian version of democracy produced a spirit of commercial and imperial aggressiveness and stimulated a rich culture. The Spartans left behind no art or architecture of consequence, nor did they develop a literary or dramatic tradition. Yet many Greek cities feared and mistrusted Athens' expansionism and looked to Sparta for leadership as Athenian power grew.

The Spartans' attachment to tradition, the austerity of their lives, and their rigorous adherence to the military ideal were widely admired. Many of the poleis were far more attracted to Spartan stability than to the democratic experiments of Athens. Powerful but staunchly conservative, the Spartans rarely undertook any kind of political initiative and therefore seemed less threatening to their neighbors. If they lived on the labor of serfs, they often lived less well, materially, than those who served them. Their standards of courage, loyalty, endurance, and honor were high, and the penalty for failing them was severe: disgrace and loss of citizenship. The Spartans deliberately contrasted their ascetic way of life with what they considered the self-indulgence and reckless individualism of the Athenians; one of their kings, Agesilaus, asked what the greatest Spartan virtue was, is said to have replied, "Contempt of pleasure."

The imperial aggressiveness of Periclean Athens finally roused the Spartans and their allies to concerted action. Military sparring commenced in the 450s, but not until 431 B.C., at Corinth's urging, did Sparta declare war on Athens. The ensuing civil war lasted for 27 years and ended with the defeat of the Athenian empire.

The Peloponnesian War

By the end of the Persian Wars, Athens was the most powerful polis in the Greek world, not least because it had played a decisive part in defeating the Persians. Moreover, its essentially democratic government had proved stable and effective. Athens organized a defensive alliance of Greek poleis to repulse any future Persian attack. This was the Delian League, so named because the money contributed by the member states was stored in a treasury on the island of Delos, sacred to Apollo and politically neutral.

Other poleis, including Sparta, Thebes, and Corinth, soon became suspicious that the league was intended primarily to enhance Athenian power. The Athenians, they believed, were transforming an association of free states into an empire. Their concerns were intensified in 454 B.C. when the league's funds were moved to Athens and some of the money was diverted to pay for an ambitious building program in Athens itself. The Greek world largely divided into competing camps, with Athens and the poleis that remained in the league arrayed against Sparta and its supporters.

Chief among Sparta's allies was Corinth, gateway to the Peloponnesus and the site of intersecting east-west and north-south trade routes. A polis of traders and manufacturers, Corinth was also blessed with fertile soil. Like Athens, Corinth attracted immigrant artisans to its thriving economy, but unlike Athens its government was oligarchic, perhaps because of Spartan influence. Both Athens and Corinth acquired impressive empires and constructed powerful navies with which to defend them. The two poleis thus had much in common, but in the end, political considerations persuaded the Corinthians to side with Sparta. By the time the war ended, both the Corinthians and the Athenians had suffered greatly for their animosity.

Conflict between the Spartan and Athenian alliances was perhaps inevitable. The Peloponnesian War, so called after the homeland of the Spartans and their principal supporters, broke out in 431 and lasted until 404 B.C., when it ended in the defeat and occupation of Athens. Although the conflict involved virtually the whole of Greece in a generation of bitter strife, it did not result in more satisfactory or more stable conditions. It served principally to hasten the decline of the independent poleis that had proved themselves incapable of coexistence. If the war seems particularly memorable in the history of the West, it is in large part because of the detailed and authoritative account left by Thucydides, who both participated in and recorded its events.

Thucydides, born between 460 and 455 B.C., had been active in Athenian politics before the war. Elected general in 424, he was responsible for the defense of Amphipolis in northern Greece. When Sparta seized Amphipolis, Thucydides was tried in absentia and exiled. Not until 404 did he return to Athens. The purpose of his *History of the Peloponnesian War* was to narrate the events of the war to 404, but he brought it down only to 411 before his death; a later historian, Xenophon, completed the account. Thucydides was not content with a

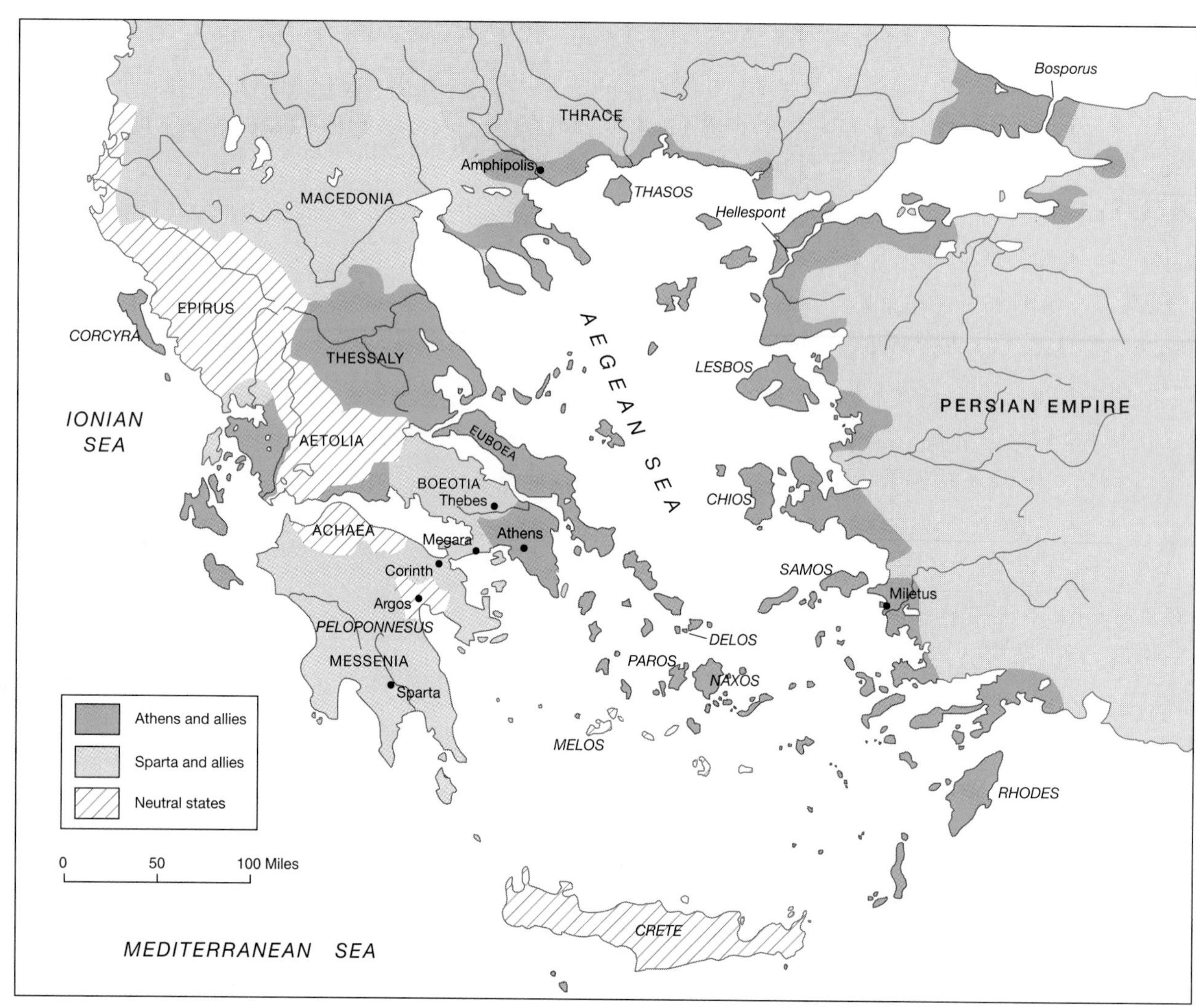

MAP 4.3 ALLIES IN THE PELOPONNESIAN WAR

mere narrative of events. Through the use of set speeches, he analyzed the motives and reactions of the principal personalities of the struggle to give future generations an understanding of its causes. At the heart of his examination was the contrast between the restless, revolutionary Athenians and the confident, conservative Peloponnesians. Thucydides was also intrigued by the contest between Athens, a naval power, and Sparta, whose strength was on land; as a military commander he laid stress on the problems of siege warfare, troop landings, and nighttime battles. Unlike Herodotus, he deliberately avoided digressions, and he made a scrupulous effort to verify his facts, though like other ancient historians he embellished the speeches of his protagonists to clarify their motives and express what he judged to be their character. As a narrative historian, Thucydides has never been surpassed. With Herodotus, he ranks as one of the fathers of historical study.

A Generation of War

The Athenian war effort went badly at first. The Persian Wars had demonstrated the power and efficiency of the Athenian navy, but no land army in Greece was a match for the Spartans. Trusting to the strength of Athens' fortifications and the richness of its treasury, Pericles allowed the Spartans to ravage the countryside outside Athens while the Athenian navy struck at the Peloponnesus.

The devastation of the farmlands around Athens, however, drove thousands of people inside the walls. In

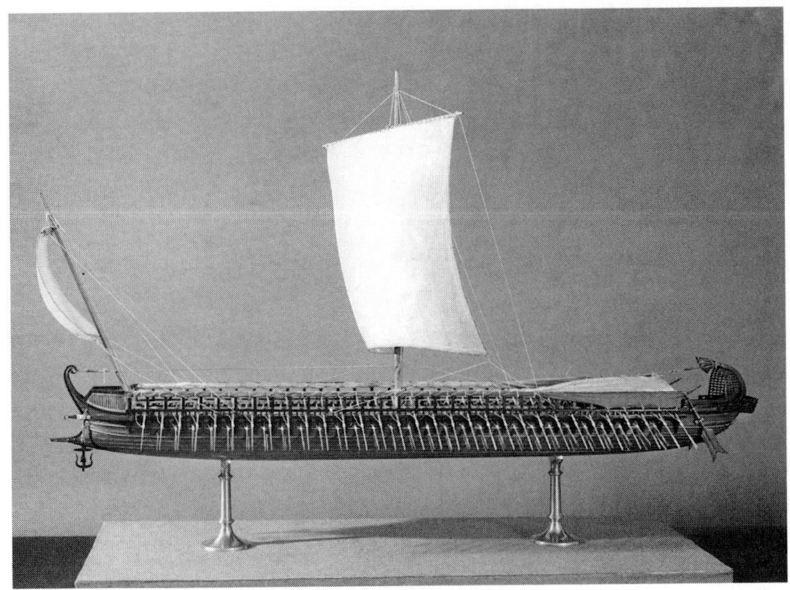

Model of a fifth-century B.C. *Greek trireme (galley) of the kind used in the Peloponnesian War. It was 120 feet long and required a crew of 200.*

430 B.C. a terrible plague, still unidentifiable, ravaged the city. Perhaps as much as a quarter of the population, including Pericles himself, had perished by the time the contagion finally abated in 427.

The Athenians found themselves without an able leader to take his place. The city split into two main factions, a war party and a peace party. After ten years of inconclusive warfare, with reverses for both the Athenians and the Peloponnesians, the peace faction at Athens gained the ascendancy. In 421 the combatants signed the so-called Peace of Nicias, which was supposed to last for 50 years.

When war erupted anew in 415 B.C., a brilliant but unscrupulous young aristocrat, Alcibiades, promoted a daring scheme to invade Sicily. The Athenians' intention was twofold: by conquering the Sicilian Greek cities, they could enrich themselves with treasures and crops; at the same time, they could disrupt Sicilian trade with the Peloponnesus, especially Corinth, thereby weakening its alliance with Sparta.

A string of disasters dogged the Sicilian expedition. When Alcibiades was recalled to Athens to answer trumped-up charges lodged by his political enemies, he defected to Sparta and helped the Spartans against his own polis. By painting a menacing picture of a growing Athenian empire in the west, he induced the Spartans to send the Sicilians a volunteer force. In the spring of 414 the Athenians found themselves trapped between local units and a Spartan expeditionary force. The Athenians dispatched more troops, but when they arrived in the spring of 413, it was too late. A rout occurred, and the expedition surrendered.

The Athenians fought on but never regained the initiative. Defeat was assured when in 405 B.C. Sparta ambushed the Athenian navy in the Hellespont. Of 179 Athenian ships only 9 escaped, and 4,000 Athenian prisoners were executed. Even then the city resisted a siege. But by the spring of 404 the situation was hopeless, and Athens surrendered unconditionally.

The long-term causes of the Peloponnesian War are to be found in the nature of Greek political life, which encouraged confrontation rather than unity. The temporary alliance against the Persians had proved only an exception to the tradition of intercommunal rivalry. The defeat of Athens was hailed as a victory for Greek independence, but it did nothing to foster unity among its divided states. Neither Athens nor Sparta ever completely recovered from the long struggle, and within 60 years a new conqueror, Philip of Macedon, would extinguish the independence of the polis for good.

SUMMARY

In the space of a few centuries the Greeks, emerging from a Dark Age characterized by a shrinking population, severe economic disruption, and cultural decline, developed one of the most brilliant civilizations in history. The core of this development was the polis, an independent sociopolitical institution that bound together the residents of a city and the surrounding territory, serving as the basis for their religious and cultural life as well as their political institutions. The ideals and the character of the respective poleis differed, ranging from the conservative, militaristic society of Sparta to the democratic, commercial, and imperialistic society of Athens. Although the latter pioneered in the development of political democracy, it limited participation to a minority of its inhabitants, excluding women, resident aliens, and slaves. Greeks of the Classical Age never solved the problem of political unity. They cooperated to repel the invading Persians, after which they organized themselves into rival alliances that ultimately took up arms against each other in the Peloponnesian War, the greatest tragedy of ancient Greek history.

By the end of the Peloponnesian War, the concept of the polis as the dominant force in the lives of its citizens, inspiring and fulfilling them, had been damaged beyond repair. The internal divisions within the Greek world ultimately produced wounds far more serious than those inflicted by the Persian invasions. In the years that followed, the Greeks moved in new political and cultural directions but failed to solve the fundamental dilemma of their disunity. That dilemma remained part of the Greek legacy, along with the magnificent achievement of its Classical Age.

NOTES

1. Herodotus, *The Persian Wars,* trans. G. Rawlinson (New York: Modern Library, 1942), pp. 587–588.
2. Xenophon, in A. Powell, *Athens and Sparta: Constructing Greek Political and Social History from 478 b.c.* (Portland, Ore.: Areopagitica Press, 1988), p. 240.

SUGGESTIONS FOR FURTHER READING

Austin, M. M., and Vidal-Naquet, P. *Economic and Social History of Ancient Greece.* Berkeley: University of California Press, 1978.

Bengston, H. *History of Greece: From the Beginnings to the Byzantine Era,* trans. and rev. by E. F. Bloedow. Ottawa: University of Ottawa Press, 1988.

Boardman, J. *The Greeks Overseas.* Baltimore: Penguin Books, 1973.

Cargill, J. *The Second Athenian League: Empire or Free Alliance?* Berkeley: University of California Press, 1981.

Charbonneaux, J., Martin, R., and Villard, F. *Archaic Greek Art, 620–480 b.c.* London: Thames & Hudson, 1971.

Demand, N. H. *Urban Relocation in Archaic and Classical Greece: Flight and Consolidation.* Norman: University of Oklahoma Press, 1990.

Dover, K. J. *Greek Homosexuality.* New York: Random House, 1980.

Dowden, K. *The Uses of Greek Mythology.* London: Routledge, 1992.

Drews, R. *The Coming of the Greeks: Indo-European Conquests in the Aegean and the Near East.* Princeton, N.J.: Princeton University Press, 1988.

Finley, M. I. *Economy and Society in Ancient Greece,* ed. B. D. Shaw and R. P. Saller. London: Chatto & Windus, 1981.

———. *Early Greece: The Bronze and Archaic Ages,* 2nd ed. New York: Norton, 1982.

Forde, S. *The Ambition to Rule: Alcibiades and the Politics of Imperialism in Thucydides.* Ithaca, N.Y.: Cornell University Press, 1989.

Garlan, Y. *Slavery in Ancient Greece,* rev. ed. Ithaca, N.Y.: Cornell University Press, 1988.

Garland, R. *The Greek Way of Life: From Conception to Old Age.* Ithaca, N.Y.: Cornell University Press, 1990.

Hood, S. *The Arts in Prehistoric Greece.* Baltimore: Penguin Books, 1978.

Hooker, J. T. *The Ancient Spartans.* London: Dent, 1980.

Hornblower, S. *The Greek World, 479–323 b.c.* London: Methuen, 1983.

Just, R. *Women in Athenian Law and Life.* London: Routledge & Kegan Paul, 1989.

Kagan, D. *The Fall of the Athenian Empire.* Ithaca, N.Y.: Cornell University Press, 1987.

Kennell, N. M. *The Gymnasium of Virtue: Education and Culture in Ancient Sparta.* Durham: University of North Carolina Press, 1995.

Lacey, W. K. *The Family in Classical Greece.* Ithaca, N.Y.: Cornell University Press, 1968.

Lintott, A. *Violence, Civil Strife, and Revolution in the Classical City, 750–330 b.c.* Baltimore: Johns Hopkins University Press, 1982.

Luce, J. V. *Homer and the Heroic Age.* New York: Harper & Row, 1975.

Manville, P. B. *The Origins of Citizenship in Ancient Athens.* Princeton, N.J.: Princeton University Press, 1990.

Marinatos, S., and Hirmer, M. *Crete and Mycenae.* New York: Abrams, 1960.

Murray, O., and Price, S., eds. *The Greek City: From Homer to Alexander.* Oxford: Clarendon Press, 1990.

Ober, J. *Mass and Elite in Democratic Athens: Rhetoric, Ideology, and the Power of the People.* Princeton, N.J.: Princeton University Press, 1989.

Oliva, P. *The Birth of Greek Civilization.* Edmonton, Alberta: Pica Pica Press, 1985.

Ostwald, M. *From Popular Sovereignty to the Sovereignty of Law: Law, Society, and Politics in Fifth-Century Athens.* Berkeley: University of California Press, 1986.

Page, D. L. *Sappho and Alcaeus.* Oxford: Clarendon Press, 1955.

Pomeroy, S. B. *Goddesses, Whores, Wives, and Slaves.* New York: Schocken Books, 1975.

Schaps, D. M. *Economic Rights of Women in Ancient Greece.* Edinburgh: Edinburgh University Press, 1979.

Sealey, R. *Women and Law in Classical Greece.* Chapel Hill: University of North Carolina Press, 1990.

Snodgrass, A. M. *Archaic Greece.* Berkeley: University of California Press, 1980.

———. *An Archaeology of Greece.* Berkeley: University of California Press, 1987.

Stockton, D. *The Classical Athenian Democracy.* New York: Oxford University Press, 1990.

Strauss, B. *Athens After the Peloponnesian War.* Ithaca, N.Y.: Cornell University Press, 1986.

Willetts, R. F. *The Civilization of Ancient Crete.* Berkeley: University of California Press, 1977.

Wood, E. M. *Peasant-Citizen and Slave: The Foundation of Athenian Democracy.* London: Verso, 1988.

Zinserling, V. *Women in Greece and Rome.* New York: Schram, 1972.

CHAPTER 5

The Greek Achievement and the Hellenistic World

The Peloponnesian War marked the end of Athens' bid for political and cultural supremacy. The ensuing period of confusion was brought to an end by the appearance of a new power, the northern kingdom of Macedon. Yet the ultimate failure of the Greek political system could not diminish the cultural achievements of Greek civilization. The Greeks were pioneers in many fields of Western culture and provided the basis for a distinctively Western tradition in areas as diverse as history and sculpture, urban planning and medicine, drama and mathematics.

The world in which Greek ideas were developed was one of war and disturbance, and the Greek concern for measure in all things must be seen against that background. The Greek conviction that the pursuit of reason could provide a basis for order in human affairs was reflected in the artistic achievements of the classical period. The essence of this classical belief was the quest for an ideal balance between mind and body and for harmony between the individual and society. The Greeks summed this up in the adage "Nothing in excess."

The Greeks believed that humans could achieve order in their lives by comprehending the causes not only of other people's actions but also of their own. This faith in reason and self-understanding was as central to Greek spiritual life as belief in divine forces. The Parthenon, the principal temple on the Athenian Acropolis, was intended to celebrate Athens as much as to honor the goddess Athena. Even in the worst of times, the belief in human potential remained central to the Greeks' vision of life. At the same time, they understood the powerful forces of the irrational that were part of human nature and had to be acknowledged and pacified. If Apollo, god

Alexander the Great in a Hellenistic bust that projects him as an image of idealized manhood. Alexander's conquests reshaped the Mediterranean world and left a legacy in central Asia as far as India.

The Doric temple of Apollo at Basae, contemporary with the Parthenon but remotely situated in Western Greece, is one of the masterpieces of classical proportion and design.

of the sun, represented clarity and order, he was balanced by the figure of Dionysus, god of wine, sexuality, and abandon.

The Greeks believed that human life was subject to uncontrollable forces. Such forces might be propitiated, but they could never be tamed. Chief among them was Nemesis, or destiny, from which there was no appeal. If the values of harmony and order were paramount in Greek sculpture and architecture, Greek fatalism found its outlet in the tragic drama. Even the plastic arts, however, reflected the Greek sense of the pathos and frailty as well as the nobility of human existence.

The Visual Arts: In Search of the Human Ideal

The buildings on the Acropolis were the culmination of classical architecture. The two principal Greek architectural styles, Doric and Ionic, were both represented on the Acropolis. Both had undergone a long development. The Doric style was widespread by 600 B.C.; the Ionic, though used in the Archaic period, was not common until the fifth century B.C.

The Doric order is austere and majestic; the Ionic order, by contrast, is more delicate and makes use of complex architectural details and decoration. When, after the Persian Wars, the Greeks collaborated to construct the Temple of Zeus at the Panhellenic shrine of Olympia, they chose the Doric order. Built between 470 and 456 B.C., it was the largest Doric temple in Greece. Libon of Elis, its designer, was concerned to render the classical sense of order in architectural form. The positioning of the columns and other architectural elements follows precise mathematical formulas. A similar concern for proportion can be seen in the temple of Apollo designed by Ictinos and built at Bassae in the western Peloponnesus around 450–425 B.C.

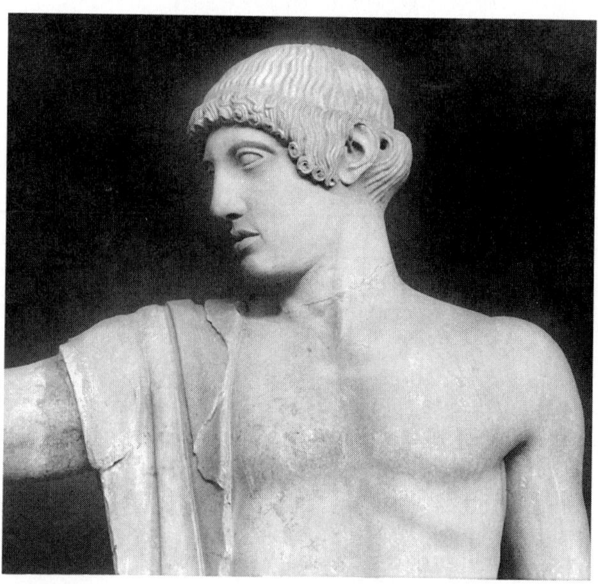

Detail of Apollo from the center of the west pediment of the Temple of Zeus at Olympia.

Sculptors of the Classical Age were particularly concerned with harmony. They sought to produce a fresh notion of human beauty by presenting the human form through the application of principles of symmetry and proportion. Polyclitus of Argos, one of the most important classical sculptors, invented a mathematical system of proportion in order to depict the ideal male form. His book, *The Canon* (c. 440 B.C.), argued that ideal beauty is achieved by an exact correspondence of proportion among all parts of the human anatomy.

One of the great achievements of fifth-century B.C. Greek sculptors was the depiction of movement. Figures such as a woman fastening her sandal or a charioteer gripping his reins convey motion in a satisfyingly natural fashion. Such figures contrast sharply with the formal, rigid statuary of the Archaic period. The classical sculptors were largely successful in this endeavor because of their careful observation of human anatomy, particularly musculature. Subjects such as Zeus hurling a thunderbolt or an athlete poised to throw a discus were obviously chosen, at least in part, to explore the artists' anatomical interests. Naturalism was heightened by the skillful depiction of bones and muscle as though under living skin. Artists had manifestly become more sensitive to and appreciative of the natural world.

Paintings on classical Greek vases commonly treated religious, military, and social themes, as in this fifth-century B.C. depiction of a warrior about to depart for battle facing a girl with a wine jug and an olive branch, the symbol of peace.

Toward the end of the fifth century B.C., both sculpture and vase painting began for the first time to exhibit an interest in portraying individuals rather than an idealized beauty. Associated with this was a more frequent depiction of aging and death as artists began to explore the psychological ramifications of mortality. Thus the subject of death and the human response to it came to be treated frequently in works of art.

The *lekythoi,* or oil flasks, used for funeral ceremonies are decorated with scenes that are among the most moving in classical art. Many show grieving figures or funerals; the background is generally white instead of the black or red favored on other painted pottery. Although the figures retain the composure of the classical style, they frequently display deep emotions. A similar individual reaction to death also characterizes the *stelai,* or grave markers, of the late fifth century, which reveal a sense of loss and resignation as well as depth of feeling.

The Athenian Acropolis

The most famous buildings of the classical period are the structures on the Athenian Acropolis. The magnificence of their design and execution is still visible. The Parthenon (447–438 B.C.) in particular is an unsurpassed example of classical achievement and remains perhaps the best-known symbol of Western culture. Construction on the Acropolis went on despite the Peloponnesian War; the Erechtheum, the last temple on the site to be finished, was completed in 406 B.C. Despite the political tensions of the classical period, the temples serve as a memorial to its highest ideals.

The natural stone outcrop known as the Acropolis made an ideal location for the temples. The site, which rises more than 400 feet above Athens, had dominated the city's life from the Bronze Age, when it was occupied by a fortress. During the Archaic period a number of temples were built there, but the Persians destroyed them in 480 B.C. The new building program was begun in 449 under the general supervision of Phidias, the leading sculptor of the day. The most important building, the Parthenon, honored the city's patron goddess, Athena, whose statue, 40 feet high and encrusted with

Grave stele from Heges.

gold and ivory, adorned the interior of the temple. Athena's legend was the focus of the exterior sculptural program as well. The east pediment—the triangular space supporting the roof—pictured her birth, the west pediment her contest with the sea god Poseidon for the territory of Attica. The bands of stone (friezes) above the outer colonnade portrayed Greeks battling mythical Amazons and centaurs in an allegorical representation of the triumph of civilization over barbarism, while another series showed the procession of the Panathenaic festival in which Athenians of both sexes ascended the Acropolis each year to present the goddess with a new robe. The Parthenon was severely damaged by bombardment in A.D. 1687, and the statue of Athena has long since disappeared. Tourism and pollution have replaced war as the chief threats to the citadel, and much of its surviving statuary and decoration have been removed for safety.

Sculpture was used in three sections of the building. The Ionic running band, or frieze, shows a ceremony that was held every four years at the time of the Great Panathenaic festival. It depicts Athenians walking and riding in procession and others at the climax of the religious ceremonies. The balance of form, motion, and rhythm in this sculpture makes it one of the most impressive masterpieces of classical art. The extant freestanding figures originally on the east and west pediments are no less striking despite their damaged condition. The group of three goddesses from the east pediment blends ideal form and natural observation, particularly in the harmony of limbs and flowing drapery. The rectangular slabs decorating the outside of the building, which are called *metopes,* show various legendary battles, including

In this detail of the west-face Parthenon frieze (c. 442–432 B.C.), the speed and vigor of the horses' movement contrast strongly with the calm, typically classical expressions of their riders.

the conflict between the Lapiths, a tribe of northern Greece, and the half-human, half-animal centaurs, which for the Greeks represented the clash of civilization and barbarism.

Work on the entrance to the Acropolis, the Propylaea, began in 437 B.C. and lasted for six years, although the war probably forced its architect, Mnesicles, to modify his original design. He used both Doric and Ionic columns, an uncommon practice for a classical building. The little Ionic temple of Athena Nike (goddess of victory), built between 427 and 424 B.C., is decorated with carvings that depict the earlier Athenian triumph over the Persians. The depiction of historical figures instead of legendary ones was no doubt intended to recall Athenian successes at a time when the city faced renewed crisis.

The Erechtheum, an Ionic temple of unusual and striking design, was begun in 421 B.C. It was the site of a variety of religious ceremonies and commemorated several gods. The Erechtheum's most famous element is the south porch, whose roof is supported by the Caryatids, statues of young women, rather than traditional columns.

Late Classical Art

Nothing comparable to the scope and ambition of the Acropolis was attempted in Greece during the century that followed Athens' defeat. The shrines at Olympia and Delphi were expanded, and new forms were devised, such as the *tholos*, or circular building. The grandest project of the age was perhaps the reconstructed Temple of Artemis at Ephesus. Many of the principal fourth-century B.C. sculptures are lost, although surviving Roman copies enable us to trace the principal stages of development in this field. The heroic, idealized facial expressions of fifth-century B.C. works gave way to a new and often inward sense of individualism. The sculptor Praxiteles, for example, was famous for the gentle melancholy of his figures, a mood aptly characterized by the *Hermes* at Olympia often attributed to him.

Tragic Drama and the Meaning of Existence

The fifth century B.C. also gave rise to the tragic drama, a form invented by the Greeks. The plays written for performance in the sanctuary of Dionysus at Athens represent classical literature at its height and the birth of theater as we know it. The three great playwrights of the era—Aeschylus, Sophocles, and Euripides—not only created a new form of human expression but also set a standard in their works that has never been surpassed.

The extant works are religious, in two senses. In the first place, the theater for which they were written was regarded as sacred to the god Dionysus, who was honored at the festival at which they were performed. In the second place, their plots, usually derived from legend, frequently deal with the interaction between mortals and gods in search of the meaning of existence. To achieve an appropriate seriousness, the style of performance was lofty and dignified. The actors, all of whom were male,

As a result of pollution and the deterioration of the stone, the Caryatids of the Erechtheum, on Athens' Acropolis, have now been moved to the Acropolis Museum.

thought of themselves as priests of Dionysus and wore masks, intricate costumes, and elevated shoes.

Greek tragedy had its origins in choral hymns honoring Dionysus and accompanying religious sacrifice, and the chorus, a group of supplemental actors who commented on the actions of the main performers, remained an important element in classical plays. In earlier works, such as Aeschylus' *Suppliant Women,* the choral group is at the center of the action. Generally, the chorus reflects on the action and its implications for the moral law, the affirmation of which is a prime function of tragedy.

The three principal dramatists illustrate the evolution of fifth-century Athenian cultural history. Aeschylus (525–456 B.C.) lived at a time when the ideals of the early classical period were still unshaken by disaster. His plays reveal a preoccupation with the corrupting influence of power; he had been a soldier at Marathon in 490 B.C. Aeschylus did not abandon his belief that justice would always prevail; he recognized, however, the difficulties of gaining knowledge, for only suffering can teach the errors of human ways. Moreover, even after the lessons have been learned, they do not alter the conclusion. Only a divinely inspired justice, represented by Zeus, chief of the Olympian gods, can determine the outcome.

Aeschylus' optimism persists even when he depicts scenes of violence and bloodshed. His greatest achievement is the trilogy known as the *Oresteia,* first performed at Athens in 458 B.C. The *Oresteia* is both the family saga of the royal house of Atreus and a historical romance that connects the Trojan wars with the founding of Athens. The central action of the drama is the slaying of King Agamemnon by his wife, Clytemnestra, in retaliation for his sacrifice of their daughter, Iphigenia. Their son Orestes is then ordered to avenge his father's death by killing his mother. Pursued by vengeful spirits who represent both outraged female deities and the torments of his own conscience, Orestes is finally cleared in a public trial in Athens in which the deciding vote is cast by Athena, the patron goddess of the city. The play thus traces the evolution of Greek society from a primitive monarchy ruled by blood vengeance to a citizen-state governed by law and justice.

Sophocles (c. 496–406 B.C.), the most renowned of the tragic playwrights, asserts that each individual is responsible for deciding between good and evil. Yet in his plays the choice is often obscured or difficult and at times impossible to make. Sophocles was more insistent than his fellow dramatists on human helplessness in the face of divine will or destiny. The play for which he is most widely known, *Oedipus the King,* has remained the most enduring symbol of classical tragic drama. First performed in 429 B.C., it combines a unity of time, place, and action with a story that moves inexorably toward a tragic conclusion.

The play tells the story of Oedipus, who is doomed before birth by divine decree to murder his father and marry his mother and who finally discovers that he cannot avoid his fate. The simplest conclusion to be drawn from Oedipus' story is that humans must meet their destinies, but it is unclear whether such fates are deserved. Oedipus does not consciously decide to kill his father or marry his mother, although unknowingly he does both. Why, then, should he bear the consequences of his actions? Perhaps the meaning of the play is that much of human life is subject to forces beyond our comprehension and control. In this sense, Sophocles chronicled the impotence of human will in the face of destiny and warned that humans should not expect self-reliance to provide a means of avoiding fate.

The plays of Euripides (c. 485–406 B.C.), Sophocles' contemporary, reflect the profound impact of fifth-century B.C. Greek political conflict and its social repercussions. Perhaps as a consequence, his work has the most direct meaning for us. Euripides was bent on exposing the social and political injustice of his time. He acknowledges that irrational forces, symbolized by the gods, affect human life, but he refuses to respect and worship them. Indeed, his open skepticism made people suspect him of impiety. The characters in his plays often reach the limits of their endurance, and his depiction of their response reveals a keen sense of psychological portraiture.

More than any of his predecessors, Euripides displays a deep sympathy for the problems of women in a male-dominated society. Characters such as Medea and Phaedra, who seek vengeance and passion outside the norms of social life, challenge many of the fundamental assumptions of Athenian society. Euripides' plays—together with the powerful creations of Aeschylus and Sophocles, including the vengeful Queen Clytemnestra in the *Oresteia* and the heroine of Sophocles' *Antigone,* who defies a royal prohibition to give her brother a proper burial—offer a gallery of female characters unsurpassed in the history of Western drama.

In a world that admired Spartan militarism, Euripides hated war and its attendant misery. His play *The Suppliant Women* was apparently written in 421 B.C., when the Peloponnesian War was temporarily halted by the Peace of Nicias. The play deals with the return of the bodies of dead warriors to their families, in particular to their wives and mothers. The scenes of mourning that he depicted were undoubtedly grimly familiar to his audience. Furthermore, the expression of grief does not terminate the violence. In the last scene, Athena announces that the heirs of the dead soldiers will launch a war of

Human Destiny: A Greek View

This chorus from Sophocles' Antigone *expresses his complex view of human destiny.*

Chorus. ***Happy the life that tastes not lamentation!***
But when with the curse of God a lineage shakes,
From generation down to generation
Comes no surcease of sorrow; so, when breaks
The Thracian tempest and the dark surge wakes,
Up from the deeps it whirls the sable sand,
While groan, in answer to the waves, the capes of the wind-vexed land.
Lo, from of old the Labdacids are stricken—
On the sorrows of their dead new sorrows fall.
Each generation sees the same curse quicken,
Some God still ruins them, helpless. In the hall
Of Oedipus one hope lit, last of all,
One root yet living. Now, this too lies slain
By Hell's red dust, by a reckless tongue, by a Fury in the brain.
Thy power, O Zeus, who can master? What pride of man's endeavor?
Sleep binds Thee not (that snares all else to rest),
Nor the tireless months of Heaven—Time leaves Thee ageless ever,
Throned in the dazzling glory of high Olympus' crest.
But for Man, from long ago
Abides through the years to be
This law, immutably—
All over-greatness brings its overthrow.
For Hope, that wanders ever, comes oft to Man as blessing;
For oft she cheats, till his giddy lusts are stirred.
Nearer she creeps, the deceiver, till he stumbles, all unguessing,
In the hot fires hid beneath him. Wise is the ancient word—
That he whom God hath planned
To ruin, in his blinded mood
Sees evil things as good—
And then the coming doom is hard at hand.

Source: F. L. Lucas, *Greek Tragedy and Comedy* (New York: Viking, 1968), p. 144.

vengeance. Euripides has rejected the optimism of Aeschylus; the cycle of violence cannot be broken.

Euripides lived long enough to see his fears fully realized. Driven from Athens by a public that had little taste for reminders of their folly, he ended his days at the court of the king of Macedon. There he wrote *The Bacchae,* a work that shows the limits of the rational mind in confronting the darkness of experience. This profoundly disturbing work, which describes the killing of Pentheus, the young king of Thebes, at the hands of his mother, acknowledges that emotion can overturn the sense of balance and proportion and that religious intoxication can release powers of destruction.

Not all Greek theater was tragic. The performances of tragedies—during festival competitions, three a day—were interspersed with bawdy farces called *satyr plays* and with spirited comedies. The master of Attic comedy, Aristophanes (c. 450–c. 385 B.C.), often treated satirically the same issues taken up by the tragic playwrights. His *Lysistrata,* produced in 411 B.C. after the failure of the Sicilian expedition, decries the futility of war no less than Euripides' *Suppliant Women,* but using the weapons of ridicule—in this case, a sex strike organized by the women of Athens to bring the menfolk to their senses—rather than pathos. It is an extraordinary mark of the openness of Athenian society that a work that mocked the war effort could be staged at the most critical point of the struggle.

The Greeks and the Physical World

Science and philosophy developed together in sixth-century B.C. Greece, laying the foundations for the Western tradition in both. Since early Greek science, or *physis* (from which our word *physics* derives), was based on speculation and casual observation rather than systematic experiment, it shaded off easily into the more general attempt to describe the nature of the world of humanity that we call philosophy. The Greeks had the benefit of existing traditions of knowledge, notably Babylonian astronomy. From the beginning, however, Greek science differed from earlier traditions in attempting to provide an essentially material description of the world without assuming the intervention of divine forces. This was a radical departure from previous thought, and more than any other factor it laid the foundation for Western science.

The Greeks were not preoccupied, as we are, with the origin of the material world. They assumed that the earliest state of the universe, which they called *chaos,* was a formless flux of elements out of which an orderly, patterned condition had emerged, the cosmos in which they lived. Classical mythology had attempted to account for the transition from chaos to cosmos by the action of the gods, but the school of science that grew up in Ionia at the beginning of the sixth century B.C. sought to explain it by material processes alone.

The Ionian School

The first major thinkers in this school, Thales, Anaximander, and Anaximenes, all residents of the city of Miletus, posed a simple yet extraordinary question: What is the world made of? The question was extraordinary because it contradicted the commonsense observation that the world is made of many quite different things. The assumption that there was a fundamental unity beneath the varied world of appearance enabled the Ionians to posit the idea of *matter,* the single, uniform stuff from which the cosmos took shape.

Thales, who lived in the early sixth century B.C. and was renowned for having correctly forecast a solar eclipse, suggested that the fundamental cosmic substance was water. Water was not only the most abundant single material in the world, it could also take solid shape by freezing and could liquefy as a gas, thus providing a basis to account for both land and atmospheric forms. What Thales' theory apparently failed to provide was a principle of transformation that could explain these successive states. Thus from the beginning Greek science was beset with the fundamental problem of change or, in physical terms, motion.

Anaximander attempted to deal with this problem by suggesting that the world represented a warring concourse of opposed qualities—hot and cold, wet and dry, and so forth. He conceived the first state of matter as an undifferentiated mass in which antagonistic elements or their properties were latent rather than distinct. This mass he called the *apeiron,* "the boundless," a notion similar to the traditional one of chaos. Anaximander solved the problem of motion by assuming it to be a primary quality of the apeiron; the universe had started not from a condition of rest but from one of turbulence and flux. This motion had gradually sorted out the apeiron into the familiar cosmos, rather like the operation of a centrifuge. The less agitated elements, being colder and wetter, had condensed into the solid earth and its oceans; the hotter and drier parts had formed the atmosphere; and those hottest of all had burst into flame, creating the sun and the starry heavens.

Anaximander boldly guessed that life had first arisen in the warm mud or slime, producing first reptiles, then land animals, and ultimately the human race. He thus hit upon the first theory of evolution, which he defended by pointing to fossilized seashells he had discovered in the mountains, and to the parallel between infant helplessness and that of certain fish species. Most remarkably, he produced a complete account of the cosmos without reference to the gods of myth; whereas earlier Greeks had used the myth of Atlas to explain how the earth could be suspended in space, Anaximander suggested that since the earth occupied the exact center of the universe, its position was maintained by an equilibrium of forces.

Anaximenes attempted to explain the existence of spirit or intelligence by positing not water but air as the primary substance. In its grosser material forms, he suggested, air constituted the basis of the physical world, whether heated into fire or condensed into earth and water; but in its most perfect and rarefied forms it was spirit, a part of which, trapped within the body, was the soul of each human and animal form. This idea of the soul as confined by the body, to be released only upon death, had a profound influence on the thought of the fourth-century B.C. philosopher Plato and through him on Christianity as well.

Pythagoras of Samos developed the idea of a spirit that survived the death of the body into a theory of the transmigration of souls similar to that taught by Buddhism (see Chapter 7), according to which souls passed into new bodies at the time of physical death. From this Pythagoras deduced the essential unity of all living things. Pythagoras also made significant contributions to mathematics and musical theory, declaring boldly that the universe exhibited the same mathematical relationships found in harmonic intervals.

Philosophy in the Fifth Century B.C.

Greek thinkers of the fifth century B.C. were dissatisfied with the theories of their predecessors, particularly with the account of motion given by the Ionians. Heraclitus (flourished c. 500 B.C.) of Ephesus, like Pythagoras a priest as well as a philosopher, rejected the idea of any moment of creation or process of evolution; the world, he said, "is, was, and ever will be" exactly what it is at the present moment. This meant not that the cosmos was static but, on the contrary, in a continuous state of flux and creation, an idea that he expressed in his famous paradox that one "cannot step in the same river twice."

Parmenides of Elea (c. 515–c. 450 B.C.) contended, against Heraclitus, that motion was impossible since the idea of an unoccupied space through which matter could pass was logically absurd. When it was pointed out to him that things did appear to move (for example, the lips of Parmenides denying that motion existed), the philosopher replied loftily that this was merely an illusion.

Empedocles (c. 493–c. 433 B.C.), a native of Akragas in Sicily who, like Pythagoras and Heraclitus, became something of a cult figure, propounded an ambitious cosmogony based on the idea of four primary elements—earth, air, fire, and water. These elements, combined in varying proportions by the twin forces of attraction and repulsion (which Empedocles called "love" and "strife"), produced physical substances. Because chance alone determined such combinations, monstrous forms had probably been created at an earlier period, but these, failing to adapt, had perished in the struggle for existence. Empedocles thus propounded an early form not only of the Newtonian principle of gravity but also of Darwinian natural selection. His theory of the four basic elements was accepted down to the seventeenth century A.D., although two later figures, Leucippus and Democritus of Abdera (c. 460–c. 370 B.C.), put forth a rival theory that stated that all physical entities were composed of tiny, undifferentiated pellets of matter, which they called *atoms* (literally, "without parts," or indivisible).

These daring thinkers of the sixth and fifth centuries B.C., often called pre-Socratic to distinguish them from the generation of Socrates and his successors, propounded many of the basic questions that Western science would later pursue. Not surprisingly, they scandalized contemporaries by their denial of the gods; Anaxagoras of Clazomenae (c. 500–428 B.C.), who lived in Periclean Athens, was expelled from the city for asserting that the sun was not a divinity but a white-hot stone, and the sanctuaries of Pythagoras' followers in southern Italy were sacked and burned and many of their number killed. By the mid-fifth century B.C., an intellectual reaction had set in against the pre-Socratics. One theory seemed to beget another, without any certain knowledge being reached. A consequence of this was the rise of a new group, the sophists.

The sophists shunned speculation about both the physical world and the gods, concentrating instead on teaching practical skills such as the arts of persuasion and rhetoric. Their professed aim was to understand not the nature of the world but how to get along in it. Their basic presumption was summed up in the motto of one of their number, Protagoras (c. 481–c. 411 B.C.), that "man is the measure of all things." The task of humans was not to describe an objective world but to shape it to their own ends.

Socrates

Parmenides, Protagoras, and many other figures of the middle and late fifth century B.C. would be brought to life in the dialogues of Plato, where their theories were argued back and forth. The chief protagonist of these dialogues, however, was Plato's own teacher, Socrates (469–399 B.C.), one of the most remarkable personalities of antiquity. The son of a sculptor and a midwife, he was a frank admirer of the Spartans, a familiar figure in the marketplace, where he held his impromptu discussions with pupils and passersby alike, and notorious enough to be satirized in Aristophanes' play *The Clouds.* Unlike the sophists, Socrates took no payment for his teaching; unlike them as well, he claimed to be wise only in realizing the extent of his own ignorance. His teaching method, the dialectic, consisted of a series of questions and responses

Platonic Love

In this extract from the Symposium, *Plato describes what has often been called platonic love.*

It is necessary for the one proceeding in the right way toward his goal to begin, when he is young, with physical beauty, and first of all, if his guide directs him properly, to love one person and in his company to beget beautiful ideas and then to observe that the beauty in one person is related to the beauty in another. If he must pursue physical beauty, he would be very foolish not to realize that the beauty in all persons is one and the same. When he has come to this conclusion, he will become the lover of all beautiful bodies and will relax the intensity of his love for one and think the less of it as something of little account. Next he will realize that beauty in the soul is more precious than that in the body, so that if he meets with a person who is beautiful in his soul, even if he has little of the physical bloom of beauty, this will be enough and he will love and cherish him and beget beautiful ideas that make young men better, so that he will in turn be forced to see the beauty in morals and laws and that the beauty in them all is related.

Source: M. P. O. Morford and R. J. Lenarden, *Classical Mythology* (New York: Longman, 1977), p. 126.

on a set theme. By exploring a subject from all sides and thereby refining his students' capacity to analyze and define it, Socrates hoped to guide them toward better understanding. For his own part, Socrates never offered answers but only further questions, believing that genuine knowledge could never be communicated, only discovered.

Socrates' intellectual fearlessness and his refusal to subscribe to popular opinion, as well as the association of several of his students with a hated oligarchy that was briefly imposed on Athens at the end of the Peloponnesian War, made him a natural target for those seeking a scapegoat for the city's military defeat. Arraigned on charges of impiety and corrupting the young, he was sentenced to death. Few citizens expected the execution to proceed, deeming the disgrace of the conviction sufficient to discredit the aged philosopher. Socrates' friends urged him to escape, and his captors apparently gave him an opportunity to do so. But he refused, arguing that his flight would be an admission of guilt and a defiance of the law. His death, dramatically described by Plato, gave intellectual freedom its first martyr in the West.

Plato

Plato (c. 427–c. 347 B.C.) was deeply affected by his mentor's death. In a unique tribute, he couched most of his writings in the form of dialogues in which Socrates has the chief role. How accurately he expressed his master's thought cannot be known, but it is safe to say that if the style is that of Socrates, the substance is surely Plato's.

The basis of Plato's philosophy is his theory of forms. All our ideas, he asserts, whether of material entities such as chairs and tables or of conceptual ones such as beauty, justice, and goodness, are intuitions of immaterial forms that are the basis of all physical and mental reality. We first perceive a physical object or intellectual category and then, through dialectical analysis, proceed to recognize the permanent form it fleetingly and imperfectly embodies.

Plato gives an example of this process in his dialogue on love, the *Symposium.* Typically, our first intuition of love is through admiration for a beautiful body, but our feeling for the person who attracts us can deepen only if we discover a corresponding beauty of soul as well. In this way we proceed from the material to the spiritual and then from the particular to the general as we gradually come to understand that what we love is the quality of goodness that manifests itself in the beloved. The beauty that attracted us at first is transitory; the basis of our permanent affection is our own aspiration to the good, and love is the desire of two persons to fulfill that aspiration in each other.

In the hierarchy of forms, goodness is the ultimate value, and later Christian philosophers, deeply influenced by Plato, would declare goodness to be the primary quality of God. If goodness is the final object of philosophy, however, the object of civil society is justice, a quest Plato pursued in his best-known dialogue, *The Republic* (c. 374 B.C.). As in other dialogues, his characters weigh various definitions of justice; some argue that it is the force of custom or the will of the strongest. Ultimately Plato settles on the idea that justice is the harmony that arises when each person is able to pursue his or her own best talent: the artisan to build, the musician to play, and the ruler to govern.

To ensure that each talent is properly developed and employed, Plato constructs a three-tiered society that resembles an idealized version of Sparta. At the top are the *guardians,* who live communally and enjoy neither family nor possessions and whose function is wisdom and rule. The guardians are assisted by *auxiliaries,* or soldiers, chosen especially for their strength and courage. The *majority,* who are permitted moderate affluence, are trained and assigned to perform the other functions of society.

Since the capacity to rule—that is, to perceive justice in its essence and apply it to the social order—is the rarest of talents, the education of the guardian elite is protracted and difficult. Only those who have demonstrated both the necessary philosophical aptitude to grasp and internalize the nature of the forms and the practical ability to apply them to affairs may be entrusted with the responsibility of the state. But since the existence of these talents, as well as the lesser ones that pertain to the lower orders, can be discovered only through time, education, and testing, it is axiomatic that all citizens, both male and female, begin on a plane of equality and be educated to the limits of their ability. Plato thus combines a radical democracy of opportunity with a radical elitism of final authority to produce a society that will exemplify, as far as humanly possible, his ideal of justice.

Plato was given an opportunity to put his utopia to the test when Dionysius II, the tyrant of Syracuse in Sicily, engaged him as a personal tutor in 366 B.C. The challenge to impart his conception of justice to a man of power was irresistible, but Dionysius soon tired of the rigors of the dialectic and Plato returned to the more receptive pupils of the Academy, the school he had founded in the groves outside Athens sacred to the hero Academus. What remained of the experiment was the warning he had given that society would not be just until kings had become philosophers and philosophers kings.

Aristotle

Aristotle (384–322 B.C.) was Plato's chief pupil. He began as a disciple of his master but broke away to develop his own philosophy and ultimately to found his own school, the Lyceum, located in the grove of Apollo Lyceius in Athens. Unlike Socrates and Plato, Aristotle was not a native Athenian. He was born in Stagira in northern Greece, returned to tutor Alexander of Macedon, and, threatened as Socrates had been with prosecution following Alexander's death, left Athens in the last year of his life, remarking that he would not permit the city to commit a second crime against philosophy.

Aristotle's philosophy is firmly rooted in the sensible world. He rejected Plato's conception of ideal forms that lacked any direct connection with material substance. Instead he suggested that form was inherent in matter itself. Every substance, he contended, consists of a mutable stuff on which change operates—the substrate—and an unchanging form, conceived as a kind of blueprint that determines its final material form. Thus, for example, the final mature form of the child is the adult, as the oak is of the acorn. Form and matter, which had long been distinct in Greek philosophy, were thereby reunited in Aristotle's conception of substance. The world was neither static nor chaotic but a dynamic process; change was neither illusory nor random but orderly and patterned.

This conception had significant implications for the study of both the material world and human society. In rejecting the material world as illusory, Plato rejected science for philosophy, the truths of observation for the truths of contemplation. Aristotle restored science by asserting the final and indivisible reality of material substance, and by conceiving the world in terms of orderly process he gave empirical knowledge a new and far more sophisticated basis.

Aristotle's own quest for knowledge was tireless. One ancient commentator numbered his works at 400, another at 1,000. He wrote on virtually every subject: metaphysics, natural science, ethics, politics, history, literature, and rhetoric. His essays on prior and posterior analytics were the founding works of Western logic, and his *Poetics* was the first systematic treatment of aesthetics. In addition, his pupils undertook a complete history of the sciences under his direction. It was no wonder that the Middle Ages called him the "master of those who know," and when the poet Dante referred to Aristotle as simply "the philosopher," readers understood at once who was meant.

Aristotle was no less interested in achieving a just society than Plato, but his approach was characteristically different. After analyzing the constitutions of some 158 Greek cities, he defined the basic types as monarchy (rule by one), aristocracy (rule by a minority), and democracy (majority rule). Each type had its own virtues and defects; the most stable form, he felt, would be one that combined the best elements of aristocracy and democracy, rewarding merit and encouraging the growth of a prosperous middle class.

Generally enlightened, Aristotle nonetheless shared some of the prejudices of his time and culture. He defended slavery, arguing that it was in the nature of some people to obey others, and unlike Plato, he held women to be naturally inferior to men. Pragmatic rather than heroic, he praised the "golden mean" in both private and political conduct and counseled against excess in any form. If his thought was less daring than Plato's, it was eminently more serviceable in the daily world. Between them, the two men set the terms for much of subsequent Western thought. The British philosopher Alfred North Whitehead remarked that Western philosophy was a mere series of footnotes to Plato, and Christianity owed much to him. As for Aristotle, it is no exaggeration to say that he created the Western intellectual curriculum, stamping and defining its various disciplines and branches of knowledge.

The Rise of Macedon

Despite the intellectual brilliance of the fourth century B.C., the Greeks failed to find a basis for political stability. No single state could fill the vacuum left by the collapse of Athenian power, and peaceful cohabitation proved as elusive as ever. The early years of the fourth century saw divisive skirmishes among Sparta, Thebes, Corinth, and Argos that invited the intervention of the Great King of Persia. By the so-called King's Peace of 387 B.C. the Greeks bought a brief respite, but the price was high; many of the Greek cities of Asia Minor, whose freedom had supposedly been achieved by the victories in the Persian Wars 100 years earlier, were handed back to Persian rule. It was not long before Thebans and Spartans were once again fighting. In 371 B.C. Thebes defeated Sparta at Leuctra and became for a few years the dominating force in Greek politics.

Such instability was bound to attract outside intervention. The Persians were too far away and had problems in their own empire. Just to the north of the Greeks, however, lay the kingdom of Macedon, hitherto a backward land of farmers and agricultural laborers. Although the Greeks considered them barbarians, the Macedonians spoke a rough Greek dialect; and if they managed to avoid becoming entangled in Greek political feuding, it was principally because they were kept occupied defending themselves from raiders from the north.

In 359 B.C. Philip became king of Macedon. Over the next 20 years he gave ample evidence of his powers as an orator, general, and statesman, but perhaps his greatest asset was his ability to manipulate and outmaneuver even the most cunning Greek politicians. By negotiating with his enemies secretly and singly, Philip soon brought virtually the whole of Greece under his sway.

Philip denied any actual plan to conquer Greece. There was even talk of an Athenian-Macedonian alliance that could unite the Greeks and lead them against Persia. Disunity in Athens, however, undermined the scheme. The pro-Macedonian faction at Athens found itself increasingly under pressure from a conservative majority that could not conceive of Athenian power subordinated to a barbarian king. The success of Philip's opponents at Athens unquestionably owed much to the fact that their principal spokesman was also the greatest Greek orator of the day, Demosthenes (384–322 B.C.).

Demosthenes proved a formidable opponent to Philip. A man of great energy and resolve, he had overcome a speech defect to become one of the foremost rhetoricians in Athens. Demosthenes persuaded the Athenians to levy taxes and pour money into military preparations to defend Greek liberty. In 341 the Athenians sent troops to northern Greece to attack Macedonian strongholds. Philip sent an army south, and at Chaeronea in 338 he defeated a combined Greek army with the assistance of his son Alexander. In a congress at Corinth the same year, a league of all Greek cities except Sparta proclaimed Philip its captain-general.

A year later Philip began plans to enlarge his empire even further by attacking Persia, but he was never to carry them out. In 336 he was assassinated under mysterious circumstances, perhaps through the jealousy of Olympias, Alexander's mother, for Philip's new wife. Alexander, tutored by Aristotle himself, succeeded him. His career was to prove even more spectacular, but the loss of Philip at so delicate a stage in the reestablishment of peace was fateful for the Greeks. The new king had little interest in establishing good terms with his Greek neighbors; he was eager to invade Asia and pursue his dreams of world conquest.

The Conquests of Alexander the Great

With the accession of Alexander (356–323 B.C.) in 336 B.C. the history of the Greeks was transferred to a wider stage. The spread of Greek culture throughout much of Asia was, in fact, one of Alexander's principal achievements and, unlike the empire he sought to build, one of long duration. Yet Alexander himself, however well disposed to Hellenic ideas, was not reluctant to use force to dominate the Greeks. When in 335 the Thebans took advantage of trouble in the north to stage a revolt, Alexander and his troops stormed the city, razed it, and sold the population into slavery. Thereafter the horrified Greeks provided no more opposition to him, and he was

A Call to Arms

Demosthenes tries to shame his Athenian audience into taking action against Philip of Macedon.

What is the cause of these events? Not without reason and just cause were the Greeks of old so ready to defend their freedom but now so resolved on servitude. Men of Athens, there was then something in the spirit of the people which is not there now, something which overcame even Persian gold and kept Hellas [Greece] free, something which admitted defeat on neither land nor sea. Now the loss of that has ruined everything and made chaos of our affairs. What was that thing? Nothing involved or tricky. It was just that one and all hated those who accepted bribes from men who aimed to rule or ruin Hellas. To be convicted of taking bribes was a most grievous crime; yes, they punished the guilty one with the utmost severity, and there was no room for intercession or pardon. Therefore the right moment for achieving each enterprise, the opportunity Fortune often extends even to the indifferent at the expense of the vigilant, could not be bought from statesmen or from generals, any more than could our mutual good will, our distrust of tyrants and foreigners, or any such thing at all. But now these possessions have been sold off like market wares, and in exchange there have been imported things which have brought ruin and disease to Hellas. And what are these things? Envy, if a man has received a bribe; laughter, if he admits it; indulgence for a man proved guilty; hatred for his critic; and all the other things that come from bribery. As for warships, troops, abundance of funds and equipment, and all else that may be held to form the strength of our cities, in every instance they are present in greater abundance and extent than in days gone by. But all this is being made useless, unavailing, unprofitable because of those who traffic in them.

Source: P. MacKendrick and H. M. Howe, eds., *Classics in Translation* (Madison: University of Wisconsin Press, 1966), vol. 1, p. 288.

free to turn his attention to the campaign against Persia. By the time of his death in 323 B.C. at the age of only 33, he had extended Macedonian rule from the Adriatic to the river Indus.

The great expedition left for Asia Minor in 334 B.C. Success came quickly with a lightning victory over the forces of the Persian governors at the river Granicus, although Alexander himself was almost killed in the confusion. Pausing only to liberate the Greek cities of Asia Minor, in 333 he pushed south into Syria, where he defeated the Persians at Issus. Most of the next year was spent in a siege of Tyre. Alexander's troops finally destroyed it in time to reach Egypt by the winter. Not only did the Egyptians give way without fighting, but the oracle of Zeus Ammon prudently greeted him as the son of God and rightful pharaoh of Egypt. While in that country Alexander founded Alexandria, later to be one of the great cities of the ancient world. In 331 he moved east of the river Tigris, where he scored one of his greatest victories at Gaugamela; although vastly outnumbered, his forces penetrated the enemy lines and drove the Persian king, Darius, into flight. At Persepolis, the old Persian capital, Alexander burned the royal palace, seized the treasury, and began to enlist the young men of Persia in his army.

Over the next three years Alexander battered the rugged northern and eastern sections of the Persian Empire into submission. In 326 he reached northwestern India, but after a desperate battle against the warrior king Porus and his forces (which included 200 elephants), his men would go no further. Even Alexander's drive would not persuade them to take on the kingdoms of the Ganges, and he was compelled to turn back to Persia. The main part of the expedition took the route they had followed on the outward journey, but Alexander, with a small contingent, set out on a perilous trip to explore the

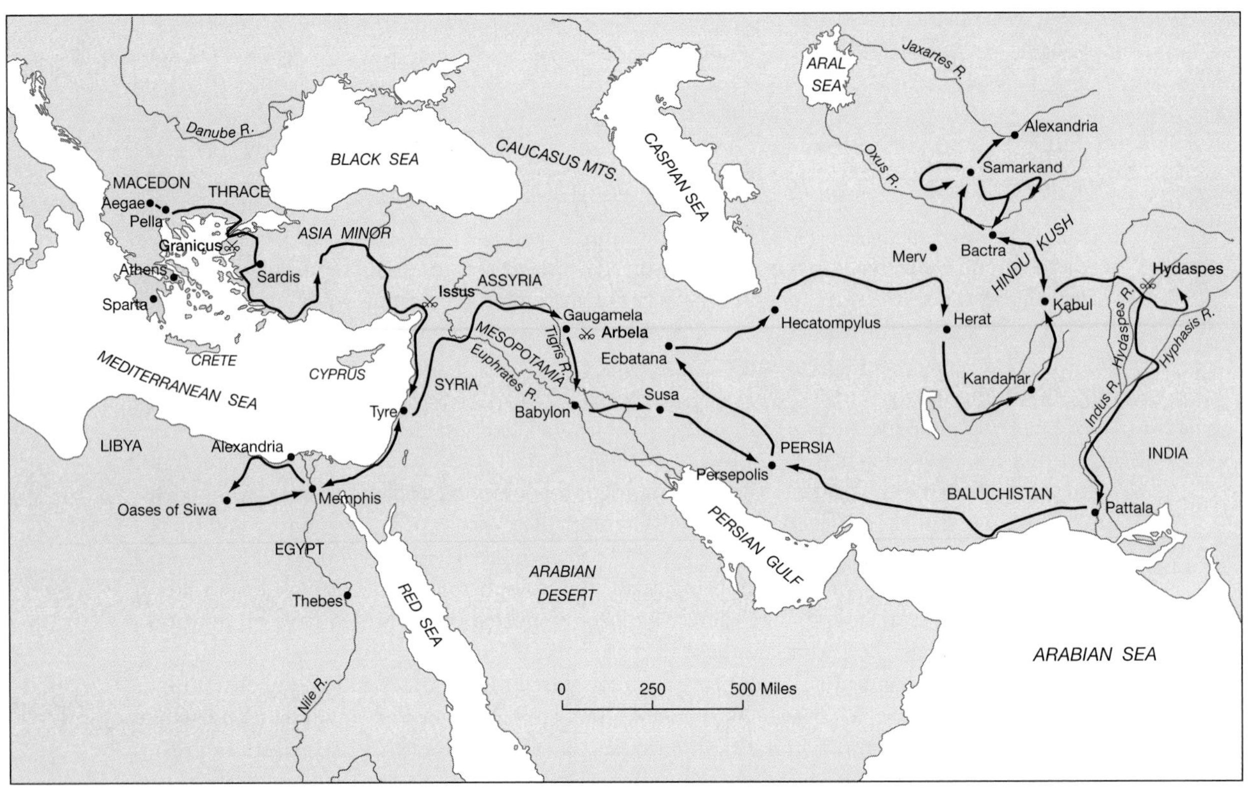

MAP 5.1 ALEXANDER'S CONQUEST OF THE PERSIAN EMPIRE, 334–323 B.C.

desert wastes of the coast while another group went by ship. Even Alexander's iron constitution was not proof against such continued ordeals. While preparing yet another campaign, against southern Arabia, he became sick and died within ten days.

Such a life was made possible in part by the remarkable personality and restless energy that characterize Alexander's portraits and that certainly marked his career. At the same time, he had other virtues. The peoples whom he conquered were encouraged to retain their native laws, religions, and customs, and he himself set an example of "the marriage of east and west" by taking a Persian bride. To unite the enormous variety of peoples involved in his conquest, he founded more than 70 cities, all embodying the principles of Greek urban planning, architecture, and institutions. Through these strongholds many of his conquests survived the confusion that followed his death.

Alexander's critics have often observed that he never seems to have paid any regard to who would succeed him or how his empire would have been ruled on a permanent and stable basis. Apart from the cities he founded, he retained, for the most part, the administrative structure of the Persian Empire. Toward the end of his life he began to adopt the Asian royal style with too much enthusiasm. To the discomfort of his Macedonian old guard, he wore Persian dress, required them to make obeisance before him, and even assigned Persian brides to them. It is by no means certain that, had he survived his illness, his empire would have been more permanent. His achievements still stand: the spread of Greek culture from a small corner of southeastern Europe to most of the Mediterranean and central Asian world and the memory of a life that became a byword for heroism and daring down through the ages.

The Hellenistic Kingdoms and the Cosmopolitan World

In the absence of a successor nominated by Alexander, disagreements among his generals after his death resulted in the breakup of the Macedonian empire. The most important of the new states were Egypt, Pergamum, Macedon, and the kingdom of the Seleucids, each of which fought the others until the Romans conquered them all. They continued to spread Greek culture and customs, a process called *Hellenization* after the Greek name for Greece, *Hellas.* But the resulting period, the Hellenistic Age, represented a hybrid civilization in which Greek and western Asian cultures were freely blended and exchanged.

The Ptolemies and the Seleucids

The Egyptian city of Alexandria remained the most significant center of Greek learning. There Ptolemy, a former officer of Alexander's, proposed the creation of an institute for study and research called the Temple of the Muses—the *Museum.* Ptolemy himself had bolstered his claim to power by snatching Alexander's body and burying it at Alexandria, although the tomb has never been discovered. In 305 B.C. he took the title of king and, on his death in 283, was succeeded by his son. The dynasty of the Ptolemies continued to rule Egypt until Rome's absorption of it after the reign of Cleopatra in 31 B.C.

Ptolemaic rule had little of the multiracial character of Alexander's original design. Egypt was run primarily by a Greco-Macedonian elite, and Greek remained the official business language. Cleopatra was the only Ptolemaic ruler who learned Egyptian.

The wealth accumulated by the Ptolemies became legendary—not surprisingly, given the elaborate taxing and licensing system of the state. Even beekeepers had to have a license from the king, and fishermen were required to pay a part of their catch to a representative of the royal treasury. Little or nothing of the money raised from the peasants in the form of such levies as taxes, death duties, sales taxes, and transit dues was used to improve their lot. Some was spent on maintaining the strongest navy in the Mediterranean, and the rest ended up in the royal coffers.

The former Persian territories in Asia were seized by the commander of Alexander's footguard, Seleucus, who by the time of his murder in 280 B.C. had sufficiently consolidated his power to be succeeded by his son, Antiochus. The Seleucids ruled until 83 B.C., when they were briefly replaced by Armenian kings and then annexed by Rome. Even Seleucus himself, however, had to give up Alexander's Indian conquests, and the Seleucid portion of the empire shrank rapidly. As early as 275 B.C. Antiochus held off with great difficulty an invasion of the Gauls, a tribe that had migrated from western Europe, only to become involved in futile wars with Egypt. The

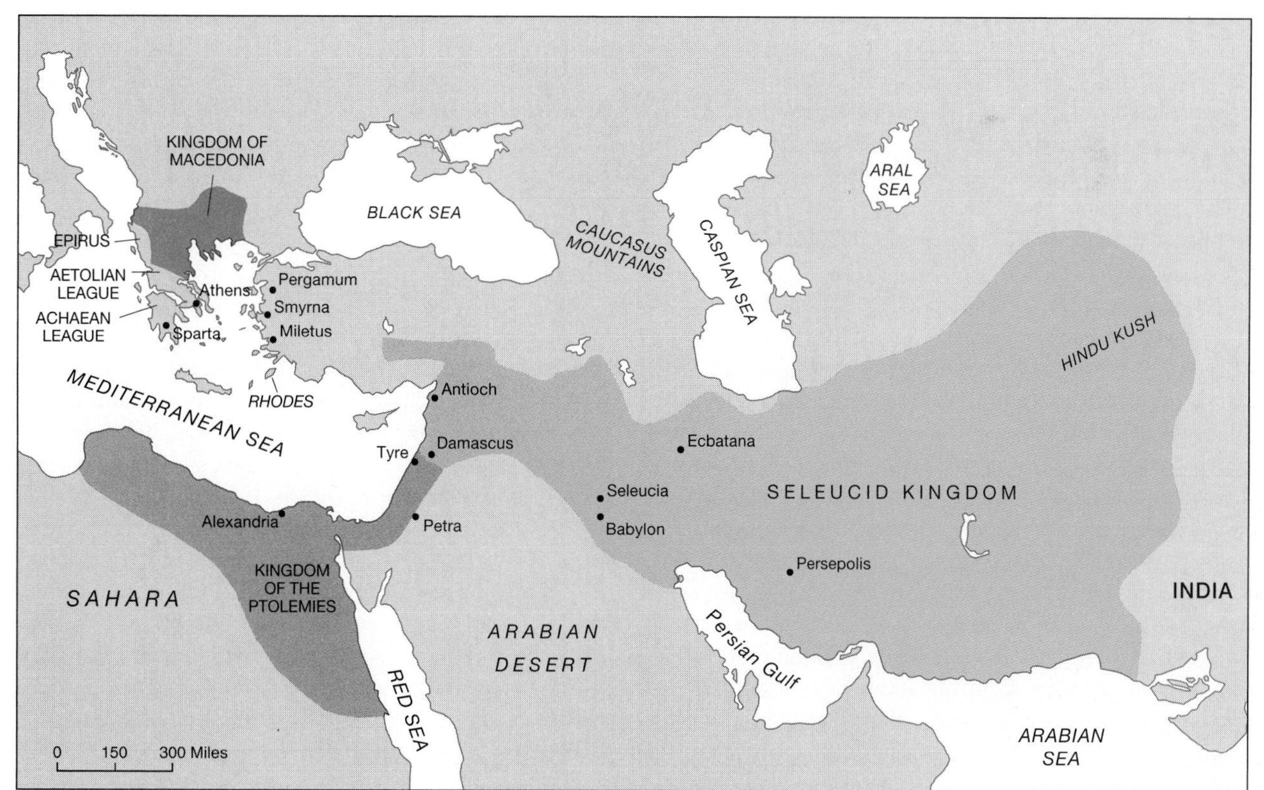

MAP 5.2 HELLENISTIC KINGDOMS, c. 275 B.C.

sheer size of the Seleucids' territory precluded the establishment of a Ptolemaic-style bureaucracy, and much of it was ruled by local governors. Antioch, the royal capital, was designed on Greek lines, and Greek continued to be spoken in Seleucid cities as far east as the river Tigris for centuries following the fall of the kingdom.

Macedon and the Hellenistic Greeks

Macedon acquired a permanent dynasty only in 275 B.C., after several generals had fought for its possession. The eventual victor was Antigonus, a grandson of one of Alexander's commanders. His successors spent most of their time fighting with neighboring kingdoms for influence in central and southern Greece, where two competing leagues of poleis, the Aetolian and Achaean, battled each other as well as external enemies.

The vision of a single great state, Hellenic in culture but multiethnic in character, did not die with Alexander but remained alive as an ideal until the Romans unified the eastern Mediterranean and western Asia two centuries later. Alexander had prayed at a celebrated banquet for a union of all hearts and a commonwealth of Macedonians and Persians; the philosopher Zeno envisioned a universal city under one divine law; and the word derived from this, *cosmopolitanism,* originally taken up by the Cynics to indicate their attachment to no state, was finally adopted in the Hellenized world to signify world citizenship. This remained (as it does today) an ideal rather than a reality, but it had some practical consequences for the old Greek poleis themselves, now under Macedonian domination but enjoying a certain degree of autonomy. Honorary citizenship was increasingly conferred on foreigners, and whole cities exchanged citizenship as a mark of friendship and alliance, as in the case of Athens and Rhodes. Arbitration was extensively adopted in the third century B.C. as a means of settling boundary claims, and foreign commissioners were frequently invited to adjudicate intracity disputes, a practice that would have been almost unthinkable among the jealously divided and fiercely independent poleis of the fifth century. Leagues grew up among cities, which shared a joint army, pursued a common foreign policy, and introduced a common system of taxes, tariffs, weights, and measures.

The best known of these leagues, the Aetolian and Achaean, developed innovative federal structures that were models of cooperation. The Aetolian League, centered in the region north of the Gulf of Corinth, granted dual citizenship, its members retaining their native citizenship along with citizenship in the league. This practice was known as *sympolity.* More distant states were linked to the league by *isopolity,* according to which their citizens enjoyed Aetolian civil but not political rights. In the Achaean League, based in the northern Peloponnesus, the mutual exchange of citizenship was rare. Members of the federation shared a common coinage and uniform standards of measurement and used a system of federal courts. Both leagues had relatively democratic constitutions, with power vested in each case in an assembly, a representative council, and an elected general. The federal governments could levy taxes, raise armies, and conduct foreign policy. These and other Greek leagues of this period illustrate a trend away from the distinctive autonomy of the polis in favor of a significant degree of cooperation and unity.

Temples and sanctuaries, such as Delphi, had long been considered neutral ground, but after 270 B.C. whole cities, including Smyrna and Miletus, proclaimed their permanent neutrality, and more and more places sought the status of *asyla* (asylums), which were immune from reprisal. Obviously, these claims were not always respected, but they had a certain deterrent force. War itself became milder, at least temporarily; the old practice of slaughtering the males in a conquered city and selling the women and children into slavery was first modified into a general sale of both sexes and finally abolished altogether; when it was revived, as against Mantinea in 223 B.C., it aroused a storm of protest. In short, international public opinion had begun to develop, at least among the older Greek cities, and the idea of a world without borders, of a universal city of the spirit, persisted through Roman times until it was given its final expression in antiquity by the fifth-century A.D. Christian philosopher Augustine in his book *The City of God.*

Pergamum and Bactria

Pergamum, an ancient Greek polis in Asia Minor, was the most influential Hellenistic kingdom in Greek affairs. For a time it had been a Seleucid possession. Its local governor, a eunuch called Philetaerus, had used the money in the treasury to hire his own army; he was succeeded by a nephew, Eumenes I (263–241 B.C.), who governed Pergamum with the support of the Seleucids' great rivals, the Ptolemies. Under later rulers Pergamum won a reputation as a great cultural and artistic center, reaching a high point in the reign of Eumenes II (197–159 B.C.). Its chief religious shrine was the immense altar to Zeus erected by Eumenes II around 180 B.C. to commemorate the victories of his father, Attalus I, over the Gauls during the preceding century. The tangled, writhing bodies of the figures on the frieze, with their intensity of gesture and facial expression, represent one of the high points of Hellenistic art. Other Pergamene rulers

Athena Slaying a Giant, *detail of a frieze in the altar to Zeus at Pergamum, shows the head of the giant Aleyoneus, whose hair is grasped by Athena.*

reinforced their reputations as champions of Hellenism by contributing money and building projects to Athens and other Greek cities.

At the eastern end of Alexander's conquests, on the northeastern frontier of India, a new kingdom, Bactria, broke off from Seleucid rule around 250 B.C. Its control of trade routes throughout central Asia lasted until the middle of the following century and brought the descendants of Alexander's Greek mercenaries into contact with the peoples of India. Even after Bactria had been overrun by central Asian nomads, Greek-style cities such as Begram and Taxila continued to exert a cultural influence: Gandharan Buddhist sculpture, the earliest monumental Buddhist art, made use of Greek styles and techniques. Thus in the two centuries following Alexander's death the various Hellenistic kingdoms each contributed to the Hellenization of vast tracts of Asia.

In the meantime, a new political force had begun to make its presence felt in the western Mediterranean: Rome. In 133 B.C. the last king of Pergamum died childless and willed his kingdom to Rome; by 31 B.C. the defeat of Cleopatra left almost the whole of Alexander's

A head of the Buddha, from Gandhara. The expression shows the influence of classical Greek art.

empire in Roman hands. Thus the history of the Hellenistic world became fused with that of Rome.

Changing Economic Patterns

Although in some ways the Hellenization of western Asia produced significant social and economic changes for both natives and new arrivals, it did not entail a complete revolution. The citizens of the newly founded cities of the Hellenistic period continued to own the land in and immediately around the city and used slaves or resident aliens to work for them. The rest of the land belonged to the king and was worked by peasants, as it had been for centuries. The basic level of agricultural production thus remained fairly constant.

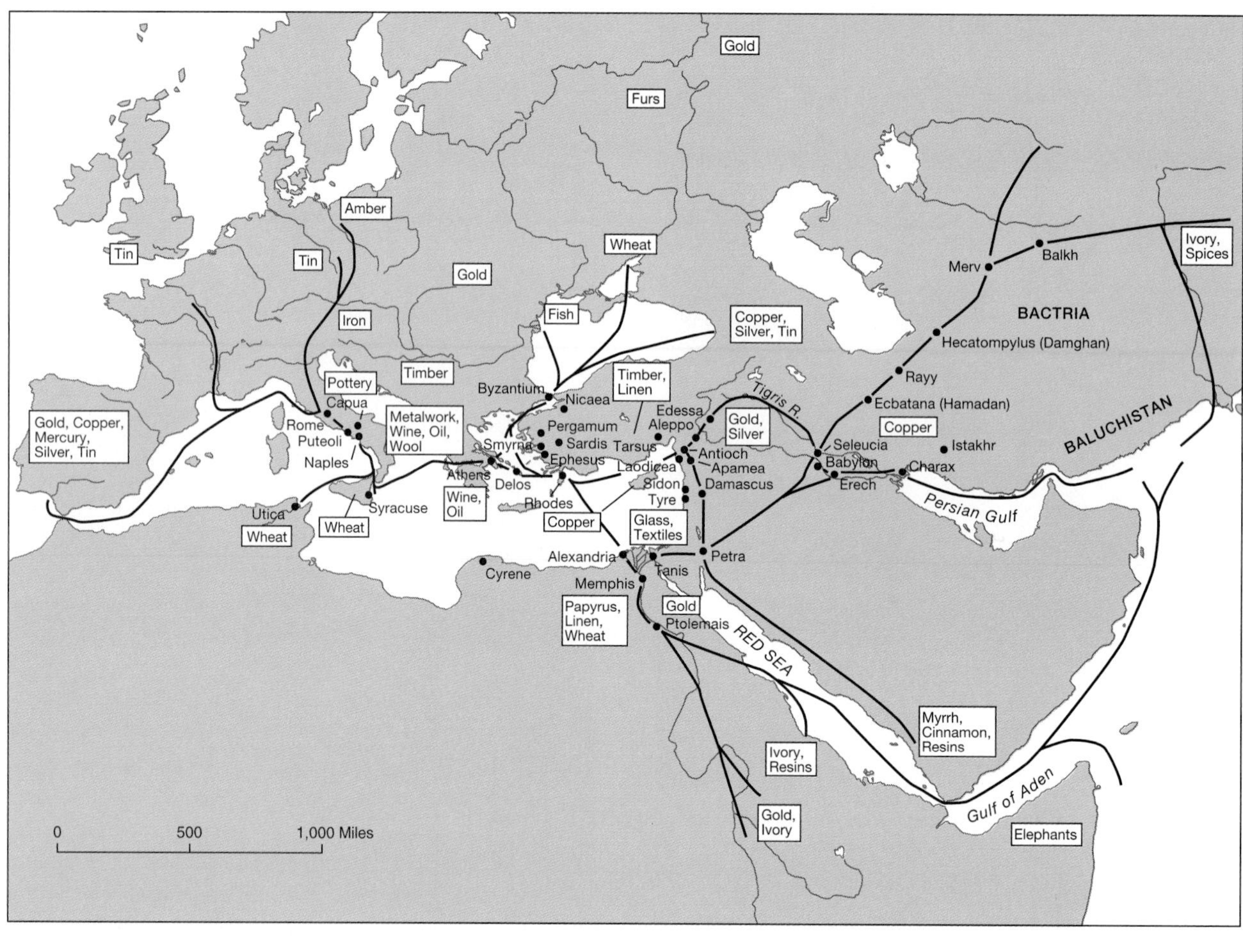

MAP 5.3 TRADE IN THE HELLENISTIC WORLD, c. 145 B.C.

Some rulers did try to make improvements. Both the Ptolemies and the Seleucids encouraged the introduction of more sophisticated agricultural equipment, such as iron plows and more efficient oil and wine presses, and introduced new fruit and crops. One of the Ptolemies' successes was a new quick-growing wheat that gave a double harvest and a higher yield. On occasion, the extra supplies were sent to feed the urban poor, although in general the kings, or their local representatives, were unwilling to subsidize the growing urban population at their own expense. In some cases the cities tried to solve the problem of subsistence on their own. Samos, for example, set up a fund for making loans; the interest on the loans was used to purchase grain, which was then distributed free to the citizens.

Within each independent city-state, industry and manufacturing developed according to the needs and abilities of the resident artisans. Sidon was famous for its glassware, Tarsus for its linen, and Antioch for its gold and silver, as might be expected of a royal capital. The volume remained small, and there is no evidence of mass production. Most businesses were family-run, with perhaps two or three slaves. Economic power was concentrated in the hands of the royal family and a small minority of wealthy landowners who, rather than providing food to the urban centers, preferred to ornament them with new temples, porticoes, and theaters that would perpetuate the memory of their donors.

In one significant respect, however, Alexander's conquests did change economic patterns. Trade, both in manufactured goods and in raw materials, became increasingly international, and the descendants of Alexander's Greeks found themselves in commercial contact with the people of the East. The kingdom of Bactria continued to serve as a center for Greek interests in central Asia, but other trade routes were also developed. Delos and Rhodes lay on the routes connecting Greece and Italy with the east and were also a conduit for the Black Sea trade in slaves, fish, fur, wheat, and timber. To the south the great caravan routes connecting the Mediterranean with Arabia, India, and central Asia passed through Phoenician and Syrian ports.

The principal route, which ran through Seleucid territory, followed the river Tigris to the Persian Gulf and then the coast of Baluchistan to the mouth of the river Indus. Although under Seleucid control, the route was used for a while by the Ptolemies, but in time they developed their own trade route, which involved sailing around the south coast of Arabia to the Gulf of Aden. Although the route was longer, it opened up the Arabian spice market as well as that of India. The Sabaeans, the ancient inhabitants of modern Yemen, produced myrrh and cinnamon, both highly regarded and expensive in the West.

More complicated was the importation of elephants. After Alexander's Indian campaign, the strategic value and prestige of having elephants in a royal army appealed to his successors. The Ptolemies had a source fairly close to home, for they captured their elephants in what is now Somalia; the Seleucids, by contrast, had to import theirs from India. Nor was this ancient form of military extravagance without its problems. On a famous occasion in 217 B.C., at a battle fought between Ptolemy IV and Antiochus III, Ptolemy's forest elephants were no match for the larger Indian elephants of the Seleucid army. Terrified by the smell and the trumpeting of these beasts, according to the Greek historian Polybius, the African elephants fled.

Trade contacts such as these were sufficiently important to the Seleucids for them to station a permanent ambassador at the court of one of the Indian kingdoms, the Mauryan empire. One of the ambassadors, Megasthenes, wrote a detailed account of India, now lost, that circulated widely in the Greco-Roman world (see Chapter 2).

Although the cultural exchange resulting from these commercial links was limited, some mutual influence undoubtedly occurred. Many of the Greek coins minted in India have an inscription in Greek on one side and in a local script on the other. Western theories of medicine and astrology were imported into India, and some Greek settlers became assimilated into the native populations. Some were said to have become Buddhists, while others were described by a later writer as the equivalent of the warrior class in Hindu society.

All such contacts throughout Asia in the Hellenistic period were originally motivated by the desire to establish trading relations, but they also awakened curiosity in some Greek minds as to the nature of the wider world. Polybius, the Greek historian, joined a military expedition that seems to have sailed down the western coast of Africa as far as southern Morocco. Another traveler, Pytheas, set off on a journey from the Greek city of Massilia (modern Marseilles) in 320 B.C. that took him as far north as the Arctic Circle. From his description he seems to have reached either Iceland or the northern coast of Norway.

Alexandria: Capital of the Ptolemies

From the time of its foundation by the great conqueror in 332 B.C., Alexandria became a natural meeting place for the cultures of Europe and Asia. Its planner was Deinocrates, like Alexander a Macedonian. Laid out on a grand scale, its main street was said to be 100 feet wide and lined with shops and bazaars. The principal building complex was the royal palace, which served both as the residence of the Ptolemies and as the seat of government. Surrounded by gardens and fountains, it was occupied for the most part by the Greek-speaking bureaucrats who administered Ptolemaic Egypt.

The center of Greek culture at Alexandria was the Museum, one of the major intellectual institutions of the ancient world. Within its walls were lecture halls, laboratories, observatories, a dining hall, a park, and a zoo. Its library was said to have contained over half a million scrolls, and its principal librarian was also the head of the whole organization and thus one of the most powerful figures in Alexandria. In some ways the Museum resembled a modern university, except that the scholars and scientists who worked there had no obligation to teach. They were supported by the Ptolemies to pursue their own research and to glorify the royal family.

At first the Greek community tried to keep out the native Egyptians, but as intermarriage became more common, Alexander's dream of fusing cultures became at least in part fulfilled. The Alexandrians came to think of themselves, and be thought of by others, as cosmopolitans, citizens of the world that revolved around their city. They were notorious for their rowdiness, always ready for a spectacle, fond of noisy demonstrations, rude to foreigners, arrogant, and opinionated. The Ptolemies kept them more or less contented by constructing race tracks and parks and by staging lavish public festivals and sports events that were often the pretext for violent street demonstrations.

Only the Jews of Alexandria, one of the largest settlements of the Diaspora (the settlement of the Jews outside Palestine), maintained their cultural independence. Ptolemy I had encouraged the establishment of a Jewish community, and by the time of Ptolemy III (246–221 B.C.) there were three synagogues in the city. The Jewish population lived together in one district of the city and had its own governing council. The Jews were given the right to be judged by their own magistrates according to their own law, a privilege that brought some hostility from Greek Alexandrians, who felt that religion was a private matter. With time the Jews came to speak Greek, and the Old Testament was translated into that language, a version known as the Septuagint. Services at the synagogues were conducted in Greek, and many Jews took Greek names, such as Theophilus ("lover of God"). The Jews of Alexandria were allowed to own land and were often employed as tax collectors but were rarely involved in trade or moneylending. On several occasions Jewish generals led Egyptian forces, and Jewish mercenaries were not unknown.

Much of the activity at Alexandria centered around the harbor, one of the most international of its times, with traffic from the Nile and the Red Sea as well as the whole of the Mediterranean. Great quays and warehouses were constructed there, as well as Alexandria's most famous monument, the Pharos. This was a vast lighthouse, named after the small island on which it stood at the mouth of the harbor. The Pharos was 440 feet tall, and the beam of light from its lantern was intensified by a series of reflectors. A marvel of the latest technology, it became an apt symbol of the city whose port it illuminated.

Few traces of Ptolemaic Alexandria remain today; owing to a change in sea level, most of the ancient city is underwater. The tomb of Alexander, a pilgrimage center for centuries, has never been found, and the Pharos was destroyed by an earthquake in the fourteenth century A.D. Yet the memory of the city's glamor and cultural activity has not altogether faded, nor has its power to fuse different cultures. One of the greatest modern Greek poets, Constantine Cavafy (1863–1933), spent his life there, and much of his work evokes the cosmopolitan world of Hellenistic Alexandria.

Hellenistic Science and Religion

By the time of Alexander, the Greeks had discovered two basic principles of science: the use of mathematics as a means of investigating natural phenomena and the idea of establishing general truths by practical research. Both of these were applied in the development of Hellenistic science, which made greater strides than the science of any comparable period before the sixteenth and seventeenth centuries A.D.

The most important advances of the Hellenistic Age were in the life sciences—Theophrastus (c. 369–c. 285 B.C.), a successor to Aristotle at the Lyceum, founded the science of botany—and in geography and astronomy, whose study was stimulated by the conquests of Alexander and the requirements of trade. By the mid-fourth century, Heraclides of Pontus (c. 390–310 B.C.) had discovered that the earth revolved daily on its axis. The astronomer Aristarchus of Samos (c. 310–230 B.C.) wrote a treatise on the size of the sun and the moon, arguing that the sun was the center of the universe. This was regarded as impiety by most of his contemporaries, to whose view of life the earth and human existence were central. An even more remarkable figure was Eratosthenes (c. 275–194 B.C.), the head of the library at Alexandria under Ptolemy III, who measured the circumference of the earth, calculated by using a shadow to determine the angle between the Egyptian cities of Alexandria and Aswan. The most influential Hellenistic astronomer, Hipparchus (c. 190–126 B.C.), proposed a rival theory involving cyclical movements of the planets and measured the lunar and solar years with considerable accuracy. Hipparchus produced the first work on trigonometry, *The Table of Chords;* discovered the irregular occurrence of equinoxes; and compiled a catalog of some 850 stars. The geocentric theory eventually received its classic statement in the *Almagest* of Claudius Ptolemy, a second-century A.D. Greek scholar.

The greatest mathematician of the Hellenistic world was the geometer Euclid (flourished c. 300 B.C.). Euclid also wrote on astronomy and music, but his major achievement was *The Elements,* the most important work on geometry in antiquity. One of the most popular textbooks of all time, it was translated into Hebrew, Latin, Arabic, and western languages and has remained useful up to our time. A little later, Archimedes of Syracuse worked on the geometry of cylinders and spheres and in the process established the mathematical value of pi (3.14), also discovered independently in India.

Archimedes of Syracuse: Practical Science in the Ancient World

Perhaps the greatest figure in Hellenistic science, Archimedes (c. 287–212 B.C.) was born at Syracuse in

Sicily. After completing a period of research at Alexandria, he returned to Syracuse to become chief scientific adviser to King Hieron II (265–215 B.C.). He wrote on geometry and calculus and considered that his greatest work was in theoretical mathematics. On his tomb was engraved the figure of a sphere within a cylinder, a symbol of his concern for pure, abstract form.

Yet Archimedes' chief claims to fame are based on the practical use to which he put his knowledge. The inventor of the science of hydrostatics, the measurement and use of waterpower, he constructed a planetarium, worked by water, to represent the movements of the sun and planets around the stationary earth. He developed pulleys and a drilling system to pump out ships and to drain the fields of the Nile delta after flooding. The archetypal absentminded scientist, he was, it was said, too forgetful to eat; and when he discovered the concept of specific gravity by noticing the water he displaced in his bathtub, it is said that he leaped out and ran naked through the streets, crying "Eureka!" ("I have found it!"). When Hieron had constructed a huge ship, the *Syracusia,* Archimedes found a way of launching it and then said to the king: "Find me a place to stand and I shall move the world."

In mathematics his achievements include the invention of a system for expressing extremely large numbers and the solution of various problems relating to the cube. Although most of his work was done at Syracuse, he corresponded with the mathematicians working at Alexandria. A letter to Eratosthenes there included a complex mathematical analysis described in the form of an elegiac poem. Like many of his contemporaries, he applied his theories to the study of astronomy, and his planetarium still survived in the time of Cicero, 200 years later.

All Archimedes' skill was needed in 215 B.C., when Syracuse was besieged by the Romans. He spent his time inventing ways to defend the city, including iron gates that caught up the Roman soldiers as they advanced toward the walls and lifted them into the air, and pulleys for raising huge stones or lumps of lead to be dropped on enemy ships. Finally, in 212 an outbreak of malaria undermined the morale of both Romans and Syracusans, and the city, which the Athenians had failed to take 200 years earlier, was forced to surrender. It is said that when Archimedes realized that his beloved Syracuse was about to fall, "he wept much." The Roman soldiers, storming the city, killed him by accident. Archimedes' career became symbolic of the achievements of the Hellenistic scientists; a profoundly original thinker, he was also famous for his patriotism.

Health and Medicine

The father of Greek medicine, Hippocrates, was born on the island of Cos in the mid-fifth century B.C. and traveled widely in the Greek world. His writings include case studies of various illnesses that show his concern with the practical details of curing invalids. Doctors still subscribe to the Hippocratic Oath, which prescribes a physician's ethical responsibility. Hippocrates' successors were more interested in research, which often involved dissection. According to the Roman scholar Celsus (early first century A.D.), who wrote a book about Hellenistic medicine, doctors not only dissected corpses to study their entrails but also practiced human vivisection on criminals. Whether this is true or not, Hellenistic doctors made important discoveries concerning digestion and the vascular system. The Alexandrian physician Herophilus, working in the early third century B.C., discovered that the brain was the center of the nervous system and that the arteries carried blood, and he was the first person to measure the human pulse. His dissections enabled him to discover the ovaries and perhaps also the fallopian tubes. His contemporary, Erasistratus, a fellow Alexandrian, distinguished between the sensory and motor nerves and discovered the heart's function in the circulation of the blood.

Ruler Cults and Mystery Religions

Interest in the workings of the body did not preclude a concern for more spiritual matters, and the Hellenistic age saw a number of fundamental changes in the nature of Greek religion. From the time of Homer, traditional beliefs had centered around the Olympic pantheon, the 12 deities, including Zeus and Athena, who were thought to live on Mount Olympus in northern Greece. The Greeks thought of their gods as like themselves, distinguished only by their powers and their immortality, and they came to symbolize various human attributes: Ares, the war god, personified aggression; Aphrodite, sexual love; and so on. Over time a wide variety of local cults sprang up, and the concept of the original deities became blurred by the variations of regional practices. By the fifth century B.C. educated Greeks had begun to doubt the existence of the traditional gods. Temples were still built and rituals celebrated, but the old beliefs began to lose their power. When the Greeks came into contact with the enormous variety of Asian religions, fundamental changes occurred.

The first major development was initiated by Alexander, who claimed to be descended from Hercules and Achilles and in 324 B.C. ordered the Greek states to pay him godlike honors. The subsequent practice of ruler

Greek Medicine

In the following extract, taken from his work on epidemics, Hippocrates describes his approach to the treatment of illness.

These are the things observed in disease from which we have learned to judge them, studying the general nature of mankind as well as the peculiarities of the individual, the disease as well as the patients, the measures taken and the physician who prescribed them. Our judgment is easier or harder in proportion to our knowledge of these matters. First of all, there is the general climate and any local peculiarities of geography and weather. Then there is the particular patient—his habits and way of life, his occupation, his age; his words, manner of speaking, talkativeness, silence; his disposition; his sleep or lack of it, the time and nature of his dreams, his gestures, his tears. Thirdly, from the onset of the disease we must consider the movements of the bowels and the urine, the spitting and vomiting; we must observe the causes of each stage in the progress of the disease, and likewise their effects, and how it finally reaches a favorable end or death. During its course we must study the patient's sweats and chills, coughs and sneezes, hiccoughs and breathing, belching and gas, and bleeding and piles. From our observation of these we must then decide what course the disease will take next.

Source: P. MacKendrick and H. M. Howe, eds., *Classics in Translation* (Madison: University of Wisconsin Press, 1966), vol. 1, p. 311.

worship became a feature of many Hellenistic kingdoms. In Egypt, where from time immemorial the people had been accustomed to think of their pharaoh as the incarnation of the sun god, Ptolemy I began by deifying Alexander, and his son deified both his father and himself. From then on the reigning monarch automatically became a god, and the Seleucids soon followed the example of their Egyptian rivals.

Clearly, these ruler cults served political purposes, reinforcing the power and prestige not only of the kings but of their dynasties as well. It is doubtful that they satisfied religious needs on any broad scale, and the conquering Macedonians and Greeks, far from exporting Greek religion to Asia, found themselves subscribing to Asian and Egyptian religions, which in many cases they carried back to Greece. The most popular cult was that of the Egyptian deities Sarapis and Isis. Sarapis was invented by Ptolemy I, who adapted the cult of Osiris, the Egyptian god of the underworld, to Greek tastes. Sarapis was a god of healing and a protector of travelers, and by the second century B.C. he was worshiped as far west as Sicily. Isis, his wife, was even more important, offering the promise of life after death to all of her initiates who had undergone certain mysterious rituals.

Other "mystery cults" also flourished, as did the practice of magic and astrology. The Greeks, with their tendency to religious eclecticism, were attracted to the mystery cults, which focused on the afterlife and offered hope in a period when the economic condition of many people had deteriorated. At the same time, one of the few Greek cults that developed and spread throughout the Hellenistic period was that of Tyche, or chance, a force beyond control or understanding that dictated the fate of human existence.

These various strands of belief, combined with the monistic world view of Aristotle and his successors, particularly Zeno of Elea, produced the philosophical conception of a single god. This god, as developed by the school of philosophy known as Stoicism, was an object of contemplation rather than worship. Nonetheless, Stoic divinity was a significant element in the development of an idea powerfully associated with monotheism, that of universal salvation.

The one people in the Hellenistic world who already practiced a monotheistic religion were the Hebrews. Following the period of Babylonian captivity described in Chapter 1, the Hebrews had scattered throughout Asia and had established settlements alongside those of other religions. Orthodox Jewish belief was essentially exclusive, however, and Hebrew communities were appalled at the concept of ruler worship, which inevitably brought them into conflict with the authorities. One of the consequences was the uprising of Judas Maccabaeus and his followers from 173 to 164 B.C. against their Seleucid rulers, a rebellion still commemorated in the annual Jewish festival of Hanukkah. Elsewhere in Asia, Jewish settlements were more peaceful. In general the Jews of the Diaspora continued to look to Jerusalem as their holy city and to pay an annual tax for the upkeep of the temple there. Nevertheless, contacts between the wide range of Hellenistic religious thought and Orthodox Judaism inevitably affected both sides; in turn, each was to play a part in the formation of Christianity.

The Changing Status of Women

As we have seen, the social life of women in classical Greek society was largely restricted to the household. By the end of the fifth century B.C., however, a number of artists had begun to show a marked interest in female subjects and some critics questioned the traditional role of women in Greek society. One of the earliest examples of this can be found in Euripides' play *Medea,* first performed in 431 B.C. It describes the vengeance of Medea upon her husband, Jason, who had abandoned her for a new, royal bride. In the eyes of an Athenian audience, Medea would have labored under two crushing disadvantages, as a woman and as a foreigner. Although she was married to a Greek by whom she had had two children, Athenian law did not recognize the issue of foreign wives as citizens. Thus Jason had no responsibility in deserting her for a Greek wife who could provide him with legitimate offspring. The abandoned Medea inveighs bitterly against her fate:

> ***We women are the most unfortunate creatures. . . .***
> ***A man, when he's tired of the company in his home,***
> ***Goes out of his house and puts an end to his boredom***
> ***And turns to a friend or companion of his own age.***
> ***But we are forced to keep our eyes on one alone.***
> ***What they say of us is that we have a peaceful time***
> ***Living at home, while they do the fighting in war.***
> ***How wrong they are! I would very much rather stand***
> ***Three times in the front of battle than bear one child.***[1]

In the end, Medea kills both her own children and Jason's intended bride in what has remained the most famous act of vengeance in Western literature.

This figurine of a woman with a fan comes from Tanagra in Boeotia, where examples of these clay statuettes were first found.

In the fine arts, sculptors had begun by the fourth century B.C. to turn to the naked female form to express concepts of ideal beauty that in the previous century had been expressed through male subjects. The most famous example was Praxiteles' much imitated Aphrodite of Cnidos. The statue combines the dignity of a goddess with a clearly erotic message. Aphrodite is depicted in the act of bathing; surprised by an unseen intruder, she covers herself modestly with one hand—thus drawing the viewer's attention to what she attempts to conceal. The female nude would remain one of the most popular artistic subjects throughout the Hellenistic age.

Women's lives also interested Hellenistic writers. In a poem set in Alexandria, Theocritus (c. 310–250 B.C.) depicts two women from Syracuse in southern Italy who have moved to the big city and become suburban housewives. Theocritus describes their walk around town on a festival day and records their casual conversation and gossip. It is hard to imagine so witty, realistic, and familiar a note having been sounded in the fifth century B.C., whose writers showed little or no interest in women's daily lives.

Improvement in the status of women was thus slow but perceptible. The old barriers to their legal and economic rights remained, but the Hellenistic kingdoms made it possible for some women of extraordinary character to achieve power. The generalship of Arsinoë II, the wife of Ptolemy II, seems to have led Egyptian forces to victory in the wars between Egypt and the Seleucids (276–272 B.C.), and she was deified. Arsinoe and other Hellenistic queens and princesses began to play an increasing cultural role as well. Berenice II, wife of Ptolemy III, corresponded with the leading poet of the day, Callimachus, and Stratonice, wife of the Seleucid king Antiochus I (ruled 280–261 B.C.), helped to build the art collection on the sacred island of Delos. Following such aristocratic examples, other women began to write and publish and even to appear in public. Aristodama of Smyrna traveled through Greece in the mid-third century B.C. giving recitals of her poetry; her brother went along as her business manager. The city of Lamia was so impressed by her compositions that she was not only awarded honorary citizenship but declared *proxenos* or informal diplomatic representative of the city.

Hellenistic Women

Two Hellenistic inscriptions throw light on the improving status of women in that period. The first records the gratitude of the city of Lamia to the poetess Aristodama for her public readings; in the second, King Antiochus III establishes a state cult in the name of his wife.

Good fortune. The people of Lamia decreed: Whereas Aristodama, daughter of Amyntas of Smyrna in Ionia, an epic poetess, came to the city and gave several readings of her own poems in which she made appropriate mention of the Aetolian nation and the ancestors of the people. . . , showing zeal in her declamation, that she be a *proxenos* [protector and informal diplomatic representative] of the city and a benefactor, and that citizenship, the right to acquire land and property, grazing rights, exemption from reprisals, and safety by land and sea in peace or in war be granted to her and her children and her property for all time together with all the grants made to other *proxenoi* and benefactors. To . . . her brother and his children there shall be rights of *proxenia,* citizenship and freedom from reprisals.

King Antiochus to Anaximbrotus, greeting. As we desired to increase still further the honor of our sister-queen Laodice . . . we have now decided that, just as there are appointed throughout the kingdom high-priests of our cult, so there shall be established in the same districts high-priestesses of her also, who shall wear golden crowns bearing her image and whose names shall be mentioned in contracts after those of the high-priests of our ancestors and of us.

Source: F. W. Walbank, *The Hellenistic World* (Cambridge, Mass.: Harvard University Press, 1982), pp. 73, 216.

Two schools of Hellenistic philosophy, discussed below, actively encouraged the participation of women at their meetings and made no distinction between the sexes: Stoicism and Epicureanism.

Hellenistic Philosophy

Plato and Aristotle saw in the polis the natural unit of the human community. The Hellenistic world of empire, with its much broader political and commercial connections, called for a philosophy that could express the changed relations among individual, state, and society.

The three major schools of thought to emerge from the Hellenistic age provided different counsel for the problems of the age. Stoicism aimed at achieving inner tranquility in a troubled world, Epicureanism advocated the cultivation of private life, and Cynicism rejected engagement with the world as such.

The most influential of the three was Stoicism. It was founded by Zeno of Elea (335–263 B.C.), who came to Athens in 313 and set up a school in the stoa or portico of the Athenian marketplace, from which the word *Stoic* derives. The Stoics believed in a ruling providence, but happiness, they emphasized, depended on avoiding desire for or dependence on things—wealth, power, fame—that were ultimately subject to the control of others. The Stoics did not advocate withdrawal from public life but rather an ideal of disinterested service and detachment from ambition. They preached a high ethical standard, including general pacifism and the recognition of universal human equality.

Stoicism was adopted by the Romans and served as the fundamental ethical system of antiquity until the rise of Christianity, which internalized much of its teachings. Among the most important Roman Stoics was Epictetus (A.D. c. 55–c. 135), a former slave. In his *Handbook* Epictetus counsels trust in providence even in the face of dire misfortune. The philosopher, in his view, speaks for that providence, "taking the human race for his children." The Roman emperor Marcus Aurelius (A.D. 121–180), a later follower, strove for serenity and detachment despite his vast responsibilities. "Tell yourself every morning," he wrote in his *Meditations*, "'today I shall meet the officious, the ungrateful, the bullying, the treacherous, the envious, the selfish. All of them behave like this because they do not know the difference between good and bad.'"

The philosophy expounded by Epicurus (341–270 B.C.) was geared to personal satisfaction rather than social duty. Epicurus adopted the Atomist theory of the fifth century B.C., which held that the universe was a purely material structure unaffected by the existence of the gods; he thus rejected the Stoic belief in providence. The soul, like the body, was mortal, and thus earthly happiness was the only goal of existence. This could best be achieved through the state of *ataraxia,* a condition neither agitated by excessive desire nor subject to avoidable discomfort and pain. To attain ataraxia, one should abstain from all things that made one vulnerable to disappointment and suffering, be it business, politics, or the pursuit of pleasure. Thus, whereas the serenity achieved by the Stoics was the result of an active life in the service of others, that of the Epicureans was premised on abstention from the public world. Epicureans were, of course, encouraged to associate with one another, and the school Epicurus himself founded in Athens in 306 B.C., which included women and slaves, shared a common life that included regular discussions and a monthly banquet.

The Cynics carried rejection of the world to a far greater extreme than either the Stoics or the Epicureans. Civilization, they contended, was a false creation that encumbered humans with arbitrary conventions and artificial needs. To regain a natural life, it was necessary to shun its social and material trappings entirely. Diogenes of Sinope (c. 400–c. 325 B.C.) taught by example the virtues of an ascetic life and an uncensored tongue; his defiance of convention won him the nickname "the Cynic" ("dog"), soon applied to all adherents of his philosophy. Cynicism was clearly a radical response to the social dislocation of the world in the fourth century B.C. Its following declined in the later Hellenistic period, but it revived during the Roman Empire and influenced early Christian monasticism.

Hellenistic philosophy derived ultimately from the Sophists, with their emphasis on a personal career in the world. It thus reflected a divorce between ethical and natural philosophy. For the pre-Socratics, there was no distinction between understanding the world and conducting oneself in it. By the late fourth century B.C., however, science had become a descriptive enterprise, and philosophy in large part a quest for meaning in a world ruled at best by an abstract providence and at worst by pure chance.

SUMMARY

The achievements of the Greeks within the relatively brief flowering of their culture were remarkable. Greek art and architecture set standards that guided subsequent artists for centuries and remain a powerful influence today. The tragic drama of fifth-century B.C. *Athens is the basis of the Western theater tradition, and its archetypal heroes and heroines remain an inspiration across the entire spectrum of Western art. Greek science and philosophy, particularly in the works of Plato and Aristotle, formed much of the Western intellectual tradition. During the Hellenistic period, Greek culture spread widely across the Mediterranean and among the older societies of Egypt and western Asia, contact with which broadened and enriched Greek thought. The Greeks experimented with various forms of government, including democracy, and created a distinctive political unit, the polis. But their inability to resolve their disputes peacefully or to find a basis for federal union undermined the independence they so jealously protected, and after repelling Persia in the fifth century* B.C.*, they fell prey to Macedon in the fourth. Only in the more cosmopolitan climate of the third century* B.C. *did the Greeks seek a wider conception of the state and the world, but the emergence of a great new power in the west, Rome, was to complete the political subjection begun by Alexander.*

NOTES

1. *Euripides I,* trans. R. Warner (Chicago: University of Chicago Press, 1955), p. 67.

SUGGESTIONS FOR FURTHER READING

Barnes, J. *Aristotle.* Oxford: Oxford University Press, 1982.

Burkert, W. *Greek Religion.* Cambridge, Mass.: Harvard University Press, 1985.

Casson, L. *Travel in the Ancient World.* London: Allen & Unwin, 1974.

Cawkwell, G. *Philip of Macedon.* Boston: Faber & Faber, 1978.

Finley, M. I., ed. *The Legacy of Greece: A New Appraisal.* Oxford: Clarendon Press, 1981.

Green, J. R. *Theatre in Greek Society.* London: Routledge, 1994.

Green, P. *Alexander to Actium: The Historical Evolution of the Hellenistic Age.* Berkeley: University of California Press, 1990.

Hammond, N. G. L. *Alexander the Great: King, Commander and Statesman.* London: Chatto & Windus, 1981.

Haynes, D. *Greek Art and the Idea of Freedom.* London: Thames & Hudson, 1981.

Kirk, G. S., and Raven, J. E. *The Pre-Socratic Philosophers: A Critical History with a Selection of Texts,* 2nd ed. Cambridge: Cambridge University Press, 1983.

Lefkowitz, M. R., and Fant, M. B. *Women in Greece and Rome.* Toronto: University of Toronto Press, 1978.

Lesky, A. *Greek Tragic Poetry,* 3rd ed., trans. M. Dillon. New Haven, Conn.: Yale University Press, 1983.

Lloyd, G. E. R. *The Revolutions of Wisdom: Studies in the Claims and Practice of Ancient Greek Science.* Berkeley: University of California Press, 1987.

MacDowell, D. M. *The Law in Classical Athens.* London: Thames & Hudson, 1978.

Marrou, H. I. *A History of Education in Antiquity.* Madison: University of Wisconsin Press, 1982.

Morford, M. P. O., and Lenardon, P. J. *Classical Mythology,* 2nd ed. New York: Longman, 1977.

Onians, J. *Art and Thought in the Hellenistic Age: The Greek World View, 350–50 b.c.* London: Thames & Hudson, 1979.

Pollitt, J. J. *Art and Experience in Classical Greece.* Cambridge: Cambridge University Press, 1972.

Rist, J. M., ed. *The Stoics.* Berkeley: University of California Press, 1978.

Staveley, E. S. *Greek and Roman Voting and Elections.* Ithaca, N.Y.: Cornell University Press, 1972.

Walbank, F. W. *The Hellenistic World.* Cambridge, Mass.: Harvard University Press, 1982.

Wycherley, R. E. *The Stones of Athens.* Princeton, N.J.: Princeton University Press, 1978.

CHAPTER 6

The Romans

The Romans left an indelible mark throughout much of Asia and North Africa as well as the West. In law, politics, religion, language, and the arts, Roman culture spread throughout an empire that stretched from the Atlantic to western Asia and from North Africa to England. The alphabet in use throughout much of the Western world was derived from the Roman alphabet, and the various Romance languages, such as Italian and French, are derived from Latin. The Western calendar is a modified form of one adapted from an Egyptian calendar by Julius Caesar in 46 B.C. Rome advanced fundamental political concepts, especially the republican form of government, that have influenced numerous modern states. The Romans developed sophisticated law and jurisprudence that served as the foundation of modern Continental European legal systems as well as those of the areas Europeans colonized, especially in Africa and Asia. Roman law had an impact on the English common law, much of which was employed in formulating the canon law of the Roman Catholic church, and modern international and maritime law is based on it. Even the road network of modern Europe and the Middle East is based on one planned and built 2,000 years ago by the Romans.

From the beginning of their rise to power the Romans envisioned their task as one of regional and ultimately world domination. In fulfilling this vision, they carried their culture throughout much of the ancient world. Through the Romanization of diverse peoples and cultures, the Romans were able to transmit ideas they had acquired from others as well as those that they developed themselves. In particular, the two great streams of Western culture, the classical and the Judeo-Christian, spread throughout the empire. In assessing their own cultural achievements, the Romans were uncharacteristically modest. They seem to have believed that their

A Roman consul administers the law from his chair of office. The scepter in his left hand symbolizes his authority.

virtues lay in efficient rule and success on the battlefield rather than in aesthetic and intellectual achievements. Rome's self-appointed task was to rule the known world.

The history of Rome began with the traditional foundation of the city in the mid-eighth century B.C., but almost at once it fell under the domination of another people of ancient Italy, the Etruscans. Rome's subsequent rise to power was made possible by the impact of Etruscan rule.

Italy Before Rome

Early in the Bronze Age the first Indo-European invaders of Italy had displaced the older inhabitants of the peninsula, who were related to the native populations of Spain and Gaul, and built their houses on platforms resting on poles. Toward the end of the Bronze Age various groups who spoke Italic dialects arrived—the Umbrians, the Samnites, and the Latins. Among the settlements of the Latins was the small village of Rome on the river Tiber, the site of which may have been inhabited as early as 1400 B.C., although its legendary founding was in 753 B.C. With the dawning of the Iron Age about 1000 B.C., a shared culture began to develop among the tribes of central Italy. This culture is called Villanovan, on the basis of artifacts discovered at the village of Villanova near Bologna. It was powerfully affected in the succeeding centuries by the arrival of Greek colonists in southern Italy and the rise of an important new culture to the north, the Etruscan.

The Etruscans

As early as Roman times scholars began to question the identity, origins, and language of the Etruscans. By 700 B.C. these people had settled in central Italy, in what was later called Tuscany. There is considerable doubt, however, as to whether they were of foreign origin or a native Italian people with a more highly developed culture. In most cases the principal Etruscan cities developed where Villanovan communities had previously existed, which would seem to support the latter theory. Yet the ancient Greeks and Romans, with few exceptions, were convinced that the Etruscans had migrated to Italy from western Asia, perhaps from the ancient kingdom of Lydia, in what is now Turkey. Much of their social life and art was strikingly Eastern in character.

As is clear from the ornate funerary objects found in tombs dating from the mid-seventh century B.C., the Etruscans were a rich and technologically sophisticated people from the beginning of their history. Their commercial connections included the Greek cities of southern Italy and the Phoenician colony of Carthage in North Africa. Indeed, throughout the seventh and sixth centuries B.C., the three principal trade rivals in the western Mediterranean—the Etruscans, the Greeks, and the Carthaginians—formed a constantly changing series of alliances. The high point of Etruscan success came in 540 B.C. when, with Carthaginian help, they defeated the Greeks at Alalia and drove them out of the island of Corsica, off the coast of Tuscany. The price of their victory, however, was that their erstwhile collaborators, the Carthaginians, obtained control of the nearby island of Sardinia, a rich source of iron and other minerals that had formerly been in Etruscan hands. The Greeks had their revenge when, in 474 B.C., a Syracusan fleet destroyed Etruscan forces off the coast at Cumae and effectively put an end to any Etruscan influence in southern Italy.

By then the Etruscans had already lost one of their strongholds in central Italy, Rome itself, which they had occupied from around 616 B.C. In 510 the Etruscan rulers of Rome were driven out by the Romans, and centuries of Etruscan decline began. The principal Etruscan cities nearest to Rome were conquered one by one: Veii in 396, Cerveteri in 353, and Tarquinia, the richest Etruscan center, in 351. The northern Etruscans submitted to the

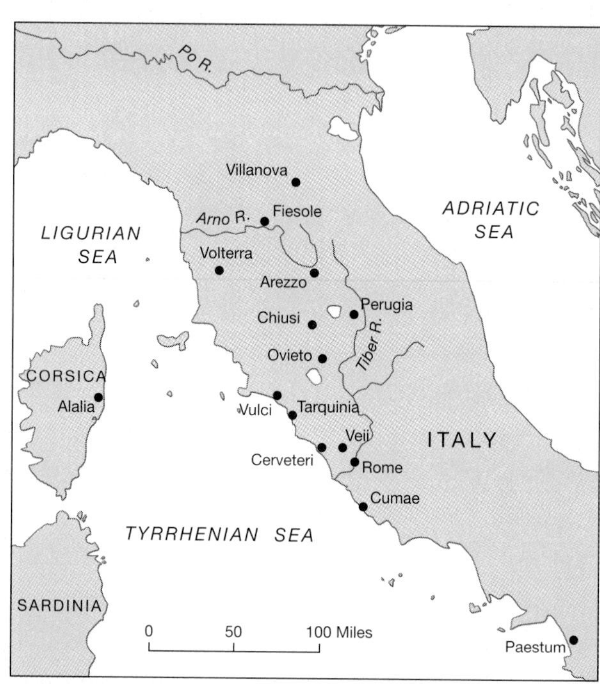

MAP 6.1 ETRURIA

Lid of an Etruscan funerary urn depicting the couple whose ashes it contains. Note the characteristic Etruscan concern for vividness of facial expression and lack of interest in proportion.

Romans without resistance, and in the wars of the third century B.C. in which the Romans fought and finally destroyed Carthage, the Etruscans provided support.

By the first century B.C. the Etruscans had been awarded the right of Roman citizenship and became absorbed into the Roman state. It is perhaps surprising that a people who had once been one of the richest and most active in the Mediterranean should have declined so rapidly. A partial explanation may be found in the nature of Etruscan society, which was divided into a small hereditary aristocracy and a large body of slaves and peasant farmers. Such a social structure, lacking flexibility, functioned successfully in the relatively stable conditions of the seventh and sixth centuries B.C. With the changing economic conditions produced by Roman expansion, however, the small number of rich Etruscan families were unable to hold their own, let alone compete against the increasingly prosperous Romans. The pronounced gloominess of late Etruscan art may suggest a sense of imminent cultural demise.

Early Rome

The early history of Rome is shrouded in legend. The Romans themselves celebrated the foundation of their city in 753 B.C. on April 21 of each year, although there were different and irreconcilable accounts of who the actual founders had been. Modern archaeological research has done much to clarify the early stages of Roman history, but uncertainties remain, and it may never be possible to establish precise chronology.

From Monarchy to Republic

Recent archaeological finds of Bronze Age pottery have shown that a small community probably existed on or near Rome's Capitoline hill in the second millennium B.C., but there is no real evidence of continuity of occupation, and the Iron Age settlements of the eighth century B.C. probably represent a new beginning. The traditional founding date of 753 B.C. coincides closely with the archaeological evidence. Like other Latins, the first Romans were probably farmers and shepherds, and the simple huts discovered on the seven hills that surround Rome are similar to those of other Latin tribes to the south and east. The fertile land below was left for grazing.

As the community grew, the slopes of the hills, which were formerly used only as burial sites, became inhabited, and by the end of the seventh century B.C. the grazing land had been partially drained and settled. There are also signs of contact with the outside world, notably the importation of pottery and metalwork from neighboring Etruscan cities. Roman historians later endowed their city with a legendary founder, Romulus, who, together with his twin brother, Remus, was said to have been born to Rhea Silvia, the daughter of a local king, and the war god Mars. For more than two centuries, according to tradition, the city was ruled by seven kings, first Latin and then Etruscan.

Rome as the Etruscans found it was a small country town. The new rulers built it up considerably. Etruscan engineers drained the marshy central valley and built temples, shrines, and roads. Etruscan craftsmen introduced and developed new skills and established guilds, including those of the bronze workers, goldsmiths, and carpenters. Most important of all, under Etruscan rule the Romans came into contact for the first time with the outside world. From the simple village life of a small community under the leadership of tribal chiefs they took their place in a larger cultural and political context that extended beyond Italy. It took only a century for the Romans to learn the principles of Etruscan technology, expel their former rulers, and begin their climb to power.

The Republic: Conflict and Accommodation

With the expulsion of the Etruscans, the Romans devised a new form of government, abolishing the monarchy and founding a republic. The entire citizen body, including both classes, was known as the *populus.* The patricians, who comprised about 10 percent of the population, were the landed, governing class, and the plebeians, who included soldiers, artisans, laborers, merchants, and farmers, were subject to their rule. The result of the patricians' monopoly of office, which included their assembly, the Senate, and the two chief magistrates, or consuls (elected by all citizens but chosen solely from the patriciate), was the growth of a patronage system that reinforced elite control. Patrons offered jobs, protection, and legal services, and within the closed ranks of the magistrates, advancement along the career ladder, or *cursus honorum,* depended on the sponsorship of senior officials.

Patronage provided a rough system of checks and balances, as did the principle of collegiality. Either of the consuls could reject the proposals of the other by pronouncing the word veto ("I forbid"); in this fashion, executive authority was limited. But as patrician factions jockeyed for popular support, the plebeians were able to wrest a series of concessions that, over a period of two centuries, successfully challenged the patrician monopoly of office and created a parallel set of plebeian institutions and magistracies.

The first of the new magistrates were the two tribunes, whose function was to represent plebeian interests in the Senate. The person of a tribune was held to be sacrosanct, and his door was to be open day and night to any citizen. In 471 B.C. the plebeians won the right to meet in their own assembly, and around 450 they compelled the promulgation of a law code, the Twelve Tables. This provided, among other things, legal recognition of the patronage system and prescribed the death penalty for patrons who violated their duties to their clients. The plebeians next won the right of intermarriage with the patricians (445) and then of admission to some of the lesser magistracies (421).

It was not until 367, with the passage of the Sexto-Licinian Laws, that plebeians could stand for the consulship. Any man elected to the office automatically ennobled his family, and a mixed patrician-plebeian aristocracy began to develop that encouraged the support of the poorer plebeians by distributing some of the land won in Rome's conquest of Italy. The final recognition of the plebeians' formal political equality came in 287, when the Hortensian Law made decisions of the plebeian assembly binding on the Senate and the Roman people. The patricians' slow and reluctant acceptance of the need for compromise had significant consequences for the growth of Roman power; without adjustment, Roman expansion abroad would have been impossible.

The Unification of Italy and the Conquest of the Mediterranean

Between 509 and 266 B.C. the Romans extended their control over the Italian peninsula, aided by a number of factors. The Etruscans failed to mount any serious or organized opposition and, as we have seen, were defeated city by city. The Greeks in southern Italy, like their fellow Greeks in the homeland, were so rent by intercity feuding that they offered little unified resistance. Finally, the Romans turned to their own advantage an event that could have proved catastrophic. In 390 B.C. the Gauls, a northern Celtic people, crossed the Alps and moved into Italy. In the course of their rampaging they laid waste much of central Italy and sacked Rome. By the speed of their recovery, particularly in comparison with their Etruscan and other neighbors, the Romans proved to themselves and their fellow Latins that only they could mount a real defense of the peninsula in the face of foreign invasion.

The Latins had signed a treaty with Rome as early as 493 B.C. The formation of the Latin League in that year guaranteed the Romans some security on their immediate borders and allowed them to deal with the Etruscans and the other peoples of central Italy. The Aequi and the Volsci were defeated in 431, and with the fall of the city of Veii in 396 the collapse of the Etruscans seemed assured.

There remained, however, one of the fiercest of Italian peoples, the Samnites. This warlike tribe came originally from the rugged mountainous country to the east of Rome, but during the fifth century B.C. they had moved south into the rich land in the region below Naples abandoned by the Etruscans after the battle of Cumae in 474 B.C. For a while both Romans and Samnites were sufficiently distracted by problems elsewhere to leave each other in peace, but conflict was inevitable. The Samnite Wars, which lasted intermittently from 325 to 290 B.C., constituted the most serious challenge Rome had yet faced to its growing power. By 290 B.C., however, the Samnites had been crushed and their principal cities turned into Roman colonies.

That left the Greeks of the south the only independent group on the peninsula. Unable to agree on a plan of common defense, they turned to outside help. The people of Tarentum (modern Taranto) invited Pyrrhus, the Greek ruler of the Adriatic Confederation of Epirus, to aid them. One of the other Greek cities in southern Italy, Thurii, appealed for Roman aid against this outside intervention, thereby giving the Romans an excuse to attack. The wars with Pyrrhus lasted from 281 to 272, and by 267 B.C. the whole of southern Italy, Greeks and native tribes alike, had submitted to Roman domination.

The Punic Wars

The unification of the Italian peninsula brought Roman power to bear on Sicily, which had been colonized by Greeks and Carthaginians and was now, after a long struggle, under the control of the latter. Carthage had been founded on what is now the bay of Tunis by

Phoenician emigrants in the mid-ninth century B.C. By the sixth century B.C. it had become the dominant power in the Mediterranean, with colonies extending as far as Spain. Rome and Carthage had generally enjoyed peaceful relations under a treaty of 509 B.C. that recognized their respective spheres of influence, with Sicily as a neutral zone. Carthage resembled Rome in certain respects. Ostensibly a republic, it was in fact an oligarchy based on wealth. Like the Romans, the Carthaginians had two chief magistrates, elected annually, but the government was run by the heads of prominent households who made up the Senate and the Council. They worshiped both Phoenician and Greek gods; a colossal statue of Apollo stood in the forum or chief square of Carthage, but the Carthaginians still sacrificed children to their older deity, Baal-Ammon.

With Rome bent on expansion, a confrontation over Sicily was inevitable. In 264 B.C. the Romans sent an expeditionary force to Messana (Messina) at the behest of its Greek population. Carthage responded, and the first of the three Punic Wars began, so called because the Latin for Phoenician is *Punicus.*

The First Punic War, which lasted from 264 to 241 B.C., proved to the Romans that the Carthaginians were formidable opponents. Fighting for the first time at sea, Roman forces suffered severe losses, and it was only the development of an effective Roman fleet that finally drove the Carthaginians to seek peace. The Romans were in no mood to negotiate a face-saving compromise. A war in which the Romans had for the first time to face the serious possibility of defeat seems to have reinforced both the best and worst aspects of their character. Brave, efficient, and self-sacrificing, they won by virtue of their persistence and determination. Having won, though, they dictated terms of peace that humiliated Carthage, demanding both the surrender of territory and the payment of a large indemnity. In the following years, moreover, the Romans did what they could to cause trouble between the Carthaginians and their allies while expanding along the eastern Adriatic shore of Illyria (modern Croatia).

In 218 B.C., hearing that a Roman expedition was marching to Spain to support a revolt against Carthaginian allies, Carthage struck back. The Second Punic War (218–201 B.C.) began with the arrival of a Carthaginian force in Italy under the leadership of perhaps the most brilliant and certainly the most famous of Carthaginian generals, Hannibal (247–c. 183 B.C.). Counting on the support of the local population, he crossed into Spain and descended on Italy over the Alps with a huge supply train, inflicting several painful defeats on Roman forces. The last, at Cannae in 216, virtually annihilated a Roman army.

Hannibal besieged Rome, but he was unable to sustain his momentum. His forces were a long way from home, and the Romans effectively blocked the arrival of reinforcements. The Italian population was still too fearful of Roman reprisals to aid Hannibal, and Rome remained a formidable opponent fighting on home territory. As a result, Hannibal and his troops spent years waiting for the formation of an anti-Roman alliance that never materialized. The Romans seized the opportunity to rebuild their forces and sent a counterexpedition to North Africa to invade Carthaginian territory under the young and ambitious general Scipio.

When the victorious Romans demanded uncompromising peace terms, Hannibal returned with his troops to reinforce the Carthaginians. In 202 the entire Carthaginian army was defeated at Zama in North Africa and forced to surrender, and peace was concluded the following year. Carthage was divested of its entire empire, including Spain, and was left with only a small strip of territory around the city itself, in modern Tunisia. It was forced to pay a crippling indemnity and permanently disband its armed forces. The once proud Carthaginians were reduced to impotence, and the expression "Carthaginian peace" entered the language, denoting a dictated settlement designed to crush an opponent permanently.

Conquests in the East

Throughout the following century the Romans continued to fight sporadically in Spain, where they established control in a series of brutal campaigns. The helpless Carthaginians, who had attracted Roman enmity by regaining some of their former prosperity, were completely destroyed in the Third Punic War of 149–146 B.C. Their city was leveled, and its inhabitants were sold into slavery.

In theory, Roman involvement in the affairs of Greece and the Asian kingdoms was for the purpose of defending and even "liberating" the Greeks from their Hellenistic rulers. Already by the end of the third century B.C., Greek art and literature had become fashionable at Rome. Victory over the Carthaginians had fed the Romans' pride and arrogance. Triumphant in the western Mediterranean, they looked to the rich kingdoms of Asia as both potential enemies and attractive conquests. Allegedly advocating the cause of Greek freedom, first in Macedon and then in Asia, Roman forces fought a series of wars to gain control there.

The first step was to secure the Adriatic Sea, which was begun in the First Illyrian War of 229–228 B.C. In the following years the Romans became involved in a series of wars with Philip V of Macedon and Antiochus III of the Seleucid empire, and by 200 B.C. they were

MAP 6.2 ROMAN ITALY

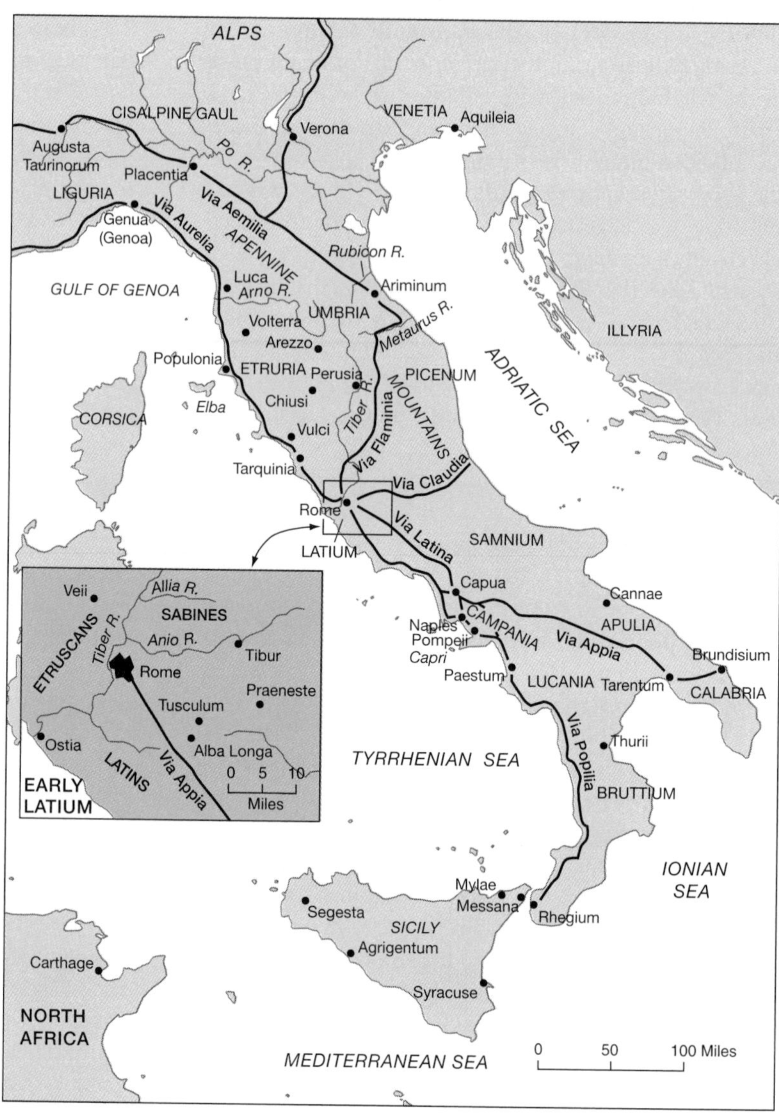

committed in the Hellenistic east on a massive scale. The next half century saw complex battles and negotiations in western Asia in which territories of the Hellenistic kingdoms either gained their independence or were merged with other states. The Greek poleis threw off Macedonian domination in 197 B.C., thanks to Roman assistance.

In the case of Pergamum, King Eumenes decided that collaboration offered better prospects than opposition. Pergamum continued to serve Roman interests in Asia as a client state until 133 B.C., when Attalus III willed it to Rome in a last attempt to win favorable treatment for his people. Any illusion the Greeks may have had that Roman campaigns against Macedon or the Seleucid empire of Syria were for their benefit was shattered when a defensive league of Greek poleis was crushed at Pydna in 168. In 146 another Greek army that refused to accept Roman "liberation" was defeated at Corinth. The Romans razed the city and shipped its artworks to Rome. Other temporary beneficiaries of Roman aid also paid with their freedom. The Romans supported the Jewish revolt of the Maccabees in 167; two centuries later, a Roman army would destroy the last vestiges of Jewish independence and burn the temple in Jerusalem.

The Crisis of the Republic

By the end of the second century B.C. the Romans had constructed a huge empire of subject regions, client states, and nominally free kingdoms that stretched from Spain to western Asia. They had failed, however, to develop effective systems of administration, and the consequences were often chaotic. Provincial governors were frequently inefficient and corrupt. Patricians and wealthy

Roman relief sculpture (164 A.D.), Altar of the Matron, monument of Vettius Severus, questor of Colonia.

plebeians, enriched by their conquests, began to compete in piling up fortunes derived either from property in Italy or from the provinces.

Rome's imperial career had also affected the constitutional balance at home. The victories in the Punic Wars had enhanced the Senate's prestige. During the many years of fighting it had been necessary for some authority to make decisions quickly and efficiently, and that task had fallen to the Senate. Among the powers it assumed was the right to prolong magistrates' terms of office when conditions of war made it necessary. Furthermore, by the end of the wars the Senate had taken control of foreign policy, and the provincial governors it appointed thus had unofficial license to extort what they could from their subjects. Laws against bribery were passed in 181 and 159 B.C., but to little effect; Rome's opponent in North Africa, King Jugurtha, was advised that "at Rome everything is for sale."

The poorer plebeians had lost rather than gained from the continued warfare. Rome's new territories had been won by citizen-soldiers, eager to return to their farms or businesses. In order to hold on to their conquests, the Romans now needed to maintain conscript troops outside Italy, but in many cases plebeians were unwilling to serve. On some occasions the tribune, as defender of plebeian rights, stepped in to arrest the consul conducting the conscription. In other cases the conscript had little choice. Many small plebeian farms had been swallowed up by the growth of large estates, or *latifundia,* whose wealthy owners bought public land and worked it by means of slaves made available by the wars. Thus the poorer plebeians who had survived economically by cultivating their plots had little choice other than to serve abroad or to join the growing number of unemployed in Rome. The urban mob that these social conditions produced was to prove a new and powerful force in Roman political life.

As the government of the empire grew ever more complex, divisions began to appear among the wealthy as well, both patrician and plebeian. Public contracts for tax collecting, construction work, or other projects were issued by the Senate. Because they were supposed to oversee the contracted work, senators were barred from appointing themselves and undertaking these contracts in their own names. The rich landowners who were not members of the Senate thus became the principal group to benefit from the large sums of money spent in and received from the provinces. This new social and economic class was known as the *equestrians,* or cavalry. The provision of a horse at public expense had been a mark of honor from earlier times; now it became a property qualification to distinguish between senators, with their inherited wealth, and the new class of equestrians. Of course, the formal exclusion of senators from lucrative work in the provinces, especially tax collecting, scarcely impeded their accumulation of wealth through bribery, payoffs, and the like. With the spoils of three continents at their disposal, the patrician and equestrian classes reaped immense fortunes. Meanwhile, the gap between the propertied elite and the poorer plebeians continued to widen.

The Gracchi

By the last third of the second century B.C. Rome faced a number of serious and interrelated problems. The great estates required increasing numbers of slave workers, while free agricultural laborers were all but disappearing as a class. There was little chance of agrarian reform as long as the members of the Senate saw it as contrary to their own interests. In 133 B.C., facing apparent deadlock, the tribune Tiberius Gracchus attempted to introduce major changes. He recommended that the government reclaim state land that had been illegally occupied, mostly by owners of large estates. A proposed commission would distribute the repossessed farmholdings to the landless. Tiberius' plan was approved by a plebeian assembly made unusually large by the crowds of poor exfarmers who had poured into Rome to vote for the measure. To achieve this, however, Tiberius had bypassed the Senate and illegally blocked the veto of a fellow tribune. Wealthy landowners claimed that he had acted unconstitutionally. He ran for a second term to implement

Hannibal: A Roman View

Livy's description of Hannibal was written some 200 years after the Second Punic War, yet it vividly conveys the Romans' wary respect for the Carthaginian general.

Hannibal was dispatched to Spain and on his first appearance attracted the interest of the army. The old soldiers thought that a younger Hamilcar had come back to them. They saw in him the same features, the same liveliness of expression, the same fire in the eyes. But shortly his resemblance to his father was only the least among their reasons for devotion to him. Never was an individual more perfectly suited both to obedience and to command. It would be hard to say whether the commander or the army loved him more. There was no one whom Hasdrubal [Hannibal's older brother] preferred to put in charge of any assignment which demanded bravery and vigor; nor was there any leader under whom the army fought with greater confidence and daring. When danger was to be faced it was Hannibal whose spirit was the boldest, and in a crisis his strategy was the shrewdest. Under no hardship did his energy wane or his spirits flag. He could face heat or cold with equal endurance. His appetite for food and drink were controlled by hunger and not by pleasure. His waking and sleeping were not fixed by day and night. What time remained after the task in hand was done he gave to sleep, and this without any need of soft bed or quiet. Many a time he could be seen lying on the ground among the sentries and pickets off duty, covered only with a soldier's cloak. His dress was no different from that of his fellow-soldiers, but his weapons and his horses were of the finest. He was the best among cavalry and infantry alike, always the first to go into battle and the last to leave any clash of arms.

These qualities were matched by equally great flaws of character: inhuman cruelty and a worse than Punic treachery which had no regard for the truth, held nothing sacred, was stopped by no fear of the gods or scruple at breach of faith. With such an endowment of faults and virtues he served for three years in Spain under the command of Hasdrubal, omitting no experience or training suitable for a man destined to become a great military leader.

Source: P. MacKendrick and H. M. Howe, eds., *Classics in Translation* (Madison: University of Wisconsin Press, 1966), vol. 2, p. 296.

the new law but was clubbed to death in street fighting on election day.

Tiberius' younger brother, Gaius, was elected tribune for 123 B.C. and again for the following year. More cautious than Tiberius, he buttressed his appeal to the plebeians by seeking the support of the equestrians. The right to collect taxes in Roman territory in Asia was for the first time put up for auction at Rome rather than meted out by the Senate, providing equestrians with the opportunity to compete for highly profitable monopolies. At the same time the membership of juries that tried provincial governors for corruption was, at Gaius' suggestion, limited exclusively to equestrians. Governors had always been drawn from the Roman Senate, and this gave the equestrians the chance to play watchdog over provincial administration and protect their own interests. Like his brother, Gaius was threatening the wealthy senatorial landowners, and despite his attempt to broaden his political base, he met with the same fate: early in 121 he and perhaps as many as 3,000 of his supporters were killed by mobs openly encouraged by the Senate.

The failure of the Gracchi demonstrated that the political system that had been devised for a small city 400 years earlier was inadequate for the governance of a vast empire. Furthermore, no ambitious politician could leave out of account two new forces on the political scene: the urban mob and the standing army. The first had been used against the Gracchi. The second, a professional fighting force whose primary loyalty was not to Rome but to whichever general led and paid it, was to play a crucial role in the careers of the next generation of politicians. Indeed, the men who struggled for power right up to the end of the republic—Marius, Sulla, Pompey, and Caesar—were all highly successful field commanders in their own right who could count on the loyalty of their troops.

Cornelia and the World of the Gracchi

In some ways even more remarkable than the Gracchi themselves was their mother, Cornelia. Born in the late 190s B.C., she was the younger daughter of Scipio Africanus, the victor of Zama, and Aemilia, whose brother Hannibal had slain. Cornelia was probably about 20 years old when she married the politically prominent plebeian Tiberius Sempronius Gracchus, who had been twice consul.

Cornelia bore Tiberius 12 children, of whom only 3—the future tribunes Tiberius and Gaius and their deformed sister Sempronia—survived. Widowed around 154 B.C., Cornelia was a diligent mother, allegedly boasting that her sons, rather than her jewelry, were her true ornaments. Cicero was impressed by the care she took with their education: "We read the letters of Cornelia," he wrote, ". . . from which it appears that they were reared more on their mother's discourse than on mother's milk." Another oft-repeated story asserted that she prodded her sons toward fame by claiming to be bored with her titles and lineage; certainly she was ambitious for them.

Controversy surrounds Cornelia's role in her sons' careers. Some contemporaries claimed that it was she who had urged Tiberius to take up the agrarian problem and to go over the Senate's head to the Assembly when his reforms were stalled. Others asserted that she and Sempronia were at least partly to blame for the murder of the latter's husband, Scipio Aemilianus, who had opposed the work of the land commissioners responsible for implementing Tiberius' reforms. Later she was accused of aiding Gaius' political activities, even to the point of hiring men to impersonate harvesters and agitate for her son. That Gaius felt obliged to respond to these attacks suggests at least some substance to the allegations.

The murders of both of her sons, and with them the hope for reform they represented, made Cornelia a tragic figure. Nonetheless she remained undaunted and continued to move proudly in Roman political circles as of old. At one point she rejected a marriage proposal from Ptolemy VII of Egypt, who wished the support of her eastern connections in his own dynastic quarrels. Toward the end of her life she lived at Misenum on the Bay of Naples, presiding over a celebrated literary salon.

Whether any of the writings of Cornelia have survived is unclear; Cicero, as we have seen, was familiar with some of her letters, although historians have questioned the authenticity of the fragments that remain. But her combination of ambition, fidelity, virtue, and personal modesty made her the archetypal Roman matron and one of the few figures of either sex in the later republic to win the general approbation of posterity.

Marius, Sulla, and the Rebellion of Spartacus

Two figures, Marius the populist and Sulla the aristocrat, dominated Roman political life from Marius' first consulship in 107 B.C. to Sulla's retirement in 79. Fierce opponents, each could claim military successes, Marius in Africa and Sulla in Italy, where the latter played a large part in crushing a revolt by Rome's Italian allies in the so-called Social War of 90–88 B.C. Marius' principal contribution to Rome was his reform of recruitment procedures. During his first consulship he abolished the need for members of the army to own property; the poverty-stricken could enlist and be armed at public expense. Men who joined did so not only for the pay but also in the hope that they would receive a grant of land at the end of their service.

Both Sulla and Marius, together with their followers, were responsible for bloody purges among their opponents, which plunged Rome repeatedly into civil war; neither provided even a temporary solution to Rome's real problems. Sulla ruled as dictator until he retired in 79 B.C. This was, in fact, a constitutional position, first created after Hannibal's victory at Cannae; the holder was appointed for six months by the two consuls, with the Senate's advice, to rule the state during an emergency. Sulla imposed a new constitution that attempted a return to the conservative and elitist concepts of the early republic. He doubled the size of the Senate and strengthened its powers, limited the tribunes' right of veto, and abolished their ability to legislate and take legal action. After Sulla stepped down, faction and class conflict resumed, including an uprising by Rome's most despised class, its slaves.

Enslaving prisoners had been a Roman practice since 396 B.C., when the citizens of the captured city of Veii were taken to Rome. Throughout the second century B.C. thousands of prisoners were shipped to Italy and put to work on the great estates. Plantation workers generally toiled in chain gangs and were locked up in underground barracks at night, but it was harder to control herdsmen, who had to be left free to tend their flocks. Slave uprisings were therefore a continuous threat and made travel through remote agricultural areas unsafe. In 73 B.C. a major revolt erupted, led by the Thracian gladiator Spartacus. An initial band of 74 men quickly swelled to an army of 70,000, and only massive intervention by the Roman army crushed the rebels. Some 6,000 of them were crucified as a warning to others.

In general, however, the Romans were liberal in granting freedom to domestic slaves, if not in their treatment of them during the years of servitude. Throughout the first century B.C. thousands of slaves were freed by their owners through a process called *manumission,* which required them to purchase their freedom. Many of them became shopkeepers, artisans, or clerks, although some practiced their skills as teachers or doctors. The freed slaves, or *liberti,* were subject to certain legal restrictions, but their children became full citizens.

Julius Caesar

The principal political contest of the generation following Sulla was between Pompey (106–48 B.C.), who called himself Pompey the Great and appointed himself defender of the Senate, and Julius Caesar (100–44 B.C.). Both men were military commanders as well as politicians. Pompey combined the virtues of his military calling—efficiency and good planning—with lack of principle, deviousness, and personal vanity. Caesar's talents were much more complex and versatile; some have called him Rome's greatest mind. A successful politician and orator and a lucid, elegant prose writer, he was also, as Pompey was not, a genuine political thinker. Caesar realized that the only sure way to achieve power was through military force. After making his mark in the politics of the capital between 65 and 62, he left Rome, first to serve as governor in Spain and then, in 58, in Gaul. He remained there for almost ten years and completed the conquest of the region, thereby bringing much of continental Europe north of the Alps into the orbit of Roman civilization.

Before leaving Rome, Caesar ensured his continuing influence by concluding a secret agreement in 59 B.C. to divide the power and patronage of the capital with Pompey and the wealthy businessman Crassus, who had made his political reputation by putting down Spartacus; this pact is known as the First Triumvirate. Pompey and Caesar cemented their alliance by the marriage of Caesar's daughter, Julia, to Pompey—a match that proved unexpectedly happy despite a considerable age difference. During Caesar's period in Gaul, however, both Crassus and Julia died, and Pompey, distrustful of the increasingly popular Caesar, forged close ties with the aristocrats in the Senate. When in January 49 B.C. the Senate commanded Caesar to relinquish his command, he illegally ordered his army to cross the Rubicon River, the boundary between Gaul and Italy.

Caesar's march to Rome with his victorious army made civil war inevitable. After a brief period of indecision, Pompey and his followers fled to Greece. Caesar followed him and defeated his forces at Pharsalus (48 B.C.). Pompey himself escaped to Egypt, whose ruler decapitated him and sent the embalmed head to Caesar as a means of currying favor. Caesar turned this to patriotic advantage by executing Pompey's murderers and erecting a statue to him in the Senate. Caesar spent the winter in Alexandria, where he entered into a liaison with the young queen of Egypt, Cleopatra. By the time he left, Cleopatra was pregnant. She named her son Caesarion and sent him to Rome. Although Caesar showered Cleopatra with presents and honors, he never returned.

By 46 B.C. Caesar had been appointed dictator, which gave him emergency powers to govern for up to six months. As dictator, he set about reorganizing the government both at home and in the provinces. Among his most lasting achievements was the creation of a unified code of civil law. Produced with the help of eminent legal experts, it served as a model for later times. His reformed calendar, based on the research of astronomers at Alexandria, was used in the West until the eighteenth century, and our present one, introduced by Pope Gregory XIII in 1582, is a modified form of it.

Caesar also launched an ambitious and wide-ranging series of reforms. He began an extensive public works program designed in part to take citizens off the welfare rolls and make them less susceptible to the violence that had become commonplace in Rome. To that end also he instituted a police force and relieved the overpopulation of the capital by sending 80,000 citizens into the provinces. He subsidized Italian farmers to restore the agricultural self-sufficiency of the peninsula and undertook the overhaul of provincial administration. To reduce political opposition, he packed the Senate with his own followers. But his plans had little time to take effect. On March 15, 44 B.C., he was assassinated by a band of senatorial conspirators led by a magistrate, Gaius Cassius, and the prominent aristocrat Marcus Brutus. The agony of the republic was to be prolonged for another 13 years.

A portrait bust of Julius Caesar made in Egypt in the late first century B.C.*, perhaps during Caesar's stay with Cleopatra.*

The End of the Republic

In the turmoil that followed Caesar's assassination, Mark Antony (83–30 B.C.), his former lieutenant, organized the attempt to avenge his death. He was joined by Caesar's young great-nephew, Octavius (63 B.C.–A.D. 14), whom Caesar had named in his will as his heir. On Caesar's death Octavius had arrived in Rome from the provinces to assume power. It was soon clear that Antony and Octavian (the name Octavius now took) were bound to clash. After the defeat of Caesar's assassins in 42 B.C. at Philippi in western Greece, an uneasy settlement placed Octavian in charge of the western provinces while Antony was dispatched to the east. To strengthen their ties and to protect Antony from the enticement of Cleopatra, whom he had met on an earlier tour of duty, he was persuaded to marry Octavia, Octavian's sister. A woman of firmness and tact, she seems to have curbed Antony's tendencies to sensuality and self-indulgence and maintained peaceful relations between her new husband and Octavian. From 39 to 37, Octavia and Antony administered the eastern provinces from their base in Athens.

Three years of domestic tranquility were enough for Antony. After a disastrous military operation in Syria, he escaped to Alexandria, where in 34 B.C. he made his union with Cleopatra official by the so-called Donations of Alexandria. This news was predictably exploited at Rome by Octavian, who depicted his rival as degenerate

THE ROMAN REPUBLIC

Period	Important events	Major writers
Early Republic (509–275 B.C.)	• Founding of the republic (509 B.C.) • Establishment of the Tribunate (494 B.C.) • Plebeian Assembly (471 B.C.) • Twelve Tables (c. 450 B.C.) • Licinian-Sextian Laws (367 B.C.) • Hortensian Law (287 B.C.) • Unification of Italy (c. 400–275 B.C.)	• Menander (Greek)
Overseas Conquest (275–146 B.C.)	• First Punic War (264–241 B.C.) • Second Punic War (218–201 B.C.) • Wars in the eastern Mediterranean (200–146 B.C.) • Third Punic War (149–146 B.C.)	• Ennius • Plautus • Terence • Cato the Elder
Late Republic (146–27 B.C.)	• Reforms of the Gracchi (134–121 B.C.) • First Consulate of Marius (107 B.C.) • Social War (90–88 B.C.) • Age of Sulla (88–79 B.C.) • First Triumvirate (59–49 B.C.) • Caesar's dictatorship (46–44 B.C.) • Second Triumvirate (43–36 B.C.) • Augustan settlement (27 B.C.)	• Lucretius • Catullus • Cicero • Julius Caesar

and corrupt. With Antony out of Rome, Octavian declared war on Egypt.

Cleopatra (69–30 B.C.) had her own ambitions. She was a Macedonian by birth and thus the descendant of Alexander the Great, and her native language was Greek. Yet she also considered herself to be the successor of the pharaohs and a descendant of the sun god Re. Like Alexander, she dreamed of uniting East and West in one great empire. Her liaison with Mark Antony was a gamble that, without the resistance of Octavian, might well have produced military success.

The end for Cleopatra and Mark Antony came in 31 B.C. at the naval battle of Actium in western Greece. When Antony's forces deserted, he and Cleopatra escaped to Egypt, where Antony committed suicide. Cleopatra attempted to ingratiate herself with Octavian, but, failing, she too took her life. Octavian was left as sole leader of the Roman world, and his victory marked the end of the republic.

Augustus and the Pax Romana

By the time of the battle of Actium, Rome had suffered more than a century of civil and external war. Political institutions had in large part ceased to function effectively, and much of Italy was in chaos. Yet when Octavian died in A.D. 14, Rome had attained political stability and commercial prosperity. Augustus—to use the title he assumed in 27 B.C.—formally inaugurated the empire, a period that lasted some 500 years in the West and nearly 1,500 in the East.

Augustus, remembering Caesar's fate, took great care to avoid the appearance of autocratic rule. He declined the title of *rex* (king) or dictator, preferring to be known simply as *princeps,* or first citizen, an honorific used for elder statesmen under the republic. At the same time, however, he was careful to retain the title of *imperator* (victor), which was granted to successful generals, and, like Caesar, he assumed the office of *pontifex maximus* (high priest) when it fell vacant. In addition, when he resigned the office of consul in 23 B.C., the Senate conferred on him the powers of a tribune for life. His successors were known by the title of imperator, which has come into English as *emperor.* It is thus with Augustus that we can speak of Rome as an empire in the political sense, that is, as possessing not merely a territorial empire but also an imperial form of government.

Augustus was careful to preserve republican institutions. Under his rule and that of his successors, the Senate met and Roman aristocrats continued to be elected to the consulship, but all decisions of importance originated with the emperor. Ostensibly, the form of Roman government was now a dyarchy (rule of two) in which the Senate and the emperor cooperated to administer the empire. In fact, the emperors made as much or as little use of the Senate as they chose. As commanders in chief of the army, they could be deposed only by military revolt or assassination.

Augustus himself restored the Senate to its former standards of birth, wealth, and conduct, gave it control of Rome's civic administration, and used its members to govern the inner provinces of the empire. He was outwardly deferential to it and claimed in his autobiography to have "transferred the state back into the hands of the Senate and the Roman people." But he never yielded to it except in trivial matters, and he ruled directly over the outer provinces of the empire. Augustus retained Egypt, the granary of the empire, as an imperial estate; he assumed the title of pharaoh and forbade any senator to set foot there without his consent.

Augustus reorganized the army, over which he likewise retained direct control. He fixed its size at 25 legions; regularized pay, pensions, and terms of service; and deployed it at key points throughout the empire. His own security force, the 9,000-man Praetorian Guard, was sworn to personal loyalty to him. Augustus skillfully used his religious authority as well. Casting himself as the champion of traditional Roman religion, he revived a number of old priesthoods, rebuilt more than 80 temples, and encouraged the worship of Venus (as the Romans had renamed the Greek goddess Aphrodite), from whom Julius Caesar had traced his lineage. Although he was careful not to present himself as a god in Italy, he tacitly permitted himself to receive divine homage in the provinces and encouraged the erection of temples, monuments, and statues to himself and to his wife, Livia, throughout the empire.

Augustus devoted considerable attention to restoring the economic and fiscal health of the empire. He introduced new censuses to assess the population, assets, and resources of the provinces, where the principal wealth of the empire lay. He staffed the financial bureaucracy with members of the equestrian class, thus reinstating them in their traditional role and providing a buffer against senatorial corruption.

The civil wars of the late republic had taken their toll in Italy, where the principal occupation remained farming. Owners of latifundia were encouraged to diversify their crops to guard against poor years or changes in the market. Many medium-sized farms specialized in the production of wine or olive oil, both of which were popular abroad and easy to export. The general rise in living standards produced by the Augustan peace led to a demand for luxury products such as peacocks and pheas-

View of the Roman Forum, with the Arch of Titus in the distance.

ants, so even a modest poultry ranch could be profitable. Augustus encouraged agriculture not only for its practical benefits but also as a symbol of the bounty guaranteed by political stability.

Italian industry flourished under Augustus, partly for obvious economic reasons and partly because the emperor seems to have favored businessmen and manufacturers rather than the ingrown, snobbish aristocracy. A style of pottery called Arretine was developed in the ceramics factories of Arezzo and other centers in central Italy; Arretine vessels were exported throughout the empire. Such demand required new, more efficient methods of production. One of the factories at Arezzo could mix 10,000 gallons of clay at a time, and similar mass production techniques were used for the extraction and working of metals. Furthermore, Augustus' building program throughout Italy stimulated demand for bricks, tiles, and other construction materials.

Augustan legislation stimulated industry and commerce throughout the provinces. Egypt, with its fine sand, became a center for glass manufacture, while Alexandria retained its importance as an international port for the buying and selling of raw materials. With a return to prosperity, the demand for luxury goods such as silk, rare fruits, and fine wines rose sharply. To some extent this could be satisfied by products from the provinces; the Greek island of Cos was famous for its silks, and dates, figs, and plums were imported from Spain. Supply stimulated yet more demand, and Roman traders found themselves exploring ever more distant markets.

In the late first century B.C., Roman sailors discovered that monsoon winds greatly aided the sea journey from Egypt to India. The trip there took some 40 days, and the speed with which commercial links grew is demonstrated by the large quantities of Arretine pottery discovered at ports on India's east coast. The Indian connection was valuable in itself, providing spices, jewels, ivory, and other exotic commodities. More important, it gave the Roman world better access to China, with its production of high-quality silk, than the dangerous overland route that passed through the territory of the warlike Parthians, the inhabitants of northeastern Persia. From the time of Augustus it was possible to transport Chinese products through Afghanistan, down the river Indus, and across the Indian Ocean to Syria and then Rome. Fashionable Romans were thus assured of luxury products, although some political leaders were concerned that the trade in luxury items seriously depleted stocks of gold and silver.

At Augustus' death the empire was peaceful, stable, and prosperous. Firm leadership and prudent reform were responsible for this. Augustus drew a clear distinction between political and administrative control. The former he kept in his own hands; the latter he dispersed as widely as the security of the empire permitted. Thus provincial autonomy and local self-government were stressed, as was respect for ethnic customs and cultures. This enabled Rome to control a very large empire with a minimum of centralized bureaucracy, and that in turn kept taxation at tolerable levels. Local self-government proved Augustus' happiest and most enduring innovation. It enabled the provinces to withstand the effects of erratic or tyrannical rulers and to prosper until the empire weakened in the third century A.D., when the Augustan system began to break down.

Social Legislation

Much of Augustus' social reform was intended to correct the general laxity that had developed during the last century of the republic. Comprehensive laws on marriage were introduced that rewarded large families and penalized the single, the childless, and people who married beyond childbearing age. Decrees were also issued to curb promiscuity and adultery, and Augustus exercised his own paternal rights directly, sending both his daughter and his granddaughter into exile for breaches of his code. In part this legislation reflected Augustus' attempt to promote the family as a social unit and his concern with the falling population of native Roman citizens. The slaves who had been freed during the previous century represented a foreign element in Italy that the emperor saw as a potential threat. Thus in addition to his encouragement of large families, he had laws passed that specifically limited the number of slaves who could be freed by their masters.

Augustus himself lived simply and unostentatiously, at least in public, and laid great emphasis on duty to the state as well as traditional values and morality. High society must have found the new austerity difficult to adapt to, and Augustus' successors were unable to maintain his high moral tone—nor, in most cases, were they much inclined to do so.

Augustan Literature and Art

A masterful propagandist, Augustus made full use of the arts to reinforce the impression of peace and prosperity. Much of the art produced at Rome during his reign was official, commissioned by the state to serve government purposes. Yet if he can justly be accused of cultural manipulation, it must be admitted that the art and literature of his age are of the highest quality.

The literary period of Augustan Rome is known as the Golden Age. Perhaps the greatest poet of the age, and one of the most influential figures of the Western literary tradition, was Publius Vergilius Maro, called Virgil (70–19 B.C.). His principal work, the *Aeneid,* an epic poem in 12 books, was commissioned to give the Romans their own national epic, worthy to stand alongside the *Iliad* and the *Odyssey.* It contains passages of patriotic fervor, recounting the mythical founding of Rome by Aeneas, son of Venus, after he fled from the ruins of Troy. Virgil consciously made his epic a Roman counterpart of Homer's works, thus firmly linking the glories of Rome to the Hellenistic cultural legacy. An earlier work of Virgil's, the *Georgics,* deals with one of the emperor's favorite themes, praising agriculture and the virtues of family life on the farm and offering practical advice on farming, forestry, and raising cattle and horses.

Among the other Roman poets of the period to praise country life was Horace (65–8 B.C.), a personal friend of both Virgil and Augustus, whose private secretary Horace became. A more worldly man than Virgil, Horace combined passion with irony to create a series of short odes that illuminated both Roman politics and his own refined sensibility. The leading prose writer of the time was Livy (59 B.C.–A.D. 17), whose *History of Rome,* also sponsored by Augustus, told the story of Rome's growth from its earliest days.

Peace and order were the goals of Augustus' administration and the subject of one of the most complex works of art produced during his reign, the *Ara Pacis,* or Altar of Peace, which combines episodes from Rome's mythic past with representations of Augustus and his family leading the way to the ceremony at which the altar is to be dedicated to the goddess Peace. In fact, beginning with Augustus' rule, Rome was to enjoy two centuries of relative civil security, known as the Pax Romana, or Roman Peace. It was an extraordinary accomplishment, but it was not without its price. The republic, despite its corruption and strife, had represented an ideal of self-government that was now abandoned. The exile of the poet Ovid (43 B.C.–A.D. 17), the witty and irreverent author of *The Art of Love,* showed the darker side of Augustus' campaign to reform morals, and the historian Livy's refusal to take his account of Rome down to his own time for fear of giving offense was no doubt only an example of the self-censorship imposed on art, scholarship, and political expression. Throughout the first decades of the empire an underground movement of political philosophers known loosely as the "Stoic opposition" continued to discuss principles of rational government and the possibility of restoring the republic. Many of the real or imagined members of this group lost their lives during the first century of the empire. Not all Ro-

MAP 6.3 THE ROMAN EMPIRE

mans, in short, succumbed to Augustan propaganda or confused order with liberty.

The Julio-Claudians

The one problem for which Augustus was unable to find a satisfactory solution was the choice of his successor. In the end he was forced to nominate his able but unpopular stepson, Tiberius (A.D. 14–37). The first five emperors, including Augustus himself, were related to one another as members of the Julian and Claudian clans. Thus the principle of hereditary succession was implicitly established, although as early as the reign of Claudius (A.D. 41–54) the right to select the family member chosen emperor was temporarily seized by the army, a precedent that was to prove dangerous.

The Julio-Claudian emperors do not make a particularly good case for the hereditary system of government. Claudius himself was effective enough. A dedicated administrator, he also achieved what even Julius Caesar had failed to do by adding Britain to the empire. Nor did Tiberius altogether deserve the hatred with which his contemporaries regarded him. Whatever his personal idiosyncrasies, which are spelled out in lurid detail by the historians Tacitus (c. 55–c. 117) and Suetonius (c. 69–c. 160), the Augustan peace was maintained throughout his reign.

The other two Julio-Claudians, however, were a very different matter. Gaius, better known as Caligula, or "Little Boots" after a childhood nickname, came to the throne in A.D. 37 amid general relief at the passing of Tiberius. By the time of his assassination in 41, he had a reputation for criminal insanity that has endured; among his more whimsical acts was declaring a horse his prime minister. If Nero (54–68) surpassed the excesses of Caligula, and in certain respects he did, the greater length of his reign is at least in part responsible. He was protected from his worst instincts during its first five years by his mother, Agrippina, but after ordering her killed in 59, he organized a reign of terror against the aristocracy. He may not have deliberately started the great fire that destroyed Rome in 64, as legend states, but he certainly took advantage of it to build an immense palace, the so-called

Golden House of Nero, and to persecute the Christians, whom he accused of starting the conflagration.

The Flavians and the "Good" Emperors

Nero committed suicide after being proscribed by the Senate. His death was followed in 69 by a year of confusion in which no fewer than four generals proclaimed themselves emperor. The final victor, Vespasian (69–79), was the first emperor to die peacefully since Tiberius. A professional soldier, hardworking and conscientious, he did much to repair the damage wrought by Nero and reasserted the Augustan policy in the provinces. He also gave Rome one of its most famous monuments by turning an artificial lake that had been made for Nero within the walls of his Golden House into the Colosseum.

Vespasian had little better luck than Augustus in finding a successor. His two sons, Titus and Domitian, were groomed to succeed him. Titus, the elder son, served his father as general in the Roman province of Judea, annexed by Rome in A.D. 6, where disturbances had broken out in the last years of Nero's reign. Vespasian himself had commanded Roman forces in 66, when the Jews of Caesarea and Jerusalem protested their lack of civil equality. The revolt at Caesarea was suppressed, but at Jerusalem the protestors remained active. In 70, Roman forces under Titus finally crushed the revolt, destroyed the temple of the Jews, and abolished the Jewish national council, the Sanhedrin.

By the time of his accession, Titus was known for his cruelty, and his well-publicized love affair with Berenice, sister of the Jewish king Julius Agrippa II, had given Rome a subject for gossip. When he came to power, he proved a modest and popular ruler, but a fever cut short his reign barely two years later. Domitian (81–96) continued his father's policies of maintaining efficient government and improving provincial defenses and administration, but, victim of his own paranoia, he constructed the apparatus of a police state, instituting a complex system of state spies and informers.

Prominent Roman political leaders could take no more. With the approval of the Senate, a group of conspirators determined that an elderly senator of unimpeachable character would be chosen to serve as immediate successor to Domitian. Aided by the Senate, he would select as his successor someone who seemed qualified for the position and adopt him as his son. The scheme worked well. Domitian was assassinated in 96 and replaced by Nerva (96–98), who was doubly qualified by his age (66) and by the fact that he was childless. Nerva, in turn, adopted one of the most distinguished generals and provincial administrators of his day, Trajan (98–117).

The Pantheon, Rome. The inscription, which dates the building from the third consulship of Agrippa (27 B.C.), must have been intended by Hadrian as a tribute to Agrippa's master and friend, Augustus.

Thus merit rather than birth or brute force was responsible for a series of outstanding Roman emperors, for Trajan, in his turn, was to adopt as his successor the able and cultivated Hadrian (117–138). The system of adoption continued in the selection of the next two emperors, Antoninus Pius (138–161) and Marcus Aurelius (161–180). With Trajan and Hadrian, they provided an extended and much needed period of stability. Under Trajan the borders of the empire expanded to their fullest extent, and Hadrian successfully consolidated them. He traveled tirelessly throughout the provinces to see that imperial defenses and administration were strengthened. The reign of Hadrian, perhaps the most gifted and complex of all the emperors, marked the high point of imperial civilization, but it was tainted by the suppression of another Jewish revolt, led by Simon Bar-Kochba ("Son of the Star"), which ended in the extermination of most of the Jewish population of Judea in 133.

Life in the Roman Capital: Imperial Pomp and Urban Squalor

By the time of Hadrian's reign Rome's center had become filled with temples, monuments, and public buildings, many of which have partially withstood the ravages of time, barbarian invaders, and Renaissance builders looking for bricks or marble for their own palaces and churches. Roman architecture and engineering had a lasting effect on later styles. In particular, the Roman use of columns, arches, and domes has been widely imitated since the eighteenth century in public building in Europe and the Americas.

One of the greatest domed buildings, the Pantheon, designed by Hadrian himself, was constructed around 126. Its imposing portico (or porch), containing 16 monolithic granite columns, leads into the central rotunda, the roof of which consists of a huge concrete dome. The building is lit only by a central *oculus,* or eye, in the top of the dome. As the sun moves across the sky, its rays travel around the inside of the Pantheon, whose form thus became symbolic of the world itself.

The Forum, where the early political life of the young republic had been concentrated, remained at the heart of the city's activities. During the empire, however, effective political control passed to the emperor and his staff, who lived on the Palatine (from which our word *palace* is derived), the hill overlooking the ancient assembly place of the people. Augustus' house there (which can still be visited) is a surprisingly, if characteristically, modest structure. Domitian, with his obsessive need for protection, began the construction of a huge imperial palace, the Domus Augustana. This palace, extended by his successors, contained its own race track and incorporated a private viewing stand from which the emperor could watch the races in Rome's main public stadium, the Circus Maximus.

According to tradition, racing and blood sports had been introduced into Rome by the Etruscans. By the time of the empire, chariot races and gladiatorial combats were held on a massive scale before a vast public; in its heyday the Circus Maximus had places for more than 300,000 people. Prizes were very large; a successful charioteer could easily amass a fortune and become the idol of a rabid fan club. There were four teams, the Reds, Whites, Blues, and Greens, each with its ardent supporters, and rivalry was intense.

Life in Imperial Rome

An embittered description of life in imperial Rome was penned by the Roman satirist Juvenal.

So the day goes by with a lovely order of business:
First, this handout; then the forum, the courts of Apollo,
And the triumphal statues, including some lousy Egyptian's,
At the base of which only pissing's permitted.
There they go, the poor souls, old clients, weary and hopeless,
Though the last hope to leave is always that of a dinner,
They must buy cabbage now, and a little kindling to cook it.
Meanwhile, all by himself, on a couch unshared, their good king will
Gobble and guzzle the choicest products of land and ocean.
Down goes a whole estate; from such luxurious tables,
Broad and antique, down goes a whole estate at one sitting.
This will kill parasites off, at least; but who can endure this
Luxury, grudging and cheap? A whole roast boar for one gullet
When good custom decrees this is the fare for a party?
You will get yours pretty soon, when you go and undress in your bathroom,
Trying to ease your gut's distending burden of peacock.
Hence come sudden deaths, too sudden for old men to make wills.
What a good laugh for the town at all of the dinner tables!
Hear the disgruntled friends cheer at the funeral service!

Source: Juvenal, *The Satires,* trans. R. Humphries (Bloomington: Indiana University Press, 1958), p. 22.

A large plastic scale model of Rome in A.D. *350 showing the Circus Maximus in the center and the Domus Augustana behind. Note the arches of the aqueduct to the front.*

The principal stage at Rome for individual gladiatorial contests was the Colosseum, which held 50,000 spectators. There were three types of gladiators: the Samnite was heavily armed with a long oblong shield, the Thracian relied on a small round shield, and the Retiarius carried only a net and dagger in one hand and a short pronged spear in the other. In general, combats ended with the death or surrender of one of the participants. In the case of surrender it was up to the crowd (or the emperor, if he was present) to decide the loser's fate. As the empire grew and the Romans had access to more exotic creatures, animal contests (either against gladiators or between animals) became increasingly popular. In the "games" of A.D. 249, fully 1,000 pairs of gladiators fought, and among the animals killed were 32 elephants, 10 elks, 10 tigers, and 60 lions. Such entertainment reveals a darker side of Roman culture.

Emperors exploited popular tastes by organizing special games, such as the one in 249, to keep the urban masses content. This policy of "bread and circuses," by which rulers attempted to control their often unruly subjects, also entailed the construction of centers for the distribution of grain and the sale of basic commodities such as wine and oil at subsidized prices. The provision of cheap grain for the Roman masses had begun as early as the tribunate of Gaius Gracchus (123–122 B.C.). By 58 B.C. free grain was being provided for any citizen who needed it, and this remained the case throughout the history of the empire. The magistracy in charge of the distribution of the grain dole, the Annona, was one of the most important public offices.

Rome was also provided with a plentiful supply of fresh water. A huge system of aqueducts connected pipes through which millions of gallons of water flowed each day; the water fed public fountains and baths as well as the private homes of the well-to-do. The street drains were covered, an improvement over the open sewers of earlier times. (After the fall of Rome, open sewers were to become the norm again until the nineteenth century.)

For all the ingenuity of its public works, however, imperial Rome was overcrowded, and life must often have been uncomfortable. Most Romans lived in apartment blocks, of which there were some 45,000. Laws regulated the height of these buildings to discourage the construction of unsound structures, but buildings sometimes collapsed, and fire was a constant hazard. The streets were crowded and noisy, and traffic jams were a frequent problem: descriptions of the squabbling and brawling between carriage drivers sound all too familiar to the modern big-city dweller. It is little wonder that at weekends and in summer, affluent Romans escaped to their rural villas. Hadrian imported all the convenience of the city to his immense villa at Tivoli, which contained libraries, theaters, baths, and quarters for hundreds of servants.

Life in the Provinces and on the Frontier

The same dependable engineering that provided the capital with water linked the city, by means of a vast road network, to the farthest corners of the provinces. Good communications were essential for maintaining efficient government, and Roman roads are the most visible remains of the Roman achievement. The main roads connecting Rome to other parts of Italy were begun in the fourth century B.C. Rome's armies included builders who surveyed and laid roads for supplies and reinforcements in conquered territories and provinces. By the time their conquest was complete, each province was thus provided with an effective network of communications. The thousands of miles of roads were well maintained and provided with milestones, and in the time of Augustus a column was erected in the Roman Forum that displayed the distances between Rome and the principal cities of the empire.

Provincial Life in Southern Europe, North Africa, and Asia

An empire as vast as that ruled by Trajan and Hadrian encompassed an enormous diversity of people, culture, language, and religion. The average Roman soldier or administrator probably felt most at home in Greece or the Greek cities of Asia Minor, where he was surrounded by art and architecture of the kind that had conditioned Roman taste. Athens, although no longer of political significance (its former rival, Corinth, was the capital of the Roman province of Achaea), was always a cultural and intellectual center. Augustus provided it with a fine new marketplace, and Hadrian had a public library built there. Even in the Greek world, however, there were cultural differences. The Greeks, for example, were fond of serious music, which held little interest for the Romans, and the Greeks showed no enthusiasm for gladiatorial contests. Even Greek theaters had to be adapted for the performance of Roman plays by the construction of a permanent stage set.

Elsewhere in the provinces, where local culture was less developed and new cities were built, the Romans created an environment more to their taste. Many cities in southern France and Spain still have their Roman amphitheaters, and Roman public baths were built throughout the empire. One of the most elaborate sets of baths were those at Leptis Magna in North Africa, which rival even those of the capital for size. Like many other public works, they were paid for by a wealthy private citizen rather than by the state.

The generally mild climate of the Mediterranean region meant that life in the Roman provinces of North Africa, Spain, or western Asia was in many respects similar to that in Italy. Large public squares were adorned with temples and public buildings such as baths and theaters, and private houses often included gardens. The best-preserved of these houses can be seen at Pompeii.

Pompeii: Life in a Provincial Town

On August 24, A.D. 79, the volcano Vesuvius, which stands above the Bay of Naples, erupted. The lava that flowed from it and the pumice and ash that were spewed out buried a number of small towns. The most famous of these is Pompeii, located 10 miles southeast of the volcano. The finds excavated there in the past 250 years provide detailed evidence about life in a provincial town of the period—from the shrines of the religious cults and the houses and gardens to the meals Pompeiians had prepared at the time of the eruption.

Lying some 150 miles south of Rome, Pompeii was a prosperous town of 20,000 people that served both as a commercial center for its region and as a holiday resort for Romans of modest means who sought to escape the heat of summer. It provides an impressive picture of the pleasant but modest lifestyle of the provinces. Houses were spacious and comfortable, and the frescoes that decorated them were often of high quality. Many houses had private gardens, sheltered from the noise of the streets. The furniture, tableware, and other household goods were often elaborately designed.

Pompeii's layout followed the Greek system of town planning, adapted to the irregularities of its hillside. Long, narrow residential blocks were separated by narrow access roads running at right angles to the main avenues. As in all town plans of this kind, there are two principal arteries: the *cardo,* running north-south, and the *decumanus,* running east-west.

The town contained three public baths, a concert hall, a theater, and an amphitheater capable of accommodating all the citizens, as well as houses of prostitution; a famous sign in the form of an erect phallus pointed to the red-light district. The main square or forum was closed to vehicular traffic; about it were grouped public buildings, including a *basilica,* or large hall, that was the setting for Pompeii's legal and financial activities. At the opposite end of the forum was the main temple, dedicated to Jupiter. Just beyond it was another temple, consecrated to the emperor Augustus, whose memory by the first century A.D. was revered throughout the empire.

Excavation at other towns buried by Vesuvius suggests that Pompeii was far from the most prosperous site in the region. Some of the villas at nearby Herculaneum are grander than anything at Pompeii, particularly the lavish waterfront homes with large windows that opened on the view. Recent excavation at Oplontis has revealed a magnificent villa.

In addition to serving the needs of tourists, Pompeii and the neighboring towns had their own commercial life. The largest building in Pompeii's forum, for example, was neither religious nor political; it was a large hall for the clothmakers and dyers that combined storage and sales facilities with a meeting place for fabric manufacturers. Nearby was a large open market, the Marcellum, at which farmers sold their produce. At its center, where fishmongers had their stands, was a pool connected to underground sewers, in which the sellers cleaned their fish; it was found filled with scales. Other shops in the city sold utensils, wine and olive oil, and bread, including flat loaves that look like modern pizza bases. In addition to the usual artisans, Herculaneum boasted a colony of artists.

A number of toilet facilities, including a communal one across from the Marcellum, were found in Pompeii. The provision of such facilities throughout the empire was one of Vespasian's contributions to Western culture. To this day in Italy a public urinal is known as a *vespasiano.*

Provincial Life in the North

The northern provinces present a different picture. In the rich farmland of northern France, life was concentrated not in cities but around country villas. The largest of these contained, in addition to farming establishments, small factories turning out pottery, bricks, ironwork, and other materials useful for the armies guarding the northeastern frontier against hostile Germanic tribes. The grain and wool produced by the smaller establishments served the farms themselves, which seem to have been run by slaves, and the neighboring troops.

Britain, one of the remotest provinces, was the northern frontier, for the Romans never gained control over what is now modern Scotland. Agricola, who governed Britain from 78 to 84, did what he could to Romanize the local population, and in the south Roman ideas and customs took root fairly quickly. The capital, Londinium (most of which lies beneath modern London), developed into a city of some size, and Roman villas and baths have been uncovered throughout southern England.

The Romans' last major extension of their frontiers is recorded in detail on the monument known as Trajan's Column. In 101 and again in 104 Trajan led expeditions to subdue the Dacians, whose territory in modern Romania lay to the east of the river Danube, previously a frontier. To celebrate Trajan's victory and the submission of the Dacians to Rome, a 125-foot column was erected in Trajan's Forum in Rome that shows the campaigns in vivid detail: the crossing of the Danube, the Roman army building camps and bridges, the harangues of Trajan, and scenes of battle and torture. Here is carved no mere celebration of Roman triumph but a vivid iconographic record of the endurance needed by emperor and foot soldier alike to create and maintain the empire.

Women in Roman Society

With the growth of empire and of contact with the Hellenized East, the position of upper-class women became freer. Wealthy and aristocratic women were able to preside over literary salons and to dabble in high politics. The salons appear to have been of some cultural importance from the days of the Flavian dynasty to the empress Julia Domna (died A.D. 217). Some women won fame as orators, and political demonstrations by women were not unknown. In 195 B.C. the women of Rome gathered to demand repeal of the Oppian Law, which, having confiscated most of their gold for the war effort against Hannibal, had been prolonged as a peacetime tax. On a similar occasion in 42 B.C., when women were taxed to pay the expenses of the civil war, a group of them burst into the Forum, and their spokeswoman, Hortensia, made an impassioned speech:

> **Why should we pay taxes when we do not share in the offices, honors, military commands, nor in short, the government, for which you fight between yourselves with such harmful results? . . . Let war with the Celts or Parthians come, we will not be inferior to our mothers when it is a question of common safety. But for civil wars, may we never contribute nor aid you against each other.[1]**

The legal position of Roman women was, as in Greece, strictly subordinate. In the intensely patriarchal culture of early Rome, the male head of the family literally had life and death powers over the members of his household. Adult males were emancipated at their father's death, but women were subject, at least in theory, to the guardianship of a male relative until marriage. Roman law assumed the incapacity of women to deal with matters of contract, property, and inheritance.

There were two kinds of marriage, with or without *manus,* the equivalent of a transfer of paternal authority to the husband. Marriages without *manus* left the bride freer but also with fewer rights. The consent of both partners was required for betrothal, but a woman could refuse a prospective husband only if she could show that he was morally unfit. With or without *manus,* the bride's father continued to exercise considerable supervision over his daughter and could, as in Greece, initiate divorce.

Divorce among the upper classes in the late republican and imperial periods was surprisingly casual. No legal reason was required for it, and unless scandal was involved, it carried no particular stigma. Despite the official exhortations to increase childbearing, infanticide and abortion were commonly practiced; in fact, infanticide did not become a moral offense until the third century A.D. Among the many advertised techniques for contraception was the suggestion that a woman hold her breath at the moment of male ejaculation.

Roman matrons were expected to master such traditional domestic skills as spinning and weaving. In practice, they left these tasks to their slaves, exercising only general supervision of the household. With little restriction on their movements, they were able to visit, shop, and attend public functions. In this and other respects they enjoyed far greater freedom than their Greek counterparts.

At the apex of the social scale, some women enjoyed extraordinary honors. The erection of statues to the women of prominent Roman families was imitated by provincial governors, who put up likenesses of their wives. Some women were granted citizenship and even held public office in late Hellenistic Greece, a practice that continued into Roman times. A number of empresses were deified after death, becoming part of the official state religion.

For the great majority of Roman women, life was quite different. Most of these women fell into three broad categories: slaves, freedwomen, and the freeborn poor. The slaves of well-to-do families were perhaps the best off economically; they were permitted to accumulate property and even to buy other slaves. Their duties were varied, including cooking, cleaning, clothesmaking, and the care and nursing of children. More specialized slaves might serve as secretaries, ladies' maids, masseuses, entertainers, and midwives. Some acquired considerable education. Because there was always more demand for male slaves, however, slave daughters were often left to die of exposure or sold. All female slaves, whatever their function, were used sexually by their masters; Cato the censor, in addition to exercising his own prerogatives, gave his male slaves access to the women of the household in return for a fee.

Slaves might buy their freedom or be manumitted through marriage. Freedwomen comprised a large part of the Roman working class, serving as laundresses, shopkeepers, waitresses, and prostitutes or working at artisanal trades or as domestics. Some attained prosperity, but many continued to work for their former masters. Freeborn women enjoyed a higher status than any slave, even slaves who worked in the imperial household, and often wielded considerable influence. They were discouraged from marrying slaves, and in A.D. 52 a senatorial decree reduced those who did to the status of slaves of their husbands' masters. Some freeborn women purchased the freedom of male slaves in order to marry them, but this practice was subsequently outlawed. Under the fourth-century ruler Constantine it was made a capital offense for a woman to cohabit with a slave, and the slave himself was to be burned to death.

Unlike notable women of the upper classes, whose lives were often commemorated, we have little biographical information about the great mass of Roman women. Their position, restricted as it was, did offer some opportunity for mobility and self-expression and in these terms compared favorably with that of the women of Han China. The epitaph of one woman, Claudia, must serve for the anonymous history of many:

> **Stranger, what I have to say is short. Stop and read it through. This is the unlovely tomb of a lovely woman. Her parents named her Claudia. She loved her husband with her whole heart. She bore two sons, one of whom she leaves on earth; the other she has placed beneath the ground. She was charming in conversation, yet her conduct was appropriate. She kept house; she made wool.[2]**

The Roman Achievement

The Romans' mission, as defined by Virgil, was to "rule the world, show mercy to the defeated, and strike down the proud." From the beginning, Roman culture was imitative rather than original. The first Roman poet of whom anything is known is Ennius (239–169 B.C.), a writer the Romans themselves called the father of Roman poetry. Ennius adapted tragedies from Greek and used Greek metrical schemes to write his *Annals,* an epic chronicle of Rome; almost all his work is lost. The first writers whose work has survived in any quantity, the comic playwrights Plautus (c. 251–184 B.C.) and Terence (c. 195–159 B.C.), turned Greek comedies into Latin and generally adapted them to Roman tastes, with results that were lively and often earthy.

The last years of the republic produced a rich body of literature. The poetry of Catullus (c. 84–c. 54 B.C.) is renowned for its uninhibited satire and eroticism, and his account of an unhappy affair with the girl he calls Lesbia is painful and candid. *On the Nature of Things,* by Lucretius (c. 99–55 B.C.), expounds the materialist teachings of Epicurus in one of the world's greatest philosophical poems. Caesar himself left us the history of his military campaigns in Gaul, written in a simple but gripping style.

Perhaps the most representative literary and political figure of the late republic was Marcus Tullius Cicero (106–43 B.C.). A successful lawyer and politician, Cicero published many of his speeches, the rhetorical power of which serves as a reminder of the Romans' cultivation of oratory. Cicero also wrote philosophical works and took an active part in politics, but he is best remembered for the personal correspondence that he kept to be published after his death. His nearly 900 letters provide an incomparable picture of the man and his world, his political judgments, his literary tastes, and his personal relations. If they often reveal Cicero's weaknesses—his vanity, his reluctance to make decisions, and his stubbornness—they confirm his humanity and sensitivity. His weaknesses proved ultimately fatal; proscribed in 43 B.C., he was assassinated, and his severed head was nailed to the rostrum of the Senate.

The Romans also paid a good deal of attention to practical matters. Cato (234–149 B.C.) published a guide to farming, as did Varro (116–27 B.C.), Rome's first public librarian, who also wrote on language and grammar. A work from the late first century B.C., Vitruvius' *On Architecture,* influenced Renaissance architects such as Bramante and Michelangelo. Sextus Frontinus (c. A.D. 30–104), who directed Rome's water system, wrote a fascinating treatise on aqueducts.

If the Augustan Age saw in Virgil the apex of Roman poetry, the so-called Silver Age that followed found its historian in Cornelius Tacitus (c. A.D. 55–c. 120). In his *Histories* and his *Annals* he vividly portrayed the corruption of the imperial court, which he contrasted with the lost virtue of the republic. His *Germania,* a description of the German tribes that had successfully resisted

Cicero on His Daughter's Death

Cicero's letter to his friend Atticus conveys the effect on him of his daughter's death.

Astura, 15 May 45 B.C.

To Atticus

I think I shall conquer my feelings and go from Lanuvium to my house at Tusculum. For either I must give up my property there for ever—since my grief will remain the same, though I shall become able to conceal it better—or if not it does not matter in the least whether I go there now or in ten years' time. The place will not remind me of her any more than the thoughts which consume me all the time, day and night. You will be asking me if there is no comfort to be derived from books. I am afraid that in this situation they have the contrary effect. Without them I might have been tougher; an educated man is not insensitive or impervious enough.

So do come as you wrote you would, but not if it is inconvenient. A couple of letters will be enough. I will come and meet you, if necessary. Whatever you can manage, so be it.

Source: Cicero, *Selected Works,* trans. M. Grant (Harmondsworth, England: Penguin Books, 1960), p. 87.

incorporation into the empire in Augustus' time, similarly contrasts their hearty independence with the decadence of imperial Rome.

The Silver Age was characterized by satire. Petronius (died A.D. 66) poked fun at the self-importance of rhetoricians and the self-indulgence of the newly rich in his comic novel *Satyricon.* Lucan (39–65) and Juvenal (c. 60–c. 127) lampooned Roman mores in verse, as did Martial (c. 40–c. 104), whose pithy epigrams spared no vice or folly:

> *You're so alike, you're matched for life:*
> *A nitwit man, his nitwit wife.*
> *(I wonder then why it should be*
> *That such a pair cannot agree?)*[3]

Rhetoric, philosophy, natural science, and history were among the chief subjects of Roman prose. Seneca (c. 5 B.C.–A.D. 65) wrote Stoic treatises as well as tragedies in the Greek style, and Quintilian (c. 35–c. 100) composed what remained the standard work on Latin rhetoric. Pliny the Elder (23–79) left behind many volumes of a natural history, and the correspondence between his nephew Pliny the Younger (c. 62–c. 113), governor of Bithynia, and the emperor Trajan offers a vivid picture of the daily life of a provincial administrator in Asia Minor. Tacitus' contemporary Plutarch (c. 46–c. 120) wrote a highly influential set of biographies called *Parallel Lives,* comparing Greek and Roman historical personalities. The practice of literature could be a dangerous profession in imperial Rome; Lucan and Seneca were both compelled to commit suicide by Nero, and Juvenal is said to have been exiled by Domitian.

In a sense, the greatest Roman contribution to literature was the Latin language itself. Latin was the language of the early writers of the Christian church and remained the common link between people of culture in the West virtually until our own time. It is still used for scientific nomenclature and remains the official language of the Roman Catholic church. It evolved into all the Romance languages, including French, Italian, Spanish, Portuguese, and Romanian, and was a root of English and German as well.

The Romans were awed by the brilliance of Greek visual art, and many of their own chief monuments are marked by a dependence on classical models. Yet in at least two major fields the Romans developed an independent style. Roman portraiture broke with the idealizing classical style. Taking their cue from Hellenistic examples, Roman artists learned to use physical appearance to convey character. Many of the best Roman portraits are revealing psychological documents; that of Cicero, for example, reveals his smugness as well as his humanity.

In architecture most of all, the Romans expressed their need to construct and to dominate. Whereas Greek buildings are generally meant to be seen from the outside, Roman buildings consciously enclose their occupants. The Pantheon is a striking example of this, as are the imperial baths and, on an even grander scale, monumental complexes such as Trajan's Forum, which could accommodate thousands of people. The invention of concrete in the first century B.C. and the growing mastery of the principles of stress and counterstress enabled architects to experiment with forms—arches and vaults—that passed into the Western architectural tradition. The theaters, stadiums, libraries, markets, temples, and other public buildings constructed on three continents are proof of the high quality of Roman engineering.

Roman Law and the Ideal of Justice

Beyond the Latin language itself, Rome's major contribution to civilization was its legal system, the principles of which still undergird the jurisprudence of most European countries, Quebec, Louisiana, and Latin America. As Roman law evolved, two fundamental concepts developed: that judicial decisions must be based on equity rather than on the rigid application of the law and that all persons of the same status enjoyed identical legal rights. Most cases were decided by a judge (*judex*), who applied the appropriate law (*jus*). The judge could seek the advice of a specialist learned in the law (*juris prudens*), who assisted him both in interpreting it and in applying it equitably to the case at hand. Their function was carried out under the watchful eyes of citizens, since trials and suits were conducted in public.

Other magistrates, especially praetors, whose main function was to act as judges in civil cases, had the power to make and shape law by issuing edicts at the outset of their annual term. In these edicts they enunciated the principles by which they intended to interpret legislation. This practice—subject to legislative review—was more efficient than amending laws in the Senate or the Assembly to conform to changing circumstances and made for speedier justice. As the empire developed, imperial edicts began to replace praetors' edicts, signaling a further consolidation of imperial power.

Like other ancient societies, the Romans at first applied their laws—the *jus civile,* or civil law—only to themselves, leaving visiting foreigners without rights in the absence of a treaty between their state and Rome.

This impeded commercial development, and magistrates built up a body of law—the *jus gentium,* or law of nations—applicable to all persons, citizen or alien. Gradually the two forms of law adopted common principles and procedures and were applied to resident aliens as well. With the extension of citizenship to most of the free population in A.D. 212, a single law covered most of the empire. Most women, as noted, were legally subordinate and subject to male guardianship, but their rights of property and consent were gradually liberalized.

The Empire in Crisis

At its height in the mid-second century A.D., the Roman Empire extended over some 3.5 million square miles and embraced a population of about 75 million people. More than 85 percent were engaged in agriculture, but Rome itself had a population of approximately 1 million, and Alexandria in Egypt and Antioch in Syria numbered several hundred thousand inhabitants each. The 1,000 cities of the empire were connected by an extensive network of roads, some of which are still in use today; water was piped in by aqueduct. Roman law, backed by Roman legions, provided stability and security, while decentralized administration and local autonomy lightened the imperial yoke.

Yet the empire suffered from structural weaknesses. The supply of cheap labor provided by conquest and slavery was a disincentive to innovation and efficiency, but when Rome's frontiers ceased to expand, that supply began to dry up. The economy slowly contracted, underscoring the fact that its strength had lain in the acquisition of new resources rather than the development of existing ones. At the same time, unrest on the frontiers stretched the imperial army and treasury. Marcus Aurelius' unwise decision to end the system of adoptive emperors destabilized the state; the reign of his deranged son Commodus (180–192) ended in assassination and civil war, with the Praetorian Guard at one point actually attempting to auction off the throne to the highest bidder.

The Severi

Order was restored by Septimius Severus (193–211), an African-born general whose accession to the throne symbolized the increasingly multiracial nature of the empire and the shift in its center of gravity from Rome. Septimius spent little time in his capital; most of his reign was devoted to pacifying the frontiers, and he died campaigning in Britain in 211. With him, the dyarchy effectively came to an end. He opened the Senate to commoners while stripping it of much of its function, making the army and the civil service the main avenues to imperial preferment. But he encouraged the codification of the law under the jurist Papinian and laid the groundwork for the general extension of citizenship throughout the empire by his son and successor Antoninus, known as Caracalla (211–217). This had, among other aims, the effect of broadening the tax rolls.

The dominant figure during the next several years was Septimius' widow, Julia Domna (c. 169–217), a woman of powerful character who was even spoken of as a candidate for the throne herself. The later Severi included the unpopular Macrinus (217–218), the profligate Elagabulus (218–222), and the adolescent Alexander Severus (222–235). Only Septimius died a natural death among the Severi, and with the assassination of Alexander by the army, the dynasty was extinguished. A period of near-anarchy ensued.

The Germanic Invasions

In the 50 years from 235 to 285, more than 25 emperors were officially recognized by the Senate. Almost all were raised to power through, and sooner or later killed by, the army. These rulers had little reason to feel loyalty to Rome. They were themselves generally not of Roman origin; selected by an army that was itself increasingly non-Roman, they were unlikely to see beyond their own interests and those of their men to the state as a whole.

The empire was now under serious threat from outside. Germanic, partly Romanized tribes such as the Goths and the Alemanni penetrated its defenses. As early as 231 marauding Franks crossed the river Rhine. In 259 the city of Rome itself was almost invaded by the Alemanni. In many parts of the empire it became clear that Rome could provide no help against invaders, and some of the provinces tried to establish themselves as independent states with their own armies. Although the attempts of Gaul in 260 and Palmyra in 267 to win their freedom were crushed, they presaged the fragmentation of the empire. By 271 the reigning emperor, Aurelian (270–275), began the construction of a defensive wall around the city of Rome, the first since the time of Hannibal. Meanwhile, in the east, Roman armies were continually involved in repelling the Persians, revived under the Sassanid dynasty.

These problems had a devastating effect on the economy. Taxes increased as the value of money plunged. The constant threat of invasion or civil war made trade difficult. What funds there were went for the

THE ROMAN EMPIRE

Period	Major emperors	Important events	Cultural highlights
Julio-Claudians (31 B.C.–A.D. 68)	• Augustus (27 B.C.–A.D. 14) • Tiberius (A.D. 14–37) • Caligula (37–41) • Claudius (41–54) • Nero (54–68)	• Principate • Founding of Christianity • Expansion into northern and western Europe	• Virgil • Livy • Ovid • Seneca • Philo of Judea • Petronius • Horace
Flavians (69–96)	• Vespasian (69–79) • Titus (79–81) • Domitian (81–96)	• Jewish revolt • Growth of autocratic government • Vesuvius eruption	• Roman Colosseum • Martial
Adoptive emperors (96–180)	• Nerva (96–98) • Trajan (98–117) • Hadrian (117–138) • Antoninus Pius (138–161) • Marcus Aurelius (161–180)	• Largest geographic extent of the empire • Bar-Kochba rebellion • Economic expansion • Economic expansion	• Pantheon • Tacitus • Plutarch • Lucian
Severi (193–235)	• Septimius Severus (193–211) • Caracalla (211–217) • Alexander Severus (222–235)	• Military autocracy	• Baths of Caracalla • Dio Cassius • Clement of Alexandria
Barracks emperors (235–284)	• 26 emperors in 49 years	• Military anarchy • Germanic invasions • Economic decline	• Origen • Neoplatonism
Late Empire (284–c. 450)	• Diocletian (284–305) • Constantine (306–337) • Valens (364–378) • Theodosius (379–395)	• Tetrarchy • Edict of Milan (313) • Origins of Byzantine Empire • Christianity becomes the state religion (378)	• Jerome • Early monasticism • Ambrose of Milan • Augustine

support of the army, and the general standard of living steadily declined. The former Hellenistic kingdoms in the east suffered less than the western provinces, since they were protected in part by their prosperity. Much of Italy's farmland ceased to be cultivated, the loss of export markets played havoc with industry, and the population of Rome diminished.

The Reforms of Diocletian

The accession of Diocletian (284–305), the son of a Dalmatian freedman, marked the beginning of a revival that would extend the life of the empire by two centuries, but on a very different basis. The days of a unitary empire ruled by a single emperor were henceforth over, to be replaced by a system known as the *tetrarchy* (rule of four). Under this system, devised by Diocletian, two senior rulers, called Augusti, would share responsibility with two junior rulers, or Caesars. When an Augustus died, he was to be replaced by his Caesar, who in turn would appoint a new junior associate. Each tetrarch had his own capital and defense perimeter, but each could issue decrees binding on the empire as a whole. None of the tetrarchs based himself in Rome, further proof of the capital's declining importance; Diocletian ruled from Nicomedia (modern Izmit) in northwestern Turkey.

Despite sharing power, Diocletian remained the dominant figure of the tetrarchy; indeed, it was only his authority that prevented immediate rivalries from breaking out. He, too, implemented the wide-ranging series of reforms that transformed the social, economic, and administrative structure of the empire. After quartering the throne, Diocletian divided the provinces, roughly doubling their number. His purpose was to tighten control, for each governor was now made responsible for the heavy new requisitions laid on the localities by the

Head of the colossal statue of Constantine from the Basilica of Constantine in Rome. Rather than the faithful likeness of an individual, this is an abstract representation of power.

central government. The cost of the new bureaucracy alone was a heavy burden for the exhausted empire, being equivalent to the furnishing of two or three legions. The army itself was considerably expanded, chiefly with conscripts but also with levies from barbarian tribes. A contemporary observer complained that the number of soldiers and officials in Diocletian's empire exceeded the number of taxpayers.

This remark, however exaggerated, summed up the paradox of Diocletian's reforms. On the one hand, the empire needed firm and expanded government if it was to recover from the disasters of the mid-third century; on the other hand, it lacked the resources to sustain such a government. Diocletian strove to maximize those resources and to stabilize the economy. He reformed the coinage, decreed regulation of wages and prices, and, to compensate for the lack of money in circulation, instituted taxation in kind. At the same time, he forbade all people listed on the tax rolls to leave their registered domicile and heaped such obligations on the *curiales* (local landowners conscripted into government service) that many fled.

The results of Diocletian's reforms were mixed. With secure borders, a measure of prosperity returned to the empire. Taxes were higher but more equitably and realistically levied, and with improved as well as intensified administration, public confidence was at least partially restored. But the burdens of taxation and service were heavy, and virtually the last trace of republican institutions—the only check on absolute autocracy—were swept away.

Diocletian never appeared in public but maintained an elaborate court ritual and sought to restore the prestige of the imperial office by reviving the traditional state cults, including emperor worship. This brought him into conflict with Christians, whom he vigorously persecuted. Diocletian retired from office in 305 to Split in his native Dalmatia, where he maintained one of his principal residences; he died there in 313, but not before witnessing a bloody struggle for power among his fellow tetrarchs.

Constantine: The Last Renewal

The division of the empire begun by Diocletian was formalized by Constantine (died 337), who was acknowledged as senior Augustus in 312 after defeating his chief rival and was recognized as sole emperor from 324. Constantine extended Diocletian's reforms of the currency and the army, but he is chiefly remembered for having changed the course of Roman and subsequent Western history in two decisive ways: He transferred the imperial capital to the great new city he built on the Bosporus, Constantinople (now Istanbul), and he adopted Christianity as his personal religion. (The growth and early development of Christianity are discussed in Chapter 7.)

Constantine's conversion to the Christian faith followed a dream he had on the eve of the Battle of Milvian Bridge (312), which established his control of Italy and his preeminence as Augustus. As he related to the Christian historian Eusebius many years later, he saw in his dream a cross of light superimposed on the sun. He thereupon ordered his men to paint a monogram of Christ on their shields and attributed his subsequent victory to the favor of the Christian God as well as that of Apollo, god of the sun. Constantine continued to regard himself as under the protection of both deities, whom he sometimes appeared to regard as distinct and sometimes as aspects of a single divine power. This calculation may have been partly political, as the solar cult was still widely popular throughout the empire. It was Christianity, however, that benefited the most. Constantine granted Christians freedom of worship in 313 by the Edict of Milan, showered favor and privilege on them, and even preached on their behalf at court. In 325 he convened a church council at Nicaea that resolved doctrinal disputes (see Chapter 7). More ominously, he also denounced the Jews for the murder of Jesus, a theme that would be echoed in the patristic literature later in the fourth century. Constantine's embrace of Christianity was decisive for the fortunes of the church. Without his support it might well have remained a minority sect, as it did in neighboring Persia. With that support it became the majority religion of the Roman Empire by the middle of the century and ultimately one of the great religions of the world.

Constantinople, which the emperor named for himself, was built on the straits that separate the Black Sea from the Mediterranean, a location purportedly revealed to him in a vision, though also of clear strategic value. The city was dedicated to the Christian faith, but it was also meant as a second inauguration for the empire itself. Temples from far and wide were stripped of their ornaments to furnish the churches and public buildings of the new capital, and residents were attracted by the offer of free land and a permanent grain supply. Rome itself was to survive little more than a century after the founding of Constantinople in 330, but the city of Constantinople would serve for 1,000 years as the capital of the Byzantine Empire that succeeded it (see Chapter 8).

The Twilight of Rome

Constantine's sons contended for control of the empire after his death. Their successor, Julian (361–363), known as the Apostate, is chiefly remembered for his attempt to revive the pagan cults and check the spread of Christianity. Julian fancied himself another Alexander and prepared an expedition against Persia. He died on the march; it was Rome's last campaign of conquest. The Persians pressed it in the east, while Germanic tribes ravaged the northern frontier and Moorish raiders attacked the cities of Africa. In 378 a Gothic host, itself in flight from the fierce central Asian nomads known as the Huns, destroyed a Roman army at Adrianople in Thrace.

Theodosius (379–395), the last ruler of an undivided Rome, made peace with the Goths and enrolled many of them in the Roman army. In 410, however, the Visigoths (West Goths), under their leader, Alaric, sacked the city of Rome itself, an event that shocked the entire Roman world. For 800 years no enemy army had entered the city. Even Christians who had lived in expectation of Judgment Day were stunned. Father Jerome lamented that the lamp of the universe, the church, had been extinguished and that in Rome's fall the whole world had perished.

Simultaneously, the Vandals, another German tribe, invaded Gaul and Spain and established a powerful seafaring kingdom in North Africa, from which they disrupted the supply of grain to Rome and harassed communications between the eastern and western halves of the empire. In the 420s two Germanic tribes, the Angles and the Saxons, settled in Britain, the first province abandoned by the empire, while the Alemanni and the Franks moved into Gaul. In 455 the Vandals invaded Italy by sea and sacked Rome once more. Finally, in 476 a coalition of German tribes deposed the young emperor of the west, Romulus Augustulus, and replaced him with their chieftain, Oadacer. By 500 the Angles and Saxons held Britain, northern Gaul was in the hands of the Frankish king Clovis, the Visigoths ruled Spain and southern Gaul, and the Vandals occupied Rome's former domains in northwestern Africa. The eastern portion of the empire survived and in the sixth century made unavailing attempts to recover the west. Thereafter, as Byzantium, it would pursue its own separate destiny. Rome was no more.

Rome in Perspective

No historical question has been more widely debated than the decline of the western empire. The historian Ammianus Marcellinus (born c. 330) attributed Rome's ills to a loss of virtue and a decline of vital energy. Edward Gibbon (1737–1794), in his monumental *History of the Decline and Fall of the Roman Empire,* saw Rome in part as the victim of Christianity, which was alien to its spirit and diverted it from pressing civil and military problems.

More recent historians have focused on social, economic, political, and demographic factors. Some have pointed to the low productivity associated with the use of slave labor, some to the increased burden of taxation and the loss of economic mobility in the empire. Others have emphasized the contingencies of Rome's situation, including the depredations of the German tribes and the pressure of the Huns. Nonetheless, certain long-standing structural weaknesses of Roman society should be borne in mind. The Romans never resolved the economic and class divisions that had destroyed the republic. The Augustan settlement papered over these divisions, but at the cost of subsidizing an unproductive urban population whose support required continuous expansion and conquest, and with an imperial system that increased rather than diminished the army's role in politics. These underlying problems left the empire ill prepared to deal with stagnation and retrenchment.

The survival of the eastern empire must be contrasted with the collapse of Roman power in the west. If

The Christian Empire

In this speech, delivered in 336 to celebrate the thirtieth year of Constantine's reign, the church historian Eusebius works out a theological justification for the existence of a Christian emperor and empire.

The divine Logos [Word], which is above, throughout and within everything, visible and invisible at once, is the lord of the universe. It is from and through the Logos that the emperor, the beloved of God, receives and wears the image of supreme kingship, and so guides and steers, in imitation of his Lord, all the affairs of this world. . . . Constantine, like the light of the sun, . . . illuminates those farthest from him with his rays . . . and harnessing the four Caesars like spirited coursers beneath the single yoke of his royal quadriga, he molds them to harmony with the reins of reason and unity, guiding his team like a charioteer, controlling it from above and ranging over the whole surface of the earth illuminated by the sun, and at the same time present in the midst of all men and watching over their affairs. . . . God is the model of royal power and it is he who has determined a single authority for all mankind. . . . Just as there is only one God, and not two or three or more, since polytheism is really atheism, so there is only one emperor. . . . He has received the image of the heavenly monarchy, and his eyes lifted on high he governs the affairs of this world in accordance with the ideas of his archetype, fortified by the imitation of the sovereignty of the heavenly king.

Source: R. Browning, *The Emperor Julian* (Berkeley: University of California Press, 1976), p. 22.

the empire's political center of gravity was the city of Rome, its economic and cultural base had always been in the eastern Mediterranean, a fact that Constantine recognized when he built his new capital on the shore of Asia. In a sense, the stronger, more viable half of the empire survived there, its history and culture continuous down to the Turkish conquest of 1453.

SUMMARY

The Roman Empire was the largest and most ethnically diverse political unit ever seen in the world up to its time. It stood for nearly 1,000 years and left the permanent impress of its law, its language, its culture, and its institutions on the subsequent history of the West.

The effects as well as the subsequent destinies of the eastern and western portions of the empire must be contrasted. From the point of view of the Hellenized east, the long centuries of Roman rule were an episode of foreign domination in a region whose civilizations stretched back thousands of years. To be sure, the passing of Rome was painfully felt, and many of its institutions were retained, but on the whole the traditions and cultures that Rome had so freely borrowed for its own only reverted to their native soil, and everyday life went on much as before. The major difference between the pre- and post-Roman periods was the advent of Christianity; the major change to come was the rise of Islam.

In the west, Rome's influence was far more formative and profound. Rome was the first civilization known to most of Europe. Its historical memory remained strong, and from medieval times down to the nineteenth century it was the chief model for Western culture, as it is still in many respects today. The classical culture of Greece remained the heritage of both East and West, but without the legacy of Rome, the Western world as we know it today would be unimaginably different.

NOTES

1. Appian, *Civil Wars,* in *Appian's Roman History,* trans. H. White (New York: Macmillan, 1912–1913), 4.33.

2. S. B. Pomeroy, *Goddesses, Whores, Wives, and Slaves: Women in Classical Antiquity* (New York: Schocken Books, 1975), p. 199.
3. G. Wills, ed., *Roman Culture* (New York: Braziller, 1966), p. 124.

SUGGESTIONS FOR FURTHER READING

Balsdon, J. P. V. D. *Roman Women.* Westport, Conn.: Greenwood Press, 1975.

Birley, A. *Marcus Aurelius: A Biography,* rev. ed. New Haven, Conn.: Yale University Press, 1987.

Bradford, E. *Cleopatra.* New York: Harcourt Brace Jovanovich, 1972.

Bradley, K. R. *Slaves and Masters in the Roman Empire.* Berkeley: University of California Press, 1987.

Brendel, O. *Prolegomena to the Study of Roman Art.* New Haven, Conn.: Yale University Press, 1979.

Christ, K. *The Romans: An Introduction to Their History and Civilization.* Berkeley: University of California Press, 1984.

Cornell, T., and Matthews, J. *Atlas of the Roman World.* New York: Facts on File, 1982.

Crawford, M. *The Roman Republic.* Cambridge, Mass.: Harvard University Press, 1982.

Cunliffe, B. W. *Rome and Her Empire.* London: Bodley Head, 1978.

D'Arms, J. H. *Commerce and Social Standing in Ancient Rome.* Cambridge, Mass.: Harvard University Press, 1981.

Deiss, J. J. *Herculaneum: Italy's Buried Treasure,* rev. ed. New York: Harper & Row, 1985.

Dixon, S. *The Roman Family.* Baltimore: Johns Hopkins University Press, 1992.

Duncan-Jones, R. *The Economy of the Roman Empire: Quantitative Studies.* Cambridge: Cambridge University Press, 1982.

Dyson, S. L. *Community and Society in Roman Italy.* Baltimore: Johns Hopkins University Press, 1991.

Feldman, L. H. *Jew and Gentile in the Ancient World: Attitudes and Interpretations from Alexander to Justinian.* Princeton, N.J.: Princeton University Press, 1993.

Finley, M. I. *The Ancient Economy.* Berkeley: University of California Press, 1973.

Gardner, J. F. *Women in Roman Law and Society.* Bloomington: Indiana University Press, 1986.

Garnsey, P., and Saller, R. *The Roman Empire: Economy, Society and Culture.* Berkeley: University of California Press, 1987.

Goodenough, S. *Citizens of Rome.* New York: Crown, 1979.

Grant, M. *Cities of Vesuvius: Pompeii and Herculaneum.* Baltimore: Penguin Books, 1971.

———. *The Etruscans.* New York: Scribner, 1981.

Hanfmann, G. *Roman Art.* New York: Norton, 1976.

Heurgon, J. *The Rise of Rome to 264 B.C.* Berkeley: University of California Press, 1973.

Hooper, F. A. *Roman Realities.* Detroit: Wayne State University Press, 1979.

Hopkins, K. *Conquerors and Slaves.* Cambridge: Cambridge University Press, 1981.

Jones, A. H. M. *The Later Roman Empire; 284–602: A Social, Economic, and Administrative Survey.* Baltimore: Johns Hopkins University Press, 1986.

Lefkowitz, M., and Fant, M. B., eds. *Women's Life in Greece and Rome,* rev. ed. Baltimore: Johns Hopkins University Press, 1982.

Luttwak, E. N. *The Grand Strategy of the Roman Empire.* Baltimore: Johns Hopkins University Press, 1976.

Macmullen, R. *Roman Social Relations, 50 B.C. to A.D. 284.* New Haven, Conn.: Yale University Press, 1981.

Millar, F. *The Emperor in the Roman World, 31 B.C.–A.D. 337.* Ithaca, N.Y.: Cornell University Press, 1977.

Pallottino, M. *The Etruscans.* Baltimore: Penguin Books, 1976.

Potter, D. *Prophets and Emperors: Human and Divine Authority from Augustus to Theodosius.* Cambridge, Mass.: Harvard University Press, 1995.

Potter, T. *The Changing Landscape of South Etruria.* New York: St. Martin's Press, 1979.

Scullard, H. H. *Roman Politics, 220–150 B.C.* Westport, Conn.: Greenwood Press, 1982.

Syme, R. *The Roman Revolution.* New York: Oxford University Press, 1960.

CHAPTER 7

The Ancient World Religions

The earliest evidence for religious beliefs dates back to the Neanderthal people of the late Paleolithic period. Even in its most primitive forms, religion helped humans explain their natural environment, to the point of providing means, such as prayer, sacrifices, or offerings, intended to control the world around them. Appeasing the gods, for instance, was seen as a way to ward off illness or famine or perhaps to enjoy the blessings of children and fertile fields. Religion also provided a way for people to relate to each other, often hierarchically within their own society, especially since priests usually enjoyed substantial social and political status. Religious beliefs could be used as well to persuade people to obey their secular rulers and perform their vocational responsibilities. Eventually, many religions developed codes of ethical conduct to guide adherents in their dealings with each other. Thus religion was often the bond that bound a society together.

All of the religions discussed in this chapter took their particular character from the environment in which they evolved. The Hindu concept of *dharma* and the Christian practice of monasticism paralleled the social and political realities of their respective societies. Most religions try to influence the nature of society, with varying success, and it is important to remember that none of them exists in a vacuum as pure theology. Yet by considering the principal world religions as entities and by comparing their aims and characteristics, it is possible to cast fresh light on some of the oldest human needs, hopes, and fears.

The great bronze Buddha at Kamakura, near Tokyo, completed in 1252 and originally housed in its own temple but now in the open and still visited by millions of tourists, daytrippers, and worshippers every year. It was built with the help of funds raised from the common people of the Kamakura domains, and shows the compassionate benevolence of the Buddha, or Amida Buddha as the Japanese say.

All of the world's major religions, including Judaism and Christianity, had their origins in Asia. All of them go back roughly 1,500 to 2,500 years, yet they still affect the lives of most people today. Most Communist states substituted a secular belief system, but in China, much of both Confucianism—like Taoism, more of a moral philosophy than a religion—and traditional folk religion survive, and in Russia and eastern Europe, traditional religion remains popular despite decades of suppression.

Hinduism

Hinduism is the oldest world religion, and India has remained the most religiously oriented of all major cultures. Hinduism is often called a way of life, which is true but not very helpful. It is hard to define; its name means simply "Indianism," and the religious element is hard to sort out from more general cultural practice. The caste system is a good illustration. It is a Hindu practice, but it is also observed by South Asian Muslims and Buddhists. Caste has some minor religious connection but is primarily a system of social organization and is discussed as such in Chapter 23. There is no single body of writings for Hinduism like the Koran, the New Testament, or Buddha's sayings, and Hinduism had no single founder.

Hindu Beliefs and Writings

In the broadest sense, we can define Hinduism as developing out of the complex of religious beliefs held by the people of the Indus civilization, which included the cult of Shiva, still the dominant god of Hinduism. The Aryans brought their own tribal gods, including the war god Indra and the fire god Agni,* but by the time the Vedas were first written down, many centuries later, Vedic religion was becoming a mixture of Harappan, Aryan, and Dravidian (southern Indian) elements. Composed cumulatively between about 1500 and 600 B.C., first orally and later written down, as a set of hymns, spells, and mystic poems used at sacrifices, the Vedas are the world's oldest religious texts still used in worship. The last of the Vedas, the *Upanishads* (seventh century B.C.), deal mainly with the nature of the universe and the place of humans in it. The *Upanishads* involve a sophisticated metaphysics that is characteristically Indian, a far cry from the earlier anthropomorphic (humanlike) gods of the Aryans. Asceticism and mysticism are seen in the *Upanishads* as paths to wisdom and truth.

The *Upanishads* deal also with good and evil, law, morality, and human duty and are often seen as the core of classical Hinduism. But Hinduism's main ethical text is the much later *Bhagavadgita* (second century A.D.), which tells the story of Prince Arjuna. Arjuna is faced with a rebellion led by disloyal friends, relatives, and teachers, people he has loved and respected. He knows his cause is just but cannot bring himself to fight and kill those so close to him. He stands in his chariot awaiting battle and talks to his charioteer, who turns out to be Krishna, an incarnation of the Vedic god of creation, Vishnu. Krishna tells him that bodily death does not mean the death of the soul and is thus unimportant. For any individual's life, what is important is duty, and action in accordance with duty, without attachment, personal desires, or ambition. Each person has a special role in society, and morality lies in faithfulness to that prescribed role.

This concept of *dharma,* the selfless execution of one's prescribed duty on earth, applied also to the faithful following of caste rules. Arjuna was a ruler and had to follow the ruler's dharma, which included the duty to fight to uphold his rightful power. Other roles in society entail their own, different dharmas, including that of lower castes to serve and defer to those above them and the rules associated with wives, students, parents, and others. *Karma* is the result or consequence of one's actions; faithfulness to one's dharma produces good karma or reward, while behavior contrary to dharma yields bad karma and punishment. There is much universal human wisdom in this, but it also clearly supported the social status quo of India and its maintenance by force if necessary. It has accordingly been much criticized, even by leading Hindus. In many ways it is inconsistent with other parts of Hinduism, especially the doctrine of *ahimsa,* or nonviolence and reverence for all life. Mahatma Gandhi, the leading religious figure of modern India, saw no conflict between the *Bhagavadgita* and ahimsa and took the former simply as emphasizing duty.

A broad variety of doctrine, however, is characteristic of Hinduism. Hinduism has cumulatively incorporated various ideas, texts, and practices and combines what may seem excessive emphasis on ritual with much genuine spirituality. But the concepts of dharma and karma have remained basic to Hinduism, as has the tradition of meditation and asceticism. Moral uprightness lies in faithfulness to dharma, and dharma is rightly different for everyone. This has helped create the tolerance for which Hinduism is noted. All faiths and all ascetic or

*Compare the Latin *ignis,* "fire," and the English *ignite.*

Creation: Hindu Views

These selections from the Rig Veda *illustrate early Hindu concepts of creation. Compare them with the biblical accounts in Genesis and John.*

Let me proclaim the valiant deeds of Indra,
The first he did, the wielder of the thunder,
When he slew the dragon and let loose the waters,
And pierced the bellies of the mountains. . . .
When Indra, you slew the firstborn of dragons,
And frustrated the arts of the sorcerers,
Creating sun and heaven and dawn,
You found no enemy to withstand you. . . .
At first there was only darkness wrapped in darkness.
All this was only unillumined water.
That One which came to be, enclosed in nothing,
Arose at last, born of the power of heat. . . .
But who knows, and who can say
Whence it all came, and how creation happened?
The gods themselves are later than creation,
So who knows truly whence it has arisen?

Source: A. L. Basham, *The Wonder That Was India* (New York: Grove Press, 1983), pp. 248, 400.

mystic disciplines are seen as paths to truth, which is held to be universal. Gandhi said he did not object to the message of Christian missionaries but wished they could be more faithful to their dharma—that is, true Christians.

Reincarnation

The belief in reincarnation and the immortality of the soul, probably first held by the Harappans, had reappeared by late Vedic times and became a further basic part of Hinduism. The karma produced by one's mortal life determined the next rebirth of the soul, which might be in a person of higher or lower status or even in an animal or insect. Special piety, meditation, asceticism, and understanding of eternal truth could bring escape from the endless cycle of birth and rebirth. The soul was then liberated from the cycle and achieved *moksha,* not a bodily heaven but a blissful spiritual rejoining with the godhead, whose essence was love.

Belief in reincarnation heightened reverence for all life. One's relative might have been reborn as a horse or a spider. Bovine animals were especially revered from Harappan times on, both for their basic usefulness to people and for the obvious relation of the cow's milk with creation and motherhood. Bulls and oxen, too, were valued natural symbols of patient strength and virility, as also in Mediterranean cultures. But to Hinduism all life is sacred, and all creatures are part of the great chain of being that manifests the divine. Accordingly, pious Hindus are vegetarians, and all but the lowest castes (and the westernized) particularly avoid eating beef. Milk, curds, clarified butter, and yogurt are also used ritually in religious ceremonies.

By late Vedic times (c. 600 B.C.) the Hindu pantheon was dominated by the trinity of Vishnu, Shiva, and Brahma, all supreme deities. There developed as well, however, a bewildering variety of consorts, divine incarnations, and lesser gods, each with his or her own cult, as Hinduism continued to incorporate regional and folk religious figures and traditions. These included, among the more prominent, Ganesh, the benevolent elephant-headed son of Shiva and of his consort Parvati; Hanuman, the monkey god; Lakshmi, wife of Vishnu and goddess of good fortune; Krishna, the human incarnation of Vishnu; and Kali or Durga, a consort or female equivalent to the grimmer aspect of Shiva, sometimes called the goddess of death. Kali was also a positive figure prayed to for help, especially by women.

Hinduism accepted the presence of evil and suffering in the world to a greater extent than other religions and recognized that people, themselves a mixture of good and evil, love and hate, petty and noble, selfish and altruistic, must come to terms with their own nature and with the nature of the cosmos. The major Hindu gods and goddesses thus represent both aspects, destroyers as well as creators, makers of suffering as well as bliss, true representations of the world as it is. Nevertheless, most devout Hindus, especially literate ones, have always been basically monotheistic, stressing the oneness of creation and the majesty of a single creative principle above the level of a humanlike god figure, to which access was possible without cults or intermediaries but through devotion, meditation, and mystical understanding of eternal truth. As a Hindu proverb put it, "God is one, but wise people know it by many names."

Jainism and Sikhism, reformist offshoots of Hinduism that arose, respectively, in the sixth century B.C. and the late fifteenth century A.D., centered on monotheism. So too did the teachings of the Buddha, in which universal truth was given no material identity, as it is not in pure Hinduism. A similar tension has existed in Christianity between concepts of the Christ as a godhead and the worship of saints and other cults.

Hinduism never developed a fixed or uniform ritual comparable with those of Christianity or Judaism. Pious Hindus recite specified prayers daily before the simple altar found in nearly all Hindu homes and may make frequent offerings of prayer, food, and flowers at one of the many temples throughout India, which are tended by people called *priests.* But there is no formal "service," no established ordination or clergy comparable with those of Christianity, and no special day for worship like the Sabbath. Brahmins—the highest and supposedly priestly caste and the exclusive keepers and reciters of the sacred rituals, mainly texts from Sanskrit Vedas and epics—are the only people who perform the rituals for death, marriage, coming of age, and intercession with the divine. These are certainly priestly functions, but such people are not seen as necessary intermediaries for laypersons. Not all Hindu Brahmins are priests, and although Hindu priests may tend temples and receive offerings, they are a far more informally constituted group than in Christianity or Judaism. There are a number of Hindu festivals, most of which are as much cultural as religious, such as the autumn Diwali, or festival of lights, and the spring festival of Holi, and there is an ancient tradition of religious pilgrimage to famous temples and sacred sites.

Hinduism is deeply rooted in the Indian tradition and in the modern sense of Indian identity, and it remains the basic guide for over 700 million people. But despite its strong elements of spirituality, Hinduism has also long recognized the importance to human life of achieving material well-being (*artha*), the responsibility of individuals to provide for their families, and the importance of interpersonal love and of sex (*kama*). Such matters are basic parts of human nature and hence accepted as good. Hinduism in effect rejects nothing that God has made but celebrates and enshrines all of life, including its creation through sex, while making much less distinction than in the West between the sacred and the profane; all are part of creation, which is divine. Hinduism's acknowledgment of the bad as well as the good things of life may perhaps have made things easier or psychologically healthier for its followers, who accept the tragedies and sufferings of life without feeling that they are somehow being punished.

Buddhism

The preoccupation of the *Upanishads* with eternal truth reflected a troubled world. A new hybrid India was emerging, and the rise of larger states brought an increase in the scale of warfare. Many people sought solace or escape from a harsh reality through otherworldly quests. The founders of Buddhism and Jainism, roughly contemporary figures in the sixth century B.C., pursued such a path, as they also reacted against the growing ritualization of Hinduism and its dominance by the priestly caste of Brahmins. Both urged independent access to truth through meditation and self-denial without the aid of priests or ritual, and both taught the equality of all in these terms, rejecting caste distinctions. But Buddhism and Jainism were developments within the tradition of Hinduism, and they also share the Hindu beliefs in dharma, karma, *samsara* (reincarnation), moksha, devotion, and nonviolence or reverence for life. Both rejected the folk panoply of Hindu gods but reaffirmed Hinduism's basic monotheism, its nonpersonalized worship of the infinite and of the "great chain of being."

Gautama Buddha, the Enlightened One

The founder of Buddhism was born around 563 B.C. in the Himalayan foothills region of Nepal, the son of a minor raja ("king"; compare the English word *royal*) of the Sakya clan. His family name was Gautama and his given name Siddartha, but he was also later called by some Sakyamuni ("Sage of the Sakyas"), as well as Gautama or Prince Siddartha. Until he was 29 years old, he led the conventional life of a prince, filled with earthly pleasures. At 19 he married a beautiful princess, and in due time they had a son, or so say the pious legends elaborated in great detail long after his death, as with so many religious figures. We know that he subsequently became an ascetic, wandered and taught for many years, acquired a number of disciples, founded a religious order, and died at the age of about 80 somewhere between 485 and 480 B.C. This is all we know of his life for certain. The later embroidered story of his life, replete with miraculous tales, is important, as it has influenced the lives of many millions among successive generations of Asians, from India eastward.

A modern sadhu, or holy man, who has renounced the world and lives by begging for food. He sits in front of a temple frieze in South India.

According to this story (in its briefest form), Prince Siddartha, filled with nameless discontent, wandered one day away from his walled palace and met in quick succession an old man broken by age, a sick man covered with boils and shivering with fever, a corpse being carried to the cremation ground (Hindus have always burned their dead), and a wandering sadhu (holy man) with his begging bowl and simple yellow robe, but with peacefulness and inner joy in his face. Overwhelmed by this vision of the sufferings of mortal life, the emptiness of worldly pleasure, and the promise of ascetic devotion, Siddartha shortly thereafter left his palace, abandoning his wife and son. He became a wandering beggar, seeking after the truth and owning nothing but a rag of clothing and a crude wooden bowl to beg the bare essentials of food. For several years he wandered, wasted from fasting, until he determined to solve the riddle of suffering through intense meditation under a great tree. After 49 days, during which he was tempted by Mara, the prince of demons, with promises of riches, power, and sensual pleasures, he perceived the truth and attained enlightenment. From this moment, he was known as the Buddha, or the Enlightened One. Soon after, he preached his first sermon, near Banaras (Varanasi) in the central Ganges valley, and spent the rest of his life as an itinerant preacher with a band of disciples.

The Four Noble Truths, announced in that first sermon, formed the basis for the new faith: (1) Life is filled with pain, sorrow, frustration, impermanence, and dissatisfaction. (2) All this is caused by desire, by wanting, and by the urge for existence. (3) To end suffering and sorrow, one must be released from desire. (4) Release from desire can be gained by the eightfold path of "right conduct." The right conduct of the eightfold path was later defined as kindness to all living things, purity of heart, truthfulness, charity, and avoidance of fault finding, envy, hatred, and violence. To these were added specific commandments not to kill, steal, commit adultery, lie, speak evil, gossip, flatter, or otherwise wander from the path.

Followers of the path may attain *nirvana,* or release from the sufferings of worldly existence through the endless cycle of rebirth, and achieve blissful reabsorption into the spiritual infinite, as the Buddha did on his death. Such perfection was, however, rare, and although the Buddha did not say so, Buddhism incorporated the Hindu concept of karma. In accordance with this, less dutiful individuals were reborn in successive existences in forms appropriate to their behavior in their most recent incarnations. Accounts of the Buddha's own teachings were recorded in a collection of texts called the Tripitaka ("three baskets"). In addition, a literature of moral tales about the life of the Buddha grew up, together with commentaries on the teachings, which are comparable in many ways to the stories of the Christian New Testament.

Like Christianity, Buddhism remained for its first several centuries a minority religion, although the difficult discipline of the original teachings was softened somewhat so as to accommodate more followers. The conversion of Emperor Ashoka (c. 269–c. 232 B.C.) helped transform it into a mass religion, and it began to spread from India, first to Ceylon and Southeast Asia and later to China, Korea, and Japan. Within India, Buddhism survived for many centuries, although its following slowly declined from a peak reached around A.D. 100. For many, its distinction from Hinduism was gradually blurred, and except for its several monastic orders and some lay devotees, Buddhism was slowly reabsorbed into Hinduism. The remaining Buddhist centers and monasteries in the central Ganges heartland were destroyed, most of the monks slaughtered, and the few survivors driven into exile by the Muslim invaders of the twelfth century. That holocaust largely extinguished Buddhism in the land of its birth.

Hinayana and Mahayana Buddhism

Soon after Ashoka's time, Buddhism divided into two major schools known as Hinayana (the "lesser vehicle") or Theravada and Mahayana (the "greater vehicle"). Theravada Buddhism remained closer to the original faith, although it too was necessarily popularized to some extent as it spread and included more scope for the doctrine of good works. By performing good works, one could acquire "merit," which could even offset bad conduct in the building of karma; thus, for example, pious donations could make up for the bad karma of unethically acquired money. Theravada was the form of Buddhism transmitted to Southeast Asia, where especially in Burma, Thailand, Cambodia, and Laos, as well as Ceylon, it has remained the dominant religion and is paid far more than lip service even today. Nearly all young men in

Buddhist Teachings

Many of the teachings attributed to the Buddha are almost certainly later additions or commentaries. Here are two rather striking passages from such Buddhist scriptures, whose closeness to the Christian Gospels is remarkable.

A man buries a treasure in a deep pit, thinking: It will be useful in time of need, or if the king is displeased with me, or if I am robbed, or fall into debt, or if food is scarce, or bad luck befalls me. But all this treasure may not profit the owner at all, for he may forget where he hid it, or goblins may steal it, or his enemies or even his kinsmen may take it when he is not on his guard. But by charity, goodness, restraint, and self-control man and woman alike can store up a well-hidden treasure—a treasure which cannot be given to others and which robbers cannot steal. A wise man should do good; that is the treasure which will not leave him.

Brethren, you have no mother or father to care for you. If you do not care for one another, who else will do so? Brethren, he who would care for me should care for the sick.

Source: A. L. Basham, *The Wonder That Was India* (New York: Grove Press, 1983), p. 284.

these countries traditionally spent two years in a Buddhist monastery, as many still do, with shaven heads, a yellow robe, and a begging bowl.

Mahayana Buddhism developed a little later, during the Kushan period in India in the second century A.D. What had begun as a spiritual discipline for a few became a mass religion for all, popularized, humanized, and provided with a variety of supports. The Buddha himself was made into a supernatural god, and there were also innumerable other Buddhas called *bodhisattvas,* saints who out of compassion delayed their entrance into nirvana in order to help those still on earth to attain deliverance. Faith in and worship of a bodhisattva also offered comfort to those who felt they needed divine help for any purpose. This, in turn, promoted the worship of images, including those of the original Buddha, and the development of elaborate rituals and cults. Such worship by itself, it was held, could produce salvation, as well as help in solving worldly problems.

Some forms of Mahayana Buddhism acquired a magic overlay. Bodhisattvas and their attendants were believed capable of flying through the air. Sanctity could be obtained, some held, merely by repeating ritual phrases or worshiping supposed relics of the Buddha. The Mahayana school also developed details of a bodily heaven to which the faithful would go, filled with recognizable human pleasures, while to match it, there was a gruesome hell, presided over by a host of demons, where the wicked or unworthy suffered an imaginative variety of hideous tortures. One may again compare this with analogous changes in Christianity. As with Christianity, the popularization of Buddhism led to extensive artistic representation in painting, sculpture, and architecture, including a number of often profoundly beautiful paintings and statues of the Buddha and his attendants and a great variety of temples. The latter included the pagoda form in the Mahayana countries and the dagoba in Theravada lands.

Mahayana Buddhism was transmitted to China (via central Asia), Korea, and Japan because by that time it had become the dominant form in India. From China it spread to Tibet and Korea and from there to Japan by A.D. 500. A number of new Mahayana monastic orders and sects that developed originally in China, including the contemplative and mystical school of Ch'an Buddhism, were diffused to both countries; in Japan, the term *Ch'an* was corrupted into *Zen,* and other schools and monastic orders of Buddhism also flourished. The growth of Japanese Buddhism accelerated greatly during the period of direct Japanese contact with T'ang dynasty China (eighth century), when many Japanese Buddhist monks visited the country. In Japan and Korea too, Buddhist art flourished in a variety of forms. In the 840s the Chinese state, concerned about and covetous of the growing wealth and power of Buddhist temples and monasteries, confiscated much of it and suppressed Buddhism except as a small minority religion within a dominantly Confucian context. That was to be its fate until modern times. But in Japan Buddhism remained proportionately far more important. Buddhism is today, at least nominally, the major religion of Japan, although most Japanese are either wholly secular or very casual followers

The great stupa (temple) at Sanchi in central India. Begun by Ashoka in the third century B.C., it was enlarged during the century after his death, when the outer ring and gateways were added. The stupa represents the universe as the great bowl of the sky. The small three-tiered structure on top became the basis for the pagoda form as Mahayana Buddhism spread from India to China, Korea, and Japan.

in their adherence to any religious faith. In Korea, Buddhism survived the T'ang persecution and remained vigorous, though losing ground in the modern period to secularism, as in Japan.

Confucianism

Many people argue that Confucianism is not a religion but merely a set of ethical rules, a moral philosophy. It is true that it specifically avoids any concern with theology, the afterlife, or otherworldly matters, and it is true as well that most Chinese, Korean, Vietnamese, and Japanese Confucianists supplemented it with Buddhism, Taoism, or Shinto (traditional Japanese animism or nature worship), which provide a greater otherworldly structure. In the end it does not perhaps matter whether one calls Confucianism religion or philosophy; it is the creed by which millions of East Asians, close to a third of the world, have lived for over 2,000 years. Confucianism has probably made more impact on belief and behavior than any of the great religions, in the sense that most East Asians accept and follow the teachings of Confucius more thoroughly than followers of the ethical teachings of any other system of belief. Those teachings contain much common sense about human relations, but they are a good deal more than that, reflecting and shaping a highly distinctive set of values, norms, and sociopolitical patterns. Confucianism has its temples too, which serve as monuments to the doctrine even though it lacks a prescribed ritual or an organized priesthood.

Confucius and Mencius

Confucius (K'ung Fu-tze, 551–c. 479 B.C.), the son of a minor official in one of the smaller states of eastern China long before the first imperial unification, became a teacher and later an adviser to various local rulers. He never had a definite official post, and he had no discernible political influence. Like Plato, he looked for rulers who might be shaped by his advice, and like Plato, he never really found one. Several of his students became his disciples, though never as organized as in Plato's Academy; after his death, they and their students began to write down his teachings and to expand on them.

The most famous of his later followers and commentators was Meng-tzu (Mengzi), Romanized to Mencius (c. 372–c. 289 B.C.). Confucius and Mencius lived in the chaotic period of warring Chinese states and sought means for restoring order and social harmony through individual morality. Society in East Asia has always been profoundly hierarchical. The social order was seen in terms of a series of status groups and graded roles, from the ruler at the top through officials, scholars, and gentlemen to the father of the family, all of whom possessed authority over those below them but also had the responsibility to set a good example. The key element was "right relationships," carefully defined for each association: father-son, subject-ruler, husband-wife, elder brother-younger brother, and so on. Confucius and Mencius provided what became doctrinal support for such a system. It left small place for the individual but at the same time stressed the vital importance of self-cultivation and education as the only true guarantee of morality, or "virtuous behavior."

A Ch'ing dynasty ink rubbing of Confucius, made over 2,000 years after the death of the sage. There are no contemporary portraits.

The Confucian View

According to Confucianism, people are born naturally good and inclined to virtue but need education and the virtuous example of superiors to stay that way. Confucius emphasized "human-heartedness," benevolence, respect for superiors, filial loyalty, and learning to prevent anarchy and to achieve the "great harmony" between self and society that was his chief objective. Force and law were no guarantee of individual virtue or of social harmony; indeed, they were seen as ineffective as well as unnecessary in a properly run society. People must want to do right, and that can be achieved only by internalizing morality. When force or punishment has to be used, the social system has broken down.

Confucianism offered a highly pragmatic, this-worldly, and positive view of people and of society; it provided little scope for metaphysical speculation, for the supernatural, or for concepts like sin or salvation. Although Confucius and Mencius were certainly conservatives and supporters of a hierarchical social order, their doctrine also allowed for individual ability and dedication. They taught that everyone is born with the seeds of virtue and that by self-cultivation and by following virtuous examples, anyone can become a sage. This concept was incorporated later in the imperial examination system and the selection of officials from the ranks of the educated, regardless of their social origins. Confucianism also reaffirmed the right of the people to rebel against immoral or unjust rulers who had forfeited the "mandate of Heaven" by their lapse from virtue. Thus loyalty to superiors was ultimately subordinate to moral principle. This often presented individuals with a severe dilemma, especially in family situations; fathers, for example, however unjust, were rarely defied.

Natural calamities like floods, droughts, or earthquakes were commonly taken as portents of Heaven's displeasure at the unvirtuous behavior of rulers and as pretexts for rebellion, especially since they disturbed the Confucian sense of order and harmony. The natural world was seen as the model for the human world. Both ran by regular rules. Nature was a nurturing power, not a hostile one, grander and more to be admired than human works, something to which people should harmoniously adjust rather than attempt to conquer. But it was not to be looked to except as a pattern. As Confucius said, "Heaven does not speak"; it merely shows us a model of order and harmony to emulate.

Such occasional references to Heaven as an impersonal force superior to humanity are about as far as Confucius went beyond the human world. When disciples asked about the suprahuman world or life after death, he merely said that we had enough to do in understanding and managing human affairs without troubling about other matters. Although he did not explicitly say so, he did approve, however, of what is rather misleadingly called *ancestor worship.* In folk religion, ancestors were prayed to as if they could intervene as helpers. Confucian practice merely extended respect for one's elders to those who had gone before, valuing them as models and performing regular rituals at small household shrines to keep their memory alive. It was the duty of the eldest son to perform rituals on the death of his father, keeping the ancestral chain intact through successive generations and thus ensuring family continuity. Mencius underlined this by saying that of all sins against filiality (respect for one's parents), the greatest was to have no descendants, by which he meant male descendants, since women left their parental family at marriage and became members of their husband's family. This attitude still militates against current Chinese efforts to reduce the birthrate.

In the twelfth century A.D. the Confucian philosopher Chu Hsi (Zhuxi, 1130–1200) went somewhat further in speculating about the nature of the universe, in whose operation he saw the working of abstract principles, rather like those of Plato, and a Supreme Ultimate, or impersonal cosmic force. From his time on it is appropriate to speak of Neo-Confucianism, which also sets before every person the goal of becoming a sage through self-cultivation. Like classic Confucianism before it, Neo-Confucianism spread to Korea, Vietnam, and Japan, where it became the dominant philosophy, especially among the educated.

Confucianism in general strikes a balance between individual self-development and achievement, on the one hand, and the subjection of the individual to the greater good of the family and society, on the other. Unfettered individualism and freedom, basic values to Americans, connote in East Asia selfishness and the absence of rules or essential constraints, the result of which is social chaos, from which everyone suffers. For Confucianism, chaos is the greatest of all evils. Though officially rejected, Confucianism remains in many ways the basis of Chinese society today. It has persisted because it works, as the ethical code of probably the world's most successful society over so long a time. It is said to be a basic factor also in the phenomenal success of modern Japan, Korea, Taiwan, Hong Kong, and Singapore.

Taoism

The second important moral or religious philosophy of traditional China was Taoism (Daoism), from the Tao (Dao), or Way. Taoism is hard to define since one of its

Sayings of Confucius

Sayings attributed to Confucius and printed in the Analects *are usually brief and pithy. Here are some examples.*

- Learning without thought is useless. Thought without learning is dangerous.
- Shall I teach you the meaning of knowledge? When you know a thing to recognize that you know it, and when you do not know to recognize that you do not know, that is knowledge.
- Not yet understanding life, how can one understand death?
- The gentleman is concerned about what is right, the petty man about what is profitable.
- The gentleman's quality is like wind, the common people's like grass; when the wind blows, the grass bends.
- If one leads them with administrative measures and uses punishments to make them conform, the people will be evasive; but if one leads them with virtue, they will come up to expectations.

The following are from the Book of Mencius.

- Between father and son there should be affection; between sovereign and minister, righteousness; between husband and wife, attention to their separate functions; between young and old, a proper order; and between friends, fidelity.
- Nature speaks not, but the ongoing of the seasons achieves the nurturing of the ten thousand things of creation. . . . [The moral laws of society] form the same system with the laws by which the seasons succeed each other. . . . It is this same system of laws by which all created things are produced and develop themselves, each in its order and system, without injuring one another, that makes the universe so grand and impressive.

Source: Translated by R. Murphey.

basic axioms is silence, even inaction. It holds that the observable, rational, human world does not matter; the far greater cosmic world of nature does. Accordingly, one must seek guidance from the cosmos, which is beyond the realm of words. The chief text of Taoism, the *Tao te Ching* ("Classic of the Way"), is a cryptic collection of mystical remarks whose meaning even in Chinese is far from clear. The famous opening line is typical and may be translated as "The name that can be named is not the eternal name" or "The Way that can be spoken of is not the true Way, which is inconstant," implying, one supposes, that truth can only be expressed in language, if at all, through riddle and paradox. Much of the content is attributed to a contemporary of Confucius' known simply as Lao-tze (Laozi, "The Old One"), although the present text is not older than the third century B.C. and was probably compiled by several hands. Lao-tze is said to have debated with Confucius and to have disappeared in old age, traveling westward, where he somehow became immortal.

On one point the *Tao te Ching* is clear: "Those who understand don't talk; those who talk don't understand." This comment may well have been aimed at the Confucians, but although Taoist figures did occasionally speak or write, it was usually in riddles or in metaphors drawn from nature. All make the point that worldly strivings, especially attempts at political control, are futile and wrong. Their message is to relax, "go with the flow," stop trying to improve things, as the Confucians were always doing. The Taoists' favorite model was water, which flows around obstructions, adapts itself to what is, and seeks the lowest places. Whatever is, they said, is natural and hence good.

The other major figure of Taoism was the philosopher Chuang-tze (Zhuangzi; died c. 329 B.C.), whose still intriguing essays and parables further expound the ideas already associated with the school. One of his most delightful stories tells that he dreamed he was a butterfly, and when he awoke could not be sure whether he was himself or was the butterfly now dreaming that it was Chuang-tze.

Taoism grew into a religion as it merged with folk beliefs, earlier animistic and nature worship, belief in the supernatural, and a variety of mystical practices. Taoist priests, temples, and monastic orders developed (however inconsistent with the earlier message), and the originally rather esoteric philosophy became a mass religion. Later Taoists, especially after the Han dynasty, practiced magic and alchemy and pursued the search for elixirs of immortality. Such activities put them in bad repute with proper Confucians, as did their habit of irresponsible hedonism or pleasure seeking. However, the Taoists' search for medicinal herbs and their experimentation contributed importantly to the growth of Chinese medicine and other technology. They deviated from their supposed founder's injunctions to accept nature without questioning and began instead to probe for its secrets.

As it acquired a mass following, Taoism also developed a pantheon of gods and "immortals" who offered help to people in trouble and eased the way to a Taoist version of the Buddhist heaven. Taoism became in many ways an important supplement to Confucianism, and Confucians often found parts of it attractive. It was aptly said that most Chinese were Confucian when things went well and Taoist when things went badly and in retirement or old age. Confucianism's activist and social reformist postures were well complemented by Taoism's passivity and inwardness. This dualism appealed to the old Chinese distinction between yin and yang, where yang is the strong, assertive, masculine principle of existence and yin is the passive, intuitive, feminine one. Taoists and Confucianists alike agreed that both nature and humans must approximate a balance of yin and yang elements and that nature should serve as a model for humanity. But where Confucians sought to shape the world through education, Taoists urged acceptance of things as they are, confident that human meddling could not improve on cosmic truth. For them, the human world was terribly petty.

Asian Religions: Some Reflections

Most East Asians have always been eclectic in religion, weaving into their beliefs and practices elements from different religious traditions. Confucianism and Taoism are dominant except in Japan, where Confucianism, Buddhism, and Shinto predominate. Shinto is similar to Taoism but remained closer to animism and nature worship. These complementary parts form a whole, representing the religion or philosophical outlook of nearly a third of the world. Each part of the combination has its undeniable appeal, and it is easy to understand why most people selected from all of them in their beliefs and practices. When Christian missionaries arrived in the sixteenth century, they found the religious ground already thoroughly occupied in Asia not only by Confucianism, Taoism, and Shinto but by Hinduism, Buddhism, and Islam as well. All were old and sophisticated religions or philosophies with long literate traditions.

All of these Asian religions recognized that there is evil in the world, and even evil people, but none of them ever developed the sharp dichotomy (or dualism) between good and evil that is characteristic of Zoroastrianism, Judaism, Christianity, and Islam. In the Indian and Chinese view, all of creation is the work of God ("Heaven," the creative principle), which thus necessarily includes what is perceived by humans as both good and bad. Consequently, there was no conception of "original sin" inherent in individuals, no Garden of Eden or early innocence from which people then fell into error and suffered punishment because they had broken God's rules. Evil was understood as part of God's created world, not as some human aberration. The Christian idea of sin thus had little meaning in Asia; as has often been said, "Eden was preserved in the East." Bad behavior was acknowledged and might be punished in this world and the next, but the basic presumption was that people were born and remained intrinsically good, not with built-in inclinations to "sin."

Misbehavior was seen as a failure of society, which God created imperfect, and as the result of an individual's straying from the teaching and model of her or his elders or superiors, as in Confucianism, or from the established rules of her or his dharma in Hinduism and Buddhism, as made clear by priests and sages. People were seen not as morally lost when they strayed from the path but as always redeemable, through education or renewed efforts at right behavior, aided by piety, meditation, and so on. Return to virtue, or "merit," might also be won by good deeds, including charity, or simply by leading (in Christian words) "a godly, righteous, and sober life," but never by having one's "sins" magically forgiven by priestly or other ritual, since no concept of sin existed. Nor was faith or the acceptance of any creed ever seen as paramount, if important at all; people were judged by their actions.

One further distinction between all of these eastern Asian religions, on the one hand, and Christianity, Judaism, and Islam, on the other, is their acceptance of the natural world as good, as part of divine creation that is greater and more powerful than humankind but like them a part of the cosmos. People occupy a humbler place in God's creation, and it behooves them therefore to adjust, while seeking in nature the image of God rather than in themselves. The sages and holy men who sought wisdom and the understanding of God or of the cosmos looked for it in nature, in the mountains, far from human distractions. There was no conception of the natural world as an enemy, to be fought against or overcome, as in later Christianity. Nature was instead seen as a nurturing mother or as an inspiring model. Adapting to it and understanding it were the keys both to earthly success and to spiritual and moral truth.

Such a thread runs deeply through Hinduism, Buddhism, Confucianism, Taoism, and Shinto and is far weaker, absent, or explicitly opposite in Judaism, Christianity, and Islam, as in the Book of Genesis call to the human world to "have dominion" over all the world of nature or in the nineteenth- and twentieth-century Western drive for the "conquest of nature." One might perhaps argue that Judaism, out of which Christianity and later Islam grew, was conceived in a harsher environment than the great religions of Asia farther east, where it may be easier to see nature as beneficent and nurturing and people as prospering by adjusting to, accepting, and admiring it. Whatever the reasons, Asia west of India followed a different religious path.

Zoroastrianism and Mithraism

We know less about Zoroastrianism, the dominant religion of ancient and classical Persia (Iran), than about any of the others described in this chapter. Zoroaster, its founder, lived long before the advent of preserved written records in Persia, probably between 800 and 600 B.C., and the incomplete texts we have on the belief and practice of the religion he founded come mainly from the thirteenth century A.D., although earlier texts existed by the sixth century B.C. The founder's name in Persian was Zarathustra (Zoroaster was the Greek version), and his teachings are recorded and embroidered in the Avesta, but the form of the Avesta we have is only a fragmentary remnant of earlier texts and includes much later material. To the Greeks and Romans, Zoroaster was famous as the founder of the wisdom of the Magi, mythical Iranian priest-kings. In his youth he reportedly had celestial visions and conversations with divine beings, after which he became a wandering preacher. Later he interested an eastern Iranian prince in his teachings; the prince became his protector and advocate, and the new religion became a state church.

Zoroastrian Beliefs

Zoroastrianism was rooted in the old Iranian or Aryan folk religion, and there are some striking similarities between it and the religion of Vedic India. Both are polytheistic (professing many gods), and both worshiped Indra as well as natural forces, especially fire. Both believed in the supremacy of moral powers and of an eternal natural law and a creative principle. The major difference lay in the pronounced dualism of Zoroastrianism, which divided creation into the powers of good and evil, light and darkness. Vedic India called all their gods and goddesses *deva,* and although many of them had destructive aspects, in general they were seen as good. Zoroastrianism used the closely related term *daeva* in Persian to refer to evil spirits only, which are opposed and kept in check by the forces of good and light, incorporated in the supreme deity, the sexless Ahura-Mazda. In one of several striking parallels with Judeo-Christian theology, Ahura-Mazda's original twin, Ahriman, was, like Lucifer, banished from heaven to hell, where he or she reigns as the principle of evil. Earlier cults, such as that of Mithras, the god of day, survived within Zoroastrianism and later spread to the Mediterranean.

Zoroaster reportedly said that he received a commission from God to purify religion, in effect by transcending the earlier cults, introducing moral laws, and constructing a theory of the universe embodying the dualist principle. By his time Iranian society was based mainly on agriculture rather than hunting, gathering, or nomadism; had developed cities and towns; and was ready for a more sophisticated theology than nature worship alone or ritual cults. Ahura-Mazda is the personification not only of power and majesty but also of ethical principles for guidance. She or he is described in the Avesta as assisted by her or his creatures, "immortal holy ones," the forces of good sense or good principle, truth, law, order, reverence, immortality, and obedience. The history of the conflict between these good forces and the forces of evil is the history of the world. Creation is divided between these two forces, whose endless conflict has as its object the human soul. People are creations of Ahura-Mazda, but they are free to decide and to act and can be influenced by the forces of evil. All human life and activity are part of this conflict. By a true confession of faith, by good deeds, and by keeping body and soul pure, any individual can limit the power of the evil forces and strengthen the power of goodness. Evil deeds, words, and thoughts strengthen the power of evil.

After death, each person is judged in heaven, according to the Book of Life in which all deeds, thoughts, and words are recorded. Wicked actions cannot be undone but can be balanced by good works. If the balance is favorable, the person enters paradise; if unfavorable, he or she suffers the eternal pains of hell. If the account is equally balanced, a kind of limbo or intermediate stage is provided, with the final lot to be decided at the last judgment. The Avesta tells us almost nothing about ceremonial worship, but it appears from early times to have centered on a sacred fire. Later development of the religion added the doctrine of repentance, atonement, and the remission of sins, administered by priests.

Zoroaster saw himself as a prophet and believed that the end of the present world and the coming of the Kingdom of Heaven were near. For most people his doctrines were too abstract; both old and new popular deities became part of Zoroastrianism in later periods, and a priesthood developed that organized and conducted worship and laid down detailed laws for the purification of the body and soul, the conduct of good works, the giving of alms, the pursuit of agriculture, and the prohibition against either burning or burying the dead. Both soil and fire, as well as water, were considered sacred and not to be defiled by death. Bodies were to be exposed in appointed places, sometimes on an elevated platform, for consumption by vultures and wild dogs. Originally Zoroastrianism apparently had no temples, but in later periods fire altars came into use, and these evolved into temples where priests performed sacrifices and other rituals. Priests were the teachers and keepers of the religion; every young believer, after being received into the religion, was supposed to choose a spiritual guide, usually a priest. Most of the changes mentioned here seem to have come about by approximately the sixth century B.C. and to have begun considerably earlier.

With the rise of the Persian Empire in the sixth century B.C., Zoroastrianism became the state religion. Under the Achemenid dynasty and its conquests, the religion spread over most of western Asia and the Turkic republics of central Asia. After the collapse of this first empire, Zoroastrianism languished and then was restored to new vigor under the Sassanids from the third to the seventh centuries A.D., when it was again the state church; the state enforced compliance with its religious laws. The Arab conquest of Persia, complete by 637, and the persecutions that followed largely extinguished Zoroastrianism in the land of its birth. In modern Iran there remain only a very few followers, now under new pressure from the rigid fundamentalism of its Muslim rulers. The chief survivors are the Parsees of the Bombay area (the name Parsee is a corruption of *Persian*), who came originally from Persia to India about the eighth century A.D., primarily to escape Muslim persecution; they still maintain most of the doctrine and practices of classical Zoroastrianism.

Zoroastrianism, as well as the cult of Mithras, which it incorporated, had a profound influence on Eastern and Western thinking during the time of its flourishing. It has obvious similarities both with Hinduism and with Judaism and Christianity, and in part even with Islam, especially its doctrines on life after death. Its basic dualistic emphasis helped shape early Christian theology, and more than traces of what was eventually labeled the "dualistic heresy" remain even in modern Christian thought, like its pre-Christian ideas about the judgment of the dead, the relationship between faith and good works, and the role of the priesthood. Arising out of more primitive cults, especially the worship of fire and of the sun, it became through the teachings of Zoroaster and his successors a sophisticated theological, cosmological, and ethical system that was known to and admired by both Eastern and Western civilizations before or during the period when they were working out their own transition from tribal cults to mature religious thought. Although Zoroastrianism largely ceased to exist nearly 14 centuries ago, many of its ideas live on in the other great religions.

Mithraism

The worship of Mithras began as early as the fourth century B.C. Originally Ahura-Mazda's chief aide in the battle against the powers of darkness, Mithras became the central figure in a cult that spread rapidly throughout western Asia and into Europe, arriving in Rome in the first century B.C. In the years following A.D. 100 it acquired many new adherents in Italy and other parts of the Roman Empire, attracting the lower classes, slaves, and soldiers, who took their religious customs with them when they served abroad; a temple to Mithras has been discovered in the Roman remains of London. By the late third century Mithraism was vying with Christianity to replace the old paganism, though Constantine's support of the Christians caused Mithraism's rapid decline.

Mithraism's broad appeal was probably due to the fact that it combined the spirituality of its origins with humanizing detail. Unlike Ahura-Mazda, the remote god of light, Mithras, god of day, was born in human form on December 25 in a cave. When he grew up, he slaughtered a mythical sacred bull, whose blood fertilized the earth. After a time Mithras returned to heaven, where he intercedes with Ahura-Mazda on behalf of his followers.

Ceremonies in honor of Mithras were held in special temples known as Mithraea, which often took the form of underground caves in memory of his birth. Among the rites of initiation was baptism in a bull's blood, which formed one of the seven stages of induction; others included the recitation of various miracles that Mithras had performed, such as ending a drought and averting a flood. It is a measure of Mithraism's appeal that Christianity adopted a number of its external characteristics, including the symbolic date of December 25 as the birthday of Jesus; the day marks the approximate period of the winter solstice, when the sun, returning from south of the equator, is "reborn." In the end Mithraism gained no lasting hold. One reason for this may be that women were not accepted as initiates and played no part in the rituals or the myths. By contrast, many early converts to Christianity were women.

The importance of the written word in Judaism is manifested in this fresco, painted in the third century B.C. *The scroll it depicts probably was intended to represent a copy of the Torah.*

Judaism

Unlike Buddhists or Christians, the Jews have maintained a strong sense of ethnic as well as spiritual identity. That this identity has survived through so lengthy and so tragic a history is an indication of the strength of Jewish convictions. From the beginning the Jews saw themselves as special instruments of a unique providence. The vision of Abraham, whose family fled from Ur around 2000 B.C., was twofold. Abraham, the traditional founder of the Jewish people, put his faith in a God who operated in the world on principles of righteousness. At the same time, he saw the Jews as appointed by God to communicate this vision to the world. To transmit their message, the Jews found it essential to maintain their separateness from the peoples with whom they came in contact. This did not preclude the possibility of others joining the Jewish nation, but those who did so had to give tangible proof of their conversion. The symbolic representation of this was the rite of circumcision, a tradition that probably goes back to the time of Abraham. In addition, as Judaism developed, customs evolved that strengthened the sense of ethnic distinctness.

The Covenant at Sinai and the Torah

Abraham's message stressed a universal obligation for the Hebrews to serve humanity as a "kingdom of priests." Moses enunciated the terms of this service in the Sinai desert after the exodus from Egypt, particularly in the Ten Commandments, which laid out the tenets of the Jewish ethical system. The first four dealt with human obligations to God and described how people were to worship Yahweh. The remaining six were concerned with relationships between peoples, parents and children, husbands and wives; they also prohibited certain crimes, such as perjury, theft, and murder. Other ancient religions produced codes governing conduct, but the Ten Commandments were unique in that they were directed not only at the Jews but at all peoples. They underlined the special character of the Jewish message, moreover, by forbidding the worship of nature or of images and by emphasizing that the piety and morality they outlined constituted a duty. All who abided by them would be rewarded; the disobedient would be punished. By subscribing to the Covenant, the Jews acquired a special historical consciousness. The Ten Commandments were universal in their application, yet the Jews alone bore the responsibility of communicating the message to the world. This sense of special identity proved crucial to the survival of Judaism, and the Jews, throughout centuries of persecution.

The teachings that evolved from the Covenant at Sinai are known as the Torah, or Law. The Torah laid out the religious and moral requirements of Judaism in prescriptions and prohibitions; one of its special characteristics was the importance laid on negative commands: "thou shalt not." Jewish law aimed to cultivate a holiness that would influence not only the spiritual life of individuals but also their relationship to society. Just as the pious Buddhist was enjoined not to wander from the path by injunctions that regulated human relationships, so the Torah taught Jews about their religious duties and their earthly responsibilities, including an injunction to "love thy neighbor as thyself" that could apply to Jews and non-Jews alike.

As in Hinduism and Buddhism, Jewish law paid special attention to the poor and the weak. The Torah forbade employers to exploit their workers. Complex regulations governed the making and repaying of loans to protect the borrower. Unlike the code of Hammurabi and the laws of the Hittites, which were intended to safeguard property, the Torah sought to protect the individual. This concern extended also to animals. Although Jews were not required to be vegetarians, as pious Hindus were, the Torah instructed them to treat oxen and other work animals with kindness and to allow them the same right as humans to rest on the sabbath, the weekly day of repose. Detailed instructions concerned the preparation and consumption of food and drink and other aspects of daily life. Dietary regulations covered both foods that could and could not be eaten and the dishes and utensils with which they were prepared and consumed. Many Jews still observe this tradition, often loosely referred to as "keeping kosher." Generally, the Torah's social legislation aimed to eliminate distinctions based on rank, wealth, or birth; in the eyes of the law, all people were equal and enjoyed the same rights. This was in strong contrast to the hierarchical caste system of Hinduism or the graded society of Confucius.

In later centuries Judaic traditions often alienated the Jews from other people. Even in cosmopolitan Alexandria, the Jewish community lived apart from the rest of the population, a tradition that, by unhappy irony, became a requirement in the ghettos of the Middle Ages in Europe. It is therefore important to remember that the Torah exhorts Jews to follow the example of their God and love all persons equally. Only by doing so, while maintaining their own Jewish character, could they truly love God. Tradition, together with the experience of prolonged exile following a brief period of nationhood, accentuated the Jews' sense of distinctiveness. Furthermore, their belief that they were divinely chosen to reveal God's love for all was often interpreted by non-Jews as a conviction of moral superiority. Yet from its beginning the message of Judaism was intended to apply to all societies.

The Prophets

The Torah's injunctions left no doubt that people who violated the Law would be punished. Formal warning was insufficient to instill righteousness, and throughout the history of the kingdom of Israel there appeared religious figures known as *prophets.* The word is derived from the Greek word *profetes,* meaning "one who speaks for another"; the prophets of the Old Testament thought of themselves as spokesmen for God. Inspired by their visions of God's will, they counseled and rebuked their contemporaries on every aspect of religious, moral, and political conduct.

The earliest prophets were probably unofficially attached to shrines or, during the kingdom, to the royal household. From the eighth century B.C., figures such as Jeremiah vigorously opposed corruption in official religion. Calling his people to a rigid observance of ethical monotheism, Jeremiah railed against the emptiness and hypocrisy of formal religious observance. Speaking on behalf of his God, he thundered: "Why have they provoked me to anger with their graven images and with their foreign idols?"[1] Other prophets, such as Isaiah, reminded the Jews of their unique historical mission: "Give thanks to the Lord, call upon his name; make known his deeds among the nations, proclaim that his name is exalted."[2]

Although the prophets affirmed their belief in the Jews' special destiny, they underlined the universal nature of their message and insisted on the necessity of rigorous monotheism. The God of Israel was the only God, destined to be the God of all people. Furthermore, their messages were directed against both religious error and social injustice. They reproved an errant people for breaking their covenant with God. In the words of Amos:

> **Seek the Lord and live, lest he break out like fire in the house of Joseph, and it devour, with none to quench it for Bethel [the northern kingdom's chief sanctuary], O you who turn justice to wormwood, and cast down righteousness to the earth!"[3]**

The prophet's role as unofficial mediator between God and humanity is a special characteristic of the Jewish religion and was partly embraced by Christianity and Islam. It profoundly influenced the life and teachings of Jesus, whose denunciations of the Jewish religious leaders of his day were in the prophetic tradition.

With the destruction of Solomon's temple at Jerusalem in A.D. 70 by Roman forces, the Jews lost the

A Prophet Calls for Social Reform

Typical of the prophetic message is the following passage from Amos, written in the eighth century B.C. The prophet is incensed by the social injustice he sees among the Hebrews.

Listen to this, you that trample on the needy and try to destroy the poor of the country. You say to yourselves, "We can hardly wait for the holy days to be over so that we can sell our grain. When will the sabbath end, so that we can start selling again? Then we can overcharge, use false measures, and fix the scales to cheat our customers. We can sell worthless wheat at a high price. We'll find a poor man who can't pay his debts, not even the price of a pair of sandals, and we'll buy him as a slave."

The Lord, the God of Israel, has sworn, "I will never forget their evil deeds. And so the earth will quake, and everyone in the land will be in distress. The whole country will be shaken; it will rise and fall like the Nile River. The time is coming when I will make the sun go down at noon and the earth grow dark in daytime. I, the Sovereign Lord, have spoken. I will turn your festivals into funerals and change your glad songs into cries of grief. I will make you shave your heads and wear sackcloth, and you will be like parents mourning for their only son. That day will be bitter to the end.

"The time is coming when I will send famine on the land.

"People will be hungry, but not for bread; they will be thirsty, but not for water. They will hunger and thirst for a message from the Lord. I, the Sovereign Lord, have spoken."

Source: Amos 8:4–11a, *Good News Bible* (New York: American Bible Society, 1976).

focal point of their worship. The temple was never forgotten; to this day pious Jews pray at the western wall of the building, known as the Wailing Wall, the only part still standing. Jewish tradition advises Jews to leave a tiny part of their house unfinished, perhaps a small piece of wall unplastered, in memory of Jerusalem and its temple. The need to remember Jerusalem underlines the sense of dispersal that has permeated the past two millennia of the Jewish Diaspora ("scattering").

Jerusalem: The Holy City

The historic center of Judaism, Jerusalem is today the crossroads of three great world religions—Judaism, Christianity, and Islam—and remains sacred to each. Jerusalem is situated dramatically on a series of hills north of the Negev desert. From its beginnings it appears to have been a sacred city; its name derives from Shalem, a western Semitic deity of the second millennium B.C. King David captured it from a local tribe, the Jebusites, about 1000 B.C. and made it the capital of Israel. His successor, Solomon, enlarged it and built a massive temple.

The temple was a thick-walled rectangular building of squared stones and cedar beams laid out from east to west, 110 feet long, 48 feet wide, and more than 50 feet high. A huge porch extended on its eastern side, and side chambers were built against the other three sides. An interior wall marked off the main hall from the sanctuary of the ark, a 30-foot cube paneled with richly carved cedar that admitted light through high lattice windows and contained a single lamp. Two cherubim carved from olive wood, each standing 15 feet high, surmounted the ark.

Over the centuries the city, and especially the temple, became the primary focus of the Jewish faith. Psalm 137 rings with the passionate sense of loss felt by the Jews during their first exile from the city during the Babylonian captivity of the sixth century B.C.:

> ***If I forget thee, O Jerusalem, let my right hand lose its cunning. If I forget thee, O Jerusalem, let my tongue cleave to the roof of my mouth.***[4]

After the return to Zion, the Jews constructed a second temple, completed around 515 B.C., on the ruins of the first. The city too was rebuilt and flourished under successive domination by the Persians, the Ptolemaic dynasty of Egypt, and the Romans. During the Hellenistic period the Jews became dispersed throughout the eastern Mediterranean world, but Jerusalem remained their spiritual capital, the site of their pilgrimages, and the direction they turned to in prayer. All pious Jews, wherever they were, sent money each year for the temple's upkeep.

Ancient Jerusalem reached the height of its splendor under the otherwise repressive rule of the Roman client-king Herod the Great (37–4 B.C.), who undertook a restoration and expansion of the temple that was completed only shortly before Romans razed both the city and the temple after the Jewish rebellion of A.D. 70. Despite Herod's unpopularity, even his Jewish subjects marveled at the reconstruction of their temple; one rabbi commented, "He who has not set eyes upon the structure of Herod has not seen a structure of beauty in his life." But the fame of Herod would rest not on his public works but on the birth, late in his reign, of Jesus of Nazareth. Jerusalem was where Jesus came to preach his gospel and where, outside the city walls, the Romans crucified him in A.D. 29.

Christianity made little headway in Jerusalem in the decades after Jesus' death and slow progress even after the city was once again rebuilt. Not until its adoption by the Roman emperor Constantine early in the fourth century were the sites associated with Jesus' life identified. The Church of the Resurrection, completed in 335, marked the beginning of Jerusalem as a Christian capital, and by the end of the fourth century it was crowded with churches, shrines, and monasteries, as well as hospices for the thousands of pilgrims who now thronged to it. Within the church Jerusalem acquired the status of a patriarchate, equal in rank to the far larger cities of Alexandria, Antioch, and the new imperial capital of Constantinople. Under the Byzantine emperors, its position was unrivaled. But after a brief Persian occupation (614–629) it surrendered to Muslim forces, ushering in the city's third phase as a religious center.

The Talmud

With the temple gone and its priests scattered, Jewish worship centered on local synagogues and their teachers, or rabbis. The term *rabbi* is often applied to individuals who have undergone special study and training in religious matters. In more recent times rabbis have come to serve as the equivalent of priests or ministers of congregations, with a wide range of social and counseling responsibilities. In its original sense, however, the term applied to anyone who impressed fellow Jews by the wisdom and insight with which he expounded Jewish Law.

The principal source of the Law was found in the biblical texts. The transformation of the written and oral

Following the Jewish revolt against Roman rule in A.D. 66, Roman troops looted Jerusalem, taking such religious objects from the temple as the menorah, or seven-branched candlestick, and the sacred trumpets. The scene is depicted here on the Arch of Titus in Rome.

accounts into a fixed canon was long and complex; the work that came to be known among Christians as the Old Testament had probably received its final form by A.D. 100. Rabbinical teachings on these biblical texts, together with legal judgments, religious duties, and other aspects of Jewish life, began to be recorded by the scattered Jewish communities of the Diaspora. By the middle of the fourth century B.C. the Jews of Palestine had compiled the religious and ethical teachings known as the Talmud, which, together with another version of the Talmud produced slightly later in Babylon, has served ever since as the single most cohesive force in Judaism. The aim of the Talmud's creators was to use biblical interpretation and discussion as the basis for religious, moral, and legal practice that could serve all Jewish communities.

The rituals of modern Judaism derive from the Talmud, as do marriage laws and other social customs. Until the nineteenth century, religious services utilized the Hebrew liturgy, which included psalms and other readings from the Bible, established by Talmudic scholars; Orthodox Jewish worshipers continue this practice today. The custom of the bar mitzvah (the confirmation of boys at age 13) and the principal holy days of the year, together with the manner in which they should be kept, derive from the Talmud. Fasting marks Yom Kippur, the day of atonement for sins, the most solemn day of the year.

Firmly anchored in a tradition that goes back to the Torah and Moses' exposition of the Covenant, the Talmud is a practical guide to conduct rather than a theological treatise. Unlike the early Christian writers, who sought to provide a sound theological basis for the principles of their religion, the Talmudic rabbis concentrated on religious practice and morality. The Talmud teaches that faith is valuable only if it leads to ethical action. In this way Judaism avoided many of the theological controversies that characterize the history of Christianity. In its insistence on God as pure spirit, Talmudic doctrine reaffirms a belief as old as Abraham. The Hebrew Scriptures, it is true, refer to God as one who addresses Moses and the prophets, but this manner of speaking is used only to make communication possible between God and humans: "We describe God by terms borrowed from the divine creation in order to make [God] intelligible to humans." Judaism is thus the only ancient religion that avoids the use of the visual arts and condemns the worship of "graven images." Centuries later Islam adopted similar strictures.

The goal to which obedience to God will lead is an age of righteousness on earth. Judaism believes that this period of universal peace will be ushered in by the Messiah, who will preside over the spiritual regeneration of humanity. In Isaiah's words:

> **Of the increase of his government and of peace there will be no end, upon the throne of David, and over his kingdom, to establish it, and to uphold it with justice and with righteousness from this time forth and for evermore."[5]**

Judaism remains a minority religion outside of Israel, but its principal religious texts, the Hebrew Scriptures, have had a profound influence on Western culture. Many of its principles have entered the mainstream of Western culture through the religion that sprang from it, Christianity.

Christianity

From the time of its adoption by Constantine, the history of Christianity has been linked with that of Western culture. During the centuries of its diffusion and transmission by missionaries throughout the world, it has taken on a variety of forms. If the range of Christian belief is less varied than that of Hinduism, it is more eclectic than Judaism or, probably, Buddhism. Yet its founder, Jesus of Nazareth, was a Jew who regularly attended the synagogue on the Sabbath and on the principal Jewish religious festivals and who declared that his purpose was not to destroy but to fulfill the Jewish Law.

Virtually all that is known about the life of Jesus is contained in the Gospels of Matthew, Mark, Luke, and John. Even the date of his birth is uncertain; most modern authorities place it between 4 and 2 B.C. The Gospel writers give little information about his early life; only Matthew and Luke describe the nativity (Jesus' birth) and his childhood. Near the age of 30 Jesus was baptized by John, "the Baptist," a religious ascetic in the style of the earlier prophets. Fervent in denouncing the ways of his contemporaries, John predicted that one greater than he would come after him as an agent of divine judgment and identified that figure as Jesus. In taking up the life of an itinerant rabbi, Jesus preached John's message that the Jews should mend their ways and return to a strict observance of the Law. He was assisted in his mission by a band of 12 male followers, who were called the *apostles.*

By the time of Jesus' baptism, Jerusalem had become the capital of the Roman province of Judea and the center for a wide variety of Jewish religious movements. The Pharisees, who advocated strict observance of the Law, were one such group. The Sadducees combined Jewish

WORLD RELIGIONS

	Hinduism and Buddhism	Chinese	Persian	Judeo-Christian
1500–600 B.C.	Vedas			Exodus (c. 1250 B.C.) Reign of David (c. 1000–c. 970 B.C.)
600–100 B.C.	Jainism (600–500 B.C.) Gautama Buddha (c. 563–c. 485 B.C.)	Confucius (551–c. 479 B.C.) Lao-tze (c. 500 B.C.) Mencius (c. 372–c. 289 B.C.) Chuang-tze (c. 350 B.C.)	Zoroaster (before 600 B.C.) Mithraism (before 300 B.C.)	Fall of Judah (586 B.C.)
100 B.C.–A.D. 320	*Bhagavadgita* (A.D. 100–200) Mahayana Buddhism (A.D. 100–200)			Jesus (c. 4 B.C.–A.D. 29) Death of Paul (A.D. 67) Destruction of the temple at Jerusalem (A.D. 70) Edict of Milan (A.D. 313)

traditions with those of the Greco-Roman world in a blend typical of the Hellenistic period, while the Zealots advocated violent revolution against the Romans. These groups were united in one respect: opposition to Jesus' teachings.

The ideals that emerge in the Gospel accounts stress the importance of love and the avoidance of anger or violence. In the Sermon on the Mount, Jesus extends the traditional Jewish sympathy for the poor and the helpless: "Blessed are the meek, for they shall inherit the earth." His teaching was explicitly based on the Law; his insistence on the importance of following its ethical content rather than merely observing its outward forms drew the Pharisees' anger. Their attempts to trap him in a simple solution to moral dilemmas are described by the Gospel writers. When Jesus was reproached for preaching against divorce, which the Mosaic Law permitted, he replied: "For your hardness of heart Moses allowed you to divorce your wives, but from the beginning it was not so."

Some of his followers interpreted Jesus' declaration that the Kingdom of God was at hand as referring to contemporary political events; they believed him to be predicting the expulsion of the Romans and the refounding of David's old kingdom of Israel. The use of David's title of Messiah (*Christos,* in Greek) by Jesus' followers thus implied that he was the successor of the great Jewish king; for this reason the high priest condemned him for blasphemy and the Romans crucified him.

The apostles' belief in Jesus' physical resurrection was the prime factor in the foundation of a church to promote his teachings. The message of the apostle Peter's first sermon was that Jesus had died and risen to be with God and that baptism marked the adherence of those who accepted his resurrection. These first Christians were Jewish by birth and continued to follow the basic Jewish Law, but their belief in the divine as well as the human nature of Jesus inevitably aroused hostility and suspicion among their contemporaries. When one early convert, Stephen, was stoned to death, many others left Jerusalem and traveled throughout Asia, preaching and seeking converts. Tradition credits one of them, Thomas, with having carried Christianity to India.

Paul and the Expansion of Christianity

The most important figure in the development and spread of Christianity was Paul (died A.D. 67), a Pharisee who had been present at the stoning of Stephen. Converted to Christianity by a vision, Paul was the first and greatest theologian of the early church. As a Jew he spoke Aramaic, the language of Jesus and his followers, but he had been raised in the Greek city of Tarsus and was at home in the world of Greco-Roman culture. His exposition of the principal beliefs of Christianity, together with his preaching in Greece and Italy, facilitated Christianity's rapid spread. The cohesion of the early church and its teachings, for which Paul is largely responsible, is in strong contrast to the variety of traditions that accumulated about the Buddha after his death.

According to Pauline doctrine, human failure to follow God's law was the consequence of Adam and Eve's disobedience, which corrupted all their descendants. Thus humans could achieve salvation not by living in accordance with any set of laws, Jewish or other, but only by divine grace. The life and death of Jesus were intended, Paul taught, as a manifestation of this grace; as

The Sermon on the Mount

The essence of Jesus' teaching is found in the Sermon on the Mount.

Now when he saw the crowds, he went up on a mountainside and sat down. His disciples came to him, and he began to teach them, saying:

"Blessed are the poor in spirit,
for theirs is the kingdom of heaven.
"Blessed are those who mourn,
for they will be comforted.
"Blessed are the meek,
for they will inherit the earth.
"Blessed are those who hunger and thirst for righteousness,
for they will be filled.
"Blessed are the merciful,
for they will be shown mercy.
"Blessed are the pure in heart,
for they will see God.
"Blessed are the peacemakers,
for they will be called sons of God.
"Blessed are those who are persecuted because of righteousness,
for theirs is the kingdom of heaven.

"Blessed are you when people insult you, persecute you and falsely say all kinds of evil against you because of me. Rejoice and be glad, because great is your reward in heaven, for in the same way they persecuted the prophets who were before you. . . . Do not think that I have come to abolish the Law or the Prophets; I have not come to abolish them but to fulfill them. . . .

"You have heard that it was said, 'Love your neighbor and hate your enemy.' But I tell you: Love your enemies and pray for those who persecute you, that you may be sons of your Father in heaven."

Source: "The Sermon on the Mount." Scripture taken from the Holy Bible: New International Version. Copyright © 1973, 1978, 1984 by International Bible Society. Used by permission of Zondervan Publishing House.

God's son, he suffered in order to show God's love for humanity. All who accepted Jesus' sacrifice through faith, said Paul, could achieve reconciliation with God.

Paul was the virtual creator of Christian theology, and his views were debated and generally accepted throughout the early church. Yet the austerity of his view of proper relations between men and women caused problems for future theologians. Women played an important part in the life of Jesus and were among his most loyal and devoted supporters; a majority of those who followed him to his crucifixion were women. Nonetheless, Paul required them to play a subordinate role. The devout man, he taught, should avoid them as much as possible: "It is well for a man not to touch a woman." Those who were single should remain so, Paul urged, as he himself did. He counseled marriage in cases where sexual abstinence was impossible, but he warned that it tended to distract from spiritual duties by tempting a couple to think in worldly terms. Yet elsewhere in his writings Paul compares marriage to Christ's relationship with the church. Paul's teachings have profoundly influenced social relations and sexual ethics in the West up to our time.

One of the earliest surviving depictions of Jesus' crucifixion and resurrection appeared in the "Rabula Gospels" (c. 460). At the foot of the cross, Roman soldiers gamble for Jesus' robe.

Paul saw Christianity as a universal religion. Unlike Judaism, it involved no traditional or ethnic barriers, and unlike Hinduism or Buddhism, its followers could become Christians only by rejecting their earlier religious beliefs. In expressing these ideas Paul used the universal language of his day, Greek, which had been spoken since the Hellenistic period from Italy to India. The use of Greek helped to transform Christianity from an offshoot of Judaism to a universal religion by placing it on the vast stage of the Roman Empire. The other crucial factor in the transformation was Paul's insistence that converts to Christianity were not bound to follow the customs prescribed in the Jewish Law or to undergo circumcision. Paul's opinion was much debated in the first century of Christianity, but its general acceptance facilitated the conversion of Gentiles to the early church. (*Gentile* is derived from a Latin word meaning "non-Roman," thus "foreign," "pagan.")

The rich and complex character of many Hellenistic cults, with their blend of ancient Greek and Asian features, had in many ways prepared the West to accept a new religion from Asia. Throughout the Roman world, as we have seen, philosophical systems of belief such as Stoicism and Epicureanism provided satisfaction only to an elite few, while traditional Roman religion was largely an instrument of the state. Provided that they said or did nothing to question the state's authority, Paul and other Christian missionaries were free to preach their doctrines in public. Nor was there any serious likelihood of Jewish opposition, since the Roman forces that destroyed the temple in Jerusalem in 70 effectively ended the city's role as a religious center. Indeed, some Hellenized Jews in the Roman world became enthusiastic converts, and the network of synagogues throughout the Mediterranean area and western Asia often provided a valuable platform for Paul and the other missionaries.

For its first decades the new movement functioned on a relatively informal basis, with preachers, teachers, and evangelists either self-appointed or selected by individual congregations. The community at Jerusalem remained "first among equals," while Paul continued to exercise supervision over the churches he founded. Conflict with the Roman authorities was usually avoided; Paul himself instructed Christians to obey the laws and pay taxes.

As Christian communities grew and became more active, the need for greater organization arose. Around the end of the first century the principal seat of religious authority moved from Jerusalem to Rome, where according to tradition Peter and Paul had founded a church. Each community had a leader, or bishop, but beginning in the fourth and fifth centuries the bishops of Rome claimed supreme authority by virtue of their reputed succession from Peter.

There was a constant need to define and explain Christian doctrine as it came into contact with adherents of other beliefs. The Gnostics, who followed a Hellenistic blend of Greek and Roman religious beliefs, posed a particular challenge. They despised the world of matter and sought salvation by escape from the flesh, like Hindu and Buddhist ascetics. Many of them eagerly adopted the belief in a divine Christ but could not accept that the divinity had become flesh in the person of Jesus. To avoid the confusion of dogma presented by Gnostic Christians and others like them, the leaders of the early church formalized their teachings.

The Christian canon evolved in response to a Gnostic opponent of the church, Marcion (died c. 160), who refused to acknowledge the Old Testament as a source of revelation. From the time that the content of the New Testament was established, this canon served as a binding force for Christians throughout the Roman Empire and has remained central to Christianity ever since. Judaism and Christianity are therefore "religions of the book" in a way that Hinduism and Buddhism are not.

The earliest Christian preachers were the apostles, who chose and ordained their successors. Throughout the history of the church, its leaders have traced their mission back to the earliest Christians, and the concept of apostolic succession represents a major difference between Christianity and Judaism. The religious ceremonies conducted by the early ministers of the church were in the vernacular, and the rites included the celebration of the sacraments, visible ceremonies intended to bestow divine grace on worthy recipients. Two sacraments are retained by nearly all Christians today in one form or another: baptism and the commemoration of the Last Supper. The precise nature and number of these sacraments, however, was the subject of long debate. The Catholic church finally established the definitive number at seven, but Protestant reformers in the sixteenth century recognized only baptism and the Lord's supper.

The Church and the Roman Empire

During the reign of Septimius Severus (193–211) figures such as Julia Domna began to take an interest in the theoretical bases of Christianity. One of the principal Christian writers of the age was Tertullian (c. 160–c. 225), who was the first to formulate the doctrine of the Trinity, whereby one God is simultaneously conceived of as Father, Son, and Holy Spirit. The detailed philosophical implications of this doctrine provided thorny problems for the church for centuries.

Two other major figures of the third century, Clement (c. 150–c. 214) and Origen (c. 185–c. 254), both of Alexandria, continued the process of synthesizing the original Jewish content of Christianity with Greek ideas and culture and making the result available to their Roman readers. Origen fell victim to the first major systematic persecution of Christians, initiated by Emperor Decius (249–251). After Decius' death, Christians were able to resume their worship, but the persecution had created a new theological issue: Should the Christians who had saved themselves by making public sacrifices to local gods be forgiven and readmitted to their congregations? To deal with such cases, a system of penance evolved that was to prove one of the most striking characteristics of medieval Christianity.

Christianity's impact on the Roman Empire during its first three centuries was through the effects of personal example and moral witness rather than systematic organization and conversion. The high moral standard maintained by most Christian leaders, coupled with the willingness of many to die as martyrs, elicited reluctant admiration. The subtleties of Christian theology attracted the interest of prominent intellectuals. Furthermore, both church and empire depended for their success on careful organization and concern for administrative detail; some church leaders saw the empire as a force for order that made the performance of their own work possible.

By the beginning of the fourth century, one out of every ten Roman citizens was at least nominally a Christian. Emperor Diocletian (284–305) attempted to control the growing faith by a series of persecutions that lasted from 303 to 311. Although the policy produced thousands of martyrs, it failed in its aim, and in 313 Diocletian's successors, Constantine and Licinius, issued the Edict of Milan, granting all citizens of the empire freedom of religious worship. Constantine later introduced legislation that protected the church. Writing in the aftermath of this new partnership between church and state, the Christian writer Eusebius (c. 260–c. 339) claimed that the empire and the church were both the work of God.

Constantine's toleration for Christianity doubtless owed much to the fact that his mother, Helena, was a Christian who devoted her influence to its promotion. As an elderly woman she visited the Holy Land and helped found numerous churches there. By the late fourth century, writers began to credit her with the discovery of the "true cross" on which Jesus had been crucified.

The Early Church and Heresy

Unlike Hinduism or Buddhism, Christianity presented a single body of doctrine, together with the requirement that adherents accept the faith in the form in which their religious superiors handed it down and interpreted it to them. Indeed, from the time of Paul the growth of Christian influence had been aided by careful, consistent leadership. With Constantine, victory had been won, but the church paid a price for its success. Its new power and security encouraged the development of alternative views about basic Christian teachings, which had to be discussed and in most cases were prohibited in church councils. Throughout the fourth and fifth centuries various theological interpretations were proposed, only to be declared heresies. The words *heresy* and *heretic* are now often used to describe an unconventional opinion and its holder; they were originally coined to describe someone whose beliefs were contrary to the teaching of the church and whose immortal soul was thus in danger. In this way early Christians defined theological orthodoxy in relationship to views that were deemed unacceptable. In contrast, Judaism never attempted to define heresy; Hinduism has always embraced seemingly inconsistent ideas; and Buddhism, Confucianism, and Taoism, in their different ways, were intended to be adapted to the individual's moral and spiritual needs.

The first dispute resulted from the problem that had occurred after the persecutions of Decius, namely, how people who had betrayed their faith at the time of Diocletian should be treated. The most delicate cases were those of priests who had, at the imperial command, surrendered the Scriptures to be burned. A group of rigid opponents to reinstatement developed at Carthage, in North Africa; they were known as the Donatists from their leader, Donatus. In an effort to solve the controversy, Constantine summoned a council of bishops in 314 at Arles in Gaul. Although the council decided against the Donatists, it was unable to enforce its opinion. The principle of using church councils to debate and rule on theological issues, however, had been established.

Among the earliest heresies to be denounced was Arianism, first propounded by a priest from Alexandria named Arius, whose teaching concerned the divinity of Christ and the relation between God the Father and God the Son. Arius claimed that Christ was divine but did not have the same nature as the Father, who had created him. In 325 the Council of Nicaea (an ecumenical rather than a regional gathering, as Arles had been) rejected the Arian view; the Nicene Creed asserted that the Father and Son were fully equal, sharing one being and, together with the Holy Spirit, constituting the Trinity. This formulation met with opposition, and the debate about the Trinity and the nature of Christ still continues.

Monasticism

Even before the establishment of Christianity as the state religion, individual Christians had turned to asceticism and solitude as a source of spiritual discipline. The tradition of withdrawal from the world to an austere life of religious devotion is also a characteristic found in Hinduism, Buddhism, and Taoism. In all three religions, monks have tended to live in communities, although solitary mystics or hermits inaugurated the Christian tradition. (*Monk* is derived from the Greek word monos, meaning "alone.") Anthony (c. 251–356), generally acknowledged as the father of Christian monasticism, spent some 20 years after 285 alone in the desert of Egypt. As the practice spread and communities began to develop, monastic life was organized according to a set pattern or rule. Such rules were established in Asia as early as 358 by Basil (330–379) and later in Italy by Benedict (480–547). Throughout the ensuing history of Christianity the religious orders of men and women who retired to monasteries and convents exerted considerable influence in secular as well as sacred matters. Monks preserved the Latin language and classical Latin texts, carefully copying them for monastery libraries.

The Papacy

No less important than monasticism for the history of Latin Christendom was the growth of the power and prestige of the bishop of Rome, more familiarly known as the *pope* (the Latin *papa* is derived from *pappas,* the Greek word for "father"). The claim to papal primacy, though based on Jesus' allusion to the apostle Peter as the rock on which the church would be built, was in fact asserted much later and only in response to the growing authority and claims of the patriarch of Constantinople. Pope Leo I (440–461), the beneficiary of an imperial Roman decree recognizing his sole jurisdiction over the Latin church, claimed to have fullness of power, presumably over the church as a whole. If the Byzantine emperors had been able to continue the expansion of their rule after the sixth century, such claims might have proved worthless. But the internal problems of the Byzantine Empire and the external challenge of the Muslims destroyed whatever chance the patriarch of Constantinople had to establish himself as universal head of the Christian church and contributed to its growing split into eastern and Latin communions. The popes' ability to maintain their independence was momentous, for they claimed to have authority superior to that of monarchs. In Eastern Orthodoxy, however, ultimate authority rested in the hands of the emperor. In practice, of course, in both east and west, challenges to the authority of emperors and popes were periodically successful.

The greatest early medieval pope, Gregory I (590–604), enhanced papal power by sponsoring a mission to convert the pagans of Anglo-Saxon England. The mission's success was due in part to his instructions that pagan festival days and shrines be adapted to Christian use rather than repudiated outright. He was concerned as well with the conversion of the Lombards and with the expansion of Christianity in Spain. Contemporaries called him "God's consul" because of his administrative reforms, particularly the reorganization of papal revenues. A monk himself, Gregory wrote a biography of Benedict, thereby helping to provide the impetus that made the Benedictine Rule the dominant form of monastic life by the ninth century.

Augustine

If Paul was the first great leader in the history of the early church, Augustine (354–430) was its culminating figure and one who influenced Christian thought for centuries after his death. His writings, which draw on Christian theology and Greco-Roman thought, deal with complex questions: human nature and destiny, the work of Christ as savior, and the relationship of the church to the world. His *Confessions,* an autobiographical account of his spiritual life, reasserted Paul's teachings, particularly the unique importance ascribed to God's mercy as a means of forgiveness. In *The City of God,* written between 413 and 426 when Roman power was crumbling, Augustine claimed that God was punishing the Romans for the violence and corruption of their empire. The new order to emerge from this chaos should, he argued, be a Christian society, governed by principles of love and justice.

Augustine, bishop of Hippo, author of The City of God, *in a detail from a painting by Simone Martini.*

A portion of Augustine's theological writing was inspired by his opposition to Pelagius, whose views had brought him a number of enthusiastic followers. The Pelagians believed that humans did not inherit original sin and that free will was sufficient to attain salvation. Divine grace was not limited to the preordained elect but was given to all persons; hence Pelagius' view of human nature was not pessimistic, like that of Augustine. In works such as *On Original Sin* and *On Grace and Free Will,* Augustine attacked the Pelagian view. To some of Augustine's contemporaries and successors, however, his argument presented an equally extreme picture: a world ruled by a God so omnipotent that lives were predestined, where individual acts of goodness were insignificant in the face of dependence on divine grace. Medieval theologians generally tried to steer a middle course between the two extremes, but the debate was to be renewed in the sixteenth-century Protestant Reformation, which saw the revival first of Augustinian and then of Pelagian views.

Augustine's views on sex and marriage have remained central to Catholic thought ever since his time. The only justifiable purpose of sexual relations, he believed, was the creation of children, and only within the institution of marriage. Marriage thus serves the divine will, even though people who abstain from sexual relations are of a spiritually higher order. This concept of the flawed state of the human condition is a fresh assertion of the Pauline belief in human sinfulness. Augustine remained unrivaled as an expositor of Christian theology until Thomas Aquinas in the thirteenth century. Augustinian principles inspired the Protestant reformers to seek fundamental changes in Christian practice. Martin Luther and John Calvin were both dedicated readers of Augustine.

Women in the Ancient World Religions

The role of women in ancient and classical religious practice was roughly consistent throughout Eurasia. Most priestly functions were reserved for men, and women were often excluded from the inner sanctum of the temple, especially in Judaism. Judaism and, to a degree, the teachings of Paul contain an underlying bias against women, seeing them as "unclean" and hence as profaning religious ritual. In many Orthodox Jewish congregations, women were obliged to sit apart from men, concealed behind a screen. In India by classical times, priests were exclusively male, and this was also true of Buddhism and most of Taoism. Confucianism, which largely lacked a priestly order, was explicitly male-dominated and preached the subjection of women to their husbands. Shinto, the Japanese partial equivalent of Taoism, similarly reflected the heavy male dominance of Japanese society. Nevertheless, some women played major religious roles, separate from the male priestly order, as soothsayers and priestesses in ancient and classical Greece and Rome and similarly in ancient and classical India. The Tantric version of Hinduism, in its celebration of sex as the embodiment of the life force and hence a celebration of the divine mystery, made a central role for women as the chief focus of its rituals and doctrine. In this, Tantrism may be seen as echoing very early religious veneration of women as symbols of fertility and life. Perhaps it was also, like the acceptance of temple priestesses and soothsayers in both East and West, an acknowledgment of the spiritual and intuitive qualities of women. Especially in the earlier periods, most religions (except Judaism and Islam) have imputed to women special access to the mysteries and special spiritual powers.

As Buddhism and Christianity developed, so did female devotion, and various orders of nuns were organized, counterparts to the monks of both religions and with a similar discipline. Women had in fact played a far more prominent part in the early growth of both religions than the established order recognized. The Buddha and Jesus seem to have paid as much attention to women as to men and apparently made little status distinction between them; both may indeed have been said to favor them or to regard them as more open to the message. For whatever reason, both religions quickly produced female saints in great numbers, of which the best known are the Virgin Mary and the Buddhist goddess of mercy, Kuan Yin (Kannon in Japanese), among a host of others to whom people prayed for help probably more often than to male saints. In our own time women generally (except in Judaism and Islam) play a more active role than men in religious faith and practice everywhere, as perhaps they have always done, and the Christian priesthood is in the early stages, at least within Protestant Christianity, of admitting them on equal terms.

Hinduism has always had more or less equal numbers of female and male deities, and even Shiva was provided with a female consort of equal powers, although by classical times the priesthood was closed to women and currently shows few signs of removing that bar. But Hindus still give at least equal attention to female deities and hence continue to acknowledge the special powers and insights of women. Confucianism has no deities, no saints, and no organized priesthood, although since Han times a small number of people calling themselves Confucian priests have tended the temples and conducted services centered on the veneration of Confucius the sage. These have always been men, and Confucianism barely acknowledges the existence of women. Women in Confucian countries seek religious involvement in Taoism or Buddhism, where their role is more accepted—another aspect of East Asian eclecticism in religion.

From very early times in China there was an explicit assertion of the need for balance in all things between yin (female) and yang (male); this was incorporated into Taoism and accepted by nearly all Chinese, including Confucians, although most Chinese followed both religious traditions. The persistence of this idea even in modern China indicates an acceptance of the equal importance of male and female characteristics and the essential role of both.

Religion seems to have evolved away from its earliest emphasis on women. With the rise of the first states and empires, the coming of bureaucracy, the increase in large-scale warfare, and the consequently greater importance of the warrior, males and male roles may have become more dominant, and religion may have changed accordingly. Most of the great religions subordinate or even exclude women, and most tend to justify male domination. Judaism, Confucianism, and Islam are probably the clearest examples, but only Judaism and Islam speak explicitly, and pejoratively, about women. Christianity, to some degree a blend of Judaism with other Eastern religious traditions, was clearly male-dominant. Only Buddhism and to some extent Taoism approach the ideal of gender equality.

SUMMARY

In spite of the obvious differences between the religions and moral philosophies discussed in this chapter, they share some important characteristics. Each continues to influence the lives of millions of people. Whereas the worship of the gods of ancient Egypt, Assyria, or Greece has largely vanished, the major religions and philosophies described here provide at least partial solutions to the problems of life for their followers, even though they originated in times and cultures remote from our own. The major world religions share a number of attitudes. Nonviolence and reverence for life are urged by Hindu and Christian doctrine alike. The important role played by the religious mystic and teacher is typical of virtually all present world religions. Moreover, each attempts to order human relationships in society as well as individually. In this, however, they share another common characteristic: the fact that the ideal visions they propose remain, for the most part, unfulfilled.

In an age of rapid communications, the ancient world religions have inevitably, and often profitably, come into direct contact with one another. Christian priests and teachers continue to work in Asia, and in India, Mother Teresa of Calcutta, herself an Albanian, has become a symbol of practical Christian charity. At the same time, Western culture has become increasingly open to the religions of the East, with their emphasis on spiritual rather than material values. In the 2,000 years since the foundation of Christianity, only one other religion has established itself on the same global scale: Islam, whose formation and growth are discussed in the next chapter.

NOTES

1. Jer. 8:19.
2. Isa. 12:4.
3. Amos 5:6–7.
4. Ps. 137:5–6.
5. Isa. 9:7.

SUGGESTIONS FOR FURTHER READING

Religions of South and East Asia

Basham, A. L. *The Origins and Development of Classical Hinduism.* Boston: Beacon Press, 1989.

Bowker, J. *Problems of Suffering in Religions of the World.* Cambridge: Cambridge University Press, 1975.

Callicot, J. B., and Ames, R. T., eds. *Nature in Asia: Traditions of Thought.* Albany: State University of New York Press, 1991.

Chamberlane, J. H. *China and Its Religious Inheritance.* London: Allen & Unwin, 1993.

Chaudhuri, N. C. *Hinduism: A Religion to Live By.* New York: Oxford University Press, 1979.

Creel, H. G. *What Is Taoism? And Other Studies in Chinese Cultural History.* Chicago: University of Chicago Press, 1970.

De Bary, W. T., ed. *Sources of Indian Tradition.* New York: Columbia University Press, 1958.

———. *Sources of Chinese Tradition.* 2 vols. New York: Columbia University Press, 1964.

Embree, A. T., ed. *The Hindu Tradition.* New York: Modern Library, 1966.

Gombrich, R. F. *Theravada Buddhism: A Social History.* London: Routledge & Kegan Paul, 1988.

Hardy, F. *The Religious Culture of India.* Cambridge: Cambridge University Press, 1994.

Harvey, B. P. *An Introduction to Buddhism.* Cambridge: Cambridge University Press, 1990.

Herman, A. L. *A Brief Introduction to Hinduism.* Boulder, Colo.: Westview Press, 1991.

Hopkins, T. *Hindu Religious Tradition.* Encino, Calif.: Dickenson, 1971.

Humphreys, C. *Buddhism.* London: Cassell, 1962.

Kohn, L. *Laughing at the Tao.* Princeton, N.J.: Princeton University Press, 1995.

Monro, K. W. *Reaching for the Moon: Asian Religious Paths.* Chambersburg, Pa.: Anima Publications, 1991.

Palmer, M., et al. *The Book of Chuang Tzu.* Harmondsworth, England: Penguin, 1996.

Schwartz, B. I. *The World of Thought in Ancient China.* Cambridge, Mass.: Harvard University Press, 1985.

Sharma, A., ed. *Women in World Religions.* Albany: State University of New York Press, 1987.

Smart, N. *Religions of Asia.* Englewood Cliffs, N.J.: Prentice Hall, 1993.

Taylor, R. L. *The Religious Dimensions of Confucianism.* Albany: State University of New York Press, 1991.

Thompson, L. G. *Chinese Religion.* Belmont, Calif.: Wadsworth, 1988.

The Judeo-Christian Tradition

Coggins, R., Phillips, A., and Knibb, M., eds. *Israel's Prophetic Tradition.* Cambridge: Cambridge University Press, 1984.

De Jonge, M. *Jesus, the Servant-Messiah.* New Haven, Conn.: Yale University Press, 1991.

Fredriksen, P. *From Jesus to Christ: The Origins of the New Testament Images of Jesus.* New Haven, Conn.: Yale University Press, 1988.

Grant, M. *The Jews in the Roman World.* New York: Scribner, 1973.

Grant, R. M. *Augustus to Constantine: The Rise and Triumph of the Christian Movement in the Roman World.* San Francisco: HarperSanFrancisco, 1990.

Hengel, M. *Acts and the History of Earliest Christianity.* London: SCM Press, 1986.

Jacobs, L. *The Talmudic Argument.* Cambridge: Cambridge University Press, 1984.

MacMullen, R. *Christianizing the Roman Empire, A.D. 100–400.* New Haven, Conn.: Yale University Press, 1984.

Meeks, W. A. *The First Urban Christians: The Social World of the Apostle Paul.* New Haven, Conn.: Yale University Press, 1983.

Renko, S. *Pagan Rome and the Early Christians.* Bloomington: Indiana University Press, 1986.

Riches, J. *The World of Jesus: First-Century Judaism in Crisis.* Cambridge: Cambridge University Press, 1990.

Sanders, E. P. *Jesus and Judaism.* Philadelphia: Fortress Press, 1985.

Segal, A. F. *Paul the Convert: The Apostolate and Apostasy of Saul the Pharisee.* New Haven, Conn.: Yale University Press, 1990.

———. *Rebecca's Children.* Cambridge, Mass.: Harvard University Press, 1986.

Smith, M. S. *The Early History of God: Yahweh and the Other Deities in Ancient Israel.* San Francisco: HarperSanFrancisco, 1990.

Watson, F. *Paul, Judaism, and the Gentiles.* Cambridge: Cambridge University Press, 1987.

Witherington, B., III. *Women in the Earliest Churches.* Cambridge: Cambridge University Press, 1988.

PART TWO
The Middle Ages

CHAPTER 8

Byzantium and Islam

While nomadic invaders were transforming western Europe after the collapse of Roman rule, the eastern half of the empire, despite initial setbacks at the hands of the Goths and the Huns, laid the foundation in the sixth century for a period of imperial brilliance. The Byzantine Empire, or Byzantium, derived its name from the former Greek colony of Byzantium, which Constantine had transformed into the site of his new capital, Constantinople, in 330. Strategically located on the Bosporus, part of the great water route between the Black and Aegean seas, the city, surrounded on three sides by water, was easily defended. It was also a natural site for a commercial center, since it was the crossroads for the great east-west trading routes that extended from Asia to Europe, as well as the north-south routes that reached from southern Russia into the Mediterranean. Byzantine culture, a distinctive fusion of Greco-Roman and Christian traditions, made a lasting impact on many peoples of eastern Europe.

After a 1,000-year history, Byzantium fell in 1453 to the Ottoman Turks, who conquered it on behalf of Islam, the youngest of the world's major religions. Islam began in Arabia in the early seventh century. From there it spread throughout the Middle East and beyond, into Iran, North Africa, the Iberian peninsula, and the Balkans. Virtually from the beginning, Islamic expansion brought the Arabs into conflict with their Byzantine neighbors, and as early as 674, Muslim armies made their first, albeit unsuccessful, attempt to conquer Constantinople. During the ensuing eight centuries hostility and periodic warfare often characterized relations between the Muslims and the Byzantines, but the peoples of the two civilizations also traded with each other and synthesized classical culture.

An aristocratic family watches games at the Hippodrome in Constantinople. Leaf from an ivory diptych, c. 355.

Byzantium

The Byzantine Empire was a remarkable achievement. The last of its emperors, Constantine XI, could trace the imperial succession back to the Roman emperor Augustus in the late first century B.C., although many of the institutions familiar to Augustus had long ceased to exist. Continuity of culture and tradition helped to make the Byzantine Empire the most durable political entity in medieval Europe. It not only preserved and enhanced classical culture but also made important contributions in law, religion, commerce, and the arts. Moreover, the empire provided a crucial buffer between waves of invaders from Asia and the peoples of western Europe as they constructed new states in the aftermath of the Roman decline and the German, Viking, and Magyar invasions.

Historical Background

In contrast to the chaos that prevailed in the Roman world in the third century, most of the ensuing 100 years was a time of peace, both externally and internally. Despite its administrative separation in the late fourth century, contemporaries still regarded the empire as a single state. Yet the roots of the future division were already present. The western part of the empire, which traditionally enjoyed political supremacy, had always been inferior to the east in terms of natural resources, population, urban centers, commerce, and industry. When it became increasingly apparent in the fifth century that the west could not defend itself against outside invaders, rulers in the east concentrated on protecting their own domains. Suspicion, conflict of interest, and jealousy were stronger than feelings of unity and responsibility, especially as the two halves of the empire evolved into separate states, each with its own laws and coinage. Even religion played a modest role in dividing the empire, as the Latin Christians found themselves at odds with the Monophysites, who emphasized Christ's divinity at the expense of his humanity and who enjoyed substantial support in Egypt, Syria, Palestine, and Constantinople.

Although the eastern half of the empire survived, it did not escape the blows of nomadic invaders. As early as 378 the Visigoths, who had received sanctuary in the empire two years earlier, defeated the emperor Valens and the Roman army of the Danube at Adrianople. The empire saved itself by allowing the Visigoths to settle in the Balkans and to govern themselves in return for serving in the Byzantine army. Faced with the threat of an invasion by the Huns in the mid-fifth century, the government at Constantinople paid the tribute demanded by Attila (died 453), the Huns' leader. When the Ostrogoths threatened the eastern empire in the late fifth century, the Byzantines persuaded their chieftain, Theodoric (died 526), to invade Italy instead. Thus by the early sixth century, when the western empire had for all practical purposes ceased to exist, the Byzantine domains still embraced the Balkan peninsula, Armenia, Syria, Palestine, Egypt, and Asia Minor, the economic heartland of the empire.

The Age of Justinian

An empire that stretched from the Nile to the Black Sea was not enough to satisfy Justinian (527–565), a strong-willed, pious emperor determined to recover conquered Roman lands. He first ended a war with the Persians on his eastern frontier, thus freeing troops to reclaim much of North Africa from the Vandals. Belisarius, the most prominent of his generals, accomplished this task in 533 and 534. The following year Belisarius overran Sicily, and between 536 and 540 he reconquered the Italian peninsula from the Goths. In 550 he sent an expedition against the Visigoths in Spain, which soon brought the southern part of the Iberian peninsula under his rule. The boundaries of the ancient Roman Empire were still a long way from being restored, and Justinian's campaigns had exacted a heavy toll. Overtaxed, the empire was on the verge of fiscal collapse, nomadic pressures had seriously undermined the defenses in the east, and the fighting with Persia had disrupted trade with India and China.

Justinian ruled as an agent of God, enjoying supreme authority over both church and state. Just as

Justinian and his entourage.

there was only one God, so there could be only one Christian empire governed by one emperor, himself subject to divine law alone. One of Justinian's contemporaries aptly stated the imperial ideal:

> **[God] has given you the scepter over terrestrial power in imitation of the celestial kingdom in order that you should teach men to cultivate justice. . . . The emperor is equal to all men in the nature of his body, but in the authority of his rank he is similar to God, who rules all. For there is no one on earth higher than he. . . . Impose on yourself the necessity of obeying the laws, since no one on earth can force you to do so.[1]**

The emperors became the focal point of a partly Persian, partly Roman court ritual designed to enhance their power and image. Over the centuries the ceremonial became increasingly elaborate, until it finally included ingenious mechanical contraptions, such as a throne that could be raised or lowered, a gold-plated bronze tree filled with gilded bronze birds, and gold-covered lions that roared when a visitor approached. Eventually, people who wanted an audience with the emperor not only had to prostrate themselves but were expected to kiss the monarch's foot and hand. Beginning in the seventh century the emperor styled himself *basileus,* or "ruler of all the world," a title analogous to the Persian notion of "king of kings," in addition to the title *autocrat,* or "sole ruler," to underscore his absolute power.

Keeping the church in order was a fundamental part of Justinian's imperial responsibility as well as a means of preserving unity. His concern extended even to the sexual behavior of his clergy; on one occasion he had two homosexual bishops arrested, castrated, and publicly humiliated. Generally, he preferred to convert dissidents to his point of view rather than impose harsh punishment. Nevertheless, the government burned a number of Manichaean heretics to death when they refused to retract their belief in a dualistic universe that identified goodness with the spirit and evil with matter. Thanks especially to the patronage of his wife the empress

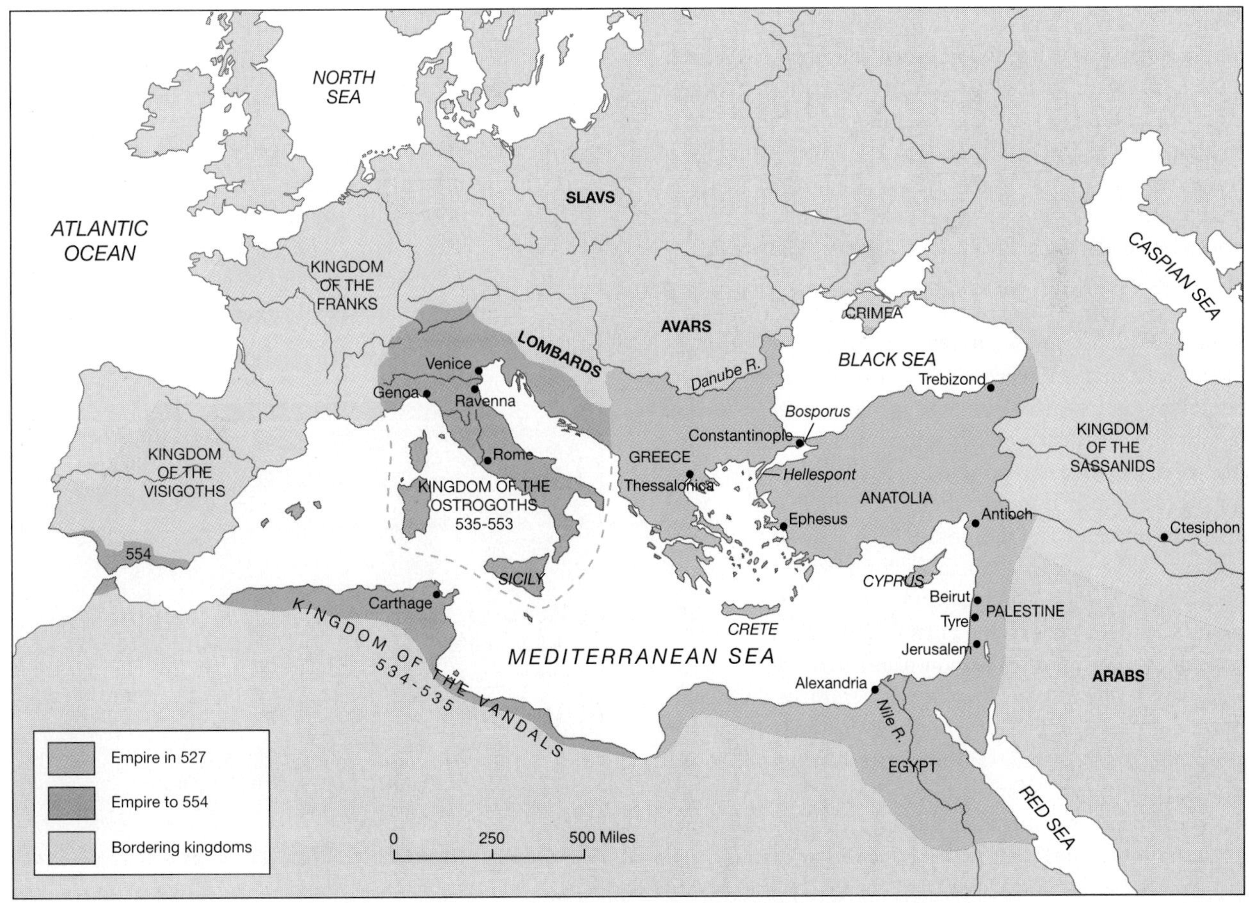

MAP 8.1 THE BYZANTINE EMPIRE UNDER JUSTINIAN

Theodora, the Monophysites, who refused to distinguish between the divine and human natures in Christ, fared much better. Justinian issued an imperial edict seeking a compromise between Orthodox Christians and Monophysites, but he also used his authority to close pagan schools in Athens. After his effort to restore unity failed, he reaffirmed his fidelity to Orthodox Christianity.

Justinian enjoyed considerable success in his reform of the law, which he deemed, like religion, a source of social and political cohesion. His goal was nothing less than

> **to attempt the most complete and thorough amendment of the entire law, to collect and revise the whole body of Roman jurisprudence, and to assemble in one book the scattered treatises of so many authors, which no one else has hitherto ventured to hope for or to expect.[2]**

Under the supervision of Tribonian, the highest judicial officer in the empire, a royal commission imposed order on the mass of surviving Roman imperial edicts, deleting repetitions and resolving contradictions. It also compiled a digest of Roman judicial opinion gleaned from 2,000 volumes. To train law students in this material, the commission prepared a handbook called the *Institutes,* which remained in use in Europe into the twentieth century. All three of these documents were in Latin, still the official language of the empire, but the government issued a volume of new laws, called *Novels,* in Greek, the language of most citizens in the east. Later, these compilations were collectively known as the *corpus juris civilis,* or "body of civil law."

Although Justinian's legal reform was intended to be a work of conservation, it offered significant improvements, including simpler ways to convey property and inheritances and the replacement in law of the extended family with a nuclear core of parents and children. The influence of the code was profound. In the twelfth century it spread to western Europe, where the principle of mutual interest—enshrined in the phrase "that which touches all concerns all"—provided much of the basis for Western medieval law, both religious and secular. This concept contributed to the development of representative institutions in the West during the fourteenth century and eventually to modern parliamentary government, although Byzantium itself remained autocratic. Justinian advanced other reforms to curtail administrative corruption, eliminate the sale of offices, and reform provincial government, but his lasting monument was his *Code, Digest,* and *Institutes,* the most significant single body of legal documents in Western history and the primary means for the preservation and transmittal of the Roman legal heritage.

Theodora: From Actress to Empress

"Whether or not a woman should give an example of courage to men, is neither here nor there. . . . Flight, even if it brings us to safety, is not in our interest."[3] With those words, the Empress Theodora persuaded Justinian not to flee from his capital in the midst of the greatest crisis of his reign, the Nika riot of 532. The Greens and the Blues, the principal rival organizations that provided charioteers and acrobats as well as avid supporters for the games in Constantinople's stadium, the Hippodrome, made common cause against the government. In support of two of their number, whom the government had unsuccessfully tried to hang, they set fire to the city and besieged the imperial palace. Shamed into action by Theodora, Belisarius ordered the imperial army to suppress the rioters. Before he called the troops off, some 30,000 people had perished, but Justinian's throne was secured.

Justinian had married Theodora, daughter of a bearkeeper, seven years earlier, when he was in his early forties and she in her late twenties. Before she became Justinian's mistress and eventually his wife, she had followed her sister onto the stage, an occupation associated with promiscuity. What little we know about these years in Theodora's life comes from the historian Procopius, her bitter enemy. The portrait he draws is one of a courtesan and striptease artist who had frequent abortions and indulged in sexual orgies. On stage, he said,

Mosaic from the church of San Vitale in Ravenna portraying the empress Theodora with her attendants.

"she would often undress and parade naked among the people, with only a girdle around her groin and genitals."[4] In pursuit of a better life she became the mistress of a bureaucrat, who took her to North Africa before tiring of her. In Alexandria she met and was probably converted by prominent Monophysite clergymen. Justinian met her after she had returned to Constantinople and taken up a trade spinning wool. Under Roman law a man of Justinian's rank could not marry an actress, but Justinian's predecessor, his uncle Justin I, issued a special edict to remove this ban. Two years after their marriage in 525, the patriarch of Constantinople crowned Justinian and Theodora.

As empress, Theodora generally acquitted herself well. She took a special interest in the prostitutes of the capital, at one point purchasing their freedom from their keepers and returning each to her parents with a gold coin. She and Justinian provided aid to Antioch after it was ravaged by an earthquake in 528 and to two other towns that were similarly victimized the following year. She also extended monetary assistance to the churches and villages of Asia Minor. In addition to her work on behalf of the Monophysites, she attempted, without success, to obtain the election of a pope who would look more tolerantly on them. Her efforts to dissuade the Persians from breaking their treaty likewise failed, but her experience in government prepared her to run it when Justinian was ill with the bubonic plague in 542. The empress died of cancer six years later; her death had a major impact on Justinian, who increasingly devoted his last years to religious pursuits.

Byzantine Economy and Society

An important part of the empire's long existence and relative stability was its economic and social structure. As long as its aristocracy was service-based, its free farmers were prosperous, and its trade was in Byzantine hands, the empire was strong. But the rise of a military aristocracy, the decline of independent farmers, and the

Theodora: A Hostile View

In his Secret History, *Procopius paints this extremely unflattering portrait of the empress Theodora.*

Theodora had a lovely face and was generally beautiful, but she was short and pale—not completely, but enough to seem pallid—and her expression was always serious and frowning. All time would not be enough for anyone who tried to record most of her past life on the stage. . . . Now I must speak briefly of what she and her husband did, for they never acted separately in their life together. For a long time they gave everyone the impression that they were constantly at odds in opinions and mode of life. But later it was realized that this was deliberately cultivated by them so that their subjects, far from joining together and rebelling against them, would all have different views about them. . . .

Of her body she took more care than was necessary, though less than she herself desired. She went very early to her bath and left it very late, and after her bath she went to breakfast. After breakfast she rested. At lunch and dinner she took all kinds of foods and drinks and would sleep for long periods from morning until night, and at night until sunrise. And after this self-indulgence for such long stretches of the day, she saw fit to rule the Roman Empire. If the emperor gave orders to someone for an action against her wishes, the man's affairs stood at such a state of fortune that soon afterwards he would be dismissed from his office in ignominy and destroyed in a most shameful manner.

Source: Procopius, *History of the Wars,* trans. A. Cameron (Boston: Twayne, 1967), pp. 311, 323.

domination of trade by Italians fatally weakened the Byzantine state.

Economic Patterns

Much of the wealth of the Byzantine Empire came from agriculture, especially commencing in the seventh century, when manufacturing and commerce began to decline as a result of continuing warfare and a decreasing population. During the fourth and fifth centuries the basic agricultural unit was a large estate worked by hundreds of sharecroppers bound to the land as *coloni,* or serfs—peasants who were legally bound to those estates. Coloni who fled their estates were hunted down, returned, and enslaved. During the sixth and seventh centuries the Persian, Slavic, and Arab invasions increased the need for higher taxes and military recruits, thus encouraging the development of a free peasantry that could provide the necessary labor and shoulder the increased financial burden. By the eighth century, coloni and slaves had virtually disappeared. In the tenth century the large lay and ecclesiastical estates began expanding again, especially when members of the landed aristocracy acquired control of the throne in the eleventh century. Landowners forced many peasants into a nearly servile status, particularly in the face of staggering taxes that left the peasants heavily in debt or bankrupt.

The abundance of grain, olive oil, wine, and cheese impressed western European visitors in this period. Byzantine farmers produced plentiful amounts of food despite the absence of technological improvements of the kind adopted in the west, such as wheeled iron plows and scythes. During the last centuries of the empire this prosperity collapsed when the state valued peasants more as sources of military manpower than as farmers. In this period the great landowners held their estates virtually tax-free in return for providing the imperial army with troops. The gross abuse of the peasantry and the consequent decline of agriculture significantly weakened the empire, whose greatest strength had been its independent farmers.

Commerce, though less important in the Byzantine economy than agriculture, played a significant role. Constantinople was the primary center of trade between the Middle East and Asia on the one hand and Europe on the other. Byzantine merchants traveled as far as East Asia and Spain in the early centuries of the empire. From Asia came Chinese silk, prized by the wealthy as an alternative to abrasive, heavy wool; spices to season and sugar to sweeten food; and jewels, pearls, and ivory, imported to adorn the rich and to beautify churches. Africa provided slaves as well as ivory, and the Black Sea region was a source of wheat, furs, hides, slaves, salt, and wine. From France and Italy came textiles and weapons.

In addition to these items, many of which passed through the empire en route to more distant locations, the Byzantines exported commodities of their own, including cotton, glassware, and enamels from Syria and timber, flax, and honey from the Balkans. The greatest Byzantine export was silk, whose manufacture the Byzantines first learned of in the mid-sixth century, thanks to two monks who smuggled silkworm eggs out of China. To prevent a small number of wealthy people from monopolizing the new industry, the state assigned the various stages of production to separate guilds, each of which operated under government regulation. Until the eleventh century, manufacturing and sales were limited to Constantinople, but in the eleventh and twelfth centuries silk production spread to Greece and Sicily. The Byzantine emperors also enjoyed a monopoly in the production of gold embroidery and purple dye. Among the most luxurious exports from the tenth century on were cloisonné enamel plaques, intricately crafted by jewelers who soldered gold wire onto a gold backing and then filled the tiny partitions, or *cloisons,* with glass tinted by metal oxides.

By the tenth century foreign merchants, particularly Italians, had taken over most of the carrying trade. These merchants generally had exemptions from the 10 percent customs tax in return for providing naval assistance to the Byzantine government. The Venetians in 1082 and the Genoese in 1261 even received their own special quarters in Constantinople with extensive trading rights throughout the empire. Thus in the later centuries of the empire the Italians received much of the profit of the extensive trade network that centered on Constantinople. This too was a factor that contributed to the empire's decline.

Merchants, Artisans, and the Aristocracy

Although Constantinople was the center of Byzantium's major industries and the hub of its international trade routes, the provincial towns were the home of artisans and merchants who plied their wares at rural fairs. The greatest of these fairs was at Thessalonica, which became second in importance only to Constantinople in the last centuries of the empire. Probably larger than its famous counterpart at Champagne in France, the Thessalonica fair attracted traders from as far as Spain and France, though most merchants were native Greeks. Merchants and artisans alike were subject to government regulation, as were bankers, lawyers, and notaries. In general, government control was designed to protect the trade guilds in the capital from nonguild artisans and peddlers and from control by powerful landowners. State inspectors monitored the quality of manufactured articles, workers' wages, shop size, and prices to ensure a stable supply at regulated prices. Guilds, in other words, served the state. Government control of the guilds declined in the twelfth century, and during the later period of the empire they became more like their counterparts in western Europe, concerned primarily with their own welfare.

The notion of service to the state was also at the root of the Byzantine conception of nobility. Aristocrats enjoyed superior social status because of their service as courtiers and government officials. Vertical mobility was a characteristic of Byzantine society, unlike the feudal societies of contemporary western Europe. Not until the tenth century did a landed, hereditary nobility emerge as the result of military needs.

Defensive requirements prompted the emperors to organize their territories into military districts, called *themes,* each of which was governed by a general in charge of civil and military affairs. Recruited locally, troops received grants of land in return for military service. These grants could not be sold but passed to the soldiers' sons, who assumed responsibility for military duty. The theme system had an adverse impact on the traditional service-based aristocracy but gave rise to a new military nobility, which in general was less educated and less culturally refined than the old aristocracy.

A civil aristocracy continued to exist side by side with the new military one; members of the former continued to function as tax collectors, judges, and heads of government offices. A number of those who served in the civil aristocracy were eunuchs—men who had been castrated, probably for criminal behavior or after being sold by destitute parents. They were popular at court because their condition precluded them from becoming emperors and because they had no independent base of power. By the eleventh century the Byzantine aristocracy included foreigners who served as officers in the military. Vertical mobility may have peaked in the middle of that century, when the state attempted to draw large numbers of merchants and foreigners living in Constantinople into the government.

Shortly thereafter, Byzantine society underwent a major transformation when the elite families in the military aristocracy banded together through intermarriage, forming a powerful "clan" linked to the Comnenian dynasty, which governed the empire from 1081 to 1185. Those who were not part of this clan found themselves excluded from the military aristocracy; some made their way into the civil aristocracy, which was henceforth deemed inferior. In the late twelfth century the civil aristocracy regained supremacy when Emperor Andronicus I (1183–1185) crushed the military elite who opposed his rule. Nevertheless, the last centuries of the empire were characterized less by the rule of a civil bureaucracy than by that of semifeudal warlords whose power was based on family networks. In general, Byzantium evolved from a highly centralized state to a virtually feudal society ruled by a military aristocracy. Western Europe developed in the opposite direction.

Women in the Byzantine Empire

The confines of the family defined the social role of most Byzantine women. From the sixth to the late eleventh centuries, the nuclear family, not the clan, was at the heart of the social structure. As a result, the social position of women was generally less than it had been in the late Roman era. There were exceptions, such as the empresses Theodora and Irene (797–802) and the women who defied traditional standards of propriety by becoming actresses, public dancers, or courtesans. Women as well as men debated issues of public import, such as the use of religious images. In emergencies women served in the common defense, as they did when a governor in Asia Minor ordered young women to dress in men's clothing and help defend the walls when an Arab fleet attacked about 825. For the most part, women spent their lives in a tightly knit patriarchal family. To preserve their honor—and that of their families—patriarchs provided special apartments in their homes for female family members. Patriarchal authority extended to the arrangement of marriages, a decision made by the immediate family and other relatives.

Byzantine laws offer insight into the status of women. Except in matters pertaining exclusively to women, they could not act as witnesses in the signing of contracts. An edict of Emperor Leo VI (886–912) explains why:

> **The power to act as witnesses in the numerous assemblies of men with which they mingle, as well as taking part in public affairs, gives them the habit of speaking more freely than they ought, and, depriving them of the morality and reserve of their sex, encourages them in the exercise of boldness and wickedness.**[5]

Yet an eighth-century law treated husband and wife virtually as equals with respect to property and stipulated that a widow with children control all the property in her capacity as the new head of the family. A fourth-century law pertaining to coloni who had escaped or been abducted provided for the return of males within a period of 30 years but established a lower limit of 20 years for women, presumably reflecting a lack of worth after their childbearing years were past. By law a free woman could be punished if she had sexual intercourse with a slave, but such activity by a free man was tolerated.

Beginning in the late eleventh century the nuclear core broadened into an extended family as the basis of social and legal order, perhaps because of the changing outlook of the ruling Comnenian dynasty, which found its primary political support in a kinship network. Educated, politically intelligent women became more active in court and aristocratic circles. Emperor Alexius I Comnenus (1081–1118) officially shared imperial power with his mother, Anna Dalassena. In the words of Alexius' daughter, Anna Comnena, Alexius acted as if he were his mother's servant:

> **He used to say and do whatever she ordered. The emperor . . . made his right hand the executor of her orders, his ears paid heed to her words, and everything which she accepted or rejected the emperor likewise accepted or rejected. . . . Alexius possessed the external formalities of imperial power, but she held the power itself.[6]**

Alexius' wife, Irene, accompanied him on his military expeditions and, like other women of the age, engaged in political intrigue. A number of prominent women, including Anna Comnena, who had a special interest in Aristotle, patronized scholarship. In the late twelfth century Empress Euphrosyne governed the empire for her husband.

The greater prominence of women was accompanied by a growing disregard for traditional standards of morality in court circles, as reflected in the open practice of adultery and incest. Among the masses, however, the traditional role of the ideal spouse as submissive and generally confined to the home undoubtedly continued. Anna Comnena, a major public figure, observed that the common women of her society still wore veils when they left the privacy of their homes. In Byzantium at least, the social mores of the elite were apparently slow to influence commoners.

Reform at the Imperial Court: Anna Dalassena

Anna Comnena describes the reforming work of her grandmother, Anna Dalassena, who virtually governed the Byzantine empire for her son, Alexius I.

The women's quarters in the palace had been the scene of utter depravity ever since the infamous Constantine Monomachos [1042–1055] had ascended the throne and right up to the time when my father [Alexius I] became emperor had been noted for foolish love intrigues, but Anna effected a reformation; a commendable decorum was restored and the palace now enjoyed a discipline that merited praise. She instituted set times for the singing of sacred hymns, stated hours for breakfast; there was now a special period in which magistrates were chosen. She herself set a firm example to everybody else, with the result that the palace assumed the appearance rather of a monastery under the influence of this really extraordinary woman and her truly saintly character. . . . Her house was a refuge for penniless relatives, but no less for strangers. Priests and monks she honored in particular: they shared her meals and no one ever saw her at table without some of them as guests. . . . She was by nature thoughtful and was always evolving new ideas, not, as some folk whispered, to the detriment of the state; on the contrary, they were wholesome schemes which restored to full vigor the already corrupted empire and revived, as far as one could, the ruined fortunes of the people.

Source: The Alexiad of Anna Comnena, trans. E. R. A. Sewter (Harmondsworth, Middlesex: Penguin, 1969), pp. 120–121.

Constantinople, Jewel of the Bosporus

Constantinople is located on a hilly peninsula between the Sea of Marmora and the Golden Horn on the boundary between Europe and Asia. With a 7-mile-long inlet and a natural harbor, it had a population of perhaps 1 million in Justinian's time. Others lived in the suburbs, which comprised outlying commercial centers, residential villages, and, along the shores of the Bosporus, resorts for the wealthy. The city was home to many peoples, including Greeks, Italians, Jews, North Africans, Syrians, Armenians, and Goths. Greek was the normal language of daily discourse, although the imperial government and the law courts used Latin. Beginning in the early fifth century mammoth walls 15 feet thick and 40 feet high protected the city.

Constantine had originally planned the capital in imitation of Rome, to the point of including seven hills within the original walls. At the heart of the city was the Augusteum, a great open square, like the Roman Forum, around which were grouped the Church of Hagia Sophia ("Holy Wisdom"), the public baths, the Senate House, and the entrances to the Hippodrome (a large oval arena) and the royal palace. The palace consisted of assorted buildings, courtyards, and gardens commissioned by various emperors and built on terraces that extended down toward the sea. A broad avenue stretched westward from the Augusteum to the Golden Gate; a second avenue branched off to the city's other principal entry, the Gate of Charisius, in the northwest. The rest of the city was a web of narrow lanes lined with houses, shops, monasteries, and hundreds of churches. The greatest of these were Hagia Sophia, where emperors were crowned, and the Church of the Holy Apostles, where they were buried.

The houses of the wealthy were multistoried structures built around circular courtyards, many of which had fountains. More modest homes might have simple patios, and those of the poor, constructed of wood, were constantly threatened by fire. The destitute, often chronically unemployed, slept in the streets unless they were fortunate enough to find temporary shelter in the hostels, hospitals, and orphanages run by the churches or under arcades and other public structures kept open by the government during the winter. The impoverished could usually find food in church kitchens, but beggars were common. All registered householders in the city could obtain bread free or at a nominal cost, and the government placed price controls on other basic foods with the exception of fish, which could not be hoarded. Distribution of free bread ended in 618, when the Persians conquered Egypt, a major grain supplier. The government's interest in maintaining stable food prices

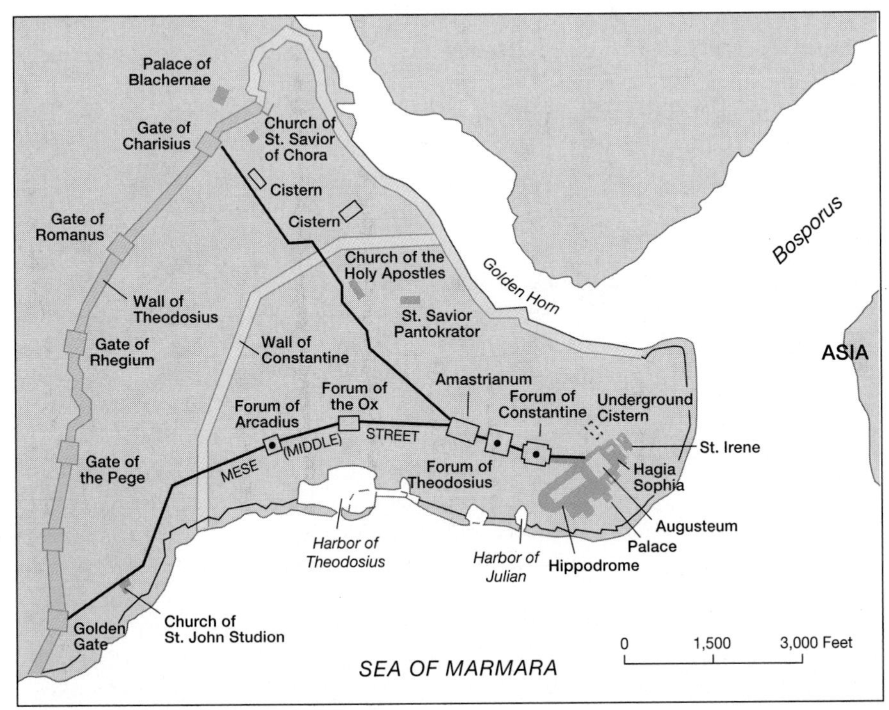

MAP 8.2 CONSTANTINOPLE IN JUSTINIAN'S TIME

The church of Hagia Sophia was completed in 535; the minarets were added 1,000 years later by the Turks.

stemmed from the need to prevent riots, not humanitarian concerns.

Rioting Greens and Blues destroyed the old Church of Hagia Sophia in 532, but its replacement, commissioned by Justinian, became the city's greatest monument. The church's distinctive feature is a soaring dome resting on four arches, a feat made possible by the use of pendentives—spherical triangles that distribute the dome's weight to the arches. The dome of the Roman Pantheon, in contrast, rests on round walls. Though the exterior of Hagia Sophia was plain, sumptuous mosaics, gold, silver, and variegated marble adorn the interior. Numerous windows, including a ring of 40 at the base of the dome, and 1,000 lamps provided lighting. As Procopius testified, "The church is singularly full of light and sunshine; you would declare that the place is not lighted by the sun from without, but that the rays are produced within itself."[7] Hagia Sophia was an architectural jewel and an appropriate focal point for the Byzantine Empire. After the Ottoman Turks conquered the city in 1453, they altered the church's appearance to meet the needs of Islam.

Byzantine Christianity and Culture

In contrast to the largely secular culture of the modern West, Byzantine society was framed in religious terms. Conflict between church and state in the modern sense was impossible because one Christian emperor ruled, in theory, both civilian and ecclesiastical government in a single Christian commonwealth. This form of government is usually referred to as *caesaropapism,* a term that underscores the unity of civil and ecclesiastical power, of emperor and patriarch, in imitation of God's rule over a universal heavenly kingdom. The Byzantine ideal might be summed up as one church, one creed, one sovereign.

Caesaropapism did not give the emperor absolute power in religious affairs. He did not possess either a priestly title or priestly functions, such as the ability to administer the sacraments. Emperors periodically faced challenges from ecclesiastical figures, particularly patriarchs (the highest ecclesiastical officials in the Byzantine church), and religious dissidents such as the Monophysites. No emperor was powerful enough to alter doctrine or liturgy arbitrarily, although the imperial position entitled him to mediate religious disputes. Yet the ideal of a Christian emperor ruling a Christian state remained a powerful one throughout the empire's existence.

Byzantine Christianity was very conservative, with an emphasis on tradition, liturgy, and pomp. All aspects of worship, from the ritual to the design and decoration of churches, were intended to promote a sense of mystery and otherworldliness. Aids to worship, such as religious images and relics, received special importance; supposed pieces of the cross, thorns from Jesus' crown, and Mary's robe and shroud were especially valued. Not only did a trade in relics thrive, but devout Christians sometimes stole them for their churches. In light of the emphasis on

An ivory panel depicting the Byzantine emperor Constantine VII being crowned by Christ.

otherworldly values, the Byzantines regarded ascetic living highly and typically held monks in great esteem.

Religious Controversy

Given the importance of religion in Byzantine society, theological disputes were virtually unavoidable. Perhaps the most serious controversy erupted around 726, when Emperor Leo III (717–741) banned the use of religious icons, such as pictures or statues of Christ and the saints, as graven images. This was the view already held by Jews and Muslims, but long before the eighth century, religious images had become commonplace in both western and eastern Christendom, largely for devotional reasons but also as political symbols and commercial objects.

Leo's ban incited a furious debate, known as the Iconoclastic Controversy, that lasted until 787 and then flared again between 813 and 843. The monks in particular opposed the prohibition even in the face of persecution; some were executed, exiled, maimed, or publicly ridiculed by having to parade through the Hippodrome hand in hand with a woman. A church council upheld the iconoclastic position in 754, but 33 years later, under the influence of Empress Irene, another council accepted icons as a channel of divine grace on the condition that they be revered but not worshiped. The empress Theodora, widow of Theophilus, settled the issue in 843 in yet another council that reaffirmed the use of religious images.

The popes' opposition to Byzantium's attempt to abolish images strained relations between the empire and the papacy. Other factors contributed to a deteriorating relationship, including an imperial decision during the Iconoclastic Controversy to transfer ecclesiastical jurisdiction over the Balkans, southern Italy, and Sicily from the pope to the patriarch of Constantinople. Theological conflict also flared when the Latin church modified the traditional creed to stipulate that the Holy Spirit "proceeds" from the Father "and from the Son" (*filioque*). In Byzantine eyes the added term *filioque* had no biblical basis and was thus unacceptable. The feuding culminated in 1054, when each side excommunicated the other, causing a schism that has never been fully healed. The fundamental cause of the breach was conflicting views over the respective roles of emperor and pope in the church.

Religion and Culture

Religious convictions and reverence for classical antiquity largely shaped Byzantine culture. The educated laity were typically trained in the Greek classics, though always within a Christian framework. The learned displayed keen interest in the relative merits of Plato and Aristotle, with the latter attracting the greater support. Virtually all students studied the Homeric epics, and scholars pursued advanced studies in philosophy, law, and medicine.

The importance of the classical tradition encouraged many writers to imitate its literary forms, such as history, satire, orations, and epigrams (short poems, usually witty or barbed in tone). Byzantine writers did not produce secular, lyrical poetry, nor were they very interested in classical drama; classical tragedies were read but not performed, perhaps because of church opposition. Generally, Byzantine authors were imitative rather than creative. This conservative tone was evident in their interest in grammars, encyclopedias, and commentaries. Some literary forms, such as sermons, hymns, and the lives of saints, were intended as religious pedagogy and composed for common people; the illiterate could have such works read to them. Although saints' lives extolled virtue, piety, and steadfastness, they usually contained more than a little adventure and psychological drama. One of the finest forms of Byzantine literature was liturgical poetry, which set religious verse to music.

The most characteristic Byzantine art form was the mosaic, which blended classical and Christian influences. Mosaics adorned the surfaces of domes, semidomes, and apses and were situated to take maximum advantage of the limited light in churches. Artists tilted the glass, ceramic, marble, or shell cubes that made up their pictures to create a shimmering effect. The mosaicists illustrated both sacred and secular themes, although the advocates of iconoclasm wanted religious art restricted to abstract symbols, animals, and plants, much as in contemporary Islamic art.

Byzantine artists were fond of painting icons, or devotional panels. These images, rendered according to strict formal rules, reflect the spiritual devotion of Orthodox Christians. The figures in the icons are traditionally painted frontally to create the impression that the subjects are communicating with the viewer about the mysteries of the Christian faith. The prevailing conservatism in the empire is reflected in art forms, which show only modest changes from the age of Justinian to the fall of the empire in the fifteenth century at the hands of Islam.

Islam and the Arabs

By 750, thanks in large measure to the appeal of its vision of society and the religious commitment of its adherents, Islam had spread from its homeland in Arabia into Persia and through the Middle East and North Africa as far as the Iberian Peninsula. The Arabs who spread the Islamic message were Semites from the Arabian Peninsula. Economically, the lives of its inhabitants depended on the camel, which facilitated trade between the Mediterranean and India. Camel caravans had played an important role in the spice trade during the Hellenistic and Roman eras and were still important in the sixth century, when Muhammad was born.

Mecca, Muhammad's native city, was strategically located at the crossroads of the caravan routes from

In Defense of Icons

John of Damascus, an eighth-century monk, wrote this argument in favor of icons around 730.

For the invisible things of God since the creation of the world are made visible through images. We see images in creation which remind us faintly of God, as when, for instance, we speak of the holy and adorable Trinity, imaged by the sun, or light, or burning rays, or by a running fountain. . . .

Worship is the symbol of veneration and of honor. Let us understand that there are different degrees of worship. . . .

Of old, God the incorporeal and uncircumscribed was never depicted. Now, however, when God is seen clothed in flesh, and conversing with men, I make an image of the God whom I see. I do not worship matter, I worship the God of matter, who became matter for my sake, . . . who worked out my salvation through matter. I will not cease from honoring that matter which works my salvation. I venerate it, though not as God. . . . Is not the most holy book of the Gospels matter? Is not the blessed table matter which gives us the Bread of Life? Are not the gold and silver matter out of which crosses and altar-plate and chalices are made? And before all these things, is not the body and blood of our Lord matter? Either do away with the veneration and worship due to all these things, or submit to the tradition of the Church in the worship of images, honoring God and his friends.

Source: St. John Damascene on Holy Images, trans. M. H. Allies (London: Burns & Oates, 1898), pp. 10–17 passim.

Main apse of the cathedral in Cefalu, Sicily, dominated by the figure of Christ as Pantocrator (Ruler of All).

Palestine and Syria to Yemen, at the southern end of the peninsula, and from Mesopotamia to Ethiopia in eastern Africa. Little manufacturing or agriculture existed in the area, but Mecca was a pilgrimage center where visitors came to worship assorted deities. The main sanctuary housed idols representing some 360 gods, including Allah (*al-ilah* means "The God"), a creator deity. Because pilgrims contributed to the local economy, commerce and religion were closely entwined.

Muhammad and Islam

Born about 570, Muhammad was orphaned as a small boy and raised by an uncle. He worked for a while as a shepherd, lived with the nomadic Bedouins, and traveled with caravans on the Syria-Yemen route. This experience served him in good stead when the wealthy widow Khadija employed him to manage her caravan business. When Muhammad was about 25, he married her; they had several children and an apparently happy relationship. A devout disciple of traditional Arabic religion, Muhammad regularly went into the hills near Mecca to pray, and there, in a cave on Mount Hira in 610, he heard a voice proclaim that he was the messenger of God. According to Muslim tradition, the voice was that of the archangel Gabriel. For some three years, however, Muhammad was not fully certain of his calling, although Khadija was sympathetic and became his first convert. Others followed, including younger sons of prominent Mecca families. Most, however, were young people of modest background who were sympathetic to the traditional ideals of family solidarity, honor, and generosity, as distinct from the profit-oriented values of the wealthy merchants.

The religion Muhammad founded is known as Islam ("submission"). A Muslim is one who submits to the will of Allah (God) and who fulfills the five duties known as the Pillars of Islam. The first of these is the sincere profession of the *Shahada,* a simple credal statement: "I bear witness that there is no god but God; I bear witness that Muhammad is the messenger of God." In time Muhammad professed strict monotheism, although at the outset of his ministry he accepted three traditional Arabic deities as lesser beings who could intercede with God on behalf of believers; he later renounced this view. Muhammad rejected the Christian doctrine of the Trinity, even while according respect to Jesus as a prophet:

> **The Messiah, Jesus son of Mary, was only the Messenger of God, and His Word that He committed to Mary, and a Spirit from Him. So believe in God and His Messengers, and say not, 'Three.' . . . God is only one God.[8]**

Similar in most of these attributes to the God of Judaism and Christianity, Allah is eternal and infallible as well as the creator and ultimate judge of all people. As his servant, Muhammad was the last and greatest of the prophets, whose number included Adam, Abraham, and Jesus. Four prophets were transmitters of divine revelation: Moses in the Torah, David in the Psalms, Jesus in the Gospels, and Muhammad in the Koran.

The second of the Pillars is *Salat,* formal prayer at five specified times each day. Following ritual purification, worshipers face Mecca and together move through a cycle of standing, bowing, prostration, and sitting. *Salat* often occurs in a mosque (an Arabic word meaning "place of prostration"). Each mosque has a niche indicating the direction of Mecca, a raised pulpit from which sermons are preached, and, normally, a minaret from which the call to prayer is made.

Almsgiving, in the form of a mandatory tax called the *Zakat* ("purification"), is the third Pillar. It renders the rest of the believer's property religiously acceptable

BYZANTIUM AND ISLAM: THE EARLY CENTURIES

Byzantines	Muslims
Constantine makes Byzantium his capital (330)	
Age of Justinian (527–565)	
• Code (529)	
• Hagia Sophia (532–537)	
	Muhammad's vision (610)
	Hejira (622)
	Origins of Sunni-Shi'ite split (late 650s)
	Umayyad caliphate (661–750)
Iconoclastic Controversy (726–787)	Invasion of Iberia begins (710)
	Abbasid caliphate (750–1258)
	Spain breaks away (756)
	Moroccan independence (788)
	Tunisian independence (800)
Iconoclastic Controversy renewed (813–842)	
	Beginning of Fatimid rule in Egypt (969)
Schism between Byzantine and Roman churches (1054)	Abbasids become puppets of the Seljuk Turks (1055)
Comnenian dynasty (1081–1185)	Mongols overrun Baghdad (1258)

and symbolizes the strong sense of community among Muslims. In effect, it is a loan to God, who will repay it many times over. The fourth Pillar consists of fasting (*sawm*) during the lunar month of Ramadan, during which time no food, drink, medicine, or sensual pleasure can be taken during daylight hours.

The final Pillar is the *Hajj*, a pilgrimage to Mecca, if circumstances allow, to visit the Kaaba, a temple that Muslims believe was built by Abraham and his son Ishmael. Some Muslims regard *Jihad* (literally, "exertion" in God's service) as a sixth Pillar. It can take two forms: the greater jihad involves an internal spiritual struggle, and the lesser jihad entails physical conflict against the enemies of Islam.

Muslims believe that the Koran (*Qur'an* in Arabic), the sacred text of Islam, contains the word of God as revealed to Muhammad. His companions established the text in its present form about 650. Proper recitation of the Koran, according to Muslims, results in a special sense of divine presence. Its pages contain social as well as religious maxims, including instructions about inheritance, dowries, and marriage. The Koran generally treats men as superior to women and allows slavery subject to restrictions on how slaves can be treated and when they should be freed.

> **Those your right hands own who seek emancipation, contract with them accordingly, if you know some good in them; and give them of the wealth of God that He has given you. And constrain not your slave girls to prostitution, if they desire to live in chastity.[9]**

Further guidance is found in the *Hadith*, sayings based on recollections of Muhammad's words and acts; Muslims have collected thousands of these. As a guide to godly living, Muslims created the *Shari'a*, or "way" of the believer, including laws governing behavior and belief.

Sunnis, Shi'ites, and Sufis

Muhammad's teachings incited opposition at Mecca, and in July 622 he moved some 200 miles north, to Yathrib, later called Medina. This event became known as the *Hejira*, or migration, the date of which became the first year of the Muslim era. There he remained, gathering followers and launching expeditions against Meccan cara-

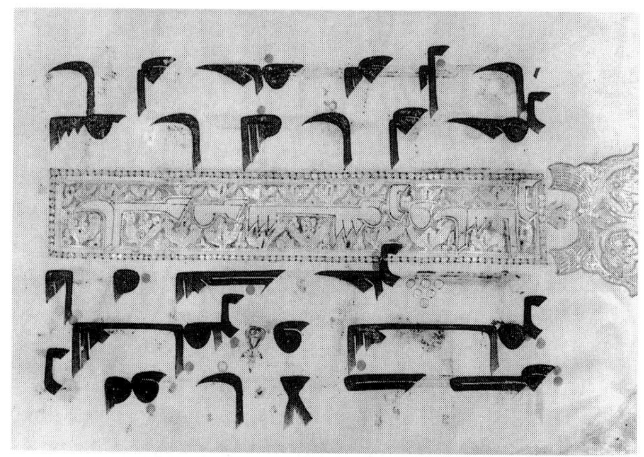

A page from the Koran, written in Kulic script.

vans, until he was powerful enough to return to Mecca in 630. He died at Medina from a fever in June 632.

Upon news of Muhammad's death his key advisers agreed that his closest friend, Abu Bakr (c. 573–634), should be the new leader, or caliph ("deputy") of the prophet. Abu Bakr and the caliphs who succeeded him had no status as prophets but functioned as the head of the Arab state, commander of the army, supreme judge, and leader of public worship. During his brief tenure as caliph, Abu Bakr imposed unity on most of the Arabian people, many of whom had reverted to their independent ways after Muhammad's death. His army challenged Byzantine control of Palestine, and his successor, Umar (634–644), eventually conquered Jerusalem. Umar's forces carried Islam into Syria, Iraq, Persia, and Egypt before assassins murdered him in 644. The new caliph, Uthman (644–656), continued the militant policy of early Islam, sending his armies across North Africa to Tunisia and northward into Armenia and Afghanistan. Muslim fleets defeated the Byzantine navy, captured Cyprus, and plundered Rhodes. Uthman died at the hands of assassins, among them Abu Bakr's son, in 656.

The rebellious Muslims in Egypt who were responsible for Uthman's murder successfully pressed for the election of Ali (656–661), Muhammad's son-in-law and cousin, as the new caliph. Ali faced a challenge from Muawiya (died 680), the governor of Syria and a member of the powerful Umayyad clan, whose army fought Ali's forces in 657. When both sides agreed to arbitration, radical idealists broke with Ali and formed their own party, the Kharijites ("seceders"). The arbitration failed, but in the aftermath of Ali's assassination by a Kharijite in 661, Muawiya had no serious rival, and Muslims proclaimed him caliph at Jerusalem. He ruled from Damascus in Syria.

The modern division of Islam into two main branches, the Shi'ites and the Sunni, had its origins in Ali's claim that he had been designated Muhammad's successor before the prophet died. Ali's party, or *shi'ah,* supported this claim. When Muawiya died in 680, Ali's son, Husayn, led the Shi'ites in a rebellion, only to die with his family at the hands of Umayyad troops the same year. In Shi'ite eyes, he was a martyr, and his death is reenacted each year in a type of passion play.

The core of the Shi'ite movement is the conviction that Ali was the true successor of Muhammad and thus the first *imam,* or caliph. Some Shi'ites expand the *Shahada* ("creed") by adding the phrase "and Ali is his comrade." Most Shi'ites eventually came to believe in a succession of 12 imams extending from Ali to Muhammad al-Muntazar (died 878), who reportedly disappeared into a cave, is still living, and will someday return as a savior (*Mahdi*). Until that time, Shi'ites accept only those laws and beliefs found in the Koran or set forth by a true imam, the beneficiary of divine revelation. In contrast, most Muslims, known as Sunni, follow the tradition (*sunna*) established by Muhammad and the Koran; they regard the latter as complete and do not attribute special religious knowledge to their leaders. Shi'ites believe that a Muslim can perform the pilgrimage to Mecca by proxy or can substitute a visit to the tomb of a Shi'ite saint, such as Ali.

As in the case of early Christianity, some devout Muslims embraced an ascetic life characterized by solitary meditation, fasting, prayer, lengthy vigils, and poverty. Some of the devout were content to wear simple woolen frocks and soon became known as Sufis, after the Arabic word *suf* ("wool"). The Sufis were mystics whose ultimate goal was union with God through love and the purification of the soul. An important means to this end is the special remembrance of God by repeating his 99 "most beautiful names," whether in a rhythmic chant, in silence accompanied by special breathing exercises, or in a dance that culminates in a swoon. In the tenth century the Sufis began organizing brotherhoods, each of which was led by a master who taught disciples and inducted them into the order. As in the case of Christian monasticism, most orders had affiliated lay members who participated in the orders' religious worship. The Sufis played a major role in the spread and popularization of Islam, in part because of their willingness to incorporate local customs and beliefs into Muslim orthodoxy.

The Umayyads at Damascus

Between 661 and 750 the Umayyad family provided the caliphs who ruled the Islamic world from their capital at Damascus. Arab conquests continued. As caliph, Muawiya continued to battle the Byzantines, especially in eastern Asia Minor. Between 674 and 678 his troops besieged Constantinople itself, but the fortifications proved too formidable. The Arabs returned again in 717–718, only to be foiled by new defenses, a harsh winter, disease, and "Greek fire," a fearsome substance (possibly made with quicklime or distilled petroleum) that ignited on contact with water.

By the early eighth century all of North Africa was in Muslim hands, and the first raids across the Strait of Gibraltar into Iberia came in 710 and 711. Because the

A detail from one of the eighth-century mosaics that line the walls of the Great Mosque at Damascus.

peninsula was already in a state of political chaos, it fell into Muslim hands before the end of the decade. With their allies, the Berber tribesmen of North Africa, the Arabs crossed the Pyrenees into the Frankish kingdom in 718. From 720 until 759 they occupied the town of Narbonne, which served as a base for plundering expeditions. Islamic penetration north of the Pyrenees might have been more extensive had it not been for the bitter fighting that erupted between the Arabs and the Berbers in Spain and North Africa between 734 and 742 and factional struggles among the Arabs themselves. Internal rivalries were more important than the military skills of the Franks in halting Muslim expansion in Europe near Tours in 732.

In the meantime, Arab armies resumed their push into Asia, reaching as far as the Indus River. In the early eighth century they established themselves in such places as Turkestan, Baluchistan, and the northwestern corner of India (now Pakistan), which to this day remains Muslim. Not until the eleventh century, however, did Turks from central Asia establish Islam as a major force in much of the Indian subcontinent.

The Umayyads organized their empire into five states, each of which was governed by a viceroy appointed by the caliph in Damascus: Iraq and the Muslim lands to the east; central and southern Arabia; eastern Asia Minor, Armenia, and the Caucasus; Egypt; and the

Sufi Mysticism

The poet Hafiz uses the analogy of a bird to express his search for mystical reunion with the divine.

My soul is as a sacred bird, the highest heaven its nest,
Fretting within its body-bars, it finds on earth its nest;
When rising from its dusty heap this bird of mine shall soar
'Twill find upon the lofty gate the nest it had before.
The Sidrah [Tree of Paradise] shall receive my bird, when it has winged its way,
And on the Empyrean's top, my falcon's foot shall stay,
Over the ample field of earth is fortune's shadow cast,
Where upon wings and pennons borne this bird of mine has passed.
No spot in the two worlds it owns, above the sphere its goal,
Its body from the quarry is, from "No Place" is its soul.
'Tis only in the glorious world my bird its splendor shows,
The rosy bowers of Paradise its daily food bestows.

Source: E. A. Reed, *Persian Literature: Ancient and Modern* (Chicago: Griggs, 1893), p. 329.

rest of North Africa and the Iberian peninsula. The speed of the Arab conquest was such that the conquerors had to rely on native bureaucrats to administer the subject areas; in Spain the Jews were particularly useful in this regard. Viceroys who governed from Damascus as well as viceroys and provincial governors who siphoned tax revenues into their personal coffers undermined administrative effectiveness in the later years of Umayyad rule. The tax structure itself became a major source of trouble. All free non-Muslims paid a poll (head) tax, and those with land paid a tax on it as well, whereas Arabs outside of Arabia did not. Converts to Islam were exempt from the poll tax but not the land tax, a situation that caused them to resent Arab landowners in their midst.

A variety of factors, including the problematic tax structure, undermined Umayyad power. No less important was the disaffection caused by the specter of an opulent court in Damascus. Shi'ites, who were strong in Iran and Iraq, and Kharijites were implacable enemies of the Umayyads, as were the Abbasids, who claimed to be the heirs of Ali and who traced their ancestry to Muhammad's uncle. The Abbasids revolted in 747, overran Iraq in 749, and seized Damascus the following year. Most members of the Umayyad family were ruthlessly slaughtered, although one fled to Spain and founded a caliphate at Córdoba. The Abbasids briefly moved the capital to Kufah in Iraq and then built a new one at Baghdad.

The Abbasids

Factional intrigue, violence, and the decentralization of power marked the Abbasid caliphate (750–1258). Abu al-Abbas (750–754), its founder, referred to himself as "the Bloodletter," an apt sobriquet in view of his slaughter of many of the deposed Umayyads. Many of his successors were no less vicious in executing Shi'ites who challenged their authority. Al-Abbas felt it necessary to surround himself with several thousand bodyguards. In the ninth century the caliphs recruited Turkish slaves, presumably more loyal to their employers, as guards, yet even they turned against the caliph, al-Mutawakkil, whom they assassinated in 861. Imperial ministers and generals openly intrigued to manipulate the succession

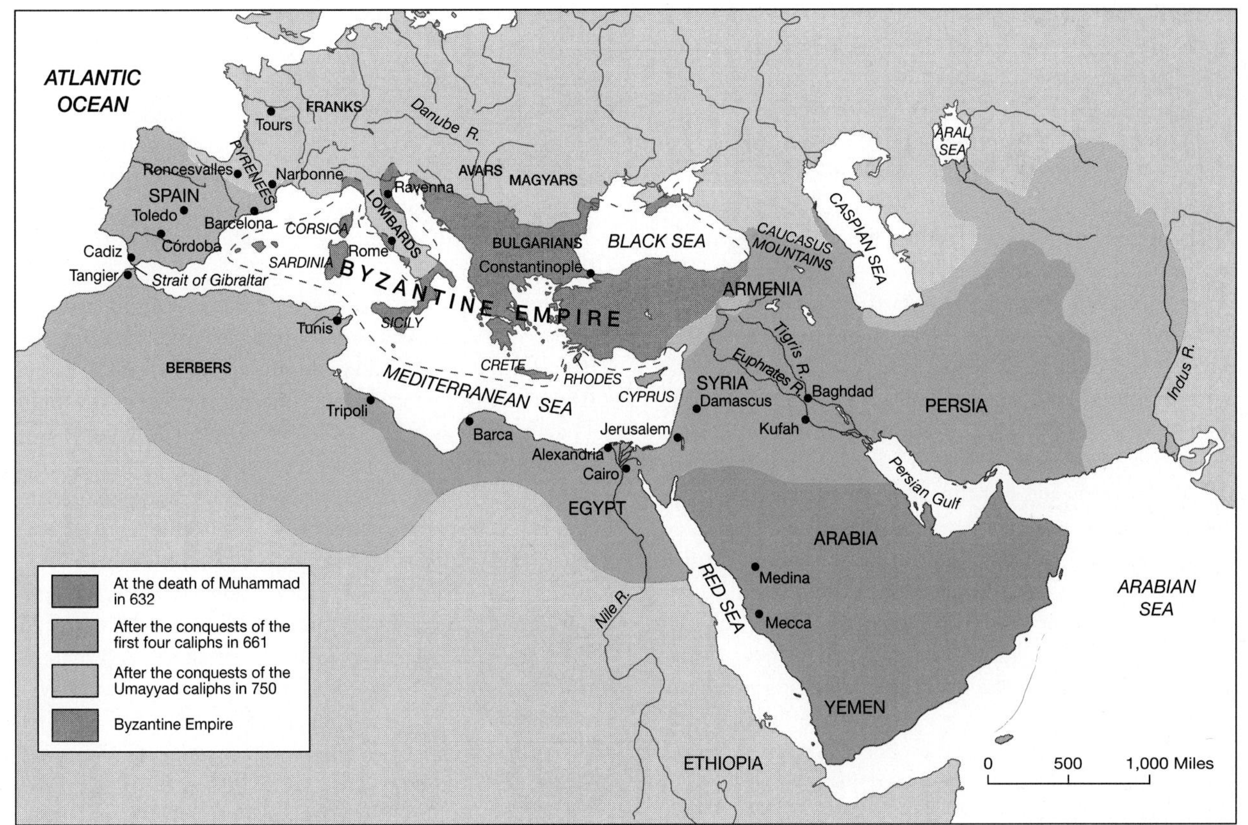

MAP 8.3 THE EXPANSION OF ISLAM

while the caliphs enjoyed court living as avidly as had the Umayyads. With tens of thousands of staff members and servants, the palace complexes in Baghdad were centers of waste, inefficiency, and decadence, their cultural splendor notwithstanding.

The decentralization of power and the breakup of the empire characterized the Abbasid period. Spain had gone its own way when the Umayyad prince, Abd al-Rahman (756–788), established an independent caliphate at Córdoba. Like its counterpart in Baghdad, it became a brilliant cultural center, only to succumb to turbulent palace guards in the mid-tenth century. The caliphate of Córdoba then fragmented into smaller Muslim states, making it easier for the Christians to begin their reconquest of the peninsula. Morocco broke away from Baghdad in 788 and was under Shi'ite rule for two centuries before succumbing to the Córdoban caliphate. Tunisia became independent in 800 and in the ensuing century conquered Malta, Sicily, and Sardinia in addition to plundering the coasts of France and the Italian peninsula. Egypt pursued its own course beginning in the mid-ninth century and in 969 fell under the dominion of the Shi'ite Fatimid family of Tunisia, which ruled from the new capital of Cairo. By 1000 the Fatimid empire embraced North Africa, Syria, and much of the Arabian peninsula, but in the eleventh century it too suffered at the hands of inept caliphs and rebellious slave armies, making possible the modest gains of Christian crusaders in the late 1090s.

The story was much the same in the east, where the aristocratic Samanid family established an independent dynasty in parts of Persia and central Asia. Revolutionary upheavals and revolts by African slaves shook Iraq in the late ninth century, and the Buyids, a Shi'ite clan from Persia, occupied Baghdad in 945. For a century thereafter the Abbasid caliphs were mere puppets of the Buyids, whose rulers claimed a variety of titles, including "emir of emirs" and "king of kings." They in turn fell in 1055 to the Seljuk Turks, originally from Turkestan. These new invaders found it useful to maintain the Abbasids as figureheads, but the caliphate perished in 1258, when Mongol invaders overran Baghdad and murdered the last caliph. From Baghdad the Turkish sultans ruled Iraq, Syria, and Persia, but not until the sixteenth century would another group of Turks, the Ottomans, extend their sway throughout most of North Africa. Never, however, would any Muslim caliph exercise sovereignty on the scale of the Umayyads in the early eighth century. The Abbasid period marks the end of Arab dominance in the Muslim world and the emergence of Islam as an international religion.

Islamic Civilization

The driving force in Islamic civilization was the teachings of Muhammad, but wherever Islam spread, it assimilated native cultures. The result was the creation of a distinctive civilization, with major centers of culture in Damascus, Baghdad, Cairo, Córdoba, and, later, Delhi and Constantinople. The economy and the culture of the Islamic world had a substantial impact on the peoples of Europe and Asia.

Economic Life

As a merchant, Muhammad gave Islam a keen appreciation of commerce and, indeed, of all forms of productive activity, provided they were carried out in an honest, charitable spirit. Sayings attributed to him in the Hadith describe merchants as "the couriers of the horizons and God's trusted servants on earth," who, if honest, "will stand with the martyrs on the Day of Judgment." Tilling and sheepherding were occupations also created and blessed by God, but "the best of gain is from honorable trade and from a man's work with his own hands."[10] Muhammad condemned moneychangers, prostitutes, hoarders, greedy merchants, and lenders who charged usury (interest). Similar ethical maxims are found in contemporary Christian teaching and underscore the common attempt to curtail acquisitiveness and dishonesty on the one hand while instilling thrift and humaneness on the other. However, contemporary Christianity did not place a comparable positive emphasis on commerce per se.

Muslim trade routes eventually extended from the Pyrenees to the Indus. Muslim traders also traveled far beyond the boundaries of Islamic states, ranging as far as India, Southeast Asia, and China. Others crossed the Sahara into western and central Africa or sailed down Africa's east coast as far as Kilwa (in modern Tanzania). They traded as well with the peoples of Byzantium, western Europe, and Russia, though much of this commerce was in the hands of Jewish and Christian merchants. Ships carried most of the trade with Europe and Asia, but the primary route with China, the "Great Silk Way," ran overland through northern Persia and Turkestan. The fact that non-Muslim merchants could live and work in Islamic states enhanced commercial growth. Around 1285, for instance, the sultan of Egypt formally welcomed merchants "who come to his realm, as to the garden of Eden, by whatever gate they may choose to enter, from Iraq, from Persia, from Asia Minor, from the Hijaz [in Arabia], from India, and from

China."[11] The absence of internal tariff barriers in the Muslim world between the eighth and twelfth centuries also fostered commercial expansion. So too did the development of bills of exchange (checks) and joint-stock companies, which enabled many people to invest in business activities, thus sharing both profits and risks.

Manufacturing in the Islamic world was extensive and varied. Linen, cotton, wool, and silk were among the products, as were glass, ceramics, metals, soaps, dyes, and perfume. Some areas were renowned for their manufactures: Córdoba for its leather, Egypt for glass and linens, Toledo and Damascus for steel, Kufah for silk kerchiefs, Baghdad and Samarkand for porcelain, and Bukhara (in central Asia) for carpets. The Muslims learned how to make paper from the Chinese in the eighth century and later founded their own mills. The widespread availability of paper stimulated scholarship and encouraged publishing.

Islamic Society

"The noblest among you in the eyes of God is the most pious," said Muhammad, "for God is omniscient and well informed." This principle could serve as a new basis for social valuation, in contrast to the traditional Arab recognition of an aristocracy based on birth and family ties. A similar position is expressed in the New Testament, but as Islam and Christianity evolved, each accommodated notions of a social hierarchy. Muhammad himself reportedly gave preeminence to the Arabs: "The best of mankind are the Arabs." "Love the Arabs," he insisted, "for three reasons: because I am an Arab, because the Koran is in Arabic, and because the inhabitants of Paradise speak Arabic."[12]

During the Umayyad period, Muslims recognized four social classes, the first of which comprised Arab Muslims, the de facto aristocracy. The government in Damascus recorded their names in a special registry and gave each Arab Muslim a regular payment from the imperial treasury. Initially, the government reserved the new garrison towns, such as Cairo and Kufah, for them alone. Arab families discouraged their female members from marrying non-Arabs.

Non-Arab Muslims made up the second class. Because they typically affiliated themselves with an Arab clan or family, they were known as *mawali,* or clients. By the early eighth century not only were they more numerous than the Arabs, but they resented their inferior status, especially since some of them were more educated than their Arab counterparts. Some mawali reacted by embracing Shi'ite views, while others claimed to have become Arabs through clientage. In time the Arabs of the conquered lands tended to intermarry with the mawali, giving rise to a broader definition of an Arab as one who spoke Arabic and embraced Islam.

The third class in Islamic society consisted of free non-Muslims, primarily Jews, Christians, and Zoroastrians. Such persons, known as *dhimmis,* or covenanted people, received personal security and substantial local autonomy in return for accepting Muslim rule and paying additional taxes. Dhimmis were free to worship according to their own rites, engage in business activities, own property, and for the most part govern themselves through their own laws and in their own courts. They could not hold public office, bear arms, testify in court against Muslims, dress in Muslim fashion, or use saddles on their horses. One such pact, dating from about the seventh century, specifically prohibited missionary activity: "We shall not manifest our religion publicly nor convert anyone to it. We shall not prevent any of our kin from entering Islam if they wish it." The same pact also made the dhimmis' inferior status very apparent: "We shall show respect toward the Muslims, and we shall rise from our seats when they wish to sit."[13] For the most part the dhimmis received more tolerance and respect than medieval European Christians accorded Jews. Periodically, repression occurred, however, as when the dhimmis' commercial success threatened the Muslims, when the latter suspected the dhimmis of collaborating with the crusaders or the Mongols, or when the dhimmis ignored the terms of their covenant.

Slaves were the lowest class in Islamic society. Although Muhammad had reservations about slavery, he accepted its legality. A saying in the Hadith may reveal his true feelings: "The worst of men are those who buy and sell men."[14] Muslims could not be enslaved, but conversion did not automatically bring manumission. Nor could masters and slaves marry, though the former could take slaves as concubines. The children of such a union were free, and their mother enjoyed a special status, could not be sold, and received her freedom when her master died. Children of slave parents, however, were born slaves.

The Islamic economy was not heavily dependent on slaves, as was the Roman Empire or the southern United States before the American civil war, but large numbers of slaves were traded and used primarily in the military or as servants. Some caliphs were the sons of slave mothers. The wealthiest Muslims possessed thousands of slaves. The Arabs enslaved prisoners, but they also purchased many slaves in markets. There were slaves of nearly all races and from a wide variety of places, including Spain, Greece, sub-Saharan Africa, India, and central Asia. So plentiful and varied was the supply that handbooks were available to guide consumers in the art of purchase. The advice included observations on the strengths and weaknesses of the various peoples: Greek women, for instance, "are good as treasurers because they are meticulous and not very generous," whereas Slavic women "live long because of their excellent digestion, but . . . are barren because they are never clean from menstrual blood."[15] Despite the popularity of slavery, Islamic teaching recommended manumission and urged that slaves be allowed to purchase their freedom.

Muslim Women

Women in traditional Arabic society, although important in the home, were subordinate to men. They could neither inherit nor claim a share of spoils won on the battlefield, and their husbands enjoyed an absolute right of divorce. In some instances baby girls were regarded with such disdain that they were buried alive at birth or killed at the age of 5 or 6. The Koran alludes to this practice—disapprovingly—in several places, as in an account of the Last Judgment, "when the buried infant shall be asked for what sin she was slain."[16]

Muhammad sought to improve the treatment of women, according them spiritual if not social equality. They were to be obedient to men, who were responsible for the management of affairs.

> **Men are the managers of the affairs of women for that God has preferred . . . one of them over another, and for that they have expended of their property. Righteous women are therefore obedient. . . . And those you fear may be rebellious admonish; banish them to their couches, and beat them.**[17]

The proper relationship between husbands and wives, according to Muhammad, entailed love. Muslims conceived of marriage in contractual terms, with each party having rights and responsibilities. According to the Koran, a man could have up to four wives, but no woman was entitled to more than one husband. In practice, the expense of supporting more than one wife generally confined polygamy to the wealthy. Behind the practice of polygamy was the conviction that procreation was a fundamental purpose of marriage. "Your women," said Muhammad, "are a tillage [cultivated land] for you; so come unto your tillage as you wish."[18] Muhammad's comment hints at Islam's recognition of the importance of sexual pleasure for both men and women, an attitude strikingly different from the medieval Christian view of sex in essentially negative terms.

The Koran exhorted women to dress circumspectly, taking special care to cover their breasts and to draw their veils around them when they left the home. Such admonitions led free-born Muslim women in the towns to veil their faces in public and to seclude themselves within their own part of the home, known as the harem. The harem system did not originate with Islam but had roots in ancient Mesopotamia and was similar to the Byzantine practice of providing private apartments for women in their own homes. The harem became a characteristic part of Islamic society by the late eighth century. The seclusion of women in harems or behind veils, the practice of polygamy, and a willingness to beat disobedient wives underscore the fact that Islam, though making important advances over traditional Arab society, was far from establishing the social equality of the sexes. This is also apparent with respect to the inheritance of property; in pre-Islamic Arabic society, women could not inherit at all. The Koran lifted this absolute prohibition but still limited women's rights in specified circumstances.

In practice, the role of women in medieval Islam varied substantially. Some played an active part in politics, including the scheming that became a regular part of determining succession to the caliphate. The wife of the Ummayad caliph al-Walid I (705–715) engaged in political activities to promote justice and encouraged her husband to enlarge mosques. One of the greatest of the Abbasid caliphs, Harun al-Rashid (786–809), apparently owed his position to his fabulously wealthy mother, Khayzuran, a former slave, who may have had a rival son assassinated. Harun's wife, Zubaydah, contributed money to build an aqueduct in Mecca and took an interest in urban development, much as aristocratic Turkish women patronized hospitals and schools. Women were de facto rulers of Egypt in the 1020s, late 1040s, and 1250s.

Muslim women participated in a wide range of cultural and intellectual pursuits. During the Umayyad caliphate they provided salons in which scholars, poets, and other educated people could gather; prominent among such women was Muhammad's great-granddaughter, Sukaina. As in pre-Islamic society, women wrote poetry, and female professionals sang elegies at funerals. Throughout the Umayyad period, women studied law and theology, while in the caliphate of Córdoba women as well as men taught in schools. Female scholars were prominent in the towns of Muslim Spain, and some lectured at the universities of Córdoba and Valencia. Women were also active in the Sufi movement. The Abbasids employed women to spy against the Byzantines

Muhammad's Teaching about Women

Muhammad outlined his view of female dependency in the Koran.

And if ye are apprehensive that ye shall not deal fairly with orphans, then, of other women who seem good in your eyes, marry but two, or three, or four; and if ye still fear that ye shall not act equitably, then one only. . . .

If any of your women be guilty of whoredom, then bring four witnesses against them from among yourselves; and if they bear witness to the fact, shut them up within their houses till death release them, or God make some way for them. And if two men among you commit the same crime, then punish them both; but if they turn and amend, then let them be. . . .

Men are superior to women on account of the qualities with which God hath gifted the one above the other, and on account of the outlay they make from their substance for them. Virtuous women are obedient, careful, during the husband's absence, because God hath of them been careful. But chide those for whose refractoriness ye have cause to fear; remove them into beds apart, and scourge them: but if they are obedient to you, then seek not occasion against them. . . . And if ye fear a breach between man and wife, then send a judge chosen from his family, and a judge chosen from her family: for if they are desirous of agreement, God will effect a reconciliation between them.

When ye divorce women . . . put them not forth from their houses, nor allow them to depart, unless they have committed a proven adultery. . . . Lodge the divorced wherever ye lodge, according to your means; and distress them not by putting them to straits. And if they are pregnant, then be at charges for them till they are delivered of their burden; and if they suckle your children, then pay them their hire . . . and act generously.

Source: The Koran, trans. J. M. Rodwell (New York: Dutton, 1909), pp. 410–430 passim.

in the guise of merchants, physicians, and travelers, which suggests that they undertook such activities in their own society.

The status of Muslim women began to decline in the late Umayyad period owing to the large increase in the number of slave women that occurred during the territorial expansion of Islam. Increasingly, men saw women as objects, the possession of which reflected wealth. During the Abbasid caliphate, government decrees increasingly regulated the public appearances and clothing of women. Women were banned from public ceremonies. In twelfth-century Seville "decent women" could not dress like prostitutes or hold their own parties, even with their husbands' permission. Some of these regulations were intended to stress female modesty. In Seville women could not run hostels because of the possibility of sexual improprieties, and they could not enter Christian churches because the priests had reputations as fornicators and sodomites. In markets they could deal only with merchants of good reputation, and they could not sit by the riverbank in the summer in the presence of men. For the most part such regulations, though patronizing, suggest concern for the protection of women in Islamic society.

The Muslim Synthesis in Medicine, Science, and Philosophy

The Muslims assimilated and advanced the medical and scientific knowledge of classical antiquity. Because Muhammad had reportedly praised the study of medicine, the subject received considerable attention from medieval Muslim scholars, especially after the works of Galen, Hippocrates, and other classical writers were available in Arabic translations. The great age of medical advance occurred in the Abbasid period, when Muslims founded schools of medicine and hospitals; Baghdad alone had 860 physicians in the year 931.

This Arabic miniature, which was painted around 1222–23, contains a recipe for cough medicine and shows an apothecary preparing it.

The contributions of two men are especially noteworthy in this field: the Persian physician al-Razi (Rhazes; died c. 925), head of the Baghdad hospital, who wrote approximately 120 medical books, including a pioneering study of smallpox and measles; and the Persian scholar Ibn Sina (Avicenna; died 1037), whose *Canon of Medicine* synthesized classical and Islamic medical knowledge, appeared in Latin translation in the twelfth century, and served as the leading medical text in Europe as late as the seventeenth century. Among the topics Ibn Sina explored were the contagious nature of tuberculosis, psychological disorders, and skin diseases. One of the keys to his success was his willingness to learn from practice: "I . . . attended the sick, and the doors of medical treatments based on experience opened before me to an extent that cannot be described."[19]

The importance of experimentation was evident in other sciences as well. Although alchemy—the attempt to transform common metals into gold and other valuable substances—failed to achieve its goal, its practitioners acquired valuable chemical knowledge and developed the world's first laboratories. Al-Razi classified all matter as animal, vegetable, or mineral and distinguished between volatile and nonvolatile substances. In the field of optics, Ibn al-Haytham (Alhazen; died 1039) of Cairo rejected the classical theory that the eye emits visual rays, arguing instead that it sees by receiving rays of light. He devised experiments to study refraction, eclipses, and the atmosphere.

The Muslim ability to synthesize is perhaps best illustrated in the field of mathematics, where Islamic scholars adopted "Arabic" numerals from India, including zero and the placement of numbers in series to denote units, tens, hundreds, and so forth, and geometry and simple trigonometry from the Greeks. One of the leading scholars in this field was Muhammad ibn-Musa al-Khwarizmi, whose ninth-century treatises on arithmetic and algebra (*al-jabr,* "integration") later influenced Europeans. Later mathematical work involved quadratic and cubic equations and led to the development of analytical geometry and spherical trigonometry.

Beginning primarily in the twelfth century, Muslim advances in mathematics and science spread to Europe through Sicily and Spain, where the Jews played a crucial role as cultural intermediaries. In the sixteenth century those achievements provided much of the foundation for the scientific revolution.

Islamic philosophy was heavily indebted to the works of Plato, Aristotle, and the Neoplatonists. No question was more basic to Muslim philosophers than the proper relationship of reason to revelation. The most prominent of the early Arab philosophers, Yaqub al-Kindi (died c. 870), attempted to reconcile Plato and Aristotle while insisting on the importance of knowing God and the universe as the key to immortality, a doctrine essentially derived from the Neoplatonists. When some philosophers insisted that reason was equal in importance to revelation as a means to acquire religious knowledge, al-Ghazali (died 1111) sought to restore the primacy of belief, thereby preventing Islamic doctrine from becoming the monopoly of an educated clique of theologians. God, he insisted,

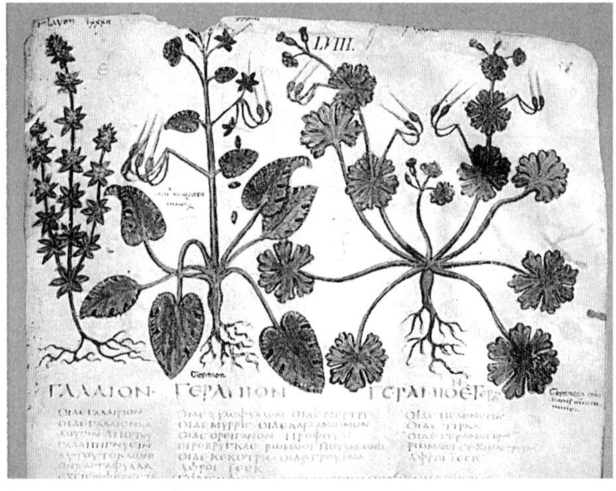

Page from a medical manuscript describing the cultivation of medicinal herbs.

could reveal divine mercy to the common people as well, for belief is

> **a light which God bestows on the hearts of His creatures as the gift and bounty from Him, sometimes through an unexplainable conviction from within, sometimes because of a dream in sleep, sometimes by seeing the state of bliss of a pious man. . . , sometimes through one's own state of bliss.[20]**

Al-Ghazali's attack on rationalist theologians prompted a defense of Aristotelian and Neoplatonic philosophy by the celebrated Ibn Rushd (Averroës, 1126–1198) of Córdoba, a judge and court physician. Like Ibn Sina, he was convinced that the truths of reason and revelation were compatible. The same truth, he argued, could be expressed either philosophically or symbolically; when, therefore, the Koran seemed to advocate an irrational belief, he resolved the apparent contradiction by interpreting the sacred texts allegorically. Through his extensive commentaries on Aristotle, which appeared in Latin translation in the thirteenth century, Ibn Rushd had a major impact on the development of scholastic thought in medieval universities. His views were equally influential in shaping late medieval Jewish philosophy, as reflected especially in the teaching of Gersonides (1288–c. 1344), a French rationalist noted for his commentaries on Aristotle. The Western religious and philosophical heritage is greatly indebted to Islam, not least for introducing European thinkers to much of Aristotle's work.

Islamic Literature

Medieval Muslims were fond of verse. Indeed, the Koran itself was written in quasi-verse form. A ninth-century Arabic scholar aptly summarized the importance of verse:

> **Poetry is the mine of knowledge of the Arabs, the book of their wisdom, the muster roll of their history, the repository of their great days, the rampart protecting their heritage, the trench defending their glories, the truthful witness on the day of dispute, the final proof at the time of argument.[21]**

Verse was the medium used by Firdawsi (c. 935–c. 1020) to compose what became the Iranian national epic, the *Shah-Nameh* ("Book of Kings"), which recounted Persian history from legendary times to 641. Nearly 60,000 verses long, it was instrumental in establishing the definitive form of the Persian language, much as the King James Bible and the works of Shakespeare did for English.

Another Iranian poet, Shams ud-din Hafiz (c. 1325–c. 1389), composed some 500 short lyric poems using simple language and proverbial expressions. Most have three levels of meaning: a reflection of contemporary life in the Persian town of Shiraz, with much to say about wine and love; an expression of tribute to Hafiz' courtly patrons; and a statement of his Sufi beliefs through images readily understood by Iranian readers. Hafiz' works reveal sympathy for the common people, dislike of hypocrisy, and preoccupation with love:

> ***When your beauty radiated on creation's morn,***
> ***The world was set ablaze by love freshly born.[22]***

Hafiz influenced another major Sufi poet, Jami (1414–1492), whose mystical lyrics explored ethics and existence. His contemporary, the Indian poet Kabir (died 1518), was also a mystic. Raised as a Muslim and influenced by Hindu teachings, Kabir taught the equality of all persons and their ability to achieve unity with God through personal devotion.

Apart from the Koran, the best-known Islamic literary work was *The Thousand and One Nights,* a collection of stories from the Middle East and Asia that were originally transmitted orally, much like the ancient Homeric epics. In their extant form, most are set against the background of Baghdad during the caliphate of Harun al-Rashid or Cairo under the Fatimids. A fragment of the work existed by the ninth century, although it was another 600 years or so before a final version emerged.

Final mention must be made of history as a literary form. The greatest medieval Muslim historian was the Tunisian Ibn Khaldun (1332–1406), a pioneer of sociological methodology in explaining the past. To write history, he insisted, required a knowledge of geography, climate, economics, religion, and culture. He called attention to the necessity of evaluating documents preparatory to writing history, since all records are likely to contain inaccuracies. These errors, he explained, are the result of partisanship, overconfidence, a chronicler's failure to grasp the meaning of what he has recorded, excessive faith in one's sources, the inability to place an event in proper context, a desire to gain favor from patrons, a reliance on myth, and exaggeration. A sense of group consciousness was basic to Ibn Khaldun's philosophy of history; a strong communal identity enabled a people to triumph, but their civilization decayed as that spirit weakened. This theory, he believed, explained the decline of the Abbasid caliphate and the triumph of two less cultured nomadic peoples, the Seljuk Turks and the Mongols.

SUMMARY

The Byzantine and Islamic civilizations, thrown together by geography, lived in troubled proximity, sometimes engaging fruitfully in a commerce of goods, ideas, and values but periodically erupting into conflict and attempted conquest. Both civilizations made incalculable contributions to Western civilization by preserving and transmitting classical culture, the Byzantines primarily in literature and the arts, the Muslims especially in science and mathematics. Religion permeated both societies, providing their foundations and shaping their outlook. The Byzantines largely inherited their religious tradition from previous centuries, while the Arabs founded a new religion, borrowing parts of the Judeo-Christian heritage. They differed as well with respect to the religious issues that most deeply divided them: Byzantines fought over religious images, whereas Muslims debated the succession to the caliphate and the relationship of faith and reason. Both cultures revered the law, the Byzantines through Justinian's epic code and the Muslims through the Shari'a. Although neither society accorded women social equality, women enjoyed certain legal rights with respect to property and were occasionally active at the highest levels of politics and in cultural pursuits. Islam, in fact, improved the position of women.

Economically, the Byzantine Empire was based primarily on agriculture, while the Muslim states were oriented toward trade. Although the two cultures shared certain manufacturing interests, such as silk, Muslim trade and production were generally more sophisticated than those of Byzantium. Indeed, a major source of Byzantine weakness in the later centuries of the empire was that it relinquished commerce to the Italians. Nor were Byzantine rulers successful in preserving the welfare of the free peasantry on whom the empire's strength rested; the rise of a military aristocracy seriously undermined the strength and stability of the empire. The Islamic states, in turn, were sapped by the periodic rebellion of slave armies. Violence, intrigue, bloated bureaucracies, and inadequate tax structures weakened both Byzantine and Muslim governments. Their conflicting imperial ambitions further undercut their strength, eventually leaving both prey to the invading Turks. The legacy of both civilizations continues to shape the lives of millions of people, particularly in southeastern Europe, the Middle East, and North Africa.

NOTES

1. D. J. Geanakoplos, *Byzantium: Church, Society, and Civilization Seen Through Contemporary Eyes* (Chicago: University of Chicago Press, 1984), pp. 19–20. The quotation is from Agapetus, a deacon in the church of Hagia Sophia.
2. Ibid., p. 74.
3. R. Browning, *Justinian and Theodora* (London: Thames & Hudson, 1971), p. 72.
4. Geanakoplos, *Byzantium,* p. 321.
5. Ibid., p. 304.
6. Ibid., p. 303.
7. Ibid., p. 196.
8. *The Koran Interpreted,* trans. A. J. Arberry (New York: Macmillan, 1955), vol. 1, p. 125.
9. Ibid., vol. 2, p. 50.
10. B. Lewis, trans. and ed., *Islam from the Prophet Muhammad to the Capture of Constantinople* (New York: Walker, 1974), vol. 2, pp. 125–129.
11. Ibid., p. 166.
12. Ibid., pp. 195–196.
13. Ibid., p. 218.
14. Ibid., p. 128.
15. Ibid., pp. 246–247, 250.
16. *Koran Interpreted,* vol. 2, p. 326.
17. Ibid., vol. 1, pp. 105–106.
18. Ibid., p. 59.
19. Lewis, *Islam,* vol. 2, p. 179.
20. Ibid., p. 21.
21. Ibid., p. 173.
22. *The Divan,* 87:1–2.

SUGGESTIONS FOR FURTHER READING

Crone, P. *Meccan Trade and the Rise of Islam.* Princeton, N.J.: Princeton University Press, 1987.

Donner, F. M. *The Early Islamic Conquests.* Princeton, N.J.: Princeton University Press, 1981.

Downey, G. *Constantinople in the Age of Justinian.* Norman: University of Oklahoma Press, 1960.

Endress, G. *Islam: A Historical Introduction,* trans. C. Hillenbrand. New York: Columbia University Press, 1988.

Esposito, J. L. *Islam: The Straight Path,* 2nd ed. New York: Oxford University Press, 1991.

Every, G. *The Byzantine Patriarchate, 451–1204,* 2nd ed. New York: AMS Press, 1978.

Haldon, S. F. *Byzantium in the Seventh Century: The Transformation of a Culture.* Cambridge: Cambridge University Press, 1991.

Hourani, A. *A History of the Arab Peoples.* Cambridge, Mass.: Harvard University Press, 1991.

Hussey, J. M. *The Byzantine World.* Westport, Conn.: Greenwood, 1982.

———. *The Orthodox Church in the Byzantine Empire.* Oxford: Clarendon Press, 1986.

Kazhdan, A. P., and Epstein, A. W. *Change in Byzantine Culture in the Eleventh and Twelfth Centuries.* Berkeley: University of California Press, 1985.

Kitzinger, E. *Byzantine Art in the Making.* Cambridge, Mass.: Harvard University Press, 1977.

Lapidus, I. M. *A History of Islamic Societies.* Cambridge: Cambridge University Press, 1988.

Le Strange, G. *Baghdad During the Abbasid Caliphate.* New York: Barnes & Noble, 1972.

Lewis, B. *Islam: From the Prophet Muhammad to the Capture of Constantinople.* New York: Oxford University Press, 1987.

Loverance, R. *Byzantium.* Cambridge, Mass.: Harvard University Press, 1988.

Maclagan, M. *The City of Constantinople.* New York: Praeger, 1968.

Magoulias, H. J. *Byzantine Christianity: Emperor, Church, and the West.* Detroit: Wayne State University Press, 1982.

Mottahedeh, R. P. *Loyalty and Leadership in Early Islamic Society.* Princeton, N.J.: Princeton University Press, 1980.

———. *The Mantle of the Prophet.* New York: Simon & Schuster, 1985.

Nicol, D. M. *Church and Society in the Last Centuries of Byzantium.* Cambridge: Cambridge University Press, 1979.

Peters, F. E. *The Hajj: The Muslim Pilgrimage to Mecca and the Holy Places.* Princeton, N.J.: Princeton University Press, 1994.

Pinault, D. *The Shiites: Ritual and Piety in a Muslim Community.* New York: St. Martin's, 1992.

Runciman, S. *The Byzantine Theocracy.* Cambridge: Cambridge University Press, 1977.

Sherrard, P. *Constantinople: Iconography of a Sacred City.* New York: Oxford University Press, 1965.

Watt, W. M. *The Majesty That Was Islam: The Islamic World, 661–1100.* New York: St. Martin's Press, 1990.

———. *Muhammad: Prophet and Statesman.* New York: Oxford University Press, 1974.

———. *Muhammad's Mecca: History in the Qur'an.* Edinburgh: Edinburgh University Press, 1989.

Wiet, G. *Baghdad: Metropolis of the Abbasid Caliphate,* trans. S. Feiler. Norman: University of Oklahoma Press, 1971.

GLOBAL ESSAY

Writing and Communication (I)

A major element in the development of civilization was the invention of writing. Its original purpose was probably to leave messages and to keep track of financial and other transactions, but the ability to accumulate and preserve knowledge transformed almost every aspect of human life. The power of the written word became vastly extended with the invention of printing, and the twentieth century has seen the discoveries of new technologies and an almost unimaginable proliferation of means of communication. These three stages—writing, printing, and mass communications—have affected the history of virtually every human civilization.

The people of Uruk (now Warka), one of the principal Sumerian city-states, devised the earliest known writing system. Late Neolithic people kept records using small tokens in the shape of disks, spheres, half spheres, cones, and other figures, some of which they marked with incisions. Usually kept in clay containers, such tokens might be used, for instance, to represent animals in a palace herd. Late in the fourth millennium B.C., as cities and large-scale trade developed, the use of tokens to maintain records became too cumbersome. The Mesopotamians substituted written images known as ideographs for the tokens. During the third millennium B.C. these ideographs evolved into wedge-shaped marks that could be impressed on a clay tablet quickly and easily with a split reed. The Sumerians also wrote on stone and metal, but clay, which was plentiful in their country and was already used for building and pottery, was much easier to make marks on. Mistakes could easily be smoothed out, and they could make the record permanent by leaving the clay to dry in the sun or baking it slowly in an oven. In this form it was light and easy to carry. The system of wedge-shaped marks on clay is known as cuneiform, after the Latin word *cuneus,* which means "wedge."

Cuneiform combined the use of pictographic signs (representing objects) and phonetic signs (representing sounds) with a total of some 350 characters. The Sumerians' Akkadian successors adopted it and it was in general use in western Asia and Persia until around the middle of the first millennium B.C. Cuneiform signs formed the basis of the earliest known alphabet, which was devised around 1400 B.C. at the Canaanite city of Ugarit. An *alphabet* is a system using only phonetic symbols. The Canaanite writing system, known as North Semitic, gave rise to a large number of later alphabets, including the Arabic, Hebrew, Greek, and Latin.

Around 3000 B.C., shortly after the Sumerian invention of cuneiform, the Egyptians introduced a system of writing known as hieroglyphics. The word means "sacred carved text," but the Egyptians used hieroglyphs for funerary and commemorative inscriptions as well as religious ones and often painted or wrote them on papyrus, a material woven from the reeds that grew along the Nile River. Whether the Sumerians directly influenced the

Statuette of the goddess Ningal from Ur, 2080 B.C. The figure can be identified by the cuneiform inscription on the side of the throne.

Egyptians is uncertain. The sudden appearance and rapid development of hieroglyphic writing suggest contact, but the Egyptians never developed a simplified sign system like cuneiform; throughout their long history they made no attempt to change the basic hieroglyphic signs, although they introduced the cursive forms of hieratic and, later, demotic (a script devised for secular use) for speedier writing with brushpen on papyrus for business, tax, and other nonmonumental purposes.

The earliest writing in India dates back to the Indus valley civilization, which flourished between 3000 and 2000 B.C. in what is now Pakistan. Small, square sealstones were carved with picture signs, often accompanied by animals. The script has never been deciphered. With the disappearance of the Indus valley culture, knowledge of writing seems to have been lost for a few centuries. By 600 B.C. the Aryan invaders of India had developed an alphabetic script. Under the Maurya dynasty (third century B.C.) the *Brahmi*, ancestor of all modern Indian scripts and of many others elsewhere, was firmly established and was used for numerous rock-carved edicts of the emperor Ashoka (269–232 B.C.).

Scholars have attempted to link the Brahmi script with the Indus valley pictograms and thus provide it with a native origin. Most experts, however, believe that a Semitic alphabet was imported into India. Given the remarkable way the alphabet was adapted to Indian needs, this must have occurred sometime before the third century B.C., although no traces of earlier inscriptions have survived. We shall look at the early history of Brahmi when we consider the other descendants of the Semitic alphabets.

The beginning of writing in China is difficult to trace. Its first surviving appearance is in the form of divination inscriptions on shells and bones worked by the Lung Shan people around 2000 B.C. and found in far greater numbers at Anyang and other Shang sites of the late second millennium B.C. The bones were carved with divinations relating to the public and private life of the ruler: building projects, military campaigns, tribute payments, sickness, royal excursions, the weather. These oracle bones were then burned, and the position of any cracks that occurred was carefully studied, since the patterns they formed and their position in relation to the inscriptions were supposed to reveal the wishes of the sacred spirits and to predict the future. The system is known as scapulimancy. It was used in a simpler form as early as the fourth millennium B.C. in China and elsewhere in the eastern Neolithic world. The Anyang rulers were the only people in Chinese history to add inscriptions; all other instances of scapulimancy were produced by drilling holes around which the cracks could form.

The writing was a highly developed series of characters related to those still in use today. It appears already well developed on the Anyang bones, and its origins are thus obscure. Simple pictures represent the objects of everyday life. A short line above or below a longer line conveyed the abstract ideas of "above" and "below." Each

Relief from the tomb of Akhti-Hotep showing hunters with hieroglyphic inscriptions above them.

character had a phonetic sound, consisting of one syllable. In time the signs came to be used phonetically, although to avoid ambiguity picture signs remained in use. Thus a sign group conveying an action includes a hand, one conveying an emotion includes a heart, and one naming a tree includes a tree.

These composite characters, combining pictographic and phonetic signs, soon became the most common type. Most of the pictographic elements were recognizable, but many of the old phonetic signs were only approximate, and the spoken language has changed completely over such a long period, as it has everywhere. Speakers of different languages or dialects sound the characters differently, but the meaning is the same. By the eighth century B.C. characters had evolved beyond simple pictographic and phonetic elements and included abstract ideas in an often multiple mix of signs or in two-character combinations. The Chinese script is accordingly best labeled "ideographic." The educated Chinese reader or writer, even of a newspaper, has to master several thousand characters to be literate. Furthermore, since each character represents a concept rather than a sound, there is a dissociation between the written and spoken language. This feature had an important benefit: the fact that the standardized written language did not vary with regional dialects proved of immense value in unifying a country of such pronounced diversity. Only in the twentieth century, with the diffusion throughout China of the standard written and spoken language of Peking (Beijing) made possible by methods of mass communication, has speech become more uniform.

The Chinese system of writing remains virtually unique in retaining its nonalphabetic form. Even cultures that borrowed Chinese characters to write their own languages, such as Korean, Vietnamese, and Japanese, added a separate phonetic system for many purposes. But the Chinese characters are still used, their meaning unaffected by differences in spoken language. Most other written languages in the world developed an alphabetic system, many of them directly or indirectly based on the earliest alphabet of all, the North Semitic.

One of the earliest decipherable inscriptions in alphabetic writing is the calendar found at the Canaanite site of Gezer, dating to the eleventh century B.C.—approximately the biblical period of Saul and David. The words, roughly scratched on a schoolchild's tablet of soft limestone, consist of a poem describing the principal agricultural occupations of the seasons.

Other Semitic languages used versions of the original North Semitic alphabet, with the exception of Akkadian, which continued to employ cuneiform. Aramaic writing goes back to the beginning of the first millennium B.C. and by 500 B.C. had become the most important and widespread script of western Asia. It served as the diplomatic writing system for the western provinces of the Persian Empire and continued to be used until around the second century A.D. The square Hebrew script still in use today derives from Aramaic. The Jews adopted the Aramaic language, the common tongue of the region, during the period of the Babylonian captivity. With their return, Aramaic became the vernacular of the Jews in Palestine.

After the conquest of Persia and the introduction of Greek as the official business language there, Aramaic scripts began to develop local variations; one of them, Nabatean, was to give birth to Arabic. The Hebrew version seems to have split off around 200 B.C. and began to attain uniformity between 30 B.C. and A.D. 70. In the subsequent period the script was widely used in the production of biblical manuscripts and occasionally for nonliterary documents such as letters and accounts. Detailed rules regulated the copying of synagogue scrolls and the manner in which they should be set out. As a result, Hebrew writing has changed little since the first century A.D.

The primary diffusers of the Semitic alphabet in the Mediterranean region were the descendants of the Canaanites, the Phoenicians, who occupied the narrow

An impression of a stone seal depicting a bull from Mohenjo-Daro, c. 2500 B.C. This seal, with its distinctive marks, may have been used as a signature.

THE VISUAL EXPERIENCE

Byzantine and Islamic Art

In this mosaic from San Vitale, Ravenna, Abel and Melchisedek offer sacrifices to God, events interpreted by Christians as foreshadowing the sacrifice of Christ.

Detail depicting Justinian, from a sixth-century mosaic in the Church of San Vitale, Ravenna, Italy.

The altar and apse of San Vitale, Ravenna, which functioned as a royal chapel for Justinian.

This mosaic shows Justinian (left) presenting the church and Constantine (right) presenting the city of Constantinople to Mary and Jesus.

The Hijra: Muhammad flees Mecca with a companion as Jesus watches. The Muslim artist is paying homage to Islam's Christian heritage.

This fourteenth-century Persian painting shows Muhammad and his disciples with the Kaaba, the black rock that is sacred to Islam.

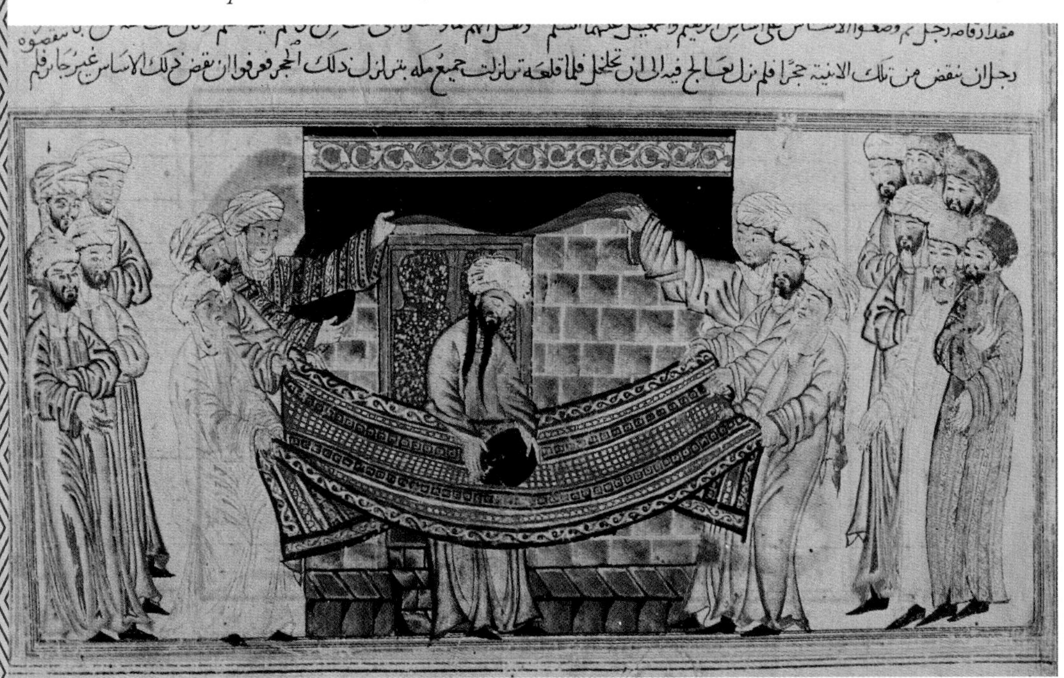

A thirteenth-century Iraqi painter depicted Arab apothecaries preparing medicine.

Interior of the lavishly ornamented mosque at Córdoba, Spain.

coastal plain of what is now Lebanon and Syria during the first half of the first millennium B.C. The greatest traders and seafarers of their time, the Phoenicians set up commercial posts from the Atlantic to the Tigris; they are even reputed to have circumnavigated Africa. To assist their financial and trading activities they developed a form of Aramaic script for the Phoenician language that they spread in the course of their commercial activities.

Among the peoples who came into contact with the Phoenicians were the Greeks. A form of writing had existed in the Bronze Age world of the Minoans and Mycenaeans (second millennium B.C.), but with the collapse of Mycenaean culture, knowledge of it died out. The earliest works of Greek literature, the epic poems attributed to Homer, had begun as oral compositions, passed from speaker to speaker without being recorded, but as Greek culture developed in the eighth century B.C., an efficient writing system became necessary. The Greeks may have learned the Phoenician alphabet from contacts in the eastern Mediterranean, but the transmission just as likely occurred in Italy. Both Greeks and Phoenicians had set up trading posts there, partly to sell to Italian customers and partly to exploit the mineral wealth of the Italian peninsula. Throughout the seventh and sixth centuries B.C. the Greeks founded colonies in southern Italy and Sicily, and the new writing system was diffused there.

Italy became an important site in the transmission of the original alphabet. Italic peoples such as the Oscans and the Umbrians used their own versions of the Greek alphabet, as did the Etruscans of central Italy. During the Etruscan occupation of Rome (616–510 B.C.) the Romans adopted the Greek alphabet and later spread it throughout their empire. Every modern European language uses a form of the Roman alphabet, with the exception of Russian, Bulgarian, and Macedonian, which employ a version of the Greek. By the fall of the Roman Empire the Greek and Roman alphabets had become standard for all Western cultures. They have remained so.

In the Arabic world little evidence exists of writing before the coming of Islam. The Nabateans, who lived in the Sinai region, used a version of the Aramaic script, but the oldest Arabic inscription in Nabatean characters dates only to A.D. 267. In the early period of their culture the Arabs had little need for writing, even though they were highly language-conscious and poetically gifted. Arab poets preferred to hand down their compositions orally, and each bard had at least two young companions whose task it was to memorize their master's works and continue the tradition.

The Gezer calendar.

With the appearance of Islam in the seventh century A.D. a writing system was urgently needed. Muslims felt it essential to record every syllable of the Koran with precision, and the ability to write became a valued skill. Furthermore, since strict Muslim law discouraged pictures, the Arabs began to develop calligraphy (fine, ornamental writing). Within less than two centuries after the time of Muhammad, Arabic calligraphy had reached a sophistication that has been surpassed only in China, where people valued it as early as the Han period and considered it a basic art form. Like Chinese calligraphy, several kinds of Arabic script were developed, ranging from monumental angular lettering, preferred for copying the Koran and other important works, to more cursive letters used for decorative displays. Today both types are in use, and in China calligraphic ability remains the mark of an educated person.

As Islam spread it carried the new writing with it. The diversity of peoples and territories that fell under Arab rule, from North Africa and parts of Spain in the west to India and the border of China in the east, encouraged the development of local forms of Arabic script. The western style is known as Maghribi ("Western"), and Muslim traders introduced a version of it into central and western Africa. Iran and Turkey adopted other forms.

When the Arabs carried their writing system to India, they found yet another alphabet descended from the Semitic, the Brahmi. Brahmi is not strictly a true alphabet, since each basic consonant is accompanied by the vowel *a.* This syllabic device is due to the fact that in the early northern Indian languages, the best known of which is Sanskrit, *a* was the most common vowel sound. Other vowels were represented either by their own signs

An eleventh-century northern Buddhist Sanskrit work written in the Nepalese version of Brahmi.

when they began a word or by signs that modified the consonants. Modern Indian scripts for the most part still use this system, although the languages of South India belong to a different family.

For the first centuries of its use, Brahmi seems to have been fairly consistent throughout India, although no manuscripts survive and the only extant examples of writing are on coins, seals, and inscriptions. Under the Gupta dynasty of the fourth century A.D., northern India developed its own version, which in due course spread to the Buddhist centers of Chinese Turkestan. Beginning under Emperor Ashoka in the third century B.C. and in subsequent centuries, versions of the Brahmi script also spread, via Buddhist texts, to Ceylon (Sri Lanka), Burma, Thailand, Cambodia, and Vietnam. Each of these countries in time developed its own form of Brahmi, alphabetical systems written with added flourishes and curves that remain in use today, although Chinese characters later displaced the Brahmi-based script in Vietnam. Thus while Muslim culture introduced one version of the Semitic alphabet into India, Buddhism was the vehicle whereby another form spread even farther east.

In the Americas the Maya had formed a complex system of hieroglyphic writing as early as the fourth century A.D. The Maya based their signs on pictures, and most of the surviving examples take the form of monumental inscriptions carved in stone. Not all of them have been deciphered, but they mostly consist of archival records or religious texts, and a number attest to the Mayan interest in astronomy and the calendar. Other Mesoamerican peoples developed their own scripts, notably the Aztecs and the Mixtecs, and used them in extended manuscripts known as *codices.* These consist of long strips of animal hide or tree bark, which were folded concertina fashion, like a modern map. Most record mythological events, and some owe their preservation to the conquering Spanish of the sixteenth century. With the arrival of Europeans the Roman alphabet replaced hieroglyphic systems.

Before the invention of printing, writing provided only limited literacy. Inscriptions erected in public places were, of course, available for all to read. The Roman Emperor Augustus wrote an autobiography, *Res Gestae* ("Things I Have Done"), shortly before his death in A.D. 14, and had copies distributed throughout the empire; it was also inscribed on the bronze doors of his tomb. Muslim rulers often used the public display of passages from the Koran as a means of spreading and reinforcing the faith.

Yet such examples confirm the general limitations of literacy. Administrators, priests, and sometimes merchants—the cultural elite—had to read, both for business and governmental purposes and for the preservation of sacred texts such as the Bible, the sayings of the Buddha, and the Koran. Plays and poems were popular in the Greek and Roman world, and authors composed a few romantic stories in Greek in the second and third centuries A.D., but little evidence survives of the circulation of written literature beyond the elite in the ancient world.

SUGGESTIONS FOR FURTHER READING

Craig, J. *Thirty Centuries of Graphic Design: An Illustrated History.* New York: Watson-Guptill, 1987.

Goody, J. *The Logic of Writing and the Organization of Society.* Cambridge: Cambridge University Press, 1986.

Gordon, C. H. *Forgotten Scripts: Their Ongoing Discovery and Decipherment,* rev. ed. New York: Basic Books, 1982.

Hosking, R. F., and Meredith-Owens, G. M. *A Handbook of Asian Scripts.* London: British Museum, 1966.

Hutchinson, J. *Letters.* New York: Van Nostrand Reinhold, 1983.

Lasswell, H. D., Lerner, D., and Speier, H., eds. *Propaganda and Communication in World History,* vol. 1. Honolulu: University Press of Hawaii, 1980.

Logan, R. K. *The Alphabet Effect: The Impact of the Phonetic Alphabet on the Development of Western Civilization.* New York: Morrow, 1986.

Roberts, C. H. *The Birth of the Codex.* London: Oxford University Press, 1983.

Sampson, G. *Writing Systems.* London: Hutchinson, 1985.

Schmandt-Besserat, D. "The Earliest Precursor of Writing," *Scientific American,* June 1978, pp. 50–59.

CHAPTER 9

The Civilizations of Early Africa

The vast continent of Africa, which covers 11.7 million miles, comprises 20 percent of the earth's land surface; only Asia is larger. The birthplace of humanity, Africa became the home of numerous cultures and civilizations, including Egypt in the north, Kush and Axum in the east, Ghana and Mali in the west, and the Swahili city-states and Great Zimbabwe in the southeast. Not until the post–World War II period and the dismantling of Western imperialism, however, was there sustained scholarly interest in the preimperial history of sub-Saharan Africa. The emergence of newly independent African states and their schools and universities sparked enormous interest in the African past. We now know how rich and varied these early African cultures and civilizations were and how much contact they had with Europe, western Asia, and India, especially through extensive trading networks that transmitted not only commercial goods but culture as well.

Early Africa

Prehistoric Africa became the center for the development of stone tools known as hand axes, which may have served for skinning and chopping up animals and other sources of food. Rich deposits of these tools have been found in eastern Africa, from whence their use spread to western Europe and India.

The African Land

Despite this early evidence of cultural diffusion, a degree of geographic isolation has always affected life in much of Africa. The Sahara was not always the formidable barrier it is today. Indeed, between 5500 and 2000 B.C. hunters,

Bearded male figure from Jenné, Mali, dating from the fourteenth century.

animal breeders, and farmers used open grassland areas now covered with sand. Even when changes of climate returned the last of these grasslands or savannas to their desert state, devoid of fish and game, caravans of traders used routes that crossed the central Sahara or made their way through Nubia and Egypt to and from the Mediterranean. Nonetheless, for most of recorded history the vast expanses of the Sahara, which eventually covered nearly a third of the continent, have hindered the movement of people or goods and kept contacts to a minimum.

Much of central and southern Africa is inaccessible by sea because good natural harbors are rare. Although Africa is three times the size of Europe, its coastline is actually shorter. Enormous sandbars along both the east and west coasts made navigation hazardous. Even within the continent, which stretches some 5,000 miles from north to south and an equal distance across at its widest point, transport from one region to another is difficult. Because of rapids and waterfalls, few rivers are navigable, nor are there any inland seas such as the Black or the Caspian to facilitate transportation. Deserts, rain forests, and the swamps east of the Sahara were additional barriers to travel.

To the difficulties presented by geography must be added other natural problems. Unlike Mesopotamia or India, which experienced a predictable alternation of dry and wet spells each year, the African climate is extremely irregular. Two or three years of drought may be followed by prolonged rainfall that erodes the soil (mostly clay) and washes away important nutrients. Furthermore, the regions that are hot and humid provide natural breeding grounds for insects such as mosquitoes, tsetse flies, and other parasites. Regular food production under such conditions poses formidable problems. Without it most of the early inhabitants of Africa were unable to establish the widespread urbanization that, as we have seen in Asia and Europe, is normally the precondition for social and economic development and technological innovation. The only place on the African continent where the introduction of farming techniques led to an early appearance of urban civilization was Egypt, where the fertility of the Nile valley made comparatively large population concentrations possible.

In sub-Saharan Africa the most habitable areas were the three major savanna (grassland) regions, one extending across the continent south of the Sahara, known as the Sudan (Arabic for "land of the black people"; it is not to be confused with the modern state of that name); a second amid the mountains of eastern Africa; and the third ranging across southern Africa above the Kalahari Desert. Between the expanses of grasslands are the tropical rain forests, parts of them virtually impenetrable and virtually all of them hazardous to humans and cattle because of such endemic diseases as sleeping sickness and malaria. Despite the often inhospitable terrain and the erratic weather, sub-Saharan Africa offered its inhabitants two distinct advantages: ample room for expansion and, until modern times, freedom from Eurasian invaders.

Agriculture and Ironworking

The earliest peoples of Africa supported themselves by hunting and gathering. Around 5000 B.C. crop farming and animal breeding were introduced to the North African coastal regions, probably from western Asia. Farming had almost certainly begun independently in Ethiopia, the central Sudan, and the upper Niger valley. In eastern Africa, particularly Ethiopia and the Nile valley in the Sudan, the people laboriously cultivated local cereals such as millet and sorghum from native wild grasses, while in the west the Bantu began to occupy the coastal rain forests, attracted there by the abundance of indigenous yams and oil palms. Animal husbandry had spread into the Sahara while that region was still lush grassland, but the emerging desert forced most of its inhabitants to migrate to the north or the south, driving their cattle with them. Many settled in West Africa and Ethiopia, and from the latter some of their descendants migrated into East Africa between 1500 and 1000 B.C. Only later did agriculture extend into southern Africa.

Throughout the whole of Africa, with the notable exception of Egypt, the transition from hunting to farming and cattle raising was very gradual, and in many regions both food systems probably coexisted for centuries. In addition to climate, two other reasons accounted for the slow growth of agriculture. First, the range of the native forest food plants was limited. Only with the importation of such crops from abroad as taro (a type of yam), sugarcane, and banana and coconut trees—all native to Southeast Asia—were dependable staple crops developed by the beginning of the first millennium A.D. The food supply also expanded with the domestication of chickens, ducks, and geese, all of which came from Southeast Asia, and pigs. Second, unlike the Chinese or the peoples of the Mediterranean and western Asia, many inhabitants of sub-Saharan Africa never worked in bronze. The peoples along the Atlantic coast—in what became Mauritania, Senegal, and Nigeria—were exceptional in this respect, though even their use of bronze was limited. Until the introduction of iron shortly before 500 B.C., most African farmers had only stone and wood tools, the use of which rarely produced surplus crops.

The Phoenicians, who founded Carthage, and the Assyrians, who conquered Egypt, introduced ironworking techniques. The ability to work in iron had reached

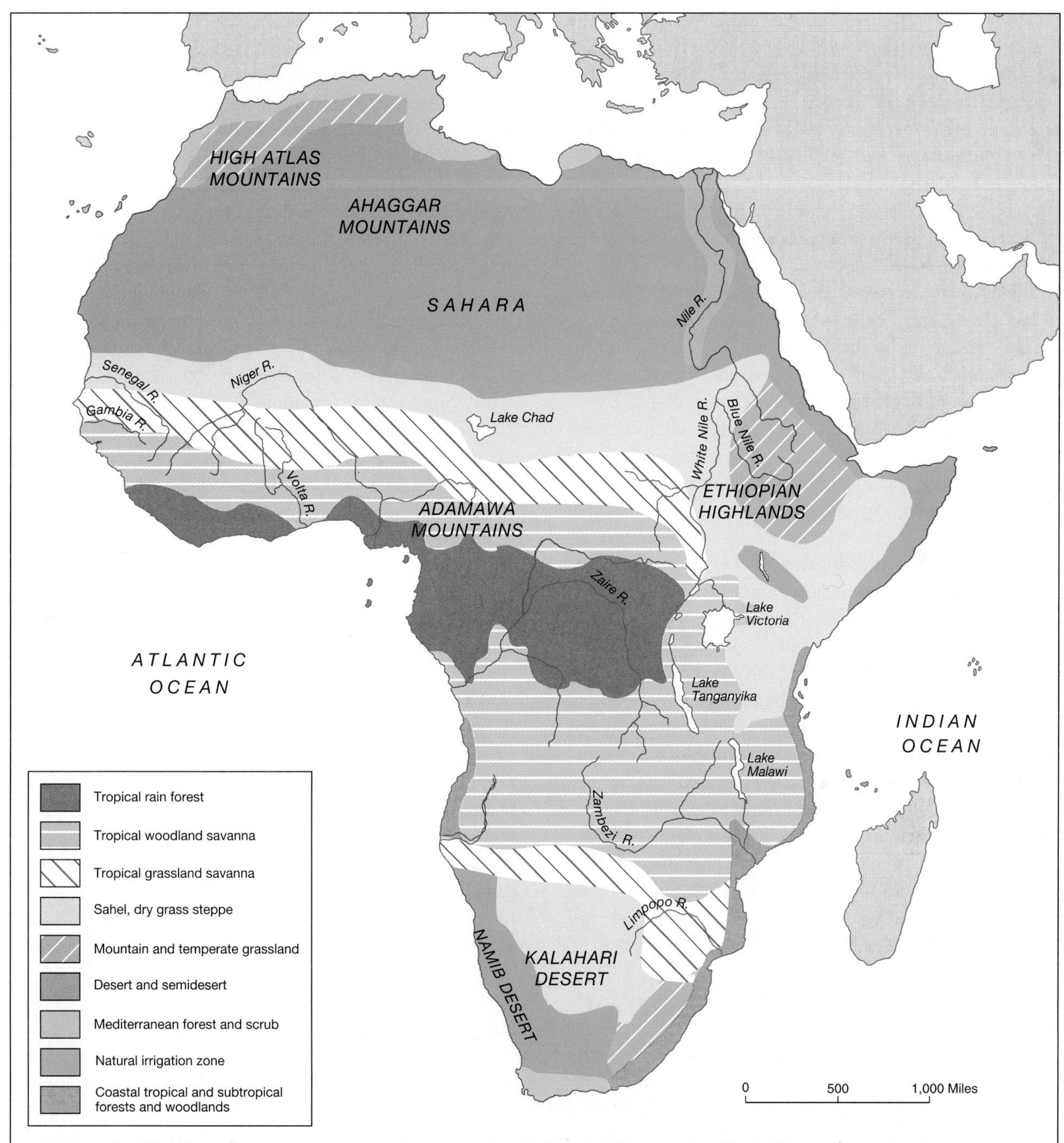

MAP 9.1 TOPOGRAPHY OF MODERN AFRICA

Meroë in the Sudan by 500 B.C., and from there it spread slowly southward. In the meantime the West Africans learned about iron from the Carthaginians. They used iron to manufacture such tools as picks, hoes, and axes as well as weapons (arrowpoints and spearheads). Africans who possessed these implements enjoyed obvious advantages in food production and in warfare.

Early African Society and Culture

The chief beneficiaries of the expanding knowledge of agriculture and ironworking were dark-skinned peoples known as the Bantu. From their West African homeland in what later came to be called Nigeria and Cameroon they migrated to the south and east over a period of two millennia until they inhabited virtually all of sub-Saharan Africa apart from the southwestern savanna, the southern jungles, and the Kalahari Desert. Those regions became the new home of the peoples dislodged by the Bantu—mostly the hunter-gatherers known as the San and the Khoikhoi. Two main factors accounted for the Bantu migrations: population growth, which the development of agriculture had sparked, and the limited ability to raise food on the central African plateau because of thin topsoil and limited water.

As the Bantu spread through most of sub-Saharan Africa, their tribes developed a good deal of cultural variety, as attested to by the more than 400 closely related Bantu languages. Diversity was apparent too with respect to inheritance, with some groups recognizing the primacy of the female line, others the male. Despite such differences, at root the Bantu shared a common heritage in which family and kinship were especially important. Extended families grouped themselves into communal units, the chieftains of which were chosen by family elders or inherited their office and ruled with the assistance of a council of elders. The chief and elders administered laws grounded in tradition; they tried violators, sometimes by ordeal if the testimony about their alleged offenses was inconclusive. A common form of trial by ordeal (used also in Europe) cast the accused into a body of water in the belief that the innocent would sink, whereas the guilty would float. Supreme loyalty was to the communal group, whose members were united not only to their families but also to subgroups based on age and sometimes to secret societies. As life became increasingly sedentary, the basis of authority began to shift from kinship to residence, so that villages and then groups of allied villages assumed greater power. The more powerful chiefs became kings, with the first monarchies apparently emerging in West Africa around the first century A.D. To substantiate their claims to authority the kings depicted themselves as descendants of divine ancestors, with special powers over fertility. Over time the monarchs employed a hierarchy of public officials to help them govern. Other societies continued to rely on the traditional communal organization, with its interlocking obligations and the importance of blood ties.

Although the Bantu economy was firmly based in agriculture and cattle grazing, other occupations developed. Miners extracted iron, copper, and gold, which skilled artisans used to fashion tools, weapons, jewelry, and other items. Spinners and weavers made clothing and blankets, carpenters constructed buildings, and potters created a variety of items. Woodcarvers and basket-weavers also produced their wares. In some Bantu societies specific family groups controlled the crafts and operated them according to strict regulations, but other societies operated more freely. As in Europe, the artisans themselves usually traded their goods, though as cities developed so too did merchants and trading organizations. With sedentary life came the notion of land ownership and the emergence of patron-client relationships, typically between landlords and tenants.

The Bantu combined a strong sense of communal responsibility with religious convictions that touched virtually every aspect of life. Like the Chinese, they believed that their deceased ancestors dwelt among them in spirit, deserved respect, and influenced their lives. With all ancient peoples they also associated the forces of nature with religious spirits, whom they sought to propitiate by traditional rituals. As agriculture developed, special rituals and festivals came to be associated with specific crops, especially those, such as yams and millet, that were basic staples. Although the Bantu were not monotheistic, many believed in the existence of a supreme but unknowable being.

One of the best examples of early Bantu culture has survived in terra-cotta (baked clay) figurines of humans and animals as well as depictions of fluted pumpkins produced by the Bantu who lived in central Nigeria between 500 B.C. and A.D. 200. They also worked in copper and bronze and created fine jewelry. Their representation of the human figure influenced West African artists for centuries, just as later generations copied the shapes of their houses and the layouts of their villages, thereby contributing to the pronounced sense of continuity that characterizes sub-Saharan African history. The high quality of Nok art, as this culture is known, is evidence of a considerable degree of patronage and social stability and thus of the existence of a well-organized, reasonably secure society.

The Ancient States of the Eastern Sudan

The eastern Sudan was the home of two of the oldest kingdoms in Africa, Kush and Ethiopia, neither of whose inhabitants were ethnically, linguistically, or culturally one with the Bantu, though commercial contacts developed between them. The people of Kush were subject to Egyptian domination during much of the New Kingdom, but as Egypt declined a Kushite state, with its capital at Napata on the upper Nile, emerged in the eleventh century B.C.

Terra-cotta sculptures from the Nok culture, such as this head, exerted a profound influence on later African art.

The Kingdom of Kush

Beginning in the eighth century B.C., Kush extended its sway over Egypt, where its rulers established the twenty-fifth dynasty. For more than 60 years the dark-skinned Kushite monarchs governed Egypt, worshipping Egyptian deities, inscribing their names on the temples, and wearing the traditional Egyptian crown as the symbol of their authority. The Kushites now reigned over an empire that extended from the Mediterranean to the borders of modern Ethiopia and possibly beyond. But these were troubled years because of Assyrian aggression, including the temporary capture of Memphis in 670 B.C. The stone and bronze arms of the Kushites were ultimately no match for the iron weapons of the Assyrians, who drove the Kushites out of Egypt a decade later. Although Egypt was no longer theirs, Kushite sovereigns retained the style and titles of the pharaohs.

In the sixth century B.C. the people of Kush moved their capital farther south to Meroë, partly for defensive reasons but also because of its advantageous location as a trading center. Not only was the Nile navigable at this point, but Meroë was situated at the western end of a caravan route from the Red Sea and also sat astride the north-south route that extended from Egypt into the heart of Africa. At Meroë the annual rainfall was greater than at Napata, with obvious advantages for farming, and the region had abundant iron ore and timber for its smelting.

The economy of Meroë was varied. The kingdom became a major center of iron production for northeastern Africa. Defeat at the hands of the Assyrians had taught the Kushites the value of iron, which was useful not only for weapons but also for axes and hoes as well as spears and arrows for hunting. Judging from surviving art reliefs, many people farmed (mostly sorghum and millet) or grazed animals, but others engaged in the manufacture of cloth, apparently from both flax and cotton. Hunting was also an important livelihood, as reflected in the kingdom's export trade. The Kushites exported ivory, ebony, leopard skins, ostrich feathers, and gold in exchange for products from the Mediterranean, India, and East Asia. From the Kushites the Egyptians obtained trained elephants for their army.

At first Egypt heavily influenced the culture of Meroë. For a time Meroë's religion and official language were Egyptian, as was its architecture, including a walled palace, great temples, and rows of pyramids in which deceased rulers were entombed. Gradually Meroë's culture became less Egyptianized. Local gods and shrines took their place alongside Egyptian deities, African animals (lions, giraffes, elephants, and ostriches) were featured in art, pyramids acquired distinctive flat tops, and a local language, called Meriotic but so far untranslated, replaced Egyptian. Meriotic culture became increasingly eclectic as the Kushites employed Hellenistic, Persian, and Indian motifs in such areas as architecture and sculpture.

The cultural indebtedness of the Kushites notwithstanding, their society was substantially different from that of their northern neighbors. Whereas the Egyptians were concentrated in a narrow floodplain, the Kushite population was scattered in small villages that dotted extensive fields watered by summer rains. Political control was therefore more decentralized, with local chiefs and clan leaders exercising a good deal of authority as long as they and their people paid tribute to the king each year. The only check on the king's authority was apparently the pragmatic need to retain the people's support; this was not automatic, since rulers who angered their subjects were periodically overthrown. When a new king ascended the throne, his mother, who enjoyed considerable prestige, provided stability and continuity. Her role probably reflects a general appreciation of women among the Kushites.

The Kushite kingdom reached its peak in the first century A.D., at which time it exchanged ambassadors

MAP 9.2 EGYPT, KUSH, MEROË, AND AXUM, 1500 B.C.–A.D. 350

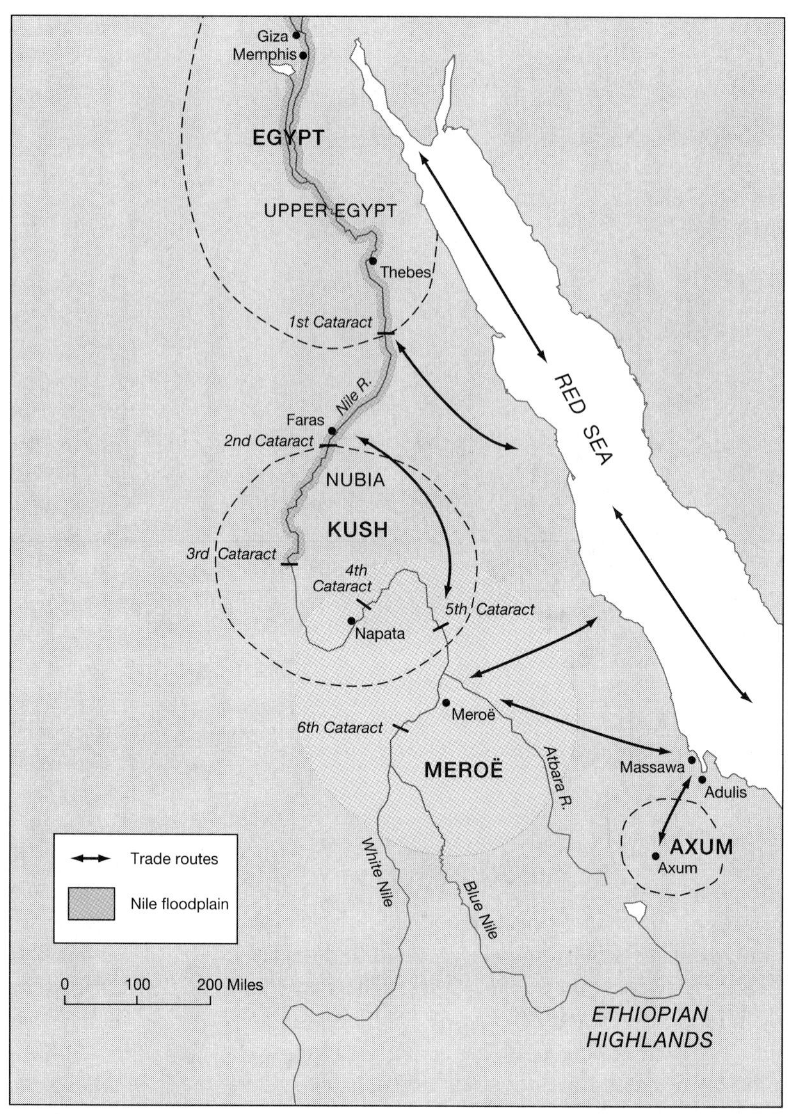

with the Roman Empire. The power of Kush began to ebb in the second century as Ethiopians and desert nomads disrupted its trade routes. The iron industry declined as the forests were depleted, and heavy farming and erosion depleted the soil's fertility. The economic problems of the Roman Empire, hitherto a major market for Kushite luxury goods, were also a factor in Meroë's decline. The kingdom fell in the fourth century to the Ethiopians, and the town of Meroë was abandoned. Kush's historic importance was based on its role as a country in which the cultural traditions of Egypt mingled with those of dark-skinned Africans and where contact existed as well with the cultures of Hellenistic Greece, Rome, Persia, and India. Kush also played a crucial role in spreading the knowledge of ironworking in Africa.

Axum, the Christian Kingdom

To the southeast of Kush lay the mountainous land of Ethiopia, where the native inhabitants were farming such grains as wheat, barley, and millet before the arrival of Semites from Yemen early in the first millennium B.C. Although the Semites had come as traders, the mountainous terrain encouraged them to take up farming. In time they intermingled with local inhabitants, creating both the ethnic and the cultural fusion that came to dis-

This relief from a stela at Meroë depicts a Kushite queen and a ram-headed god. Note the Egyptian influence.

tinguish Ethiopia. The language of these Semites, Sabaean, gradually merged with the local tongues to form Geez, the classical Ethiopian tongue.

The Sabaeans brought with them the knowledge of writing and Hebrew religious traditions, including the observance of the Sabbath and Jewish dietary regulations. The best-known example of this influence is the tradition that the Ethiopian royal line can be traced back to Menelik, son of Solomon and the queen of Sheba, and that Menelik brought the Ark of the Covenant with him to Ethiopia. The story is recounted in *The Glory of the Kings,* the most famous work in Ethiopian literature; parts of it date to the fourth century A.D. The Sabaeans had probably acquired Jewish influences when the Hebrew kingdom of Solomon expanded, sending emigrants into southern Arabia.

The state that the Sabaeans established became known as the kingdom of Axum, from the name of its capital. Taking advantage of their strategic location on the shores of the Red Sea, the Axumites profited from the trading network that extended from the eastern Mediterranean and the East African coast to Arabia and India. Like Kush, Axum had extensive contacts with Egypt and was subject to its influence. The heart of this contact was trade, since the Egyptians looked to Axum for spices, incense, and precious stones from India as well as ivory, gold, ebony, myrrh, rhinoceros horns, and elephants from sub-Saharan Africa. The traders of Axum also exported locally produced spices, frankincense (used in burials), and luxury goods made of glass, brass, and copper; most of these goods went to Egypt and the Byzantine Empire.

As Egypt declined, Axum's power increased, until by the mid-fourth century A.D. its sway extended from Kush, which overran King Ezana (c. 320–c. 350), to the edge of the Horn of Africa. Axum was now the most powerful state in East Africa and the hub of the region's trade. Unlike the earlier kingdom of Kush, Axum minted its own coinage, a symbol of its political and commercial strength. In the sixth century Axum annexed the portion of the Arabian peninsula that is now Yemen, but before the century was over, Axum's principal trade rival, Persia, had driven it from this territory.

Christianity began to make inroads in Axum as a result of trade with the Byzantine Empire, and Ezana, influenced by his tutor, a Syrian Christian named Frumentius, made it the state religion in 350. However, it took centuries for the new religion to be diffused effectively among the common people. Ethiopian Christians followed the Egyptians in embracing Monophysite theology, with its belief that the human and divine natures of Christ were fused in the Incarnation. Axum's close religious ties to Egypt were also reflected in the appointment of the first bishop of Axum by the patriarch of Alexandria. The adoption of Christianity gave the kingdom of Axum a historical identity that set it apart from its African neighbors and enabled it to conduct its wars in the name of religion. The Judeo-Christian tradition made Ethiopians unique among Africans; after the Muslim conquests of the seventh and eighth centuries, only Nubia and Axum remained Christian.

Weakened by internal strife and cut off from its Mediterranean trading partners by the advance of Islam, Axum experienced economic stagnation and political chaos. The Muslims destroyed Adulis, Axum's principal port, in 710 and took over its trade routes. Moreover, much of the commerce that had once passed through the Red Sea shifted to the eastern Mediterranean and the Persian Gulf; Axum had been bypassed. Environmental factors—the depletion of forests and the erosion of soil—probably contributed to Axum's decline. The kingdom itself survived, thanks to its mountainous terrain, though it would be essentially isolated from the outside world for a millennium. Many of the Ethiopian people remained faithful to their Coptic Christianity into the twentieth century.

Trading Patterns, Slavery, and Urban Development

The trading routes that extended between Egypt and its southern neighbors, Kush and Axum, were but one example of regional networks developed by Africans. West Africa was the site of others well before trans-Saharan trade began to grow dramatically in the seventh century A.D. Iron, copper, and gold as well as foodstuffs were featured objects in this commerce. Farm wives bartered goods in village markets held at regular intervals, while merchant families organized trade on a broader basis, shipping goods in canoes, on donkeys, or on the heads of porters.

As early as the first millennium B.C. daring traders, most of them desert dwellers, occasionally used horse-drawn chariots to carry goods across the Sahara. The two-month journey required knowledgeable guides, bribes to the nomads who roamed the desert, stamina to endure blinding sandstorms and limited water supplies, and patience to deal with the scorpions and the lice that lived around the oases. Much of this trade was in the hands of the Garamantes, who lived on the northern fringes of the Sahara in what is now Libya and hunted black Africans to sell into slavery, and of the Berbers, indigenous nomads who lived in the western and central regions of North Africa. The introduction of the camel into northern Africa from central Asia revolutionized the trans-Saharan trade. The camel could go for several days without food or water while carrying 500-pound loads and traveling as much as 20 miles a day. But camels could carry these loads only four months a year without endangering their health. So valuable were camels that in the Sahara people calculated their wealth in terms of the number of camels they owned.

Enterprising traders developed a network of caravan routes between North Africa and the Sudan between A.D. 200 and 700. Over these routes fine silk, cotton, copper (for the bronze industries), steel, glass beads from Venice, salt, figs, dates, and horses for the royal cavalries were shipped southward. Returning caravans transported gold, pepper, ivory, kola nuts, leather, cotton cloth, and slaves from West Africa. Outfitting a caravan involved great expense, including the cost of the camels and the merchandise, fees for the guide, wages for the drivers and outriders, "protection" money, and heavy tolls at both ends of the journey. The larger the caravan, the greater the need for security. By the fourteenth century some caravans included as many as 12,000 camels. Substantial

The tallest of the obelisks still standing at the East African city of Axum is nearly 70 feet high.

Christianity in Africa

In the early sixteenth century a Portuguese visitor, Father Francisco Alvares, described the practice of Christianity in Axum.

As they say the church of Axum is the most ancient, so it is the most revered of all Ethiopia, and the services are well conducted in it. In this church there are 150 canons, and as many monks. It has two head men; one is named nebrete of the canons, which means teacher, and the other nebrete of the monks. These two heads reside in the palaces which are within the great enclosure and circuit of the church; and the nebrete of the canons . . . is the principal one, and the more respected. He has jurisdiction over the canons and the laity of all this country; and the nebrete of the monks only hears and rules the monks. Both use kettledrums and trumpets. They have very large revenues [renderings of praise], and besides their revenues they have every day a collation [light meal] which they call maabar of bread and wine of the country, when mass is finished. The monks have this by themselves, and the canons also, and this maabar is such that the monks seldom eat other food than that. They have this every day except Friday of the Passion [Good Friday], because on that day no one eats or drinks. The canons do not take their maabar within the circuit of the church, and are seldom there, except at fixed hours; neither is the nebrete in his palace, except at some chance time when he goes to hear cases. This is because they are married, and live with their wives and children in their houses, which are very good and which are outside. Neither women nor laymen go into the enclosure of this church [but worship elsewhere].

Source: *Africa in the Days of Exploration,* ed. R. Oliver and C. Oliver (Englewood Cliffs, N.J.: Prentice Hall, 1965), pp. 77–78.

risks could be rewarded with enormous profits, as in the case of a fifteenth-century merchant whose fortune was estimated at 12,500 ounces of gold.

Salt, gold, and slaves were the most important items in the trans-Saharan trade. The salt, which was in great demand in West Africa, came mostly from sites in the mid-Sahara such as Taghaza, some 500 miles north of Timbuktu, where the houses themselves were built of salt blocks. At places like Taghaza slaves quarried the salt in 200-pound blocks for shipment south. Muslim merchants in the north controlled much of the salt trade, shipping most of it to central Africa in return for gold, slaves, ivory, and ostrich feathers. Some of the salt found its way to northern markets, and the Bantu transported the rest of it to the east and west, carrying it on their heads (the average porter could carry 55 pounds) or across lakes in canoes. In central Africa humans consumed most of the salt, with the remainder going to animals. Yet because of its expense the people used very little salt in their diet, which was dominated by yams, millet (a cereal grass), and, for those near lakes and rivers, fish.

Most African gold came from what is now Ghana, Nigeria, and Senegal. Men dug alluvial soil from pits or underground shafts and floated it in huge trays to the mineheads, where women extracted the gold by panning. From the mines the gold was normally transported in hollow feather quills to trading centers for conversion into ingots, coins, or jewelry and for transshipment across the Sahara. By the eleventh century as much as 9 tons of gold was sent northward each year. Not surprisingly, the mining and shipment of gold was the leading industry in black Africa.

Second only in importance to gold as an export were black slaves. From an average of 1,000 per year in the late seventh and eighth centuries, the number grew until it peaked at 8,700 per year in the tenth and eleventh centuries; by the fifteenth century it had declined to 4,300 per year. Traders transported small numbers of white slaves in the opposite direction for sale to the royal courts of West Africa. Most slaves were kidnapped or seized in armed raids or warfare, often from the communal groups that had not organized into states, though some rulers sold their own subjects. Monarchs desirous of increasing

The Trans-Saharan Crossing

Ibn Battuta provided a vivid description of his trek across the Sahara in a caravan in 1352.

At Sijilmasa I bought camels and a four months' supply of forage for them. Thereupon I set out . . . with a caravan including, amongst others, a number of the merchants of Sijilmasa. After twenty-five days we reached Taghaza, an unattractive village, with the curious feature that its houses and mosques are built of blocks of salt, roofed with camel skins. There are no trees there, nothing but sand. In the sand is a salt mine; they dig for the salt, and find it in thick slabs, lying one on top of the other. . . . No one lives at Taghaza except the slaves of the Massufa tribe, who dig for the salt. . . .

We passed ten days of discomfort there, because the water is brackish and the place is plagued with flies. Water supplies are laid in at Taghaza for the crossing of the desert which lies beyond it, which is a ten-nights' journey with no water on the way except on rare occasions. . . . Truffles [an edible underground fungus] are plentiful in this desert and it swarms with lice, so that people wear string necklaces containing mercury, which kills them. . . .

We came next to Tasarahla, a place of subterranean water-beds, where the caravans halt. They stay there three days to rest, mend their waterskins, fill them with water, and sew on them covers of sackcloth as a precaution against the wind. . . . The desert is haunted by demons; if the takshif [an advance agent] be alone, they make sport of him and disorder his mind, so that he loses his way and perishes. For there is no visible road or track in these parts—nothing but sand blown hither and thither by the wind. You see hills of sand in one place, and afterwards you will see them moved to quite another place. . . . Thus we reached the town of Iwalatan [Walata] after a journey from Sijilmasa of two months to a day.

Source: Ibn Battuta, *Travels in Asia and Africa, 1325–1354,* trans. H. A. R. Gibb (London: Routledge, 1929), pp. 317–319.

The introduction of the camel around A.D. 200 revolutionized trans-Saharan trade.

the size of their armies captured neighboring peoples and traded them into slavery for horses; by the fifteenth century, a horse was worth 7 to 15 slaves in Senegal. Attractive girls and eunuchs fetched the highest prices, and female slaves were generally more valuable than their male counterparts because of the high demand for harems and household servants. The human cost of the slave trade was enormous, as fatalities sustained in raids and subsequent confinement and transportation resulted in as many as five to ten deaths for every slave who reached North Africa. The Africans themselves retained many slaves for use in the fields, construction work, mining, porterage, the military, and royal harems.

The growth of the trans-Saharan trade stimulated urban development on the northern fringes of the savanna. Chief among the emerging frontier cities was Kumbi, with a population of 15,000 to 20,000 in the eleventh century.

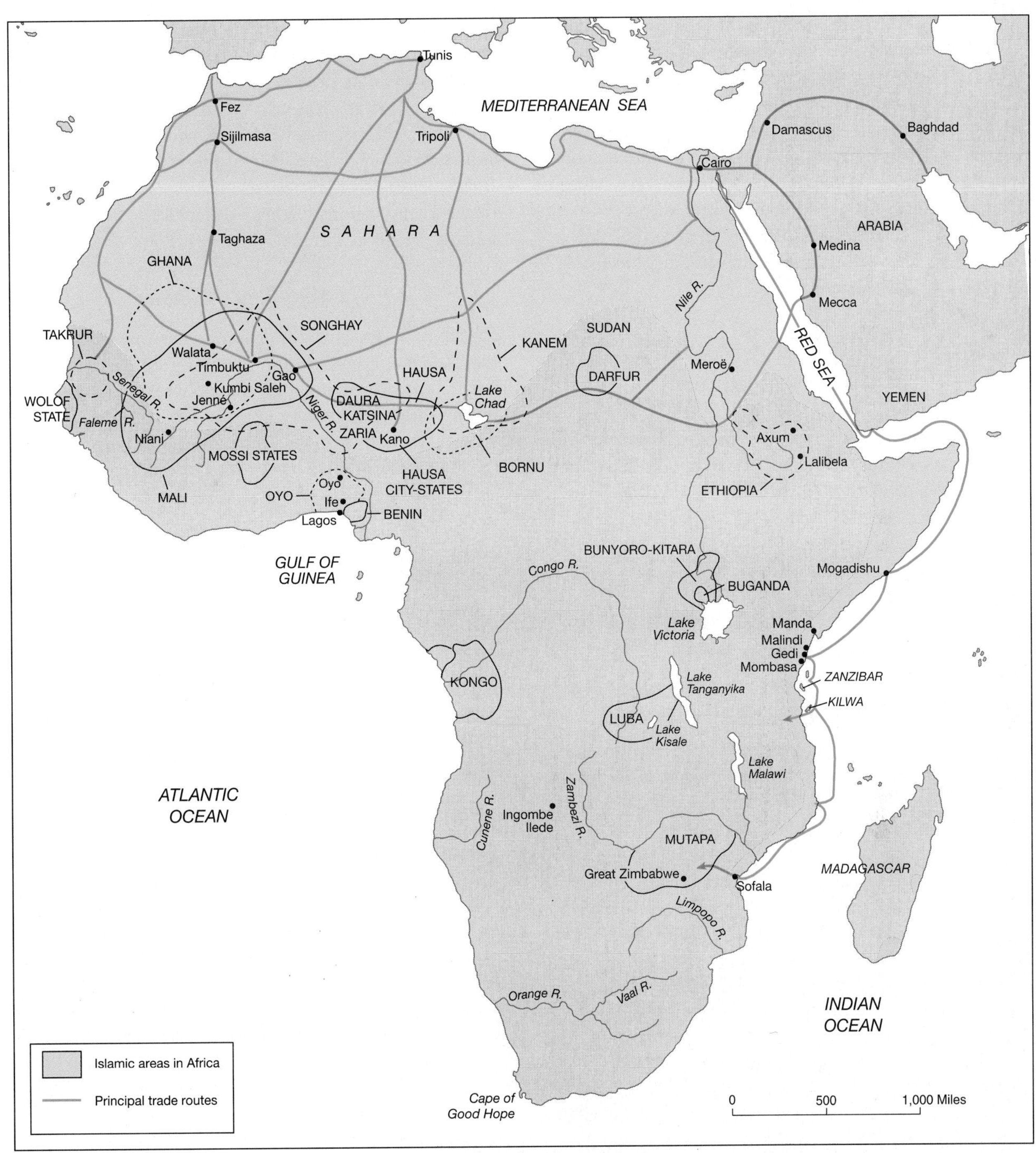

MAP 9.3 AFRICA, 1000–1500

Timbuktu, Walata, Jenné, and Gao also became notable cities, each of which, like Kumbi, was a commercial center with a cosmopolitan population in which Muslims and Jews mingled with black Africans. These cities were the main gateways for the expansion of Islamic culture and technology into sub-Saharan Africa, as exemplified by the construction of mosques, the introduction of writing to the western Sudan (a skill known much earlier in Kush and Axum), and, commencing in the fourteenth century, the manufacture of bricks. Muslims advised Sudanese rulers, and scholars introduced West Africans to the rich culture of the Islamic world. Koranic schools and universities were founded, the most noted of which was Timbuktu's University of Sankoré. Graduates of these schools were especially useful to the rulers of the West African states, providing them with bureaucrats whose primary loyalty was to their sovereign rather than to their kin or their village. The importing of Islam was crucial to the development of sub-Saharan Africa.

The States of the Western and Central Sudan

For hundreds of years before the arrival of Europeans in the fifteenth century, a series of impressive kingdoms governed the peoples of the western and central Sudan. Monarchs proclaiming themselves divine ruled from splendid courts with the aid of councils of ministers, few of whom held their offices on a hereditary basis. The kings were therefore able to tap men of talent to administer their realms, the wealth of which derived largely from taxes and tribute. But in the end the administrations could not keep pace with territorial expansion, and disputed successions further weakened the kingdoms, as in early medieval Europe.

The Kingdom of Ghana

By the time the Muslims arrived in the mid-eighth century, Ghana, known as the "land of gold," was prosperous. Located on the upper Niger River, it had emerged by the early fifth century out of a federation of farming villages. It soon developed into a powerful kingdom with the ability to dominate vassal states on its frontiers. Both economically and culturally the kingdom impressed

Slave Raids and Their Victims

The twelfth-century Arab geographer Al-Zuhri describes contemporary raids by the Muslims of Janawa (Ghana) to capture and enslave the Amima, a loosely organized migrant group living in interior Africa.

From this country desert slaves are imported. The people of Ghana make raids on the land of Barbara and Amima and capture their people as they used to do when they were pagans. Amima are a tribe of Janawa who live on the coast of the Great Sea in the west. They follow the religion of the Majus [infidels]. On account of their paganism no-one enters their country and no merchandise is imported into it. They wear sheep skins. They have plenty of honey and live in the sand without any building except tents which they make from desert grasses. The people of Ghana make raids on them every year. Sometimes they conquer and sometimes they are conquered. These people have no iron and fight only with clubs of ebony. For this reason the people of Ghana overcome them, for they fight them with swords and spears. Any slave of them can run on his own legs faster than a thoroughbred horse. . . .

The people of Zafun [a town in eastern Ghana] take captives from the people of Amima, a tribe of the Janawa who live in the eastern part of the desert . . . near the Nile of Egypt. They are people who profess Judaism. . . . They are the poorest of the Janawa. They read the Torah. Silk and saffron and manufactured goods and tar are imported to them from the Maghrib and al-Andalus and the desert. . . . They have also the magic stone, which is a stone shaped like a human being in whole or in part, as in the shape of a hand or leg or heart; but stones of complete [human] form are found. Anyone who acquires a complete stone can bewitch with it kings and *amirs* [commanders] and all mankind.

Source: *Corpus of Early Arabic Sources for West African History,* trans. J. F. P. Hopkins and ed. N. Levtzion and J. F. P. Hopkins (Cambridge: Cambridge University Press, 1981), pp. 98–100.

Muslim visitors. An Arab writer of the tenth century referred to a trade contract for 20,000 gold coins, and a century later the Muslim chronicler al-Bakri, who lived at Córdoba in Spain, noted the customs duties levied by the king of Ghana on goods exported from or imported into the country. Ghana's commercial sophistication impressed the Arabs, themselves expert traders.

The capital was located at Kumbi Saleh, in reality two adjacent towns, one for the monarch and his court and the other dominated by an enclave of foreign merchants and Muslims. The mosques and houses of the merchants in the latter were made of stone, in contrast to the mud-built structures of the native population that surrounded the royal palace. In spite of continual contact with the world of Islam, Ghana maintained its cultural and religious independence until the eleventh century. Although al-Bakri noted that many of the king's advisers were Muslims (though the monarch himself was not), he described the religion of Ghana as "paganism and the worship of idols." The picture he provides is of an aristocratic society, dominated by the king and his court, that was the focus of elaborate rituals. Reflecting Ghana's role as a supplier of gold, on formal occasions both the monarch and his retainers dressed in garments of fine cloth and bedecked themselves with gold ornaments, giving Ghana's ruler a reputation among many Africans as the "richest monarch in the world." Guarding the royal dwelling were horses whose bridles were decorated with gold and whose blankets were woven with gold thread. When the king summoned his subjects to an audience, they approached him on their knees and with dust on their heads to express their respect. According to al-Bakri, the king maintained his power with the support of a 200,000-man army. Although this figure was surely exaggerated, Ghana's army, the core of which was an effective cavalry, was impressive.

The fundamental importance of the king, both in life and in death, is reminiscent of similar cultural patterns in ancient Egypt. According to al-Bakri, when a king died, a huge dome of wood was constructed over the site of his tomb. Buried within it were the deceased's weapons and ornaments and his plates and cups, which were filled with various foods and beverages.

The women of Kumbi Saleh and other trading cities in the western and central Sudan were respected, and some of them held positions in the government. They wore collars and bracelets, an honor accorded among males only to the king. In the cities, public nudity was common for women of all ranks, but as a matter of freedom rather than license. In the caravan town of Walata, near Kumbi Saleh, the heir apparent to the throne was the son of the king's sister rather than the king's own son, a custom known as uterine descent. Walata wives were free to take lovers. Outside the cities, the women of the western and central Sudan spent much of their time in the fields. The men typically cleared the land and prepared the fields for planting, but women did the threshing, winnowing, and milling and raised vegetables in small family plots.

The reasons for Ghana's decline in the twelfth century are murky. In the late eleventh century an invasion by the Almoravids, a strict Muslim sect of northwestern Africa, disrupted trade and damaged agriculture, but the kingdom survived until 1203, when a vassal state destroyed it. Shortly thereafter, Mali annexed its territory.

The Empire of Mali

The chaos that followed the collapse of Ghana enabled the people of Mali, former vassals to Ghana, to impose their domination over the western Sudan. The empire of Mali remained the most powerful force in West Africa for two centuries (c. 1250–c. 1460). Its founder, Sundiata (c. 1235–c. 1260), initially put together a federation in which local governors maintained their positions while acknowledging Sundiata as their monarch. With the conquest of adjacent territory by Sundiata and Uli, his son and successor, the new kingdom combined the southern half of Ghana with Mali and parts of what is now Guinea. Uli thus controlled not only the major gold-producing areas but also the communications network provided by the upper Niger River and its tributaries. From Timbuktu, the great trading city on the southern fringes of the Sahara, to the Atlantic coast, Mali had established a secure base for economic prosperity.

Although Sundiata owed much of his authority and success to his exploitation of traditional beliefs in his spiritual powers, he was nominally a Muslim and enjoyed the support of the predominantly Muslim merchant class. So too did Uli, a devout Muslim. The key to Mali's prosperity was the success of the merchants. Taking their cue from Muhammad, himself originally a merchant, they used their pilgrimages to Mecca and the other holy cities of the Muslim world as a means of building trade connections. Mali's products were sold through North African outlets in European markets around the Mediterranean.

Above all, the economy of Mali benefited from the fact that since the twelfth century most European communities had begun to replace copper and silver with gold as the principal unit of currency. The Christian kings of northern Spain began to use gold in imitation of the Almoravids who had settled in southern

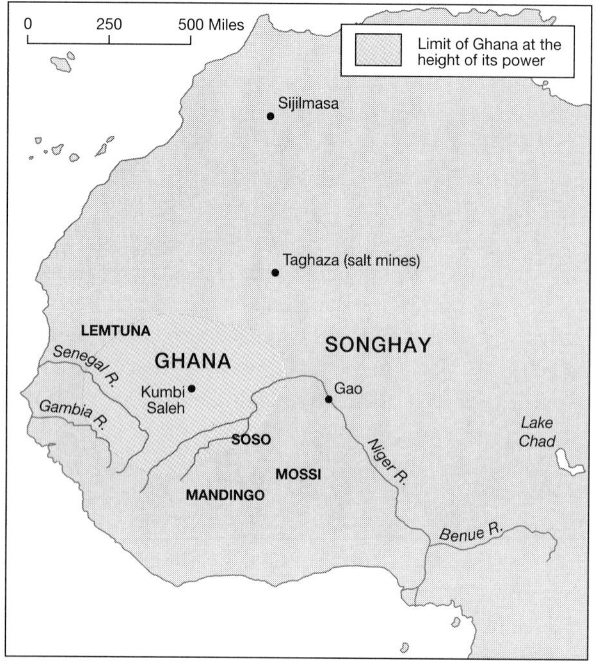

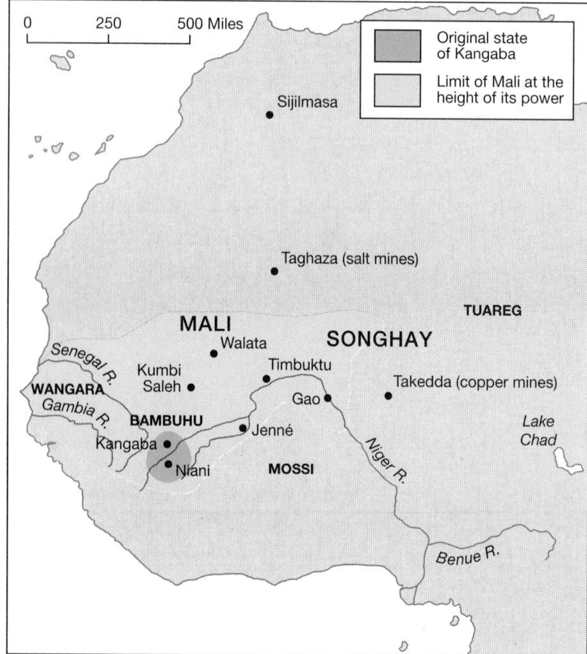

MAP 9.4 ANCIENT KINGDOMS OF THE WESTERN SAHARA

Iberia, and during the thirteenth century most major banking centers of western Europe adopted gold coinage. At least two-thirds of the gold that made this possible was mined in territory controlled by Mali. To facilitate commerce, Mali devised a currency system that used standardized weights of gold dust for large amounts and imported cowrie shells for everyday transactions.

The account of Ibn Battuta, an Arab traveler who visited Mali in 1352–1353, is invaluable. Sophisticated and tireless, Ibn Battuta was no casual sightseer; by the time he made his tour of Mali, he had already visited China. Among other things, he was struck by the general safety of traveling conditions among the Malian people, asserting that there was "complete security in their country." The Malians, he said, had a greater horror of injustice than any other people and showed no mercy to those guilty of it. Part of this could presumably be ascribed to the influence of Islamic law, and Ibn Battuta comments on the zeal with which law and theology were studied. On visiting the chief judge of Niani at his home, he saw the judge's children in chains, from which they could win release only by reciting the Koran from memory. Ibn Battuta did not approve of all aspects of life in Mali. The elaborate court ceremonials, with their hymns in praise of the king and the ritual groveling of the courtiers, met with his contempt.

Ibn Battuta sheds light on the role of women in Malian society. They were free, he noted, to circulate as they chose, without wearing a veil, and to select their

Terra-cotta equestrian figure from Mali, thirteenth to fifteenth century.

companions. He was startled that the female slaves of the king and the provincial governors wore no clothing. Although there is no concrete historical evidence that women played an important role in Mali's political and economic life, his observations suggest a substantial difference between traditional Islamic society and that of sub-Saharan Africa.

Mansa Musa, Caliph of "The Western Parts"

Mali was just past the zenith of its powers when Ibn Battuta saw it. Under Mansa ("Emperor") Musa (1312–1337), Mali's greatest ruler, it extended from Lake Chad to the shores of the Atlantic and from the Sahara to the edge of the tropical rain forest. Both north and south, local kingdoms paid regular tribute and in some cases accepted Malian governors, some of whom were members of Musa's family. Among the lands over which Musa held sway was Songhay to the east, whose market town of Gao played a crucial role in the trans-Saharan trade. Indeed, the key to Mali's power was its domination of both trade and the gold fields in the western Sudan. Altogether, Musa ruled perhaps 8 million people.

A devout Muslim, Musa has been acclaimed by Islamic historians for his grand pilgrimage to Mecca in 1324–1325. During his journey he made a spectacular visit to Cairo, where the sultan of Egypt greeted him. Musa entered the city with a magnificent entourage that included 100 camels, each laden with 300 pounds of gold, and 500 slaves carrying golden staffs. His lavish almsgiving and purchases in the city's bazaars reportedly sparked a serious inflation that lasted years. As a result of

Journey to Mali

The following passage comes from Ibn Battuta's account of his travels in West Africa to visit the Muslim rulers there.

I was at Malli during the two festivals of the sacrifice and the fast-breaking. On these days the sultan takes his seat on the pempi [ceremonial chair] after the midafternoon prayer. The armor-bearers bring in magnificent arms—quivers of gold and silver, swords ornamented with gold and with golden scabbards, gold and silver lances, and crystal maces. At his head stand four amirs [attendants] driving off the flies, having in their hands silver ornaments resembling saddle-stirrups. The commanders . . . and preacher sit in their usual places. The interpreter Dugha comes with his four wives and his slave-girls, who are about a hundred in number. They are wearing beautiful robes, and on their heads they have gold and silver fillets, with gold and silver balls attached. A chair is placed for Dugha to sit on. He plays on an instrument made of reeds, with some small calabashes [gourds] at its lower end, and chants a poem in praise of the sultan, recalling his battles and deeds of valor. The women and girls sing along with him and play with bows. Accompanying them are about thirty youths, wearing red woollen tunics and white skull-caps; each of them has his drum slung from his shoulder and beats it. Afterwards come his boy pupils who play and turn wheels in the air, like the natives of Sind. They show a marvellous nimbleness and agility in these exercises and play most cleverly with swords. Dugha also makes a fine play with the sword. Thereupon the sultan orders a gift to be presented to Dugha and he is given a purse containing . . . gold dust, and is informed of the contents of the purse before all the people. The commanders rise and twang their bows in thanks to the sultan. The next day each one of them gives Dugha a gift, every man according to his rank. Every Friday after . . . prayer, Dugha carries out a similar ceremony to this that we have described.

Source: Ibn Battuta, *Travels in Asia and Africa, 1325–1354,* trans. H. A. R. Gibb (London: Routledge, 1929), p. 328.

Musa's pilgrimage, the wealth of the Sudan became legendary throughout the eastern Mediterranean.

Musa's journey had a lasting impact on West Africa. When he returned to Mali, he brought with him an architect and poet from Andalusia who introduced Arabic architectural styles to the western Sudan. A new mosque was constructed at Timbuktu, and the one at Gao was remodeled. Henceforth major buildings were normally constructed of brick rather than pounded clay. With Musa also came Islamic scholars, many of whom took up residence in Timbuktu, making it the leading cultural center in West Africa and a hub of the book trade. Under Musa's patronage, Timbuktu, Jenné, and Niani became internationally acclaimed centers of theological and legal scholarship.

Under the leadership of Musa and the Islamic faith he championed, Mali made great strides. Islam helped Musa develop a literate bureaucracy, facilitated diplomatic contacts with Muslim states in North Africa, and contributed to royal authority by establishing new lines of power. Yet Musa observed the rights of local chiefs and retained many traditional African customs, including an elaborate court ritual that included magic. Musa's pride in his people is reflected in a story he told about his predecessors, who had reputedly dispatched two expeditions, one consisting of 400 ships and the other of 2,000 ships, to cross the Atlantic; only one vessel, he said, had returned from this daring feat of exploration. Mali's reputation reached Europe, thanks in part to the work of a cartographer from Majorca, who in 1375 drew a map that depicted the ruler of Mali seated on his throne, a gold nugget and a scepter in his hands, as a Berber trader approaches.

The Guinea Coast: The Yoruba and Benin

To the southeast of Mali were the so-called forest states of the Guinea coast. Much of this region is savanna, and the peoples of this area did not inhabit the forests until population pressure forced them to do so. The most intriguing of these peoples were the Yoruba, who founded a state at Ife in the eleventh century. As its artistic remains indicate, it was a thriving, sophisticated state, most of whose trade was in the hands of women. The fertile soil and abundant rainfall of the region enabled the people to produce surplus cereal and root crops, leaving them with ample time and wealth to develop artistic and craft skills. The bronze and terra-cotta portraits of Ife's rulers, strikingly naturalistic, have suggested to some scholars a dependence on the art of the ancient Nok culture. Artists probably made the terra-cotta and metal castings for funeral ceremonies. The people of Ife presumably exported food, kola nuts (used medicinally as a stimulant), and ivory to obtain copper for their artistic endeavors from the Sahara.

In the forests southwest of Ife, most Edo-speaking peoples lived in small villages, but around the eleventh century some of them established a city-state at Benin. By the time the Portuguese arrived in 1485, the walled city of Benin governed a prosperous state whose territory extended westward from the Niger delta to Lagos on the Atlantic coast. A Dutch visitor to the city around 1600 compared its houses and wide streets favorably with those in Amsterdam. The city was about a mile square, with additional walled enclosures extending for miles beyond, but some of this area was intended to provide shelter for animals as well as people. As at Ife, Benin probably originated as a sanctuary for people seeking protection from human and animal predators. Like Ife, Benin produced superb sculptures in bronze, terra-cotta, ivory, and

The imposing mosque at Jenné reflects the success of Islamic expansion in West Africa.

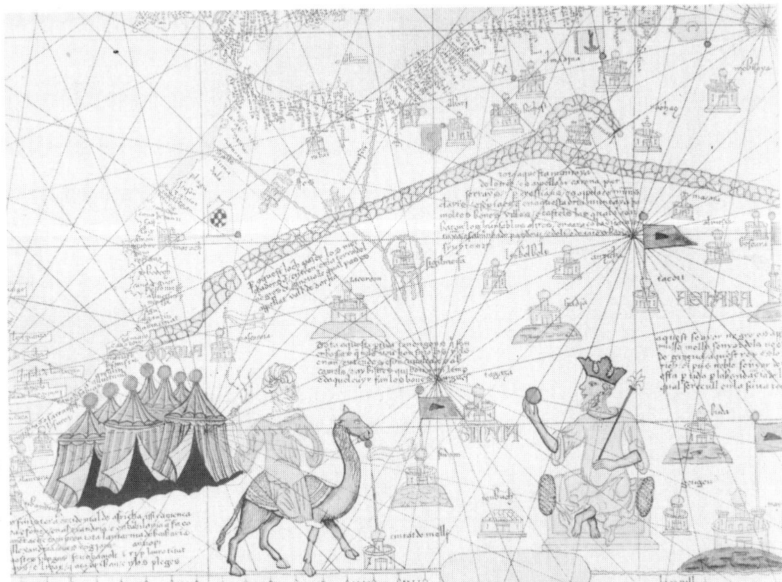

This detail of a map of Africa drawn in 1375 depicts Mansa Musa on the throne of Mali.

wrought iron, though its figures were more conventional and stylized than those of Ife. Much of the art from both states exalts their monarchs. Benin continued to expand until the early sixteenth century, at which time it ceased to have captives to sell into slavery. Not until the eighteenth century did Benin again sell Africans—this time its own citizens—as slaves, bound now for the Americas.

Central Africa

Central Africa was the scene of significant political, economic, and social developments in the centuries after 1000. Our knowledge of this region is very uneven, owing in part to the absence of written records until the nineteenth century but also in part to the scarcity of other materials, such as archaeological remains, for areas such as the land northwest of Lake Victoria where Bantu farmers lived. Sometime between 1350 and 1500 a people known as the Luo migrated southward into this region and took over the Bantu kingdoms of Kitara (henceforth known as Bunyoro) and Buganda. Although the Luo invented a legend of their peaceful acquisition of the palaces, herds, and wives of the Bantu, a tradition from an area further south that the Luo did not conquer indicates that the takeover was violent. But for the most part the rest of central Africa, extending from Kongo in the west to eastern Zambia and Malawi in the east, experienced centuries in which the people improved their farming techniques and developed their manufacturing. Local regions began to specialize in mining, metal manufacturing, agriculture, or hunting. As largely self-sufficient communities declined, trade between regions grew.

The centuries after 1000 were also a time when village-based communities began to merge into larger political units. As in western and central Sudan, territorial chiefs, whose authority derived largely from their religious functions, acquired greater power and influence. Their enhanced status may have owed something as well to such factors as their domination of trade, their expertise in manufacturing metals, or their hunting skills. Whatever role such factors may have played, the chieftains based their claim to rule on their role as spiritual mediators or their reputed ties to deceased ancestors. The people revered the chiefs as religious leaders. In turn the chiefs provided protection and leadership in battle as well as food in times of scarcity and guards for the increasingly important trade routes.

In the west, Kongo, situated on the lower Zaire River, was an area of fertile land and ample rainfall, enabling its Bantu residents to produce surplus food to trade. Most of the inhabitants were farmers, and their religion understandably focused on the spirits of the land. The river was not only a source of fish but also an avenue of transport. Copper, iron, and salt had to be imported, but not over long distances. By 1400 the communities of Kongo had united into a kingdom, the capital of which was Mbanza Kongo. As trade grew, so did the manufacture of cloth made from palm fibers, highly developed pottery, and metal goods. Such items were traded to people along the Atlantic coast for salt and seashells; the latter served as currency.

Luba, in the heart of central Africa, was situated around Lake Kinsale in what is now Zaire. Like Kongo it

EARLY AFRICA

	Eastern Sudan	Western and Central Sudan	East Africa	South Africa
Before A.D. 300	Kingdom of Kush (before 1000 B.C.–A.D. 330)		Arrival of the Bantu (after A.D. 1)	
300–1000	Peak of Axum's power (300–710)	Kingdom of Ghana (c. 400–1203)		Arrival of the Bantu (after A.D. 300)
1000–1600		Empire of Mali (c. 1250–c. 1460)	Golden Age of Swahili city-states (c. 1200–c. 1600)	Great Zimbabwe (c. 1000–c. 1500)

was blessed with fertile soil and adequate rainfall. The people raised cereal crops, hunted for game in the abundant woodlands, and fished in lakes and rivers. They too produced a surplus of food, including dried fish. Canals cut through swamps facilitated travel and communications, enabling the residents of Luba to import and distribute salt from the north and copper from the south. Expert Luba artisans crafted copper necklaces, rings, and bracelets. As the population expanded, competition for resources became a problem, apparently encouraging local chieftains to merge into the Luba kingdom by 1400.

Eastern Zambia and Malawi, a major region for cattle raising, was also important for its copper manufacturing, ivory hunting, and commerce. As in other areas of central Africa, copper had minimal utilitarian value because iron was in ample supply, but copper was a sign of

Typically realistic bronze sculpture of a king of Ife.

Yoruba mother and children; the mother, a religious devotee, holds an offering bowl in the form of a cock. A second child is on her back.

Bronze sculpture of a king of Benin.

status and was used for ornaments as well as in ritual observances. The leading trading center of this region, Ingombe Ilede ("the place where cows lie"), located on the Zambesi River near its junction with the Kafue River, may have been less a permanent town than a large, wealthy trading camp. Residents of the region wove cotton, carved ivory, made copper jewelry, and worked in gold and iron. They traded salt and probably surplus food to southern Africa in return for copper. (Archaeologists have found thousands of copper bangles mostly made of fine wire on the arms and legs of skeletons.) Most of this area's commerce was with East Africa, where the traders obtained glass beads, shells, and probably salt and cloth in return for metalware, gold, and ivory. Ingombe Ilede was abandoned during the 1400s when immigrants from Great Zimbabwe established the more powerful Mutapa kingdom to the southeast.

The City-States of East Africa

Unlike remoter regions to the west, the coast and offshore islands of East Africa were visited by Phoenician, Greek, Roman, Arab, and Indian traders well before the Bantu settled in the region during the first centuries A.D. The earliest traders sought ivory and tortoise shells from the indigenous Africans and in time founded their own settlements along the coast, partly to trade, partly to fish. By the early seventh century the mostly Arab merchants in these towns were shipping black slaves to Persia. The Bantu began residing in the coastal communities some 300 years later, at which time some of them apparently converted to Islam. Fresh waves of immigrants—mostly Arabs, Persians, and Indonesians—arrived in the eleventh and twelfth centuries and intermarried with the Africans. The culture that evolved in these cities was a mixture of Bantu and Islamic traditions. The primary language was Kiswahili (*Swahili* means "people of the coast"), a Bantu tongue that incorporated large numbers of Arabic words and came to be written in Arabic script.

The leading Swahili city-states—Mogadishu, Kilwa, Malindi, Manda, and Mombasa—thrived on their commerce in the thirteenth, fourteenth, and fifteenth centuries. Gold (mined by the Bantu in the region of Zimbabwe), ivory, slaves, leopard skins, tortoise shells, cotton cloth, and mangrove poles (for the construction of homes around the Persian Gulf) were the main exports, in return for which the Swahili merchants imported Indian and Chinese cloth, Persian ceramics, Chinese porcelain, glassware, and beads. The slaves, captured from interior villages by raiding parties, were shipped as far afield as the Persian Gulf, India, and China. The cities also traded with the hinterland, sending such items as fish and shell beads in return for ivory and foodstuffs.

Swahili society was organized into three principal classes, the chief of which comprised the sultan and his family, high-ranking government officials, and prominent merchants. Generally wealthy, they were Muslims who were typically descended from Arab or Persian immigrants. They derived most of their wealth from overseas trade, though most of them owned sizable farms, and some of the merchants were also involved in the manufacture of cotton cloth and glass beads. Below the upper class were artisans, minor government officials, and ship captains. Like those higher in the social scale, most of them were Kiswahili-speaking Muslims; unlike the upper class, however, they were native Africans. At the bottom of the social hierarchy were the slaves, who did much of the farming and manufacturing.

East African women were generally subordinate to men. A woman had the right to refuse to marry a particular man, but men made most decisions concerning marriage, including whether or not polygamy would be practiced, because they controlled the bulk of the material possessions. In a polygamous household, the wives enjoyed equal authority with their husband only if they were unanimous in their view. Men decided where and what to farm, cleared the land, and then left the women to do most of the agricultural labor while the men hunted, fought, or tended to local affairs.

The greatest of the nearly 40 Swahili city-states, Kilwa, was situated on two offshore islands to the south of Zanzibar. Around 1200 they were united under the rule of Abi bin Hasan, whose name appears on the copper coinage minted by the new state, the first of its kind in East Africa. The principal town, Kilwa Kisiwani, was constructed during his reign; its buildings, many of them stone, include a great mosque and a royal palace. A new dynasty, the Mahdali, remained in power from the end of the thirteenth century until the arrival of Portuguese colonizers two centuries later. Mahdali rulers initiated elaborate building programs, enlarging the great mosque and constructing a vast palace, its great courtyard illuminated by hundreds of oil lamps. Large warehouses were built to store the cargoes shipped through Kilwa. In 1331 Ibn Battuta visited Kilwa, which impressed him as "one of the most beautiful and well-constructed towns in the world."

For much of the period before the Europeans' arrival, the main centers of East Africa formed part of a Muslim commercial network that stretched to India and China. By the mid-thirteenth century the Muslims had consolidated their commercial monopoly in the Indian Ocean. Kilwa and other centers maintained Muslim influence in the western zone of this trading empire while also acting as a link between Islam and the indigenous peoples of Africa.

Southern Africa

Unlike the other regions of Africa we have surveyed, southern Africa was not exposed to foreign peoples until the Portuguese came in the late fifteenth century. The earliest inhabitants of the region were people who spoke a language unrelated to Bantu called Khoikhoi. Hunter-gatherers, they depicted both themselves and their prey in rock paintings that are among the finest achievements of prehistoric African art. The Bantu reached southern Africa by the fourth century A.D., bringing with them new agricultural techniques and a knowledge of ironworking. At the artificial cave of Castle Cavern in Swaziland, pottery, smelted iron, and iron-mining tools have been found that date to the early fifth century. This and other proof of metalworking south of the Limpopo River (including iron mines) indicate that Bantu farmers and smiths had begun to make their way down the continent relatively early, coexisting with rather than conquering the hunting and gathering peoples whom they found there.

By the eleventh century hundreds of villages occupied the high plateau of the Transvaal. Some were still inhabited in the nineteenth century and were seen by early missionaries to southern Africa. The buildings, made of stone, were circular, as were the fences that surrounded each house and the outer walls of the villages. Archaeologists have learned a good deal about the widespread trading patterns of this region. Copper ingots, iron implements, and salt were important items of commerce, as were such minerals as red hematite, which Africans used as cosmetics. The discovery of cowrie shells from the Indian Ocean indicates how far the trading networks extended.

Great Zimbabwe: Capital of South Africa's First State?

North of the great bend in the Limpopo River was Great Zimbabwe ("stone houses"), the capital of several successive Bantu kingdoms. The site, strategically located on the southern edge of the Zimbabwe Plateau, had been occupied since the fourth century A.D. What may have been South Africa's first state developed in the eleventh century in large measure because it was the center of gold mining and the resulting trade with the coastal communities of East Africa. Great Zimbabwe also benefited from relatively fertile land, superb building materials, adequate supplies of game, and minimal exposure to crop-devouring locusts and the tsetse flies that endangered humans and cattle.

Between the eleventh and fifteenth centuries the rulers of Great Zimbabwe constructed enormous complexes of stone buildings. The most impressive was 300 feet long and 200 feet wide with a unique conical tower. Oval walls surrounded the structure, and the entire complex was encircled by an elliptical stone wall up to 32 feet high and as much as 17 feet thick. This complex housed the elite and served as a place for the ruler and tribal representatives to intercede with ancestral spirits. After a German explorer rediscovered Great Zimbabwe in 1871, incredulous Europeans were reluctant to accept the fact that the magnificent city was the work of Africans and instead hypothesized that it was the creation of Solomon and Sheba or of the Phoenicians.

Beyond the walls the commoners lived in huts so crowded together that their eaves virtually touched.

The conical tower and part of the ruins of Great Zimbabwe.

Great Zimbabwe's population may have been as large as 18,000. For all but the elite, living conditions were harsh. The absence of sanitation facilities would have meant prevalent disease, and the smoke from thousands of cooking fires would at times have enveloped the city in smog. The population's basic dietary staples were sorghum and millet, supplemented by beans and squash. The more fortunate residents also ate meat, usually beef, although some lamb, goat, and wild game were available.

By the thirteenth century the society of Great Zimbabwe had become specialized. Some people farmed; others spun cloth or mined gold (from alluvial deposits and quartz reefs), iron, copper, and tin; artisans made pottery, carved soapstone and ivory, or constructed buildings. The principal building material was granite, available locally in convenient thin slabs. Zimbabwean artisans also used a sturdy plaster known as *daga,* made of clay derived from decomposed granite; *daga* enabled the artisans to create smooth, polished surfaces as well as intricate patterns. The skill of Zimbabwean builders can still be seen in the city's walls, constructed without mortar and wherever possible without sharp corners. Other residents engaged in commerce. Through their East African trading partners the people of Great Zimbabwe imported glass from western Asia, ceramics from Persia and China, and salt and copper from neighboring Africans; in turn they exported gold and gold ornaments, as well as weapons and iron tools.

Great Zimbabwe began to decline in the fifteenth century, apparently as the cumulative effect of declining trade, depleted soil, overgrazing, and dwindling supplies of wild game. Late in the century, a new dynasty moved the capital to a site near the Zambezi River. At that point the empire, which the newly arrived Portuguese called the Monomotapa, extended from the Zambezi to the Limpopo River and from the Indian Ocean to the Kalahari Desert in the west. Like its predecessor's, the wealth of the kingdom was based primarily on the area's gold deposits, which were now mined in open pits. Weakened by court intrigue, the empire soon splintered, leaving its people exposed to Portuguese encroachments. Great Zimbabwe remained, its buildings and walls but one reminder of the rich cultural accomplishments of the African peoples in the centuries before 1500.

SUMMARY

The early civilizations of Africa manifest striking diversity. Originally hunter-gatherers, the Africans, like many other ancient peoples, learned to raise a wide range of grains, root crops, and other vegetables. Taking advantage of such natural resources as gold, copper, ivory, ebony, and prized animal skins, they developed extensive trading networks that linked them to western Asia, India, and Europe. Urban centers emerged in the northwest, the northeast, and the southeast; some, such as Niani and Meroë, became the capitals of states, while others, such as Kilwa and Mogadishu, were loosely allied with other cities. Skilled artists, especially in Ife and Benin, carved magnificent bronze portraits, and talented sculptors throughout much of Africa worked in ivory, wood, and—especially in Great Zimbabwe—soapstone. Architects blended native motifs with designs adapted from the Egyptians, the Persians, and the Arabs. Wherever Islam spread, learning flourished; the theological and law schools of Timbuktu, Jenné, and Niani acquired international reputations. African achievements were indeed significant long before the Europeans arrived.

African civilizations also had their share of problems. Many Africans made minimal use of metal tools, probably because of discouraging geographic factors, including less fertile soils and severe climate. Moreover, they tended to abuse the environment, depleting forests, overgrazing pastureland, and exhausting the soil, all of which encouraged erosion. Many Africans depended heavily on the export of gold and slaves rather than on manufactured goods. The introduction of Islam may have reduced the slave trade, but the practice remained widespread. All civilizations, of course, have mixed records. Slavery in early-nineteenth-century America, for instance, was harsher than it was in Africa, and virtually all societies have failed to protect the environment. The arrival of the Europeans in sub-Saharan Africa beginning in the fifteenth century was not responsible for introducing slavery to the continent, but mounting Western demands for cheap labor greatly intensified the slave trade.

SUGGESTIONS FOR FURTHER READING

Ade Ajayi, J. F., ed. *The UNESCO General History of Africa,* vols. 1–4. Berkeley: University of California Press, 1980–1988.

Asante, M. K. *Afrocentricity,* rev. ed. Trenton, N.J.: Africa World Press, 1988.

Clark, J. D. *The Cambridge History of Africa,* vol. 1: *From Earliest Times to 500 B.C.* Cambridge: Cambridge University Press, 1982.

Cockcroft, L. *Africa's Way: A Journey from the Past.* New York: St. Martin's Press, 1990.

Connah, G. *African Civilizations: Precolonial Cities and States in Tropical Africa: An Archaeological Perspective.* Cambridge: Cambridge University Press, 1987.

Crowder, M., and Ade Ajayi, J. F., eds. *A History of West Africa.* New York: Columbia University Press, 1972.

Curtin, P., et al. *African History,* rev. ed. New York: Longman, 1984.

Davidson, B. *Africa: History of a Continent.* New York: Macmillan, 1972.

Diop, C. A. *Civilization or Barbarism.* Brooklyn: Hill, 1991.

Dunn, R. E. *The Adventures of Ibn Battuta: A Muslim Traveler of the Fourteenth Century.* Berkeley: University of California Press, 1987.

Fage, J. D. *A History of Africa,* 3rd ed. New York: Knopf, 1995.

Horton, M. *The Swahili.* Oxford: Blackwell, 1996.

July, R. W. *A History of the African People,* 3rd ed. New York: Scribner, 1980.

———. *Precolonial Africa: An Economic and Social History.* New York: Scribner, 1975.

Levtzion, N. *Ancient Ghana and Mali.* London: Methuen, 1973.

Mokhtar, G., ed. *Ancient Africa.* Berkeley: University of California Press, 1980.

Olaniyan, R., ed. *African History and Culture.* Ikeja, Nigeria: Longman, 1982.

Pouwels, R. L. *Horn and Crescent: Cultural Change and Traditional Islam on the East African Coast, 800–1900.* Cambridge: Cambridge University Press, 1987.

Shaw, T. *Nigeria: Its Archaeology and Early History.* London: Thames & Hudson, 1978.

Shaw, T., Sinclair, P., Andah, B., and Okpoko, A., eds. *The Archaeology of Africa: Food, Metals, and Towns.* London: Routledge, 1993.

Shillington, K. *History of Africa.* New York: St. Martin's Press, 1994.

Trimingham, J. S. *A History of Islam in West Africa.* New York: Oxford University Press, 1962.

———. *Islam in East Africa.* Oxford: Clarendon Press, 1964.

CHAPTER 10

The Americas to 1500

The first people in the Americas were hunter-gatherers who came from Siberia across the land bridge that is now the 56-mile-wide Bering Strait. The periodic expansion of ice sheets over much of the Northern Hemisphere had lowered sea levels worldwide as much as 300 feet, making it possible to walk from Siberia to Alaska during much of the period from about 75,000 to 10,000 years ago. Skeletal remains have enabled scholars to estimate that migrants first moved into North America more than 20,000 years ago. Southward migration brought their descendants to Mexico around 18,000 B.C., Peru by 11,000 B.C., and the tip of South America by 9000 B.C.

The pressure of expanding population and the search for food encouraged the movement of these peoples. They supported themselves by hunting, but where natural food supplies were rich, they gradually formed settlements. The transition from a nomadic existence to agricultural communities was far more gradual than that in Europe or Asia. During the period from about 8000 to 2000 B.C., which American archaeologists call the Archaic, different regions adapted to their environmental resources. On both the Atlantic and the Pacific coasts of North America and on the coasts of what are now Brazil, Peru, and Chile, fishing communities began to grow. Elsewhere, as in the woodlands of eastern North America or the Andes Mountains of Peru, hunting remained the principal means of support. Although some agricultural techniques may have developed in certain regions, survival throughout the Archaic period depended on wild food.

Around 5000 B.C. or shortly thereafter the people of Mexico were growing maize (corn), beans, pumpkins, squash, chili peppers, plums, and avocados. By 2000 B.C. (and possibly much earlier) the Amerindians of Peru were raising manioc (tapioca) and potatoes. Contact between the various Amerindians enabled agricultural

Mogollon ritual figure, c. 1150, composed of wood, feathers, fiber, and earth pigments.

information to spread. Those living in Peru learned about peanuts from the lowlands of the Amazon and maize from Mesoamerica (Mexico and Central America), while the Amerindians of Mexico acquired the cultivation of manioc from the tribes of Peru. Around 1500 B.C. maize was being cultivated in what is now the southwestern United States by the ancestors of the Pueblo Indians, and sometime after 300 B.C. Amerindians in eastern North America had acquired this ability, long after they knew how to raise sunflowers, artichokes, and grasses.

As elsewhere in the world, the development of agriculture encouraged population growth. This was especially so in the fertile regions of Mesoamerica and Peru, as opposed, for example, to the arid lands of the American southwest. Nevertheless, permanent villages did not appear in Mesoamerica until about 2500 B.C., several thousand years after the beginning of agriculture. This was probably because it took a long time for maize plants to become sufficiently developed to produce more per acre than wild plants. In time, reliance on maize and potatoes had the advantage of requiring less labor than raising grain. Surplus labor could therefore be harnessed, as in ancient Egypt and Mesopotamia, for the construction of temples and palaces as well as for the creation of sizable armies with which to expand and defend the state.

Early Mesoamerica: The Olmecs

The first major center of civilization in the Americas developed on the hot, humid, forested lands of the Mexican Gulf Coast. The site now called San Lorenzo Tenochtitlán was first settled on a plateau around 1500 B.C.; on all sides the people extended the plateau with clay, rock, and sand. By 1200 B.C. San Lorenzo had become a major ceremonial center for the Olmecs ("rubber people," a name later bestowed on them by the Aztecs). The settlement consisted mostly of religious and governmental buildings, to be used only on formal occasions, interspersed with approximately 60 stone ornaments and carved heads. An estimated 1,000 people lived in San Lorenzo, and another 1,250 in the environs.

Following the destruction of San Lorenzo around 900 B.C., probably by invaders, the Olmecs made La Venta their ceremonial center. Founded a century earlier, the settlement at La Venta occupied an island surrounded by swamps. The principal structure was a stone pyramid 110 feet high. The other buildings, spread out over a mile and a half, were decorated with elaborate stone carvings, the material for which had to be transported a considerable distance. Among the objects found in this vast temple complex were fine jade carvings, presumably left as religious offerings. When the Olmecs abandoned La Venta between 600 and 500 B.C., Tres Zapotes to the northwest became the final Olmec center, a status it enjoyed until they forsook it too at the beginning of the first century A.D.

The Olmecs' love of sculpture, which led them to seek such raw materials as jade, serpentine, and basalt, brought them into contact with other peoples and transmitted their culture. Olmec pottery and figurines have been found as far north as northern Mexico and as far south as present-day Salvador and Costa Rica. The best-known examples of Olmec art are mammoth heads, some 9 feet high and sculpted out of basalt, that probably depicted Olmec chiefs. Olmec architecture, steles (stone-slab monuments), and altarpieces were also monumental, reflecting the fact that they were produced by highly centralized states in which a small hereditary elite exercised political authority.

Olmec religion seems to have foreshadowed that of the Maya. A motif that frequently recurs and is later found among the Maya is a half-human, half-jaguar figure. Olmec deities included gods of wisdom, rain, death, fire, and spring, all of whom the successors of the Olmecs worshipped. A number of Olmec sculptures indicate that these people may have sacrificed humans, probably war captives but perhaps children and dwarfs as well. Judging from the remains of split, charred human bones in the refuse deposits at San Lorenzo, the Olmecs were probably cannibalistic. The religion, art, and architecture of the Olmecs left a profound impression on later Mesoamerican culture, as perhaps did their systems of

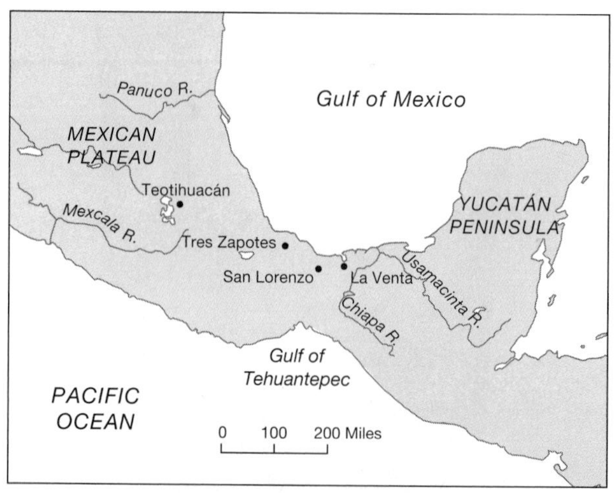

MAP 10.1 MESOAMERICA AND THE OLMECS

This stone figure of a woman and child is a representative example of Olmec sculpture.

writing and calculating dates, although we know little about these.

Teotihuacán: The First Great City in the Americas

Following the Olmecs' decline, other major centers of civilization developed in Mexico. One of these was at Teotihuacán, on the high plateau of central Mexico, 20 miles from modern Mexico City. The Maya created another, the heart of whose territory was the Yucatán peninsula and Guatemala. Throughout most of the period from A.D. 100 to 750, Teotihuacán was the dominating force in much of Mesoamerica. Shortly before 600, when it was at its height, the city covered 8 square miles and housed a population possibly as large as 200,000, greater than any contemporary European city. Construction had begun in the first century A.D., when planners laid out two great avenues at right angles to each other, dividing the area into quarters. The Aztecs later called the north-south road the Avenue of the Dead. As the city grew, it was laid out on a grid plan based on the two main arteries, with the chief ceremonial structures on the Avenue of the Dead. At the southern end stood the Pyramid of the Sun, 250 feet high and 650 feet square at its base. Its name derives from the Aztecs, who believed it to be the sun's birthplace, although it may have had a different significance for the people who built it. Recent exploration indicates that there may be a huge tomb at its base, though this has never been excavated; other scholars suggest that this was a natural cave associated with a creation myth. At the opposite end of the Avenue of the Dead stands a similar construction, the Pyramid of the Moon, approximately half the size of the Pyramid of the Sun.

Almost at the center of the city is a sunken courtyard known as the Citadel, which is surrounded by temples. The chief deity was a goddess who bestowed such gifts as water and seeds and who was also associated with conquest and human sacrifice. In the middle of the square is another temple, dedicated to Quetzalcoatl, the sides of which are decorated with representations of the Feathered Serpent, together with the Fire Serpent, bearer of

Teotihuacán ceramic mask from an incense burner, c. 300–600.

the sun across the sky. The presence of more than 20 temple complexes in the city suggests that it was governed by a priestly elite, possibly in cooperation with secular officials who employed a military force to requisition the necessary labor. Square residential compounds lined much of the Avenue of the Dead. Within the simple walls were luxurious dwellings, probably the homes of the ruling class; in them, rooms decorated with murals of ritual processions and animals such as jaguars and coyotes were ranged around a central courtyard. Workers and artisans lived on the outskirts of the city in more crowded conditions, and some of the outlying districts were reserved for foreigners. The city had canals that brought drinking water to the housing compounds and a sewer system.

Among the finest of Teotihuacán's manufactured goods are cylindrical vases, often covered with plaster and painted. Small figurines were mass-produced by means of clay models, and examples of both have been found throughout Mesoamerica. Much of the city's commercial preeminence came from its control of obsidian mines near the modern city of Pachuca, which supplemented the stone mined near Teotihuacán. In addition to production for home use, knives, blades, scrapers, and dart points were manufactured for export, and the obsidian itself was a major export item. The city had more than 400 workshops that specialized in obsidian and another 100 that manufactured ceramic, shell, and groundstone items. Artists sculpted life-size masks out of such materials as basalt and jade. Hieroglyphics found on pottery and murals suggest that the people of Teotihuacán were literate, but if they produced written documents, none have survived.

The city's vast scale, coupled with the presence of Teotihuacán culture over a geographic area that includes most of Mexico and Guatemala, indicates a people with expansionist aims. Future archaeological work may indicate whether they ruled an empire or whether their influence was limited to the adoption of their culture by neighboring peoples. They apparently built no forts, depots, or roads to administer an empire, but neither did the Aztecs, who were unquestionably imperialistic. Teotihuacán culture influenced both the Toltecs and the Aztecs. Both the people of Teotihuacán and the Aztecs cremated their dead and worshiped some of the same deities, including Tlaloc, the rain spirit, and Quetzalcoatl, the Feathered Serpent, god of the wind. By the fourteenth century, in fact, the name Teotihuacán meant "place of the gods" in the Aztec language.

Invaders, probably from the city-state of Cholula to the southeast, sacked Teotihuacán about 750, burning its great houses. Yet the remnants of the city, its temples abandoned, continued to be inhabited for centuries. People lived in hovels constructed in corners of the former palaces, and the pyramids became a place of pilgrimage for the Aztecs.

Aerial view of Teotihuacán, which at its peak in the late fifth century may have had a population of 200,000, much larger than any European city.

The Maya

Around the time of the early building at Teotihuacán, Maya civilization began to develop in southern Mexico and Central America. The area controlled by the Maya, which had a population of perhaps 14 million, was divided into districts, each dominated by a primary center that exercised authority over a descending hierarchy of progressively smaller sites. The primary centers, of which there could be only four at any given time (one for each compass direction), varied substantially in size. Tikal, which covered 50 square miles (including residences and shallow lakes), probably housed 40,000 to 80,000 people, and El Mirador, a later center, was home to 80,000. The primary sites were religious and ceremonial centers dominated by the hereditary elite, around which were numerous house-mounds.

The so-called palaces, large structures divided into many small, cramped rooms, were uncomfortable and damp. They apparently housed the elite. The other structures were almost exclusively religious: stone processional ways, temples, stairways decorated with painted stucco masks, and the pyramids that are the most famous characteristic of Maya architecture. The enormous ceremonial sanctuaries made use of vaults (arched roofs), an architectural feature not employed elsewhere in Mesoamerica. At Tikal the highest pyramid is 229 feet tall and decorated with sculptures of Maya warlords. The only constructions of importance at Tikal besides the temples, pyramids, and palaces are ball courts and tombs.

Ball courts became a common feature of Amerindian cities and towns in ancient Mexico and the southwestern region of what would later become the United States. Teams of players wearing pads on elbows, wrists, and knees tried to drive a hard rubber ball through one of the stone rings in the side walls of the court. Large crowds of enthusiastic spectators cheered their favorites. The games were extremely physical and demanded considerable skill, since the balls had to be struck without being handled. Judging by surviving artwork, the games involved recreation and religious ritual; some scenes depict the death god presiding over the games. For many Amerindians this form of sport was indeed sacred.

Maya Society, Religion, and Culture

The archaeological evidence for Maya life includes written and carved texts. The Maya devised a complex system of writing based on 850 characters, some representing pictorial objects, some concepts, and others syllables. With it they recorded historical, religious, and astronomical information organized by means of an elaborate

MAP 10.2 THE MAYA, THE AZTEC, AND THE INCA

calendar more accurate than its European counterpart. The urge to record the passing of the seasons seems to have been common to many Mesoamerican peoples, but the Maya calendrical system outstrips the others in intellectual complexity. It was based on various cycles, the so-called long count, including a 365-day solar year, a 360-day lunar year, and a 584-day year of Venus. There was also a 260-day cycle, formed by joining 20 day names to 13 numbers—a ceremonial year, unrelated to the lunar or solar calendar and apparently antedating both. The solar year comprised eighteen 20-day months and one 5-day month. The Maya recorded the births, marriages, and military triumphs of the rulers and their ancestors, as well as religious myths.

The importance of the Maya elite continued after their deaths. Virtually every pyramid contains a tomb in its base, presumably of an aristocrat. Ancestor worship seems to have played a major role in Maya court religion, each ruler being associated with the god from whom he claimed descent. Maya warlords launched military campaigns with the help of these divine patrons, not so much to seize enemy territory as to capture prisoners for slavery and sacrifice.

The lives of the peasants, some free, others bound to the land, were very different from those of the ruling class. Indeed, measurement of the skeletons found in royal tombs and in simple village graves shows that the nobility were much taller than their farm laborers. This may reflect a difference in ethnic origin or result from superior nutrition; for the Maya it was proof that the gods created rulers and ruled separately. The villages that have been studied had no elaborate ceremonial sanctuaries, although they did have shrines. In the countryside around Tikal, for every 50 to 100 dwellings there was a small religious center, dividing the residential areas into zones. Because most land was swampy, the Maya drained it with canals and in some cases mounded soil to raise the fields above the wetlands. Some Maya farmers used slash-and-burn agriculture: they cut and burned trees and brush, the ashes from which fertilized the soil for such crops as maize, beans, peppers, and squash.

Maya women were sometimes prominent. At least two women—Kan Ik (583–604) and Zac Kuk (612–615)—ruled the center at Palenque, and in other centers women periodically governed in their own right or acted as regents. As in medieval and early modern Europe, leaders of centers established alliances with each other through marriage; in the Maya world this usually took the form of an alliance between a primary and a secondary center. In reckoning their lines of descent, Maya aristocrats emphasized whichever line, female or male, was more prestigious. A matchmaker often arranged marriages, sometimes while the prospective couple was very young. The Maya were monogamous, but divorce was easily accomplished, with either spouse having the right to repudiate the other.

The Maya manufactured and exported cotton textiles to the other peoples of Mesoamerica in return for

Temple I at Tikal, with nine levels (perhaps an allusion to the nine levels of the underworld), is a superb example of Maya architecture.

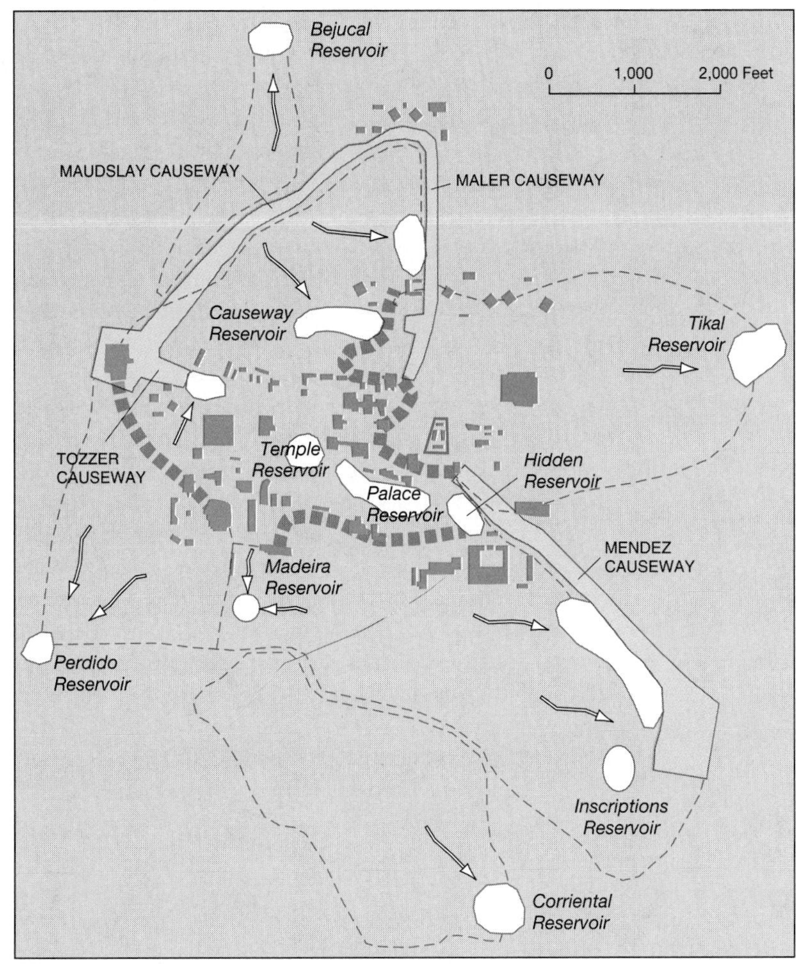

MAP 10.3 CEREMONIAL CENTER AT TIKAL.

Recent archaeological research suggests that Maya power was based in part on effective management of water supplies. This map shows the reservoirs (black), which were filled by catchment areas (dotted lines), raised causeways, and drainage ditches.

such items as jade and cacao (chocolate), the latter not only a drink for aristocrats but also a medium of exchange. Artisans made ceramics, metalware, and jewelry, while others engaged in weaving and matmaking. Seagoing canoes were used in long-distance trading.

Maya painting, pottery, and sculpture are strikingly different from those of their neighbors. The Maya style is elaborate and complex, and surviving stone and wooden carvings often feature scenes of nobles accompanied by their divine protectors, together with lengthy inscriptions; the gods are highly stylized. Maya painting, unlike that at Teotihuacán, is naturalistic, showing an interest in portraiture and the aristocrats' lives. The narrative murals at the temple in Bonampak depict a Maya raid, the capture and sacrifice of prisoners, and a ritual dance.

The stone processional ways at Tikal and elsewhere were symbolic of the divine roads that led from the "green tree of abundance," which stood at the center of the earth; they formed a setting for ceremonies in praise of the gods. The supreme deity was Itzamna, creator of the world and lord of fire, who is frequently depicted as a snake. The most commonly portrayed Maya deity, recognizable by his large nose and the axe or smoking cigar in his forehead, was Bolon Tzacab, a manifestation of Itzamna. The Maya worshipped the Feathered Serpent of the Teotihuacán people and the Aztecs under the name of Kukulcán. Numeric subdivisions played an important role in Maya religion: there were four world directions, each with its own color and with a tree on which sat a particular bird; the heavens were divided into 13 layers and the underworld into 9. Gods associated with the jaguar, a symbol of night, ruled the sinister Maya underworld. To provide companions and attendants in the next world for their rulers, the Maya sacrificed humans, using prisoners. The most common method was decapitation following torture. The Maya also practiced self-mutilation, drawing blood from wounds in ear, penis, or tongue and splashing it on pieces of bark as offerings to the gods.

A Maya woodcarving of a moustachioed dignitary or priest.

The Collapse of Maya Civilization

Around the year 800 this conservative, elitist culture went into decline. The last inscribed Maya calendar date was the equivalent of 909, by which time most sites had been abandoned and their populations scattered. Scholars still debate the causes. Overpopulation and misuse of agricultural land by overplanting or excessive burning may have been contributing factors, possibly causing this savage fighting. Yet by themselves they are insufficient to account for so precipitous a collapse. The complex developments that triggered the decline probably commenced with the fall of Teotihuacán, which prompted rival Maya city-states to fight each other for control of the trade routes. Needing more people to serve in their armies and to construct monuments to intimidate their rivals, Maya rulers must have encouraged population growth and increased food production. The resulting situation was probably compounded by social and political unrest, leading to attacks on the elite. As the economic system broke down, large-scale agriculture collapsed and famine ensued (as reflected in the fact that skeletons of this period, including those of some aristocrats, reveal the effects of malnutrition). Many peasants died or migrated elsewhere. Around 820 savage fighting resulted in the burning of cities, villages, and crops and the decapitation of young men, contributing to the catastrophic decline in population. Recent research also indicates that rainfall sharply decreased between 800 and 1000, suggesting that drought and famine contributed to Maya decline.

The Toltec Empire

The decline of Teotihuacán enabled a new power, the Toltecs ("reed people"), to emerge in Mesoamerica. Their capital, Tula, covered 3.5 square miles and had a popula-

A portion of the reconstructed mural from Bonampak depicting the Maya ruler in the center holding a spear.

THE VISUAL EXPERIENCE

Art of Early Africa and the Americas

The lasting impact of Christianity on Ethiopia is vividly represented in this seventeenth-century painting of St. George slaying a dragon, a traditional Christian theme.

A Maya ruler from the seventh or eighth century is dressed in distinctive regalia associated with warfare and spiritual struggle.

Bronze leopard, c.1750, Nigeria (Benin).

This illustration from an Aztec manuscript depicts Emperor Montezuma II surrendering to Hernando Cortés. (Coloring has been added.)

In this mural from the Temple of the Warriors at Chichén Itzá, an advance party of Toltecs reconnoiter a Maya town from their boats. The god Quetzalcoatl watches from the upper right.

This diorama depicts the Inca in the Urubamba Valley near Cuzco on the eve of their conquest by the Spaniards. Terraces enabled them to farm in the Andes, and the transportation of goods was by pack trains that traversed suspension bridges.

The quarter-mile-long Great Serpent Mound near Cincinnati, Ohio, is a vestige of the Adena culture, the earliest of the Mound Builders. The dead were buried in log-lined tombs and earthen crematory basins at the center of effigies like that shown here. Other effigies were built in the shape of eagles, bears, and alligators.

This crown of the Yoruba is made from vegetable fiber, iron, cotton, and glass beads.

This mask of an Eskimo shaman depicts the spirit of a sea mammal.

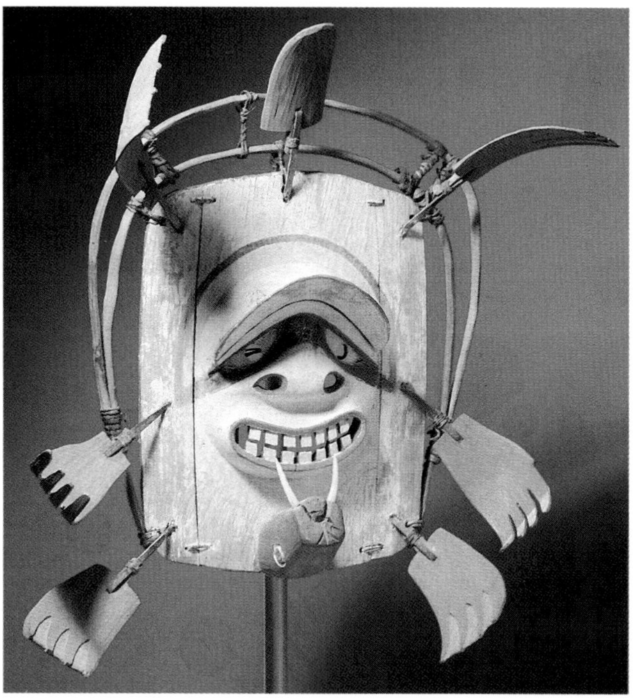

tion estimated between 30,000 and 60,000, with another 60,000 farmers living in surrounding villages. Immigrants from other areas flocked to the city between 750 and 950. Tula included pyramids, a temple with sculpted stone columns, great halls, and individual statues in the form of reclining men holding sacrificial knives and round dishes on their stomachs; some scholars speculate that the hearts of sacrificial human victims were deposited in these dishes. Like the later Aztecs who admired them so much, the Toltecs displayed the skulls of their victims on wooden racks. Compared with those of Teotihuacán, Toltec artists were more preoccupied with human sacrifice, war, and death. Their chief deity was Quetzalcoatl, the Feathered Serpent. The Toltec empire consisted of small, semi-independent kingdoms. The Toltecs demanded tribute from their neighbors, ruling an empire that extended throughout most of central Mexico from coast to coast. Evidence of Toltec influence has been found as far away as Mexico's Oaxaca valley and Guatemala.

The Toltecs' best-known ruler, Topiltzin (c. 980–999), appropriated Quetzalcoatl's name as his own, apparently as part of an unsuccessful campaign to reform religion and abolish human sacrifice. Legend has it that Topiltzin's unpopular views led to his overthrow and flight from Tula. Around A.D. 1000 the Toltecs seized the Maya center at Chichén Itzá in the Yucatán and thereafter carried out a building program patterned on that in Tula; this was done, according to the Maya, by "Kukulcán," the Maya name for Quetzalcoatl, raising the possibility that the conqueror of Chichén Itzá was Topiltzin. Legend also has it that as Topiltzin left Tula, he promised to return in 1519. When the Spanish conquistador Hernando Cortés (1485–1547) landed in Mexico that year, the stunned Aztecs were unsure whether or not he was Topiltzin.

Colossal columns from Pyramid B at Tula, showing costumed warriors ready for battle.

The Toltec empire collapsed in the mid-twelfth century, and Tula was put to the torch. By this time the empire had been weakened by factional strife, poor harvests, and conflict with neighboring states, including Cholula, and it could not cope with large numbers of immigrants who sought refuge from a catastrophic drought to the northwest. Toltec influence lived on, chiefly among the Aztecs, who pillaged Tula and carried off many of its art works to Tenochtitlán, their capital.

The Aztec Empire

The Aztecs were originally an agricultural tribe from western Mexico forced by drought or population pressures to migrate into the Basin of Mexico. Aztec histories describe their ancestors as the chosen people of the sun god, destined to conquer and rule in his name. In the uninhabited swampy lands near Lake Texcoco they founded the twin towns of Tenochtitlán (the present Mexico City) and Tlatelolco in 1325 or 1345. In 1428 they began to expand their territory until their realm included much of Mexico. By 1500 the Aztec empire controlled a territory of some 125,000 square miles with a population of about 10 million people.

The century or so of the Aztec empire is well documented, both by Spanish visitors and missionaries and by the Aztecs' own books, or codices, some of which escaped destruction. The latter include calendars, historical texts, works on geography and religion, and a magnificent botanical volume with drawings of medicinal plants. Extensive records of Aztec legal disputes also survive, and Spanish administrative records provide further information.

Tenochtitlán was the largest city in Mesoamerica, with a resident population in 1519 estimated at 150,000 to 200,000, but the greater metropolitan area numbered 400,000, some five times as large as contemporary London. When the Spanish arrived, King Montezuma II (1502–1520) lived in a palace of 300 rooms, the grounds of which occupied 10 acres and included the royal living quarters, law courts, administrative offices, an arsenal, a prison, a concert hall, a zoo and an aviary, and quarters for 3,000 workers and servants. The city contained hundreds of temples, including the central complex comprising three huge pyramids. Atop the largest, which soared to a height of 200 feet, were twin temples to the rain and sun gods. The sacred precinct also included smaller temples, housing for the priests, racks to display the skulls of

Topiltzin's Ouster and Prophecy

The story of the overthrow of Topiltzin, the ruler of Tula, was widely recounted by the Aztecs. In retelling the story, the sixteenth-century Dominican friar Diego Durán praised him for his piety and his prophetic role in preaching a New Law. Durán misidentified the Toltecs as Topiltzin's disciples.

Topiltzin . . . was a venerable and devout person, held in deference, honored and revered as one would a holy man. . . . I saw a picture of him on an ancient paper. . . . This document showed Topiltzin with a venerable appearance: as an old man with a long red beard turning white. . . .

I have heard it affirmed that a great persecution arose against Topiltzin and his disciples and that a bitter war was waged against them, since the number of people who had accepted the New Law was great. . . . The Toltecs were not allowed to settle in any town . . . until Topiltzin made his home in Tula, where he reposed for some years, until the persecution began anew. Finally, weary of being harassed, he and his followers decided to give in to their persecutors and to depart.

Having come to this decision, Topiltzin called together the people of Tula and all his disciples. He thanked them for having allowed him to live among them and then bade them farewell. . . . He prophesied the arrival of strangers who would come to this land from the east. They wore unusual and multicolored clothing from head to foot. They used head coverings. This was the punishment which God was to send them in return for the ill-treatment which Topiltzin had received and for the shame of his banishment. In this chastisement young and old were to perish.

Source: Diego Durán, *Book of the Gods and Rites and the Ancient Calendar,* trans. and ed. Fernando Horcasitas and Doris Heyden (Norman: University of Oklahoma Press, 1971), pp. 57, 61–62.

Stone statue of a reclining warrior with a bowl to hold sacrifices, found at Chichén Itzá in 1875.

tens of thousands of sacrificial victims, and a large ball court. The capital's main streets were actually canals laid out in a grid pattern; the Spaniards who witnessed this were reminded of Venice. The city also had two main markets, one of which was larger than those in Rome and Constantinople and, according to Spanish observers, accommodated 60,000 buyers and sellers on a busy day.

The most intensive Mesoamerican farming system supported the high density of population in the capital and in other cities. The Aztecs used plant and animal fertilizers to enrich the soil and developed complex irrigation systems using terraces and canals. Especially in the area of their capital the Aztecs reclaimed swamplands and drained lakes to create productive agricultural terrain. The resulting farmland was sufficiently fertile to feed six to eight people per acre. The Aztecs' homeland was not rich in natural resources, and a principal motive for conquest seems to have been to gain possession of

Aztec statue of the god Quetzalcoatl in the form of a feathered serpent with a human head.

commodities such as maize and other foodstuffs, cotton cloth, incense, metal, and—the most prized of all—jade. Thus military aggression as much as trade was the primary means of economic development. The only large-scale industry that manufactured objects for export made tools of obsidian.

Aztec Society

Like other early tribes of Africa and the Americas, the Aztecs were originally organized along kinship lines, but by the early 1500s Aztec society was stratified. At the top of the hierarchy was the king or emperor. Unlike most European monarchies, the eldest son was not the automatic heir. Instead an inner circle of nobles and high priests chose the successor from among the ruler's legitimate sons or, if necessary, his brothers or nephews. Unlike Topiltzin of Tula, who in theory was both divine and human, the Aztec kings depicted themselves as intimate representatives of the gods but not personally divine. In this respect they were like some of the African rulers discussed earlier. The Aztec empire was a militarized state, and its kings were thought of, above all else, as warriors. By the mid-fifteenth century a new ruler customarily launched his reign with a major military campaign. The rulers were also the preeminent figures in the state religion.

Below the king were the nobles, who comprised approximately 5 percent of the population. In addition to their own hereditary estates they derived income from lands bestowed on them in return for service to the crown. From this class came the provincial governors and judges who administered the empire and the generals who preserved its security and extended its frontiers. They lived in large stone residences, wore luxurious clothes and jewelry, and ate a wide range of imported foods.

Beneath the nobility were the warriors, whose status derived from their conquests, the source of sacrificial victims and essential commodities. The status of warrior was earned when a young soldier captured his first prisoner, and advancement to the nobility could be attained by later killing or capturing four enemy soldiers. Failure to complete this assignment in several campaigns resulted in demotion to the laboring class, or *macehuales.*

The macehuales belonged by birth to one of 20 *calpullis.* Originally clans, the calpullis eventually became administrative districts. Each had its own ward in the city, its own jointly owned farmland on the outskirts, its

This drawing of an Aztec marriage shows the symbolic union of the couple by the knotting of their cloaks; at the bottom, a matron carries the bride over the threshold.

own schools (concentrating on agriculture and military training, for boys only), and its own temple. In time of war, each district provided its own military unit. Each of the calpullis specialized in a particular craft. Unlike nobles, priests, and slaves, the macehuales had to pay taxes, but in turn they received a portion of the tribute collected from subject peoples. Although women played no formal part in running the clan's affairs, they had a crucial role in farming. Because large numbers of men engaged in military campaigns, women helped plant the fields and cared for the land during the growing period, camping by the fields in brushwood huts, clearing the weeds, and driving off animal predators. Female participation in agricultural labor was undoubtedly reflected in the worship of the great earth goddess, Coatlicue, and the goddess of maize, Xilonen, who also protected the home.

Below the macehuales were the *mayeques,* mostly conquered peoples who lived as tenant farmers on the nobles' estates; like serfs, they were bound to the land, but they were also subject to military service. At the bottom of Aztec society were slaves, whose ranks were filled by captives, debtors, thieves, and conspirators. Aztec slaves could acquire possessions, including slaves of their own, and purchase their own freedom. Manumission was automatic if an escaped slave took sanctuary in the royal palace. The children of male slaves and free women were born free. Aztec slavery was less restrictive than that later practiced in the United States.

Families, each of which paid a dowry, arranged Aztec marriages. If the girl's family expected compensation for the loss of a household helper and a potential potter or weaver, the boy's parents had to do without their son's services as a worker or a soldier who would bring home plunder. After marriage the couple's relatives helped them build and furnish their house. Husbands and wives were expected to be faithful: husbands physically punished wives accused of immorality, and prostitution was permitted only in military camps. Prostitutes were strangled as soon as they showed signs of illness or weakness, and their corpses were thrown into the swamps.

The Gods of Human Sacrifice

The final segment of Aztec society comprised the priests. Entry to the priesthood was open to commoners, and even the two highest priests did not have to possess noble blood. Priests operated religious schools in which they educated future priests as well as the nobility, and they marched in the vanguard of the Aztec armies, possibly engaging in the fighting. Although required to be celibate, they were free to leave the priesthood and marry. The priests spent much of their time involved in soothsaying as they tried to answer the myriad questions posed to them by the people, including queries about whom to marry. So great was the demand for their services that soothsaying specialists had developed by the end of the fifteenth century. A third priestly duty involved their responsibility to control foreign deities, a task they performed by studying the idols of conquered peoples at Tenochtitlán and subordinating them to their own gods in a conscious act of religious imperialism.

Aztec priests are best known for their role in human sacrifice, a ritual previously practiced by the Olmecs, the Maya, the people of Teotihuacán, and the Toltecs, but never on the massive scale of the Aztecs. The dedication of the great temple at Tenochtitlán in 1487 included the sacrifice of between 20,000 and 80,000 prisoners, three entire tribes captured for the purpose in central Mexico. Four columns of prisoners stood in lines stretching $2^1/_2$ miles waiting for two priests to rip their hearts from their bodies; the exhausted priests finally collapsed. During the last decades of Aztec rule at least 15,000 humans a year were ritually sacrificed. The Aztecs met the demand for victims by conquest, thus placing a premium on capturing rather than slaying their foes. When the Aztecs confronted the Spaniards, this put them at a decided disadvantage.

Two factors explain the Aztecs' practice of sacrificing humans on such a scale. In part this stemmed from their conviction that the deities—especially Huitzilopochtli, the tribal warrior god and representative of the sun—responded primarily to nourishment rather than to prayer, more traditional rituals, or asceticism. Without such nourishment the "fifth sun," under which the Aztecs thought they lived, would perish, ending sunlight and with it the world. The analogy was simple and direct: "Just as men go to the market to find their warm tortillas so shall our god come to market with his army,

An Aztec priest removes the heart of a sacrificial victim.

Human Sacrifice

This description of Aztec sacrifices was written by Bernard Díaz del Castillo, who accompanied Cortés to Tenochtitlán in 1519. The victims are captured members of Cortés' expedition.

When we had retired almost to our quarters, across a great opening full of water, their arrows, darts, and stones could no longer reach us. . . . The dismal drum . . . sounded again, accompanied by conches, horns, and trumpet-like instruments. It was a terrifying sound, and . . . we saw our comrades who had been captured in Cortes' defeat being dragged up the steps to be sacrificed. When they had hauled them up to a small platform in front of the shrine where they kept their accursed idols we saw them put plumes on the heads of many of them; and then they made them dance with a sort of fan. . . . Then after they had danced the [Aztecs] laid them down on their backs on some narrow stones of sacrifice and, cutting open their chests, drew out their palpitating hearts which they offered to the idols before them. Then they kicked the bodies down the steps, and the Indian butchers who were waiting below cut off their arms and legs and flayed their faces, which they afterwards prepared like glove leather, with their beards on, and kept for their drunken festivals. Then they ate their flesh with a sauce of peppers and tomatoes. They sacrificed all our men in this way, eating their legs and arms, offering their hearts and blood to their idols as I have said, and throwing their trunks and entrails to the lions and tigers and serpents and snakes that they kept in the wild-beast houses.

Source: J. J. Norwich, ed., *A Taste for Travel* (London: Macmillan, 1986), p. 305.

to buy sacrifices and human beings, which he can eat."[1] No less important was the use of human sacrifice to strike terror into the Aztecs' enemies, whether soldiers seized in battle, unsuccessful generals, corrupt administrators, or slaves. The Aztecs ate the arms and legs of their victims, not for normal sustenance but as part of a religious ritual, a communion with the gods, and donated the hearts and blood to their deities.

Montezuma II and the Decline of the Aztecs

The reign of Montezuma II, who succeeded his uncle as emperor in 1502, provides an intriguing case study of imperial conquest, human sacrifice, and despotic rule. An autocratic, imposing man, his skill as a military commander and his status as a priest in the temple of Huitzilopochtli won him the crown, but 17 years later Aztec power had so weakened that the Spaniards were able to overrun much of his empire. Four principal reasons accounted for this, all of which stemmed from Montezuma's attempt to consolidate and stabilize his realm. First, although Montezuma conquered the Mixtecs in Oaxaca and won other victories, these brought in less wealth than previous Aztec campaigns. He expended effort as well to repress rebellion within the empire, again with no significant material gain other than fresh supplies of humans for the altars of Tenochtitlán. Second, under Montezuma the long-standing rivalries with the neighboring Tlaxcaltecs and Tarascans intensified, increasing military expenditures with nothing to show for them but more captives.

The third factor involved a loss of confidence in Montezuma's regime occasioned by the outbreak of a major famine in 1505 and the policies Montezuma implemented to deal with it. Since 1454 the Aztecs, trying to cope with an expanding population, had gone to great lengths to prevent famine through massive public works projects that entailed the subjugation of millions of people. In 1505 it became apparent that these efforts were inadequate to protect even the privileged population of Tenochtitlán. Unable to meet the needs of his people from outsiders, Montezuma demanded increased tribute from neighboring city-states in the valley of Mexico, prompting revolt.

Finally, within Tenochtitlán itself Montezuma's consolidation measures provoked discontent. As the conquests and the accompanying patronage diminished, Montezuma removed from their posts all high officials who were not of noble blood and executed many, thereby making more room for the hereditary nobility. By blocking the advancement of men of talent to high office, he rigidified the class structure. Merchants who were critical of Montezuma, in part because of growing restrictions on their trade, had their property confiscated, and they too were sometimes killed. Montezuma distributed some of their property to old soldiers in a bid for popular support. This was also the reason behind his abolition of slavery for debt, which had mushroomed because of the famine; this step won him acclaim among the poorer peasants.

Montezuma tried to disguise his increasingly despotic rule by depicting himself as a god-king. Those approaching him did so with head and eyes lowered, and his chief advisers could eat in his presence only if they stood and did not look at him. As he moved through the streets, his people had to stand motionless and stare at the ground. When Cortés observed all this, he remarked that the customs of the royal court were more splendid than those of an Asian potentate. Yet never did Montezuma enjoy absolute power; he could not launch military campaigns without the approval of his war council, though it was reduced in most respects to an advisory role.

The Spanish arrived in Tenochtitlán on November 8, 1519, the ease of their entry made possible in part by Montezuma's uncertainty as to whether or not Cortés was the returning deity Quetzalcoatl; playing it safe, he sent Cortés the regalia of Quetzalcoatl and two other gods. Although Montezuma died in an Amerindian uprising a year later, the empire lasted until 1521. Dissension within the Aztec empire alone cannot account for the collapse. Although the Aztecs were so despised by some of their Mexican neighbors, including the Tlaxcaltecs, that the latter refused to join them against the Spaniards, others, including the people of Tula, sustained heavy losses fighting the Europeans. The Spanish also possessed superior weapons—artillery in the early battles, swords and crossbows in the later ones. In August 1521 the Spaniards razed Tenochtitlán, ending Aztec rule.

Early Peru: The Chavín Culture

By 2500 B.C. the inhabitants of fishing villages on the Peruvian coast had begun to raise cotton, squash, beans, and guavas. Approximately 500 years later these communities developed into chiefdoms, their centers dominated by large, presumably ceremonial buildings. Typically, these centers had populations of about 1,500 and were surrounded by smaller villages—a pattern later used by

The Famine of 1454

The following account describes the 1454 famine. Food shortages subsequently plagued the Aztecs.

In this year of disaster there was widespread death and thirst. And then there arrived . . . frightful packs of boars, poisonous snakes, and vultures as well. And the hunger was so great that the imperial Mexicans sold themselves, and others hid themselves away in the forest, where they lived as wood people. In that region there was nothing to eat for all of four years, so that two separate parties of the Mexicans sold themselves into slavery. It was mainly to buy slaves that the Totonacs came to Mexico with maize. . . . Before that the Mexicans had not used maize to make loaves. They crawled into holes and died anywhere. The vultures then ate them, and no one buried them.

Source: G. Brotherston, ed., *Image of the New World: The American Continent Portrayed in Native Texts* (London: Thames & Hudson, 1979), p. 213.

the Maya. At the largest of these sites, El Paraíso, archaeologists have found the remains of huge masonry platforms that were once part of a temple complex. To build these platforms, workers from nearby villages quarried and transported 100,000 tons of rock, whether by forced or voluntary labor is unknown.

Around 1800 B.C. these communities began to expand inland. The greatest of the new settlements was begun at Chavín de Huantár around 850 B.C. Some 10,600 feet above sea level in the north Peruvian Andes, Chavín was a ceremonial center, like San Lorenzo and La Venta in Mesoamerica. The buildings consisted of temple platforms containing interlinked galleries and chambers on different levels. In the oldest part of the complex was a stele depicting one of the two main Chavín deities, the Smiling God, a figure in the form of a jaguar-man with catlike fangs and locks of hair shaped like snakes. The other Chavín deity, also with feline-human features but holding staffs in his hands, has been dubbed the Staff God. Lintels, gateways, and cornices were decorated with similar carvings, and stone human and jaguar heads were fastened on the outside wall of one of the temple platforms. The prominence of the jaguar in the Chavín cult has led some scholars to suspect that it was an offshoot of Olmec religion; a few suspect Chinese influence.

Chavín stirrup-spout vessel, ceramic, fifth to second century B.C.

Over the succeeding centuries the Chavín cult spread throughout central and northern Peru, both in the mountains and on the coast. Chavín motifs and jaguar designs appear on the pottery and textiles of this region. Whether people embraced the new faith by choice or compulsion is not known, but the most likely explanation is that it was linked with maize crops and spread as more people began raising corn. Like the Olmecs in Mesoamerica, the Chavín cult served as a unifying force and influenced the art and religion of later Peruvian peoples. Chavín culture had vanished by 300 B.C. for unknown reasons.

The Inca

The history of the Inca in South America paralleled the development and collapse of Aztec civilization in Mexico. Like their contemporaries to the north, the Inca dominated their neighbors to form a sizable empire under authoritarian rule, but it too would fall quickly to European conquerors. Shortly after Cortés' conquest of Mexico, another Spanish soldier of fortune, Francisco Pizarro, arrived in Peru. The Inca empire he found there in 1527 stretched along the Pacific coast and through the Andes Mountains to central Chile, covering an area of more than a million square miles—twice the combined size of France, Spain, and Italy—and embracing a population estimated at between 6 and 16 million. Unlike the major civilizations of Mesoamerica, that of the Inca was not urban. Most people lived in villages or small towns that seldom had more than 1,000 inhabitants, and even Cuzco, the capital, housed only the court and a number of priests.

The most powerful of all South American peoples, the Inca passed on their history verbally from generation to generation by means of professional memorizers. The Spanish-written versions of these traditional accounts form the basis for a study of Inca history, but they need to be treated with care, since the oral tradition of the Inca produced a selective version of the facts to buttress the power of the ruling classes, and the Spanish accounts are often inconsistent.

The Rise of the Inca

The Andes region, where the Inca originated, has varied resources. Fertile river valleys supported the cultivation of maize, beans, peppers, squash, and tomatoes; potatoes grew on the slopes; and the high mountain

THE EARLY AMERICAS

	Mesoamerica	Peru	North America
before 300 B.C.	Olmecs (c. 1500 B.C.–c. A.D. 1)	Chavín culture (c. 850–c. 300 B.C.)	Adena and Hopewell cultures (c. 800 B.C.–c. A.D. 600)
300 B.C.–A.D. 100			Mogollon culture (c. 300 B.C.–A.D. 1350)
100–750	Dominance of Teotihuacán (c. 100–c. 750) Maya empire (c. 100–909)		Beginning of Anasazi culture (c. 300) Beginning of Mississippian culture (c. 500–600)
750–1300	Toltecs (c. 750–c. 1150)		Navaho migration (after 1000) Apache migration (c. 1200)
1300–1600	Aztecs (c. 1325–1521)	Inca expansion (c. 1350–1493) Fall of Cuzco (1533)	Founding of the Iroquois League (c. 1570–1600)

plateaus provided grazing land for llamas and alpacas. The early Inca were nomads who settled throughout the Cuzco valley, moving from village to village in search of fertile land. Legend colors the history of the early rulers, but archaeological evidence confirms that the mid-fourteenth century was marked by Inca expansion beyond the Cuzco valley. The cause may have been related to a global weather change in the mid-fourteenth century, a period known as the Little Ice Age. A diminution of rainfall in the Andes area prompted the Inca to seek land elsewhere. At the same time, they began to raid more distant peoples in search of plunder. By the mid-fifteenth century such casual raids had been converted into a policy of conquest.

Subdued territories were governed by Inca officials and garrisons. Family rivalries within the ruling class led to further conquest, and the Emperor Topa Inca Yupanqui (1471–1493), one of the most powerful Inca rulers, led his armies into what is now the Peruvian coast, highland Bolivia, northern Chile, Ecuador, and most of northwestern Argentina. The last years of his reign were spent traveling throughout the territory he had conquered, establishing local administrations and organizing systems of tribute.

State and Society Under the Inca

Inca society was highly stratified. The noblest aristocrats claimed descent from an emperor and were called "Inca by blood." The emperor, who ruled by divine right, was allegedly descended from Inti, the sun god, and his mummified body became the object of a cult after his death. Like the Egyptian pharaohs, he married his sister but simultaneously had many wives and concubines. In an attempt to ensure a peaceful succession, one of the emperor's sons was crowned during his father's lifetime. He was expected to construct his own palace and appoint his own servants. When the reigning monarch died, his widows, concubines, and servants, all thoroughly inebriated, were killed, which had the practical effect of reducing the opportunities for opposition against the new ruler. As in Montezuma II's reign among the Aztecs, Inca sovereigns demanded extreme forms of deference, including the duty of subjects to kneel and avert their gaze as they passed, a requirement also imposed by Japanese emperors on their subjects. Even the advisers of an Inca ruler had to speak to him through a screen. In theory, his authority was limitless, but in practice custom undoubtedly imposed restraints.

Inca government was hierarchical. Immediately beneath the emperor, from whom all authority derived, were the four prefects of the principal territories of the empire. Often members of the imperial family, they lived in Cuzco, from where they supervised the work of the provincial governors, typically drawn from the hereditary Inca nobility. The chieftains beneath them were generally Inca nobles or leaders of the states the Inca had conquered. The sons of the latter were often taken to Cuzco to be trained in administration, thereby providing a constant supply of personnel while guaranteeing their fathers' loyalty. At the bottom of the bureaucracy were men selected for their ability, but all positions in the upper levels of the government were reserved for those of aristocratic birth.

The central government imposed two forms of taxation. The first consisted of service in the army or labor on public works projects; the second, called the *mit'a*, involved agricultural work, either in the fields or tending

Inca Royal Marriages

Marriage customs and the status of concubines at the Inca court were described by Pedro Cieza de Léon, who participated in the Spanish campaigns against the Inca and then spent three years interviewing the Inca before writing a book on their culture.

It was ordained by them that he who became king should take his sister, being the legitimate daughter of his father and mother, as his wife, in order that the succession of the kingdom might by that means be confirmed in the royal house. It appeared to them that by this means, even if such a woman, being sister of the king, should not be chaste, and should have intercourse with another man, the son thus born would still be hers, and not the son of a strange woman. They also considered that if the Inca married a strange woman, she might do the same and conceive in adultery, in such a way that, it not being known, the child would be received as a natural born son of the lord. For these reasons, and because it seemed desirable to those who ordained the laws, it was a rule among the Incas that he amongst them all who became emperor should take his sister to wife. . . . If by chance he who became lord had no sister, it was permitted that he should marry the most illustrious lady there was, and she was held to be the principal among all his women. For none of these lords had less than 700 women for the service of their house and for their pleasure. So that they all had many children by these women, who were well treated, and respected by the people.

Source: Pedro Cieza de Léon, *The Second Part of the Chronicle of Peru,* trans. and ed. C. R. Markham (London: Hakluyt Society, 1883), pp. 26–27.

flocks, manufacturing, or mining. The Inca had no medium of exchange, unlike the Indians of Mesoamerica, who used the cacao bean. People paid taxes and tribute in kind. Portions of the crops and manufactured goods went into state warehouses for use by the government, the nobility, and the army, but the state also stored reserves to feed the people in times of famine, as in China.

The army enforced public order. Numbering 200,000, with auxiliary labor and supply units, it was efficient and disciplined. Permanent garrisons maintained order, and revolts met with fierce reprisals. The skulls of rebels were fashioned into drinking cups, and drums were made from their skins. Rebellious peoples faced transportation to more distant parts of the empire, and docile subjects received their lands. As the empire expanded, rebellions became more common, and many of the peoples whom the Inca conquered later supported the Spanish.

The need for soldiers and workers was such that the state required marriage and endorsed polygamy. Young people who neglected to take mates had them selected by

The Inca city of Machu Picchu was built around the time of the arrival of the Spanish.

local officials, who annually paired off young men and women as they lined up in village plazas. The marriage ceremony involved the joining of hands (a custom also popular among European peasants) and the exchange of sandals. At the ensuing wedding feast the bride and groom each received two sets of clothing from the government, one for everyday use and the other for special occasions. The major exception to the principle of required marriage involved the "chosen women." Each year several thousand attractive girls aged 8 or 9 were selected for entry to temple schools that trained them for approximately five years in domestic activities and the performance of religious rites. Later taken to Cuzco, some became imperial concubines or wives of the nobles, but most received assignments to temples and were called Virgins of the Sun.

Among Inca achievements was the creation of a network of paved roads that spanned nearly 19,000 miles and linked the provincial centers to the capital. As an engineering achievement, they surpassed the roads of the Roman Empire or anything constructed in Europe until the Napoleonic Age. Two main roads ran from north to south through the empire, one along the coast and the other in the highlands; several crossovers connected the two. Suspension and pontoon bridges spanned rivers, tunnels shortened distances, and stone steps or zigzags enabled travelers to navigate steep slopes. Every few miles there was a storehouse or shelter. Government runners posted along the roads carried messages or goods, but access to the roads was limited, since the Inca rulers discouraged mobility. The roads were constructed primarily for people on foot and animal traffic, since the Inca did not use wheeled vehicles.

The Inca had no system of writing, yet they maintained records concerning troops, work forces, and other bureaucratic matters. They did this with a special group of officials, each of whom memorized the details for which he was responsible by using knotted cords. To a main rope or string were attached smaller strings of varying colors; the judicious use of sets of these strings in combination with knots enabled the officials to keep detailed records. The same officials memorized Inca history and myths. The Inca measured time by a calendar that divided the year into 12 months of 30 days grouped into ten-day weeks. They devoted the remaining five days to religious ceremonies at the middle and end of the year.

Much of Inca culture centered around religious ritual, which involved an elaborate priesthood and nearly omnipresent temples, shrines, and holy places. All peoples of the empire had to worship the state deities, the highest of which, the sun god, was the ancestor of the royal family. The Inca incorporated the gods of conquered tribes into the state religion, making it possible for subject peoples to continue worshiping familiar deities. The priests sacrificed humans, but normally only on such occasions as the coronation of a new ruler or the commencement of a military campaign. Boys and girls around ten years of age were taken to Cuzco for a special ritual and then returned to the provinces to be sacrificed.

The Decline of the Inca

On the eve of the Spaniards' arrival, feuds once again racked the Inca royal family. Atahualpa (1532–1533) challenged his brother, Emperor Huáscar (1525–1532). The latter maintained control of the southern part of the empire, while his brother ruled Ecuador and parts of northern Peru. In the ensuing civil war Atahualpa's troops defeated the imperial army outside Cuzco in April 1532, capturing Huáscar and executing his entire family as well as his generals and officials. Within months Atahualpa, who assumed that Pizarro was the creator-god Viracocha, fell victim to the Spaniards and was strangled. After a brief interval, Pizarro and his men began conquering the Inca empire, capturing Cuzco in November 1533. By 1535 the Spaniards drove the last rulers of the Inca into the remote mountains of the interior, where their independent state lasted until 1572.

Like the Aztecs, the Inca, weakened by internal strife and perhaps territorially overextended, proved easy victims for the better-armed Spanish. Their conquest marked the beginning of the subjugation of South America and its indigenous peoples. Nonetheless, vestiges of earlier times survive within westernized forms. In particular, popular Christianity has preserved something of the color and fervor of pre-Hispanic times, and in the remoter regions tribes continue to speak a language descended from Incan.

The Amerindians of North America

None of the hundreds of Amerindian tribes that settled throughout what is now the United States and Canada achieved civilization on the magnitude of the Maya, the Aztecs, or the Inca, but at least some of them developed impressive cultures. As early as 3000 B.C. Amerindians in what is now southwestern Florida established the first known permanent coastal villages in North America; the residents ate fish, shellfish, wild grains, berries, and nuts and buried their dead in ceremonial mounds more than

20 feet high. Most Amerindians north of the Rio Grande lived in relatively small temporary settlements. Virtually all of them hunted and fished, although the relative absence of large game in the southwest meant that the early tribes in that region concentrated on gathering wild foods. In time agriculture developed as the knowledge of crop raising spread northward from Mesoamerica. The men typically cleared the fields (often by burning) while the women tended the crops. Some tribes began constructing sizable permanent settlements, especially in the Ohio, Mississippi, and Rio Grande valleys.

The Ohio Valley: The Adena and Hopewell Cultures

The Adena and Hopewell cultures were the creation of a large, complex Amerindian population who lived between 800 B.C. and A.D. 600 or later. Both were centered in what is now Kentucky and Ohio, though the influence of the somewhat later Hopewell culture extended from New York to the Gulf Coast and from eastern Kansas and Nebraska to the western Carolinas. The Adena people lived in round houses constructed of poles covered with woven mats, with thatched roofs, whereas the Hopewell Amerindians built round or oval houses of posts, with coverings of skins, bark, mats, or clay and thatch. Both societies expended great effort on burials, the Adena placing their dead in conical earthen mounds surrounded by earthen ramparts as much as 500 feet in diameter. Often the deceased had first been cremated, and the remains, at least of the important people, were interred with carved stone tablets, lumps of pigment, stone smoking pipes, polished stones, and similar items. Hopewellian practices were similar but sometimes grander, at least for important persons.

Based on these rather elaborate burial practices and evidence of public works projects, archaeologists believe that the Hopewell rulers controlled a sizable population. The ceremonial center at Newark, Ohio, for instance, occupied 4 square miles. The food supply must have been adequate, although there is little evidence that maize was grown. Instead the people relied on nuts, wild grapes, and plants now considered weeds as well as fish and game. The Hopewell people either traded with or possibly extracted tribute from other Amerindians extending throughout much of what is now the United States, importing obsidian from Wyoming, copper from the northern Great Lakes, shells from the Gulf Coast, and mica (used to create silhouettes) from the southern Appalachians. In return they exported tools, figurines, pottery, and copper ornaments.

A stone pipe from the Adena culture of the Ohio River valley.

The Mississippian Culture

Around A.D 500 or 600 the Mississippi valley saw the development of another major culture, the origins of which are still under investigation. These people lived in wattle-and-daub (clay over lath) houses of varying shapes in large villages. Influenced by the cultures of Mesoamerica, they raised maize, beans, and squash and embraced a religion with planting rituals. They sometimes buried their dead in distinctive pyramidal mounds with flat tops; the pyramids were arranged around plazas, often with palisades or earthworks surrounding the entire complex. The largest of these, at Cahokia, Illinois (near St. Louis), was gradually built up between about 900 and 1150; with a base of more than 18 acres, it reached a height of 100 feet. Altogether 85 mounds have been found at Cahokia, where the village was some 6 miles long. Burials could also be in cemeteries, in urns, or even beneath the floors of homes. Burial practices and domestic architecture indicate considerable variations in Mississippian culture. Eventually this culture dominated much of the southeast and midwest, remaining influential through the seventeenth century.

Around the thirteenth century some Mississippian communities developed a highly ritualistic religion

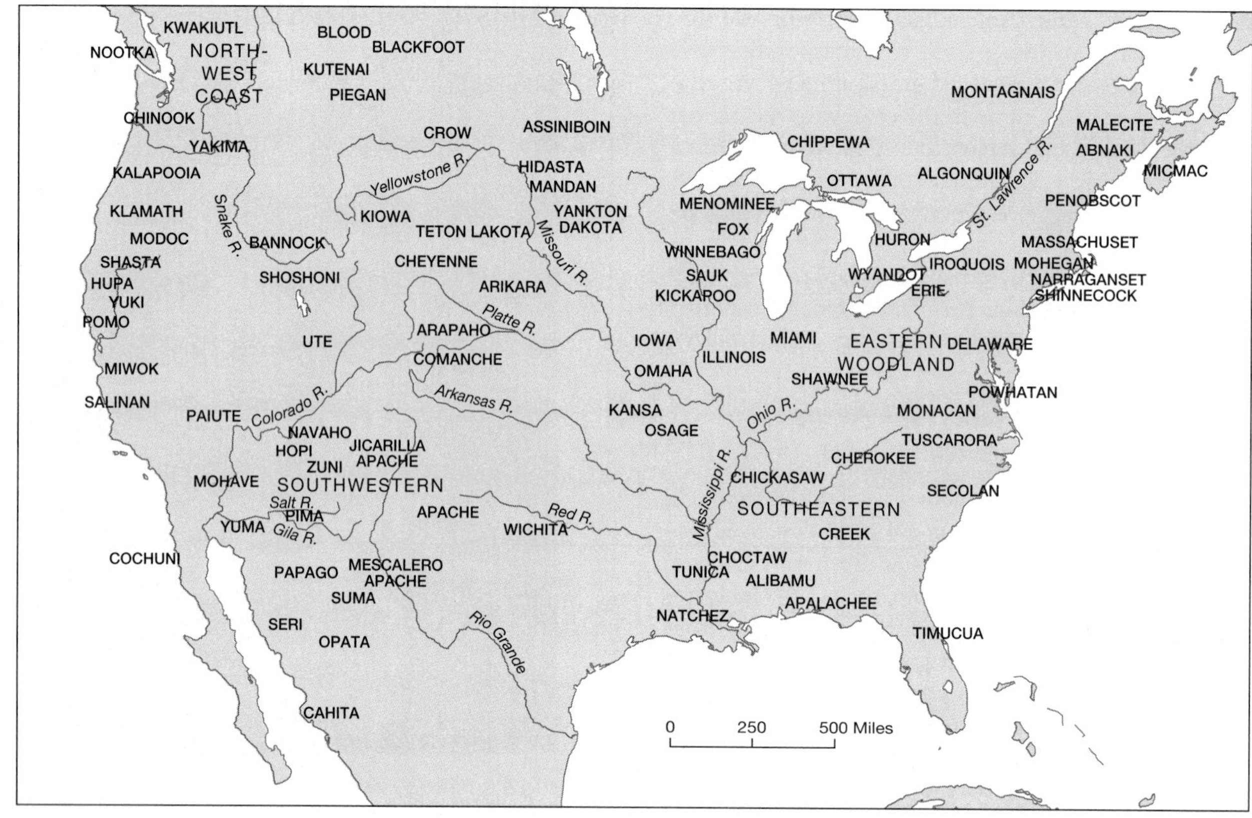

MAP 10.4 AMERINDIAN TRIBES, C. 1500

scholars have called the Southern Cult. They worshiped in large temples filled with such ceremonial objects as copper plates, maces, and monolithic stone axes. Among the most common symbols were the cross, the sun disk, an arrow flanked by semicircles, a human hand with an eye in the palm, and a sunburst. Artists influenced by this cult engraved mythological scenes depicting such exotic creatures as bird-people, animal deities, and plumed and winged rattlesnakes. Effigy jars often have depictions of human faces, sometimes with painted designs or tattoos, and others show the heads of sacrificial victims. Here too human sacrifice was practiced, possibly including infants. The artifacts point to a cult that apparently had a sophisticated mythology and served the needs of a well-developed society.

The Southwest: The Mogollon, Hohokam, and Anasazi Cultures

The Amerindians of the American southwest shared one basic cultural tradition, albeit with regional variants. Each group grew maize, beans, and squash; used masonry in building its homes; and crafted superb pottery. After about 1100 A.D. even the differences faded through cultural interchange as people migrated. The fact that two of the southwestern cultures—the Hohokam and Anasazi—existed primarily on farming in a region inhospitable to it because of the water shortages indicates that they were technologically advanced.

The earliest of the three major Amerindian cultures of the southwest, the Mogollon, existed from about 300 B.C. to A.D. 1350. The heart of Mogollon territory was southwestern New Mexico. Mogollon villages, typically scattered along the summits of ridges, generally consisted of large underground ceremonial buildings and pit houses. By the eleventh century these Amerindians were constructing towns on level ground. More than other contemporary Amerindians, they based their existence fairly equally on hunting, gathering, and agriculture, probably because of the difficulties of farming in this area. Over the long course of their history they displayed little interest in innovation; Mogollon culture was highly conservative. Some scholars believe that the modern Zuni are descendants of the Mogollon.

Hohokam culture, which developed slightly later than the neighboring Mogollon, was centered in the Salt and Gila valleys. These Amerindians too lived in pit houses, though of a different type; unlike the Mogollon, who simply put a roof over a hole, they built entire houses inside the pits. The principal Hohokam achievement was the construction of a vast network of irrigation canals, using dams to channel water from the Salt and Gila rivers. Some canals extended more than 30 miles and were as much as 6 to 10 feet deep and 15 to 30 feet wide. Construction and maintenance of the canals required a large workforce and indicates effective social organization. The influence of Mesoamerican cultures on the Hohokam is manifest in their stepped pyramids and ball courts. The modern descendants of the Hohokam, the Pima and Papago Amerindians, live in Arizona.

The Mogollon and Hohokam cultures may have influenced the Anasazi or Pueblo cultures, which emerged around A.D 300, although the Anasazi are more remarkable for their unique development. Their earliest homes—beehive domes constructed of logs and mud mortar—were unlike anything created by contemporary Amerindians, as were their elaborate storage chambers; they grew a different variety of maize; and their pottery, unlike that of the Hohokam and Mogollon but similar to the Mississippian, was flamboyant in design. Sometime after 700 the Anasazi began growing cotton and weaving on looms. Their religious rites included ceremonies to repel storms and crop damage and encourage fertility. By the eleventh century they too had begun to build towns, the characteristic feature of which were homes constructed in the shape of squares, ells, or semicircles. In succeeding years they used mud, stone, and wood to build impressive cliff dwellings and terraced apartment houses. The largest one, containing some 500 units, was the biggest residential building in North America until an apartment complex built in New York City in 1882. To grow crops they used both flood irrigation (by terracing the hills and erecting dikes) and subsurface irrigation (by constructing sand dunes at the foot of hills to hold runoff and disperse it slowly to small garden patches). At the peak of their influence Anasazi culture extended as far north as the present Idaho-Colorado border, but by 1300 the Pueblo Amerindians had been forced southward by drought, fighting between towns, and the arrival of the Navaho and Apache. Descendants of the Anasazi still live in northern New Mexico and Arizona and parts of Utah and Colorado.

These cliff dwellings at Mesa Verde, Colorado, were constructed by the Anasazi around 1200.

Later Native Cultures of North America

Well before Europeans began exploring North America, other Amerindians resettled, often coming under the influence of the cultures just described. The Navaho, now the largest Amerindian tribe in the United States, migrated from the north to the southwest, possibly as early as the eleventh century, after which they borrowed heavily from the Pueblo. Somewhat later the Apache, who are close linguistic relatives of the Navaho, also began migrating to the southwest, and by the late sixteenth century they had settled in parts of what is now Arizona, Colorado, and New Mexico; both the Pueblo and the Navaho have influenced them. Another major tribe, the Mandan, who would later be prominent in the fur trade, had moved from the east to the Missouri valley by the fourteenth century. In fact, Amerindians inhabited all regions of what is now the United States, however sparsely, by 1500.

Two Amerindian groups can be singled out for their advanced forms of political organization, surpassing the loosely knit confederations previously established by various earlier tribes, including the Huron. In the southeast the Creeks organized a confederacy that united their towns according to essentially democratic principles. The towns were grouped into two divisions, the red and the white, and peace was maintained within the confederation by ball games played by towns in opposite divisions. To the north, in what is now western New York, the Iroquois developed a well-organized military confederacy, known as the Iroquois League, that impressed Europeans. According to tradition, it was founded between 1570 and 1600 with the aid of Hiawatha for the purpose of promoting peace, law, and righteousness among the five Amerindian nations that were its original members. The Dekanawidah epic, which was transmitted orally from generation to generation, records the story of its founding.

The Iroquois Remedy for Anarchy

The following article, from the Iroquois Ritual of Condolence, was recited when one of the chiefs of the member nations of the confederacy died and was replaced. The key point is that death threatens unity, the cure for which is order and compassion.

Is not what has befallen thee then so dreadful that it must not be neglected? For, at the present time, there are wrenchings without ceasing within thy breast, and also within thy mind. Now truly, the disorder now among the organs within thy breast is such that nothing can be clearly discerned. So great has been the affliction that has befallen thee that yellow spots have developed within thy body, and truly thy life forces have become greatly weakened thereby; truly thou dost now suffer. . . . In ancient times it thus came to pass that the Federal Chiefs, our grandsires, made a formal rule, saying, "Let us unite our affairs; let us formulate regulations; let us ordain this among others that what we shall prepare we will designate by the name Water-of-pity or compassion which shall be the essential thing to be used where Death has caused this dreadful affliction, inducing bitter grief."

Source: G. Brotherston, ed., *Image of the New World: The American Continent Portrayed in Native Texts* (London: Thames & Hudson, 1979), p. 252.

The Far North: Inuit, Aleuts, and Athabaskans

The origin of the Inuit (Eskimos) is disputed, with some scholars suggesting that they are descendants of a very early maritime people and others contending that they evolved in Alaska after the last ice age. Linguistically, the Inuit are related to the Aleuts, whose origin is similarly disputed. Both groups, which diverged at least 4,000 years ago, are more closely related, both physically and linguistically, to Asians than are the Amerindians. Whereas the Aleuts confined themselves largely to what we now call the Alaska peninsula and the Aleutian islands, the Inuit spread themselves thinly across a region extending from the Bering Strait to Greenland and as far south as the Yukon.

Both peoples supported themselves by hunting and fishing. In small kayaks made of skins the Aleuts hunted seals, sea lions, and otters, and they fished for salmon in the streams. The Inuit developed a more diverse economic base, hunting for both land and sea mammals and fishing in fresh and salt water. Caribou, musk-oxen, walruses, whales, and fish were the staples of the Inuit diet. In addition to kayaks, the Inuit transported themselves in canoes and on dogsleds. In the early centuries A.D. the Inuit developed a large skin boat known as an *umiak* that served as a floating platform from which they could hunt sea mammals with harpoons.

By the end of the first century B.C. the Inuit had constructed substantial settlements near the Bering Sea. One of these, near Cape Nome, Alaska, contained approximately 400 homes; the typical house was excavated up to 20 inches deep and covered with poles and sod for insulation against the arctic cold. Some communities included large buildings in which the Inuit performed religious rites under the direction of shamans who claimed the power to heal and to predict the future. Inuit artists carved elaborate harpoon heads, knife handles, and arrow points made from antlers and later from slate.

South of the vast expanse of tundra occupied by the Inuit stretched the subarctic boreal forest, with its spruce, birch, and poplar. This was the homeland of Amerindians who spoke Athabaskan languages and lived primarily as nomadic hunters. Their numbers were small—perhaps only 35,000 by the sixteenth century, owing probably to difficulties in finding and developing a dependable subsistence base. In this respect they were unlike the Inuit, with whom they normally had poor relations. For their food supplies the Athabaskans depended primarily on caribou and moose, though they also ate musk-ox, rabbit, and

This decorated object, thought to be a stabilizer for a spear shaft, was produced by an Inuit artist before 500.

fish. Whereas the Inuit could safely store their meat throughout the year because of permafrost, the Athabaskans had to smoke or dry theirs for use during the summer. They also ate berries, wild vegetables, sap, and the tender shoots of plants such as the willow.

The Athabaskans organized themselves into bands, each of which was a socioeconomic unit typically headed by a chief hunter. Kinship and dependency bound members together. Hunting was the province of the men, while women, children, and the elderly gathered fruits and vegetables or fished. Canoes, dogsleds, and snowshoes were the principal means of travel. The Athabaskans lived in tents made of skins and, during the winter, log huts. From antlers they fashioned arrowheads and dart points, and they used copper to manufacture knives and spearheads. The Athabaskans traded with the Eskimos to obtain bone and ivory knives. Athabaskan artists applied geometric designs to canoes, paddles, and moccasins and played music using drums and rattles made from caribou hooves. The Apache and Navaho who migrated into what is now the United States were part of the Athabaskan linguistic group.

SUMMARY

In the Americas as in Africa, prosperous and sophisticated civilizations developed well before the arrival of Europeans. Some of those in the Americas were larger than the states of Europe, just as Tenochtitlán was bigger than any European city. The more advanced societies of the Americas, like those in Africa, engaged in long-distance trade, the construction of colossal temples and pyramids, and the production of fine works of art. The social welfare program of the Inca was comparable to advanced Asian systems and generally superior to the treatment of the poor in Europe. The Amerindians demonstrated the ability to organize their societies for mammoth public works projects, including swamp drainage for the construction of Tenochtitlán and the extensive canals of the Hohokam. Not surprisingly, the Amerindian cultures impressed the Spaniards, just as the coastal cities of Africa impressed the Portuguese. The once popular tendency to regard the peoples of the Americas—and of Africa—as primitive natives in need of civilization was thus erroneous.

We must nevertheless avoid the temptation to lavish excessive praise on early American civilizations. Although Amerindians domesticated crops, many of which were later exported to Europe, they lagged significantly in the development of farming implements, preferring to use their metal primarily for ornaments rather than tools. Nor did they develop wheeled vehicles or substantial oceangoing vessels (as distinct from rafts and dugout canoes). The practice of human sacrifice by some Amerindian cultures was appalling by modern standards.

The study of the peoples of Africa and the Americas underscores much common experience. They developed from hunter-gatherers to farmers, which encouraged sedentary life, the gradual emergence of towns, the growth of a merchant class, and the expansion of trade. These developments also affected art and religion, as the upper classes obtained sufficient leisure to engage more extensively in such pursuits. Religious beliefs focused on the relationship between humans and the natural world, and the priesthood, which claimed unique powers to deal with the gods, grew in importance. The significance of religion to Africans and Amerindians, as to most other peoples, was reflected in their art and architecture as well as in their burial practices. Intriguing comparisons can also be made between Roman, Chinese, and Inca roads; the canals of Venice, China, and Tenochtitlán; the calendars of the Europeans and the Maya; the Vestal Virgins of Rome and the Inca Virgins of the Sun; and the pyramids of Egypt, Kush, and the Amerindians.

Europeans overran the Americas long before most of Africa, perhaps because the Amerindians, unlike many Africans, had been isolated from European culture before the arrival of Columbus. Aztec and Inca leaders were overawed by the Europeans, whereas Africans, who had long traded with outsiders, were not. The African continent, moreover, offered considerable protection to its peoples because of its deserts and rain forests and the difficulty of gaining access to the interior. Parts of Africa remained virtually untouched before the nineteenth century, whereas in the Americas the arrival of the Europeans produced massive changes that in a matter of decades substantially affected both conquered and conquerors.

NOTES

1. F. Katz, *The Ancient American Civilizations,* trans. K. M. L. Simpson (New York: Praeger, 1972), p. 164.

SUGGESTIONS FOR FURTHER READING

Brodo, J., Carrasco, D., and Moctezuma, E. M., eds. *The Great Temple of Tenochtitlán: Center and Periphery in the Aztec World.* Berkeley: University of California Press, 1987.

Cobo, B. *A History of the Inca Empire.* Austin: University of Texas Press, 1979.

Coe, M. D. *The Maya,* 4th ed. London: Thames & Hudson, 1987.

———. *Mexico,* rev. ed. London: Thames & Hudson, 1984.

Conrad, G. W., and Demarest, A. A. *Religion and Empire: The Dynamics of Aztec and Inca Expansionism.* Cambridge: Cambridge University Press, 1984.

D'Altroy, T. N. *The Incas.* Oxford: Blackwell, 1995.

Davies, N. *The Aztec Empire: The Toltec Resurgence.* Norman: University of Oklahoma Press, 1987.

———. *The Toltec Heritage.* Norman: University of Oklahoma Press, 1980.

———. *The Toltecs: Until the Fall of Tula.* Norman: University of Oklahoma Press, 1977.

Dumond, D. E. *The Eskimos and Aleuts,* rev. ed. London: Thames & Hudson, 1987.

Fagan, B. M. *The Great Journey: The Peopling of Ancient America.* London: Thames & Hudson, 1987.

Fiedel, S. J. *Prehistory of the Americas.* Cambridge: Cambridge University Press, 1987.

Hammond, N. *Ancient Maya Civilization.* New Brunswick, N.J.: Rutgers University Press, 1982.

Miller, M. E. *The Art of Mesoamerica: From Olmec to Aztec.* London: Thames & Hudson, 1986.

Morley, S. G., and Brainerd, G. W. *The Ancient Maya,* rev. R. J. Sharer. Stanford, Calif.: Stanford University Press, 1983.

Schele, L. *A Forest of Kings: The Untold Story of the Ancient Maya.* New York: Morrow, 1990.

———, and Miller, M. E. *The Blood of Kings: Dynasty and Ritual in Maya Art.* Fort Worth: Kimball Art Museum, 1986.

Smith, M. E. *The Aztecs.* Oxford: Blackwell, 1996.

Soustelle, J. *The Olmecs: The Oldest Civilization in Mexico.* Garden City, N.Y.: Doubleday, 1984.

Zantwijk, R. A. M. van. *The Aztec Arrangement: The Social History of Pre-Spanish Mexico.* Norman: University of Oklahoma Press, 1985.

CHAPTER 11

Medieval India and Southeast Asia

From the mid-tenth century, about 300 years after the collapse of the Gupta dynasty and the death of Harsha, North India endured a long period of disunion, conflict, and renewed invasions from central Asia. This era culminated in 1526 with the establishment of the Mughal Empire and a new flowering of unity and cultural brilliance. The medieval centuries of disorder and conquest, comparable in some ways to the situation in Europe after the decline of the western Roman Empire, were, however, in no way a period of universal disaster. Invasion and conquest were limited to relatively short periods of disturbance in the northern half of the subcontinent. Most people in most parts of India went on with their lives in the usual way most of the time. These centuries also saw the vigorous continuation of the Indian artistic tradition patronized by the Guptas and by Harsha, including the construction of a great many magnificent temples and their sculpture, especially in the south. Trade flourished, particularly with Southeast Asia; wealthy merchants subsidized temple complexes and the arts in the rich urban culture of medieval India, and great literature continued to be produced. The south remained largely peaceful, but in much of the north, invasion, conquest, and warfare brought periodic misery.

Early Islamic Influence

The new invaders from the north were part of the general expansion of Islam, and they brought with them an often harsh and intolerant version of the new religion. But they also brought Islamic and, in particular, Persian culture, including many educated Iranians, who served as

Goddess applying Kohl (dark coloring) around eyes. Part of frieze from the Parsunath Temple at Khajuraho in central India. This is representative of the plastic achievement of Indian rock sculpture (c. 1000 A.D.)

scribes for the largely illiterate conquerors as well as administrators, artists, writers, and other elites. India, with its wealth, numbers, and sophistication, was an irresistible target, and both Hinduism and Buddhism were seen as pagan creeds, to be conquered by the faith of the Prophet. The invaders' early motives and ruthless behavior were similar to those of the sixteenth-century Portuguese and Spanish invaders of Asia and Latin America in their search for riches, such as gold and spices, and for converts to Catholic Christianity. For the Muslim invaders of India, Hinduism, with its "idolatrous" worship of many gods, its tolerance, and its lack of precise scriptural doctrine, was seen as an evil to be eliminated. Their attitude to the closely related faith and practice of Buddhism was much the same. Probably the chief original motive for their invasion of India was, however, simple plunder. Many of these central Asian groups contented themselves at first with pillaging India's wealth and slaughtering "infidel" victims before withdrawing across the passes with their loot.

In time, however, Muslim kingdoms with a largely Persian courtly culture were established in much of northern India, which had far more to attract and support them than their dry, barren, and mountainous homelands. In time this new infusion of alien vigor blended with older strands of the Indian fabric.

Since the time of Ashoka and the first Buddhist missions (see Chapter 2), there has been a close connection between India and Southeast Asia. We know very little about Southeast Asian systems before this time. It is possible that Indian influence there began before Ashoka, but our earliest data for Southeast Asian kingdoms come from the centuries after his reign and show a political, literate, and religious or philosophical culture already Indianized. Following the Muslim conquest of northern India, Islam was also carried to insular Southeast Asia by converts among Indian traders. These and other aspects of Indian civilization were, however, overlaid onto a well-developed preexisting base whose character was distinctly different.

Indian and Chinese influences have continued to operate on Southeast Asia up to the present. But this immense area, which embraces the present-day nations of Burma, Thailand, Laos, Cambodia, Vietnam, Malaysia, Indonesia, and the Philippines, has retained, despite regional differences, its own indigenous social and cultural forms. These evolved separately before the coming of Indian and Chinese elements. Only writing and various literary, artistic, political, and religious forms came in from India, Vietnam, and China. The social base and most other aspects of culture were less affected and indeed helped shape many aspects of the new culture. The latter part of this chapter deals with the civilization of Southeast Asia during the medieval period, after the fall of the Gupta Empire in India, when we can see for the first time in any detail the evolution of separate kingdoms and cultures in that region.

Approaches to the Khyber Pass near the eastern border of Afghanistan. The Hindu Kush mountain range is a formidable barrier, but it is penetrable at several passes. Through them have come a long succession of invaders of India, including the Turco-Afghan carriers of Islam and various Persian cultures. This is also a sample of central Asian landscapes.

The Muslim Advance

India at first lay beyond the wave of Islamic conquests of the seventh century, which engulfed most of the Middle East and North Africa, but Arab traders continued to bring back samples of Indian wealth. Sind, the lower half of the Indus valley, was conquered by Arab forces in the eighth century, primarily as a rival trade base. But the major advance came nearly three centuries later, from the newly converted Turks of central Asia, who had been driven westward and into Afghanistan by earlier Chinese expansion under the Han and the T'ang dynasties.

The Turkish leader Mahmud of Ghazni (971–1030), known as the "Sword of Islam," mounted 17 plundering expeditions between 1001 and 1027 from his eastern Afghan base at Ghazni into the adjacent upper Indus and western Punjab, destroying Hindu temples, sacking rich cities, killing or forcibly converting the inhabitants, and then returning to Ghazni with jewels, gold, silver, women, elephants, and slaves. By the eleventh century his remote mountain-ringed capital became a great center of Islamic culture, thanks in part to stolen Indian riches. Pillage and slaughter in the name of God did not make a good impression for Islam among most Indians, but the austere new religion, with its promise of certainty and of equality, did appeal to some. And India attracted Mahmud's successors, as well as rival central Asian Turkish groups.

The military effectiveness of these invaders depended importantly on their mastery of cavalry tactics, true to their nomadic heritage, and their use of short, powerful compound bows of laminated wood, horn, and sinew that they could fire on horseback at a gallop. The Rajputs of Rajasthan, on the flank of the Islamic invasion route, fought relentlessly from their desert strongholds and fortified cities against these Turco-Afghan armies, which the more peaceful inhabitants of Hindustan were less able to resist. Some of the Rajputs had central Asian origins too, some centuries earlier, and hence shared an originally nomadic tradition of mounted, mobile warfare, but all Rajputs were part of a military culture of great tenacity, nurtured in the desert of Rajasthan. They were never completely overcome, but most of the rest of the north, seriously weakened by continual political division and internal conflict, was progressively conquered.

By the end of the twelfth century, Punjab and most of Hindustan (the valley of the Ganges) had been incorporated into a Turco-Afghan empire with its capital at Delhi. Delhi controlled an easy crossing place on the Jumna River where a range of hills stretched southwest and provided protection. Northward lay the barrier of the Himalayas; westward, the Thar Desert of Rajasthan. Eastward the broad Ganges valley led into the heart of Hindustan, but for access to it and for routes southward, Delhi had first to be secured; all invaders from the northwest, the repeated route of entry via the Punjab, were obliged to maintain control of Delhi. Bengal was overrun in 1202, and in 1206 the Delhi sultanate was formally inaugurated. As a series of successive Islamic dynasties, it was to dominate most of North India for the next 320 years, until the rise of the Mughal Empire in 1526.

Bengal had prospered as a separate kingdom after the fall of the Gupta order. It remained the chief Indian center of Buddhism, including a great university and monastery at Nalanda, where some 10,000 monks lived and studied, and similar Hindu centers of learning and piety. Both religions and their followers were targets for the Muslim invaders. Tens of thousands of monks and other Hindus and Buddhists were slaughtered and the universities and monasteries destroyed. This catastrophe marked the effective end of Buddhism in the land of its birth. The few surviving Buddhists fled from the slaughter to Nepal and Tibet. Hindu monuments also suffered, for they violated Islamic principles forbidding the artistic representation of divine creation, including the human form.

Unfortunately for its people, northern India remained hopelessly divided among rival kingdoms, most of them small and nearly all of them in chronic conflict. In total, their armies were huge, but they seem never to have considered a united or even partially united stand against the invaders who, like Alexander before them, defeated the forces sent against them one by one. Even after Mahmud and his successors had established their rule over most of the north, little opposition was organized against them or against their repeated efforts to spread their conquests southward into central India and the Deccan.

The Delhi Sultans

Successive Turco-Afghan rulers were more accepting, if not of Hinduism, then of Hindus, who remained the vast majority of the Indian population. But Hindus were treated as decidedly second-class citizens and forced to pay a special tax as "infidels" if they refused, as most did, to convert. This was an improvement on the atrocities of the earlier raiders and followed the original Islamic practice of recognizing in other established religions a justified but inferior status.

There was no shortage of Hindu religious texts, and it was not hard in time to accept Hinduism as a sophisticated religion, not simply as "paganism." With more knowledge it was also recognized that Hinduism was basically monotheistic, like Islam, and could not be judged only on the basis of the many gods of Indian folk religion. This distinction was comparable to that between unadorned Christianity and folk practice involving many saints and local cults, as, for example, in Latin America. The head tax (*jizya*) paid by protected non-Muslims (dhimmis) was heavy—about 6 percent of an individual's total net worth annually—but it bought a degree of freedom to practice one's own religion. Moreover, the later Delhi sultans agreed to leave many of the original Hindu Indian local rulers and petty rajas in control of their domains. The sultanate thus slowly became more an Indian order and less an alien occupation. It came in time to depend increasingly on the support of India's indigenous people and, under the best of its rulers, to try to govern rather than merely to exploit.

Raids and plundering expeditions went on under the stronger rulers of the Delhi sultanate into the Deccan,

MAP 11.1 MEDIEVAL INDIA

south of the Ganges plain of Hindustan, but no permanent position was ever won there or elsewhere in the south. The landscape favored the Hindu defenders, beginning with the double row of mountains that mark the northern edge of the Deccan—the Vindhya Mountains and the Satpura Range—and including the Narbada and Tapti rivers, which run, respectively, in the valleys south of each range.

The Deccan itself is deeply eroded and in many areas cut up into steep ravines and river valleys, with easily defended hills or smaller mountains in almost every part. It has seen many bloody campaigns but never a complete or permanent victory for any of the successive invaders from the north, including both the Delhi sultanate and the Mughal dynasty as well as the Guptas and Mauryas long before. The chief and most consistent Hindu de-

Marco Polo on India

Marco Polo visited South India on his way back from China by sea in 1293. Given his fulsome descriptions of the wealth and splendor of China, it is notable that he nevertheless called India "the noblest and richest country in the world." His account of what he saw and heard otherwise has the ring of truth and is easily recognizable as an accurate picture of many aspects of Indian society and culture.

The people go naked all the year round, for the weather here is always temperate. That is why they go naked, except that they cover their private parts with a scrap of cloth. The king wears no more than the others, apart from certain ornaments: a handsome loin cloth with a fringe set with precious stones, so that this scrap of cloth is worth a fortune. . . . It is his task every day, morning and evening, to say 104 prayers in honor of his idols. Such is the bidding of their faith and their religion. . . . He also wears bracelets of gold studded with precious stones, and three anklets adorned with costly pearls and gems.

Another of their customs is that they wash their whole body in cold water twice a day, morning and evening. . . . In this kingdom justice is very strictly administered to those who commit homicide or theft or any other crime. . . . It is a proof of the excellent justice kept by the king that when a nocturnal traveller wishes to sleep and has with him a sack of pearls or other valuables—for men travel by night rather than by day because it is cooler—he will put the sack under his head and sleep where he is; and no one ever loses anything by theft.

Source: R. Latham, trans., *The Travels of Marco Polo* (Baltimore: Penguin, 1959), pp. 233–252.

fenders against the Muslim attackers were the warlike Mahrathas of Maharashtra, the arid northwestern quarter of the Deccan. They were protected by their strategically located plateau base and its mountain fringes and, like the Rajputs, had a proud martial tradition of resisting northern invasions.

The Delhi sultanate was also weakened by internal power struggles and political intrigues, which similarly plagued their Ottoman Turkish cousins later in their far larger empire. Most of the Delhi sultans were absolute rulers who tolerated no dissent and demanded total submission; most of them consequently provoked chronic revolts and plots against them, and many died by assassination, by poisoning, or in the dust of a coup or a civil war. There was no agreed method of succession, and the death of each sultan was the occasion for fighting among rivals for power.

The armies of the sultans, like those of the Ottomans and other Turkish states, owed their strength in large part to mamelukes, usually Turks bought in their youth as slaves and then trained as full-time professional fighters. They were an outstandingly disciplined force, but like many lifetime mercenaries, they were not above an interest in power and its rewards. Their commanders were often formidable contenders for political power. The ruthlessness and frequent cruelty of many of the sultans provided additional motives for revolt.

In general, the sultanate succeeded only fitfully in becoming an effective administration for the areas it controlled in the north. The records we have tell of power rivalries, intrigues at court, taxation, coups, civil wars, and abortive efforts to invade the south, but we have little evidence of the effect of these affairs on the lives of ordinary people. Political power was highly concentrated in Delhi, leaving much of the sultanate's domains under local rulers who had a good deal of autonomy. It seems likely that after the first half century or so of ruthless plunder, conquest, slaughter, and intolerance, most people in North India were left largely to themselves as long as they paid both land taxes and the *jizya.*

The main impact of the sultanate on India was probably to implant a deep mistrust of politics, government in general, and Islam in particular, where it was used as the basis of state policy. Few monuments remain from this period of northern Indian history. In broader cultural terms, however, these centuries did witness a fusion of originally Hindu elements with the Iranian influences brought in by the Turkish conquerors. Like the Mughals who followed them, they were the agents of a largely Persian culture whose richness and variety found acceptance among many Indians. What we now think of as "traditional" Indian language, poetry, music, architecture, and painting in fact took their present forms from this fusion. Islam, and Hindu-Muslim differences, proved not to be either a bar to such cultural hybridization or a source of conflict, except where it was made an issue in political and military matters. Religious differences were ultimately far less important than other aspects of culture and proved no barrier to cultural mixing.

Islam was progressively Indianized, and over the centuries it won some converts on its own merits and through the agency of a long line of Sufi mystics (see Chapter 8) whose vision was broad enough to appeal to the Indian mystical tradition.

Ala-ud-din Khalji, Oppressive Sultan

The power of the Delhi sultans was severely tested by the Mongol invasion of the early fourteenth century. By this time the Turco-Afghan invaders had been partly Indianized, like so many conquerors before them, and depended more on the support of the indigenous people. It was fortunate that on the throne of Delhi was a capable ruler, Ala-ud-din Khalji (1296–1316), who, augmenting his forces with mameluke troops, drove the Mongol horsemen back into Afghanistan in a rare Mongol defeat. Ala-ud-din had usurped the throne by having his uncle murdered, after raiding the Deccan and bringing back loot, which he used to buy the loyalty of those around his uncle, Sultan Jalal-ud-din.

Ala-ud-din paid his army officers in cash and kept tight personal control over his forces. He could neither read nor write and had no tolerance for intellectuals, sophisticated courtiers, or other elites. He abolished all regular stipends and grants to the Muslim nobles, eliminating their political influence and leaving them wholly dependent on him. He outlawed wine-drinking parties, which were in any case against Muslim doctrine, fearing that revelers might plot against him. Ala-ud-din's power base was fueled by a land tax, which he raised to 50 percent of the value of each crop, and by new taxes on milk cows and houses. The crop tax tended to impoverish especially Hindus, most of whom were engaged in agriculture. Barani, the fourteenth-century Arab historian of India, quoted Ala-ud-din as saying:

> **I am an unlettered man, but I have seen a great deal. Be assured that Hindus will never become submissive and obedient until they have been reduced to poverty. I have therefore given orders that just enough shall be left them of grain, milk, and curds from year to year, but that they must not accumulate hoards or property.[1]**

Hindus were also forbidden to possess any weapons or to ride horses. Loyalty and conformity with the sultan's decrees were further ensured by a network of spies, harsh penalties, and intricate court duplicities. He also imposed wage and price controls in Delhi and prohibited the private hoarding of gold and silver, while at the same time requiring all merchants to be licensed and their profits restricted. Peasants could sell their crops only to licensed merchants and at set prices and could retain only fixed amounts for their own use. These measures kept most prices low enough to permit soldiers and workers to live adequately on their pay, at least in the Delhi area, though merchants and peasants everywhere resented them bitterly. But the controls and taxes made it possible for Ala-ud-din to field an army that could meet and repulse the Mongol invasion.

With the Mongols defeated, Ala-ud-din resumed his looting raids in the Deccan, overcoming even some of the Rajputs and penetrating briefly as far as Pandyan territory farther south. But at his death in 1316 not only these efforts but his own family line as well came to an end; his first son was murdered by his own soldiers, and a second son abandoned all efforts at maintaining the controls established by his father and gave himself up to pleasures at court. Ala-ud-din, ruthlessly cruel and oppressive, was understandably hated and feared. His system died with him, but during his lifetime it permitted Hindustan to avoid the fate of subjugation by the Mongols. His economic controls were remarkable for their thoroughness and extensiveness, but they rested on absolute power and severe taxation, both bound to provoke resistance and ultimately to destroy them. He had bought and murdered his way to the throne with the help of the plunder brought back from his Deccan raids, but he and his successors failed to hold any part of the south or its wealth. They could maintain their authoritarian rule in the north only by

The Mongols: An Eyewitness Account

Even the Turco-Afghan rulers of the Delhi sultanate were appalled by the Mongols, whose invasion of India they managed to repel. Here is a description of them by a Turkish eyewitness.

Their eyes were so narrow and piercing that they might have bored a hole in a brazen vessel. Their stink was more horrible than their color. Their faces were set on their bodies as if they had no neck. Their cheeks resembled soft leather bottles, full of wrinkles and knots. Their noses extended from cheek to cheek and their mouths from cheek bone to cheek bone. Their nostrils resembled rotten graves, and from them the hair descended as far as the lips.

Source: H. G. Rawlinson, *India: A Short Cultural History* (New York: Praeger, 1965), p. 224.

bleeding the agricultural base of the economy—a prescription for ultimate disaster.

The Tughluqs

With the collapse of Ala-ud-din's order, a new Muslim dynasty succeeded to power in the Dehli sultanate, the Tughluqs, whose founder was the son of a Turkish court slave and a Hindu woman. His son and successor, Muhammad Tughluq (1325–1351), came to the throne when a pavilion he had erected for his father collapsed, killing the father. Muhammad's regime of strict piety and his renewed efforts at carrying Islam southward may be interpreted as an attempt to expiate his sense of guilt. He ordered everyone to observe the Koranic ordinances for ritual, prayers, and Islamic doctrine and forced large numbers of troops and officials to man his drive into the Deccan, where he briefly established a secondary capital.

The endless campaigns, and taxes to support them, provoked growing rebellion as well as southern resistance. From 1335 to 1342 North India endured a seven-year drought and famine, one of the worst such periods in its history, but Muhammad was too busy with fighting, tax collecting, and the promotion of strict Islam to respond, and there was no organized effort by the state to provide tax relief or food distribution. Well over a million people died, and revolts became even more widespread, in the north as well as in the south and even in Delhi itself. Bengal broke away and declared its independence in 1338, retaining it for the next three centuries.

Muhammad was killed fighting a rebellion in Sind in 1351, and his cousin Firuz Tughluq claimed the throne, which he held until his death in 1388. Firuz proved a more constructive ruler, who largely abandoned the earlier efforts at conquest and warfare and concentrated instead on rebuilding Delhi, with splendid new gardens, mosques, hospitals, and colleges for the study of Islam. He also supported the construction of new irrigation schemes, including dams and reservoirs, that brought new land into production. Although a Muslim zealot like Muhammad, he cut back the sultanate's system of spies and informers, abolished torture, and tried to improve the material welfare of his subjects. But his Islamic orthodoxy and intolerance, his insistence on payment of the *jizya* tax by all "infidels," and his clear message that Hindus were second-class citizens alienated the majority. Soon after his death, the sultanate's domains broke up into warring factions.

This chaos in North India invited, as so often before, a catastrophic invasion by central Asian armies, this time led by the brutal Tamerlane (1336–1405), a Turkish leader who had already ravaged much of central Asia and the Middle East. After looting the Punjab, he entered Delhi in 1398 and systematically slaughtered whatever inhabitants he did not take away as slaves or force to carry his booty. Famine and pestilence followed in his wake. The Delhi sultanate never fully recovered from this devastating blow, and its political fragmentation accelerated. Gujarat declared its independence in 1401 and flourished under its own rulers, especially in the Gujarati capital of Ahmedabad. Gujarat had always depended on its maritime trade, westward across the Arabian Sea and the Indian Ocean and eastward to Southeast Asia, and this trade now increased still more. Many Gujaratis, including their rulers, had converted to Islam, which proved useful in trade connections both westward and eastward and made Gujarat prosperous. With their commercial profits the Gujaratis built luxurious new palaces and mosques in Ahmedabad.

Sikandar Lodi and Ibrahim

In what remained of the Delhi sultanate, an Afghan clan, the Lodis, took the throne in 1450 and produced an effective ruler, Sikandar (1489–1517). A patron of culture and a poet, Sikandar encouraged scholarship and the compilation of books on medicine and music. Though a highly orthodox Muslim, he fell in love with a Hindu princess, and his reign saw the continued blending of the Islamic and Hindu mystical traditions. Sikandar himself was not, however, an adherent of Sufism, and perhaps to prove himself orthodox despite having a Hindu wife, he continued the Muslim policy of destroying temples and other Hindu religious art.

In North India, Sikandar's successor, Ibrahim (1517–1526), was a far less compelling figure than his father had been and was confronted by revolts in many parts of the remaining sultanate territories. The rival Rajput Confederacy grew and threatened to extinguish the sultanate altogether. Lahore, chief city of Punjab, was in rebellion, and its governor unwisely invited a new group of central Asian Turks to strengthen his hand against Sultan Ibrahim. This was the army of Babur (1483–1530), known as "the Tiger," who claimed descent from Tamerlane through his father and from Chinghis Khan through his mother. For 20 years, as his own account of his life tells us, he had "never ceased to think of the conquest of Hindustan." India's wealth and its political divisions chronically tempted Afghans, Turks, and others. Babur's outnumbered but brilliantly led forces defeated those of Ibrahim at Panipat, northwest of Delhi, in 1526, and in the next year similarly vanquished the Rajput Confederacy, now plagued by internal divisions. North India was again under alien domination, but the Mughal dynasty that Babur founded was to reach new levels of splendor and imperial achievement.

Bhakti and Sufi: A Religious Revival

In the troubled centuries after 1000, with their shifting and periodically disastrous political changes, punctuated by invasion and bloody warfare, it is understandable that people turned even more fervently to religion. A new Hindu movement known as *bhakti* ("devotion") developed in the south in the tenth century, spread gradually north, and by the fourteenth century reached Bengal, where at the ancient sacred city of Banaras on the Ganges a latter-day disciple, Ramananda, preached the bhakti message of divine love. Its universal appeal as well as its solace attracted a mass following in all parts of India, including many Muslims, with its emphasis on the simple love of God and the abandonment of sectarian or rival causes. This was the Sufi message also, and Sufi Muslims helped spread the bhakti movement while they also increased the appeal of a more humane yet more mystical Islam. It was celebrated by a long series of poet-saints, probably the most beloved of whom was the blind and illiterate Muslim weaver-poet Kabir of Banaras (died 1518), a disciple of Ramananda whose moving verses on the bhakti theme have inspired many millions since his time.

MEDIEVAL INDIA

	North India	South India
A.D. 1–1000		Chola kingdom (c. 200–1279) Pandyan kingdom (before 300–c. 1550) Pallavan kingdom (c. 300–c. 880)
1000–1316	Muslim invasions begin (1001) Delhi sultanate founded (1206) Reign of Ala-ud-din Khalji (1296–1316)	
1316–1565	Tughluq dynasty (1316–1388) Invasion of Tamerlane (1398) Reign of Sikandar (1489–1517) Invasion of Babur (1526)	Empire of Vijayanagar (1336–1565)

Hindu Devotion

Here are some samples of the Hindu bhakti devotional literature of medieval South India.

I am false, my heart is false, my love is false, but I, this sinner, can win Thee if I weep before Thee, O Lord, Thou who art sweet like honey, nectar, and the juice of sugar cane. Please bless me so that I might reach Thee. . . . Melting in the mind, now standing, now sitting, now lying, and now getting up, dancing in all sorts of ways, gaining the vision of the Form of the Lord shining like the rosy sky, when will I stand united with and entered into that exquisite Gem? . . . The lamb brought to the slaughterhouse eats the leaf garland with which it is decorated. The frog caught in the mouth of the snake desires to swallow the fly flying near its mouth. So is our life. . . . He who knows only the sacred books is not wise. He only is wise who trusts in God.

Source: W. T. de Bary, ed., *Sources of Indian Tradition,* vol. 1 (New York: Columbia University Press, 1964), pp. 349–352.

South India

Most of India remained in fact under native control during the Delhi sultanate, including the ancient kingdoms of Pallava, Pandya, and Chola, whose rule, cultures, and literary and artistic traditions continued largely unbroken. In much of the Deccan and the south, however, with the exception of the Chola kingdom, central state control was relatively loose, and the Hindu monarchies were organized on a semifeudal basis. Lands were held by lords as fiefs, in return for military assistance, payments in kind, and periodic attendance at court, a system similar to that in Chou dynasty China and medieval Europe. Rulers also granted tax-free estates as rewards for service. In India, as in medieval Europe, the tax burden was made heavier by grants of tax-free domains to religious orders, monasteries, and temples. These were often in fact the richest groups in the country and also received large voluntary donations, especially from merchants eager to demonstrate their piety.

The chief cities of medieval India, as of Europe, served as religious centers, grouped around a complex of temples, although supported by profits from trade, farming, and the production of artisans. The great Indian tradition of monumental architecture and sculpture flourished during these centuries, especially in the south. The major southern kingdoms alternated in their efforts to dominate all the south, but trade continued between South India and Southeast Asia. Commercial ties served, as they had since Mauryan times, as a channel for Indian influence in the parts of Southeast Asia close to the sea. There was also some settlement by Indian colonists, who brought both Hinduism and Buddhism together with other aspects of Indian culture.

Preoccupation with the violent political scene in the medieval north, for which we have more detailed records, should not obscure the unbroken continuance and evolution of indigenous Indian civilization in the south. The south remained politically divided and periodically involved in warfare among contending states, but such problems were chronic in most societies of the time elsewhere, as in Europe. The medieval South Indian record of temple building alone, including many immense and beautiful complexes, tells a more positive tale of agricultural and commercial prosperity, a relatively orderly society and government, and a continuing emphasis on religion. Much of the urban culture was supported by merchants, and this too provides some evidence of the scope and wealth of commerce, including the maritime trade with Southeast Asia from a series of ports on the southeast coast.

The Temple Builders

The history of South India during these centuries is in fact recorded largely in the building of temples and their records and inscriptions. Through them we know the outlines of rival and successive kingdoms; their conquests, rise, and decline; and the names of rulers and rich donors. Perhaps the greatest temple builders were the

The Bhakti Synthesis

Kabir, the blind Muslim weaver-poet of the fifteenth century, is the best-known representative of the Hindu-Muslim fusion in the bhakti movement.

O servant, where dost thou seek me? Lo, I am beside thee.
I am neither in the temple nor in the mosque,
Not in rites and ceremonies nor in yoga and renunciation.
If thou art a true seeker thou shalt at once see Me;
Thou shalt meet Me in a moment of time.
It is needless to ask of a saint the caste to which he belongs,
For the priest, the warrior, the tradesman and all the other castes
Are all alike seeking God. The barber has sought God,
The washerwoman, and the carpenter.
Hindus and Muslims alike have achieved that end,
Where there remains no mark of distinction.
O Lord, who will serve Thee?
Every supplicant offers his worship to the God of his own creation;
None seek Him, the perfect, the Indivisible Lord.
Kabir says, "O brother, he who has seen the radiance of love, he is saved."
Look within your heart, for there you will find the true God of all.

Source: W. T. de Bary, ed., *Sources of Indian Tradition,* vol. 1 (New York: Columbia University Press, 1964), pp. 355–357.

Pallavas of the western and central Deccan, who reigned from the fourth to the tenth centuries, but all the South Indian kingdoms built temples. It was an age of faith, like the European Middle Ages, and as in Europe, Indian builders worked in stone, although many of the temples were hewn out of solid rock and consist of a series of adjoining caves, ornately decorated and with ceilings supported by carved stone pillars.

The best-known and most extensive of these rock-cut temples is the complex of 27 caves at Ajanta in the central Deccan, which stretch in a crescent across an entire mountainside, and the nearby 34 cave temples at Ellora, both constructed between the fifth and the eighth centuries. The Ajanta caves were partly buried by a landslide and were rediscovered in the early nineteenth century in excellent condition by British amateur archaeologists, who marveled at the beautifully ornate friezes, sculptures, bas-reliefs, monumental figures of elephants and deities, and wall paintings.

The Pallavas and other southern dynasties who also patronized the arts built a great number of other temples. Many of them were freestanding, including the enormous complex at Madurai built by the Pandyan kingdom, the temples at Tanjore built by the Cholas, and similar clusters in other South Indian cities in a variety of styles.

Revenues from trade and productive agriculture, plus donations from the pious, helped make this extensive building possible. They also supported political power and imperial ambition. The Cholas were the most successful conquerors, fanning out from their base in southeastern peninsular India. Their economic strength depended in part on their organized success in constructing a system of excavated tanks or reservoirs to hold the monsoon rains and then distributing water to fields via canals during the long dry periods. Originally a feudatory dependency of the Pallavas, the Cholas emerged as the dominant power in South India by the tenth century and even absorbed much of the earlier Pandyan kingdom, including its capital at Madurai. They further developed the Pallavan style of temple building. The revived Pandyan kingdom continued the tradition when it supplanted Chola domination after the thirteenth century, and in the seventeenth century it completed the Madurai temple complex in the form we see today.

Throughout the classical and medieval periods, temples were the scenes of frequent festivals that included music, drama, elaborate processions, and dance. These forms of religious worship were also often combined with markets, as in the fairs of medieval Europe, and offered attractions for secular as well as religious interests. Pilgrimages to temple centers were popular, with the same mixture of devotion or piety and social entertainment, complete with storytellers and itinerant actors and jugglers as well as vendors of food, trinkets, and religious objects. Chaucer's *Canterbury Tales* could have been set in medieval South India, and pilgrimages and religious festivals of much the same sort remain an important feature of modern Indian culture.

The Cholas

What gave the Cholas additional power for expansion during their centuries of dominance was their profitable involvement in maritime trade and their navy. Chola armies conquered most of South India, from the central Deccan to the tip of the peninsula. The Chola navy was the greatest maritime force of the surrounding oceans. It even defeated the fleet of the Southeast Asian empire of Sri Vijaya in 1025, intervening again in 1068 to defend the Malayan dependencies it had acquired.

With the help of their navy, the Cholas also invaded the northern half of Ceylon and occupied it for more than 50 years in the eleventh century. The Cholas were finally driven out of Ceylon by a great revival of Sinhalese power, which lasted until the thirteenth century. The Sinhalese capital was moved from its classical site at Anuradhapura to a new monumental capital at Polonnaruwa, and its armies in turn briefly invaded the Tamil country of the Cholas and temporarily occupied Madurai in the late twelfth century. The Sinhalese took advantage of a Pandyan revolt against the Cholas, which in itself symptomized the overall decline of Chola power and of the resurgence of rival South Indian kingdoms. By the thirteenth century Chola power had faded and the south resumed its more typical pattern of political fragmentation, although a reduced Chola kingdom remained and continued to patronize Tamil culture and to prosper economically. The kingdom's administration was remarkable for the role played by village and district councils, which were under central supervision but retained a large measure of local autonomy.

The development of bronze casting and sculpture reached new levels of perfection in medieval South India, especially in Chola domains. The famous and exquisite figure of the dancing, many-armed Shiva was cast in eleventh-century Chola, and the form was widely copied by other Indian artists. Other pieces from this period have the same grace and beauty. These artistic accomplishments bespeak the wealth and confidence of the period. But until modern times Indians have never deemed most events of the everyday world important enough to record. Consequently, we have few accounts of day-to-day life beyond inscriptions and temple records. Indian writers concentrated on religion, philosophy, and literature. In comparison with the eternal questions, politics and material details seemed of little consequence.

The rock-cut Kailash temple, part of the large complex at Ellora in central India (sixth to eighth centuries A.D.)

Vijayanagar, Empire of Victory

Recurrent raids into the Deccan by the Delhi sultanate, which began in the thirteenth century, helped stimulate the rise of a new Hindu kingdom in 1336, the empire of Vijayanagar ("city of victory"). Having organized to resist the sultanate's incursions southward and the pressures of their Muslim associates in the northern Deccan, the founders of Vijayanagar went on to unify most of the peninsular south under their rule. Their capital, which bore the same name as their empire, impressed European travelers in the fifteenth and early sixteenth centuries as the most splendid in India, both larger and more populous than contemporary Rome. The capital depended on a huge excavated reservoir and was adorned with numerous magnificent temples. A textbook on government written by the last great Vijayanagar king, Krishna Deva Raya (1509–1529), suggests part of the reason for the empire's success in its advice on how to deal with minority subjects: "If the king grows angry with them, he cannot wholly destroy them, but if he wins their affection by kindness and charity they serve him by invading the enemies' territory and plundering his forts."[2]

Thirty-six years after the king's death, in a great battle in 1565, a coalition of the Islamic sultanates of the northern Deccan defeated Vijayanagar with the help of the new Mughal conquerors of North India, sacked and destroyed its capital city, and ended its period of greatness.

Shiva as Lord of the Dance, cast in the eleventh century in the Chola kingdom of South India. With one foot crushing the demon dwarf, the god is poised in the cosmic dance of life, holding in one hand the drum of awakening and in another the fire of creation as well as destruction. With still another hand he gives the gesture whose meaning is "fear not."

Classical Indian sculpture: figures on a wall in the temple complex at Kajuraho in central India, c. 1000.

The Eastward Spread of Islam

Buddhism and trade provided the links between India and Southeast Asia in the classical and early medieval periods, and both served as vehicles for the spread of Hinduism and other aspects of Indian civilization. But Arab traders had been active in inter-Asian trade well before the time of Muhammad and had extended their commercial networks throughout most of maritime Southeast Asia and as far east as the China coast. However, Indian converts to Islam after the founding of the Delhi sultanate were primarily responsible for carrying the new religion to insular Southeast Asia, following the long-established trade routes by sea, where they had long played a more important role than the Arabs. This included Indian merchants from Gujarat on the northwest coast and its major ports of Surat and Cambay, which had probably been India's principal base for overseas trade since at least Mauryan times, including the trade with the Hellenic and Roman world.

These enterprises continued under the Delhi sultanate, which for some two centuries ruled Gujarat and converted some of its inhabitants to Islam. Many mer-

Islamic Ideals

Key to Paradise, a guide to the good Muslim life, was compiled in the fourteenth century as an aid to newly converted Indians.

The Prophet said that whoever says every day at daybreak in the name of God the Merciful and the Compassionate, "There is no god but Allah and Muhammad is his Prophet," him God most high will honor with seven favors. First, He will open his spirit to Islam; second, He will soften the bitterness of death; third, He will illuminate his grave; fourth, He will show the recording angels his best aspects; fifth, He will give the list of his deeds with His right hand; sixth, He will tilt the balance of his account in his favor; and seventh, He will pass him over the eternal bridge which spans the fire of hell into Paradise like a flash of lightning. . . . Keep your lips moist by repeating God's name. . . . The servant of God should make the Qur'an [Koran] his guide and his protection. On the day of judgment, the Qur'an will precede him and lead him toward Paradise. The Prophet said that on the night of his ascent to heaven he was shown the sins of his people. He did not see any greater sin than that of him who did not know and did not read the Qur'an.

Source: W. T. de Bary, ed., *Sources of Indian Tradition,* vol. 1 (New York: Columbia University Press, 1964), pp. 386–387.

chants, eager for official favor, probably chose conversion for their own financial benefit. In Southeast Asia, while there was resistance to conversion by Arabs, the long tradition of learning from Indian civilization meant that Islam was more readily accepted from Indian hands. In any case, both Indian and Arab traders spread Islam eastward along the sea routes, as earlier Indian merchants had spread Hinduism and Buddhism. Burma, Siam (Thailand), Cambodia, and Laos on the mainland remained dedicated to Buddhism, but the coastal areas of peninsular Malaya as well as insular Indonesia and the southernmost Philippines, where trading fleets had easier access, were gradually converted to Islam.

Local merchants in many of these Southeast Asian kingdoms also adopted Islam as an advantage in dealing with Muslim traders from India. In several cases local rulers were converted or chose Islam, perhaps for similar reasons, and their subjects were obliged to do likewise. Insular Southeast Asia became a patchwork of Islamic sultanates. By the late fourteenth century, Indian and Arab Muslims largely controlled the trade of this enormous area and made converts first in Sumatra and Malaya, closest by sea to India, and in coastal ports throughout the far-flung archipelago. Malacca, on the west coast of Malaya, where it dominated the routes through the Malacca Strait, became a great center of commerce and a spearhead for the advance of Islam eastward. Nearly all trade eastward from India has always passed through the strait as the shortest and safest route, avoiding the treacherous southwest coast of Sumatra and the difficult Sunda Strait between Sumatra and Java.

In the course of the fifteenth century the new religion incorporated most of Malaya, north coastal Java, and coastal parts of the rest of the archipelago, including Mindanao, the southernmost large island of the Philippines, where it seems to have arrived early. Islam's further spread was checked in part by the almost simultaneous arrival of the Spanish in the Philippines and of the Portuguese and the Dutch in Indonesia, although away from the coast, inland Java remained Hindu-Buddhist for another century or so, even under some nominally Muslim rulers.

By the sixteenth century only a few small and isolated areas of Indonesia outside Java retained their original animism or tribal religion, while the island of Bali, east of Java, remained Hindu, as it still is. The very different context of Southeast Asian culture, however, softened some of the more rigid aspects of Islam. This was particularly the case with regard to the treatment of women, for Southeast Asia has always been closer to gender equality than any other major culture. At the same time Islam brought, as in India, a new emphasis on the equality of all before God. In India, the Islamic practice of purdah (literally, "curtain"), whereby women must not be seen by men outside the family and must cover themselves completely when outside the house, spread

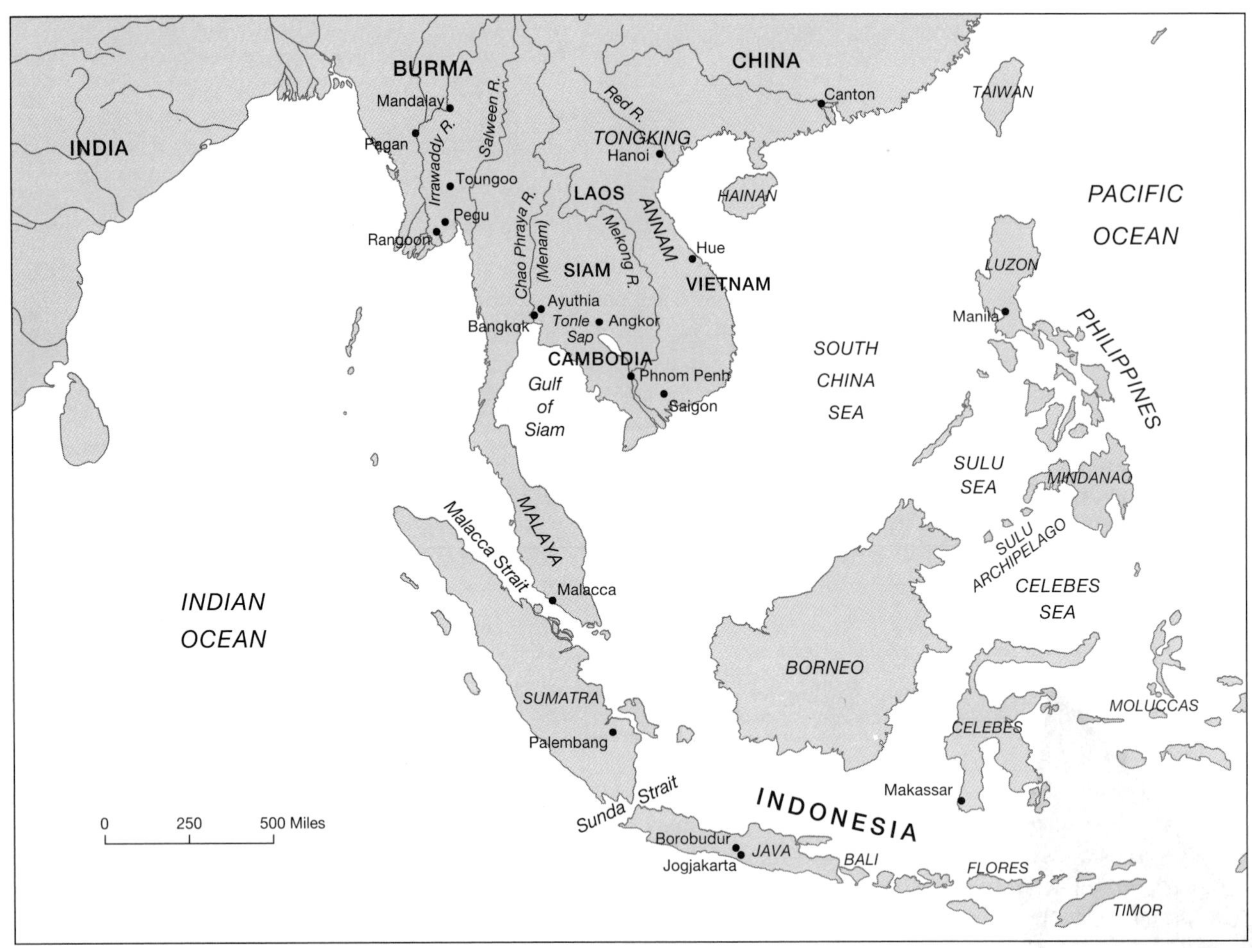

MAP 11.2 SOUTHEAST ASIA

also to Hindus in many parts of the north ruled by Muslim conquerors. In Southeast Asia, with its far more open society and its tradition of female equality, this custom was rejected. Many other Koranic injunctions were modified in practice, including dietary prohibitions, strict fasting during Ramadan, and rigid observance of the rule to pray five times a day facing Mecca. Indonesia has for some time been the world's largest Muslim country, but the Indonesian (and much of the Malaysian) practice of Islam is recognizably different from that in Saudi Arabia, Iraq, or Iran.

Medieval Southeast Asia

Indian forms of dance, music, literature, art, and dramatic versions of the great Hindu epics, the *Mahabharata* and the *Ramayana,* dominated the culture of insular Southeast Asia during the medieval period, as they still do. Meanwhile, Chinese traders became more active and more numerous from the tenth century on, especially in the eastern half of the area, and founded permanent settlements of merchants in the major port cities of the Philippines and Java. Peninsular Malaya at this period was very thinly settled, and although Malay-related languages and culture were widespread throughout the archipelago, Malays remained a small group on the mainland. The traditional Buddhist monarchies of Burma, Siam, and Cambodia, centered in the productive cores of their economies in the mainland deltas and lower valleys of the great rivers, were more self-contained. They too built magnificent temple complexes in the Indian-Buddhist style, such as those in the later abandoned Cambodian capital of Angkor built by the Khmer Empire, which flourished from the ninth to twelfth centuries.

Burma and Siam

The people of Burma and Siam include large infusions of stock originally from south China, where many of their close ethnic relatives still live. The spoken languages of both countries are distantly related to Chinese but written with an Indian-derived script. The majority inhabitants of Siam, the Thais, probably moved down over many centuries into the delta from a homeland that originally straddled the mountainous border zones of China. The origins of the people of northern Burma and to a lesser extent the lowland Burmans are similar. The civilization of both countries has been profoundly shaped, however, by the Indian models that spread to them from Ashoka's time on, including not only Buddhism but also Indian systems of writing, art, literature, philosophy, kingship, and government.

Burmans became the dominant inhabitants of Burma only after 800 and the Thais of Siam after about 1100, each displacing earlier groups who had followed the same migratory route southward from China and Tibet. These earlier inhabitants were either assimilated or remained as minorities, a problem particularly severe in Burma and still a source of chronic tension. The Burmans and Thais occupied the productive lowlands and floodplains of the Irrawaddy in Burma and the Chao Praya (Menam) in Siam, where they founded successive capitals. Indian cultural influences were welcomed, especially since they came without political conditions or ambitions. Local rulers invited Indian advisers, priests, and administrative councillors as well as philosophers, artists, and musicians. Trade was an important source of revenue along the sea routes, but in the great river valleys of the mainland, agriculture and its revenues were the heart of the economy and the chief support of the state. The early medieval capital of Burma was at Pagan, founded about 850 in the central Irrawaddy valley, which by 1057 had incorporated the Irrawaddy basin and an upland perimeter within its boundaries.

Included in the new empire were several minority groups. Some of these were in fact culturally more advanced, especially those in the south, which had been influenced by Indian culture. The most important among them were the Mons, who gained dominion over the court and culture at Pagan until the late twelfth century and played a prominent role in Burma's overseas trade. It was via the Mons that Theravada Buddhism spread to the Burmans, together with the rest of the Mon legacy of Indian civilization. But the Pagan kingdom was utterly destroyed by the Mongol invasion of the 1280s. New waves of migrants and raiders poured into Burma, and rival kingdoms struggled against each other for control after the Mongols had withdrawn. A new Burmese dynasty emerged in the early sixteenth century at Toungoo in the southwest. By 1555, after prolonged civil wars, Toungoo had brought most of the country again under one rule.

Successive kingdoms in Burma were strongly Buddhist after the region's initial conversion, and kings competed, as in Siam, in building temples and endowing religious enterprises. Their piety did not prevent them from engaging in internal military struggles, efforts at territorial expansion, and brutal campaigns against alleged heretics, followers of Buddhist sects that were considered unorthodox. From the sixteenth century there was chronic warfare as well between Burma and Siam. But despite the denial by monarchs and armies of the Buddha's teaching of reverence for life, most people in both countries were genuinely committed to Buddhism as a culture as well as the path to personal salvation.

The Toungoo dynasty was vigorously expansionist, mainly at the expense of the Thais. The rising importance of maritime trade, in which lower Burma played a growing role, provided increased revenues to fuel conquests, and the locus of political authority shifted toward the coast. Improved guns brought in by the Portuguese gave new and often devastating firepower to Burmese expansionism. But the Toungoo order proved fragile and overextended. Its capital, now at Pegu in lower Burma, fell to rebellion and invasion in 1599, and later Toungoo rulers abandoned their claims to Thai territory, although Thai-Burmese warfare continued intermittently.

Meanwhile, the Thais had formed a state that grew in power, began eventually taking over much of the decaying Khmer Empire, and in 1431 captured the Khmer capital at Angkor. Thais had probably spilled southward across the present border of southwestern China before 1200, but the trickle became a flood after the Mongol conquest of their homeland in the late thirteenth century. By the fourteenth century they were the dominant inhabitants of the Chao Praya basin. They pushed southward and eastward against the Khmers, from whom they adopted Indian art forms, writing, and political systems while accepting Buddhism from Burma and from the earlier Mon inhabitants of the Chao Praya basin. The Thai capital was established in the mid-fourteenth century at Ayuthia on the edge of the delta, then close to the Khmer frontier and with easy access both to the Gulf of Siam and to the Mon area of lower Burma.

Ayuthia consolidated its hold on the delta and continued the Thai push southward into the thinly settled Malay peninsula and eastward into Khmer Cambodia. Thais were also a major part of the invasion that sacked the Toungoo capital at Pegu in lower Burma in 1599, but for the next two or three centuries Burmese armies generally had the upper hand in their wars with the Thais and finally sacked and destroyed Ayuthia in 1767.

After a period of disorder and confusion, a new Thai dynasty, the Chakri, emerged in 1782 with a new capital at Bangkok; the same dynasty still rules present-day Thailand. Bangkok, near the seaward edge of the delta, was originally a place of marshes and tidal creeks on the Chao Praya, and the site was chosen in part because of the protection it offered against Burmese raids. With the rapid growth of maritime trade in the nineteenth century, it became a major economic center as well as the chief Thai city.

Cambodia and Laos

The Khmer people had also probably come originally from southwestern China (or northeastern Himalayan India) and were ethnically related to the Mons. They followed the Mekong River into what is now Cambodia, probably by 100 B.C., but before they had had any lasting contact with Chinese or Indian civilizations. In Cambodia they may have founded Funan, which is described as a kingdom in Han Chinese records but was partly Indianized as well. By the third century A.D. Funan seems to have covered what is now southern Vietnam, eastern and central Thailand, northern Malaya, and southernmost Burma. Its large fleets dominated the sea lanes and carried much of the trade moving eastward from India to China, of which it became a tributary state. Funan was probably several small, loosely organized states that were overthrown by a later group of Khmers in the seventh century. They inherited its domains and in the ninth century began to build a magnificent capital and temple complex at Angkor Thom, which for several centuries thereafter was the most important city in Southeast Asia.

Angkor: City of Monumental Splendor

The Khmer king Yasovarman I (889–900), who began building the new capital, designed it with the help of Brahmans invited from India to legitimate his claim to divine kingship. The plan of the city reflected the structure of the world according to Hindu cosmology. It was surrounded by a wall and a moat, as the universe was thought to be encircled by rock and ocean. In the exact middle of the city, on an artificial mound, a pyramidal temple represented the sacred Mount Meru in the high Himalayas, where Shiva was said to be perpetually meditating for the eternal maintenance of the cosmic order. Numerous other temples were grouped on and around the mound, which was regarded as the center of the universe. The king declared himself Ruler of the Universe, a title, together with attendant symbols and rituals, passed on to his successors. Angkor Thom reached its final and completed form at the beginning of the thirteenth century, after the Khmers and their rulers had adopted Mahayana Buddhism. New Buddhist temples and sculptures were added, but the earlier Hindu elements remained, and the Khmers seem to have accepted both religious traditions and symbols. The financial drain of such large-scale building probably contributed to the decline and conquest of the empire only a few decades later.

The whole urban complex was a symbol of the union between king and God and of harmony between the human and divine worlds, and it was intended to ensure prosperity for the kingdom and its people as well as the authority of the ruler. Water, a further life-giving symbol, was led from the Mekong to keep the moat full and was in turn part of a much larger system of irrigation. The city formed a square about 2 miles on each side, enclosed by its walls and moat, and was entered by five huge monumental gates. Inside was the large royal palace as well as the temple complex, but little evidence remains of the other buildings, which housed the court, its officials, clerks, engineers, workers, artisans, and other inhabitants of the city. We know from surviving inscriptions that there was a large and highly organized bureaucracy.

Less than a mile to the south Suryavarman II (1113–1150) built another major temple complex a century later known as Angkor Wat (*wat* means "temple"), which replicated the arrangement and style of the temples at Angkor Thom and like them was surrounded by a moat, although Angkor Wat was smaller than the capital. Both sites were largely abandoned after the Thai invasion of 1431, and Angkor Thom itself was left in ruins. Angkor Wat was better preserved, since it was not so central a target, and remains one of the chief monuments of Southeast Asian art and architecture, reflecting the glory of the Khmer Empire at its height.

The city, and Cambodia as a whole, may have had a larger population in the thirteenth century than in the twentieth. The Mekong floodplain's fertile alluvial soil was made still more productive by an intricate hydraulic network of canals, dams, and dikes for both irrigation and flood control. Fish from the nearby Tonle Sap lake in the middle Mekong valley added to the food supply. The monsoon rains were heavily concentrated in a short summer season, when the Tonle Sap tended to overflow, leaving much of the rest of the year too dry. Flood prevention works, storage tanks, and reservoirs were carefully engineered, and canals were constructed to direct water to rice fields while protecting them from too much water. Canals were also used to transport the stone used to build Angkor Thom and Angkor Wat. The construction and maintenance of these extensive works required enormous amounts of planning and controlled labor. As the authority of the Khmer kings began to weaken and the country was invaded, dams, tanks, and canals could not be maintained. Without the productive agriculture they made possible, the kingdom's economic base was severely reduced. The collapse of the Khmer kingdom suggests comparison with the fall of the Sinhalese kingdom in the Dry Zone of Ceylon two centuries earlier (see Chapter 2). In 1434, three years after the capture of Angkor, the capital was moved to Phnom Penh on the lower Mekong. The Khmer Empire never recovered its former power and glory, however, and jungle invaded the ruins of Angkor Thom and Angkor Wat. They were revealed again when French explorers stumbled on them in the late nineteenth century and the French colonial government later cleared the sites.

The southern part of the landlocked and mountainous state of Laos had been included in the Khmer Empire during its centuries of power. Laos then came under Thai domination until the whole region was absorbed by the French colonial empire at the end of the nineteenth century. The dominant population groups of Laos are related to the Thais and the Burmese. Like these, the Laotians originally migrated from southwestern China and adopted Buddhism, but their language and culture are distinctive. The three small Lao states had to contend with Thai, Burmese, and Vietnamese incursions. Buddhism spread to Laos from Mon and Khmer sources, but Laos was chronically squeezed between expansionist states on all sides.

Vietnam: Expansion to the South

The northern part of Vietnam, known as Tongking, in the productive basin of the Red River with its capital at Hanoi, had been part of the pre-Han South China kingdom of Nan Yueh, or Nam Viet, which included the Canton area and was then incorporated in the Han and T'ang empires. It thus acquired a heavy overlay of Chinese civilization, becoming the only Southeast Asian state to be Sinified rather than Indianized. Below the elite level, however, Vietnamese culture remained distinctively Southeast Asian and maintained its identity.

Vietnam regained its independence after the fall of the T'ang dynasty, although it had to repel efforts at reconquest by the Mongols, the Ming, and the Manchus. During these centuries the Vietnamese were engaged in their own expansion southward, down the narrow coastal

The temple complex at Angkor in Cambodia, dating from the twelfth century.

plain of Annam and eventually into the agriculturally rich delta of the Mekong in what is now southern Vietnam, a process that took nearly 1,000 years. Southward movement took place at the expense of the Indianized Champa kingdom in Annam with its capital at Hue and then of the Khmers, who originally controlled the Mekong delta and the surrounding plain.

In this long struggle, the Vietnamese drew strength from a fervent nationalism originally engendered by their efforts to resist and finally to throw off Chinese control, a 2,000-year ordeal of chronic war. But their growing empire was managed on Chinese bureaucratic lines, and their later rulers even adopted the title of emperor, although they prudently accepted the status of tributary to China. Like the Koreans and the Japanese, the Vietnamese accepted aspects of Chinese culture while resisting Chinese political control. By the early nineteenth century their empire included essentially all the modern state, including territories conquered or detached from Cambodia and Laos, with the central and southern areas ruled from subsidiary capitals at Hue and Saigon. The deltas of Tongking in the north around Hanoi and of the Mekong around Saigon, as well as the coastal plain of Annam joining them, were fertile and became highly productive under a Chinese-style system of intensive irrigated agriculture. This lent further strength to the state, helping it maintain control over a mountainous western borderland inhabited by a variety of non-Vietnamese tribal minorities in addition to Laotians and Khmers.

Malaya, Indonesia, and the Philippines

Malay-style culture and the Malay language family are dominant not only in the Malay peninsula but also in most of insular Southeast Asia, especially the coastal areas easily accessible by sea. The peninsula itself, however, has never supported a very large population, especially compared to the larger and more productive areas of Indonesia and the Philippines, and probably did not reach half a million until the late nineteenth century. Its mountainous and rain-forested landscape contained no extensive river valleys or productive agricultural plains, and settlement was most concentrated on the coast, where small ports were engaged in regional trade. There is no evidence of a highly developed indigenous civilization until the rise of Malacca in the fifteenth century, and Malacca itself was part of a larger system in greater Malay Southeast Asia. During the medieval period most of Malaya was first controlled by the Indonesian trading empire of Sri Vijaya, with its capital on nearby Sumatra, and later by the Thai state. Malaya was politically unified only under twentieth-century British colonial control, and most of its growth dates only from the tin and rubber booms of the same period.

In Indonesia the central island of Java, with its richly productive volcanic soils, has remained the heart of the sprawling island country. Rival kingdoms based on agriculture arose in Java, while larger empires based on maritime trade grew to control and profit from the sea lanes. The first and most enduring of these was the empire of Sri Vijaya, with its capital at Palembang on Sumatra, from which it could dominate the Malacca Strait, the crucial passage between east and west. It was the chief power of the archipelago from the seventh to the thirteenth centuries, despite a brief conquest by the Chola navy from southern India in the eleventh century. Buddhism spread early to Sri Vijaya, and Palembang became a major center of Buddhist learning. Meanwhile, in central Java the Sailendra dynasty in the eighth century built a land-based state on prosperous agricultural revenues, which were also used to construct one of the world's great architectural monuments, the immense Buddhist temple at Borobodur, completed by around 825.

Borobodur, like Angkor, was a symbolic representation of the sacred Mount Meru, built up in a series of nine terraces some 3 miles in circumference and including about 400 statues of the Buddha. Indian artists and sculptors were probably involved, along with Javanese artisans. Other Javanese states built many similar temples, which combined Buddhist and Hindu iconography and symbols, as at Angkor. Interstate rivalry and the final blow of the Mongol invasion broke the empire of Sri Vijaya in the 1290s, though it survived in Sumatra. But a resurgent new Javanese state expelled the Mongols and founded the empire of Majapahit in the early fourteenth century, which succeeded to the far-flung commercial interests of Sri Vijaya and at the same time unified much of eastern and central Java. Majapahit's military success was accompanied by a cultural and literary renaissance.

Majapahit was the last of the great Hindu-Buddhist states of insular Southeast Asia. Within a century it faced aggressive competition from the new trading state of Malacca and newly Islamicized ports on the north coast of Java, which soon wrested from it control of the strait and nibbled away at its domination of the maritime trade eastward and of Majapahit client states in the archipelago. Islam had earlier spread to Sumatra along the trade routes from India, and the rulers of Malacca and north coastal Java adopted the new religion as a means of enhancing their commercial connections, through which

The eighth-century Buddhist stupa at Borobodur in central Java, chief remaining monument to the Indianization of Southeast Asia before the arrival of Islam.

they made further converts. Majapahit became merely one of many small Javanese states.

The recorded history of the Philippines begins only with Magellan's voyage in 1521, in which he claimed the islands for Spain, although a settlement was not made on Luzon, the main island, until 1565. The Philippines consist of 7,000 islands, many more than Indonesia's 3,000. Although speakers of Malay-related languages have long been dominant in the Philippines, other and probably earlier cultural groups remained in relative isolation, especially in the mountainous and heavily forested parts of the larger islands. Differences of dialect, language, and culture divided the inhabitants of most of the islands, and until recent times they lived in largely separate worlds despite some interisland trading. No recognizable state emerged in any area before Spanish times, and there was no well-established or widely used form of writing, although Indian writing systems and some aspects of the Hindu tradition did have a minor effect over many centuries.

There was also trade contact with China, probably from Han times, but little cultural evidence remains from that early period, apart from Chinese coins and pottery shards. Islam penetrated most of Mindanao in the south, but until the Spanish occupation the religious pattern of the rest of the Philippines was dominated by a great variety of local animistic cults in the absence of any text-based religious tradition. This and the lack of anything approaching Filipino national coherence or identity made for ready conversion to Islam and to Christianity and contributed to the relative ease of the Spanish conquest. Four and a half centuries of Spanish control left the Philippines in many ways culturally, socially, and politically closer to Latin America than to Asia.

Central Asia

Like China but to a greater degree, India was chronically involved with invasion and conquest from the great central Asian world of steppe and desert. The world's largest area of semiarid steppe and desert covers the middle of the Eurasian continent, from the Ukraine and what is now eastern Turkey, across the southern half of the former USSR, most of Iran, Afghanistan, and what is now Pakistan, Mongolia, and most of China north of southern Manchuria and east of about 110° east longitude. Tibet belongs in the same category but at high altitudes. Throughout most of this vast Eurasian area, permanent field agriculture is possible only in a few favored spots where water is available as supplementary irrigation, as in the few widely scattered oases. Central Asia has long been occupied by a variety of peoples, the most important of which are Turkish and Mongol, who supported themselves primarily by pastoral nomadism, using animals to extract sustenance from grazing and living in turn on their meat and milk.

The typical pastoral nomad grouping was the tribe, and although many tribes might share a common language, racial stock, and culture, there was rivalry and often warfare among them. Conflicts centered on disputes over grazing rights. Grass was the indispensable and finite resource of all pastoral nomads, the means for sustaining the herds from which they lived. Each tribe worked out a more or less fixed pattern of movement whereby any given pasture area would be grazed only as frequently as was compatible with maintenance of permanent yield. Any one part of a tribe's claimed grazing area would be out of use for long periods, often several years, while the tribe and its flocks might be hundreds of miles away. This invited poaching by other tribes and resulted in chronic small-scale wars, in which the nomads developed their particular fighting skill.

As with arid areas everywhere, rainfall varied widely, as much as 40 percent between extremes; in drier years competition for grazing was intensified. The low productivity of pastoral nomadism kept human populations very low. The Mongol tribes consolidated by Chinghis (Genghis) Khan in the twelfth century totaled at most about 1 million, about the same total as in the twentieth century, in an overall area about as large as western Europe. Tibet's totals were similar, in an area only slightly smaller, and Turkish tribes probably came to only a little more.

The animals that made the nomadic way of life possible were primarily sheep and goats, native to the central Asian steppe and very little altered from their wild forms, able to survive on sparser pasturage than would be needed to sustain cattle. Given their habit of close cropping, however, they quickly exhaust any pasturage and have to be moved on before they destroy its capacity to recover. The horse was used mainly to help herd and drive the animals in their cyclical search for pasture. Sheep move slowly but can be hastened by a mounted rider, who can also mount mobile guard against predators and scout the route ahead.

The nomads became masters of horse riding and horse breeding and brought the art of horsemanship to its peak of perfection. Males spent most of their waking hours from an early age in the saddle. Most horses were small steppe ponies, also native to the area, which were not only extremely hardy and able to survive on grass that would not support larger animals, but also able, because of their shaggy coat and general endurance, to withstand the harsh winters of extreme cold and high winds of their native habitat. The invention of the stirrup in China by the fourth century B.C., and probably soon thereafter by the Saka invaders of India, greatly increased the usefulness of the horse for both peaceful and martial activities. Riders could now load, aim, and fire their arrows at a gallop and could stand to fire sideways or even backward, the so-called Parthian shot. They also mastered the technique of firing volleys on command by wheeling companies of mounted archers.

Mounted archery became the great nomad weapon. Their bows were adapted for use on horseback by shortening them in a double reflex like a Cupid's bow but without losing power, range, or accuracy. The bows were composites of laminated wood, horn, and sinew, materials readily available to the nomads. Throughout central Asia the camel was also used, not for herding but for carrying and for travel. Camels were native to the area and wonderfully adapted to its harsh environment, able to live for extended periods by drawing on fat and moisture in their humps, but also able to subsist on thorny, tough, or bitter vegetation and on brackish water, both rejected even by goats. The camel also has a secondary transparent eyelid so that it can see in the frequent dust or sandstorms. This animal was the dominant carrier of trade within central Asia. Arabs and Turks also used camels as military cavalry, although this was not common farther east.

The nomads' economy centered on their animals, as sources of food and clothing and materials for shelter, made mainly of felt (matted fibers of wood, fur, or hair), which gave excellent insulation. The black tent, supported on poles, was the major form in western areas, while in the eastern half, with its far colder winters, felt and hides were used to form the *yurt,* which had a hemispherical shape to minimize wind resistance, and was supported on light wicker frames and anchored with a net of guy ropes of braided wool, leather, or sinew. Despite its color, the black tent was well designed to shield occupants against the sun, but both tents and *yurts* were made for quick and easy disassembly and packing onto horse or camel back with each move to new pasture areas. Furniture was minimal: basic cooking equipment, tools, weapons, and spare clothing, with some cushions or piled hides to sit on. Some of the richer and more sophisticated nomads wove magnificent wool rugs with natural vegetable dyes, but most rugs were woven by oasis dwellers and, like wool, could be sold or bartered in trade. In the eastern areas meat and milk products were supplemented in the diet by *tsamba,* barley flour mixed with rancid butter in a paste, to which the nomads added tea by the tenth century.

Along many of the borders of central Asia the environmental zone between areas where agriculture is possible and those where it cannot be permanently successful without irrigation is quite broad. Across this zone the contest between pastoral nomads and sedentary farmers has flowed back and forth for millennia. It has been resolved in favor of the farmers, backed by the support structures of the modern state, only in the present century with railways, roads, power equipment, dams, wells, pumps, new agricultural techniques, and the enhanced power of national and international markets. Relations in the past between the nomads and the sedentary empires around them were usually hostile. Nomads looked to the agricultural areas for most of what little they needed to buy or barter: some grain, salt, metal goods, some wood, tea, and porcelain. To pay for what they needed they bartered wool, hides, horses or other livestock, and furs. But it was tempting to the nomads simply to take what they wanted, or to raid the trade caravans that ran through their domains carrying high-value goods like silk, gold, or lacquer that could be bartered. The scattered oases, also occupied by farmers, supported markets crowded with a variety of goods. There too the nomads could often obtain what they wanted in lightning raids.

Their great weapon against the far larger sedentary empires surrounding them was their mobility, and hence unpredictability, through the striking power of mounted warriors. Each warrior made his own bows and arrows. Men and horses moved in unison in response to signal flags. Each rider could discharge a volley of four or five arrows at short range and high velocity, then wheel away to reload and return for another charge. They would often try to draw their opponents out in pursuit and then turn in their saddles and shoot their pursuers or lead them into a prepared ambush. With such tactics they were nearly irresistible, but most of their conquests were short-lived, and they had little talent for or interest in administration. In India and in the case of the Manchus in China, those who remained as conquerors and rulers tended over time to be absorbed culturally in the far greater mass of Indian or Chinese civilization. Although they are clearly a separate people from the Chinese, Tibetans have been overwhelmed by the modern Chinese state, as have the Mongols and the Turkic people of Sinkiang, like their brothers and sisters across the border in the former USSR. Their modern fate parallels that of other central Asian people farther west and that of the American Indians, as their cultures and people were conquered and absorbed by the United States and by the states emerging out of the Spanish and Portuguese conquests in Latin America.

SUMMARY

From the late tenth century to the foundation of the Mughal dynasty in 1526, India was divided as waves of invaders from the north brought in both a new religion, Islam, and a new cultural infusion. It was nevertheless a period of great artistic creativity, especially in the south, and though the records we have tell mainly of battles, kings, and conquests, they tell also of monumental building, a flourishing of the arts, and growing and profitable trade. Surpluses from this trade helped support these creations as well as the political structures and armies of numerous states. Southeast Asia was similarly divided and engaged in chronic warfare, but there too these centuries saw the building of majestic temples and the flowering of the arts, supported as in India by extensive maritime commerce and the taxes on yields from the fertile river valleys and deltas of the mainland and the rich volcanic soils of Java. Religion too was periodically a source of conflict, as Buddhism developed new sects and Islam spread eastward over India and most of insular Southeast Asia, profoundly changing its social and cultural character.

NOTES

1. D. P. Singhal, *A History of the Indian People* (London: Methuen, 1983), p. 168.
2. A. L. Basham, *The Wonder That Was India* (New York: Grove Press, 1959), p. 198.

SUGGESTIONS FOR FURTHER READING

Andaya, B., and Andaya, L. *A History of Malaysia.* New York: St. Martin's Press, 1982.

Adshead, S. *Central Asia in World History.* New York: St. Martin's Press, 1993.

Auboyer, J. *Daily Life in Ancient India.* New York: Macmillan, 1965.

Aung-Thwin, M. *Pagan: The Origins of Modern Burma.* Honolulu: University Press of Hawaii, 1985.

Barfield, T. J. *The Perilous Frontier: Nomadic Empires and China.* Oxford: Blackwell, 1989.

Basham, A. L. *The Wonder That Was India.* New York: Grove Press, 1959.

Briggs, L. *The Ancient Khmer Empire.* Philadelphia: American Philosophical Society, 1951.

Chandler, D. P. *A History of Cambodia.* Boulder, Colo.: Westview Press, 1983.

Coedes, G. *The Indianized States of Southeast Asia,* ed. W. F. Vella. Honolulu: East-West Center Press, 1968.

Gesick, L., ed. *Centers, Symbols, and Hierarchies: Essays on the Classical States of Southeast Asia.* New Haven, Conn.: Yale University Press, 1983.

Groslier, B. P., and Arthaud, J. *Angkor: Art and Civilization.* New York: Praeger, 1966.

Hall, K. R. *Maritime Trade and State Development in Early Southeast Asia.* Honolulu: University Press of Hawaii, 1985.

Lieberman, V. *Burmese Administrative Cycles: Anarchy and Conquest, 1580–1760.* Princeton, N.J.: Princeton University Press, 1984.

Osborne, M. *Southeast Asia: An Illustrated Introductory History.* New York: HarperCollins, 1991.

Reid, A. *Southeast Asia in the Age of Commerce, 1450–1680.* New Haven, Conn.: Yale University Press, 1988.

Richardson, H. E. *Tibet and Its History.* New York: Random House, 1990.

Ricklefs, M. C. *A History of Modern Indonesia.* Bloomington: Indiana University Press, 1981.

Sar Desai, D. R. *Southeast Asia, Past and Present,* 2nd ed. Boulder, Colo.: Westview Press, 1989.

Shaffer, L. N. *Maritime Southeast Asia, 300 B.C. to A.D. 1528.* Armonk, N.Y.: M. E. Sharpe, 1993.

Singhal, D. P. *A History of the Indian People,* 2nd ed. London: Methuen, 1989.

Sinor, D., ed. *The Cambridge History of Central Asia.* Cambridge: Cambridge University Press, 1990.

Stein, B. *Peasant, State, and Society in Medieval South India.* Berkeley: University of California Press, 1980.

Taylor, K. W. *The Birth of Vietnam.* Berkeley: University of California Press, 1983.

Thapar, R. *A History of India,* vol. 1. Baltimore: Penguin, 1969.

Van Leur, J. C. *Indonesian Trade and Society.* The Hague: Van Hoeve, 1955.

Vlekke, B. *Nusantara: A History of Indonesia.* The Hague: Van Hoeve, 1960.

Wolters, O. L. *Early Indonesian Commerce: The Origins of Srivijaya.* Ithaca, N.Y.: Cornell University Press, 1967.

Woodside, A. *Vietnam and the Chinese Model.* Cambridge, Mass.: Harvard University Press, 1971.

Wyatt, D. *Thailand: A Short History.* New Haven, Conn.: Yale University Press, 1984.

Yazdani, G., ed. *The Early History of the Deccan.* London: Oxford University Press, 1960.

CHAPTER 12

A Golden Age in East Asia

The period from the sixth to the fourteenth centuries saw the reunification of China following a long period of division. After 600 years of renewed imperial splendor under the T'ang dynasty and its successor, the Sung (Song), China was overrun by the Mongols and ruled as part of their short-lived empire from 1279 to 1368, when a new Chinese dynasty, the Ming, restored Chinese power. During the same period, Korean civilization matured, produced a series of effective dynasties, and added innovations to the Chinese culture it had adopted from the earlier Han dynasty in China. In the eighth century Japan evolved a literate civilization on the model of T'ang China and in subsequent centuries produced a highly sophisticated court culture. Japan slowly dissolved into chronic fighting between rival clans until unity was reimposed by the founders of the Tokugawa shogunate by 1600.

Reunification in China

For nearly four centuries after the fall of the Han dynasty in 220 China was divided into many separate kingdoms, with much of the north under barbarian control. Buddhism flourished, perhaps as a response to the troubled times, and was promoted also by the Sinicized rulers of the north. The chief such kingdom, known as the Northern Wei, controlled most of North China from 386 to 534. It built a number of splendid Buddhist cave temples with statues of the Buddha and his devotees

Emperor T'ang T'ai-tsung (626–649) was a brilliant field commander whose campaigns reestablished Chinese control over Sinkiang and northern Vietnam, conquered Tibet, and even extended imperial rule into central Asia. An astute administrator, T'ai-tsung also restored and extended the imperial bureaucratic system of the Han.

whose style, though Chinese, reveals Indian influence, as do the many pagodas, a temple form adapted from the Indian stupa.

The Chinese cultural and political tradition proper was carried on by a succession of rival dynasties vying for supremacy in the south, which was enriched by a flood of wealthy and educated refugees from the north. Nanking (Nanjing) was the chief southern capital and major urban center, but none of the southern dynasties or kingdoms was able either to unify the region or to provide strong government. Literature, philosophy, and the arts continued vigorously despite the absence of political unity, and Buddhism also became popular in the south. This was the period of both Indian Buddhist missions to China and Chinese pilgrim visits to India; it was also a time of new technological achievements, including gunpowder, advances in medicine, refinements in the use of a magnetized needle for indicating direction (the forerunner of the compass), and the use of coal as a fuel.

Most politically conscious Chinese wanted to see the Han model of greatness restored, but first the country had to be reunified and the imperial machine rebuilt. This was primarily the work of the short-lived Sui dynasty, which in 589 welded contending Chinese states together by conquest. Interestingly, the Sui base was the same Wei valley from which the Ch'in had erupted, and like the Ch'in, the Sui built roads and canals to connect their empire, radiating out from their capital at Ch'ang An.

The second Sui emperor, Yang Ti (604–618), heady with new power, is often compared to Ch'in Shih Huang Ti. He too rebuilt the Great Wall, at a cost of an additional million lives, and reconquered northern Vietnam as well as much of Sinkiang and Mongolia, although his campaign in Korea was defeated by fierce resistance. Yang Ti built a magnificent new capital at Loyang, following the model of the Chou and the Han, but at heavy expense. Perhaps his most notable project was the building of the Grand Canal, from Hangchou (Hangzhou) in the south to Kaifeng in the north, to bring rice from the productive Yangtze delta for troops and officials in semiarid northern China. But his megalomaniacal behavior caused great suffering to his exhausted troops, forced laborers, taxpayers, and tyrannized officials. Rebellion spread, as in the last years of the Ch'in, and Yang Ti was assassinated by a courtier in 618 after only 14 years on the throne. A frontier general swept away the pretensions of the Sui heir and proclaimed a new dynasty, the T'ang. Although the new dynasty was to last nearly 300 years, it owed its success in large part to the foundations laid by the Sui, as the Han had rested on those of the Ch'in.

The T'ang Dynasty

Under T'ang rule China achieved a new high point in prosperity, cultural sophistication and greatness, and imperial power. The cosmopolitan T'ang capital at Ch'ang An (Qangan), where the Han had ruled, was the world's largest city, with about 2 million inhabitants. The imperial civil service and the examination system were reestablished, and learning and the arts flourished.

The rebuilding of the empire exacted a price, for all its glory. Most of the Han-ruled territories were reclaimed by conquest after they had fallen away at the end of the Sui, including northern Vietnam, but Tibet, Sinkiang, Mongolia, and southern Manchuria were wisely left as tributary regions, after their inhabitants had been defeated in a brilliant series of campaigns by Emperor T'ang T'ai-tsung (Tang Taizong, 626–649). Korea again fought the Chinese armies to a standstill but accepted tributary status, and much of the mountainous southwest, home of the Thai and other groups, remained outside imperial rule. T'ai-tsung is remembered as a model ruler who fostered education and encouraged conscientious officials. In his cosmopolitan time, Buddhism was still tolerated and widely popular.

In the late seventh century a beautiful concubine of T'ai-tsung's named Wu Chao (Wuzhao) was made a consort and empress by his successor Kao-tsung (Gao-zong), whom she soon came to dominate. After his death in 683 she ruled alone or through puppets and then proclaimed herself emperor of a new dynasty, the only female emperor in Chinese history. She struck at the old aristocracy, her chief opposition, and ordered many of them executed. She drew support from the Buddhist establishment, which she strongly favored and which declared her a reincarnation of the Bodhisattva Maitreya, the Buddhist messiah. Wu Chao had become a Buddhist nun after T'ai-tsung's death in 650, but she soon grew restless without greater scope for her talents. Empress Wu, as she is called, was denounced by Chinese historians, although their criticism has clear sexist overtones. She was a strong and effective, if ruthless, ruler, obviously opposed to the Confucian establishment and promoting its rival, the alien faith of Buddhism. Her being a woman in addition was just too much for her opponents to deal with, and she was deposed in a palace coup.

The gradual Sinification of the originally non-Han south below the Yangtze valley continued under the imperial momentum. By the late T'ang most of the empire's revenue came from the more productive south, including the Yangtze valley, and most Chinese lived in that area. The north, where the empire had been born, suffered as always from recurrent drought, erosion, and the silting of its vital irrigation works. But now the south, progressively cleared of its earlier forests, more than made up the difference. Agricultural techniques were slowly adapted to the wetter and hillier conditions and the far longer growing season of the south. The increasing use of human manure ("night soil") improved the less fertile soils outside the alluvial river valleys, supporting a continued increase of population, which thus provided still more night soil. Many northerners had fled south after the fall of the Han dynasty; now they and their descendants were joined by new streams seeking greater economic opportunity than in the overcrowded and often marginal north. Imperial tradition and the defense of the troublesome northwest frontiers kept the capital in the north, but the south was the empire's principal economic base.

Renewing their contacts with more distant lands westward, the Chinese found no other civilization that could rival the Celestial Empire. The Son of Heaven, as the emperor was called, was seen as the lord of "all under heaven," meaning the four corners of the known world, within which China was clearly the zenith of power and sophistication. Did not all other people the Chinese encountered acknowledge this, by tribute, praise, and imitation of Chinese culture, the sincerest form of flattery?

In fact, even beyond the world the Chinese knew, they had no equal. Rome was long gone, and the Abbasid caliphate was no match for the T'ang or its great successor, the Sung. A coalition of Arabs and western Turks did repulse a T'ang expeditionary force at the battle of the Talas River near Samarkand in 751, but the battle is perhaps more significant in that some captured Chinese transmitted the recently developed T'ang arts of printing and papermaking to the West. The mass production of paper dated from the late first century A.D., although it had been invented a century earlier. Printing, which began about 700, was first done from carved wooden blocks a page at a time, but by 1030 the Chinese, and only slightly later the Koreans, had developed movable-type printing, with individual characters made of wood, ceramics, or metal. Only in the fifteenth century would this technique reach Europe.

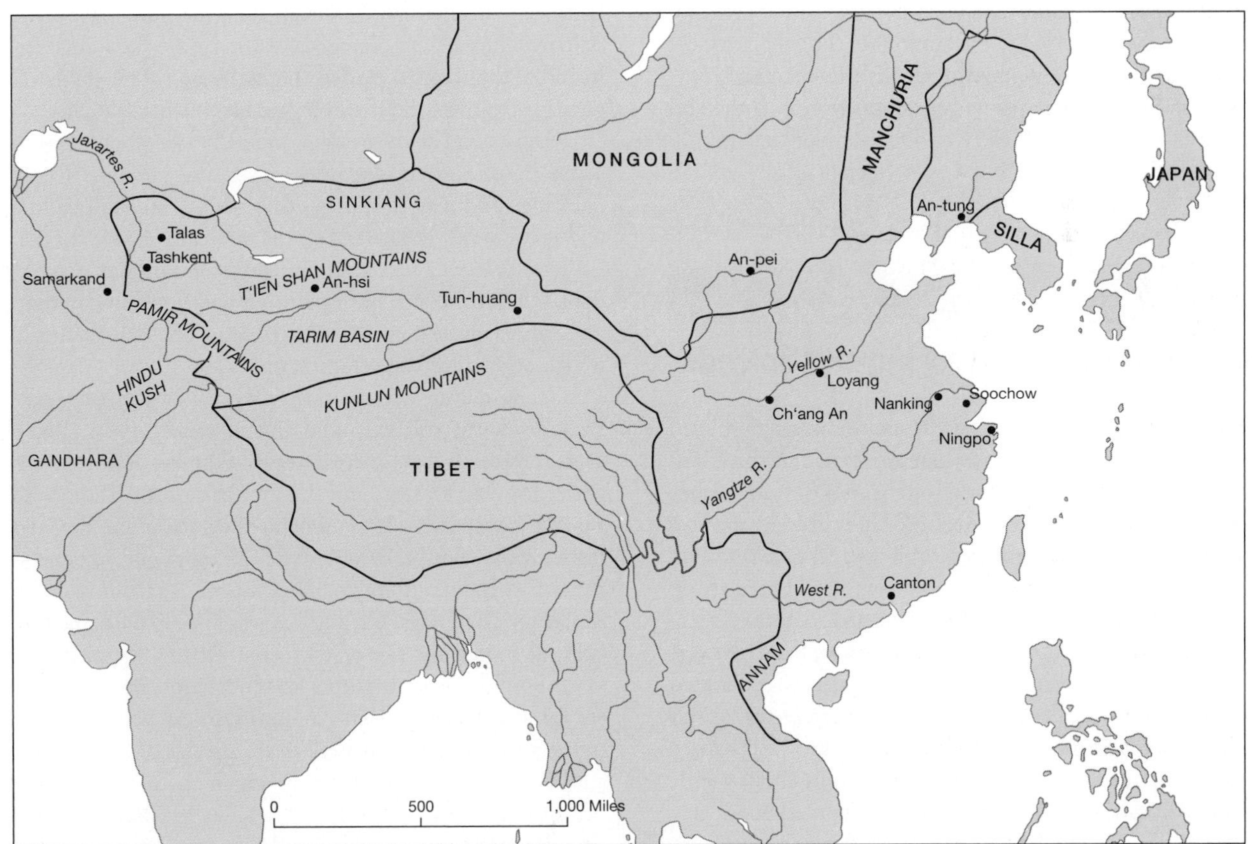

MAP 12.1 CHINA UNDER THE T'ANG

Paper and printing were typical creations of the Chinese, with their love of written records and of learning, literature, and painting. They were only two of China's basic gifts to the West, along with cast iron, the crossbow, gunpowder, the compass, the use of coal as fuel, the water wheel, paper currency, the wheelbarrow, wallpaper, and porcelain, to mention only a few. Porcelain had matured by T'ang times, and from it were made objects of exquisite beauty whose refinement was never matched elsewhere. Porcelain, silk, and later tea became China's chief exports.

The secret of making silk had been supposedly smuggled out of China by two monks at the time of the eastern Roman emperor Justinian (527–565) in the form of cocoons concealed in hollow walking sticks. But later Western silk production in Italy and France never equaled the Chinese in quality, just as European porcelain, developed in the eighteenth century, never reproduced the perfection of form and finish of the Chinese models.

Tea was introduced from Southeast Asia as a medicine and an aid to meditation and began to be drunk widely in fifth-century China. It became the basic Chinese drink during the T'ang, grown in quantities in the misty hills of the south. By the eighteenth century it was a major item of export to the West. Seeds and cuttings of the tea plant were smuggled out of China by the English East India Company in 1843 to start plantation production in India and Ceylon, and tea became the world's most popular drink.

Ch'ang An in an Age of Imperial Splendor

The splendor of the T'ang and its empire was symbolized in its capital at Ch'ang An, where the Han and the Ch'in had also ruled. It was the eastern terminus of trade routes linking China with central Asia and lands beyond and also presided over the largest empire the world had yet seen, exceeding even the Han and Roman empires. People from all over Asia—Turks, Indians, Persians, Syrians, Vietnamese, Koreans, Japanese, Jews, Arabs, and even Nestorian (eastern) Christians—thronged its streets and added to its cosmopolitan quality. It was probably also the largest wholly planned city ever built, covering some 30 square miles and including within its massive walls about a million people. The imperial census also recorded nearly another million living in the urban area outside the walls.

Like all Chinese administrative centers, Ch'ang An was laid out on a checkerboard pattern, with broad avenues running east-west and north-south to great gates at the cardinal compass points. These were closed at night, and the main avenues leading to them divided the city into major quarters. These were further subdivided by other principal streets into groups of 110 blocks, each constituting an administrative unit, with its own internal pattern of alleyways. The emperor's palace faced south down a 500-foot-wide central thoroughfare to the south gate, the one used by most visitors and all official envoys and messengers. This arrangement was designed to awe and impress all who came to Ch'ang An with the power and greatness of the empire. Kaifeng and Peking were later designed similarly, and for the same purpose.

Within the city, people lived in rectangular wards, each surrounded by walls with gates closed at night. The West Market and the East Market, supervised by the government, occupied larger blocks to serve their respective halves of the city. There and elsewhere in the city, in open spaces and appointed theaters, foreign and Chinese players, acrobats, and magicians performed dramas, operas, skits, and other amusements. Women of fashion paraded their fancy clothing and coiffures. For men and women alike, one of the most popular pastimes was polo, which had been adopted from Persia; T'ang paintings showing polo matches make it clear that women played too. As later in India, the wealthy prided themselves on their stable of good polo ponies and their elegant turnout for matches.

Artists and sculptors also found horses popular subjects; despite their apparent mass production, T'ang paintings and clay figurines of horses are still full of life and movement. Another favorite subject for art was the endless variety of foreigners in this cosmopolitan center, depicted faithfully in both painting and figurines, so that one can easily recognize, by dress and physical features, which people are being represented.

T'ang culture was worldly, elegant, and urbane, but Buddhism was still in vogue and in official favor. Buddhist temples and pagodas also gave Chinese architects an outlet for their talents, and the first half of the T'ang was a golden age of temple architecture and sculpture, the latter showing clear artistic as well as religious influences from the Indian home of Buddhism. A cosmopolitan center for all of Asia, Ch'ang An was also, like China, the cultural model for the rest of East Asia. Official emissaries and less formal visitors and merchants or adventurers came repeatedly from Korea, Japan, and lesser states to the south and west to bask in the glories of Ch'ang An and to take back with them as much as they could for building their own versions of T'ang civilization.

Persian Zoroastrians, Muslims, Jews, Indian Buddhists and Hindus, and Nestorian Christians and Byzantines from the eastern Mediterranean, representing

Tax Reform: A Chinese View

Yang Yen (727–781), a high official of the T'ang dynasty, wrote a memorial to the throne proposing tax reforms, which were carried out and lasted several centuries.

When the dynastic laws were first formulated there was the land tax, the labor tax on able-bodied men, and the cloth tax on households. But enforcement of the law was lax; people migrated or died, and landed property changed hands. The poor rose and the rich fell. The Board of Revenue year after year presented out-of-date figures to the court. Those who were sent to guard the frontiers were exempted from land tax and labor tax for six years, after which they returned from service. Yet as Emperor Hsuang-tsung was engaged in many campaigns against the barbarians, most of those sent to the frontier died. The frontier generals, however, concealed the facts and did not report their deaths. Thus their names were never removed from the tax registers. When Wang Kung held the post of Commissioner of Fiscal Census during the T'ien Pao period [742–755] he strove to increase revenue. Since these names appeared on the registers and yet the adults were missing, he concluded that they had concealed themselves to avoid paying taxes. . . . The way to handle all government expenses and tax collections is first to calculate the amount needed and then to allocate the tax among the people. The income of the state would be governed according to its expenses. All households would be registered in the places of their actual residence, without regard to whether they are native households or not. All persons should be graded according to their wealth. . . . Those who have no permanent residence and do business as travelling merchants should be taxed in whatever prefecture they are located at the rate of one-thirtieth of their wealth. All practices which cause annoyance to the people should be corrected. . . . Everything should be under the control of the President of the Board of Revenue and the Commissioner of Funds.

Source: W. T. de Bary, ed., *Sources of Chinese Tradition* (New York: Columbia University Press, 1960), pp. 414–416.

nearly all the great world religions, were among the city's permanent residents, all welcomed in this center of world culture and all leaving some evidence of their presence. Ch'ang An flourished for two and one half centuries, from the early seventh to the mid-ninth, when the capital, like the empire, fell into chaos. But from 618 to around 860 it shone with a cosmopolitan brilliance perhaps never equaled until modern times.

Cultural Achievement and Political Decay

The T'ang is still seen as the greatest period of Chinese poetry, especially in the work of Li Po (Li Bo, 701–762) and Tu Fu (Du Fu, 712–770). Some 1,800 samples of Li Po's 20,000 poems survive, including these lines:

Beside my bed the bright moonbeams glimmer
Almost like frost on the floor.
Rising up, I gaze at the mountains bathed in moonlight:
Lying back, I think of my old home.
A girl picking lotuses beside the stream—
At the sound of my oars she turns;
She vanishes giggling among the flowers,
And, all pretense, declines to come out.
Amid the flowers with a jug of wine
The world is like a great empty dream.
Why should one toil away one's life?
That is why I spend my days drinking. . . .
Lustily singing, I wait for the bright moon.
I drink alone with no one to share
Raising up my cup, I welcome the moon. . . .
We frolic in revels suited to the spring.

The legend, almost certainly untrue but appealing, is that Li Po drunkenly leaned out of a boat to embrace the reflection of the moon and drowned, happy in his illusion.

The poet Li Po (701–762) is perhaps the most appealing T'ang figure. His poetry is still learned and quoted by successive generations of Chinese.

Tu Fu was a more sober poet than Li Po, but equally admired. Here are some samples of his lines:

> ***Frontier war drums disrupt everyone's travels.***
> ***At the border in autumn a solitary goose honks.***
> ***Tonight the hoar frost will be white. . . .***
> ***I am lucky to have brothers, but all are scattered. . . .***
> ***The letters I write never reach them.***
> ***How terrible that the fighting cannot stop.***
> ***Distant Annam* sends the court a red parrot,***
> ***Gaudy as a peach blossom and as talkative as we are.***
> ***But learning and eloquence are given the same treatment:***
> ***The cage of imprisonment. Is one ever free?***
> ***The capital is captured, but hills and streams remain.***
> ***With spring in the city the grass and trees grow fast.***
> ***Bewailing the times, the flowers droop as if in tears.***
> ***Saddened as I am with parting, the birds make my heart flutter.***
> ***Army beacons have flamed for three months.***
> ***A letter from home now would be worth a king's ransom.***
> ***In my anxiety I have scratched my white hairs even shorter.***
> ***What a jumble! Even hairpins cannot help me.***

Relatively little T'ang painting or literature has survived, apart from a few tomb walls and a few texts, but we have many accounts of the great painters of the time and of fiction writers of whose work we have only a few samples. What have survived in great abundance are the magnificent glazed pottery figures used to furnish tombs and adorn houses and palaces, probably the best-known aspect of T'ang art. Learning and the arts enjoyed a further blossoming under Emperor Hsuan-tsung (Xuanzong, 712–756) and at his elegant court. But in his old age Hsuan-tsung became infatuated with a son's concubine, the beautiful Yang Kuei-fei, who with her relatives and protégés gained control of the empire but ran it badly. Rebellion resulted, and the capital was sacked in 755. Hsuan-tsung fled south with Lady Yang, but his resentful guards strangled her as the cause of all the empire's troubles, and Hsuan-tsung abdicated in sorrow. The rebellion was finally put down, and order was restored.

Although there were to be no more outstanding T'ang emperors and the power of court factions and great families grew, the economy thrived and culture flourished. A Confucian revival occurred in the ninth century, and partly as a result, the state moved to confiscate the wealth and destroy the political power of Buddhist temples, monasteries, and monks in the 840s. Most temple and monastic properties and tax-free estates, which had grown to immense size, were taken over by the state, and most monasteries were destroyed. The move was similar to that undertaken by King Henry VIII of England seven centuries later, and with similar motives—the need to regain undivided power and control over lost revenues (see Chapter 17). Chinese Buddhism never recovered from this blow and remained thereafter a small minority religion in a Confucian and Taoist society (see Chapter 7). Buddhism was also resented by many Chinese because of its foreign origins, especially orthodox Confucianists and dedicated Taoists, as Christianity was to be later. Its association with Empress Wu did not help.

Like its Han predecessor, the T'ang dynasty lost effectiveness over time and was weakened by corruption. A series of rebellions broke out after 875, prompted first by a great drought in the north but spreading quickly among disaffected subjects all over the country. Rival generals or their puppets succeeded one another on the throne after 884, and in 907 the dynasty dissolved. After a period of confusion, a young general proclaimed a new

*Annam is central Vietnam, beyond the empire's direct rule, but, as implied here, tributary.

dynasty in 960, the Sung, which was to last more than three centuries.

The Sung Dynasty

In many ways, the Sung is the most exciting period in Chinese history. Later Chinese historians have criticized it because it failed to stem the tide of barbarian invasion and was ultimately overwhelmed by the hated Mongols. But it lasted from 960 to 1279, roughly the 300-year average for most dynasties, and presided over a period of unprecedented growth, innovation, and cultural flowering. For a long time the Sung policy of defending the empire's essential territories and appeasing neighboring barbarian groups with money and flattery worked well. It made sense to give up the exhausting Han and T'ang effort to hold Sinkiang, Tibet, Mongolia, Manchuria, Vietnam, and even the more marginal arid fringes of northern China. These areas were all unprofitable from the Chinese point of view; they never repaid, in any form but pride, the immense costs of controlling them. Most of them were arid or mountainous wastelands thinly settled by restless nomads who took every chance to rebel and who were very effective militarily.

Vietnam and Korea had been chronic drains on China's wealth and military strength; both were determined to fight relentlessly against Chinese control but willing to accept a more or less nominal tributary status, which satisfied Chinese pride and avoided bloody struggles. The Sung wisely concentrated on the productive center of Han Chinese settlements south of the Great Wall and even accepted barbarian control of what is now the Peking area and a similar arrangement with another barbarian group in the arid northwestern province of Kansu (Gansu). Little of value was lost by these agreements, and the remarkable flowering of Sung China had much to do with its abandonment of greater imperial ambitions. What remained under Chinese control was still roughly the size of non-Russian Europe and, with a population of some 100 million, was by far the largest, most productive, and most highly developed state in the world.

The Sung capital was built at Kaifeng, near the great bend of the Yellow River. In addition to its administrative functions, it became a huge commercial entrepôt and a center of manufacturing, served in all respects by the Grand Canal, which continued to bring rice and other goods from the prosperous south. There was a notable boom in iron and steel production and metal industries, using coal as fuel. China in the eleventh century probably produced more iron, steel, and metal goods than the whole of Europe until the mid-eighteenth century and similarly preceded Europe by seven centuries in smelting and heating with coal. Kaifeng was better located to administer and to draw supplies from the Yangtze valley and the south than Ch'ang An, whose role in frontier pacification was in any case no longer so necessary. The Sung army was large, mobile, equipped with iron and steel weapons, and well able for some time to defend the state's new borders. Kaifeng probably exceeded a million inhabitants, with merchants and artisans proportionately more important than in the past, although there were also swarms of officials, soldiers, providers, servants, and hangers-on of various sorts.

The early Sung emperors prudently eliminated the power of the court eunuchs and the great landed families and reestablished the scholar-officialdom as the core of administration. Civil servants recruited through examination had no power base of their own but did have a long tradition of public service and could even check the abuses of the powerful. To ensure their loyalty to the empire, their local postings were changed every three years, and they never served in their native places, lest they become too identified with the interests of any one area. In each county and at each higher level the emperor appointed both a civil administrator—a magistrate or governor—and a military official, each with his own staff, who with other officials such as tax collectors and the imperial censors or inspectors had overlapping jurisdictions and could check on each other. It was an efficient system that ensured good administration most of the time. The spread of mass printing promoted literacy and education and opened wider opportunities for commoners to enter the elite group of the scholar-gentry from whom officials were recruited or to prosper in trade.

The eleventh century was in many ways a golden age of good government, prosperity, and creativity. Paper promissory notes and letters of credit, followed by mass government issue of paper currency, served the growth of commerce. Government officials distributed printed pamphlets and promoted improved techniques in agriculture: irrigation, fertilization, ingenious new metal tools and mechanical equipment, and improved crop strains. Population grew even beyond the T'ang levels. Painting had a glorious development, often supported by rich urban merchants as well as by the Sung court. Literature also flourished, aided by the spread of cheap printing. Fiction proliferated, some now in the vernacular. The most famous Sung literary figure is the poet-painter-official Su Shih (Su Tung-p'o, Su Dongpo, 1037–1101), perhaps the best known in China's long tradition of poetic nature lovers. It was a confident, creative time.

Su Shih was, like so many of the scholar-gentry, a painter as well as a poet. In several of his poems he tries

The "Ever-Normal Granary" System

Po Chu-i (772–846), one of China's greatest poets, was also a T'ang official. While serving as an imperial censor in 808 he wrote a memorial criticizing the "ever-normal granary" system.

I have heard that because of the good harvest this year the authorities have asked for an imperial order to carry out Grain Harmonization so that cheap grain may be bought and the farmers benefitted. As far as I can see, such purchases mean only loss to the farmers. . . . In recent years prefectures and districts were allowed to assess each household for a certain amount of grain, and to fix the terms and the date of delivery. If there was any delay, the punitive measures of imprisonment and flogging were even worse than those usually involved in the collection of taxes. Though this was called Grain Harmonization, in reality it hurt the farmers. . . . If your majesty would consider converting the taxes payable in cash into taxes payable in kind, the farmers would neither suffer loss by selling their grain at a cheap price, nor would they have the problem of re-selling bales of cloth and silk. The profit would go to the farmers, the credit to the emperor. Are the advantages of that commutation in kind not evident? . . . I lived for some time in a small hamlet where I belonged to a household which had to contribute its share to Grain Harmonization. I myself was treated with great harshness; it was truly unbearable. Not long ago, as an official in the metropolitan district, I had responsibility for the administration of Grain Harmonization. I saw with my own eyes how delinquent people were flogged, and I could not stand the sight of it. In the past I have always wanted to write about how people suffered from this plague [but] since I was a petty and unimportant official in the countryside, I had no opportunity to approach your majesty. Now I have the honor of being promoted to serve your majesty and of being listed among the officials who offer criticism and advice. [If] my arguments are not strong enough to convince . . . order one of your trustworthy attendants to inquire incognito among the farmers. . . . Then your majesty will see that my words are anything but rash and superficial statements.

Source: W. T. de Bary, ed., *Sources of Chinese Tradition* (New York: Columbia University Press, 1960), pp. 423–425.

to merge the two media, inviting the reader to step into the scene and be immersed in a mind-emptying union with the great world of nature. He also used dust as a symbol for both official life (dead files and lifelessness, as in our own culture) and the capital on the dusty plains of the north, where he served for many years as an official.

Foggy water curls and winds around the brook road;
Layered blue hills make a ring where the brook runs east.
On a white moonlit shore a long-legged heron roosts.
And this is a place where no dust comes.
An old man of the stream looks, says to himself:
"What is your little reason for wanting so much to be a bureaucrat?
You have plenty of wine and land;
Go on home, enjoy your share of leisure!"

A boat, light as a leaf, two oars squeaking frighten wild geese.
Water reflects the clear sky, the limpid waves are calm.
Fish wriggle in the weedy mirror, herons dot misty foreshores.
Across the sandy brook swift, the frost brook cold, the moon brook bright.
Layer upon layer like a painting, bend after bend like a screen.
Remember old Yen Ling long ago—"Lord," "Minister"—a dream, Now gone, vain fames.
Only the far hills are long, the cloudy hills tumbled, the dawn hills green.
Drunk, abob in a light boat, wafted into the thick of flowers,
Fooled by the sensory world, I hadn't meant to stop here.
Far misty water, thousand miles' slanted evening sunlight,
Numberless hills, riot of green like rain—
I don't remember how I came.

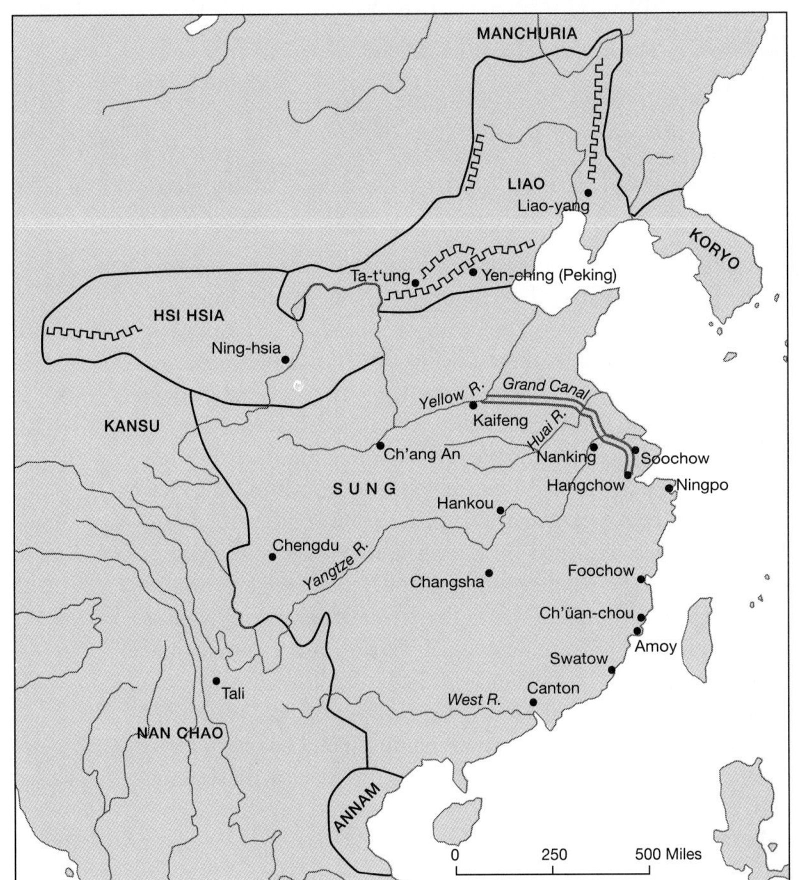

MAP 12.2 CHINA AND KOREA IN 1050

Defeat in the North

But trouble was brewing on the northern frontiers. A barbarian group, the Jurchen, spilled over from their homeland in southern Manchuria in the early twelfth century. In alliance with the Sung, in 1122 they defeated another barbarian group that had ruled the northeastern border area, returning it to Chinese control. The warlike Jurchen were not overly impressed by the army of their Sung allies, and the Sung foolishly treated them as inferiors. The Jurchen advanced southward, besieged Kaifeng, which was heavily defended, and sacked the city in 1127 after the Chinese failed to pay them an extravagant indemnity. The war continued for a decade, with Jurchen armies briefly penetrating south of the Yangtze. But the Sung armies regrouped and drove them back into northern China, finally concluding a treaty that left the Jurchen in control of the area north of the Yangtze valley with the Sung as a tribute-paying vassal. Now called Southern Sung, the dynasty built a new capital at Hangchou (Hangzhou) at the southern edge of the Yangtze delta. The Sung had lost the north, but now they could concentrate on China's heartland, the Yangtze valley and the south. Another century of brilliance and innovation ensued, with no loss of momentum.

The Southern Sung Period

Cut off from normal overland trade routes through the northwest, the Sung turned in earnest to developing sea passages to Southeast Asia and India. Permanent colonies of Chinese merchants grew in many Southeast Asian trade centers, and ports on China's southeast coast, from Hangchou south, flourished. These included large numbers of resident foreigners, mostly Arabs, who lived in special quarters under their own headmen. Foreign accounts agree that these were the world's largest port cities at the time. Taxes on maritime trade provided a fifth of the imperial revenue, an unheard-of proportion that betokened new commercial prosperity. There was a striking advance in the size and design of oceangoing ships, some of which could carry over 600 people plus cargo, far larger than any elsewhere until modern times.

The Confucian Revival

The Sung poet, official, and historian Ou-yang Hsiu (1007–1070) was one of several leading figures who promoted the revival of Confucianism and criticized Buddhism as alien.

Buddha was a barbarian who was far removed from China and lived long ago. In the age of Yao, Shun, and the Three Dynasties [the golden age of China's remote past], kingly rule was practiced, [and] government and the teachings of rites and righteousness flourished. . . . But after the Three Dynasties had fallen into decay, when kingly rule ceased and rites and righteousness were neglected, Buddhism came to China, [taking] advantage of this time of decay and neglect to come and plague us. . . . If we will but remedy this decay, revive what has fallen into disuse, and restore kingly rule in its brilliance and rites and righteousness in their fullness, then although Buddhism continues to exist, it will have no hold upon our people. . . . Buddhism has plagued the world for a thousand years. . . . The people are drunk with it, and it has seeped into their bones and marrow so that it cannot be vanquished by mouth and tongue. . . . There is nothing so effective in overcoming it as practicing what is fundamental. . . . When the way of Confucius [is] made clear, the other schools [will] cease. This is the effect of practicing what is fundamental in order to overcome Buddhism. . . . These days a tall warrior clad in armor and bearing a spear may surpass in bravery a great army, yet when he sees the Buddha he bows low and when he hears the doctrines of the Buddha he is sincerely awed and persuaded. Why? Because though he is indeed strong and full of vigor, in his heart he is confused and has nothing to cling to. . . . If a single scholar who understands rites and righteousness can keep from submitting to these doctrines, then we have but to make the whole world understand rites and righteousness and these doctrines will, as a natural consequence, be wiped out.

Source: W. T. de Bary, ed., *Sources of Chinese Tradition* (New York: Columbia University Press, 1960), pp. 442–445.

The compass, an earlier Chinese invention, was a vital navigational aid, and these ships also pioneered in the use of multiple masts (important for manageability as well as speed), separate watertight compartments (not known elsewhere until much later), and the stern-post rudder, which replaced the awkward and unseaworthy steering oar. In all these respects, Sung ships presaged modern ships by many centuries. Ironically, they helped make it possible much later for Europeans to undertake the sea voyage to Asia using the compass, rudder, and masts—plus gunpowder—originally developed by China and to record their conquests and profits on Chinese-invented paper.

Domestically too commerce and urbanization flourished. The Yangtze delta and the southeast coast had long been China's commercial centers, thanks to their high productivity and the easy movement of goods by river, sea, and canal. An immense network of canals and navigable creeks covered the Yangtze and Canton deltas, serving a system of large and small cities inhabited increasingly by merchants managing a huge and highly varied trade. The capital at Hangchou, with its additional administrative role, grew to giant size and may have reached a million and a half in population, making it one of the world's largest cities before the age of railways. Water transport made this possible for Hangchou and other big cities, including Pataliputra, Rome, Ch'ang An, Istanbul, Edo (Tokyo), and eighteenth-century London. The proliferation of Chinese cities included for the first time several as big as or bigger than the capital and many only slightly smaller. Suchou (Soochow, Suzhou) and Fuchou (Foochow, Fuzhou) each had well over a million people, and according to Marco Polo, there were six other large cities in the 300 miles between those two. Chinese medicine became still more sophisticated, incorporating even the practice of vaccinating

Advice to a Chinese Emperor

The Sung official Ssu-ma Kuang (1019–1086) was also part of the Confucian revival and wrote a monumental general history of China. Here is part of one of his memorials to the emperor, urging the abolition of Wang An-shih's reforms.

Human inclinations being what they are, who does not love wealth and high rank, and who does not fear punishment and misfortune? Seeing how the wind blew and following with the current, the officials and gentry vied in proposing schemes, striving to be clever and unusual. They supported what was harmful and rejected what was beneficial. In name they loved the people; in fact they injured the people. The crop loans, local service exemptions, marketing controls, [the] credit and loan system, and other measures were introduced. They aimed at the accumulation of wealth and pressed the people mercilessly. The distress they caused still makes for difficulties today. Besides, there were frontier officials who played fast and loose, hoping to exploit their luck. They spoke big and uttered barefaced lies, waged war unjustifiably, and needlessly disturbed the barbarians on our borders. . . . Officials who liked to create new schemes which they might take advantage of to advance themselves . . . changed the regulations governing the tea, salt, iron, and other monopolies and increased the taxes on families, on business, and so forth, in order to meet military expenses. . . . They misled the late emperor, and saw to it that they themselves derived all the profit from these schemes. . . .

Now the evils of the new laws are known to everyone in the empire, high or low, wise or ignorant. Yet there are still some measures which are harmful to the people and hurtful to the state. These matters are of immediate and urgent importance, and should be abolished. Your servant will report on them in separate memorials, hoping that it may please your sage will to grant us an early decision and act upon them. . . . The best plan is to select and keep those new laws which are of advantage to the people, while abolishing all those which are harmful. This will let the people of the land know unmistakably that the court loves them with a paternal affection.

Source: W. T. de Bary, ed., *Sources of Chinese Tradition* (New York: Columbia University Press, 1960), pp. 487–489.

against smallpox, learned from Guptan India but unknown in the West until 1798.

We know a good deal about Hangchou, both from voluminous Chinese sources and from the accounts of several foreigners who visited it, including Marco Polo, who saw it only under Mongol rule after its great period had long passed. Nevertheless, he marveled at its size and wealth and called it the greatest city in the world, by comparison with which even Venice, his hometown and probably then the pinnacle of European urbanism, was, he says, a poor village. The great Arab traveler Ibn Battuta, 50 years later in the fourteenth century, says that even then Hangchou was three days' journey in length and subdivided into six towns, each larger than anything in the West. His approximate contemporary, the traveling Italian friar John of Marignolli, called Hangchou "the first, the biggest, the richest, the most populous, and altogether the most marvelous city that exists on the face of the earth."

These were all men who knew the world; even allowing for the usual hyperbole of travelers' tales, they were right about Hangchou. Its rich merchant and scholar-official community and its increasingly literate population of shopkeepers, artisans, and the upwardly mobile supported an exuberance of painting, literature, drama, music, and opera, while for the unlettered there were public storytellers in the ancient Chinese oral tradition. Southern Sung (and the Yuan or Mongol dynasty that followed it) is the great period of Chinese landscape painting, with its celebration of the beauties of the misty mountains, streams and lakes, bamboo thickets, and green hills of the south.

Innovation and Technological Development

The Southern Sung period was also a time of technological innovation. The philosopher Chu Hsi (Zhuxi, 1130–1200), the founder of what is called Neo-Confucianism, was in many ways a Leonardo-like figure, interested in and competent at a wide range of practical subjects as well as philosophy. This was in the tradition of the Confucian scholar-gentleman, but Chu Hsi and some of his contemporaries carried what Confucius called "the investigation of things" still further into scientific inquiry. Chu Hsi's journals record, for example, his observation that uplifted rock strata far above current sea level contained marine fossils. Like Leonardo, but three centuries earlier, he made the correct deduction and wrote the first statement of the geomorphological theory of uplift. But Chu Hsi was primarily concerned with personal development. He argued that through the Confucian discipline of self-cultivation, every man could be his own philosopher and sage, a doctrine similar to Plato's.

Rapid developments in agriculture, manufacturing, and transport led to a great variety of new tools and machines for cultivation and threshing; for lifting water (pumps); for carding, spinning, and weaving textile fibers; and for making windlasses, inclined planes, canal locks, and refinements in traction for water and land carriers. Water clocks were widespread, as were water-powered mills, to grind grain and to perform some manufacturing functions. Superficially at least, thirteenth-century China resembled eighteenth-century Europe: commercialization, urbanization, a widening market (including overseas trade), rising demand, and hence both the incentive and the capital to pursue mechanical invention and other measures to increase production.

Would these developments have led to a true industrial revolution, with all its profound consequences? We will never know, because the Mongol onslaught cut them off, and later dynasties failed to replicate the conditions of late Sung society. The great English historian of early modern Europe, R. H. Tawney, warns us against "giving the appearance of inevitableness by dragging into prominence the forces which have triumphed and thrusting into the background those which they have swallowed up."[1] It is tempting to think that if the Sung had had just a little longer—or if Chinghis Khan had died young (as he nearly did many times)—China might have continued to lead the world and modern Europe might never have risen as it did.

The Mongol Conquest and the Yuan Dynasty

The Mongols overran Southern Sung because they were formidable fighters, but they were aided by some serious Sung errors. The Mongol leader, Chinghis (Genghis) Khan (1155–1227), first attacked the Jurchen territories in the north and then the other non-Chinese groups in the northwest. In 1232 the Sung made an alliance with the Mongols to crush the remnants of the Jurchen and within two years reoccupied Kaifeng and Loyang. A year later they were desperately defending northern China against an insatiable Mongol army, other wings of which had already conquered Korea, central Asia, the Near East, and eastern Europe.

For 40 years the fighting raged in the north, where the heavily fortified Chinese cities were both defended and attacked with the help of explosive weapons. Gunpowder had been used much earlier in China for fireworks and for warfare too as an explosive and a "fire powder." Fire arrows using naphtha as fuel and part pro-

EAST ASIA, 600–1500

	China	Korea	Japan
c. A.D. 600–900	Sui dynasty (589–618) T'ang dynasty (618–907)	Paekche kingdom (c. 220–660) Koguryo kingdom (c. 220–669) Silla kingdom (c. 220–935)	Nara period (c. 710–794) Heian era (794–1185)
c. 900–1200	Sung dynasty (960–1279) Jurchen invasion (1120s) Chu Hsi (1130–1200)	Koryo kingdom (935–1218)	
c. 1200–1500	Chinghis Khan (1155–1227) Yuan dynasty (1279–1368)	Mongol rule (1218–1364) Yi dynasty (1392–1910)	Kamakura period (1185–1333) Ashikaga shogunate (1333–1573)

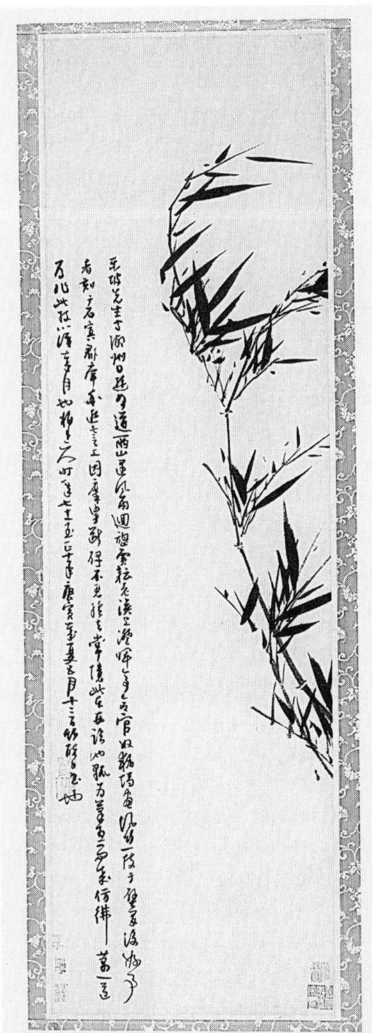

Bamboo, by Wu Chan (Yuan dynasty). Chinese artists loved to paint the graceful fronds of bamboo, each leaf created with a single stroke of the brush, in black ink. The techniques of bamboo painting were akin to those of calligraphy, and hence such paintings often include gracefully written text.

pellant had been known in early Han times, and by the tenth century fire lances, spear-tipped bamboo tubes filled with a gunpowder propellant, were in use. In the struggle between the Chinese and the Mongols, cast-metal barrels using gunpowder to propel a tight-fitting projectile appeared, marking the first certain occurrence of cannon in warfare. This devastating new technology, especially helpful in sieges, quickly spread to Europe and was in use there by the early fourteenth century.

The Sung were fatally weakened by divided counsels and inconsistent strategies, worsened by factionalism. By 1273 the Mongols had triumphed. They soon poured into the south, where Hangchou surrendered in 1276. Resistance continued in the Canton area until 1279, when the Sung fleet was defeated in a great sea battle. During much of the long struggle it was touch and go, but the Mongols made few mistakes and the Sung many, although they put up a far longer and more effective resistance to the Mongols than any of their many other continental opponents except the Delhi sultanate of Alaud-din Khalji and his mameluke troops. (The Mongols' seaborne expeditions to Japan and Java left them at a serious disadvantage; their fleet was twice scattered by major storms at critical points, and their invasion attempts were abandoned.)

The Mongols could indeed never have conquered China without the help of Chinese technicians, including siege engineers, gun founders, artillery experts, and naval specialists. Chinghis died in 1227, but he had already planned the conquest of Sung China, which was completed by his grandson Kubilai (1260–1294), who fixed his capital at Peking as early as 1264 and adopted the dynastic title of Yuan. Korea, northern Vietnam, and the previously non-Chinese southwest were also conquered; southern Vietnam, Siam, Burma, and Tibet were forced to accept tributary status as vassals. The Mongol conquest of China's southwest included the defeat of the Thai kingdom of Nan Chao based at Tali (Dali) and forced a major wave of Thais out of their homeland southward into Siam, where they joined earlier migrants (see Chapter 11).

China, for all its size, constituted only a small part of the vast empire built by the Mongols (see Chapter 13). It is astounding that an area of such extent was conquered by a people who probably numbered only about a million, supplemented by a few other steppe nomads. The simple reason is that they were uniquely tough warriors, almost literally born in the saddle, used to extreme privation and exposure, and welded into an unbeatable fighting force by the magnetic leadership of Chinghis Khan, who consolidated the many warring Mongol and related tribes into a single weapon. Chinghis was born clutching a clot of blood in his tiny fist. The Mongols in his time were shamanists (animists and believers in magic), and his mother hurriedly called a soothsayer, who declared, "This child will rule the world."

The Mongols' great military advantage was mobility. Their brilliant use of cavalry tactics, controlled by the ingenious use of signal flags, plus the short but powerful compound reflex bow, which they could load and fire from a gallop, maximized their striking force. They could cover 100 miles a day in forced marches, unencumbered by a baggage train since they carried their spartan rations of parched grain and mare's milk in their saddlebags. They always traveled with spare horses, and they knew how to open a vein in the necks of the wiry steppe ponies and drink some blood, closing it again so that horse and rider could continue. Through Kubilai's time, the Mongols rarely lost an engagement, even more rarely a campaign. Men who resisted were commonly butchered and their women and children raped, slaughtered, or enslaved.

The terror of the Mongols' record demoralized their opponents, who described them as inhuman monsters. They were expert practitioners of psychological warfare and even employed spies or agents to spread horrifying stories of their irresistible force and their ruthlessness toward resisters. Chinghis, as a true steppe nomad, especially hated cities and city dwellers and made a series of horrible examples of them, often leaving no one alive. The Mongols loved the violence and pride of conquest but had little understanding of or interest in administration, and their empire began to fall apart within a few years of its acquisition.

The period of the Mongols' rule in China, the Yuan dynasty (1279–1368), lasted a little longer only because by that time the Mongols had become considerably Sinified and had realized as well that they could not manage China without employing many thousands of Chinese. They also used many foreigners whom they felt they could trust, including the Venetian Marco Polo, who served as a minor official in China from 1275 to 1292. He and others of his contemporaries were able to reach China in this period because for the brief years of the Mongol Empire, unified control was imposed on most of Eurasia and people could travel more or less safely across it.

Marco's famous journal, like all medieval tales, includes some supernatural stories, and it was dismissed by many because it speaks in such extravagant terms about the size and splendor of Yuan China. Indeed, he soon became known as "*Il milione,*" someone who told tall tales of millions of this and that. But when his confessor came to him on his deathbed and urged him to take back all his lies, Marco is said to have replied, "I have not told the half of what I saw."

Yuan China

The Mongols ran China largely through Chinese officials, aided by a few Sinified Mongols and foreigners. The Chinese bureaucratic system was retained, leaving only the military entirely in Mongol hands. For the years of Mongol rule, Chinese culture continued its development on Sung foundations, once the country had recovered from the profound devastation of the Mongol conquest. A number of new Chinese artists restored and extended the glories of Sung landscape painting, and drama and vernacular literature flourished anew. People, especially of the scholar-gentry-official group, were understandably disheartened by the political scene and turned for solace to art and literature. Mongol rule from the new capital at Peking was exploitive and often harsh. The Mongols rebuilt the Grand Canal, neglected since the fall of the Northern Sung, and extended it to feed and supply Peking, but at a heavy cost in lives and revenue.

Kubilai proved an able ruler of his new empire but concentrated on China and became almost entirely Chinese culturally. Marco Polo gives a flattering account of his sagacity, majesty, and benevolence, a portrait that was probably no more or less accurate than his more general accounts of Yuan China. But Kubilai was followed on his death in 1294 by increasingly inept figures. Smoldering Chinese hatred of the conquerors had flared into widespread revolts by the 1330s, and by 1350 the Mongols' control of the Yangtze valley was lost, while factions of their once united front fought one another in the north. A peasant rebel leader welded together Chinese forces, chased the remaining Mongols back into the steppes north of the Great Wall, and in 1368 announced the foundation of a new dynasty, the Ming, which was to restore Chinese pride and grandeur.

Chinese Culture and the Mongol Empire

By the late T'ang period, Chinese culture had largely acquired its present form. With the occupation and Sinification of most of the south, begun under the Han dynasty and completed under the aegis of the Mongols in the southwest, the state also assumed essentially its modern form. Tibet was more permanently incorporated by the Ch'ing (Qing or Manchu dynasty) in the eighteenth century, which also added Manchuria to the empire. By Sung times, the institutions of government and society had taken on outlines that persisted until the twentieth century. Civil administration was divided among six ministries, plus the censorate, and a military administration under ultimate civil control. At the top of the pyramid was the emperor, assisted by high officials. The empire was divided into provinces within the Great Wall, 18 of them by the seventeenth century, each under a governor and subdivided into prefectures and counties.

Paper flowed to and from the capital, transmitted along a network of paved roads and canals. Most decisions ultimately had to be made or approved by the emperor, which often created a bottleneck at the top. An equally important limitation was the small number of officials of all ranks. Probably no more than 30,000 governed an area the size of Europe and a population that had reached 100 million by Sung times. These administrators were indirectly augmented by unofficial but effective gentry leadership and management, even in the vast rural areas, which were beyond the power of the county magistrate to govern alone.

Still more important in the ordering of society was the family, which not only controlled people's lives but also settled most disputes and ensured harmony by virtuous example. Government controls were thus less essential. A peasant proverb summed up the self-imposed discipline of Chinese society: "Work when the sun rises, rest when the sun sets. The emperor is far away." Dynasties rose and fell, but the fundamental order of Chinese civilization persisted.

Chinese history can be readily divided into dynastic periods in what is called the dynastic cycle. The typical dynasty lasted about three centuries, sometimes preceded by a brief whirlwind period of empire building such as the Ch'in or the Sui. The first century of a new dynasty would be marked by political, economic, and cultural vigor, expansion, efficiency, and confidence; the second would build on or consolidate the achievements of the first; and in the third vigor and efficiency would wane, corruption would mount, banditry and rebellion would multiply, and the dynasty would ultimately fall. A new group would come to power from among the rebels but would rarely attempt to change the system, only its management and supervision.

Chinese culture was continuous, even during the political chaos that followed the fall of the Han. By T'ang times most of the elements of contemporary Chinese society were present. Rice was the dominant food in the diet, supplemented or replaced in the more arid parts of the north by wheat noodles, which Marco Polo is said to have brought back to Italy in the thirteenth century in a form later to become spaghetti, and steamed bread or, among poorer people, millet. Food was eaten with chopsticks, a technique adopted early by Korea and Japan, while the rest of the world ate with its fingers.

Given the size and density of population and the consequent pressure on land, poultry, eggs, meat, and fish were relatively scarce. The diet consisted largely of rice or wheat and a variety of vegetables, including beans and bean products such as curd (tofu) as a source of protein. Oxen or water buffalo were needed for plowing and were usually eaten only when they died naturally. Pigs, chickens, ducks, and fish, however, could scavenge for their own food and thus could be more easily raised.

The Chinese cuisine is justly famous, including as it does such a wide variety of foods (the Chinese have few dietary inhibitions), flavors, and sauces. Ingredients were sliced small so as to maximize and distribute their flavor and so that they would cook very quickly over a hot fire. As the burgeoning population cut down the forests, fuel became scarce and people were reduced to using twigs, branches, and dried grass for cooking. The universal utensil was the thin cast-iron saucer-shaped pot (*wok* in Cantonese), which heated quickly but held the heat and distributed it evenly in a technique we now call "stir frying."

The Chinese landscape was more and more converted into an artificial one of irrigated and terraced rice paddies, fish and duck ponds, and market towns where peasants sold their surplus produce or exchanged it for salt, cloth, tools, or other necessities not produced in all villages. From T'ang times, teahouses became the common centers for socializing, relaxation, gossip, and the negotiation of business or marriage contracts. Fortunetellers, scribes, booksellers, itinerant peddlers, actors, and storytellers enlivened the market towns and cities, and periodic markets with similar accompaniments were held on a smaller scale in most villages. All this made it less necessary for people to travel far from their native places, and most never went beyond the nearest market town. Beyond it they would have found for the most part only more villages and towns like those they knew, except perhaps for the provincial capital and of course the imperial capital.

In the south most goods and people in the lowlands moved by waterways, in the dry north by pack animals, carts, and human porters, which also operated in the mountainous parts of the south. The wheelbarrow and the flexible bamboo carrying pole were Chinese inventions that greatly enhanced the ability to transport heavy weights, carefully balanced as they were to enable porters to wheel or trot all day with loads far exceeding their unaided capacity. All these and many other aspects of Chinese culture remain essentially unchanged today.

Korea

Korean culture, though adopting much from China, added its own innovations and retained a strong sense of separate identity, together with a fierce determination to

Life along the river near Kaifeng at spring festival time. These two scenes come from a long scroll that begins with the rural areas and moves through suburbs into the capital, giving a vivid picture of the bustling life in and around Kaifeng, at the time the largest city in the world. The painting, by Chang Tse-tuan, was done in the early twelfth century.

preserve its political independence. The Korean peninsula, set off from the mainland of Asia, is separated by mountains along its northwestern frontier adjacent to Manchuria and by the gorge of the Yalu River, which marks the boundary. The Korean people probably came originally from eastern Siberia and northern Manchuria, as their spoken language, which is unrelated to Chinese, suggests. They brought with them or evolved their own culture, which was already well formed before they were exposed to heavy Chinese influence at the time of the Han occupation in the late second century B.C.

Rice, wheat, metals, written characters, paper, printing, lacquer, porcelain, and other innovations spread to Korea after they appeared in China. As in Vietnam, literate Chinese-style culture in Korea was an elite phenomenon that rested on an already developed indigenous cultural base that remained distinctive. A Chinese-style state arose in the north around P'yongyang in the century before Han Wu-ti's conquest. On the withdrawal of the Chinese military colonies after the fall of the Han in A.D. 220, Korea regained its freedom and was thenceforward self-governing (except for the brief Mongol interlude) until the Japanese takeover in 1910, although Chinese cultural influence continued and was openly welcomed.

Three Kingdoms: Paekche, Silla, and Koguryo

Three Korean kingdoms arose after 220: Paekche in the southwest, Silla in the southeast, and Koguryo in the north, the largest and closest to China. Confucianism and Chinese forms of government, law, literature, and art spread widely throughout the peninsula, followed by Buddhism as it grew in China. But Korea's long tradition of a hereditary aristocracy in a hierarchically ordered society of privilege prevented the adoption of China's more open official system of meritocracy based on examinations. Like the Japanese, the Koreans departed from the Chinese pattern in providing an important place for a military aristocracy.

In 669, with help from the T'ang, Silla succeeded in conquering Koguryo, after having earlier demolished Paekche. With its now united strength, Silla repelled T'ang efforts at reconquest, a remarkable feat given the power and proximity of T'ang China. As a formal Chinese vassal, Silla presided over a golden age of creativity. T'ang culture was a natural model, but in many respects Korean adaptations were at least the equal of their Chinese models. Korean ceramics, fully as accomplished as anything produced in China, had a magnificent development, particularly in pottery and fine porcelain. This included the beautiful celadon ware, with its subtle milky green jade-colored glaze, whose secret formula was admired and envied by the Chinese, though it was extinguished by the Mongol conquest of the thirteenth century and never recovered. Silla Korea also went beyond Chinese written characters and began a system of phonetic transcription, derived from the sound of characters but designed to reproduce spoken Korean. By the fifteenth century this had been further refined into the *han'gul* syllabary.

Silla control weakened by the tenth century. The kingdom was taken over by a usurper in 935, who named

This masterpiece of Korean art in bronze, depicting Maitreya, the "Buddha of the future," dates from the Silla period, sixth or seventh century A.D.

his new united state Koryo, an abbreviation of Koguryo and the origin of the name Korea. The Koryo capital at Kaesong, just north of Seoul, was built on the planned imperial model of the T'ang city of Ch'ang An and incorporated most of the Chinese system of government. Interest in Buddhism and its texts, as well as a refinement of Sung techniques, stimulated a virtual explosion of woodblock printing in the eleventh century, and magnificent celadon pieces were again produced. Koryo rule dissolved into civil war on the eve of the Mongol invasion, and Chinghis Khan easily overran the peninsula in 1218. The Mongols exacted heavy tribute and imposed iron rule, even forcing Koreans to aid them in their later expeditions against Japan. But in the 1350s the Mongol empire collapsed, and in 1392 a new dynasty arose, the Yi, which was to preside over a united Korea until 1910.

The Yi Dynasty

Under the Yi dynasty Korea continued the adaptation of Chinese civilization to a greater extent than any of its predecessors, including the incorporation of the imperial examination system, the Confucian bureaucracy, and the division of the country into eight centrally administered provinces on the Chinese model. Although Confucian ideology spread, in practice officeholding was still dominated by hereditary aristocrats. From their capital at

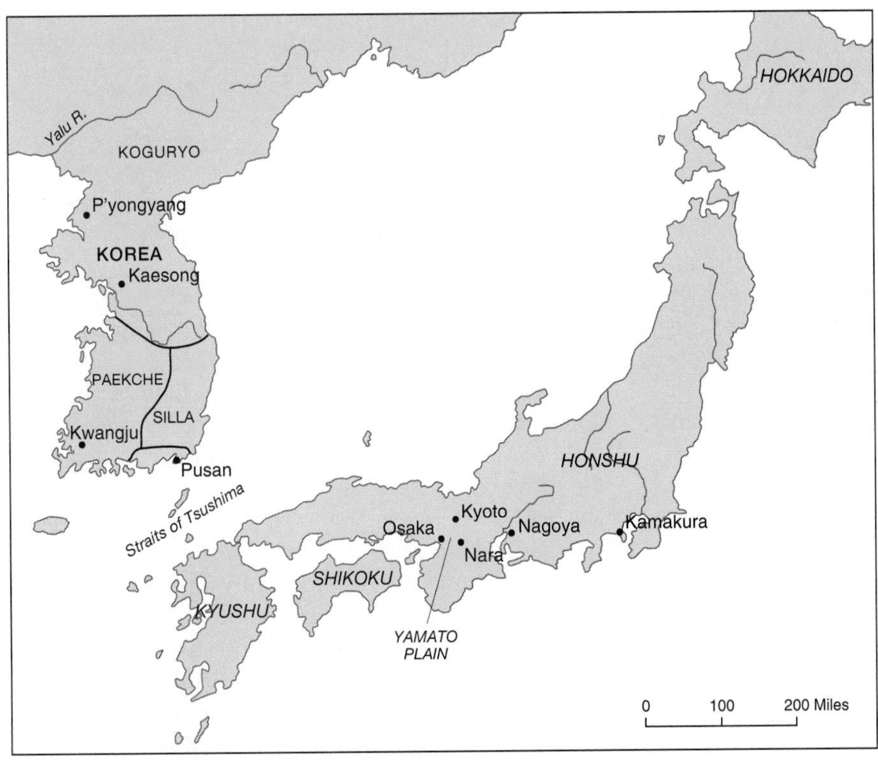

MAP 12.3 KOREA AND JAPAN, c. 500–1000

Seoul, Yi rulers continued to accept the formal status of a Chinese tributary state, a relationship that both parties spoke of amicably as that between "younger brother and elder brother." Buddhism declined almost completely, while Confucianism and Chinese-style painting and calligraphy flourished. A group called the *yangban,* originally landowners, acquired most of the functions and status of the Chinese gentry as an educated elite but remained a hereditary class, providing both civil and military officials, unlike the Chinese model.

Korean economic development was retarded by the country's mountainous landscape, which, like that of Japan and Greece, is divided into separate small basins, and by its long harsh winter, especially severe in the north. Only about one-seventh of the total land area could be cultivated, and trade and concentrated urban growth were also disadvantaged. But although most Koreans remained materially poorer than most Chinese, elite culture, technology, and the arts prospered in distinctively Korean styles, including the still superb ceramics. Korean dress, house types, diet, lifestyles, marriage and inheritance customs, and the volatile, earthy, robust, spontaneous Korean temperament remained their own as well. Food was flavored by the peppery pickled cabbage called *kimchi,* as it still is. Korea's indigenous cultural fabric was basic and showed through the Chinese overlay. There was thus no risk that Korea would be absorbed into Chinese culture, and Koreans remained proud of their independence and of their own sophisticated cultural tradition.

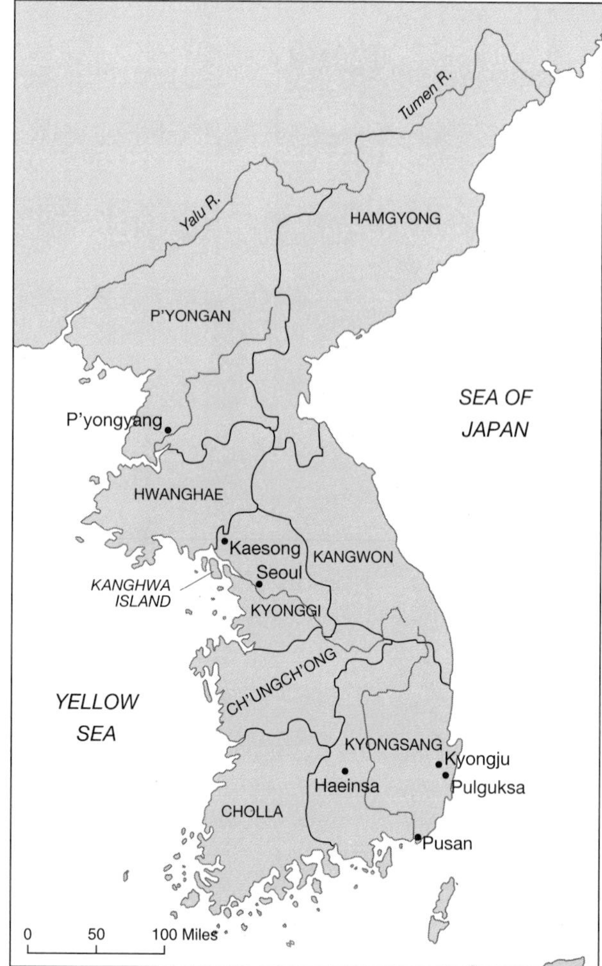

MAP 12.4 YI DYNASTY KOREA

The first century or so of Yi rule was a brilliant period in Korean and East Asian history. The fifteenth century saw a new explosion of printing, now vigorously supported by a Confucian state that put a high value on texts and learning. The Koreans further perfected the art of movable metal type, which was used among other things to reproduce the libraries burned by the Mongols and the wooden plates from which those books had been made. Eight other ambitious printing projects were carried out between 1403 and 1484. This was the first extensive use of movable type anywhere in the world. The technique originated in eleventh-century Sung China and was further developed in Korea a century or so later. In contrast, movable-type printing began in Europe only in the mid-fifteenth century.

The same century in Korea also saw important new developments in mathematics and in the manufacture of astronomical instruments. More closely related to printing was the perfection of the *han'gul* alphabet and syllabary, not only to write Korean but to give the Korean pronunciation of Chinese characters as well. Traditional characters continued to be used for official documents and elite literature, but the development and popularity of *han'gul* was an affirmation of Korea's proud and confident distinctiveness.

The vigor of the Yi order was slowly weakened by bureaucratic factionalism, which the throne never really overcame. Factionalism already had a long and disruptive history in Korea, from the time of the three early kingdoms, and it progressively eroded the effectiveness and authority of the Yi state. No strong rulers emerged after the early sixteenth century, and toward its end a divided and enfeebled Korea had to face the invasion of the Japanese warlord Hideyoshi between 1592 and 1598. His army overran and ravaged the country until, with aid from China, the invaders were driven back almost to the coast and stalemated there. The gifted Korean admiral Yi Sunsin then repeatedly defeated Japanese naval detachments and disrupted their supply lines with his ingenious "turtle ships." These vessels, covered with overlapping plates of iron and copper and armed fore and aft with beak-shaped metal prows that could ram and sink any ship, were the first armored warships. They were powered by rowers protected by the outer "turtle shell." The invasion was abandoned when Hideyoshi died in 1598, but Korea never fully recovered from its devastation.

The Yi dynasty continued, plagued by perennial factional fighting, although it still supported learning, the arts, and major new printing projects. Considerable economic growth resulted from improved agriculture and a rising commercial sector, and population probably doubled between 1600 and 1800. Merchants began to buy their way to *yangban* (gentry) status, as did prosperous farmers. Korea thus followed the path of Sung, Ming, and Manchu China and of Tokugawa Japan. But its political and administrative health was poor, ultimately inviting Japanese intervention after 1894.

Japan

Composed of four main islands off the southern tip of Korea, Japan had been both protected by its insularity from turmoil on the Asian mainland and to a degree also isolated from its development. The Straits of Tsushima between Korea and Japan are approximately 120 miles wide, and although Japan has been periodically involved with the mainland, the connection has never been as close as that between China and other areas of East Asia or between Britain and Europe. Japan has had the advantage of a clearly separate identity and as a result of its insularity has been able to make its own choices at most periods about what it wanted to adopt from abroad. Like Korea, Japan is mainly mountainous, and settlement has remained heavily concentrated on the narrow coastal plain between Tokyo and Osaka, an area roughly equivalent to the coastal corridor between Boston and Washington, D.C. All in all, Japan is about the size of California, but the northernmost island of Hokkaido was settled by the Japanese on a major scale only in this century. Mountains also retarded Japanese economic development and political unification. As in Korea, only a little over a seventh of the country is cultivated even now, although the climate, conditioned by the surrounding sea, is far milder and better watered. Coastal sea routes have also helped link settled areas and carry trade.

Early Culture and Development

The spoken language of the Japanese, unrelated to Chinese but in the same linguistic group as Korean, suggests that they too came originally from the Asian mainland north of China via the sea passage from Korea, although other migrants and cultural influences may have come into Japan from the tropical Pacific. The migrants slowly defeated, displaced, or absorbed the islands' original inhabitants, including a physically very different group called the Ainu, who now live as a tiny and dwindling minority on reservations on the northernmost island of Hokkaido. Early Japanese history is cloudy, in part because written records do not begin until the eighth century A.D., after Japan had adopted the Chinese art of writing from Korea. We have no firm dates before that time and can only guess when the people we now call Japanese arrived or when they emerged as a separate culture, but it was probably sometime between the third century B.C. and the first century A.D., partly through interbreeding with earlier inhabitants. Earlier preliterate and premetallic cultures had developed in Japan, producing pottery perhaps as early as in any part of Asia. Bronze tools and weapons from China entered via Korea about the first century B.C., and implements made of iron, a technology also imported from Korea, were being produced by around A.D. 200.

It seems clear that Korea played an important role in Japan until the fifth century A.D. By the time of the first Japanese records in the eighth century, a third of the nobility claimed Korean or Chinese descent, and clearly such lineage was perceived as a mark of superiority. Close interaction with Korea continued, with large numbers of Korean artisans, metallurgists, and technologists living in Japan, as well as Korean nobles and perhaps even rulers. There were also invasions and raids in both directions, until by about 400 such violent interactions faded and the Japanese continued to move northward from the southernmost island of Kyushu, closest to Korea, onto the main island of Honshu. There they established a central core on the Yamato Plain in the Nara–Kyoto–Osaka area, where it was to remain for approximately the next 1,000 years. The imperial capital, however, was not moved northeast to Tokyo until 1868, and the frontier with the Ainu lay just north of Kyoto for centuries.

The Nara Period

Chinese cultural infusions continued from Korea, including, sometime before 500, Chinese written characters and an increasing knowledge of Chinese culture and of Buddhism. By the end of the sixth century and increasingly in the seventh, missions were dispatched to China to observe and to bring back to Japan as much of Chinese civilization as possible. In the mid-seventh century a sweeping series of measures called the *Taika* ("Great Reform") began the process of transforming Japan and the Japanese imperial administration into a version of China's. By 710 the first permanent capital was inaugurated at Nara, a smaller-scaled copy of Ch'ang An, which presided over a modified Chinese-style government.

The ensuing century (until 794) is known as the Nara period, during which the transplantation of Chinese civilization continued, helped by successive Japanese missions to China. Currency and coins on the Chinese model were introduced. The Chinese scholars' habit of recording everything they observed was transmitted too, and important accounts of T'ang China come from Japanese sources of this period, as well as the first official histories of Japan. Buddhism spread, but Confucianism also entered from China and became important for the upper classes. As Taoism was retained in China, the original animistic and naturalistic Japanese religion of Shinto remained, in part no doubt as an assertion of Japanese distinctiveness but also because of its close connection with the imperial family. Beautiful wood-crafted Shinto shrines remain in "natural" areas even in contemporary Japan.

Artistic styles, gardens, court and official clothing, and sophisticated tastes all strove to replicate the Chinese model, and although they slowly diverged from that standard, Japanese high culture still retains the unmistakable marks of its seventh- and eighth-century Chinese origins. Even the straw mats *(tatami)* that still today cover the floor in traditional Japanese rooms, the prominence of raw fish and pickled vegetables in the diet, and the tea ceremony all came from T'ang China. Korean and Chinese artists, artisans, and technicians remained important in the Nara period as teachers and implementers of cultural reform. But Japan was a very different place, and the cultural transplant was never complete, nor did it ever penetrate very deeply into the mass of the people, most of whom remained peasants until the late nineteenth century. Unlike Chinese society, but as in Korea, descent and inherited status continued to be important, and society as a whole remained more tightly organized and more hierarchically controlled. Feudal-style lords and hereditary nobles remained the chief wielders of power. Japan tried the Chinese examination system, but, as in Korea, hereditary aristocrats undercut it by reserving most official positions for themselves. The Japanese emperor, considered divine and hence the bearer of a sacred mandate, was above politics or even administration.

Traditional Japanese stone garden at the Ryoanji Temple, Kyoto. Originally from T'ang China, this orderly and peaceful form of landscaping became characteristically Japanese and is still widely practiced.

The Heian Era

In 794 a vigorous young emperor, Kammu, moved the capital to Kyoto (then called Heian), in part to break away from the growing influence of Buddhist institutions in Nara. With the support of the powerful Fujiwara family, he and his successors began to modify or discard some aspects of the Chinese model so enthusiastically adopted earlier. Art and architecture increased their characteristically Japanese concern for textures and the use of natural materials. T'ang China was in turmoil, and Japanese missions stopped going there, while new interest arose in indigenous cultural patterns. Chinese written characters were increasingly supplemented and later somewhat displaced by a phonetic system known as *kana*. Most of its symbols combined a consonant and a vowel and made it possible to transcribe spoken Japanese accurately, as Chinese characters could not do. Chinese characters remained important among the educated elite and for official use, but the *kana* system was understandably preferred for most purposes, including popular literature.

The effort to follow Chinese patterns of government was largely given up, and power came increasingly into the hands of the Fujiwara clan and its appointees or hereditary officeholders. Because the new capital was called Heian, the centuries from 794 to 1185 are called the Heian era. The period is famous for its aristocratic and court culture, where noble gentlemen and ladies devoted their lives to aesthetic refinement. The best-known Heian work is Lady Murasaki's *Tale of Genji*, considered the world's first psychological novel.

Lady Murasaki and Heian Court Literature

Lady Murasaki's birth date is not known precisely, though it was probably around A.D. 978, nor are we sure of the date of her death, though it was probably around 1015. We do not even know her real name, since in Heian Japan it was considered improper to record the personal names of aristocratic women outside of the imperial family. It is known that she came from a junior branch of the great Fujiwara clan and that her father was a provincial governor. The name Murasaki may derive from that of a major figure in her novel, *The Tale of Genji,* or from its meaning of "purple," a pun on the *Fuji* of Fujiwara, which means "wisteria." She was far from alone as a woman author; mid-Heian period literature is dominated by women, who, particularly at court, were apparently less conventional than men. The absence of harems and extensive concubinage in Japan left women freer to express their talents in other ways.

Lady Murasaki's journal is our only source of information about her life. It records that she was a precocious child and became literate early:

> **My father was anxious to make a good Chinese scholar of [my brother], and often came to hear him read his lessons. . . . So quick was I at picking up the language that I was soon able to prompt my brother. . . . After this I was careful to conceal the fact that I could write a single Chinese character.[2]**

But she acquired a wide knowledge of both Chinese and Japanese works and also became a talented calligrapher, painter, and musician, attainments considered suitable for an aristocratic girl. At about age 21 she was married to a much older man, a distant Fujiwara cousin, and bore a daughter. The next year her husband died, and in her grief she considered becoming a Buddhist nun but turned instead to reflection on the problem of human happiness, especially for women. Around that time, approximately the year 1001, she began work on her masterpiece, *The Tale of Genji,* which was probably nearly finished when, some six years later, she became a lady-in-waiting at the imperial court.

Her journal describes the refined and colorful life at court, as well as its less glamorous rivalries and intrigues. Both are the subject of her great novel, which combines a romantic as well as a psychological approach with realistic detail and subtle insight into human behavior. *Genji* is still praised as the masterpiece of Japanese literature. Her people are real, despite the highly mannered world in which they lived, and through her journal we also have a picture of her as an extraordinarily alive, imaginative, and compelling person. A collection of her poems has also survived, which further mark her as an accomplished stylist.

The Tale of Genji deals with the life of a prince and his seemingly endless affairs with various court ladies. It includes careful attention to manners, dress, and court politics—perhaps not the most rewarding of subjects, but in the hands of Lady Murasaki they become not mere details but a means of revealing character. Although the hero is idealized, this is far more than a conventional romantic tale, and the portrayal of Genji as he grows older is a subtle one. Toward the end of her journal, Lady Murasaki gives us a candid glimpse of herself: People think, she wrote, that "I am very vain, reserved, unsociable . . . wrapped up in the study of ancient stories, living in a poetical world all my own. . . . But when they get to know me, they find that I am kind and gentle."[3] Perhaps she was all these things. Bold as she was in her writings, when describing herself Lady Murasaki still felt compelled to present her character in terms of the traditional "feminine" virtues.

Political Disorder and the Rise of Feudalism

Heian court culture was delightful, no doubt, but may suggest a lack of adequate Fujiwara concern with the real world of politics. Elite life at the capital was deeply involved with elegance, refinement, and aesthetic sensitivity but gave little thought to increasingly pressing economic problems, the poverty of most Japanese, or growing political disorder. In the end Fujiwara power was undermined and finally destroyed by new families who used their private armies to become de facto rulers over lands they had originally guarded for noble families. Some of these armies, and the new group of warriors *(samurai),* with their pronounced military ethic, had developed out of frontier wars as Japanese settlement spread slowly northeastward beyond the Yamato area after the ninth century. Armed followers of Buddhist temples increasingly took part in political struggles. Armies began to interfere in factional conflicts at court or were called in by different factions, including clans within the Fujiwara family. By the twelfth century, armies had become the real powers.

The Kamakura Period

In 1185 one of the warrior lineages, the Minamoto clan, set up a rival capital in its then frontier base at Kamakura (now a southern suburb of Tokyo). The refined culture and court-based politics of Heian were now supplemented by a less cultivated but far more politically effective system based on a combination of new bureaucratic methods, military power, and the security offered by the samurai. The samurai leaders were hereditary aristocrats who became both literate and educated and were more administrators than fighting men. Through them and other educated aristocrats Heian culture spread and in time influenced even the warrior clans. However, the rise of noble families and the samurai armies under their control led to the emergence of Japanese feudalism, a phenomenon parallel to that of medieval Europe but different from the imperial civil bureaucracy and meritocracy of China.

The emperor became increasingly a figurehead during this period, and real power rested with whoever could grasp and hold it—first the Fujiwara and then the Minamoto and other military clans. The Kamakura-based administration presided over a feudal hierarchy of warriors and nobles who were bound in fealty assured by oaths, financial and service obligations, and promises of military support. In return, the Kamakura ruler, or *shogun,* the emperor's chief military commander and agent, granted his vassal-lords hereditary rights to their lands. As in medieval Europe, this was a symptom of limited central state power, an arrangement of mutual convenience, but it was also inherently unstable as ambitious or upstart vassals sought to improve their positions or rebel against the shogun's authority. Political power was seldom unified under any single control for long. Each vassal maintained both his own group of samurai and his army, but the loyalty of these forces could not always be ensured, whether to local lords or to the shogun. The patterns that emerged in the Kamakura shogunate (1185–1333) were to dominate Japan until the nineteenth century.

In 1268 the Mongol emperor Kubilai Khan demanded the submission of the Japanese, and when they refused, the Mongols forced the recently conquered Koreans to build and man a fleet for the invasion of Japan, which arrived in 1274. Soon after the first landings a great storm wrecked many of the invaders' ships and forced their withdrawal. The Japanese executed subsequent Mongol envoys, and in 1281 a far larger expedition manned by both subject Koreans and Chinese arrived, only to be swept away by an even greater storm. This storm was typical of the late summer typhoons along the coasts of East Asia, though the Japanese can perhaps be forgiven for attributing their double deliverance to a "divine wind," or *kamikaze.* However, the costs of meeting the terrible Mongol threat and of the preparation that went on against an expected third expedition drained Kamakura resources and diverted large numbers of people from productive occupations. With the weakening of Kamakura power, political divisions and open revolts multiplied. In 1333 an unusually active emperor, Go-Daigo, whom the dominant faction at Kamakura had tried to depose, gathered support and attracted dissidents from the crumbling Kamakura structure. One of his commanders overran Kamakura and ended its power. But another of his supporters turned against him, put a different member of the imperial line on the throne, and had himself declared shogun.

The Ashikaga Shogunate

The Ashikaga shoguns, who established themselves in Kyoto from 1339, were never able to build effective central control. A rival faction supporting another member of the imperial family remained in power in southwestern Honshu and could not be dislodged, while Kyushu continued under the control of one or more other groups. Civil war became endemic, and as one consequence feudal lords beyond the reach of central control supported highly profitable piracy along the coasts of China. This caused chronic trouble between the Ashikaga and the Ming dynasty. The government tried to suppress piracy, but its power to do so was inadequate. For a time the Chinese felt obliged to abandon large stretches of their own coast and pull settlements back to more easily protected sites up rivers and estuaries. From the mid-fifteenth century, political chaos in Japan was endemic, despite the country's small size and the even smaller dimensions of its settled areas. By 1467 effective Ashikaga rule was ended and much of Kyoto had been destroyed, although the emasculated shogunate continued in name. Rival Buddhist sects and their monasteries also fought bloody wars against each other with armed monks as troops. Peasant revolts and bitter conflicts among petty feudal lords continued to ravage the countryside.

Yet despite the growing political disorder, especially after 1450, the last century of the Ashikaga shogunate saw a remarkable flowering of culture. In part this was the result of a conscious fusion of aristocratic Heian traditions with those of the newer samurai culture. Millions also

Troubled Times in Japan

Political conflicts in Ashikaga Japan were echoed in literature but did not prevent continued cultural growth. This period saw the development of the haiku poetic form, evolved from an originally Chinese model but becoming in time a distinctively Japanese mode, still much used. Here are some samples, spanning roughly a century but all reflecting troubled times.

In the hills the cries of deer,
In the fields the chirping insects.
In everything
What sadness is apparent
This autumn evening.
NIJO TOSHIMOTO *(1320–1398)*

The clouds still possess
Some semblance of order:
They bring the world rain.
SHINKEI *(1407–1475)*

To live in the world
Is sad enough without this rain
Pounding on my shelter.
SOGI, *a pupil of Shinkei (1421–1502)*

Source: J. W. Hall, ed., *Japan in the Muromachi* (Berkeley: University of California Press, 1977), pp. 254, 257.

found solace in popular Buddhist sects, including Shin, Nichiren, and Zen, originally Chinese but adapted to Japanese tastes and styles. These popular and egalitarian or, in the case of Zen, contemplative and mystical approaches concentrated on salvation, self-cultivation, and the apprehension of eternal truths rather than on the turmoil of political life. The discipline of Zen appealed to the warrior class but also stressed unity with nature, a traditional Japanese interest. Less detached but clearly related to a turning away from worldly strife was the further blossoming of temple and palace architecture, consciously and ingeniously integrated with peaceful natural settings, of landscape gardening, and of nature painting, much of it in the Southern Sung mode. The literature of the period, meanwhile, commented on the shifting fortunes of politics and the foibles of people grasping for power or gloried in the simple beauty of nature and the joys of untroubled rural life. The shogunate patronized Zen as it supported art and literature, continuing the Heian tradition.

Even more specifically Japanese was the Ashikaga evolution of the tea ceremony as a graceful, soothing, contemplative, and aesthetic ritual. Although its origins too were in T'ang China, it became and remains a distinctively Japanese assertion of cultural identity and personal serenity. Delicate teahouses set in naturally landscaped gardens in unobtrusive elegance provided havens of tranquillity and aesthetic enjoyment for samurai and other members of the elite, who took additional pleasure from the exquisite beauty of the teacups. It was a striking and thoroughly Japanese counterpart to the bloody and often ruthless life of the times.

Finally, the Ashikaga era saw the evolution of traditional dances into a stylized and distinctively Japanese form, the *Noh* drama. This subtle, Zen-inspired blending of dance, gesture, speech, and costume evolved into a unique theatrical style capable of communicating rich meaning and emotion. Every step and every movement are precisely measured to achieve a state of controlled tension, a slow-moving, concentrated experience of understatement and disciplined expression.

The production of artisans too—including, appropriately, the making of fine swords—developed still further. The arrival of the Portuguese early in the sixteenth century stimulated trade, already growing for some time, as the Europeans' more powerful vessels supplanted those of local pirates.

The Ashikaga shogunate dissolved completely into still more chaotic civil war in the 1570s, and Japan was torn by rival clans and their armies until the end of the century. In 1568 a minor but able and determined feudal lord, Oda Nobunaga (1534–1582), won control of Kyoto. He broke the military power of the major Buddhist monasteries and their fortified strongholds in the capital region, including the great fortress of the Shin sect at Osaka. As a counterweight against Buddhism, Nobunaga encouraged Portuguese and other Jesuit missionaries, but his tactics against opponents were ruthless, including the burning alive of captives and the slaughter of noncombatants.

When Nobunaga was murdered by one of his own commanders in 1582, his chief general, Toyotomi Hideyoshi (1536–1598), seized power and by the early 1590s controlled most of Honshu, Kyushu, and Shikoku, thus unifying most of Japan for the first time. A peasant by birth, Hideyoshi tried to disarm all nonsamurai to ensure that commoners were kept down and unable to challenge his authority. He nationalized and centralized the taxation system and further separated warriors from cultivators. As a self-made man, he feared the possible rivalry of others like him. His famous "sword hunt" among all commoners, in which houses were searched and all swords confiscated, reestablished rigid class lines and was accompanied by new laws prohibiting farmers or common soldiers from becoming merchants or even laborers. Hideyoshi rose to power in a period of change and instability; he saw this instability as a threat and tried to stop it. Hideyoshi seems ultimately to have succumbed to megalomania, as evidenced by his grandiose plan for the conquest of China, for which he carried out an invasion of Korea as a first step in 1592. The story of that misadventure has already been told.

Hideyoshi at first welcomed the Christian missionaries and the profitable trade with the Portuguese, but suddenly he turned against all foreigners. He seems to have feared that Christianity was becoming a disruptive factor in Japanese society and a political menace as the foreigners, already rivals among themselves, became involved in internal conflicts and as Japanese converts developed loyalties to a foreign pope. Hideyoshi placed a ban on missionaries in 1587, but this was not strictly enforced until 1597, when he crucified nine Catholic priests and 17 Japanese converts as an example.

In the chaos following Hideyoshi's death in 1598, Tokugawa Ieyasu (1542–1616), originally a vassal and ally of Nobunaga and then of Hideyoshi, emerged victorious in 1600 to found the far more effective and lasting order of the Tokugawa shogunate, which was to rule Japan under a centralized feudal administration until 1868.

SUMMARY

This chapter has summarized the renaissance of Chinese civilization after the time of troubles following the fall of the Han dynasty in 220 and the golden ages of the T'ang and the Sung until those impressive developments were cut off by the Mongol conquest late in the thirteenth century. Despite Mongol brutality, Chinese civilization continued under alien domination, and the hated invaders were eventually thrown off. Korean culture had arisen before the Han conquest and retained its distinctiveness. It borrowed heavily from Chinese civilization at the elite level while creating innovations in ceramics and printing by movable type and shaping institutions adopted from China to Korean tradition. Korea was first unified by the Silla dynasty from 669 to 995 and continued under the Koryo dynasty until it was destroyed by the Mongol invasion in 1218. Yi dynasty Korea from 1392 to 1910 saw a new burst of cultural and technological growth, although its political vigor was slowly eroded by factionalism.

Japanese civilization, having been largely created on the Chinese model and with Korean help, in time asserted its own separate cultural identity and produced a graceful elite culture that coexisted with rural poverty and chronic political division and conflict. Japanese feudalism and the role of the samurai evolved after the Heian period (794–1185) under the Kamakura and Ashikaga shogunates (1185–1568), but such methods were unable to unify the country or to end endemic civil war until the emergence of the Tokugawa clan in 1600. Despite political turmoil, Japan also produced great art, literature, and architecture and a refined culture for the upper classes. Chinese influence on the major East Asian societies was thus limited. Koreans and Japanese made what they took from China their own and went on to modify or develop it further in distinctive ways while retaining and building on their own indigenous culture.

NOTES

1. R. H. Tawney, *The Agrarian Problem in the Sixteenth Century* (London: Longman, Green, 1912), p. 177.
2. All quotations from Lady Murasaki's journal are taken from Arthur Waley's introduction to his translation of *The Tale of Genji* (New York: Doubleday, 1955), pp. ix, xxi.
3. Ibid., p. xxi.

SUGGESTIONS FOR FURTHER READING

China

Allen, T. T. *Mongol Imperialism.* Berkeley: University of California Press, 1987.

Carter, T. F., and Goodrich, L. C. *The Invention of Printing in China and Its Spread Westward.* New York: Ronald Press, 1955.

Chaffee, J. W. *The Thorny Gates of Learning: A Social History of Examinations in Sung China.* Cambridge: Cambridge University Press, 1995.

Dawson, R. S. *Imperial China.* London: Oxford University Press, 1972.

De Crespigny, R. *Under the Brilliant Emperor: Imperial Authority in T'ang China.* Canberra: Australian National University Press, 1985.

Dien, A. E., ed. *State and Society in Medieval China.* Stanford, Calif.: Stanford University Press, 1990.

Franke, H. *China Under Mongol Rule.* Aldershot, England: Varioram Press, 1994.

Gernet, J. *Daily Life in China on the Eve of the Mongol Invasion,* trans. H. M. Wright. London: Macmillan, 1962.

Hymes, R. *Statesmen and Gentlemen: Elites of the Southern Sung.* New York: Cambridge University Press, 1986.

Lo, W. W. *An Introduction to the Civil Service of Sung China.* Honolulu: University Press of Hawaii, 1987.

McKnight, B. *Law and Order in Sung China.* New York: Cambridge University Press, 1993.

McMullen, D. L. *State and Scholars in T'ang China.* Cambridge: Cambridge University Press, 1987.

Olschki, L. *Marco Polo's Asia.* Berkeley: University of California Press, 1960.

Rossabi, M. *Kubilai Khan: His Life and Times.* Berkeley: University of California Press, 1988.

Spuler, B. *History of the Mongols.* Berkeley: University of California Press, 1972.

Waley, A. *The Poetry and Career of Li Po.* London: Allen & Unwin, 1960.

Weinstein, S. *Buddhism Under the T'ang.* New York: Cambridge University Press, 1988.

Korea

Deuchler, M. *The Confucian Transformation of Korea.* Cambridge, Mass.: Harvard University Press, 1993.

Henthorn, G. *History of Korea.* Glencoe, Ill.: Free Press, 1971.

Lee, K.-B. *A New History of Korea,* trans. E. Wagner. Cambridge, Mass.: Harvard University Press, 1985.

Japan

Berry, M. E. *Hideyoshi.* Cambridge, Mass.: Harvard University Press, 1986.

Dunn, C. J. *Everyday Life in Traditional Japan.* London: Batsford, 1969.

Duus, P. *Feudalism in Japan.* New York: Knopf, 1969.

Elison, E., and Smith, B., eds. *Warlords, Artists, and Commoners: Japan in the Sixteenth Century.* Honolulu: University Press of Hawaii, 1981.

Hall, J. W., ed. *Japan Before Tokugawa.* Princeton, N.J.: Princeton University Press, 1986.

Hane, M. *Japan.* New York: Scribner, 1972.

———. *Premodern Japan,* 2nd ed. Boulder, Colo.: Westview Press, 1990.

Keene, D. *No: The Classical Theatre of Japan.* Stanford, Calif.: Stanford University Press, 1966.

Mass, J. P. *Warrior Government in Early Medieval Japan.* New Haven, Conn.: Yale University Press, 1974.

Morris, I. *The World of the Shining Prince.* Oxford: Oxford University Press, 1964.

Reischauer, E. O. *Japan: The Story of a Nation.* London: Duckworth, 1970.

Tiedemann, A. E., ed. *An Introduction to Japanese Civilization.* New York: Columbia University Press, 1974.

Totman, C. *Japan Before Perry: A Short History.* Berkeley: University of California Press, 1981.

CHAPTER 13

The Rise of Europe

The development of a distinctively European civilization occurred during the period that extended from the Germanic invasions of the Roman Empire to the establishment of the first European empire by Charlemagne in the early ninth century. The need to defend against further Muslim attacks, as well as Magyar and Viking incursions, caused major social and political changes in Europe. After surviving the challenges of the early Middle Ages, Europeans embarked in the eleventh century on an era of vigorous growth, the basis of which was economic expansion, urban development, political unification, and religious renewal. But the High Middle Ages (c. 1050–c. 1300) were also a time of bitter conflict—between popes and sovereigns, monarchs and feudal lords, Muslims and Christians, and Christians and Jews. The clash of cultures, religions, and political ideals profoundly changed the Western world.

Migration and Transformation

Generally, the invasions that transformed Europe between the fifth and ninth centuries pitted nomads against the inhabitants of settled communities and were thus a clash of distinctive lifestyles and cultures. Nomads threatened much of Europe and Asia; only remote southern China and southern India eluded their grasp. The impact of the incursions was greatest in the West, partly because the nomads tended to migrate westward, where the land was more fertile and water was more plentiful and partly because the more advanced cultures of China and India resisted transformation.

The eastern Roman Empire, with its well-defended capital at Constantinople, its thriving economy, and its strong navy, survived the invasions, but by the end of the fifth century its western counterpart was gone, its lands

Clovis, King of the Franks.

fallen into the hands of Germanic rulers: the Visigoths in southern Gaul and Spain; the Ostrogoths in Italy; the Franks in northern Gaul; the Angles, Saxons, and Jutes in England; the Burgundians in the Rhône valley; and the Vandals in North Africa and the western Mediterranean.

Unlike the Romans whom they conquered, the Germans were at first organized in social units, as tribes based on kinship, rather than as citizens of a state founded on political rights and obligations. German laws, unlike those of the Romans, were unwritten and grounded in custom. German families were responsible for the conduct of members of their household and thus played a crucial role in upholding the laws. The Germans elected their kings or tribal leaders as well as the chiefs who led the warriors into battle. In return for serving those chiefs, the warriors received weapons, subsistence, and a share of any spoils.

When the Germans lived as nomads, their livelihood revolved around cattle raising, but as they settled on their new lands they began raising grain, beans, peas, and other vegetables. Over time the Germans assimilated some aspects of classical culture, including Roman language, law, and principles of government, thus creating a distinctively European society. Because the Visigoths, Ostrogoths, and Vandals had begun to embrace Christianity before they migrated into western Europe, the fusion of Germanic and classical elements was eased. These groups were disciples of Arian Christianity, however, and not until about 500 did the Nicene Christianity of the Latin church begin to make headway among the Germans following the conversion of Clovis, king of the Franks (481–511). With the support of the Gallo-Roman population, which was loyal to Nicene Christianity, Clovis expanded the Frankish kingdom until it extended from the Pyrenees to the Rhine and beyond.

The Franks

The dynasty Clovis founded, called the Merovingian in honor of a legendary ancestor, attempted to govern the new state by reaching agreements with powerful nobles, who received the title of count in return for serving as royal officials. Frequently, however, their primary loyalty was not to the king but to their own interests. Merovingian attempts to challenge the power of the landed magnates by making counts of talented but landless men proved unsuccessful. The dynasty also declined because of the physical weakness of his successors. With kings too young to rule, aristocratic mayors of the palace exercised authority. Civil war plagued the kingdom throughout much of the sixth and seventh centuries. Unity had been restored by the early eighth century, when new invaders, the Islamic Moors from North Africa, threatened western Europe. By 711 the Iberian peninsula was theirs. Turning next to Gaul, the Moors were finally rebuffed by the Frankish mayor of the palace, Charles Martel ("the Hammer"), near Tours in 732. The battle was less significant for the Muslims, who in crossing the Pyrenees had overextended themselves, than for the Franks, whose military prowess attracted papal attention. At least in part their victory was the result of their adoption of the stirrup, a Chinese invention that enabled a rider to take advantage of the horse's momentum to strike his enemy with greater force.

Although Charles had recruited powerful men by offering them grants of land seized from the church, the papacy needed an alliance with the Franks, who could protect Rome from the Byzantine emperor and the Lombards. Thus the stage was set for a historically significant relationship between the Franks and the papacy. In 751 Charles' son and successor, Pepin the Short (751–768), deposed the Merovingian monarch and claimed the Frankish throne as his own. After the fact, he obtained papal approval for his action to make his usurpation seem legitimate. He repaid the debt in 754 by defending Rome from Lombard aggression and in addition granted certain Italian lands to the papacy. By this "donation" Pepin laid the foundation for a papal state in central Italy.

Charlemagne

The dynasty Pepin founded became known as the Carolingian (from Carolus, Latin for Charles). Its greatest ruler was Pepin's son Charlemagne ("Charles the Great," 768–814), who established an empire larger than any in Europe between that of Rome in the third century and that of Napoleon in the nineteenth. Charlemagne crushed the Lombards and claimed their crown for himself when they tried to regain the land Pepin had given to the papacy. Against the Moors his gains were modest but strategic, consisting of a *march,* or frontier district, on the southern slopes of the Pyrenees. Campaigns against the Saxons gave him control of much of what is now northern Germany, and in the southeast he overran Bavaria and pushed back the nomadic Avars. Impressed, the Abbasid caliph in Baghdad sent him gifts that included spices, monkeys, and an elephant.

Because Charlemagne had no capital to rival Baghdad or Constantinople, he determined to create a "second Rome" at Aachen (Aix-la-Chapelle) in the heart of his

MAP 13.1 THE EMPIRE OF CHARLEMAGNE

kingdom. Its layout and principal buildings were inspired by Rome, and its royal chapel by the Byzantine church of San Vitale in Ravenna. The new capital became the center of a cultural renaissance Charlemagne sponsored to enhance the reputation of his realm and to improve the quality of the clergy. To direct his palace school, Charlemagne recruited one of the foremost scholars of the age, Alcuin (c. 735–804), from England. Alcuin employed a curriculum inspired by classical Rome and refined by European writers that became the model for education throughout medieval Europe. The seven liberal arts were divided into the *trivium,* comprising grammar, rhetoric, and logic, and the *quadrivium,* consisting of arithmetic, geometry, music, and astronomy. Charlemagne, who could read but not write, acquired legal and religious manuscripts for his scribes to copy and distribute to monasteries. His sister, Gisela, supervised a convent at Chelles, near Paris, that took a special interest in copying manuscripts. His scholars issued new editions of learned works and even developed a new, more readable script, called the Carolingian minuscule, from which modern scripts are derived. Much of what we know about Charlemagne comes from a biography by Einhard (c. 770–840), a leading palace scholar. The manuscripts produced by these writers were studied by fifteenth-century scholars and thus influenced that later, more famous renaissance.

Charlemagne's apparent interest in being the equal of the Byzantine emperor culminated in 800. Three years earlier the emperor's mother, Irene, had blinded her son in order to rule herself. Charlemagne and Pope Leo III (795–816) seem to have regarded the Byzantine throne as vacant on the basis of Irene's sex. Charlemagne apparently gave some thought to marrying Irene, though nothing came of it. After the pope's political enemies temporarily kidnapped him in 799, he sought Charlemagne's help to restore his control in Rome. Thus it was that the Frankish sovereign was in Rome on December 25, 800, when, following mass, Leo crowned him emperor of the Romans. The coronation strained relations with Constantinople, which claimed the imperial title solely for its own ruler. Not until 813 did both parties agree that Charles would be recognized as emperor of the Franks and the Byzantine sovereign as emperor of the Romans. For the West, the significance of the Christmas coronation was the revival of the imperial tradition in the West and the question of ultimate authority raised by the pope's bestowal of the crown on the emperor.

Disintegration and Invasion

Hoping to preserve most of the empire intact, Louis I (814–840), Charlemagne's successor, designated his eldest son heir to the imperial title and, following the Frankish custom, promised his other two sons royal titles and the territories of Aquitaine and Bavaria. Unsatisfied, the younger sons revolted against their father. By the time peace was made in the Treaty of Verdun (843), Louis was dead and the empire was irrevocably fragmented. Between the western and eastern kingdoms, out of which eventually emerged France and Germany, was a middle kingdom that retained the imperial title and extended from the modern Netherlands into Italy. The Carolingian dynasty continued until 987, a pale reflection of its grandeur under Charlemagne.

As the Frankish states struggled to survive, new waves of invaders struck Europe. From North Africa, Arab raiders attacked the islands of the Mediterranean, southern France, Italy, and the Alpine passes. The revived militance stemmed from newly independent Muslim states in Egypt, Tunisia, and Spain following the decline of the Baghdad caliphate. Before the ninth century was over, the Mediterranean was virtually a Muslim lake.

Byzantine miscalculation was responsible for the invasion of eastern Europe by the Magyars, a nomadic people from central Asia. In 896 the Byzantines encouraged the Magyars to attack the troublesome Bulgars, but the latter outwitted the Byzantines by persuading the Pechenegs, Turkic nomads from the area around the Volga River, to attack the Magyars. Instead of fighting the Bulgars, the Magyars moved west, invading Germany, France, and Italy and plundering virtually at will. Not until 955 did the army of the German king, Otto I, defeat them, but they retained control of the Hungarian plain. There they established their own kingdom and converted to Christianity.

A third group of invaders, the Norsemen or Vikings, came from Scandinavia in swift, mobile ships. As early as 793, Viking raiders destroyed the monastery at Lindisfarne, which had been instrumental in converting northern England to Christianity. In the century that followed, the Vikings sacked the coastal regions of Europe and sailed up rivers to reach such cities as Paris and Hamburg. They even plundered the Muslim city of Seville in Spain and Italian towns reached by ships that sailed into the Mediterranean. Vikings sailed the Atlantic to Iceland and Greenland, both of which they settled, and North America. The reasons for this activity varied: some Vikings sought land for new settlements, but others apparently regarded the raids as a prelude to a settled life or as a means to establish new trade routes. Norsemen from Sweden used the rivers of Russia to contact the Byzantines and the Persians. The Vikings established settlements at Kiev in Russia, on the coast of Ireland, in northeastern England, and in northwestern France, a region later known as Normandy. In the eleventh century descendants from that area seized control of southern Italy and Sicily, and in 1066 William, duke of Normandy, conquered England. As the Normans settled, they embraced Christianity and European culture.

Feudal Society

The breakup of the Carolingian empire and the impact of the invasions caused changes in European lifestyles and governments. As royal authority ebbed, landowners turned elsewhere for protection, thereby providing the nobility and other powerful men with the opportunity to increase their power. The nobles ruled their districts with miniature governments of their own, dispensing justice, collecting fees, raising troops, and sometimes minting money. The heart of this way of governing was the personal bond: whereas in modern society we owe allegiance to a state, in the early medieval world people rendered

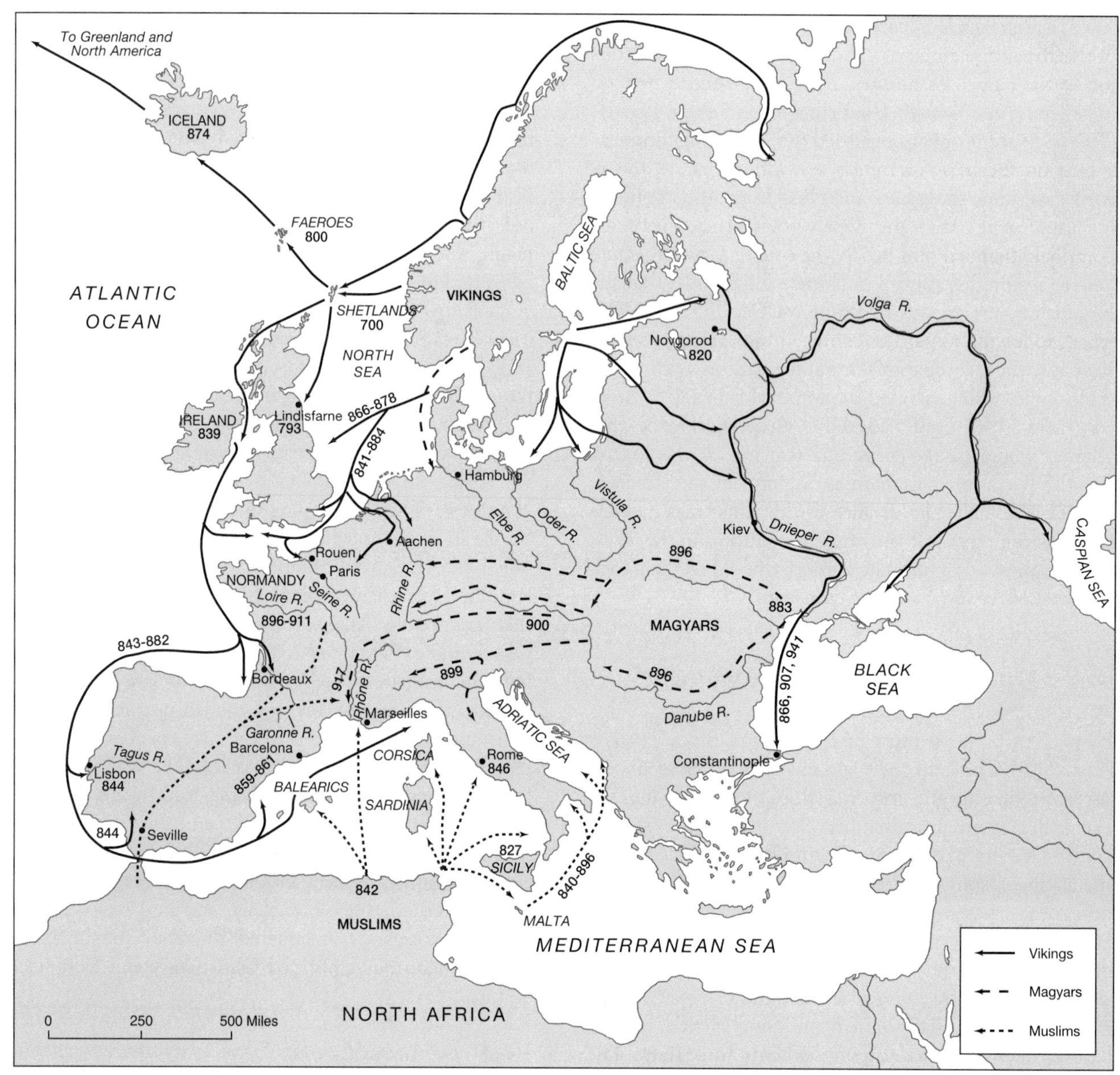

MAP 13.2 VIKING, MAGYAR, AND MUSLIM INVASIONS

allegiance to a person, and that person was in turn bound to fulfill his or her part of the contractual arrangement.

Lords and Vassals: The Feudal Aristocracy

In the Merovingian age free landowners sought protection by offering their lands to more powerful men whom they agreed to serve. The former were known as vassals. In return for their service, they lived in the lord's household or received money or the use of land, called fiefs. Normally, the most important service was military, for together the vassals comprised the lord's private army, which protected its collective members. Vassals were expected to perform other duties, such as serving on the lord's court or providing him with hospitality. As these feudal arrangements developed, various safeguards were added. In eleventh-century France, for example, the normal amount of military service required of a vassal each year was 40 days. A vassal could receive fiefs from several lords, thereby raising the question of which lord had first claim on his obedience. The solution was the designation of a liege lord as the one to whom primary obedience was due. Vassals with substantial landholdings could have vassals of their own. The feudal order was not a neat hierarchical arrangement but a complex web of loyalties and obligations, the total effect of which was to decentralize power.

Because fiefs were normally inherited, they could be acquired by women. Yet a woman could not perform the necessary military service, so she had to have a husband. Younger sons, who normally had no fief to inherit, often married such heiresses to acquire a place in the feudal order. Women exercised an important role in feudal society, managing the family estates while their husbands were away and sometimes defending their castles or fortified manor houses if they were attacked. Legally, a woman could not buy or sell property or even appear in court in her own right. Yet as the wife of a noble or a knight, she enjoyed status in the community and could normally expect the deference of her social inferiors, male or female.

People who held fiefs comprised the landed aristocracy, a hereditary group that ranged from the least significant vassals to powerful dukes and magnates. Wherever they ranked in this spectrum, nobles and knights were characterized by a devotion to fighting, jousting, and hunting; a lifestyle based on the labor of others; and distinctive social customs, such as the ritual dubbing of knights. A few nobles were so powerful as to be virtually independent, but most nobles and all knights owed obligations to monarchs or princes; at the same time, all aristocrats exercised authority over others, including the peasants. The nobles could raise and command troops, and some could even coin money. All members of the landed aristocracy had the right to hold courts, even if it was only at the manorial level for the knights. In return for these privileges the nobles and knights were supposed to protect both the church and the common people. The values espoused by the landed aristocracy included courage, loyalty, physical strength, and generosity. They measured their status in terms of the number, size, and wealth of their fiefs and the amount of authority they exercised over others, especially vassals. Their homes, ranging from castles to fortified manor houses, were another indication of their status.

The impact of the feudal order on monarchs was considerable. Although kings were normally the most substantial landowners, with vassals who owed them military and other forms of service, in some states the nobles were more powerful than their monarchical lords. In such places a king was only as dominant as his great vassals allowed him to be: if they collectively refused his bidding, he had no other army to enforce his will. In Germany the substantial size of the Magyar armies meant that the nobles could not marshal adequate defenses; hence the kings actually increased their influence, as exemplified by Otto I's revival of the imperial tradition. In western Europe, by contrast, the smallness and swiftness of the Viking raiding parties enhanced the power of local lords, who could respond more quickly to the threat than the kings could. Japan experienced a similar development beginning in the twelfth century, as the emperors increasingly lost power to hereditary warrior-aristocrats; the latter's power was based, as in Europe, on the vassals who comprised their armies. In both systems, the personal bond of loyalty was crucial, and the power of the central government was clearly limited.

The Early Medieval Peasantry

Beyond their impact on government, the invasions altered the economy of Europe. Muslim domination of the Mediterranean did not eliminate Europe's trade with the East, but it substantially reduced shipping and profits. This in turn adversely affected European towns, particularly in coastal areas. The population of early medieval Europe became overwhelmingly rural, with peasants accounting for up to 90 percent.

Seeking protection and a livelihood from the large landowners, free peasants gradually lost their lands and became dependent. Many peasants worked on large estates or manors, which became the basic social and economic unit at the local level. These manors were essentially descended from the Roman *latifundia* (see Chapter 6). In return for labor services for the owner, peasant families received the right to till tracts on the manor for their own sustenance and profit. Such arrangements allowed them considerable security—housing, land, and food—but bound them to the land; serfs could not leave the manor without permission from their lord. In addition to the agricultural labor and other services that peasants owed, they had to pay fines (often in produce or livestock) to the lord of the manor for the opportunity to marry someone from another manor, for a son to inherit the right to his father's lands on the manor, or for the use of the lord's mill to grind grain.

The conditions of peasant life varied greatly. Many peasants retained their freehold farms and their freedom and were quite prosperous, while numerous others possessed few rights and endured abject poverty. The peasant diet was simple, with black bread the primary staple. There was normally little meat, though poaching wild game was fairly common, and the more fortunate peasants periodically ate pork. Fish was available fresh to those who lived near water, or otherwise in salted form. The basic vegetables were beans, cabbage, peas, carrots, turnips, and onions; fruit, apart from wild berries and nuts, was scarce. Peasants lucky enough to have sheep, goats, or cows could make cheese, and those with chickens could eat eggs. Southern Europeans normally drank wine, whereas their northern counterparts quenched their thirst with beer, perhaps three gallons a day or more for peasants toiling in the fields.

The typical peasant household consisted of a nuclear family—a parent or parents and children. Most peasants seem to have married in their early twenties and, with the church's encouragement, tried to raise families. Better-off peasants lived in houses with several rooms, but the poor had to make do with one-room, earthen-floored cottages. Normally constructed of mud or clay, such homes had a thatched roof, a fireplace, and no windows. The living space sometimes had to be shared with animals, and peasants lived in the knowledge that their lords had the right to raze their houses and move them elsewhere. Most peasants probably never left their village, the focal point of which was the parish church, site of most of life's major events—baptism, marriage, feast days, and funerals. The peasants had no say in the selection of their priest, a function normally exercised by the manorial lord, but most priests worked in the fields and thus had some bond with their parishioners. In time many villages organized confraternities, religious societies that combined devotion with the provision of charity and care for the sick. The church and the manorial lord determined standards of peasant behavior; aside from religious obligations, manorial customs were the only law most peasants knew. But rural society was neither static nor uniform, and regional variations could be considerable. As new lands were opened up, usually by clearing forests or draining swamps, landowners lured peasant settlers by offering them improved living conditions, but for most peasants life was undoubtedly harsh.

Peasant women not only had to perform the typical child-rearing and household duties but also worked in the fields with the men and cared for the animals. On the manors the women did everything but plow. Their chief obligations in life were to bear and rear children; produce, prepare, and serve food; and manage the family's resources to enable it to exist from harvest to harvest. Women endured a life of hard toil with little amusement other than drinking, perhaps watching cockfights, and amusing themselves on the numerous holy days that dotted the church calendar. Their lives, like those of their families, must in some cases have begun to improve, however marginally, as the result of better economic conditions in the High Middle Ages.

New Foundations: Economic Expansion

The dramatic achievements of the High Middle Ages—urban growth, the organization of guilds and universities, the construction of majestic cathedrals and guildhalls, and the revival of monarchical authority—were possible only because of the large-scale economic expansion that grew out of an agricultural revival that began in the tenth century. That revival was largely spurred by population growth, which probably resulted from a decline in the prevalence of fatal disease. The development of the three-field system and crop rotation; the use of horses, properly harnessed and shoe-clad, and of fertilizer; the recovery of new land by deforestation and drainage; and the increased use of heavy wheeled plows, metal tools, and windmills permitted Europeans to produce more food with less human labor. This in turn opened up possibilities for some people to specialize in manufacturing or commerce and for some landowners to plant crops, such as flax and hemp, that were not needed for basic sustenance. Others converted their land from tillage to pasturage, specializing in sheep, cattle, or horses, sometimes even cross-breeding to improve their stock.

Agricultural and pastoral developments spurred both a rise in population and the growth of manufacturing and commerce. In the year 1000 the population of Europe, including Russia, was approximately 38 million—small in comparison to Sung China's 100 million. By the early fourteenth century, however, Europe's population had doubled. No town in western or central Europe, with the exception of several in Muslim Spain, had as many as 50,000 people in the year 1000, though in the East, Constantinople had a population of some 300,000. In the ensuing three centuries agricultural and commercial advances and the economic boom fostered by the crusades made it possible for towns to develop rapidly throughout Europe. Europeans again began to participate extensively in the trade routes that extended from England and Scandinavia to India and China, especially the commerce that had developed in the Mediterranean in the tenth and eleventh centuries. Byzantine, Muslim, and Jewish merchants remained active throughout much of Europe, but western Europeans, especially Italians, soon surpassed them.

Much of the commerce of the High Middle Ages took place at annual fairs that lasted up to six weeks. Local markets handled weekly retail sales; the international

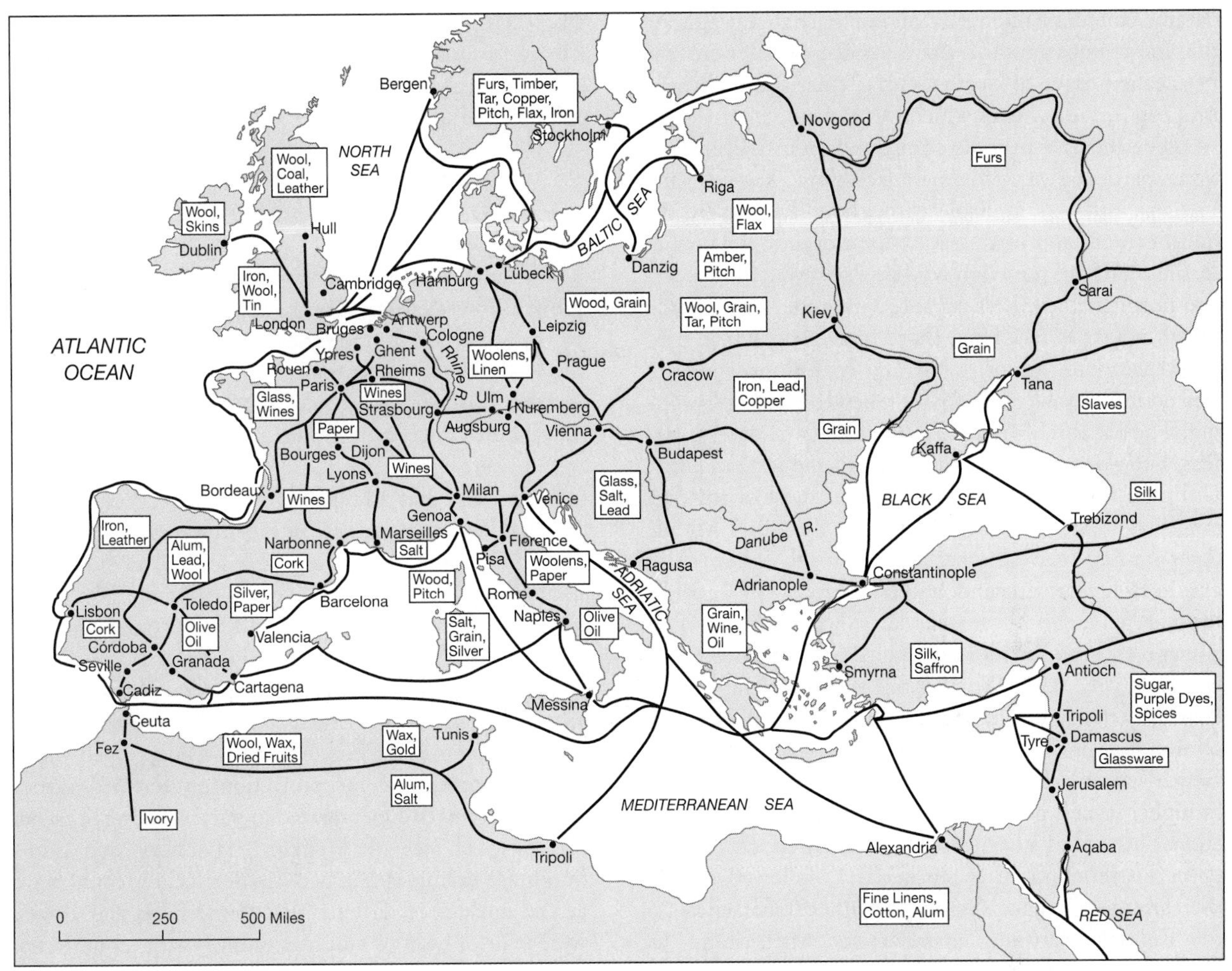

MAP 13.3 PRIMARY TRADE ROUTES OF EUROPE, c. 1300

fairs involved primarily wholesale transactions and were carefully regulated. The most influential of these convened under the protection of the counts of Champagne six times a year. Merchants found these fairs attractive because of their strategic location at the crossroads of the European trade routes and the protection offered by the counts. Transactions at the fairs required the development of more sophisticated business practices, including the use of standard weights and measures, and the evolution of an international mercantile law.

Because the fairs were international in scope, moneychangers were needed. Customarily seated on benches (*bancs*), these exchange specialists became known as bankers. They accepted deposits and were instrumental in instigating the use of paper credit, which facilitated the distribution of goods over long distances and encouraged commercial transactions when bullion and coins were in short supply. Eventually, governments found it advantageous to finance some of their activities by credit. These developments collectively led to the emergence of capitalism.

Commercial expansion stimulated the development of new organizations to meet the demand for products and to facilitate international trade. Partnerships became commonplace despite one serious limitation: the responsibility of each partner for the total indebtedness of the firm in the event of default. Because of this drawback, partnerships such as the Bardi and Peruzzi of Florence were usually formed only by family members, perhaps with a few close associates. An alternative was the *commenda,* a business association in which an investor provided capital to a merchant in return for a share of the profits but which limited the investor's potential loss to the funds he had invested. Merchants and artisans also organized in guilds. On a much larger scale, beginning in the twelfth century, various cities joined forces in commercial leagues to promote their interests. On occasion such a league, or *hansa,* became embroiled in political and military affairs. Among the most important of these confederacies were the Hanseatic League of North German cities and the Rhenish League, the leader of which was Cologne.

The increase in trade stimulated industrial production, particularly cloth manufacturing. English and Frisian cloth was available throughout Europe by the ninth century and in Russia by the eleventh. The major textile centers of the High Middle Ages were in Flanders and northern Italy. Less advanced than the sophisticated metal industries in China, those in Europe, which produced weapons, armor, tools, and cutlery, expanded in this period, thanks especially to renewed interest in mining. The old Roman mines had had shafts as deep as 500 feet, but work in them had ceased in the sixth century. Until the tenth and eleventh centuries most of the digging was in shallow pits, but during the High Middle Ages mining revived, especially along the eastern Alps and in Bohemia, England, and northern Spain. In addition to gold and silver—crucial for the expansion of coinage—European mines produced tin, copper, mercury, iron, and coal. The adoption of such technological devices as pulleys, cranks, and pumps and the harnessing of waterpower to crush the ore improved productivity. Larger supplies of bullion made it possible to mint coins in higher values; pennies were increasingly coined out of copper instead of silver. Gold coins were issued by Emperor Frederick II in Sicily in 1231, followed shortly thereafter by Florence, Genoa, and other Italian cities.

European artisans manufactured such items as leather goods, paper (primarily in Italy and Spain, although it was a Chinese invention), plate and blown glass (especially in Venice), and stained glass (France). Maritime states had shipbuilding industries, and some coastal cities produced salt by evaporating seawater. Throughout Europe the food industry developed as people specialized in salting fish, curing meat, brewing, making wine, and milling grain. The building industry flourished, particularly beginning in the eleventh century, when it became fashionable north of the Alps to use stone instead of wood and plaster for major construction.

The manufacture of textiles and metals as well as the construction of large buildings required capital, reliable transportation, adequate supplies of raw materials, and a skilled labor force. All this was possible only in a climate that could offer reasonable security and legal protection; hence industrial expansion and the reappearance of reasonably stable governments went hand in hand. Trade and industry provided the revenues without which effective governments could not exist, and the authorities, in turn, had to maintain conditions conducive to the further development of commerce and manufacturing. The High Middle Ages achieved dramatic progress because of the fortunate combination of agricultural expansion, technological and commercial development, and increasing political stability.

Urban Development and Town Life

The High Middle Ages witnessed extraordinary urban growth in western and central Europe prompted largely by the expansion of trade and manufacturing to meet the needs of a rising population.

No single factor accounts for the sites on which medieval cities developed. Some, such as Rome and Marseilles, were rebuilt on the decayed foundations of old Roman cities and administrative centers. Ports such as Pisa and Genoa recovered in the aftermath of Lombard and Arab domination. Many were located at the sites of natural harbors, such as Barcelona or Naples; on major rivers, such as London (on the Thames) and Cologne (on the Rhine); or at strategic locations astride major trade routes, such as Milan, Prague, and Vienna. Some cities, such as Bruges and Cambridge, emerged where key bridges crossed rivers. Many towns developed where people congregated for protection in fortified settlements, a trend commemorated in names ending in *fort* or *furt, burg,* or *borough:* Frankfurt, Hamburg, and Edinburgh are examples. An ecclesiastical center could serve as the nucleus of an emerging town; Paris and Rouen were seats of bishops and sites of important monasteries.

The largest medieval cities—Paris, Venice, Florence, Naples, Milan, and Genoa—probably never exceeded 100,000 inhabitants in the High Middle Ages, and the Flemish cities of Bruges, Ghent, and Ypres, as well as London and Cologne, were roughly half their size. Apart from Cologne, the largest German towns, such as Hamburg and Augsburg, had fewer than 30,000 people. Asian cities were much larger: in the twelfth century, China had 52 cities with more than 100,000 *households!* Ch'ang An, the imperial capital of T'ang China, the world's largest city, had some 2 million residents. In the Middle East, Cairo's population reached 500,000 by 1300, and the largest Muslim cities of late medieval Spain were nearly as big.

The traditional description of medieval European cities as overcrowded is often an exaggeration, though space within the city walls came to be at a premium. Beyond the walls residents could farm or build homes in the open space adjacent to the city. Some cities erected new walls as necessary, but their construction and maintenance were costly. Vertical expansion was also possible, and medieval builders often made each successive story wider than the one below, with the result that many streets received little sunlight. Pollution was common, as residents routinely dumped refuse of all types, including human excrement, in the streets. Horses, dogs, and oxen added their own dung. The popularity of ale was no doubt partly due to the prevalence of contaminated water (a phenomenon sometimes blamed on Jews because of the myth that their shadows polluted wells). Fires were a severe hazard wherever wooden buildings were common. In the absence of urban planning, medieval cities were like mazes, their winding streets and narrow alleys a mixture of fortified houses, shops, and the shanties of the poor.

The towns were the achievement of a new social order, the burghers or bourgeoisie—the urban merchants who took their place beside the aristocracy, the clergy, and the peasants. In some circles the newcomers were not welcome: a fourteenth-century English preacher thundered that "God made the clergy, knights, and laborers, but the devil made townsmen and usurers." The traditional social orders had little understanding of the merchants' role in the economy. Although many merchants and artisans originally came from humble backgrounds, in time some of them acquired substantial wealth and eventually rivaled the aristocracy. Wedded to the land and steeped in tradition, most nobles treated the merchants with disdain, though in Italy the lesser aristocracy moved to the towns and allied with their inhabitants against the greater nobility and the bishops.

The lure of the towns was due in no small measure to the privileges set forth in their charters. These were usually granted by nobles or monarchs interested in tax revenues or income from the sale of charters. In cities such as Cologne, Mainz, and Liège, however, the townspeople had to rebel to secure their charters. The heart of the typical charter was the assurance of personal freedom for anyone who lived in the town for a year and a day. Charters typically guaranteed the people the right to hold markets and often to govern themselves, even to the point of making and enforcing their own laws to regulate commerce. Towns normally had to pay a stipulated sum

The Rights of a French Town

The attractiveness of medieval towns was based in large part on the charters that set forth their privileges. A representative sample is found in the charter granted to the French town of Lorris, near Orléans, by Louis VII in 1155.

1. Every one who has a house in the parish of Lorris shall pay . . . sixpence only for his house, and for each acre of land that he possesses in the parish.
2. No inhabitant of the parish of Lorris shall be required to pay a toll or any other tax on his provisions; and let him not be made to pay any measurage fee on the grain which he has raised by his own labor.
3. No burgher shall go on an expedition, on foot or on horseback, from which he cannot return the same day to his home if he desires. . . .
4. No person while on his way to the fairs and markets of Lorris, or returning, shall be arrested or disturbed, unless he shall have committed an offense on the same day. . . .
5. No one . . . shall exact from the burghers of Lorris any tallage, tax, or subsidy. . . .
6. No one shall be detained in prison if he can furnish surety that he will present himself for judgment. . . .
7. Any person who shall dwell a year and a day in the parish of Lorris, without any claim having pursued him there, and without having refused to lay his case before us or our provost, shall abide there freely and without molestation.

Source: F. A. Ogg, *A Source Book of Mediaeval History* (New York: Cooper Square, 1907), pp. 328–330.

to their overlords each year, but usually the citizens determined the taxes they would levy on themselves.

Although townspeople were personally free, urban governments were not democratic. Power customarily rested with the prosperous merchants and master artisans. Town councils and guilds, which were organizations of people pursuing the same economic activity, exercised control. Merchants first organized guilds in the eleventh century and artisans in the 1100s. As the craft guilds developed, they insisted on at least sharing city government with the merchant guilds. Because guilds were so well organized, they dominated government affairs, particularly since they could vote as a bloc and thereby elect their own leaders to city offices.

The guilds were designed to protect the interests of their members by restricting membership, limiting competition, and setting prices. In effect, a guild enjoyed a monopoly over a particular craft or trade and controlled prices; consumers benefited too in that the guild regulated quality. Guilds trained apprentices to become journeymen and possibly master craftsmen and guild members, and some guilds educated members' children. The guilds aided needy members or their families, providing health care and financial assistance, particularly for victims of fire and flood as well as for widows and orphans. Some guilds, especially those involved with textiles or brewing, included women. Religion often played an important part in guild life, whether in activities honoring their favorite saints, in donations to churches, or in the construction and maintenance of their own chapels. Guilds rivaled the church in their pageantry, particularly their great feasts and public processions.

The guilds could not absorb all who wished to enter. Hence as peasants kept flocking to the towns, many could find employment only as unskilled laborers. Poorly paid, devoid of political rights, and often barely able to survive, they constituted the proletariat. Although these people were nominally free, few had any chance of improving their social status.

The Growth of Monarchy: England and France

No sovereigns made more effective use of the improved economic conditions to enhance their power than the rulers of England and France, particularly through their efforts to establish internal security and their interest in legal reform. In both countries the dominant political theme of the High Middle Ages was the crown's struggle to establish a position of authority reasonably secure from the claims of the church on the one hand and the powerful feudal aristocracy on the other. Political developments in this period also laid the foundation for the bitter conflict between the two countries that lasted for centuries.

From the Norman Conquest to the Angevin Empire

One of the most significant dates in English history is 1066, the year William, duke of Normandy, defeated the last Anglo-Saxon monarch, Harold, at the battle of Hastings to seize the English crown. The Norman Conquest brought fundamental changes to England, principally the imposition of a Norman-French feudal aristocracy that owed military allegiance directly to the new king and was thus more centralized than its French counterpart. The Anglo-Saxon nobility disappeared, and Normans henceforth governed England. William retained most Anglo-Saxon laws and institutions, including some of the traditional courts and the sheriffs. However, William replaced the royal council, the Witenagemot (or Witan), with the Great Council, an advisory body and court of feudal law, and its nucleus, the Small Council, composed of the king's principal advisers and officials. One of William's most remarkable accomplishments was a detailed survey of landed property in England—the Domesday Book—probably undertaken to aid tax collection. William also extended royal control over the church, gradually replacing Anglo-Saxon bishops and abbots with Normans.

During the reign of William's great-grandson, Henry II (1154–1189), the territory in France under English control increased dramatically. In addition to Normandy, Henry inherited Maine, Touraine, and Anjou from his father, the count of Anjou, and added Aquitaine and Poitou by virtue of his marriage to Eleanor, duchess of Aquitaine. The Angevin empire, as all this was called, stretched from the Scottish border to the Pyrenees and included more than half of France. In feudal terms, Henry held his French lands as a vassal of the French king.

Eleanor of Aquitaine: Court Politics and Courtly Love

In her life Eleanor linked several of the major themes of the High Middle Ages—the political struggles of France and England, the crusades, and the courtly love tradition.* Born in 1122, Eleanor, the daughter and heiress of William X, duke of Aquitaine, inherited the ducal title at the age of 15. Her guardian, King Louis VI, arranged her marriage to his son, who succeeded to the French throne as Louis VII in 1137. When Louis, a deeply pious man, set out on the Second Crusade in 1147, Eleanor too "took the cross" of the crusaders, as her grandfather, William IX, had done in the First Crusade. At Antioch, Eleanor shocked Louis by announcing that their relationship was illegitimate because of their blood ties. Whether Eleanor was now sexually unfaithful, as the king's friends charged, is impossible to prove, but Louis forced her to remain with him, and she undoubtedly was with the crusaders when they reached Jerusalem.

Papal intervention kept the royal couple together until 1152, when the church finally annulled their marriage. Happy to be rid of Louis, who was "more monk than king," Eleanor married Henry Plantagenet two months later. When Henry succeeded to the English throne in 1154, she was crowned queen of England. Having already had two daughters by Louis, she bore Henry eight children, among them two future kings of England, Richard I and John. A political force to be reckoned with during her first decade in England, Eleanor served as regent when Henry was out of the country. Beginning in 1163, her functions were largely ceremonial, and in 1168 Henry dispatched her to Aquitaine to govern her duchy. Eleven years her junior, Henry was now free to pursue an affair with his mistress. Eleanor schemed to use her children to get revenge on him. Unwittingly, he played into her hands in 1169 by dividing his continental lands among his sons, giving them a base from which to oppose him. An exasperated Henry finally placed Eleanor in captivity in 1174, thus keeping her from actively supporting her sons when they rebelled against him in 1183. Henry seems to have toyed with the notion of forcing her into a convent. She appeared in court on rare occasions in the mid-1180s, but her official release came only when Henry died in July 1189.

At Poitiers in the 1160s Eleanor presided over the beginnings of the courtly love tradition, with its exaltation of women. Although experts debate the extent of her role as a patron of literature and art, the roots of courtly love were undoubtedly in her court. The tradition flourished for the first time at the court of her eldest daughter, Marie of Champagne, patroness of Chrétien de Troyes, author of five Arthurian romances. The emphasis on love, music, and poetry was something of a

*The crusades are discussed later in this chapter, the courtly love tradition in Chapter 14.

Effigy of Eleanor of Aquitaine at Fontevrault Abbey, Normandy.

family tradition that dated back to Eleanor's grandfather, William IX, reputedly the first troubadour. The troubadours who gathered at her court to sing her praises eventually spread their passionate lyrics throughout much of France, England, Spain, and Sicily.

Eleanor virtually governed England until Richard I (1189–1199), who had been estranged from his father, arrived in the country. Close to Richard, she exercised considerable power throughout his reign, especially after he was captured while returning from the Third Crusade. In addition to raising funds for his ransom, she called on the pope to help free Richard, whom she depicted as "the soldier of Christ." In June of 1194, four months after Richard's return, she retired to Fontevrault Abbey in western France. She was buried there ten years later in a nun's habit.

Law and Monarchy in Norman and Angevin England

Henry I and Henry II undertook significant reforms in law and administration. The former shifted administrative authority from barons to men of lesser rank who operated under the direction of a new official called the justiciar. The justiciar's court, known as the Exchequer, served as the royal treasury and the government's accounting arm. The two kings were instrumental in the emergence of common law, a body of legal principles based on custom and judicial precedents, uniformly applicable throughout England and administered by royal judges. In contrast, the civil law that increasingly prevailed throughout much of the European continent was derived from Roman law, especially Justinian's *Corpus Juris Civilis.* English royal justice was not only legally superior to that dispensed in the local courts but more popular as well, and people were willing to purchase writs (legal orders) to have their cases decided by panels of jurors over which the crown's judges presided. In addition to operating a court at Westminster, the kings dispatched justices on regular circuits throughout the country. Because of the crown's role as the source of justice, the itinerant judges claimed the right to intervene in both feudal and local courts, thus furthering the notion of a common law. Henry II required residents to appear before these justices to report alleged criminals, a practice that later evolved into the modern grand jury. Henry also instituted the grand assize, which gave persons whose land titles were challenged an opportunity to have their cases judged by a jury in a royal court rather than by compurgation (the oaths of neighbors) or trial by combat in a feudal court.

Henry II's knights murder Thomas à Becket in Canterbury Cathedral in 1170.

Henry II's efforts to impose legal reforms on the church provoked a major confrontation. He was troubled that the clergy had the right to be tried and sentenced in church courts, where the penalties were less severe than those imposed in secular courts; a bishop's court, for instance, did not impose the death penalty. The Constitutions of Clarendon, which he issued in 1164, prohibited legal appeals to Rome without the king's permission, required that clergy convicted of a secular crime be sentenced in a royal court, and provided basic rights to laity tried in church courts. Thomas à Becket (1118–1170), whom Henry had appointed archbishop of Canterbury, rejected any notion of clerics' being subject to a secular court. After spending six years in exile because of his opposition, Becket returned to England, only to incur more of Henry's wrath when he excommunicated bishops loyal to the king. When Henry, in a fit of anger, asked whether no one would rid him of "this troublesome priest," four knights murdered Becket in Canterbury Cathedral. In the storm of outrage that ensued, Henry had to yield on two crucial points: clergy would be tried and sentenced in church courts, and appeals could still be made to the papal court.

The church and the barons each won a major victory during the reign of King John (1199–1216), who quarreled with Pope Innocent III (1198–1216) over a disputed election to the archbishopric of Canterbury. The pope, rejecting the candidates of both the king and the cathedral chapter at Canterbury, insisted on the appointment of a third candidate, Stephen Langton. When John balked, Innocent excommunicated him and placed England under an interdict, severely restricting religious services to the people. Faced with widespread unrest and the threat of a French invasion, John capitulated and made England a papal fief, thereby winning the pope's support.

With the church controversy settled, John determined to invade France to regain territory seized by Philip II. Although John had the support of the Holy Roman Empire and Flanders, his French vassals refused to fight against Philip, their supreme lord, and Philip crushed the imperial and Flemish forces at Bouvines (1214). The financial demands of the war had forced John to use extreme measures to raise money, thereby violating the feudal rights of his barons. In June 1215 the barons compelled John to accept the Magna Carta. Far from being a charter of rights in the modern sense, the Magna Carta served as an affirmation of feudal principles, though some of its provisions touched the clergy, the peasants, and the townsfolk. Among other things, the charter limited feudal payments, promised the

The Magna Carta

The Magna Carta, to which King John of England affixed his seal, guaranteed the rights of nobles and others in a largely feudal society, but subsequent centuries interpreted the passages quoted here as guarantees of fundamental legal rights for all.

1. In the first place, we have granted to God, and by this our present charter confirmed for us and our heirs forever, that the English church shall be free, and shall hold its rights entire and its liberties uninjured. . . .

12. No scutage [tax] or aid shall be imposed in our kingdom save by the common council of our kingdom, except for the ransoming of our body, for the making of our oldest son a knight, and for once marrying our oldest daughter; and for these purposes it shall be only a reasonable aid. . . .

13. And the city of London shall have all its ancient liberties and free customs. . . . Moreover we will and grant that all other cities and boroughs and villages and ports shall have all their liberties and free customs. . . .

20. A free man shall not be fined for a small offense, except in proportion to the gravity of the offense; and for a great offense he shall be fined in proportion to the magnitude of the offense, saving his freehold [i.e., except for the land he held without servile obligations]; and a merchant in the same way, saving [except for] his merchandise; and the villein shall be fined in the same way, saving his wainage [harvested crops set aside for seed], if he shall be at our mercy; and none of the above fines shall be imposed except by the oaths of honest men of the neighborhood. . . .

39. No free man shall be taken, or imprisoned, or dispossessed, or outlawed, or banished, or in any way injured . . . except by the legal judgment of his peers, or by the law of the land.

40. To no one will we sell, to no one will we deny or delay, right or justice.

Source: J. H. Robinson, ed., *Readings in European History,* vol. 1 (Boston: Ginn, 1904), pp. 234–237.

church freedom from royal interference, restricted fines on peasants, and confirmed the special privileges of London and other boroughs. Although John himself later ignored the charter—with Innocent III's blessing—his medieval successors repeatedly had to confirm revised versions of it. The significance of the Magna Carta was its embodiment of the principle that monarchs are subject to the law and can be constrained if they violate it. Beginning in the seventeenth century, creative interpreters argued that it contained such principles as due process of law and the right of representation for those being taxed.

Edward I (1272–1307) established another important legal precedent in 1295, when he broadened the Great Council of nobles and prelates by summoning knights and representatives from the towns. The purpose of this Parliament, as it came to be called, was to approve taxes to fund a war against France. Edward justified his decision to consult this wider group on the basis of a principle used by the church in convening a general council: "What touches all should be approved by all." This principle also influenced the development of representative bodies in France and elsewhere.

Capetian France

When Hugh Capet became king of France in 987, the country was a patchwork of fiefs that were largely independent of royal authority. Hugh's own territory, the Île de France around Paris, was considerably smaller than that of the two vassals who flanked him, the duke of Normandy and the count of Champagne. Hugh, however, had two advantages over his vassals: his lordship over them in feudal theory and his consecration by the church in the coronation ceremony. The Île de France, moreover, was centrally located and the site of Paris, which in time became the greatest medieval city north of the Alps. The early Capetian monarchs improved their political fortunes by cultivating the church's support and by having their heirs crowned and given some governmental responsibility before assuming the throne. The Capetians were fortunate in that they produced male heirs, most of whom reigned for relatively long periods. Although early Capetian authority in France was hardly extensive, it was stable. Beginning in the twelfth century the kings began to rely less on the greater nobles for their officials, preferring lesser nobles, clerics, and burghers whose loyalty to the throne was stronger.

By the time Philip II (1180–1223)—Philip Augustus, as he was called—became king, the English posed the gravest threat to the monarchy because of their extensive holdings in western France. Philip devoted much of his attention to reducing English influence, an endeavor made easier by King John's domestic problems. French troops forced John to surrender everything but Aquitaine and Gascony, more than trebling the territory under Philip's control. John's hope of winning his lands back with the help of imperial and Flemish allies perished on the battlefield at Bouvines in 1214.

Philip's domestic policies contributed significantly to the growth of monarchical power. Earlier kings had conferred land on local officials in return for their service, thus making many of their offices hereditary; many subsequently became venal and self-seeking. Philip restored greater royal control over local affairs by appointing new officers—known as bailiffs in the north and seneschals in the south—who worked for a salary and could be replaced as necessary. Moreover, they reported directly to Philip. He was careful to insist that local customs be respected, a characteristic of French law until the nineteenth century. To fund his enlarged government, the king insisted that his vassals pay their feudal dues in full. By the end of his reign, his increase of royal revenues was no less impressive than his enlargement of the royal domain. He further enhanced his authority by issuing 78 town charters, thereby forging strong links between the townsfolk and the crown.

Philip's grandson, the saintly Louis IX (1226–1270), was distinguished by his devotion to Christian principles, symbolically represented by his washing of lepers' feet during Holy Week and his bestowal of alms to the poor. Few rulers have been as dedicated to justice, both in the workings of the royal courts and in his personal capacity as the source of French justice. One of the endearing images of medieval Europe is that of Louis sitting under an oak tree or in his Paris garden dispensing justice to all comers. More formally, Louis encouraged appeals from lower courts to the Parlement of Paris, which the king recognized as the highest tribunal in France. A concern for justice and good government prompted Louis to appoint special commissioners to monitor the work of the bailiffs and seneschals. When conflict between wealthy merchants and artisans erupted in the towns, he intervened to preserve order, an action that resulted in a decrease in the number of privileges the towns enjoyed. Louis made effective use of *ordonnances,* or royal decrees, to prohibit private warfare and dueling and to require the acceptance of royal money throughout France. But for all his accomplishments, Louis failed to continue Philip II's policy of reducing English influence in France.

Louis' grandson, Philip IV (1285–1314), "the Fair," sought to expand monarchical authority, in part by using itinerant members of Parlement to extend royal justice throughout the realm at the expense of feudal courts. He also resumed hostilities against England, prohibiting Flemish towns from importing English wool. This endeavor failed when Philip's army proved unable to defeat the rebellious Flemish cities. As military expenses mounted, Philip imposed forced loans, debased the coinage, and taxed the clergy.

This last policy sparked an explosive controversy with Pope Boniface VIII that pitted French national interests against traditional claims of papal supremacy. Philip not only expelled Jews and Italian moneylenders as a pretext to confiscate their property but also launched a vicious assault on the Knights Templars, a crusading order that had prospered from the donations of the pious and its involvement in banking activities. Accusing the Templars of assorted crimes ranging from heresy to black magic and homosexuality, Philip extracted confessions by torture and had the leading Templars burned at the stake. Although the papacy refused to allow Philip to take the Templars' lands, he avoided having to repay the substantial debts he owed them.

The need for funds was also behind his decision to summon urban representatives to meet with his council of nobles and clergymen in 1302, thus marking the beginnings of a more representative assembly that later became known as the Estates General. In contrast to the English Parliament, the Estates General never became powerful enough to establish permanent control over the levying of taxes and thus to serve as an effective check on monarchical power. By the early fourteenth century the French monarchy had largely centralized authority at the expense of the feudal nobility, and in England, despite the success of the nobles in checking the growth of royal power in the 1200s, legal reform had done much to lay the foundation of a unified state.

The Holy Roman Empire and the Church

Unlike their French and English counterparts, the German emperors of the High Middle Ages failed to lay the foundations of a unified German state. In part this was due to the strength of the feudal nobility and the emperors' quest to dominate Italy, but perhaps the most crucial factor was a furious struggle with the papacy that culminated in the disintegration of the Holy Roman Empire. The church's victory was the result of reforms in the tenth and eleventh centuries that gave it new vigor and a stronger claim to moral leadership (see Chapter 14).

Germany and the Imperial Revival

When the Carolingian empire declined in the ninth century, essentially independent duchies emerged in the eastern Frankish lands. Out of this territory the Saxon duke Henry the Fowler founded the medieval German monarchy, which he governed as Henry I (919–936). His success in controlling the dukes was due partly to the freedom he allowed them in their duchies and partly to his ambitious foreign policy. He annexed Lorraine, strengthened Saxon defenses against the Magyars and Vikings by encouraging the building of fortified towns, and urged Saxon expansion in the Slavic lands beyond the Elbe River.

The policies of Henry's son, Otto I (936–973), were basically an extension of his father's, but on a grander scale. His efforts to centralize royal power incited four rebellions, all of which he repressed. When the Magyars took advantage of the civil strife to invade Germany, Otto crushed them at Lechfeld, near Augsburg, in 955. Like his father, he appointed churchmen to offices of state, knowing they could not undermine royal authority by passing their positions to their sons. The clergy, moreover, were better educated. The church welcomed the alliance with the state, which brought greater influence and grants of land. The churchmen who held those estates were responsible for providing Otto with many of his soldiers and much of his revenue.

When political turmoil in Italy offered Otto an excuse to intervene in 951, he claimed the Lombard throne as his own. Renewed conflict brought a call for his assistance from Pope John XII (955–964), who rewarded him with the imperial crown in 962. That crown had several advantages, including the legal title to the Carolingian middle kingdom and reinforcement of Otto's supremacy over the German dukes, but it also thrust his successors into an untenable relationship with the head of a church that they had to dominate to maintain their power. The imperial policy of relying on ecclesiastical officials as the primary servants of the crown was effective as long as the

THE MAJOR MEDIEVAL STATES, 900–1300

England	France	Holy Roman Empire
Anglo-Saxons unite England politically (by 954)	Beginning of the Capetian dynasty (987)	Henry I, the Fowler (919–936) • Founding of the German monarchy Otto I (936–973) • Founding of the empire (962)
Norman Conquest (1066) • William I (1066–1087) • Domesday Book		Henry IV (1056–1106) • Lay investiture controversy begins
Henry II (1154–1189) • Constitutions of Clarendon (1164)		Frederick I, Barbarossa (1152–1190)
Richard I (1189–1199) • Third Crusade John (1199–1216) • Magna Carta (1215)	Philip II, Augustus (1180–1223) • Victory at Bouvines (1214)	Henry VI (1190–1197) • Acquisition of Sicily Frederick II (1212–1250)
Edward I (1272–1307) • Expansion of the Great Council	Louis IX (1226–1270) Philip IV, the Fair (1285–1314) • Origins of the Estates General	Great Interregnum (1254–1273) Beginning of the Habsburg dynasty (1273)

Gregory VII on Papal Authority

The principles on which Pope Gregory VII and his supporters acted to reform the church and assert the supreme authority of the papacy are set forth in the Dictatus papae *("Sayings of the Pope"), which was probably composed about 1075.*

> ***The Roman church was founded by God alone.***
> ***The Roman bishop alone is properly called universal.***
> ***He alone may depose bishops and reinstate them.***
> ***His legate [direct ambassador], though of inferior grade, takes precedence, in a council, of all bishops and may render a decision of deposition against them. . . .***
> ***The pope is the only person whose feet are kissed by all princes.***
> ***His title is unique in the world.***
> ***He may depose emperors.***
> ***No council may be regarded as a general one without his consent.***
> ***No book or chapter may be regarded as canonical without his authority.***
> ***A decree of his may be annulled by no one; he alone may annul the decrees of all.***
> ***He may be judged by no one.***
> ***No one shall dare to condemn one who appeals to the papal see.***
> ***The Roman church has never erred, nor ever, by the witness of Scripture, shall err to all eternity.***
> ***He may not be considered Catholic who does not agree with the Roman church.***
> ***The pope may absolve the subjects of the unjust from their allegiance.***

Source: J. H. Robinson, ed., *Readings in European History,* vol. 1 (Boston: Ginn, 1904), pp. 274–275.

papacy did not insist on appointing only those who had its approval.

Beginning in the late eleventh century the papacy attempted to assert the church's independence from secular control. The first of these popes, Leo IX (1049–1054), deposed corrupt bishops and reasserted papal supremacy over all the clergy. In 1059 a church council took a major step in freeing the papacy itself from imperial control by establishing the right of the College of Cardinals to elect future popes, a practice still in effect. In 1075 Gregory VII (1073–1085) attempted to restore the election of bishops and abbots to the church by ending lay investiture—the bestowal of the insignia of a church office by a layperson. Practically speaking, lay investiture entailed the right of the laity, such as emperors or kings, to select bishops and abbots, though this violated church law and tradition. A reformed church could hardly be established if lay rulers selected its key officials with a view to political, monetary, and family considerations rather than to spiritual qualifications and if the loyalty of such officials was ultimately to the sovereign who had appointed them rather than to the pope.

The immediate target of Gregory's decree was the emperor Henry IV (1056–1106), who enjoyed the support of his bishops but not of the German territorial princes. The latter stood to gain by any reduction of imperial power. Recognizing the implications of the decree, Henry had his prelates declare Gregory deposed. The pope responded by excommunicating Henry, absolving his subjects from their duty to obey him, and depriving the imperial bishops of their offices. Delighted with this turn of events, the renegade princes in Germany called for a council, over which Gregory would preside, at Augsburg in February 1077; its task would be to ascertain the validity of Henry's claim to the imperial crown. Unprepared to cope with a rebellion, the emperor intercepted Gregory at Canossa in Italy to seek absolution. As a priest, Gregory had to forgive the penitent Henry, thereby giving the emperor the upper hand in the civil war that ensued in Germany. Henry was in a much stronger position when Gregory again excommunicated him in 1080. Four years later Henry's troops occupied Rome, driving Gregory into exile and installing a rival or "antipope," Clement III, on the papal throne.

The investiture struggle dragged on until 1122, when Henry V (1106–1125) and Pope Calixtus II (1119–1124) agreed in the Concordat of Worms that the church would henceforth give prelates their offices and spiritual authority but that the emperor could be present when German bishops were elected and invest them with fiefs. In theory the clergy were now more independent of secular control, though in practice their selection and work were still very political. The real winners in the investiture struggle were the powerful territorial princes, who consolidated their hold over their own lands while imperial attention focused on Rome, and the emerging urban communes of northern Italy, which seized this opportunity to achieve a semi-independent status. In the end the biggest losers were not only the emperors but the German people, who were increasingly subjected to feudal conflict at a time when the French and English were laying the foundations of unified states.

Papal Triumph and the Imperial Challenge

The papacy reached the zenith of its political power in the thirteenth century, but only after a renewal of its struggle with the empire. Emperor Frederick I (1152–1190), called "Barbarossa" because of his red beard, made domination of northern Italy (Lombardy) a cornerstone of his policy. Together with Burgundy, which he acquired by marriage, and his native Swabia, Lombardy would give him a solid territorial base from which to dominate Germany and Italy. Recognizing this, the papacy joined with the cities of the Lombard League and the Normans in Sicily to thwart Frederick's ambitions, an end they achieved in the Peace of Constance (1183), which forced Frederick to relinquish virtually all meaningful power in the Lombard cities. The imperial cause in Italy received new life when Barbarossa's son, Henry VI (1190–1197), married Constance, heiress of Sicily and southern Italy. The papacy was now caught in the imperial vise, but rather than solidifying his Italian holdings, Henry prepared to attack the Byzantine Empire. Simultaneously, he gave many of the German princes hereditary rights to their fiefs in return for their recognition that the imperial crown would likewise be hereditary rather than elective, a scheme the papacy bitterly opposed.

Innocent III (1198–1216), arguably the most powerful medieval pope, took advantage of the chaos that followed Henry's untimely death to undermine the link between Germany and Sicily. Germany plunged into civil war when Otto of Brunswick challenged the leading Hohenstaufen candidate for the imperial throne, Philip of Swabia, Henry VI's brother. Although Innocent crowned Otto in 1209, the latter's attempt to control Sicily prompted the pope to excommunicate him. At the urging of the French king, Philip Augustus, Innocent recognized the hereditary claim of Henry's son, Frederick II, as king of the Romans in 1212. Philip's victory over Otto at Bouvines (1214) decided the struggle in Frederick's favor, though Frederick continued to fight with the popes over Sicily for the rest of his reign.

Innocent III enhanced papal authority in decrees that spelled out the pope's powers in clear legal terms. The "plenitude of power" that he asserted (as had Pope Leo the Great) did not claim temporal world power but supreme spiritual sovereignty, including the right to

Innocent III, perhaps the most powerful of the medieval popes, made King John of England his vassal and helped establish Frederick II as Holy Roman emperor. This portrait is a thirteenth-century fresco in Sacro Speco Church, Subiaco, Italy.

intervene in secular affairs when the faith or morals of the church were affected. Monarchs rightly reigned, in his view, only if they served the pope as Christ's vicar. As we have seen, he acted on these principles when he humbled England's King John. In a quarrel that lasted two decades he also forced Philip Augustus to take back his wife after Philip had rejected her the day following their wedding. Innocent strengthened the church in numerous other ways, including approval for new religious orders (see Chapter 14) and attention to the restoration and decoration of various churches.

After Frederick's death in 1250, the papacy encouraged civil strife in Germany so successfully that between 1254 and 1273 there was no generally recognized emperor. Moreover, the Hohenstaufen line died out in 1268. The Great Interregnum, as the period without a recognized emperor was called, marked the triumph of the papacy over the empire—a victory achieved with French support. Yet half a century after the interregnum began, the French monarchy delivered a crippling blow to papal power and prestige.

Boniface VIII and the End of Papal Hegemony

The century between the pontificates of Innocent III and Boniface VIII (1294–1303) witnessed a dramatic change in the political fortunes of the major European states, with France and England now the dominant powers. Boniface, a short-tempered, elderly man, blundered seriously when, in 1296, he issued the bull (or edict) *Clericis laicos,* rejecting the right of monarchs to tax the clergy without papal authorization. Neither Philip IV nor Edward I, who were on the verge of war with each other, would tolerate such a challenge. Edward denied legal protection to clerics who refused to pay, and Philip prohibited the export of funds from France to Rome, crippling papal finances. Boniface retreated, allowing Philip the right to tax the clergy in an emergency and canonizing Louis IX for good measure.

Emboldened by the jubilee in 1300, when tens of thousands of pilgrims flocked to Rome, Boniface was ready when a new crisis erupted in 1301. When Philip had a French bishop tried in a royal court on charges of heresy and treason, the pope protested that this violated the clergy's privilege to be judged in a church court and warned Philip to submit to his authority as the vicar of Christ. Philip countered by summoning the first Estates General (1302), which protested to Rome. Boniface responded with a new papal bull, *Unam sanctam* (1302), in which he argued that God had given the church two swords: the church retained the spiritual sword, which was superior, but bestowed the temporal on secular authorities to wield on behalf of the church and at its direction. The bull also asserted that "submission on the part of every man to the bishop of Rome is altogether necessary for his salvation."

Whether *Unam sanctam* was a desperate ploy or the logical culmination of medieval papal claims is debatable, but Philip was undaunted. He dispatched agents to Italy to arrest the pope, whom Philip intended to try on fabricated charges ranging from heresy to sodomy and sorcery. Italian loyalists rescued Boniface, but not before he had been physically abused and the prestige of the papacy badly tarnished. In a matter of weeks Boniface was dead, and with him perished the heady days of papal supremacy. A French pope, Clement V (1305–1314), formally praised Philip's devotion, heralding the beginning of a long period in which the papacy found itself in the shadow of the French monarchy.

The Waning of the Byzantine Empire

While western Europe was achieving remarkable political progress in the High Middle Ages, internal decay and external assault plagued the Byzantine Empire. In many respects the eleventh century was pivotal in its decline. Emperor Basil II (976–1025) had secured the frontiers and brought the Balkans under Byzantine domination by defeating the Bulgars. From 1028 to 1056, however, the empire was ineffectually governed by Basil's nieces, Zoe and Theodora, who unwisely allowed imperial military strength to be sapped by supporting large landowners in their acquisition of smaller holdings. The result was the growth of a body of powerful magnates capable of fielding their own armies and posing a threat to imperial control. In effect, the empire was being feudalized.

In 1056, when the Macedonian dynasty died out, civil strife erupted until the military aristocrat Alexius I Comnenus (1081–1118) finally imposed control. In addition to weak emperors, much of the internal instability of the eleventh century resulted from a fierce power struggle between the bureaucratic elite and the aristocracy, the effects of which weakened the army and undermined the government's financial stability. The lavish expenses of the imperial court and the increasing exemption of the aristocracy from taxation forced the government to devalue its coins in the mid-eleventh century.

The internal crises made it difficult for the Byzantines to cope with the pressure on their frontiers. The peoples of west-central Asia, particularly the Pechenegs who lived along the northern coasts of the Black Sea,

A Call to Crusaders

The crusades to bring the Holy Land under Christian control were launched by Pope Urban II's speech to the Council of Clermont in November 1095. Note the appeal to spiritual, material, and racial motives as well as the emotional tone.

From the confines of Jerusalem and from the city of Constantinople a grievous report has gone forth and has been brought repeatedly to our ears; namely, that a race from the kingdom of the Persians, an accursed race, a race wholly alienated from God, . . . has violently invaded the lands of those Christians and has depopulated them by pillage and fire. They have led away a part of the captives into their own country, and a part they have killed by cruel tortures. They have either destroyed the churches of God or appropriated them for the rites of their own religion. They destroy the altars, after having defiled them with their uncleanness. . . .

On whom, therefore, rests the labor of avenging these wrongs and of recovering this territory, if not upon you—you, upon whom, above all other nations, God has conferred remarkable glory in arms, great courage, bodily activity, and strength to humble the heads of those who resist you? Let the deeds of your ancestors encourage you and incite your minds to manly achievements. . . . Let none of your possessions restrain you, nor anxiety for your family affairs. For this land which you inhabit, shut in on all sides by the seas and surrounded by the mountain peaks, is too narrow for your large population; nor does it abound in wealth; and it furnishes scarcely food enough for its cultivators. Hence it is that you murder and devour one another, that you wage war, and that very many among you perish in civil strife. . . .

Enter upon the road of the Holy Sepulcher; wrest that land from the wicked race, and subject it to yourselves. . . . Undertake this journey eagerly for the remission of your sins, with the assurance of the reward of imperishable glory in the kingdom of heaven.

Source: F. A. Ogg, *A Source Book of Medieval History* (New York: Cooper Square, 1907), pp. 284–287.

regularly raided Byzantine territory. The Seljuk Turks destroyed a Byzantine army at Manzikert in 1071, resulting in the loss of eastern Anatolia and Armenia. In the same year the Normans of Sicily drove the Byzantines out of southern Italy and attacked western Greece. Alexius Comnenus regained some of the lost territory by allying with the Venetians against the Normans and by successful military campaigns against the Pechenegs and the Turks. His military needs were so great, however, that he appealed to the papacy for volunteers to fight the Turks, thus setting the stage for the crusades.

The Clash of Faiths: Muslims Against Crusaders

The Turks had moved from the Asian steppes into the Islamic empire to serve in its armies. By 1055 one group of Turks, the Seljuks, had established themselves as the real rulers of the Abbasid caliphate. In the two centuries that followed their victory at Manzikert they extended their control over most of Asia Minor, changing it from a Christian to an Islamic civilization. Turkish domination extended into Armenia and Palestine, making it difficult for Christian pilgrims to visit the Holy Land. The Byzantine emperor Michael VII appealed to Pope Gregory VII for western assistance in 1073, and though the pontiff was willing to proclaim a holy war, not least because it might reunite Christendom under his authority, the outbreak of the investiture controversy delayed the plan.

Twenty-two years later, against a background of alleged hostilities against Christian pilgrims, Byzantine envoys from Alexius Comnenus urged Pope Urban II (1088–1099) to dispatch military aid. At the Council of Clermont (1095) in southern France, the pope proclaimed a crusade to liberate the holy places from a "pa-

A Muslim's View of the Crusaders

The Syrian-born Usamah (1095–1188), a warrior, poet, and friend of Saladin, provides an Islamic perspective on the crusaders. Often scornful of European ways, he nevertheless suggests that Muslims and Europeans who had lived in the Middle East for some time got along reasonably well.

When one comes to recount cases regarding the Franks, he cannot but glorify Allah . . . , for he sees them as animals possessing the virtues of courage and fighting, but nothing else; just as animals have only the virtues of strength and carrying loads. . . .

In the army of King Fulk . . . was a Frankish reverend knight who had just arrived from their land in order to make the holy pilgrimage and then return home. He was of my intimate fellowship and kept such constant company with me that he began to call me "my brother." Between us were mutual bonds of amity and friendship. When he resolved to return by sea to his homeland, he said to me: "My brother, I am leaving for my country and I want thee to send with me thy son . . . to our country, where he can see the knights and learn wisdom and chivalry. When he returns, he will be like a wise man." Thus fell upon my ears words which would never come out of the head of a sensible man; for even if my son were to be taken captive, his captivity could not bring him a worse misfortune than carrying him into the lands of the Franks. . . .

Everyone who is a fresh emigrant from the Frankish lands is ruder in character than those who have become acclimatized and have held long association with the Muslims. Here is an illustration of their rude character.

Whenever I visited Jerusalem I always entered the Aqsa Mosque, beside which stood a small mosque which the Franks had converted into a church. When I used to enter the Aqsa Mosque, which was occupied by the Templars, who were my friends, the Templars would evacuate the little adjoining mosque so that I might pray in it. One day I entered this mosque, repeated the first formula, "Allah is great," and stood up in the act of praying, upon which one of the Franks rushed on me, got hold of me and turned my face eastward saying, "This is the way thou shouldst pray!"

Source: *An Arab-Syrian Gentleman and Warrior in the Period of the Crusades: Memoirs of Usamah Ibn-Munqidh,* trans. Philip K. Hitti (New York: Columbia University Press, 1929), pp. 161, 163–164.

gan race," free the persecuted Christians of the East, and acquire wealth and power in a land of "milk and honey."

The motives of the church and the crusaders varied. For the papacy the crusades offered the possibility of leadership in Europe and the opportunity to heal the breach between the eastern and western churches that had been formalized in 1054. While spiritual considerations, including the promise of a plenary indulgence, moved some crusaders, others were motivated by stories of atrocities purportedly inflicted on pilgrims by the Muslims, the hope of material gain, the lure of adventure, or the desire to participate in an activity that quickly became fashionable. Most crusaders came from France, Italy, and Germany.

Alexius wanted western knights trained and equipped to fight, but instead the first group of crusaders, some 15,000 to 20,000 strong, were largely commoners, including women and children, devoid of military experience or suitable weapons. Inspired by faith, they looked to Peter the Hermit for leadership. Alarmed Byzantine officials hurriedly shipped the unruly force from Constantinople to Asia Minor. A Muslim army annihilated or enslaved most of the crusaders, leaving the bones of some as a grisly warning to others who might follow. Fired by hopes of founding the New Jerusalem, the Peasants' Crusade ended in disaster, not only for the crusaders but also for the thousands of Hungarians and

Crusaders besieging Nicaea in 1097 catapult human heads at their enemies.

Jews they killed en route and the Byzantines they robbed or whose homes they burned.

Later in the same year, 1096, some of Europe's most illustrious princes—including Godfrey of Bouillon, duke of Lower Lorraine; Raymond II, count of Toulouse; Robert, duke of Normandy and brother of the English king, William II; Hugh, count of Vermandois and brother of King Philip I of France; and Stephen, count of Blois and son-in-law of William the Conqueror—launched the Crusade of the Princes, traditionally called the First Crusade. In all there were 5,000 to 10,000 knights, more than 25,000 soldiers, and at least that many noncombatants, both male and female, including servants, pilgrims, and prostitutes.

The crusaders captured the ancient Syrian cities of Edessa and Antioch, and in July 1099 Jerusalem itself fell. The crusaders massacred the inhabitants, whether Muslims or Jews, sparing neither women nor children. It was, the victors thought, a "splendid judgment" of God. The crusaders offered the crown of Jerusalem to Godfrey of Bouillon, who agreed only to serve as protector in deference to the kingship of Christ. Following Godfrey's death in 1100, his brother Baldwin became king of Jerusalem and nominal overlord of the three other crusader states, Edessa, Antioch, and Tripoli, which together formed a 500-mile strip along the eastern Mediterranean coast. Feudal knights defended this outpost of European civilization, but at the cost of developing a strong central government. The crusaders built imposing castles and founded military orders in which the knights took the monastic vows of poverty, chastity, and obedience while dedicating their lives to the defense of the Holy Land. The Knights Hospitalers and the Knights Templars wore distinctive dress, defended castles, and generally distinguished themselves as warriors. German crusaders established a third order, the Teutonic Knights, in 1198, though most of its efforts were devoted to campaigns in Hungary and the Baltic region.

The conquests of the first crusaders were possible largely because the Muslims had been disunited. In the early twelfth century the Muslims regrouped. Their capture of Edessa in 1144 sparked the call for the Second Crusade (1147–1149), which King Louis VII of France and the German king Conrad III led. Muslims annihilated most of the crusaders as they moved through Asia Minor, and the remnant, without the effective support of the suspicious defenders already in the Holy Land, failed to capture Damascus. Instead the Muslims conquered the city, which had been an ally of the crusader states, in 1154. After Saladin (1138–1193) established himself as the master of much of the Muslim Middle East, he launched a holy war of his own to recover Palestine, taking Jerusalem in 1187. By 1189 the Christians held only Antioch, Tripoli, and Tyre.

The loss of Jerusalem roused Europe to launch a formidable crusade (the third) led by Emperor Frederick Barbarossa, France's Philip II, and England's Richard I. But Frederick drowned in Asia Minor and Philip returned home after the crusaders captured the port of Acre, leaving Richard "the Lion-Hearted" to negotiate an agreement with Saladin permitting Christian pilgrims to visit Jerusalem. This was not enough for Pope Innocent III, who called for the Fourth (1202–1204). In return for food and transport, the crusaders helped Venice reconquer the Dalmatian port of Zara, an act that resulted in their excommunication because Zara was a Catholic city. The crusaders then embroiled themselves in a disputed succession to the Byzantine throne that ended with their sack of Constantinople and the establishment of a Latin kingdom there that lasted until 1261.

Among the later crusades, only the Sixth (1228–1229), led by Frederick II, enjoyed any success, thanks to the emperor's diplomatic skills and rapport with the Muslims. A treaty with the Egyptian sultan left Jerusalem in Christian hands, but Frederick's running feud with the papacy forced him to return to Italy. Turkish forces in the employ of Egypt recaptured Jerusalem in 1244. Later crusades failed to regain the Holy Land, and in 1291 the Muslims won the last of the crusader possessions, Acre.

In terms of their stated objective—the conquest of the Holy Land—the crusades were a failure. The heavy expenditure in lives and resources as well as the undercutting of spiritual motives by worldly considerations cast a pall over the movement. One of the most significant long-term legacies was the incitement of deep-seated religious hostility between Christians and Muslims and of Christians toward Jews. Nor did the crusades heal the breach between eastern and western Christendom. In the short term the papacy probably enhanced its prestige as the spiritual leader of the West, but in the end its use of crusades to eradicate heresy in France and its deepening involvement in secular affairs began to erode its influence. European monarchs improved their position by gaining the right to levy direct taxes to obtain crusading funds, and Europe may have experienced less fighting because so many lords and knights directed their militancy against the Muslims.

The crusades had economic and cultural benefits. The heightened contact between Europe and the Middle East stimulated commerce, especially in such commodities as fine textiles, spices, and perfumes. Expanded commerce in turn encouraged improvements in ship-building and banking, including greater use of letters of credit and bills of exchange. The Venetians in particular benefited from the crusades, which enabled them to become the leading shippers in the eastern Mediterranean. Although Islamic culture was already spreading to the West through the Iberian peninsula and Sicily, the crusades fa-

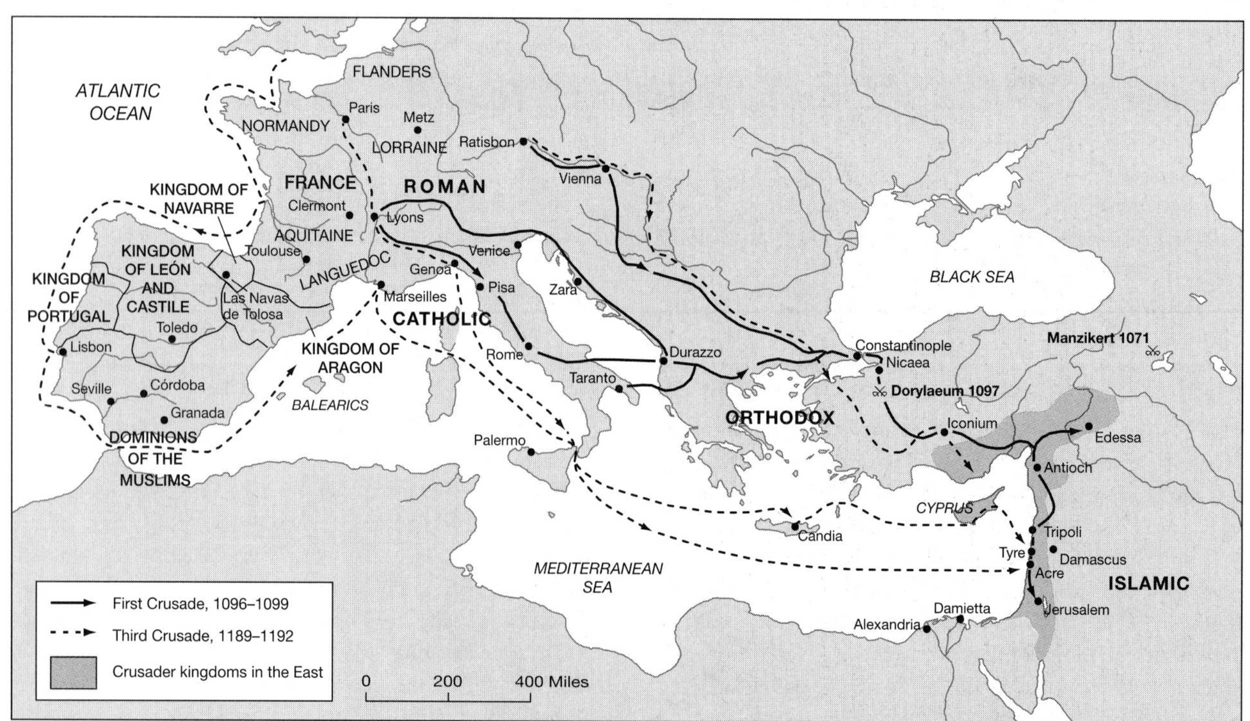

MAP 13.4 CRUSADER ROUTES

cilitated the exchange of ideas and the increase of geographic knowledge. The notion of "crusading" for a worthy cause lived on well past the last crusade and is still a common concept, usually in secular guise; the Islamic notion of the *jihad* is similar. The crusades were also significant as a chapter in the history of Western expansion and the backdrop for the great voyages of exploration that began in the fifteenth century, in part as a means of renewing the crusading movement.

Byzantium After the Crusades

While the Europeans ruled Constantinople as a Latin kingdom, Greek refugees established a rival government at Nicaea in Asia Minor. In 1261 the Nicaean regime, aided by the Genoese, who were jealous of the privileges the Latin kingdom accorded to the Venetians, regained Constantinople. The restored Byzantine Empire, however, was territorially smaller and economically weaker than it had been in 1200.

The empire survived for two more centuries, during which time its economy eroded and bitter social divisions sapped its strength. External threats were a recurring problem. A revived Latin kingdom was averted only by accident in 1282 on the eve of Charles of Anjou's planned assault. The younger brother of King Louis IX of France, Charles wanted to establish a Mediterranean empire by combining the kingdom of Sicily, which he already ruled, with the Byzantine Empire. The Sicilians dashed Charles' hopes by massacring his French supporters during an uprising known as the Sicilian Vespers. With Byzantine financial support, an Aragonese fleet from Spain seized Sicily, ending Charles' threat to the empire. But the Byzantines were unable to repel the incursions of the Serbs in the west and the Turks in the east. Their diminished territories meant fewer resources and workers, and debilitating civil wars in the 1300s further weakened the government at Constantinople. Perhaps the greatest cause of the Byzantines' decline was their inability to recover their once phenomenal prosperity, in no small measure because much of their commerce had fallen into the hands of Italian merchants.

The Iberian Peninsula and the Reconquista

Although the crusaders failed to regain the Holy Land, a much longer campaign against the Muslims for the control of the Iberian peninsula was succeeding. The *reconquista* ("reconquest") had begun in the ninth century, but by the dawn of the High Middle Ages only a thin band across the north of the peninsula was in Christian hands. Three centuries later the Muslims held only Granada at the peninsula's southern tip. Christian gains were due largely to the collapse in 1031 of the caliphate of Córdoba, which had been torn by internal dissension among Arabs, Jews, Berbers, and native Spaniards. As the caliphate, once the most prosperous state in Europe, disintegrated into petty principalities, the Christians' task was simplified.

During the course of the High Middle Ages, three major Christian kingdoms developed in the peninsula: Castile, the largest; Aragon, in the northeast; and Portugal, in the west. In addition, the tiny Basque kingdom of Navarre existed in the north. During the reign of Sancho the Great of Navarre (1005–1035), Christian Spain was largely united, but Sancho, viewing his state in personal terms, divided it among his four sons. Out of their inheritances eventually emerged the kingdoms of Navarre, Castile, and Aragon. The kingdom of Portugal was the result of a decision by Alfonso VI of Castile (1065–1109) to reward a Burgundian count in 1095 for his services against the Muslims. In 1143 Alfonso VII and the papacy officially recognized the count's son as a king, and Portugal henceforth pursued its own historical path. The reconquista proceeded more rapidly there than in the other Iberian kingdoms, the most crucial event being the capture of Lisbon in 1147 with the aid of an English fleet.

The reconquista became a holy crusade in 1063, more than 30 years before Urban II proclaimed a crusade to regain the Holy Land. In 1085 Alfonso VI conquered Toledo, the ancient Visigothic capital. Large numbers of Muslims, Jews, and Mozarabs, or Christians who had adopted Arabic culture, were incorporated into the kingdom of Castile, which promised Muslims the right to practice their religion and preserve their customs. Although Alfonso intended to be tolerant, the prospects of a Christian-Moorish civilization similar to the one that existed in thirteenth-century Sicily were doomed when the militant Almoravids invaded southern Spain from North Africa in 1096. Relations between Christians and Moors became embittered, in part because French Cluniac monks inflamed Spanish emotions and pressured Alfonso to adopt a harder line toward the Muslims. The spread of crusading zeal contributed to the Christian victories, which culminated in 1212 when the forces of Castile, Aragon, Navarre, and Portugal routed the Muslims at Las Navas de Tolosa. As in the battle for the Holy Land, the crusades led to the creation of military orders in Spain. The knights of the Calatrava, Santiago, and Alcantara orders took the vows of poverty, chastity, and obedience but interpreted them in the loosest possible manner; chastity, for example, did not mean abstinence from sexual relations but marital fidelity. The orders acquired considerable power during the High Middle Ages.

The reconquista not only provided the context in which the Iberian kingdoms emerged but also helped shape their ideals and institutions. Iberian culture, especially in the Spanish states, combined Arabic influence with a religious zeal born in northern Spain of the crusading spirit. The need for troops and the funds to support them during the long campaign against the Muslims resulted in the appearance of representative institutions, or Cortes, in León (1188), Castile (1250), and Portugal (1254), although they never acquired the power of the English Parliament. In Castile, which supplied the bulk of the men for the reconquista, the need for urban support also brought charters for the towns. Above all, the reconquista paved the way for the establishment in the fifteenth century of a unified Spain, which concluded the reconquest with the acquisition of Granada in 1492.

Granada, the "Gardens of Paradise"

Situated on the slopes of the Sierra Nevada and the banks of the Genil River, the Islamic city of Granada developed rapidly after the disintegration of the caliphate of Córdoba in 1031. As late as the ninth century Granada had been little more than a fortified village distinguished by its large Jewish population. Blessed with fertile soil and a Mediterranean climate, the population of the city rose from 20,000 in the tenth century to 26,000 in the eleventh century, about one-third the size of neighboring Seville. As the reconquista picked up speed, Muslim refugees fled south to Granada, enriching the city with an influx of artisans and merchants. When the monarchs of Castile and Aragon expelled thousands of Muslim agricultural workers in the 1260s, many moved to the kingdom of Granada. By the fifteenth century the population of the state had probably reached 350,000, of whom at least 50,000 resided in the capital, by then the wealthiest city in Spain.

The development of Granada began in earnest after the fall of the strife-ridden Zirids, a dynasty of North African Berbers from Tunis who had governed Granada for most of the eleventh century. Their successors were two dynasties of Berbers, the Almoravids (1090–1154) and the Almohades (1154–1228), the latter of which began the construction of major new fortifications. The city reached the peak of its glory during the rule of the Nasrid dynasty (1231–1492), which conquered Granada in 1238 and made it the capital of a new kingdom. For two and a half centuries Granada remained the only Islamic state in Iberia, but only by becoming a vassal of Castile, which exacted a tribute of 20 to 50 percent of the royal revenues and also required the Nasrid sovereigns to provide military assistance to Castile, even in the work of the reconquista. Thus the Granadans were forced to help the Castilians end Muslim rule in Seville in 1248.

As the city expanded, the role of the Jews declined. Their influence had peaked in the early eleventh century,

The Court of the Lions in the Alhambra is not only an exquisite walled garden but also a symbol of paradise. The four waterways that converge at the fountain represent the four rivers of paradise; the 12 lions on the fountain symbolize the signs of the zodiac.

when many Jews held fiscal and administrative offices and were prominent in the merchant community. Two Jewish financiers—Samuel ibn-Naghrilah and his son Yusuf—served as viziers, or key administrators, for Zirid kings in the eleventh century. In 1066 a violent reaction to Yusuf and other Jews in government office resulted in the massacre of as many as 4,000 Jews. Unlike Mozarabs, Jews were still tolerated in Granada, though their numbers were small by the fifteenth century.

Throughout the medieval period, Granada retained the appearance of a Middle Eastern city; one contemporary likened it to Damascus. Because of the influx of immigrants in the Nasrid period, it was extremely crowded; devoid of planned open spaces, most of its maze of streets were no more than 3 to 4 feet wide. The narrow, crooked streets at least offered some protection from the intense sunlight, as did an abundance of shady gardens and courts. Aqueducts brought water to the city, including its numerous Roman-style baths. Artisans, who were grouped according to their craft in distinct quarters or streets, produced linen and silk, much of it for export. Merchants exported fruits, sugarcane, and almonds to pay for the grain that had to be imported to supplement domestic crops.

The Nasrids patronized education and the arts, and their court attracted numerous learned Muslims. Mathematics, science, medicine, and literature flourished. A university and a hospital for the physically and mentally ill were founded in the mid-1300s, and the city had three important libraries. The greatest monuments of Granada's golden age are the Alhambra and the Generalife. The Alhambra, constructed mostly between 1238 and 1358, was a palatial fortress replete with barracks, stables, mosques, and gardens. Built on a terrace overlooking the city, the palace is richly decorated in an ornate Arabesque style with colored tiles and marble, geometric figures, and floral motifs. Its horseshoe arches, delicate columns, and graceful arcades are the culmination of Islamic architecture in Iberia. The nearby Generalife beautifully illustrates the description of paradise in the Koran as "a garden flowing with streams." Intended for summer use, the Generalife, with its pools, fountains, and trees, perfectly blends building and landscape architecture. A fourteenth-century observer justifiably described Granada in glowing terms: "No city can be compared to it as to its exterior or interior, and no country is like it with respect to the extent of its buildings, and the excellence of its position."[1]

Russia and the Mongol Conquest

While Christians were launching their crusades against the Muslims in Iberia and Palestine, the Mongols invaded Russia, which they ruled for two centuries. Just as the internal weaknesses of their Muslim enemies facilitated the initial success of the crusaders in Palestine and the advances of the Christians in Iberia, so Russian disunity made the Mongol advance easier. The last great Kievan prince, Yaroslav the Wise (1019–1054), had been an effective ruler, extending the territory of his state; issuing the first written codification of East Slavic law, building numerous churches, including the Kiev Cathedral; and supporting the translation of religious literature from Greek into Slavic. He had also strengthened ties between Russia and western Europe, in part by marrying his daughter Anna to the French king, Henry I. But Yaroslav made a fatal mistake by implementing the rota system to determine succession to the throne. According to this system, the crown passed to the senior member of the ruling family rather than to the eldest son of a deceased ruler; in other words, brothers normally had preference over sons. Moreover, each prince was assigned to a town suitable to his place in the line of succession. When the grand prince died, each prince was supposed to move up one step to the next highest town. Instead of providing for the peaceful succession of experienced rulers, the rota system fostered dissension and occasionally violent feuding. Rather than evolving into a centralized state, Russia disintegrated into a loose confederation of essentially independent principalities.

Long before the Mongols struck, the assaults of the militant Cumans, a nomadic people who lived in the steppes, crippled Kiev. Their attacks, which began in the 1060s, eventually severed Kiev's access by the Dnieper River to the Black Sea and trade with Byzantium. In 1203 the Cumans sacked Kiev, already weakened by the ravages of a rival Russian prince in 1169. These attacks had the effect of directing Russian expansion to the forests of the north and west, away from the steppes and from ties to the Byzantine Empire. By 1200 the Russians were experiencing less and less contact with the rest of Christian Europe.

Commonly called Tartars or Tatars, the Mongols who invaded Russia in the early thirteenth century were militant nomads from Mongolia who had been united into a powerful confederation by Chinghis Khan (1155–1227). They had already launched assaults on China and Korea, while other military units pushed westward until they attacked the Cumans in southern

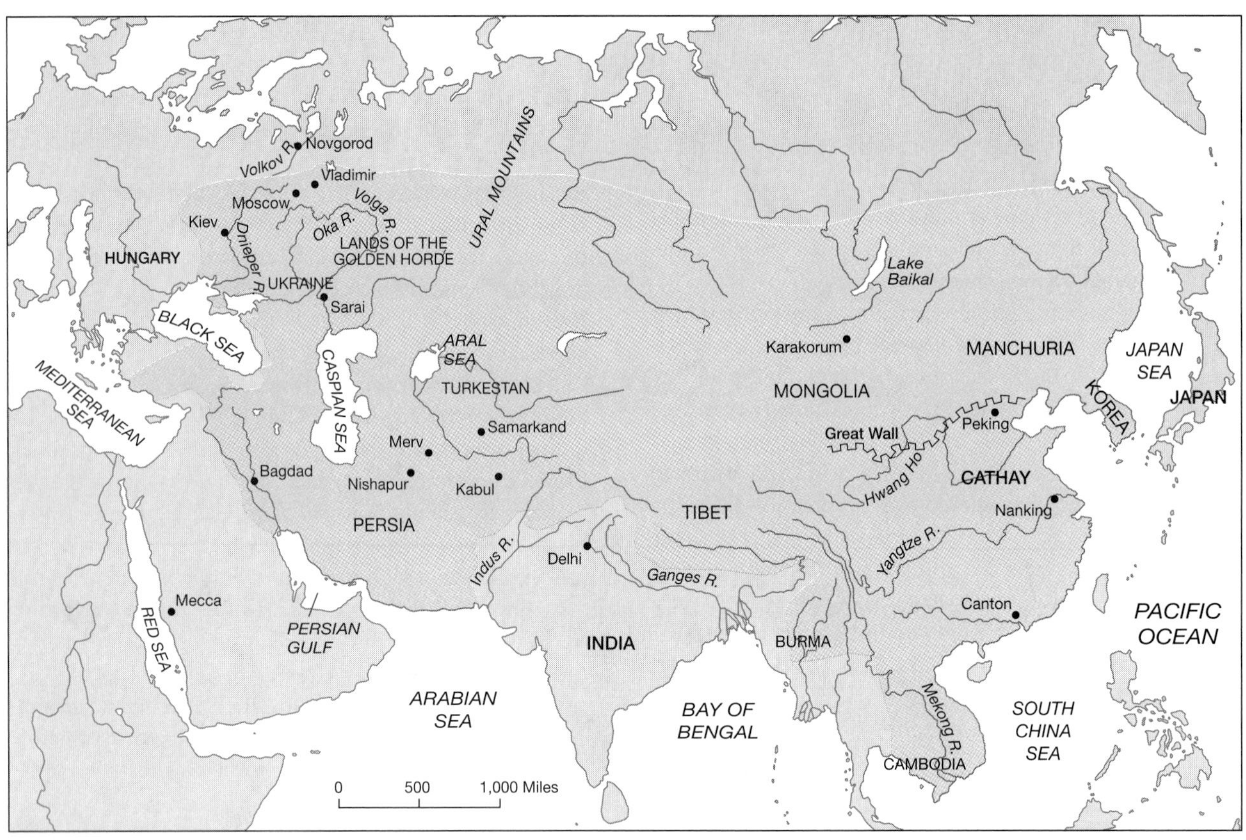

MAP 13.5 MONGOL EMPIRE, c. 1300

Russia. In 1223 the Mongols defeated a joint Cuman–Russian army, after which they held a victory banquet on a platform beneath which they crushed the captured Russian princes. At the death of Chinghis Khan the Mongols withdrew to their homeland to participate in the selection of his successor, but in 1237 they returned under Chinghis' grandson, Batu, who had an army of 50,000 Mongols and 50,000 auxiliaries, mostly Turks. By 1240 they had overrun Russia, slaughtering all who resisted. From there they invaded Poland, Silesia, Bohemia, Moravia, and Hungary, only to pull back to Russia when another khan died in 1241. In the late thirteenth century, under the leadership of Kubilai Khan, another of Chinghis' grandsons, the Mongol Empire included Russia, Persia, China, and part of Southeast Asia—the largest empire known to this time. Within its borders new possibilities existed for peoples of different cultures to communicate with and learn from each other.

The Mongols established their western capital at Sarai on the Lower Volga River, north of the Caspian Sea. The princes of southern and eastern Russia had to pay tribute to the khans, but in return they received charters, or *yarliks,* authorizing them to act as deputies of the khans. In general, the princes enjoyed considerable freedom to rule as they desired. One of them, Alexander Nevsky (died 1263), prince of Vladimir, acquired heroic status as the result of major victories over the Swedes, the Teutonic Knights, and the Lithuanians.

The Mongol incursions destroyed the last remnants of Kievan power, and henceforth medieval Russia was essentially divided into four regions. The Mongols dominated the southern steppes but exercised only moderate control over Great Russia, the region between the Volga and Oka rivers, which included the principalities of Vladimir and Moscow. Western Russia, including the Ukraine, freed itself of Mongol control in the late medieval period, only to fall under the sway of Lithuania. The Mongols had the least influence over the vast principality of Novgorod in northern Russia. Novgorod enjoyed the advantage of a strategic commercial site on the Volkov River, but most of its territory was thinly populated because of its poor soil. Immigrants who left southern Russia to escape the Mongols gravitated mostly to the northeast, where the soil was better and the rivers were more conducive to commercial development. This region provided the nucleus of the modern Russian state in the late medieval period. By that time the Mongols had left their impact on the Russians in such areas as military dress and tactics, labor levies, and the development of new trade routes. Eastern influence remained strong well into the eighteenth century, when Russian rulers attempted to westernize their country.

SUMMARY

In political terms the Middle Ages witnessed the transition of England and France from decentralized feudal states to emerging national monarchies, but the course of German and Italian history was strikingly different because of the imperial ambitions of the German rulers and the determination of the papacy to rejuvenate the church by controlling episcopal appointments. Although the popes won the struggle, destroying the Hohenstaufens in the process, they in turn succumbed to growing secular concerns and the forceful resistance of the French and English monarchs.

The century between the pontificates of Innocent III and Boniface VIII, though one of brilliant cultural achievement, nevertheless saw the beginnings of a process that eroded papal prestige and power over secular rulers. The change in papal fortunes was mirrored in the history of the crusading movement over which they tried in vain to preside. The early successes were more than offset by later failures as well as by the increasingly materialistic motives of the participants. In the end, only the Iberian crusades achieved their objectives. The accomplishments of the High Middle Ages were nevertheless significant, not only with respect to the political achievements in France and England and the reforms in the church but also in terms of commerce and urban development, the founding of universities, scholastic and scientific thought, and the construction of majestic cathedrals. It is to these religious, intellectual, and cultural achievements that we turn in Chapter 14.

NOTES

1. A. G. Chejne, *Muslim Spain: Its History and Culture* (Minneapolis: University of Minnesota Press, 1974), p. 156.

SUGGESTIONS FOR FURTHER READING

Abulafia, D. *Frederick II.* New York: Oxford University Press, 1992.

Baldwin, J. W. *The Government of Philip Augustus.* Berkeley: University of California Press, 1986.

Barlow, F. *The Feudal Kingdom of England, 1042–1216,* 4th ed. New York: Longman, 1988.

Bartlett, R. *The Making of Europe: Conquest, Colonization, and Cultural Change, 950–1350.* Princeton, N.J.: Princeton University Press, 1993.

Brooke, C. *Europe in the Central Middle Ages, 962–1154.* New York: Longman, 1987.

Chazan, R. *European Jewry and the First Crusade.* Berkeley: University of California Press, 1987.

Davis, R. H. C. *A History of Medieval Europe from Constantine to Saint Louis.* New York: Longman, 1988.

Day, J. *The Medieval Market Economy.* Oxford: Blackwell, 1987.

Duby, G. *France in the Middle Ages, 987–1460,* trans. J. Vale. Oxford: Blackwell, 1991.

Fossier, R. *Peasant Life in the Medieval West.* Oxford: Blackwell, 1988.

Hanawalt, B. A. *The Ties That Bound: Peasant Families in Medieval England.* New York: Oxford University Press, 1986.

Harvey, A. *Economic Expansion in the Byzantine Empire, 900–1200.* Cambridge: Cambridge University Press, 1990.

Haverkamp, A. *Medieval Germany, 1056–1273,* trans. H. Braun and R. Mortimer. New York: Oxford University Press, 1988.

Hillgarth, J. N. *The Spanish Kingdoms, 1250–1516,* 2 vols. Oxford: Clarendon Press, 1976–1978.

Hohenberg, P. M., and Lees, L. H. *The Making of Urban Europe, 1000–1950.* Cambridge, Mass.: Harvard University Press, 1985.

James, E. *The Franks.* Oxford: Blackwell, 1988.

Logan, F. D. *The Vikings in History,* 2nd ed. London: Routledge, 1992.

Lopez, R. S. *The Commercial Revolution of the Middle Ages, 950–1350.* Cambridge: Cambridge University Press, 1976.

Mayer, H. E. *The Crusades,* 2nd ed., trans. J. Gillingham. London: Oxford University Press, 1988.

Morgan, D. *The Mongols.* New York: Blackwell, 1986.

Morris, C. *The Papal Monarchy: The Western Church from 1050 to 1250.* New York: Oxford University Press, 1989.

Mundy, J. H. *Europe in the High Middle Ages,* 2nd ed. New York: Longman, 1991.

Nicholas, D. *The Evolution of the Medieval World: Society, Government and Thought in Europe, 312–1500.* New York: Longman, 1992.

Owen, D. D. R. *Eleanor of Aquitaine: Queen and Legend.* Oxford: Blackwell, 1993.

Postan, M. M., and Miller, E. *The Cambridge Economic History of Europe,* vol. 2: *Trade and Industry in the Middle Ages,* 2nd ed. Cambridge: Cambridge University Press, 1987.

Reuter, T. *Germany in the Early Middle Ages, 800–1056.* New York: Longman, 1991.

Riché, P. *The Carolingians,* trans. M. I. Allen. Philadelphia: University of Pennsylvania Press, 1993.

Rossabi, M. *Khubilai Khan: His Life and Times.* Berkeley: University of California Press, 1988.

Sayers, J. *Innocent III.* New York: Longman, 1994.

Turner, R. V. *King John.* New York: Longman, 1994.

Wood, I. *The Merovingian Kingdoms, 450–751.* New York: Longman, 1993.

CHAPTER 14

Life and Culture in Medieval Europe

The culture of Europe blended Judeo-Christian values, classical ideals and concepts, and Germanic traditions. As it developed, European culture also owed much to the Islamic world. By the High Middle Ages, European culture was vigorously creative. Commercial developments were instrumental in shaping the new outlook, as the burgeoning cities became the setting for the cathedral schools and the first universities as well as for the Romanesque and Gothic cathedrals. Troubadours, university professors and students, affluent merchants, and crusaders took their place in a Europe hitherto largely confined to feudal aristocrats, peasants, and parish clergy. This was an age of spiritual renewal, as reflected in the growth of papal power, the founding of new religious orders, and the intellectual brilliance of scholastic thought. Theologians such as Thomas Aquinas attempted a synthesis of all knowledge, both earthly and spiritual, for the greater glory of God. But it was no less an age whose darker side boded ill for Jews. If love, service, and civic pride inspired the building of the great cathedrals, bigotry and hate found their outlet in ruthless anti-Semitism. Nor did the status of women appreciably improve, despite their contribution to the age.

The Medieval Church

Although Christianity was the dominant religion in medieval Europe, its adherents struggled to overcome a widespread belief in primitive natural forces and magic. Early medieval priests were missionaries in their own parishes, though in time they won at least nominal adher-

Hildegard of Bingen. At the age of 42 she experienced (in her own words) "a fiery light of great brilliancy streaming down from heaven [which] entirely flooded my brain, my heart, and my breast, like a flame that flickers not but gives glowing warmth."

ence to Christianity. With its warnings of eternal damnation and its message of salvation through the sacraments, the church gradually shaped a code of conduct and a basic system of belief that became a unifying force.

In their efforts to win the people's hearts, church leaders periodically clashed with their secular counterparts. Yet they were commonly allies in maintaining control over their subjects. Most rulers governed with the church's blessing, while lay authorities protected the church and assisted it in carrying out its policies. When conflicts did erupt, church leaders could seek support from their secular allies or employ two spiritual weapons, excommunication and the interdict. Excommunication technically prohibited an offender from participating in church rites or maintaining contact with other Christians, and if the sentence was not lifted prior to one's death, the offender was eternally damned. An interdict, imposed on a particular area, could bar all church services with the exception of baptism and extreme unction (last rites). To be effective, these penalties required popular support and could not be overused.

Monastic Communities

A characteristic feature of medieval Christianity was the founding of religious communities in which men and women lived in relative isolation from the rest of society. Such communities initially developed in Egypt and then spread throughout the Roman Empire. The first monastic communities in the West appeared in the late fourth and fifth centuries, the most famous of them being the two John Cassian (385–440) founded near Marseilles in Gaul. Other monastic experiments were tried as far afield as Spain, England, and Ireland, but a monastery founded in Italy in 529 by Benedict of Nursia (480–547) eventually had the greatest impact on European monasticism.

As a guide for the monks who joined him at Monte Cassino, south of Rome, Benedict wrote a rule designed to provide for an orderly existence conducive to the dedication of one's life to God. Unlike some of the other early monastic leaders, Benedict did not call for extreme forms of self-denial but insisted on moderation in a life of prayer, contemplation, study, communal worship, and labor. Monks vowed to follow a life of poverty, to be chaste, to obey their superiors, and not to leave the monastery without permission. An abbot, elected for life by the monks and consecrated by a bishop but accountable only to the Rule and to God, directed the monastery. Each monastery was intended to be self-sufficient; hence its members had to perform a variety of tasks that ranged from farming to making clothes. To educate novices and provide service books, Bibles, and other religious literature the monks also had to teach and copy manuscripts. By the seventh century there were communities for Benedictine nuns, who regarded Benedict's sister Scholastica as their patron. Like the monasteries of the men, their convents spread throughout Europe in the ensuing centuries. In time the standards of some monasteries became lax as they accumulated material possessions, often the gifts of pious laity.

Apostolic Renewal: The New Religious Orders

A new monastic order provided the foundation for religious reform beginning in the tenth century. Although the imperial revival under Otto I in the middle of that century threatened the independence of the papal office, a contemporary reform movement helped to restore its vigor and spiritual leadership. In 910 Duke William "the Good" of Aquitaine founded a monastery at Cluny in Burgundy, with a charter guaranteeing independence from secular control. By this time control over other monasteries had fallen into the hands of feudal lords, who stripped their revenues and sold their monastic offices. To prevent this from happening at Cluny, William placed the monastery under papal protection; henceforth its abbots owed their allegiance only to Rome. They insisted on major reforms in the church, including renewed emphasis on the Rule of Benedict and the monastic liturgy, an end to the sale of church offices, and the enforcement of clerical celibacy, which, though widely disregarded, had been church policy since the fourth century, in keeping with the examples of Jesus and Paul. The call to reform received a stunning response: new foundations and converted Benedictine houses swelled the total of institutions based on the Cluniac model to more than 300, all of which were administered by priors subordinate to the abbot of Cluny. The renewed sense of spiritual devotion radiated well beyond the cloister as the Cluniac monks inspired lay believers. The heightened devotional interest was manifested in the appearance of the first prayer books for the laity.

The Cluniacs were the first wave of a series of reform-oriented monastic movements that swept the Latin church in the High Middle Ages. The Cistercians, founded in the twelfth century, were a Benedictine reform movement that emphasized individual devotion rather than public worship, and agricultural labor rather than other forms of work. The Cistercians tended to settle in remote areas to avoid corruption by secular influences. With austerity as their ideal, the Cistercians followed a rigorous vegetarian diet. They seldom spoke, and they worshiped in churches devoid of ornamentation. The Cistercians earned a well-deserved reputation for their skills in making marginal lands productive. The movement reached its peak under the leadership of Bernard of Clairvaux and his successors. Nearly 350 Cistercian abbeys were functioning by the time Bernard died in 1153, and more than 700 by 1300. Like other monastic orders, the Cistercians were less than enthusiastic about the thousands of women who wanted to become Cistercian nuns, though in the end the church resolved the issue by placing the convents under monastic supervision as a subordinate branch of the male order.

The richness of medieval Christian religious life is illustrated in the variety of orders. The Carthusians were more rigorous than the Benedictines, insisting that each monk live in a separate cell, fast every Friday, and eat with his fellow monks only on Sundays and the major holy days. In contrast to this solitary life, "canons regular" such as the Augustinians combined the monastic concept of living according to a rule with the duties of secular priests. Unlike the Benedictines and Cluniacs, the canons regular refused to amass large endowments and impressive buildings, preferring instead to follow a humble lifestyle and aid the needy.

A third form of religious vocation originated in the thirteenth century with the founding of mendicant or begging orders, so called because their friars depended on alms for their living. Like the monks and canons regular, they took vows of poverty, chastity, and obedience, and they lived in communities; unlike the monks, they devoted their lives to ministering to the laity. The Spanish Augustinian Dominic (1170–1221) founded one of the principal mendicant orders to fight the spread of heresy in southern France. The Dominicans, formally constituted in 1216, combated heresy by preaching, education, and holy living.

Francis of Assisi (1182–1226), the son of a well-to-do Italian cloth merchant, established the other major mendicant order, the Franciscans. Motivated by a religious vision, Francis sold many of his father's possessions, gave the proceeds to the church, and renounced material goods. Francis and his followers, whose ideal was absolute poverty and humility, obtained papal approval for their order in 1209. The friars devoted themselves to the spiritual and material needs of the lowly, particularly in the towns. At first the Franciscans shunned learning in preference to apostolic simplicity, but their growing competition with the Dominicans gradually persuaded them to engage in scholarly endeavors. Both mendicant orders became prominent in the universities and engaged in missionary work among the Muslims and the Mongols.

Portrait of Francis of Assisi by Peter Paul Rubens, c. 1615.

For most women attracted to the new religious movements, the lure was undoubtedly spiritual, though some may have been drawn to the religious life because they had little prospect of marriage, shunned the dangers of childbirth, or sought spiritual status to compensate for their declining role in medieval society. But churchmen were generally troubled by the prospect of separate female orders. How could they support themselves? Because women were excluded from the priesthood, who would provide cloistered convents with pastoral care? Women, moreover, were thought to be unusually susceptible to heresy. The problem became acute by the early thirteenth century as female groups began to organize, particularly in Italy and Flanders.

Clare of Assisi is the best-known founder of one of these new women's orders. Born into a pious aristocratic family at Assisi in 1194, she was influenced by a mother known for her charitable deeds and pilgrimages. While her parents were arranging her marriage, Francis of Assisi secretly met with Clare to persuade her to pursue a more rigorous spiritual life. One night in 1212, at the age of 18, she fled to a nearby chapel, where Francis received her vows to lead a life of poverty and to imitate Christ and Mary. The "Poor Clares" or "Poor Sisters" date their origins from that event. The sisters lived and worked in the church and convent of San Damiano, near Assisi, where Clare formally acquired the title of abbess in 1216, a position she retained until her death in 1253.

The problem of procuring a rule for her order, already difficult because of antifemale sentiment, was compounded by the decision of the Fourth Lateran Council in 1215 not to allow any new orders. Francis had given Clare only verbal advice and a brief "way of life," but this had not been officially recognized. In 1219, therefore, Cardinal Ugolino, the future Pope Gregory IX, provided a rule based on Benedictine and Cistercian principles: an austere life, strict seclusion from the world, and the right of the community as a whole to own property. Ugolino's intent was to place all female groups under papal protection, with a single uniform rule and with pastoral care provided by the Franciscans. Francis, however, refused to be associated with any female community apart from that of Clare at San Damiano: "God has taken away our wives, and now the devil gives us sisters," he fumed, afraid that Ugolino's scheme would ruin his order. Despite Francis' reluctance to accept pastoral responsibility for convents, he maintained close relations with Clare, who seems to have been his confidant. As she lay dying in 1253, she was visited by Pope Innocent IV, who at last approved the rule she had sought for more than three decades, which embraced a concept of poverty that allowed neither personal nor communal possessions apart from enough land on which to grow food.

Hildegard of Bingen

One of the most remarkable figures of medieval Europe was Hildegard of Bingen (1098–1179). Born near Mainz, Hildegard claimed to have had her first mystical vision before she was 5 years old. At the age of 8 her parents sent her to a nearby Benedictine nunnery, and at 15 she took her vows. Eventually she became head of her convent, but not until midlife did she experience the radical illumination, typical of medieval mystics, that freed her remarkable creativity. As Hildegard expressed it:

Holy Poverty: The Ideal of Francis

The ideals of Francis of Assisi are clearly reflected in his will, prepared shortly before his death in 1226. His emphasis on holy poverty contrasts with the growing wealth of the church.

When the Lord gave me the care of some brothers, no one showed me what I ought to do, but the Most High himself revealed to me that I ought to live according to the model of the holy gospel. I caused a short and simple formula to be written, and the lord pope confirmed it for me.

Those who presented themselves to follow this kind of life distributed all they might have to the poor. They contented themselves with one tunic, patched within and without, with the cord and breeches, and we desired to have nothing more. . . . We loved to live in poor and abandoned churches, and we were ignorant, and were submissive to all. I worked with my hands and would still do so, and I firmly desire also that all the other brothers work, for this makes for goodness. Let those who know no trade learn one, but not for the purpose of receiving the price of their toil, but for their good example and to flee idleness. And when we are not given the price of our work, let us resort to the table of the Lord, begging our bread from door to door. The Lord revealed to me the salutation which we ought to give: "God give you peace!"

Let the brothers take great care not to accept churches, habitations, or any other buildings erected for them, except as all is in accordance with the holy poverty which we have vowed in the Rule; and let them not live in them except as strangers and pilgrims.

Source: J. H. Robinson, ed., *Readings in European History,* vol. 1 (Boston: Ginn, 1904), pp. 393–394.

> **And so it came to pass in the eleven hundred and forty-first year of the incarnation of Jesus Christ, Son of God, when I was forty-two years and seven months old, that the heavens were opened and a blinding light of exceptional brilliance flowed through my entire brain. And so it kindled my whole heart and breast like a flame, not burning but warming, . . . and suddenly I understood the meaning of the expositions of the books, that is to say of the psalter, the evangelists, and other catholic books of the Old and New Testaments.[1]**

The same vision commanded her: "O fragile one, ash of ash and corruption of corruption, say and write what you see and hear." At first Hildegard felt unequal to the task and fell ill. Encouraged by her abbot, she recorded her visions, which so impressed the Catholic world that Pope Eugenius I (1145–1153) read them aloud before his cardinals and commanded her to continue.

For the next 30 years Hildegard pursued an extraordinary career, traveling, preaching, performing exorcisms, and founding two new convents. Her life was not without tribulation and conflict, and a contemporary biography attests that she was deeply wounded when her favorite assistant left her. However, she enjoyed a freedom, authority, and prestige unprecedented among the women of her time, corresponding and negotiating with popes and monarchs and receiving a charter of personal protection from Emperor Frederick I. These extraordinary marks of favor had a single source: the compelling nature of her visions and prophecies, which she continued to record in her *Book of Life's Merits and Book of Divine Works.* The status of prophet and ultimately of saint, which she enjoyed through popular veneration although the church never formally canonized her, lifted her beyond the reproach of exceeding the limits prescribed for her sex and the suspicion of heresy that might otherwise have attached to her writings and activities. To this day a cult of Hildegard is active in parts of Germany and elsewhere, and the inscription on the shrine altar of her church at Rüdescheim reads "Saint Hildegard, pray for us."

Hildegard wrote extensively not only on divinity but also on the natural world, including detailed works on medicine, cosmology, and natural history. The creative power that was evident in the descriptions of her visions, which included elaborate and often intertwined images of architecture, natural scenery and fauna, angels, the cosmic hierarchy, and God, also manifested itself in musical composition. The 77 sacred songs that compose her cycle, the *Symphonia,* are among the masterpieces of medieval chant, and the musical drama that comprises one of its sections, *The Play of the Virtues,* is considered the earliest surviving medieval morality play.

Not only is Hildegard's work the most varied and extensive body of writing and art to come down to us from a medieval woman, but it is unique as well in the attention it pays to the emotional, moral, physical, and sexual needs of women. She rebutted the notion, common in her day, that women were more lustful than men and that they experienced greater pleasure in sexual intercourse. Unlike many of her male contemporaries, she admitted women to church while menstruating but barred men who had experienced nocturnal emissions. Her mystical metaphor for the church was of a beautiful and powerful woman. If Hildegard did not challenge the male-dominated hierarchy of the church, she nonetheless forced it to accept her on her own terms and forcefully reminded it of the essential place of women in the divine plan.

Dissidents and Heretics

The spirit of reform that swept the church increased lay interest in religion, but one unintended result of this was the rapid growth of beliefs the church considered heretical (unorthodox). In the 1170s the French merchant Peter Waldo of Lyons attracted disciples by emphasizing poverty and simplicity as well as attacking the moral corruption of the clergy. The Waldensians insisted on the right of laymen to preach, rejected some of the sacraments, accepted the Scripture alone as authoritative in religion, and, like the Franciscans, embraced the ideal of apostolic poverty. Moreover, they wanted translations of the Bible in the language of the people. Although the pope excommunicated them in 1184, they remained popular in southern France and northern Italy.

The Albigensians, so called because their center was the town of Albi in southern France, posed a more serious threat to the church. Their teaching viewed the universe in terms of a struggle between the forces of good and evil.* The Cathari, or "pure ones," were supposed to abstain from most material things, including marriage, worldly possessions, and meat, in their quest to attain perfection. Some rejected the mass, infant baptism, and even the church itself; voluntarily starving oneself to death was highly praised. Not only did the church condemn the Albigensians, but Pope Innocent III even called for a crusade to exterminate them. Knights from

*Such views were called Manichaean, after the third-century Mesopotamian prophet who advocated such a dualistic view of the universe.

northern France rallied to the call, interested more in the possibility of seizing land than in uprooting heresy. The worst fighting lasted 20 years (1209–1229) and ultimately eradicated many of the heretics.

Another weapon to combat heresy was the Inquisition, which Pope Gregory IX (1227–1241) instituted in 1231. The inquisitors' task was to convert the heretics if possible, but in any case to prevent the deadly "disease" of heresy from spreading. The Inquisition embraced the principles of Roman law, including the use of torture, such as the rack or holding the feet of the accused to hot coals. Suspects had no right to counsel, no opportunity to question witnesses, not even the right to know the charges against them. Those who refused to relinquish their heretical beliefs or were convicted a second time faced severe penalties, including imprisonment, loss of property, or burning at the stake. Although some inquisitors were notoriously severe, such as a Dominican who had 180 people burned on a single day in 1239, most of the accused escaped execution. Because the inquisitors were not allowed to shed blood, the state carried out the executions, but the church nevertheless left itself open to condemnation by relying on force rather than moral suasion to maintain its spiritual supremacy.

The World of Learning

The need to staff expanding governments with educated officials and the growth of towns, with their increasingly sophisticated businesses, their law courts, and their collection of taxes and fees, led to a greater demand for literate people. This was a major cause of the educational revolution of the late eleventh and twelfth centuries, as was the Gregorian stress on the importance of a better-educated clergy. Previously, the monasteries and a few cathedral and secular schools had provided most schooling in Europe. These early schools were insufficient, both in number and in curriculum, to meet the needs of the towns, the expanding royal courts, and the growing ecclesiastical bureaucracy. The monastic schools, with a curriculum oriented toward biblical interpretation and commentary, were never intended to serve society as a whole.

Urban developments not only increased the demand for educated people but also made cathedral schools more accessible, particularly to sons of the laity. The better cathedral schools, such as those at Chartres, Rheims, and Paris, included a music school, a school for the seven liberal arts (grammar, rhetoric, logic, arithmetic, geometry, astronomy, and music), and an advanced school for theological studies. Some church schools provided education in law, medicine, philosophy, and the natural sciences. At a humbler level, various parish priests taught reading, writing, mathematics, and the other liberal arts. The church's growing interest in education was evident in the late twelfth century, when it became mandatory for every cathedral to have a school and for each to receive funds sufficient to educate the children of the poor without charge. In Italy, Germany, and the Netherlands merchants took the lead in establishing municipal schools. Surgeons, barbers, dentists, lawyers, notaries, architects, and artists could also train young people as apprentices.

The educational revolution of the High Middle Ages involved curricular changes. Before the eleventh

CHURCH AND STATE, 440–1302

Religious orders	Major popes	Church-state relations
	Leo I (440–461)	Papacy claims fullness of power
Benedictines (529)		
	Gregory I (590–604)	
Cluniacs (910)		
	Leo IX (1049–1054)	Right of College of Cardinals to elect popes (1059)
Carthusians (1084)	Gregory VII (1073–1085)	Lay investiture controversy (1075–1122)
Cistercians (1098)	Urban II (1088–1099)	Call for crusaders (1095)
	Calixtus II (1119–1124)	Concordat of Worms (1122)
Franciscans (1209)	Innocent III (1198–1216)	
Dominicans (1216)		
Poor Clares (1219)		
	Gregory IX (1227–1241)	
		Culmination of the papacy's struggle with the Hohenstaufens (1250)
	Boniface VIII (1294–1303)	*Clericis laicos* (1296)
		Unam sanctam (1302)

century the curriculum was heavily oriented toward biblical studies, but thereafter the emphasis shifted to logic. As more Latin translations of Arabic and Greek works on philosophy and natural science became available, these subjects too were the object of greater attention. Writers such as the Augustinian friar Egidio Colonna, author of *On the Governance of Rulers,* called for a comprehensive curriculum that included the seven liberal arts, classical and Christian literature, philosophy, politics, economics, natural science, and etiquette. Colonna also advocated the education of women. The educational revolution increased lay literacy, though only a small minority could read and even fewer could write.

Scholarly Guilds: The Medieval University

As growing numbers of students traveled to cities such as Paris, Bologna, and Salerno in search of the best teachers, formal organization became necessary to secure the rights and privileges of students and teachers. There was also a need for some form of academic recognition—a "degree"—that would enable qualified persons to teach in other cities. In a society accustomed to craft and merchant guilds, the natural solution was an academic guild, a *universitas* or corporation, that could protect the interests of faculty and students as well as issue licenses to teach. Organization was essential to ensure academic standards, provide protection from townspeople inclined to overcharge students for board and room, and obtain the right of faculty and students to be tried in church rather than in local courts. In southern Europe universities were initially guilds of students; in northern Europe, guilds of teachers.

The earliest universities emerged at Bologna and Paris in the mid-twelfth century, and Salerno had a medical school. Bologna's reputation as the leading center of legal studies originated with the work of Irnerius, who wrote commentaries on contemporary legal codes based on his familiarity with the Byzantine *Corpus Juris Civilis,* and of Gratian, whose *Decretum* became the standard text for the study of canon (church) law. At Bologna students first organized into regional groups called "nations," and these in turn united to form the University of Bologna, chartered by Emperor Frederick Barbarossa in 1158. Students established regulations to govern the number, length, and content of lectures and fined or boycotted teachers who failed to cover the specified material or missed classes. The faculty controlled the granting of degrees and, because of their permanence, gradually increased their authority in the university.

At Paris teachers formed a guild to control the granting of licenses to teach, at least in part because the chancellor of the archdiocese of Paris had been selling them to unqualified individuals. After a "town-gown" conflict in which several students perished, King Philip II gave the university its charter in 1200. Paris was famous for its teachers of logic, philosophy, and theology. English students were among those attracted to Paris, but in 1167 worsening relations between England and France forced King Henry II to order them home. They settled at Oxford, which had its own chancellor by 1214. The growing demand for educated people in church and state, national and urban rivalries, and the search for more hospitable environments led to the founding of more universities—more than 20 by 1300 and more than 75 by 1500. A number of these were royal or papal foundations; others were the result of migrating students, as in the case of Cambridge (from Oxford) and Padua (from Bologna).

Most universities were organized into four faculties: the arts, which comprised the trivium (grammar, rhetoric, and logic) and the quadrivium (arithmetic, geometry, astronomy, and music), theology, medicine, and civil and canon (church) law. The standard form of instruction was the lecture, which consisted of reading and expounding on a Latin text. A typical student listened to lectures for about seven hours a day, beginning at 5 or 6 A.M. Formal debates were also standard, but because of the expense universities had few books and no libraries. Students were not tested at the conclusion of a series of lectures but at the end of a program of study, when examinations were oral and usually public. A bachelor of arts degree typically took three to six years of study and qualified one to instruct others under a master's supervision. A license to teach required several more years of study. To lecture as part of the arts faculty one had to become a master of arts, which required the preparation and defense of a thesis. Substantial additional study was necessary for a doctorate in law (up to 7 years) or theology (up to 15 years).

At first, universities had no permanent campuses or buildings but used rented rooms. To assist needy students, benefactors endowed residence halls or "colleges," and these eventually acquired their own instructional staff. Among the best known are the Sorbonne, founded at Paris in 1257 or 1258, and Merton College, established at Oxford around 1263 by Robert Merton. Such colleges provided the nucleus of a permanent campus. By the end of the thirteenth century the number of students—all male—at Paris exceeded 4,000, while Oxford had more than 2,000. As centers of learning, the universities attracted some of the greatest minds of the High Middle Ages.

Paris: Monks, Merchants, and Students in the Royal City

By the time the University of Paris received its charter in 1200, the city was growing dramatically. At the beginning of the eleventh century its outskirts were still in ruins as the result of ninth-century Viking raids, but by 1300 the city's population had reached 100,000 and gloried in a majestic new cathedral, imposing new walls, and a flourishing commerce in addition to its university. In part the growth reflected the increasing power of the French monarchy, in part the city's strategic location at the crossroads of the trade routes between southern Europe and Flanders, and, by way of the river Seine, between eastern France and the English Channel. Because the Capetian monarchs made Paris their capital, the city attracted both the nobility and ecclesiastical and educational institutions, thereby increasing the demand for luxury items and other goods. Parisian artisans produced a wide range of jewelry, swords, saddles, linens, and wine barrels. Merchants traded these goods at the Champagne fairs for Flemish and Italian woolens, Asian spices and sugar, Byzantine silks, Spanish leathers, and English tin.

The heart of Paris was the Île de la Cité, an island in the Seine. Dominating its western half were the royal

MAP 14.1 MEDIEVAL UNIVERSITIES

palace and the exquisite Gothic chapel of Sainte-Chapelle, which Louis IX built to house a collection of relics that allegedly included the crown of thorns, a piece of the cross, and a sample of Christ's blood. The eastern portion of the Île de la Cité became the site of the magnificent Gothic cathedral of Notre Dame ("Our Lady"), begun in 1163. The city's commercial center, site of its guilds and principal markets, was on the right (north) bank of the Seine, extending in a rough semicircle from the Grand Pont, the great bridge, to the Île de la Cité, on which Jewish and Lombard moneychangers had their shops. To the south, the Left Bank, or Latin Quarter, was the home of the university and of several religious orders, including the Dominicans, the Augustinians, and the Carmelites. The Roman walls, which were still standing in the twelfth century, enclosed only some 25 acres and were inadequate for the burgeoning city. Philip II ordered the construction of new ramparts on both banks. The resulting walls, which enclosed approximately 625 acres, were up to 20 feet high and 10 feet thick and featured 33 towers on the north bank and 34 on the south. Just beyond the wall, where the rampart met the river, stood the Louvre, a fortified palace that also functioned as a treasury, an armory, and a prison. Philip's ambitious building program also included three new hospitals to care for the needy and three aqueducts to supply the city with fresh water. He even launched a project to pave the city's main streets with 3-foot-square blocks of sandstone.

Paris was a colorful amalgam of the secular and the sacred, the royal and the common. Law enforcement was the responsibility of the provost of Paris, whom the crown appointed, but in general a municipal council presided over by the master of the corporation of river merchants handled city affairs. Despite the presence of the crown and major religious orders, Paris was far from a puritanical city. Prostitutes were so abundant that two streets were named after them, the Rue Val-d'Amour

MAP 14.2 PARIS IN THE THIRTEENTH CENTURY

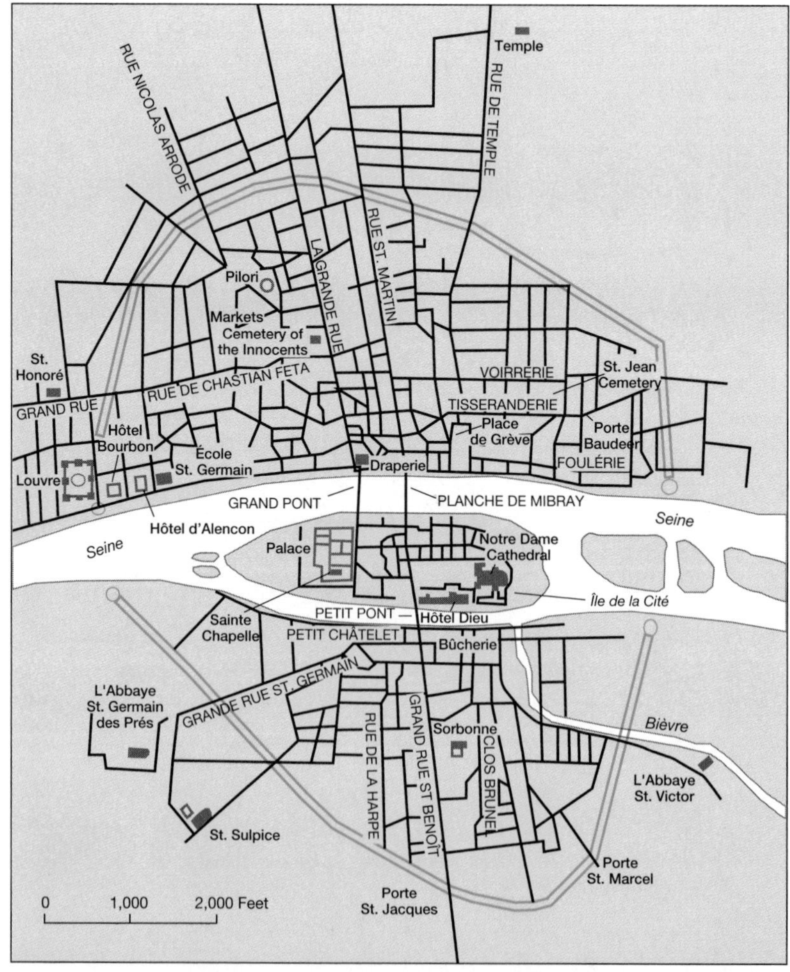

and the Rue Pute-y-muce ("whore-in-hiding"). The churchmen of Paris sometimes behaved bawdily, and in 1212 a council convened in the city tried to curtail their more outlandish behavior, including the keeping of mistresses, the Feast of the Drunken Deacons on December 26, and the Feast of Fools on January 1, when they parodied the liturgy, burned old shoes instead of incense, and marched through the streets in grotesque costumes.

In the thirteenth century, university students added to the local color, particularly when they demonstrated on behalf of a favorite cause, battled with the civic guards, or fought with the townsfolk or among themselves. Although lectures began at 5 A.M. and continued, with appropriate breaks, well into the afternoon, students had time in the evening for conversation and a few drinks in a tavern before retiring to modest rooms, typically in the attics of Left Bank houses. Classes met in rooms rented by the faculty, and only gradually did the university begin to acquire buildings, notably the privately endowed colleges, such as the Sorbonne, established to house, teach, and control the students. Although these were arduous years, the students lived in one of the most exciting European cities and studied under the foremost educators of their day.

The Scholastics

Well before the evolution of the first universities, the schoolmen, or scholastics, of western Europe were engaged in heated debates. The scholastics, who used Aristotelian methodology and adopted the Aristotelian world view, concerned themselves with three fundamental and intimately related problems: the proper study of theological knowledge, the nature of ultimate reality, and the relationship of faith and reason.

Although the roots of Christian theology go back to the first century, only in the 1100s did the discipline of systematic theology emerge through the application of logic to fundamental religious questions. The leaders in this endeavor were Peter Abelard (1079–1142) of Brittany, a master in the cathedral school at Paris, and his disciple Peter Lombard (c. 1095–1160). Their technique, known as the dialectical method, juxtaposed seemingly contradictory statements to encourage students to seek a logical resolution. Abelard applied this technique to theology in his book *Sic et Non* ("Yes and No"), a compilation of contradictory statements by early church fathers on various religious issues. Teachers encouraged students to resolve the conflicts by taking into account the way words change meaning over time, the possibility of inaccurate texts, historical context, and the need to weigh the credibility of different authorities. Peter Lombard used the same method in his *Four Books of Sentences,* which analyzed such doctrines as the Trinity, creation, the Incarnation, and the sacraments. From the thirteenth century to the sixteenth, Peter Lombard's book served as the standard theological text in the universities. Traditionalists, however, condemned the logical approach to theology on the grounds that human reason could not probe divine mysteries.

The debate over the nature of reality reflected the scholastics' indebtedness to classical Greek philosophy. In the eleventh century the French scholar Roscellin rejected the Platonic notion that universal concepts are real and instead insisted that reality consists only of individual things. Individual men and women are real; humanity is simply the name (*nomen*) for a mental category or concept. Roscellin and his followers thus came to be called nominalists. Because they attached primary significance to the experience of individual things through the senses, the nominalists radically altered traditional theology, which had relied heavily on philosophical concepts. Nominalists asserted most religious beliefs solely on the basis of faith and biblical teaching, not rational demonstration.

In contrast to the nominalists, realists such as the Italian monk Anselm (1033–1109) argued that individual things are knowable only because they reflect universal ideas, which are accessible by reason. Realists agreed that initially an act of faith is required for things beyond the reach of the senses. "I believe," said Anselm, "so that I may know." Once beyond this, reason could demonstrate the existence of universal ideas and even of God. It is impossible, Anselm argued, to conceive of a being greater than God. A being who exists is greater than a being who does not exist; therefore the idea of God must include the existence of God. The importance Anselm attached to reason did not negate Scripture but helped make logic and philosophy a fundamental part of the new systematic theology.

A group of moderate realists that included Abelard advocated a middle ground in the debate over universals. Influenced by Aristotle, they accepted the reality of both individual things and the general ideas upon which they were patterned. The idea of humanity was thus as real as the experience of individuals. The leading moderate realist, Thomas Aquinas (c. 1225–1274), taught that each particular thing has the universal within it; the universal gives the particular its essence. By studying individual things, one can rationally discover their essence and thus formulate valid general concepts.

At the heart of the debate over universals and the dialectical method was the question of the relationship between faith (or revelation) and reason. The scholastics generally agreed that theology and philosophy are intimately related, but Franciscan and Dominican thinkers disagreed over the nature of that relationship. The great Franciscan theologians Alexander of Hales (died 1245) and his pupil Bonaventure (1221–1274), both of whom taught at the University of Paris, stressed the primacy of revelation. To them faith was an act of the will by which one accepts revealed truth; reason is useful only to explain the truth gleaned from revelation. The leading Dominican theologians, Aquinas and his teacher Albertus Magnus (died 1280), who also taught at Paris, accorded reason a greater role than the Franciscans in the discovery of knowledge but stopped short of making revelation subordinate to reason. Because faith and reason are complementary paths, Aquinas believed that reason can lead an unbeliever to the point of believing.

Alexander of Hales and Aquinas wrote lengthy *summae* (summations) in which they analyzed major theological issues rationally through a process that included the meticulous refutation of opposing viewpoints. The blending of theology and philosophy is evident in Aquinas' *Summa Theologica,* particularly in the sections devoted to rational proofs for the existence of God, such as the argument from an orderly universe to the existence of a Great Designer or the argument from motion to the existence of a Prime Mover, derived from Aristotle. Aquinas' work represents the culmination of the attempt to synthesize the revealed tenets of Christianity with the rational principles of classical philosophy. Christian scholastics such as Aquinas, Jewish theologians such as Maimonides, and Muslim philosophers such as Averroës

Proving That God Exists

The compatibility of faith and reason in scholastic thought is reflected in Thomas Aquinas' arguments to prove the existence of God.

God's existence can be proved in five ways. The first and clearest proof is the argument from motion. It is certain, and in accordance with sense experience, that some things in this world are moved. Now everything that is moved is moved by something else. . . . We are therefore bound to arrive at a first mover which is not moved by anything, and all men understand that this is God.

The second way is from the nature of an efficient cause. We find that there is a sequence of efficient causes in sensible things. . . . We are therefore bound to suppose that there is a first efficient cause. And all men call this God.

The third way is from the nature of possibility and necessity. There are some things which may either exist or not exist, since some things come to be and pass away, and may therefore be or not be. . . . We are therefore bound to suppose something necessary in itself, which does not owe its necessity to anything else, but which is the cause of the necessity of other things. And all men call this God.

The fourth way is from the degrees that occur in things, which are found to be more and less good, true, noble, and so on. . . . There is therefore something which is the cause of the being of all things that are, as well as of their goodness and their every perfection. This we call God.

The fifth way is from the governance of things. We see how some things, like natural bodies, work for an end even though they have no knowledge. . . . There is therefore an intelligent being by whom all natural things are directed to their end. This we call God.

Source: Thomas Aquinas, *Nature and Grace,* trans. and ed. A. M. Fairweather. *Library of Christian Classics,* vol. 11 (Philadelphia: Westminster Press, 1954), pp. 54–56.

reflect the basic human quest to order existence and reaffirm basic ideals through the use of reason.

Law and Political Thought

Other scholars revived the study of Roman law in the late eleventh and early twelfth centuries. The revival began in southern France and northern Italy as teachers and attorneys turned to the *Corpus Juris Civilis* of Justinian for guidance. At Bologna, Irnerius and his successors lectured on the *Corpus* using the dialectical method popularized in theology by Abelard. Their work was largely confined to glosses or comments on the *Corpus,* but legal scholars soon began exploring the general principles on which the laws were based and adapting the laws to the conditions of their own time and locale. A gradual blending of ideas in Roman and customary law thus transpired. Roman influence was especially evident in the work of codifying and systematizing the law, but it also resulted in the reintroduction of judicial torture. The impact of Roman law was greatest in the Italian states and the Iberian peninsula.

Roman principles and procedures heavily influenced the development of church or canon law, which Gratian, a monk who taught at Bologna, codified in the twelfth century. His text, the *Decretum* (c. 1140), used the dialectical method to organize and reconcile approximately 3,900 laws. Canon law in this period involved not only such religious matters as sacraments and church property but also slander, libel, morals, tithes, wills, and oaths. Gratian's codification was the prelude to an increasingly judicial relationship between the church and its members.

Interest in political theory grew in large measure because of issues raised in the investiture controversy. Theorists who were sympathetic to the papacy claimed ever broader papal powers until at last they asserted the pope's right to intervene in secular matters as part of his responsibility to supervise temporal sovereigns. This was unacceptable to secular rulers, whose theorists extended the claim of royal authority until it included the duty to intervene in ecclesiastical affairs should the papacy prove incapable of reforming the church. Whereas papal writers contended that temporal sovereigns received their right to govern through the church as a divine agency, monarchical theorists insisted that God directly bestowed such power on the rulers. Manegold of Lautenbach (died 1085) went so far as to argue that God's agency was not the church but the people, who were therefore entitled to withdraw their support from a tyrannical ruler. Although Manegold's theory had democratic implications, no medieval thinker advocated a philosophy of popular government. Most would have accepted Aquinas' assertion that monarchy is preferable to other forms of government because it is the most stable.

The scholastic theologian Thomas Aquinas was influenced by Aristotle (lower left) and Plato (lower right) as well as by the earlier Christian thinkers shown above him. The Islamic philosopher Averroës lies vanquished at his feet.

Depicting society in organic terms made monarchical government seem natural. The English scholar John of Salisbury (c. 1115–1180) developed the notion of the body politic, in which the sovereign is the head; the judges and governors are the ears, eyes, and tongue; the magistrates and soldiers are the hands; and the peasants are the feet. As an apologist for papal supremacy, John then argued that the church is the soul of the body. John accepted the people's right to overthrow a tyrannical ruler on the grounds that tyranny was an abuse of the power God had bestowed on a ruler. Despite the democratic implications of this theory, John refused to make rulers responsible to their subjects; if tyrants were overthrown, people acted as divine agents, not in their own right. In general, medieval thinkers preferred monarchical government but expected sovereigns to rule justly in accord with divine law. They tended to see society and government in positive, natural terms: the state, said Aquinas, was a natural institution, not a necessary evil as Augustine had taught in the fifth century.

Science and Medicine

Although medieval thinkers failed to free science from its subservience to theology, they pointed the way to a more accurate understanding of the physical universe. Scientific knowledge came to be seen not only as a reflection of divine handiwork but also as a means to improve living conditions. The increased availability of Greek and Arabic treatises on science in Latin translation gave strong impetus to scientific study in Europe. One of the earliest interpreters of Arabic science was the twelfth-century English scholar Adelard of Bath, whose translation of Euclid's *Elements* from Arabic became the principal textbook for the study of geometry in the West. His own *Natural Questions* gave European students an insight into Arabic knowledge in such fields as astronomy, botany, zoology, and meteorology.

One of the most important contributions of medieval science was a growing awareness of the significance of observation and experiment as the best means to acquire knowledge of the physical world. Among the early advocates of this methodology were Albertus Magnus of Paris and Robert Grosseteste (c. 1175–1253) of Oxford, both of whom were influenced by Aristotle. Grosseteste was convinced that optics, or the study of vision, was the foundation of all other scientific knowledge because light was the most basic physical substance. Accordingly, he employed an early form of the experimental method to study the rainbow. His famous pupil, the English Franciscan Roger Bacon (c. 1220–1292), proposed the dissection of pig and cow eyes to understand optical principles. Bacon learned that light travels faster than sound, and he was interested in the use of magnifying glasses and eyeglasses. He is noted more for his advocacy of experimental study than for specific contributions to scientific knowledge. Bacon's oft-quoted anticipations of airplanes, submarines, and machine-powered ships were flights of fantasy, not concepts based on scientific principles, like those of Leonardo da Vinci two centuries later. However, medieval scientists such as Grosseteste and Bacon made a significant contribution by advocating the importance of the experimental method and mathematics as keys to understand the natural world.

Medical knowledge too depended on translations of Greek and Arabic works, among them the Arabic treatises of the Jewish physician Maimonides (1135–1204) and Avicenna, whose *Canon of Medicine* went through numerous editions. Arabic doctors had made major advances in the use of drugs, and this knowledge passed to Europeans, especially through the medical school at Salerno. Until Montpellier in France surpassed it about 1200, Salerno was the leading center of medical education in Europe, thanks largely to the presence of Greek and Arabic physicians. Among those who taught at Salerno were a number of women, including Trotula, author of the treatise *On Feminine Disorders*. Students at Salerno learned surgical techniques, though medieval operations were generally crude affairs using modified butchers' instruments; amputation was common. Although anesthetics were coming into use, many patients suffered through operations deadened only by alcohol or opium. Death from shock or infection was common. The Muslim Abul Kasim of Córdoba, Spain (c. 936–c. 1013), wrote the first illustrated guide to surgery, but no handbook of anatomy was available until 1316, when Mondino de' Luzzi, who taught at Bologna, prepared one. The advance of medicine was reflected in the growth of hospitals; England had 18 in 1123 but 428 by 1300. Doctors introduced quarantine in 1346. Because of the interest in optics, eyeglasses became fairly common in Italy in the thirteenth century, and surgeons even operated for cataracts. Much medieval practice was still grounded in superstition, such as the belief that sexual intercourse with a virgin would cure a man of various illnesses. Medicine remained primitive, not least because of its reliance on the ancient Greek theory of disease, according to which illnesses resulted from imbalances in the four basic "qualities" (hot, cold, wet, dry) and the four "humors" (blood, phlegm, and black and yellow bile). Folk doctors who used herbal remedies and commonsense practices often administered the best treatment.

The Medieval Vision

Between the eleventh and the fifteenth centuries European artists developed new styles that reflected not only their Christian faith but also the outlook first of the monastic and feudal orders and then of the expanding cities. The Vikings, Normans, and Magyars had destroyed many wooden churches; hence the eleventh and twelfth centuries had ample incentive to rebuild—in stone wherever possible. Perhaps even greater motivation to build stemmed from the expanding economy, the need to provide churches for pilgrims on their way to holy places, and the pious spirit engendered by the religious reforms. The cathedrals and abbey churches erected in the High Middle Ages are eloquent monuments to the faith, resolve, and urban pride of medieval Christians.

The Age of the Romanesque

The monastic revival and the militant ideals of the feudal order largely shaped the artistic style of the eleventh and twelfth centuries. The monastic reforms that commenced in the tenth century revitalized the church, giving it a new resolve to glorify God. The new style was later called Romanesque because of its similarities to classical Roman architecture. The abbey churches that epitomize this style reflect the monastic values of order, simplicity, and otherworldliness. The religious revival also led to a substantial increase in the number of people who undertook pilgrimages to the shrines of the saints, such as that of St. James at Compostela in northwestern Spain. The churches along the pilgrimage routes had to be larger than the traditional basilicas to accommodate throngs of pilgrims. In the aftermath of the Viking and Magyar invasions, the people also desired to make the churches stronger, with stone instead of wooden ceilings and with façades that were sometimes reminiscent of feudal castles. Some Romanesque churches, such as that of Notre-Dame-la-Grande in Poitiers, look almost like fortresses because of their towers and thick walls.

The nave and choir of the pilgrimage church of St. Sernin in Toulouse, France (c. 1080–1120), were built using a barrel, or tunnel, vault. The interior lighting is dim and indirect.

Romanesque churches are found throughout Europe, the greatest number being in France. Regional differences emerged as the form developed, but Romanesque (Roman-style) buildings shared basic characteristics, including a floor plan in the shape of a cross, the use of round arches and barrel (tunnel) vaults, and heavy buttresses to support the legs of the arches. The weight of the stone ceiling made it virtually impossible to cut windows into the sides of the barrel vault; hence the interiors of early Romanesque churches were dark. Later Romanesque architects revived the Roman principle of the groined vault, by which intersecting arches distribute the ceiling's weight to specific points along the wall. These points must be heavily buttressed, but windows can then be cut in the intervening spaces to illumine the church's interior.

To adorn the churches, Romanesque artists revived the technique of stone sculpture, which had largely been forgotten during the eighth and ninth centuries. The figures they sculpted were intended to teach as well as to adorn, a function especially significant in an age when the overwhelming majority of the population was illiterate. Rich in symbols easily remembered by the faithful, Romanesque sculpture was a visual reminder of the fundamental teachings of the church. One of the most common locations for Romanesque sculpture was the semicircular space, called a tympanum, above the door of a church, which was often used to show Christ at the Last Judgment. Carved capitals depicting everything from vegetation to monsters adorned the columns of churches and cloisters. To some of the godly, the artists had gone too far: "I say naught of the vast height of your churches," thundered the Cistercian monk Bernard of Clairvaux, "their immoderate length, their superfluous breadth, the costly polishings, the curious carvings and paintings which attract the worshipper's gaze and hinder his attention."[2]

The monastic spirit of the Romanesque was also manifest in the paintings of the period, the most important of which were either murals in abbey churches rendered in a Byzantine style or miniatures that "illuminated" (illustrated) manuscripts. The latter were the work of monks and nuns. Most of the identifiable manuscript illuminators in the Middle Ages were in fact nuns. Already in the sixth century the convent at Poitiers specialized in training nuns to copy and decorate manuscripts, and 200 years later two sisters, Harlinde and Relinde, founded a religious community at Maaseyck in Flanders that achieved fame for its

The Romanesque sculpture in the tympanum of St. Trophime in Arles, France, is symbolic rather than naturalistic. The winged figures around Christ represent the four evangelists, Matthew, Mark, Luke, and John.

illuminated manuscripts and gold- and jewel-bedecked tapestries. Some miniaturists depicted religious scenes, while others created intricate capital letters. Some of their work reveals a sense of humor, as in the case of the nun who depicted herself swinging on the tail of an elaborate *Q*. The miniatures served as models for murals and later for the stained glass windows that decorated Gothic churches.

The Gothic Achievement

The world of the Gothic* artist was not primarily that of the monastic and the pilgrim but rather that of the city and the scholastic theologian. Gothic cathedrals were triumphs of the urban spirit, a testimony to the civic pride that manifested itself in rivalries between the cities. The Gothic achievement was equally a testimony in stone to the synthesis of theology and philosophy that the scholastics were forging. Just as reason became the servant of faith to bridge the gap between heaven and earth, so the soaring spires and lofty vaults of the Gothic cathedral carried the vision of the worshiper logically and compellingly heavenward. The principles of scholastic theology and Gothic architecture share the conviction that reason and nature are not stumbling blocks but pathways to spiritual truth. In the Romanesque the material and the spiritual exist in an uneasy tension; in the Gothic they unite in praising God.

The principles of the Gothic style were initially worked out in the abbey church at St. Denis, near Paris, in the 1130s and 1140s. Under the direction of Abbot Suger, the goal was a church that "would shine with the wonderful and uninterrupted light of most luminous windows."[3] The key was to construct a skeletal framework strong enough to support the stone roof yet airy enough to permit the extensive use of stained glass. By using pointed instead of round arches, the architects could achieve greater height and enclose rectangular as well as square spaces. At Beauvais the groined vaulting with its supporting ribs soared to the height of 157 feet, only to collapse and have to be rebuilt. The Gothic architect also introduced the flying buttress, a support that carried the horizontal thrust of the arch to heavy piers outside the church. The purpose was twofold: placing the massive piers outside the church created a more spacious interior, and the flying buttress, like the pointed arch, guided the eye of the beholder heavenward.

The abundant stained glass windows, some of which may have been the work of women, give the interior of a Gothic cathedral an ethereal quality. One writer of the period likened the windows to the Bible: "Since their brilliance lets the splendor of the True Light pass into the church, they enlighten those inside."[4] Like sculpture, the windows had a pedagogical as well as an aesthetic function, and to the degree that they encouraged worship, they had a liturgical role as well. To create a window, the artist first sketched a design in chalk and then fit together cut pieces of glass. Details, such as facial features, were created by using metal oxides on the glass and firing them in a kiln. The artist then joined the pieces of glass with lead strips and strengthened the window by adding black iron bands, which also separated the colors to keep them from blurring in the viewer's eye. The windows took the place of the mosaics and murals that had decorated earlier churches. The windows were costly, but royalty, nobility, prelates, and guilds donated them as marks of their piety.

As in the Romanesque period, sculpture adorned the cathedrals, only more lavishly. The cathedral at Chartres, for instance, has more than 2,000 carved figures. In keeping with the attempt to unite the physical and the spiritual, Gothic statuary became more naturalistic in its representation of people and its rendering of plants and animals. Unlike their Romanesque predecessors, Gothic artists, some of whom were women, began to use human models for their statues so that their work captured elements of individual personality. Simultaneously, conven-

*The term *Gothic* was introduced in the fifteenth century to describe medieval architecture. Later critics liked the term because it was evocative of the spirit of the "barbaric" Goths who had sacked Rome. The accusation was unjust, but the term stuck.

tion required the continued use of traditional symbols, which restricted artistic freedom but assured that viewers could interpret the art's religious meaning. The range of subject matter was more extensive than that of the Romanesque era, so much so that Gothic cathedrals, with their myriad statues and surrounding stained glass, may be likened to visual encyclopedias. In its comprehensive treatment of the natural and spiritual worlds, the Gothic cathedral was akin to the ambitious *summae* of Thomas Aquinas.

Medieval Religious Music

As in architecture, music evolved in the Middle Ages from simple to increasingly complex forms. During the early medieval period the worship services of the Catholic church incorporated chants named in honor of Pope Gregory the Great. Single melody lines sung by male voices in unison and without instrumental accompaniment, Gregorian chants accorded primary emphasis to religious texts rather than melodic lines. Two monks—Odo of Cluny in the early tenth century and Guido of Arezzo 100 years later—made significant contributions to music that allowed for more elaborate forms. By arranging the tones of the scale from A to G, thus providing the first effective system of musical notation in the West, Odo enabled singers to read music instead of memorizing lines by rote. Guido improved on this system by recording the notes on a musical staff (five lines with intervening spaces), thus making it possible for musicians to reproduce increasingly complex music accurately over space and time.

Commencing in the ninth century, medieval musicians began to develop polyphony ("many voices"), at first by adding a second line five tones below the original chant, and then a third line four tones above the original chant (a full octave above the second line). Finally, they added a fourth line an octave below the first. These steps gave the chant a vertical dimension to enhance the original horizontal movement. Around the same time composers began embellishing the chants by inserting melodic phrases called tropes. At the beginning of the Gothic period, composers added a degree of complexity to their music by introducing contrapuntal lines: instead of moving parallel to the main line, the second line now moved in opposition to it; when one line ascended, the other typically descended, effectively creating two separate melodies. Taking this development one step further, composers stretched out each note in the main line to great lengths while having one or two other voices sing melodies at a traditional tempo. The complexity increased as composers assigned a different text to each line, sometimes, beginning in the thirteenth century, using vernacular texts in the second or third lines while the original line preserved the Latin text. The result was the motet, in which the original chant, played or sung as the lowest line, was treated melodically and given a repeated rhythmic pattern while other melody lines were sung above it. The interplay of musical sound effectively paralleled the interplay of soaring arches, majestic stone

A view of the apse of the Gothic cathedral at Amiens. Tiny chapels radiate around the exterior.

columns, vaulted ceilings, and beautiful stained glass in Gothic churches.

Vernacular Culture and the Age of Chivalry

Apart from the Anglo-Saxon tradition, the literature of the early medieval period was largely in Latin, though a rich oral tradition created and preserved stories and poems in the vernacular, the language of the people. The most important vernacular work from the early medieval period is *Beowulf,* a poem about a Swedish hero who saved the Danes from a monster and its mother. Written in England by a monk around the eighth century, *Beowulf* reflects the values of the period: loyalty, valor, and aristocratic worth. About the same time, Bede (c. 673–735), a Benedictine monk commonly called "the Venerable" because of his piety and learning, wrote the *Ecclesiastical History of the English Nation,* the primary source of our knowledge about English history from the time Christianity was introduced in 597 until 731. King Alfred the Great (871–899) and the scholars at his palace school translated Bede's classic from Latin into Anglo-Saxon. During Alfred's reign scholars compiled another major historical source, a vernacular collection of documents known as the *Anglo-Saxon Chronicle.*

The story of Roland's heroism in battling the Muslims as recounted in the Song of Roland was a favorite theme in medieval art. Roland is shown here about to be ambushed by the Muslims at the lower right.

During the High Middle Ages much of the material that had only been transmitted orally was written down, still in the vernacular; to this body of material were added new works, both secular and religious. The richness of this body of vernacular literature is reflected in the fact that it appeared in no fewer than eight major literary forms: heroic epics, minstrel songs, courtly romances, allegorical romances, mystery and miracle plays, pious writings, historical works, and popular stories. Latin was the language of the learned—of lawyers, ecclesiastics, and scholastics—but beginning in the eleventh century the vernacular tongues increasingly became the language of literary entertainment. Although literacy rates remained low, these works undoubtedly reached wide audiences as the literate read them aloud to others.

The Gothic statuary on the exterior of the Rheims Cathedral is more naturalistic than that of the Romanesque period (compare St. Trophime). At the left, the archangel Gabriel informs Mary that she will give birth to the Messiah; at the right, Mary visits Elizabeth, mother of John the Baptist.

The earliest heroic epics were the *chansons de geste*—"songs of heroic deeds"—composed in the northern French vernacular. In oral form they hark back to the ninth and tenth centuries, when they entertained pilgrims traveling to the religious shrines of southern France and northern Spain. The most popular is the *Song of Roland,* the legendary account of a Muslim attack on Charlemagne's rear guard as it retreated across the Pyre-

Courtly Love

One of the most intriguing documents in the courtly love tradition is the treatise on love, De amore, *by Andreas Capellanus, who was associated with the court of Eleanor of Aquitaine's daughter, Marie de Champagne. There is considerable debate as to whether this twelfth-century work was intended to be taken seriously or humorously.*

1. Marriage cannot be pleaded as an excuse for refusing to love.
2. A person who cannot keep a secret can never be a lover. . . .
3. If one of two lovers dies, love must be foresworn for two years by the survivor. . . .
4. It is not becoming to love those ladies who only love with a view to marriage. . . .
5. Too easy possession renders love contemptible. But possession which is attended with difficulties makes love valuable and of great price. . . .
6. A new love affair banishes the old one completely. . . .
7. When one of the lovers begins to entertain suspicion of the other, the jealousy and the love increase at once. . . .
8. Too great prodigality of favors is not advisable, for a lover who is wearied with a superabundance of pleasure is generally as a rule disinclined to love.

Source: J. F. Rowbotham, *The Troubadours and Courts of Love* (New York: Macmillan, 1895), pp. 245–247.

nees in 778. The poem exalts feudal virtues: personal loyalty, Christian faith, and individual honor. Because Roland failed to summon help in time to save his men, he won praise for his valor and loyalty but not for his wisdom. The conflict with Islam is also the setting for the famous Spanish *chanson* of the twelfth century, the *Poem of My Cid,* the fictionalized account of a chivalric lord who conquered Valencia. The majestic German epic *Nibelungenlied* (c. 1200) recounts the mythical quest for a hoard of Rhine gold in an atmosphere of love, treachery, and violence. Although the written version has a Christian veneer, at root it reflects pagan Germanic mythology. In spirit it is akin to the twelfth- and thirteenth-century Scandinavian *Eddas,* which recount the stories of pagan gods and heroes. The counterpart of these works in Kievan Russia was the twelfth-century *Song of Igor's Campaign,* another account of heroic exploit. Such works represent a simple historic interest in a largely mythical past dominated by valiant heroes and heroines.

French poets took the lead in composing minstrel songs, particularly in the south, where troubadours sang their lyrical lines in the Provençal dialect. These *chansons d'amour,* or "songs of love," were popular in the twelfth and thirteenth centuries throughout western Europe. Nearly 2,500 Provençal lyrics survive. Whereas the *chansons de geste* helped to establish the code of knightly conduct called chivalry, the *chansons d'amour* popularized the concept of courtly love. The key to this concept is the exaltation of women and love, sometimes in a platonic rather than a physical sense. The minstrels encouraged the adoration of the wife of someone of a higher social degree, expecting in return at least simple kindness and inner joy if not physical pleasure. Eleanor of Aquitaine, wife of the English King Henry II, presided over a cult of courtly love at Poitiers, as did her daughter, the Countess Marie, at Champagne. The Germans had their counterpart to the troubadours in the *Minnesingers* ("love singers"), whose lyrics were more spiritual than those of the French *chansons.* Women wrote romantic lyrics, though they did not exalt men as the male poets did women in the literature of courtly love.

The courtly love of the minstrels joined with the *chansons de geste* to create the courtly romance, the most famous of which are the late-twelfth-century works of

Chrétien de Troyes about King Arthur. In these stories, the adventurous knight sought his identity in the dangerous world beyond the royal court. Cistercian influence in the thirteenth century led to the addition of the theme of the Holy Grail, purportedly the chalice used by Christ in the Last Supper and later taken to Britain. Thus as the Arthurian legends spread throughout Europe, knights such as Sir Galahad and Perceval were recognizably Christian heroes. In the 1200s two French authors, William de Lorris and Jean de Meun, combined allegory and satire with the romance to create the popular *Romance of the Rose.* William's portion treats traditional troubadour themes of love in an allegorical mode, but Jean satirizes everything from women to clerical celibacy.

Although most religious literature was still written in Latin, vernacular works began to win a wider audience. Mystery plays—religious dramas about biblical subjects, especially Christ's life—were often in Latin and in fact originated as part of the Latin liturgy. With the addition of fictitious matter, the plays acquired a separate identity, opening the way for vernacular versions. Beginning in the fourteenth century, these plays were no longer the province of the clergy but became community productions typically performed, by women as well as men, during church festivals. A variation of the mystery play, the miracle play, took as its theme the life of a saint; one such was the twelfth-century English drama about St. Catherine. The miracle and mystery plays gave rise to morality plays, such as *Everyman,* which personified vices and virtues in the context of a struggle for the soul. Writers also composed a variety of pious literature in the vernacular during the High Middle Ages, including Francis of Assisi's *Canticle of the Sun,* a lyrical praise of God for creation.

The vernacular literature of this period included several historical works of note. Geoffrey of Monmouth's *British History* retells the legendary stories of King Arthur and other fictitious tales and thus hardly qualifies as history. In contrast, Geoffrey de Villehardouin provided a historical account of the capture of Constantinople by the crusaders in 1204, which he titled *The Conquest of Constantinople,* and Jean de Joinville wrote the *History of St. Louis,* the story of the French King Louis IX. Various German chroniclers also wrote in the vernacular. French writers recorded popular tales—*fabliaux*—that had long been current in oral form. Alternately satirical, coarse, and amusing, the intent was usually to entertain, though some stories had a didactic purpose as well. Some were animal fables, such as the *Romance of Reynard the Fox.*

The variety of vernacular literature provides a healthy corrective to the common notion that medieval people were overly concerned with religious issues. Instead they demonstrated a pronounced interest in such themes as chivalry, courtly love, and the mythical and mysterious past, and in bawdy stories and tales of violence and romance.

Medieval Jewry

No discussion of medieval life and culture can fail to acknowledge the significant contribution of the Jews. During the period of the Roman Empire they migrated throughout Europe as far afield as Spain, France, Dalmatia, and the Crimea. Small Jewish communities also established themselves to the east, from Arabia and Persia to India and China. Many of the earliest Jewish settlers in the West were farmers, an occupation in which they continued for centuries in southern Europe, but most of the Jews who settled farther north engaged in commerce as town life developed. Charlemagne welcomed Jewish immigrants by granting them charters that guaranteed protection and privileges. The Capetian kings of France continued this policy, making France a center of medieval Jewry. Immigrants from France and southern Europe founded the German Jewish communities beginning in the ninth century. Few Jews emigrated to Scandinavia, and England was the last major European country where they settled, mostly after the Norman Conquest in 1066. The extensive Jewish settlements in Europe and their contributions to Jewish culture ensured that in the future the Jews would be fundamentally European in outlook.

Interior of the synagogue at Worms, Germany, built in 1034.

As Europeans turned increasingly to commercial activities in the High Middle Ages, Jewish merchants were slowly squeezed out of commerce and into moneylending. Because the Christian church prohibited usury (lending money for profit), many people had to obtain their loans from Jewish businessmen. When the Lombards introduced systematic banking, many Jewish moneylenders were forced to become pawnbrokers.

The crusades had a devastating impact on European Jews, as various church leaders incited hatred against non-Christians in general. The Jews were a tempting target, particularly to Christians inflamed by charges that Jews had murdered Christ and were sacrificing Christian children at the Passover feast. The first persecution occurred at Metz in Lorraine and then spread from the Rhineland into France and England. Christian bigotry reached as far as Palestine, where the crusaders burned an entire synagogue full of Jews in 1097. Some Jews preferred to die with swords in their hands, but many committed suicide rather than die at the hands of Christians. In the English city of York in 1189, Jewish men killed their wives and children before turning their swords on themselves. The pattern of persecution was reinforced in the 1300s when Jews became scapegoats for the Black Death, for which they continued to be blamed well into the sixteenth century.

The Third and Fourth Lateran Councils furthered the climate of hostility against the Jews. Despite the fact that the councils' decrees were not thoroughly implemented, Gentiles were not supposed to be servants of Jews, nor were they allowed to live in the same districts, a regulation that encouraged the development of separate Jewish quarters. Jews had to wear identifying badges and attend Christian sermons designed to convert them. Christian officials censored or confiscated Jewish books and forced Jews to be present at public disputations intended to demonstrate the errors of their ways. English authorities seized synagogues on trumped-up charges that Jewish chanting disrupted Christian church services. The Holy Roman Empire

The Expulsion of the Jews from France

The animosity of medieval Christians toward Jews is apparent in this account of Philip II's expulsion of the Jews from France in 1182.

When the faithless Jews heard this edict some of them were born again of water and the Holy Spirit and converted to the Lord, remaining steadfast in the faith of our Lord Jesus Christ. To them the king, out of regard for the Christian religion, restored all their possessions in their entirety, and gave them perpetual liberty.

Others were blinded by their ancient error and persisted in their perfidy; and they sought to win with gifts and golden promises the great of the land . . . that through their influence and advice, and through the promise of infinite wealth, they might turn the king's mind from his firm intention. But the merciful and compassionate God . . . so fortified the illustrious king that he could not be moved by prayers nor promises of temporal things. . . .

The infidel Jews, perceiving that the great of the land, through whom they had been accustomed easily to bend the king's predecessors to their will, had suffered repulse, and astonished and stupefied by the strength of mind of Philip the king and his constancy in the Lord, . . . prepared to sell all their household goods. The time was now at hand when the king had ordered them to leave France altogether, and it could not be in any way prolonged. Then did the Jews sell all their movable possessions in great haste, while their landed property reverted to the crown. Thus the Jews, having sold their goods and taken the price for the expenses of their journey, departed.

Source: J. H. Robinson, ed., *Readings in European History,* vol. 1 (Boston: Ginn, 1904), p. 428.

asserted proprietary rights over its Jews, making them virtually the property of the crown, and other states followed suit. Many Jews fled to Poland and Lithuania, only to become the legal property of the nobility. In practice, proprietary rights had little effect on Jewish life or freedom of movement, but they provided the justification for special taxes and finally for the expulsion of the Jews from much of Europe. When Edward I banned the Jews from England in 1290, as many as 16,000 emigrated. Louis IX had decreed their exile from France in 1249, but the order was not implemented then. In 1306, however, Philip IV ordered their arrest, the confiscation of their property, and their ouster from France. Twice they were allowed back, only to be banned again in 1394. Because of political disunity in Germany, there was no general expulsion, but many local governments forced the Jews to flee. Spain and Sicily followed suit in 1492, Portugal in 1497, Naples in 1510 and again in 1541, and Milan in 1591. The expulsions forced the Jews eastward, particularly to Poland—where King Boleslav the Pious granted them a charter in 1264 to guarantee their liberties—and to the Ottoman Empire.

Between Two Cultures: The Jews in Spain

One of the principal centers of Jewish culture in the medieval era was Spain, where Jewish colonists and traders who followed in the wake of Arab conquests strengthened the pre-Islamic community. Jews enjoyed considerable freedom in Islamic Spain, mostly because of their key role in commerce and their intellectual attainments. One of the key patrons of Jewish learning was Hasdai ibn-Shaprut (c. 915–970), himself a Jew and the confidant of two caliphs. Trained in medicine and skilled in Latin as well as Arabic, Hasdai supported Jewish poets and Hebrew scholars, initiating a brilliant era of Jewish culture. The poetic revival culminated in the hymns to Zion by the physician Judah ha-Levi (1086–1141). Jewish scholars translated Greek classics into Arabic and from Arabic into Latin, paving the way for advancements in mathematics, medicine, astronomy, and cartography. The more enlightened Christian rulers, such as Emperor Frederick II and Alfonso the Wise, king of Castile, recognized the significance of these contributions and extended their patronage to Jewish scholars. Thus one of the principal avenues for the revival of classical learning in Europe came by way of the Arabs and the Jews.

The greatest medieval Jewish scholar was Moses ben Maimon (1135–1204), popularly known as Maimonides. A native of Córdoba, Spain, he spent most of his life in Cairo, where he served as court physician. As a philosopher he made contributions to Judaism comparable to those of Thomas Aquinas in Catholic theology. His major work, the *Mishneh Torah* ("Repetition of the Law"), was a *summa* of Judaism—a systematic presentation of rabbinic teachings that earned him the reputation of being a second Moses. Maimonides' approach to religion was highly rational, reflecting the views of Aristotle and Avicenna. His *Guide to the Perplexed* includes rational arguments for the existence of God, among them the thesis that there must be an Unmoved Mover. Although his views influenced Christian scholastics, conservative rabbis finally persuaded the Dominicans that Maimonides' works endangered the Christian faith, and they were banned in 1234.

Medieval Judaism also embraced a mystical tradition. In the twelfth and thirteenth centuries Jewish mystics known as *Hasidim* ("Pietists") were active in the Rhineland. Probably influenced by Christian monks, they combined a penitent's life with the conviction that God can be found through humility rather than visions. Much of the opposition to Maimonides came from mystics in Provence and Spain known as Cabalists ("Traditionalists"), who believed that every letter of the Law has a mystical meaning that can be revealed only to the initiated. Jewish and Christian mystics were one in their conviction that the deepest meaning of religion is profoundly spiritual and cannot be attained by rational processes. Christianity and Judaism were thus strikingly similar in their search for a rational synthesis and the ensuing reaction of those who favored a mystical approach to God.

Women in Medieval Society

Although medieval women were rarely subjected to the kind of persecution the Jews experienced,* their social position began to erode around the late eleventh century. In the early medieval period, wives of clergymen and warriors often enjoyed substantial social prominence and economic responsibility because they managed their households or estates while their husbands were away. Women often owned land, particularly in southern France and Spain, where there were no legal restrictions on a woman's right to administer family property. Within the feudal order, the development of the chivalric ideal reinforced the role of women as managers of domestic and estate affairs by stressing the male's role as a warrior and a vassal. This was truer in France and Ger-

*The main exception was the persecution of women in southern France during the Albigensian Crusade.

many, where chivalry had the greatest impact, than in Italy, where chivalric ideas were slow to win acceptance.

Throughout the medieval era women tended to enjoy greater power and prominence in periods of heavy military activity or vigorous expansion into new regions. The military campaigns of Charlemagne, the crusades to the Holy Land, and the reconquista took men from their homes for lengthy periods and exposed them to the hazards of war and disease. During such periods substantial amounts of property were in the care of wives and sisters as well as the church. Against the background of the crusades, western Europeans developed the cult of courtly love and troubadours exalted aristocratic ladies.

Simultaneously, however, religious and political developments began to undermine the position of clerical wives and women of the feudal order. In religion the decline was sparked by the Gregorian reforms of the late eleventh century, which had an adverse effect on women by insisting on clerical celibacy, thereby weakening the role of women in parish activities, and by seeking to curtail the ability of the laity to nominate candidates for church offices. These reforms were not fully effective until well beyond the medieval period, but the attempts to enforce them boded ill for women. So too did the growing importance of the bishops in the High Middle Ages, a development intimately related to the growth of urban life. Bishops had no female counterparts, whereas during the period when the church had been dominated by monasteries women had achieved positions of leadership as prioresses and abbesses. Monastic life continued but power gradually shifted into the hands of the bishops. The growth of cathedral schools and universities, neither of which were open to females, encouraged the trend toward more exclusively male leadership. Unless they had private tutors, girls could hope for education only in the convents, but from the twelfth century on, these establishments were interested primarily in religious rather than academic pursuits.

The church's repressive attitude toward women became especially apparent in the thirteenth century, by which time thousands of them had organized themselves into religious communities. The male orders reluctantly agreed to provide some form of discipline, but female orders remained subservient branches of their male counterparts. In general this was because women were thought to be undisciplined, prone to heretical ideas, and less than serious in their commitment to the religious life. The Franciscans, Dominicans, and Cistercians bitterly resisted the attachment of subordinate convents, though the papacy overruled them. Faced with a church hierarchy determined to relegate them to subordination

Women: A Western Medieval View

The tendency of Christian thinkers to regard women as inferior is reflected in the influential Decretum *of the jurist Gratian, written about 1140.*

Women should be subject to their men. The natural order for mankind is that women should serve men and children their parents, for it is just that the lesser serve the greater. The image of God is in man and it is one. Women were drawn from man, who has God's jurisdiction as if he were God's vicar, because he has the image of the one God. Therefore woman is not made in God's image.

Woman's authority is nil; let her in all things be subject to the rule of man. . . . And neither can she teach, nor be a witness, nor give a guarantee, nor sit in judgment.

Adam was beguiled by Eve, not she by him. It is right that he whom woman led into wrongdoing should have her under his direction, so that he may not fail a second time through female levity.

Source: Gratian, *Corpus iuris Canonici,* in *Not in God's Image,* ed. J. O'Faolain and L. Martines (New York: Harper Torchbooks, 1973), p. 130.

in all things spiritual, some women joined heretical groups such as the Waldensians, in which they could preach and administer the sacraments.

The influence of Christianity on medieval women was in other respects positive, as in the attention given to the Virgin Mary, whose influence extended throughout the High and late Middle Ages. The devout exalted Mary as the Universal Mother whose love for her son was a manifestation of her love for humanity and on whose behalf she acted as an intermediary with God. The faithful credited her with performing miracles and commemorated her life with special festivals. Revered as the queen of heaven, Mary symbolized the dignity to which women could aspire. Pilgrims flocked to her shrines, many churches were dedicated to her, and numerous other churches had lady chapels in her honor. Expressions of love to the Virgin increasingly paralleled those to aristocratic women in the literature of courtly love; the practical effect of both movements was a tendency to idealize women.

In the secular realm the development of stronger governments blocked women from many areas of political involvement. As long as state governments were ineffectual and real power resided in the great aristocratic families, women had an opportunity to assert themselves in political affairs. But as state governments revived, they required the services of lawyers and clerks to staff their treasuries and courts, and women had no access to the training that prepared people for such positions.

Changing inheritance laws also adversely affected women. A woman in the feudal order could generally inherit a fief, subject to her ability to meet the feudal obligations. In practice this meant the lord's right to arrange her marriage to a suitable vassal. Because a fief typically involved military responsibilities, her husband usually assumed control of the estate. But aristocratic families were increasingly determined to preserve their power by excluding females and younger sons from any substantive inheritance in order to keep their estates intact. They accomplished this by the principles of primogeniture and the indivisibility of patrimony, according to which an estate had to pass to the eldest son. Daughters received dowries and dowers, the latter being the assurance of an income during widowhood, but they were excluded from inheriting a portion of the family estate. If she had no brothers, the eldest daughter could usually inherit the estate. In the thirteenth century the French awarded two-thirds of an estate to the eldest son and allowed the other children to divide the remaining third. In varying degrees, most women of the propertied order were victims of legal discrimination.

For women of humbler status, economic needs often mandated a relative equality between men and women, particularly those in rural areas who worked beside their husbands in the fields or who devoted some of their time in the home to brewing ale or making cloth to sell. In the countryside women regularly hired themselves out to bailiffs on the greater estates, where they performed virtually every form of labor except heavy plowing. Much of the sheepshearing was done by women, as were the dairy and poultry chores. In the towns women worked in virtually all crafts—as butchers and bakers, haberdashers and shoemakers, goldsmiths and embroiderers. Masters' wives were active in many guilds, often training female apprentices. Widows regularly carried on their husbands' crafts, and those who had been married to merchants sometimes took over their business dealings.

In medieval society the range of occupations in which women engaged was extensive. Some women worked in the coal and iron mines, although their pay was less than that of the men. Many women toiled in domestic service; others managed their own shops. Urban life clearly expanded career opportunities for women, whether married or single. Whereas a landed aristocrat might leave directions in his will to place his daughter in a convent or find her a suitable spouse, an artisan was more likely to leave funds to train his daughter in a trade, usually because he could afford neither a dowry nor the funds to place her in a convent. Many women continued to pursue their crafts after marriage, even when their husbands engaged in a different occupation. The female labor force was crucial to the medieval economy. The scholastic Peter Lombard may have reflected the sentiments of the commoners when he observed that God created Eve from Adam's rib rather than his head or foot because they were intended to be companions.

SUMMARY

The High Middle Ages was a period of intellectual and cultural achievement. The growth of cathedral schools and the rise of universities invigorated European life and made possible the training of better-educated clergy and government officials. Scholastics made a daring attempt to synthesize all knowledge, a development that focused attention on natural science. The growth of medical schools set the stage for improved health care. Virtually all these developments occurred in the context of an urban revival sparked by an expanding economy. The cities provided the setting for brilliant artistic achievements, particularly the age of the Gothic, which owed much to the Romanesque era. The Gothic cathedrals, resplendent with their towering spires, soaring vaults, flying buttresses, and stained glass, were the perfect visual symbol of the age of faith.

But for two groups—women and Jews—the High Middle Ages brought a relative deterioration in their position. Excluded from the cathedral schools and the universities, women increasingly found themselves shunted aside in politics as well. Law and theology were forbidden areas, and women were banned from the parsonages they had once served as priests' wives. The exalted status women received in the courtly love tradition was scant compensation. The Jews, whose intellectual accomplishments influenced and were the equal of scholastic thought, found themselves in a nightmarish world of expulsion, exile, and massacre.

NOTES

1. S. Flanagan, *Hildegard of Bingen, 1098–1179: A Visionary Life* (New York: Routledge, 1989), p. 4.
2. E. G. Holt, ed., *Literary Sources of Art History* (Princeton, N.J.: Princeton University Press, 1947), p. 17.
3. E. Panofsky, *Abbot Suger on the Abbey Church of St. Denis and Its Art Treasures* (Princeton, N.J.: Princeton University Press, 1951), p. 101.
4. H. Gardner, *Art Through the Ages,* 7th ed., ed. H. de la Croix and R. G. Tansey (New York: Harcourt Brace Jovanovich, 1980), p. 337.

SUGGESTIONS FOR FURTHER READING

Amt, E., ed. *Women's Lives in Medieval Europe: A Sourcebook.* New York: Routledge, 1992.

Artz, F. B. *The Mind of the Middle Ages,* A.D. *200–1500,* 3rd ed. Chicago: University of Chicago Press, 1980.

Berman, H. *Law and Revolution: The Formation of the Western Legal Tradition.* Cambridge, Mass.: Harvard University Press, 1983.

Black, A. *Political Thought in Europe, 1250–1450.* Cambridge: Cambridge University Press, 1992.

Bogin, M. *The Women Troubadours.* New York: Paddington, 1976.

Bony, J. *French Gothic Architecture of the Twelfth and Thirteenth Centuries.* Berkeley: University of California Press, 1983.

Bumke, J. *Courtly Culture: Literature and Society in the High Middle Ages.* Berkeley: University of California Press, 1991.

Burns, J. H., ed. *The Cambridge History of Medieval Political Thought, c. 350–c. 1450.* Cambridge: Cambridge University Press, 1988.

Bynum, C. W. *Holy Feast and Holy Fast: The Religious Significance of Food to Medieval Women.* Berkeley: University of California Press, 1987.

Cobban, A. B. *The Medieval Universities: Their Development and Organization.* London: Methuen, 1975.

Cohen, M. R. *Under Crescent and Cross: The Jews in the Middle Ages.* Princeton, N.J.: Princeton University Press, 1994.

Davis, B. *The Thought of Thomas Aquinas.* New York: Oxford University Press, 1992.

Dodwell, C. R. *The Pictorial Arts of the West, 800–1200.* New Haven, Conn.: Yale University Press, 1992.

Duby, G. *Love and Marriage in the Middle Ages,* trans. J. Dunnett. Chicago: University of Chicago Press, 1994.

Ennen, E. *The Medieval Woman.* Oxford: Blackwell, 1990.

Flanagan, S. *Hildegard of Bingen, 1098–1179: A Visionary Life.* New York: Routledge, 1989.

Grodecki, L., and Brisac, C. *Gothic Stained Glass, 1200–1300.* Ithaca, N.Y.: Cornell University Press, 1985.

Gurevich, A. *Medieval Popular Culture: Problems of Belief and Perception,* trans. J. M. Bak and P. A. Hollingsworth. Cambridge: Cambridge University Press, 1988.

Keen, M. *Chivalry.* New Haven, Conn.: Yale University Press, 1984.

Knowles, D. *The Evolution of Medieval Thought,* 2nd ed. New York: Longman, 1988.

Lawrence, C. H. *Medieval Monasticism,* 2nd ed. New York: Longman, 1989.

Lynch, J. H. *The Medieval Church.* New York: Longman, 1992.

Moore, R. I. *The Formation of a Persecuting Society: Power and Deviance in Western Europe, 950–1250.* New York: Blackwell, 1987.

Murray, D. C. *A History of Heresy.* New York: Oxford University Press, 1989.

Peters, E. *Inquisition.* Berkeley: University of California Press, 1989.

Petroff, E. A. *Body and Soul: Essays on Medieval Women and Mysticism.* New York: Oxford University Press, 1994.

Radding, C. M., and Clark, W. W. *Medieval Architecture, Medieval Learning.* New Haven, Conn.: Yale University Press, 1992.

Shatzmiller, J. *Jews, Medicine, and Medieval Society.* Berkeley: University of California Press, 1994.

Sirat, C. *A History of Jewish Philosophy in the Middle Ages.* Cambridge: Cambridge University Press, 1990.

Stow, K. *Alienated Minority: The Jews of Medieval Latin Europe.* Cambridge, Mass.: Harvard University Press, 1992.

GLOBAL ESSAY

Death and the Human Experience (I)

To every thing there is a season . . . :
A time to be born, and a time to die.

ECCLES. 3:1, 2

Throughout history death has been defied or embraced, an object sometimes of fear, sometimes of hope. The earliest human ritual of which we have a record, developed by Peking man some 500,000 years ago, was associated with death, perhaps in the hope of preserving the memory of the deceased and soliciting their assistance for the living. More than 50,000 years ago Neanderthal people prepared elaborate funeral rites to deal with the needs of those who had died and presumably lived in some afterlife. Bodies were interred in graves filled with shells and ornaments made of ivory and bone, while the skin or bones of the deceased were colored with red ocher, apparently to commemorate life. They buried corpses in a fetal position, possibly to facilitate rebirth or to restrict the movements of the dead and prevent them from returning to haunt the living. Thus the first human societies sought to explain death and in the process developed primitive conceptions of an afterlife.

The earliest civilizations coped with death in strikingly different ways. The Mesopotamian *Epic of Gilgamesh* (c. 2000 B.C.) suggests that the people of that region conceived of a hinterworld below the surface of the earth, a House of Darkness in which the dead were made of clay, ate dust, and endured a wretched existence. This world was neither heaven nor hell but a place bereft of light where ghostly beings, dressed like birds, fluttered their wings. To prevent the spirit of the dead from haunting the living, the Sumerians buried the corpse and provided food and drink in the grave. They rendered offerings and prayers to their deities, but these were intended to benefit the living rather than to obtain access to a decent afterlife. To escape his destiny in the shadowy underworld, Gilgamesh searched—without success—for immortal life. The sense of resignation before death was reflected in the Mesopotamians' willingness to embrace a life of physical pleasure; as Gilgamesh is advised in the poem, it is best to live the merry life, dancing and playing night and day, for old age and death are inevitable.

The Egyptians too believed in life after death, as reflected in the Pyramid Texts of the third millennium B.C., the Coffin Texts of around 2000 B.C., and later papyrus inscriptions, documents collectively known as the *Book of the Dead*. Here we find the earliest expression of belief in a divine judgment after death. The Pyramid Texts relate the story of Osiris and his resurrection, but by the time of the Coffin Texts belief in the notion of a general judgment after death was widespread. Convinced that specific fates awaited people, the Egyptians came to fear death because of the uncertainty of their position in the afterlife. The specter of divine judgment spurred some to moral living and encouraged the development of elaborate funeral rituals designed to influence the final verdict. These included lengthy prayers repudiating sin as well as artwork stressing the deceased's goodness. One of the most common symbols of Egyptian funerary art was the scale of judgment, depicting the soul as pure enough to balance the feather of truth. Christian art later employed a similar symbol.

The earliest Greeks viewed death as the separation of the soul (or "shade") and the *thymos*—the seat of emo-

A Neanderthal skeleton discovered in France in 1909 reveals that corpses were interred in the fetal position.

tions—from the body. At death the *thymos* disappeared, leaving the soul to enter Hades, the Land of the Dead, once the corpse had been buried or had decomposed. Existence in Hades was thought to entail anything from a senseless state to associations akin to those in life. The earliest Greeks accepted death as an inescapable evil. One could hate but not fear death, which was part of the community's life cycle. There was no reason to dread either contact with the deceased or one's own death.

The Greek attitude began to shift in the seventh and sixth centuries B.C. The tightly knit communities broke up, a sense of individuality developed, philosophers speculated about salvation and a last judgment based on morality, and economic expansion and political upheaval increased feelings of insecurity and disorder. Consequently, the specter of death caused anxiety and stimulated a concern to perpetuate one's memory, often by inscriptions or by gravestones or other monuments. At first the depictions of the deceased on statues and gravestones followed conventional types, but gradually these evolved into portraits of the dead, reflecting the heightened interest in the individual that characterized later Greek art.

The Greeks initially believed that only a few aristocratic heroes escaped Hades, but over time they broadened the idea to include others, until finally a happy afterlife was possible for all who lived morally or were initiated into the mystery cults associated with such gods as Dionysus. Increasingly, they perceived death as less a part of the community's cycle of existence than a threat to the individual.

Grappling with the meaning of death produced equally varied responses among Asians. In ancient India the Vedas and the epics offered two conflicting views of death. On the one hand, death was seen as inescapable, its rule over everyone invincible. On the other, death's hold was only conditional, for each person could in theory choose from among a variety of means to attain *moksha*—release from the cycle of rebirth. All but a few sages were thought to be bound to the endless wheel of such rebirth. The nature of each reincarnation was determined by the individual's behavior in the present life and could be favorably influenced by such things as an ascetic life, the acquisition of wisdom, sacrifices, and the pursuit of morality. At the very least, adherence to such means enabled the Hindu to avoid "death in life"—living in perpetual fear of death. The Hindu sages occasionally linked death with evil—a theme common in later Christianity—but in general, death was accorded a natural and indispensable role in the cosmic order, for without it there would be no room for new life. Death should therefore

This depiction on a fifth-century B.C. tombstone of a woman holding her grandchild underscores the extent to which the Greeks, unlike the Egyptians, concentrated primarily on the beauty of life.

be celebrated, the Hindus felt, not mourned, "for death is a certainty for him who has been born, and birth is a certainty for him who has died. Therefore, for what is unavoidable thou shouldst not grieve."[1]

The ability to embrace death, or at least quietly to resign oneself to it, was complicated by the Hindu belief in *samsara,* the transmigration of souls through reincarnation, which is first explicitly stated in the *Upanishads* (c. 800–c. 500 B.C.). According to this concept, death is followed by rebirth in another worldly existence, although whether this is to be viewed in positive or negative terms was largely a personal matter. Certainly for many Hindus, *samsara* was tantamount to endless "redeath." Most Hindus sought to improve their status in the next round of existence by embracing morality and social responsibility, whereas some sought escape from physical existence through asceticism. For them, death could be the culmination of the journey along the Way of the Gods to the world of Brahma, the absolute. This quest for release and

The Hindu god Shiva and his wife, Parvati, aided by their sons, string together the skulls of the dead. One of Shiva's responsibilities was to preside over cremation grounds.

the joyful union with the infinite in *nirvana* subsequently became a dominant theme in Buddhism.

Perhaps none have been more willing to embrace death than the Taoists in China, for whom the death of an individual was insignificant in the face of the workings of the universal cosmos. Seeing themselves as a mere part of the unity of all things, they could accept death tranquilly as a manifestation of the ongoing operation of nature. "If one once recognizes his identity with this unity, then the parts of his body mean no more to him than so much dirt, and death and life, end and beginning, disturb his tranquility no more than the succession of day and night."[2]

Most Chinese explained death in the context of an extended family group that embraced the deceased, the living, and the generations yet unborn. Because the dead were seen by some to have the same needs as the living, they must be provided for, and their activities in the afterlife could in turn aid the living. Funeral ceremonies were supposed to ease the passage of the spirits into the next world, yet they would symbolically dwell in graveyards, in ancestral shrines in the homes, and in temples dedicated to specific clans. The living had to make offerings to the memory of the dead, undertake pilgrimages to their places of burial, and worship or commemorate them as a family. Ancestor worship, as it is somewhat misleadingly called, was by no means unique to China but was practiced by peoples as diverse as Persians, Indians, Russians, Scandinavians, and the Bantu of southern Africa. Ancestor worship prevented death from cutting the ties between the deceased and their families; hence the dead could be dealt with in traditional human ways, such as paying respect or making offerings. Unless the dead were thought to be angry or vindictive, the continuation of the familial relationship eased both the physical separation imposed by death and apprehensions about what lay beyond the grave.

The ideas discussed to this point treat death in one of three ways: as an inevitable part of the natural process, following which souls exist in a shadowy and normally unpleasant underworld; as part of an endless cycle of rebirth; or as part of an ongoing familial relationship between past, present, and future generations. A fourth way of viewing death, which originated in Judaism and was later adopted by Christianity and Islam, associated it

This fourteenth-century A.D. *Japanese Buddhist scroll shows the Buddha, lying on a bier, ready to enter nirvana as he is mourned by gods, humans, and animals.*

with resurrection and the notion of salvation. Like the Sumerians, the early Hebrews thought of the dead as existing in a shadowy underworld, called *sheol,* commonly linked with the tomb. Originally this was the common fate of all, good or bad, Jew or Gentile, apart from the patriarch Enoch, who "walked with God," and the prophet Elijah, who was said to have been carried to heaven in a chariot of fire. But in the late eighth century B.C., the prophet Isaiah proclaimed the resurrection of all the righteous, and nearly six centuries later the Book of Daniel asserted that even the wicked would be resurrected to face judgment. For the Jews, death became a temporary state, less important than the judgment that followed the resurrection. Thus the Hebrews, like the ancient Egyptians but unlike the Mesopotamians, stressed the importance of moral living as the necessary preparation for death and the afterlife.

Early Christianity built on this Judaic foundation, making death and resurrection the prelude to an eternal heaven of blissful existence for the saved and endless torture in hell for the damned. Death was a foe to be conquered, but the victory came with the physical resurrection of Christ, belief in which became a cardinal tenet of Christianity. Because of that triumph, wrote the apostle Paul, "the dead shall be raised incorruptible. . . . O death, where is thy sting? O grave, where is thy victory?"[3] For those who died alienated from God, death and judgment were the fearful prelude to eternity in a lake burning with fire and brimstone.

Apart from the idea of Christ's resurrection, Islam adopted the essential features of the Christian belief in death, judgment, and reward or punishment. Muslims viewed death as a divinely determined act, executed by an Angel of Death or other messengers of Allah. Death was akin to sleep, though for unbelievers this involved agony. At the appointed time the dead would be awakened, the godly to receive the pleasures of paradise and the unbelievers to face a torment so unbearable that they would plead to be destroyed. Thus Islam, like Judaism and Christianity, regarded death as a transitory state for which the proper preparation was righteous living.

Attitudes toward death affected the disposal of corpses. Cremation was common in India, Burma, and Japan, though not in China, where the people preferred to be buried in their native soil. The Etruscans, Greeks, and Romans practiced cremation (though not exclusively), but in the West it died out as the Christian belief in the physical resurrection of the body took hold. Not until the late nineteenth century did the practice revive in Europe and America.

Christianity also introduced changes with respect to burial. The Romans, like the other peoples of antiquity, kept the dead apart to prevent them from contaminating the living. The people of Rome and Pompeii buried the deceased outside the gates or beside the roads leading into the cities, but close enough to maintain the tombs and make the requisite offerings. Roman law, the early Germanic Theodosian Code, and the teachings of the early Christian theologian John Chrysostom prohibited burial within towns.

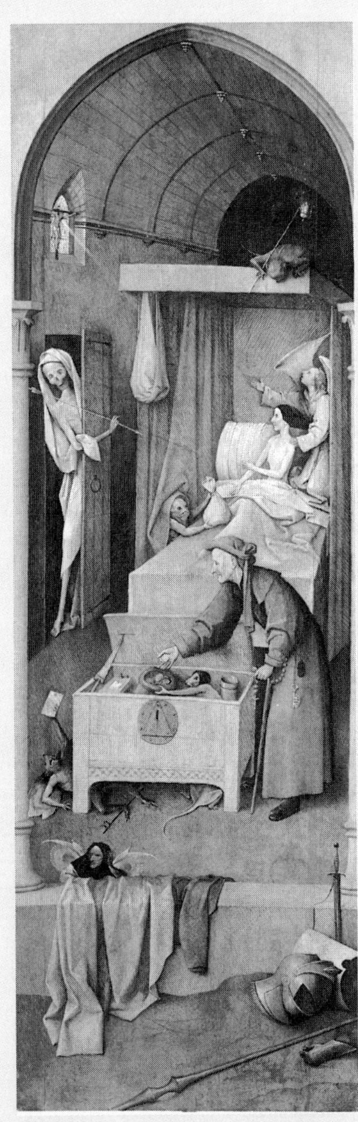

In Death and the Miser, *Hieronymus Bosch (c. 1450–1516) depicts the futile efforts of an angel to persuade a dying knight to forsake his riches for Christ. The painting reflects the medieval preoccupation with death and judgment.*

This prohibition began to change as Christians faced martyrdom in North Africa. Buried in the traditional necropolises outside town walls, their tombs soon became the sites of basilicas where devout pilgrims worshiped. Other Christians wanted to be buried nearby, thus leading to the association of churches and burial plots. By the mid-sixth century it was possible to inter a corpse within a church, thus reversing the ancient attempt to separate the living from the dead. In medieval Europe cemeteries became not only places of burial but also, because the adjacent churches themselves were social centers, sites for dancing, gambling, concerts, and business transactions. Some people even built homes in cemeteries. The proximity of the living and the dead in medieval Europe was also manifest in charnel houses, normally galleries that bordered churchyards and housed skulls and bones stacked neatly or arranged artistically for the living to contemplate.

Such customs point to a society in which life and death were viewed harmoniously—a society willing to accept the inevitability of death rather than depict it as a frightening event. The calmness of the deathbed ritual reflected faith in the church's ability to care for the souls of the deceased and in the ultimate triumph of resurrection over death. A leading historian has called this view "tamed death," an attitude prevalent among the common people of the West into the nineteenth century.

Beginning in the eleventh and twelfth centuries a new attitude began to take hold among the intellectual and social elite. In part this stemmed from a desire to have funerals reflect material wealth and status. More important, the new outlook in Europe manifested growing attention toward individuals, as reflected in the revival of funeral inscriptions, which had fallen into disuse around the fifth century; the popularity of requiem masses for individuals; and the reappearance of effigies and death masks. Individual responsibility was also emphasized, as stress was placed on the Last Judgment, with the deeds of each person weighed on the great scales. Accompanying this outlook was a change in funerary art, as decomposing cadavers—worm-ridden corpses—began to appear, mostly in the fifteenth century. Against the background of the Black Death, there was thus a new horror of dying and a longing for earthly life that had been rare in the medieval West. This preoccupation with the individual's fate has been called the "death of the self," an attitude that persisted in elite circles until the eighteenth century.

NOTES

1. *Bhagavadgita* 2:27, in *Religious Encounters with Death: Insights from the History and Anthropology of Religions,* ed. F. E. Reynolds and E. H. Waugh (University Park: Pennsylvania State University Press, 1977), p. 92.
2. Chuang-tze, 2:48, in H. G. Creel, *What Is Taoism? and Other Studies in Chinese Cultural History* (Chicago: University of Chicago Press, 1970), p. 42.
3. 1 Cor. 15:52, 55.

SUGGESTIONS FOR FURTHER READING

Ariès, P. *The Hour of Our Death,* trans. H. Weaver. New York: Knopf, 1981.

———. *Images of Man and Death,* trans. J. Lloyd. Cambridge, Mass.: Harvard University Press, 1985.

Brandon, S. G. F. *The Judgment of the Dead: A Historical and Comparative Study of the Idea of a Post-Mortem Judgment in the Major Religions.* New York: Scribner, 1967.

Creel, H. G. *What Is Taoism? and Other Studies in Chinese Cultural History.* Chicago: University of Chicago Press, 1970.

O'Shaughnessy, T. *Muhammad's Thoughts on Death.* Leiden: Brill, 1969.

Paxton, F. S. *Christianizing Death: The Creation of a Ritual Process in Early Medieval Europe.* Ithaca, N.Y.: Cornell University Press, 1990.

Reynolds, F. E., and Waugh, E. H. *Religious Encounters with Death: Insights from the History and Anthropology of Religions.* University Park: Pennsylvania State University Press, 1977.

Strocchia, S. T. *Death and Ritual in Renaissance Florence.* Baltimore: Johns Hopkins University Press, 1992.

Vermeule, E. *Aspects of Death in Early Greek Art and Poetry.* Berkeley: University of California Press, 1979.

Whaley, J., ed. *Mirrors of Mortality: Studies in the Social History of Death.* London: Europa, 1981.

CHAPTER 15

Crisis and Recovery in Europe

Famine, pestilence, war, and death—the four horsemen of the Apocalypse—ravaged Europe in the fourteenth century. The devastation inflicted by the bubonic and pneumonic plague, recurring famine, and the Hundred Years' War contributed to serious economic decline and a change in people's outlook. The prestige of the papacy suffered too when its headquarters shifted to Avignon, which proved to be the prelude to the most scandalous schism in the history of the western church. About 1450 Europe began to revive as population growth resumed, commerce and manufacturing expanded, and the states of western Europe and Russia attained greater unity and built strong central governments. In Italy, Germany, Hungary, and Poland, however, territorial princes and cities prevented the growth of centralized states. Europe in the fourteenth and fifteenth centuries moved from an age of adversity to one of recovery and in doing so laid the foundations for the early modern era.

Famine and the Black Death

From the late tenth through the thirteenth centuries the population of Europe grew as farmers expanded the amount of land under cultivation and increased the supply of food. But neither the population growth nor the food supply increased uniformly, and marginal settlements, where the possibility of extreme hunger was always high, arose throughout Europe. Even in the more prosperous agricultural regions, poor distribution facilities often resulted in pockets of famine. By 1300 the population had expanded so rapidly that most Europeans faced grave peril should unfavorable changes in the weather patterns disrupt the fragile agricultural economy.

The slaughter of rebellious French peasants on the bridge at Meaux during the Jacquerie in 1358.

The warming trend that characterized the mid-eighth to the mid-twelfth centuries was reversed as Europe entered what climatologists call the Little Ice Age, which lasted approximately two centuries. In the late thirteenth century heavy rains and unexpected freezes began to wreak havoc with the food supply. The threat of famine, which became more pronounced in the 1290s, culminated between 1315 and 1317 in the greatest crop failures of the Middle Ages. Soaring grain prices placed food beyond the reach of many, especially in urban areas, where sometimes as many as one in ten died from starvation or malnutrition. Marginal lands had to be abandoned as the poor sought relief in towns or in more productive regions, thereby increasing the strain on the food supply. As famines recurred throughout the fourteenth century, the most serious consequence was the debilitating effect of chronic and severe malnutrition on much of the population. Physically weakened, most Europeans were highly vulnerable to disease, especially tuberculosis.

The bubonic plague is caused by bacteria that live in an animal's blood or a flea's stomach and is thus easily transmitted, particularly by fleas on rats. The first symptom in a human is a small, blackish pustule at the point of the flea bite, followed by the swelling of the lymph nodes in the neck, armpit, or groin. Then come dark spots on the skin caused by internal bleeding. In the final stage the victim, convulsed by severe coughing spells, spits blood, exudes a foul body odor, and experiences severe neurological and psychological disorders. Bubonic plague was not always fatal, especially if the pus was thoroughly drained from the boil; up to half its victims survived. A more virulent form of the plague—the pneumonic variety—was transmitted by coughing and was nearly always fatal. Both forms devastated Europe.

Plague had ravaged the Byzantine Empire in the 540s and eventually extended from central and southern Asia to Arabia, North Africa, and the Iberian peninsula and north as far as Denmark and Ireland. Some 200,000 people may have died in Constantinople alone between the fall of 541 and the spring of 542. When this outbreak finally ended in 544, more than 20 percent of the people of southern Europe had died. Further outbreaks followed for another 200 years, after which Europe was free of most epidemic diseases until the mid-fourteenth century. But the bacterial strains responsible for the plague survived in the Gobi Desert of Mongolia. From there nomadic tribesmen, perhaps forced to move their flocks to new regions when hot winds began drying up the pastures of central Asia, transmitted the plague both east and west.

The plague reached epidemic proportions in the Gobi Desert in the late 1320s and from there may have spread first to China. The Chinese had already been weakened by famine brought on by drought, earthquakes, and then flooding in the early 1330s. The Black Death followed, reducing the population nearly 30 percent (from 125 million to 90 million) before the end of the century. By 1339 the plague had begun its westward march, carried by migrating central Asian rodents and by traders along the caravan routes and shipping lanes.

The impact on Asia and the Middle East was devastating. According to one chronicler, "India was depopulated; Tartary, Mesopotamia, Syria, [and] Armenia were covered with dead bodies; the Kurds fled in vain to the mountains."[1] The plague struck Constantinople and Alexandria in 1347; both cities suffered heavy losses, the latter witnessing perhaps 1,000 deaths a day in early 1348. It was worse in Cairo, one of the largest cities in the world with its population of 500,000; there some 7,000 probably died each day at the peak of the plague. By 1349 it had spread throughout the Muslim world, killing a third of the people and possibly as many as half of those who lived in towns.

The Black Death arrived in western Europe when a Genoese ship carrying infected rats from the Crimea docked at Messina, Sicily, in October 1347. Within months the plague struck the ports of Venice and Genoa, then spread throughout the rest of Italy, devastating Florence. By the end of 1348 most of France and the southern tip of England had been hit, and a year later the infected areas stretched from Ireland and Norway to Würzburg and Vienna. The plague moved relentlessly through northern Germany and Scandinavia, finally reaching western Russia in 1351 and 1352. Severe outbreaks again struck Europe in 1362 and 1375. Until the end of the fifteenth century no decade passed without at least one outbreak, and the plague continued to pose a serious threat to Europeans for two centuries after that. Surviving records are inadequate to determine accurate mortality figures, but the Black Death of the late 1340s probably claimed 25 million lives, perhaps a third of Europe's population. No war in history has destroyed so large a percentage of the people.

Europeans had no knowledge of the cause of the plague, though many attributed it to something mysterious in the atmosphere; many Christians believed it was divine punishment for their sins. Some people fled from the towns to the countryside, where the pestilence was less frequent. Officials of port cities tried in vain to turn away ships carrying signs of the infection, and some towns barred visitors in the hope of keeping the plague at bay. Reaction among the people varied considerably. Convinced of imminent death, some pursued sensual pleasures, while others turned to ascetic extremes, such

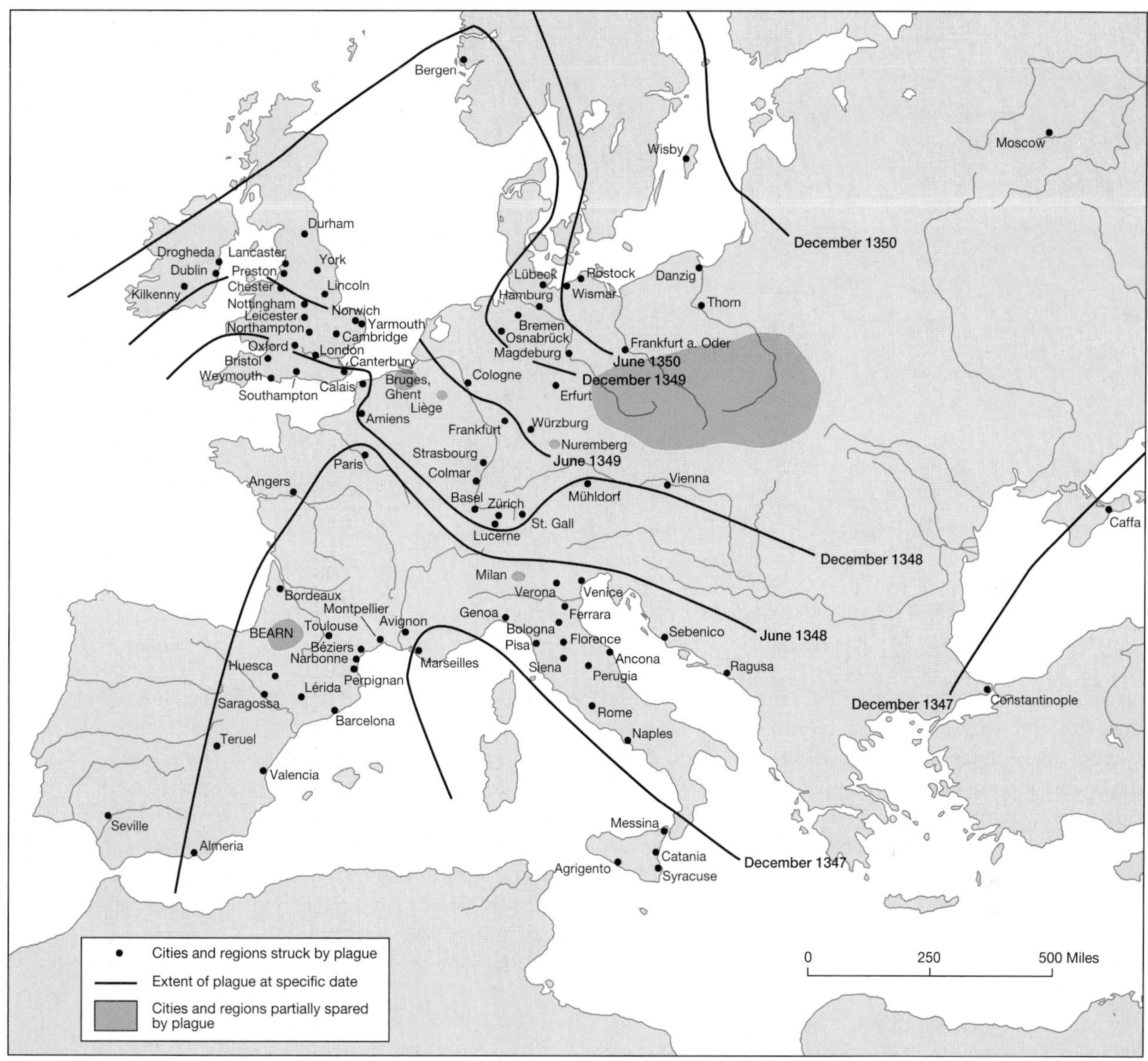

MAP 15.1 SPREAD OF THE PLAGUE IN EUROPE

as the itinerant flagellants, who whipped themselves, wore penitential dress, and bore crucifixes. Others turned to black magic and witchcraft, while some shunned anything Asian or blamed the Jews, many of whom they massacred. At Basel the bodies of slain Jews were floated down the Rhine in wine casks; 2,000 perished in Strasbourg, 600 in Brussels. People who tried to cure the sick relied on bleeding, cauterizing the boils, applying assorted substances to draw off the poison, and administering soothing potions. Many physicians fled, so the clergy often ministered to the sick and thus suffered extensively themselves. Entire Dominican friaries in Tuscany and Languedoc were decimated, and perhaps a third of the German clergy died.

The social and economic effects of the plague were profound. In several respects the Muslim response to the Black Death differed from that of Christians. Whereas the latter were preoccupied with guilt and fear, Muslims tended to regard the plague, like the *jihad,* or holy war, as an opportunity to achieve martyrdom and thus as a vehicle of divine mercy. "Their wounds had been similar" to those of holy warriors, said one Islamic tradition, "so they joined the martyrs."[2] Unlike the Christians, the Muslims therefore thought it was wrong to flee from a

A procession of flagellants during the Black Death. Note the bare backs and the whips.

plague-stricken area, though in part this may also have involved some realization that flight could spread the disease. Theologically, however, Muslims denied that the plague was contagious, inasmuch as it was supposed to be divinely bestowed on a community deserving of special favor. Europeans, in contrast, were convinced that the plague was infectious. The practical result was that Christians feared the Black Death, whereas Muslims tended to accept it as they accepted such disasters as droughts and floods.

In the Middle East the immediate effect of the plague was a sharp rise in wages for laborers and a decrease in rents and income for the propertied classes. Yet there was no long-term improvement in the living standards of rural workers, particularly in Egypt and Syria, because a large increase in military needs to defend the region meant heavier taxes. Only in the case of urban workers did income rise sufficiently to bring an increase in real wages. In Europe hundreds of villages were severely depopulated or disappeared altogether, reducing the value of land and driving up wages as the labor supply plummeted. As in the Middle East initially, peasants who survived found their services in greater demand and could obtain better terms from their landlords or find more accommodating ones elsewhere, while others moved into the towns as artisans. Falling rents and rising wages prompted landowners to seek legislation fixing wages at low levels and restricting access to urban occupations. A French ordinance of 1351 limited wage increases to no more than a third of the preplague level, while the more ambitious English Statute of Laborers of the same year fixed wages at the pre-1349 rates and prohibited the employment of cheap female workers in place of men. Spanish, Portuguese, and German governments made similar attempts to control wages, but none was very effective. The French and the English also enacted measures to curtail the rising cost of food.

Catastrophe and Rebellion

In Europe the dislocation caused by the plague, coupled with restrictive measures against peasants and artisans, contributed to explosive unrest in the late fourteenth century. In 1358 many peasants in northern France joined in uprisings known as the Jacquerie (*Jacques* was a name nobles used to address a peasant). Already embittered by efforts to limit their wages, the peasants were angry because of heavy financial exactions to support French forces in the Hundred Years' War and the actions of marauding bands of mercenaries from whom the nobles offered no protection. The peasants killed, raped, burned, and destroyed castles. They had, however, neither strong leaders nor a program of reform. Priests, artisans, and lesser merchants joined them before the nobles ruthlessly suppressed the rebellion. In the end, some 20,000 people died.

Social revolt erupted in England in 1381, fueled by the peasants' resentment at efforts to restrict their economic advances, bitterness over aristocratic cruelty toward them, and governmental efforts to impose a poll or head tax to pay for the war against France. Peasants in the south, where the rebellion broke out, were also upset by French raids on their lands. Led by the priest John Ball and the journeyman Wat Tyler, the revolt soon spread throughout much of the country as urban workers joined the peasants. The killing and destruction subsided only when the young king, Richard II (1377–1399), met with the rebels and promised reform. Instead the nobles regrouped and carried out a campaign of retribution. Radical rebel demands—the equality of all men before the law, the granting of most church property to the people, and the end of mandatory peasant labor on the lords' personal lands—were not met, though the government ceased collecting the head tax.

The Jacquerie and the Wat Tyler rebellion are but the most famous examples of the revolts that swept parts of Europe in the century after the Black Death first appeared. The peasants of Languedoc rose up in 1382 and 1383, Catalonian peasants were frequently in arms, and peasants and miners rebelled in Sweden in 1434. Much of the unrest erupted in the cities, where artisans demanded more political power and where repressive guilds chained the working poor in poverty. The greatest urban revolt was that of the *ciompi* (cloth workers) in Florence in 1378, but uprisings occurred as well in Paris and Rouen in France, at Ghent in Flanders, at Brunswick and Lübeck in the Holy Roman Empire, and at Barcelona and Seville in Spain. No other period in the Middle Ages experienced as much social unrest as the century 1350–1450.

The Hundred Years' War

Between 1337 and 1453 the English and the French engaged in a series of armed conflicts collectively known as the Hundred Years' War, though in fact they spent less than half of this period in actual fighting. Each side went to war because it felt the other threatened its security and blocked its rightful ambitions. The war began when King Edward III of England (1327–1377) claimed the French throne as his own. The last three Capetian monarchs, the sons and heirs of Philip IV, had died without leaving a male heir. Although Edward III, Philip's maternal grandson, was the closest male heir, the French nobles supported the claim of Philip of Valois, a cousin of Philip IV's sons. At first Edward accepted the decision and swore the vassal's oath of fealty to Philip for his holdings in Aquitaine. English involvement in France, however, stood squarely in the way of the ambition of the French sovereigns to extend their authority throughout the country. No less important as a cause of the war was Anglo-French rivalry over Flanders. Its count was Philip's vassal, but Flemish towns depended on English wool for their textile industry. English support for the Flemings when they rebelled against their count threatened French domination in the region, whereas French control jeopardized English trade. Another grievance was France's support for the Scots, which prevented the English from exercising lordship over their northern neighbors.

As the two sides embarked on war, France was seemingly the stronger, with greater wealth and a population three times the size of England's. The French had the advantage of fighting on terrain they knew, but this subjected their peasants to the ravages of war. The French kings, moreover, had to cope with the fact that some of their own subjects—the Burgundians, the Flemish, and the Gascons of Aquitaine—allied with the English at various times during the war. For most of its duration the French monarchs were unable to provide either strong military leadership or sound fiscal policies to finance the fighting. The English, despite the popular support marshaled by Edward III and a string of military victories, were unable to defeat France because they had neither the troops nor the funds to dominate such a vast land. In the end the English were largely reduced to a policy of intimidation, which failed in the face of renewed French resolve.

England's early victories were the result of the military superiority of its longbowmen, who could lay down a barrage of arrows powerful enough to pierce French armor at a distance of up to 200 yards. The English archers demonstrated their effectiveness at Crécy in 1346, at Poitiers a decade later, and at Agincourt in 1415. Although the French also had longbows, they failed to use them effectively. The turning point of the war came in 1429 as the English besieged Orléans. Charles, the dauphin (crown prince), his plight desperate, gambled on an illiterate peasant girl who claimed to have been sent by heavenly messengers. Accompanied by fresh troops dispatched by the dauphin, Joan of Arc, though only 17, inspired the French with a vision of victory. The English in any event were on the verge of withdrawing from Orléans, but Joan's sense of divine mission and the dauphin's decision to accept the royal crown as Charles VII in May 1429 gave the French new life. When the Burgundians captured Joan a year later, the English

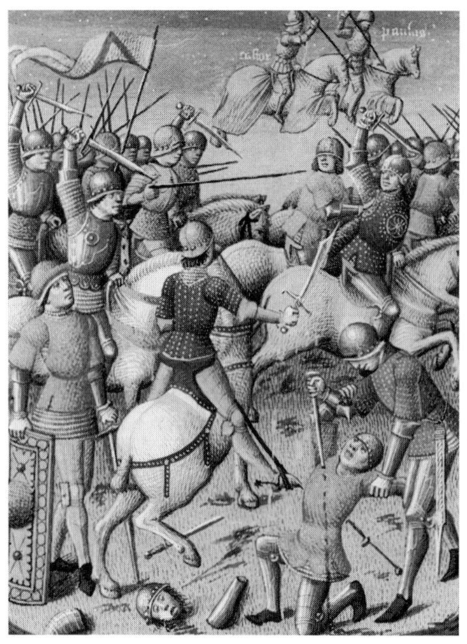

English archers slay French troops at Agincourt.

hoped to discredit her by having her tried and executed as a heretic, but instead they created a martyr. A posthumous trial found her innocent in 1456, and in 1920 the Catholic Church canonized her as a saint. In the years that followed her death in 1431, the French, with the Burgundians at their side after 1435, relentlessly drove the English out of France, leaving them in 1453 with only Calais.

The growth of national feeling and the effective use of gunpowder and heavy artillery facilitated the French victory. The new cannons were useful in besieging fortifications and they demoralized enemy forces and frightened their horses. In the end the war benefitted the French monarchy, for during its course the kings acquired both a monopoly on the sale of salt, the *gabelle* or tax on which became a major source of royal income, and the right to impose other taxes, including a direct tax called the *taille,* without the approval of the Estates General. These funds were necessary to support the standing army introduced in the war. In contrast, the English monarchs repeatedly had

The Trial of Joan of Arc

Accused, among other things, of receiving revelations from St. Catherine and St. Margaret and wearing men's clothing, Joan of Arc recanted at her trial on May 24, 1431. Four days later she again donned male dress, claiming it was appropriate because she was confined with men, and once more insisted she had received revelations.

As we her judges had heard from certain people that she had not yet cut herself off from her illusions and pretended revelations, which she had previously renounced, we asked her whether she had not since Thursday heard the voices of St. Catherine and St. Margaret. She answered yes.

Asked what they told her, she answered that they told her God had sent her word through St. Catherine and St. Margaret of the great pity of this treason by which she consented to abjure and recant in order to save her life; that she had damned herself to save her life. She said that before Thursday they told her what to do and say then, which she did. Further her voices told her, when she was on the scaffold or platform before the people, to answer the preacher boldly. The said Jeanne declared that he was a false preacher, and had accused her of many things she had not done. She said that if she declared God had not sent her she would damn herself, for in truth she was sent from God. She said that her voices had since told her she had done a great evil in declaring that what she had done was wrong. She said that what she had declared and recanted on Thursday was done only for fear of the fire.

Asked if she believed her voices to be St. Catherine and St. Margaret, she answered yes, and they came from God.

Source: *Joan of Arc: Fact, Legend, and Literature,* ed. W. T. Jewkes and J. B. Landfield (New York: Harcourt, Brace, 1964), p. 40.

to seek parliamentary approval for taxation, thereby making Parliament an indispensable part of the government. By the war's end the principle was established that neither taxes nor other forms of legislation could be implemented without parliamentary approval. Moreover, Parliament had taken the first steps to hold royal officials accountable to them or risk impeachment. England and France thus began to follow different paths of monarchical government, the former eventually culminating in constitutional monarchy, the latter in absolute rule.

The war's social consequences were profound. In both countries the rural economy suffered because of the loss of men in the fighting. The English, moreover, murdered thousands of French civilians. The war brought higher taxes and disrupted trade. The change in the manner of fighting had significant long-term effects. Both the longbow and the use of guns enhanced the value of commoners on the battlefield and thus encouraged the development of larger armies. Those armies in turn required greater financial support from the state in contrast to the smaller feudal forces. The use of cannons required major changes in the construction of city walls, which had to be much thicker. At the same time, siege trains capable of attacking towns were generally beyond the means of all but sovereigns and the greater princes; the military changes thus contributed to the evolution of more unified states. Economically, the demand for cannons, guns, and ammunition sparked the growth of the armaments industry and the mining companies that provided it with raw materials. In the long run the socioeconomic effects of the war were more important than its territorial consequences.

Joan of Arc as she may have looked, shown here holding a banner with the fleur-de-lis, the royal emblem of France.

The Spiritual Crisis of the Late Medieval Church

Against a backdrop of misery caused by famine, pestilence, and war, scandal and division rocked the church in the late fourteenth and early fifteenth centuries. The French king, Philip IV, emboldened by his earlier victory over Pope Boniface VIII, pressured Pope Clement V (1305–1314), himself French, to move the seat of the papacy from Rome to Avignon in 1309. Although an imperial city under papal control, Avignon was on the French border and was French in language and culture. The papacy remained at Avignon until 1377, a period usually referred to as the Babylonian Captivity, an allusion to the period in which the ancient Hebrews were captives in Babylon. Avignon had the advantage of freeing the popes from the turmoil then disrupting Rome and the Papal States, but it also placed the papacy under greater French influence. Of the 134 cardinals appointed during the Avignon period, 111 were French. The English, the Germans, and many Italians were displeased at the specter of a papacy in the shadow of French power, and Rome was particularly hard hit because its economy had rested so heavily on papal revenues. Perhaps most of the resentment against the Avignon popes stemmed from their efforts to create new sources of income to offset decreased revenue from the Papal States. The collection of annates, usually the first year's income from an ecclesiastical position, or expectatives, fees for the right to be appointed to a particular ecclesiastical position when it became vacant, created the impression that the popes were more concerned with material than spiritual matters.

Disillusion with the papacy became more pronounced as a result of the schism that scandalized the church from 1378 to 1417. In 1377 Pope Gregory XI (1370–1378), persuaded by Catherine of Siena and Bridget of Sweden, moved the papal court back to Rome. When he died a year later, Roman mobs intimidated the cardinals to elect an Italian pope who would keep the papacy in Rome. The cardinals obligingly chose Urban VI (1378–1389), but five months later a group of mostly French cardinals declared Urban's election void and elected a rival pope, Clement VII, a cousin of the French king, Charles V. Europeans had witnessed schisms before, but nothing like the spectacle that now divided Christendom, largely along political lines. Clement, ruling from Avignon, had the support of France and its allies, Castile, Aragon, Naples, and Scotland, whereas England, Portugal, Flanders, and the Holy Roman Empire backed Urban. The Bohemians, Hungarians, Poles, and Scandinavians also supported the Roman pope. As each pope claimed to be the true vicar of Christ and condemned the other, the schism raised serious questions about the authority of priests and the sacraments they administered. In addition to casting disrepute on church leaders, the schism encouraged the spread of heresy and mysticism, which stressed the inner life of the spirit.

Reformers called for a church council to end the scandal, contending that such a body exercised authority superior to that of a pope. Conciliar theory drew on a controversial intellectual tradition. In 1324 Marsiglio of Padua, rector of the University of Paris, had argued in his *Defender of the Peace* that because the people are the ultimate source of authority in church and state, a church council is superior to the pope. Marsiglio insisted that the church's power was restricted to spiritual matters; hence the pope had no claim to temporal authority. By reducing the church to a community within the state, he challenged its traditional claim to superiority. Although the church condemned Marsiglio's theories in 1327, his ideas provided a useful arsenal for those intent on disputing papal primacy. Among the most important of these were theologians at the University of Paris, especially Jean Gerson and Pierre d'Ailly, who espoused Conciliar arguments as the means to end the papal schism.

With the support of most monarchs, a group of cardinals representing Rome and Avignon summoned a council to meet at Pisa in 1409. It deposed both popes and chose a new one, but because neither pope accepted the council's action, three men now claimed Peter's chair. The embarrassing schism was resolved only when a new council met in the German city of Constance beginning in 1414. It took three years and the support of Sigismund, the Holy Roman Emperor, to restore unity through the election of an Italian cardinal as Martin V (1417–1431). One of the three feuding popes resigned, but the council had to depose the others. The church later regarded the Roman popes as the legitimate line. In addition to ending the schism, the Council of Constance issued two decrees supporting Conciliar views, the first of which asserted that a general council of the church derived its authority directly from Christ and thus could compel the obedience of popes "in matters pertaining to the faith, the extinction of the schism, and the form of the church." The second decree called for the next two councils to meet after intervals of five and seven years and subsequent ones every decade.

Against the background of the Babylonian Captivity, William of Ockham (c. 1290–1349), an English Franciscan theologian, challenged prevailing scholastic teachings. A nominalist, he asserted that only individual things, not essences or universals, were real and knowable. Knowledge was therefore attainable by direct experience rather than philosophical speculation. Contrary to the scholastics, he argued that the principal doctrines of Christianity, such as the existence of God and the immortality of the soul, were incapable of rational proof and had to be affirmed by faith alone. By removing the rational basis for Christian belief, Ockham opened the way to skepticism, a path some of his disciples followed. Ockham's principles convinced him that popes could not possess absolute authority, even in matters of faith; hence he contributed to Conciliar theory by insisting on the supremacy of general councils.

Mystics, who urged the importance of seeking God within oneself, also challenged the rational and institutional approach to Christianity. One of the most influential mystics was the Dominican friar Meister Eckhart (c. 1260–1328), a German, who taught that the union of the human and the divine could be achieved in the soul through divine grace. Because the views of Eckhart and Ockham challenged traditional teaching, they had to defend themselves against charges of heresy before the papal court at Avignon, and Eckhart had to recant. Among the more influential mystics was Bridget of Sweden (c. 1303–1373), founder of the Brigittine order, and Catherine of Siena (1347–1380), both of whom experienced powerful religious visions.

The strength of late medieval mysticism was among the laity, particularly in Germany and the Netherlands. The Dutchman Gerhard Groote (1340–1384) founded a movement known as the *devotio moderna* ("modern devotion"), which combined a strong sense of morality with an emphasis on the inner life of the soul rather than liturgy and penitent acts such as fasting and pilgrimages.

After his death his followers established the Brethren and the Sisters of the Common Life—lay believers who lived in strictly regulated religious houses and devoted themselves primarily to the education of young boys. Some of the most influential religious leaders of the late fifteenth and sixteenth centuries, including Erasmus, studied in these schools. The literary classic of this movement, Thomas à Kempis' *Imitation of Christ,* was a devotional handbook that emphasized personal piety and ethical conduct. Its message that "a humble husbandman who serves God is better than a proud philosopher" reflected a widespread desire among the laity to find relief from the material problems of their age through simple piety.

The Challenge of Heresy: Wyclif and Hus

Symptomatic of the church's problems in the fourteenth and early fifteenth centuries was the enthusiastic reception in England and Bohemia of ideas that challenged the very core of orthodox teaching. The Oxford professor John Wyclif (c. 1330–1384) not only denied papal claims to temporal power, as Marsiglio of Padua had done, but also demanded that cardinals and bishops relinquish their political offices and that the church divest itself of its property. In the tradition of Francis of Assisi, he insisted that the clergy should devote themselves to poverty and piety. Wyclif insisted that authority rested in the Bible alone, which should be in the language of the people, and he therefore began preparing an English version of Scripture. He also called for the abolition of many traditions, including pilgrimages, the sale of indulgences, the veneration of saints, and the doctrine of transubstantiation—the belief that the substance of the bread and wine miraculously becomes the body and blood of Christ in the Eucharist. Convinced that the true church is composed only of people divinely predestined to believe in God, Wyclif asserted that salvation was independent of the sacraments. He denied both papal and clerical power to excommunicate the righteous from the true church. Wyclif's distinction between the spiritual church of true believers and the corrupt temporal institution presided over by the popes appealed to Christians disgusted by the events of the 1300s. Wyclif enjoyed powerful support among English aristocrats, who saw in his teachings the possibility of acquiring the church's wealth. The church

Marsiglio on the Power of the People

In his Defender of the Peace, *Marsiglio of Padua makes a strong case for the people as the fundamental source of authority and the maintenance of peace as the primary task of a government.*

The authority to make laws belongs only to the whole body of the citizens . . . or else it belongs to one or a few men. But it cannot belong to one man alone . . . for through ignorance or malice or both, this one man could make a bad law, looking more to his own private benefit than to that of the community, so that the law would be tyrannical. For the same reason, the authority to make laws cannot belong to a few; for they too could sin . . . in making the law for the benefit of a certain few and not for the common benefit, as can be seen in oligarchies. . . . Since all the citizens must be measured by the law according to due proportion, and no one knowingly harms or wishes injustice to himself, it follows that all or most wish a law conducing to the common benefit of the citizens. . . .

It is hence appropriate . . . that the whole body of citizens entrust to those who are prudent and experienced the investigation, discovery, and examination of the standards, the future laws or statutes. . . . After such standards, the future laws, have been discovered and diligently examined, they must be laid before the assembled whole body of citizens for their approval or disapproval. . . . The laws thus made by the hearing and consent of the entire multitude will be better observed, nor will anyone have any protest to make against them.

Source: Marsilius of Padua, *Defensor pacis,* trans. A. Gewirth (Toronto: University of Toronto Press, 1980), pp. 48, 54–55.

condemned many of his ideas, and Oxford expelled him. Wyclif's followers, known as Lollards, kept his ideas alive well into the sixteenth century despite heavy persecution. Ultimately they helped prepare the ground for the Protestant Reformation.

Czech students studying at Oxford and members of the household of Anne of Bohemia, who married King Richard II of England in 1381, carried Wyclif's ideas to Bohemia. The leader of the Bohemian reformers, John Hus (1369–1415), rector of the University of Prague, embraced some of Wyclif's teachings, especially his concept of the true church as a body of saints and the need for sweeping reforms. Hus' views struck a responsive chord among Czech nationalists resentful of the domination of foreign churchmen. When Emperor Sigismund offered Hus a guarantee of safe conduct to discuss his views at the Council of Constance, Hus accepted, though the church had already excommunicated him. The council, which had previously condemned Wyclif's tenets, accused Hus of heresy. The church tried and convicted him and imperial authorities burned him at the stake in 1415; promises made to heretics, the church assured Sigismund, were not binding. Hus' militant followers, inspired in part by Czech patriotism, mounted a fierce rebellion that lasted from 1421 to 1436. In the end the Bohemians exercised considerable authority over their own church, an example that was not lost on Martin Luther a century later as he pondered the need for reform in the German church.

The Late Medieval Outlook

The crises of the fourteenth and early fifteenth centuries had a striking effect on people's outlook: famine, plague, and war influenced the cult of death and decay; the Hundred Years' War affected the cult of chivalry and the growth of national literature; and the Babylonian Captivity and the papal schism prompted social criticism and the views of nominalists and mystics.

The Cults of Death and Chivalry

The preoccupation with death induced by the massive fatalities resulting from famine and plague manifested itself in various ways. The pious accorded greater attention to the Last Judgment, a popular motif in art and literature. Others found solace in the Pietà, a depiction of Mary holding the dead Christ in her arms—a poignant symbol for grieving parents who shared her sense of personal loss and the hope of resurrection. Painters commonly drew figures of death, and sculptors placed skeletal figures in-

A Corrupt Clergy: Wyclif's Indictment

John Wyclif's attack on the moral evils of the clergy struck a responsive chord among many Englishmen.

We should put on the armor of Christ, for Antichrist has turned his clerks [clergymen] to covetous and worldly love, and so blinded the people and darkened the law of Christ, that his servants be thick, and few be on Christ's side. And always they despise that men should know Christ's life, . . . and priests should be ashamed of their lives, and especially these high priests, for they reverse Christ both in word and deed. . . .

O men that be on Christ's half, help ye now against Antichrist! for the perilous time is come that Christ and Paul told [of] before. . . . For three sects fight here, against Christian[s]. . . . The first is the pope and cardinals, by false law that they have made; the second is emperors [and] bishops, who despise Christ's law; the third is these Pharisees [i.e., friars]. . . . All these three, God's enemies, travel in hypocrisy, and in worldly covetousness, and idleness in God's law. Christ help his church from these fiends, for they fight perilously.

Source: J. H. Robinson, ed., *Readings in European History,* vol. 1 (Boston: Ginn, 1904), pp. 497–498.

This sixteenth-century Flemish illustration depicts the churchyard of the Church of the Innocents in Paris. On its walls was a painting of the Dance of Death, below which skulls and bones were neatly stacked for public viewing.

stead of traditional effigies on tombs. Nothing, however, more graphically reveals the fascination with death than the *danse macabre,* the dance of death that was not only portrayed in art but also acted out in eerie drama and celebrated in poetry. The *danse macabre* may be related to the psychological and neurological disorders that accompanied the plague. A recurring theme in these representations is the equality of all persons in death, a sharp counterpoint to a society preoccupied with social hierarchy. There was no more vivid reminder of this than the Churchyard of the Innocents in Paris, where heaps of skulls and bones lined the cloister walls.

Juxtaposed with this cult of death and decay, with its democratic implications, was another cult, more positive in outlook and restricted in its social appeal—the cult of chivalry. Here was a code for knights and nobles, the last gasp of a way of life and warfare being pushed into the shadows by new methods of fighting, the rising mercantile order, and a gradual shift in importance from ancestry to talent as the key to a successful political career. The cult of chivalry, with its idealized knights and ladies, was the swan song of the old order. The chivalric code exalted war, but there was nothing particularly glorious when England's peasant archers cut down the cream of French knighthood at Crécy, Poitiers, and Agincourt. Efficiency, technology, and discipline replaced bravado, loyalty, and dignity on the battlefield, a change that ultimately revolutionized and depersonalized warfare by shifting the burden from the landed elite to the masses. As if to protest the passing of the old order, the aristocracy emphasized the trappings of chivalry: pageants and tournaments. When Francis I of France and Henry VIII of England met in 1520, chivalric trappings were so extravagant that contemporaries described the scene as a "field of cloth of gold." Extravagance was indicative of the fact that chivalry, once primarily a military code of conduct, had been transformed into an elegant charade, a form of escapism.

National Literatures

The late Middle Ages witnessed the further development of national vernacular literature. The contributions of Dante, Chaucer, and Villon were critical in shaping national languages out of regional dialects. All three writers sharply criticized late medieval society and the church.

Dante Alighieri (1265–1321), who held various civic offices in his native Florence before a rival political faction forced him into exile in 1301, spent the last two decades of his life traveling throughout Italy in search of patrons. Embittered by the divisiveness of the Italian states, Dante used these years to defend the vernacular and to compose his epic poem *The Divine Comedy,* so named because it progresses from a fearsome vision of hell in the first part, the *Inferno,* to a happy ending as the reader is guided through purgatory to paradise. Dante uses the scenes from hell, peopled with everyone from popes and priests to politicians and queens, to condemn such evils as ecclesiastical corruption, political treachery, and immorality. On other levels the journey is an allegory of the Christian life and a pictorial *summa* of medieval ethical and religious teachings akin in spirit to the scholastic *summae* of Thomas Aquinas.

Disenchantment with contemporary society, especially the church, is also reflected in Geoffrey Chaucer's *Canterbury Tales.* The son of a wine merchant, Chaucer (c. 1340–1400) fought in the Hundred Years' War before serving as a royal official. It was probably on a mission to Florence that he learned of Dante's work, which influenced his own writings. Many of his poems, such as *The Legend of Good Women,* deal with the theme of love, while others, such as *The Parliament of Fowls,* may reflect contemporary political events. In the characters, anecdotes, and moral fables of *The Canterbury Tales* he probed English society, making incisive and satirical comments about the foibles and hypocrisy of ecclesiastics. The thrust is similar in a nearly contemporary work titled *The Vision of Piers Plowman,* usually attributed to William Langland (c. 1330–c. 1400). The work's 11 poetic visions reflect the crises of the 1300s, especially as they affected the peasants, and are critical of the failings of the church even while reaffirming faith in Christian principles.

The poetry of the Frenchman François Villon (1431–c. 1463) is the voice of the downtrodden and criminal element in a society thrown into turmoil by the Hundred Years' War. A convicted murderer and thief as well as a graduate of the University of Paris, Villon was in and out of jail and was for a time under sentence of death. The themes of his ballads range from the ways of the Parisian underworld and his drinking companions to meditations on the beauty of life. The specter of death stalks much of his work, reflecting the popularity of this theme in the fifteenth century.

Economic Recovery

Europe recovered from the calamities of the fourteenth and early fifteenth centuries in large measure because of renewed population growth, economic diversification,

Death and Decay

François Villon's poetry reflects not only his own experiences among the lowly and the criminal in France but also the fifteenth century's fascination with death and decay.

Death makes one shudder and turn pale,
Pinches the nose, distends the veins,
Swells out the throat, the members fail,
Tendons and nerves grow hard with strains.
O female flesh, like silken skeins,
Smooth, tender, precious, in such wise
Must you endure so awful pains?
Aye, or go living to the skies.

The following lines were written while Villon was under sentence of death; he describes the fate that awaits his body.

The rain has washed us through as through a sieve,
And the sun dried us black to caricature;
Magpies and crows have had our eyes to rive
And made of brows and beards their nouriture.
Never we pause, no moment's rest secure,
Now here, now there, as the winds fail or swell,
Always we swing like clapper of a bell.
Pitted as thimble is our bird-pecked skin.
Be not of our ill brotherhood and fell,
But pray to God we be absolved of sin!

Source: The Complete Works of François Villon, trans. J. U. Nicolson (New York: Covici Friede, 1931), pp. 32, 108.

and technological inventions spurred by the labor shortages resulting from the Black Death. As the population began to return to its former levels in the late fifteenth and sixteenth centuries, there was once again an abundant labor supply as well as improved productivity and greater economic diversification. Merchants increasingly branched out into fields as varied as banking, textile and weapon manufacturing, and mining. The Germans modernized the mines by harnessing horsepower and waterpower to crush ore, operate their rolling mills, pump water from mine shafts, and run the lifts. New blast furnaces made cast iron. Dutch fishermen learned to salt, dry, and store their fish while at sea, thus enabling them to stay out longer and increase their catch. The Hundred Years' War, as we have seen, stimulated the armaments industry, and the introduction of movable metal type led to the printing industry and encouraged paper manufacturing.

The textile industry grew in this period. The production of woolens in Flanders and the cities of northern Italy, however, declined in the fifteenth century, primarily because English monarchs built up their native wool industry by imposing low export duties on cloth and high ones on raw wool. Woolen manufacturing expanded in France, Germany, and Holland, and new textile industries such as silk and cotton developed. In Venice some 3,000 persons were involved in the production of silk, 16,000 in the manufacture of cotton. Several thousand found employment in the Venetian arsenal, the greatest shipyard and probably the largest industrial establishment in Europe.

The growth in manufacturing went hand in hand with a dramatic increase in commerce and the rise of great merchants and their organizations. The latter included the seven major guilds in Florence, the six merchant corporations known as the *Corps de Marchands* in Paris, and the 12 livery companies in London. Firms in Europe's leading commercial centers established branch offices in other cities, and exchanges or bourses opened to facilitate financial transactions. Banking houses developed rapidly; Florence had 33 in 1472. State banks operated in such places as Genoa, Venice, Augsburg, Hamburg, and Barcelona. As rulers as well as merchants needed loans, the demand for credit grew, undermining the medieval church's hostility to most interest charges. The Genoese pioneered the development of insurance, especially for merchants engaged in seaborne trade. The most stable coins of this period were Florentine florins and Venetian ducats, which helped northern Italians exercise a dominant role in banking.

Ships in the Mediterranean trade called at the Italian ports of Pisa and Genoa as well as at Marseilles and Narbonne in France and Barcelona in Aragon, but the heart of this commerce was Venice. Its 3,300 ships, some of them capable of carrying as much as 250 tons of cargo, plied the waters from the North Sea and Spain to North Africa, Syria, and the Black Sea. Genoa, itself a major maritime power, had 2,000 ships. Merchants traded European cloth in the East for spices, dyes, sugar, silks, and cotton. Shipping in northern Europe was mostly the province of the Hanseatic League, whose members included Lübeck, Danzig, and Hamburg. Their ships ranged from Scandinavia and Russia to England, Flanders, and northern Italy. From the states of the Baltic and the North Sea they obtained fish, timber, naval stores, grain, and furs in exchange for wine, spices, and cloth. Much of the commerce moved through the ports of the Low Countries; in 1435 an average of 100 ships a day docked at Bruges. In the late fifteenth and sixteenth centuries the influence of the Hanseatic League began to wane, partly owing to internal problems but mostly because of the growing power of states such as England and Denmark, whose merchants demanded an end to Hansa privileges and a greater role in the carrying trade.

Political Renewal: The Quest for Unity and Authority

The development of relatively strong centralized states in western Europe and Russia accompanied the economic revival. The political crises had increased the need for state governments to raise substantial tax revenues. Such income made it feasible to think in terms of a professional army rather than a feudal levy, but this in turn increased the costs of government. So too did the growth of royal bureaucracies, which were essential to raise the revenue and administer the realms. Greater unity generally benefitted the business community; hence the monarchs typically found important allies in the towns. Urban support translated into tax revenues (though many French towns enjoyed exemptions), an enlarged pool from which government officials could be selected, and political backing in the drive for sovereignty.

The decline of particularism—the dominance of local and regional authorities rather than a central government—was in most respects a blow to the landed aristocracy, but exemptions from most taxes and frequent appointments to political office generally appeased the aristocrats. Members of the landed elite were prominent in the national assemblies, where they enjoyed power and prestige greater than those of urban delegates. The achievement of national sovereignty was possible in large measure because the landed aristocracy's power was not so much crushed as altered: in the new system, many aristocrats became staunch supporters of the crown. In Russia and Spain, the development of a centralized state occurred as part of a drive to expel hitherto dominant invaders—the Mongols in Russia and the Muslims in Spain.

The Rise of Muscovy

During the period of Mongol domination, Russia was a conglomeration of feudal principalities, but in the fourteenth century the princes of Moscow began to "gather the Russian land" by expanding their borders through marital alliances, inheritance, purchases, and conquests. Three factors aided them: the strategic location of Moscow near tributaries of the Volga and Oka rivers, Mongol reliance on the Muscovites to collect tribute from other Russians, and the support of the Russian Orthodox church, whose metropolitan (archbishop) made Moscow the religious capital of the Russians in the fourteenth century. As Mongol power declined late in that century, the Muscovite princes ceased to be agents for the Mongols and took up the mantle of patriotic resistance. Their new role was evident when Grand Prince Dimitri defeated the Mongols in 1380 at Kolikovo, southeast of Moscow. The war of liberation continued well into the fifteenth century, during which time Moscow experienced numerous sieges. Even after the Mongols were driven out, their influence pervaded many areas of Russian life, including military organization, criminal law, the system of tax collection, and above all the principle of unqualified obedience to the state. In a very real sense, Russian sovereigns ruled much as the Mongol khans had.

The foundation of a strong Russian state was the work of Ivan III, known as Ivan the Great (1462–1505), who was determined to prevent the recurrence of the factional struggles that had plagued his father's reign. To counterbalance the power of the hereditary boyars (nobles), Ivan created a class of serving aristocracy by offering them lifetime grants of land in return for their service. Ivan enhanced his status by his marriage to Zoë, niece of the last Byzantine emperor, Constantine XI (died 1453). Henceforth Ivan referred to himself as the successor of the Byzantine emperors, adopting the Byzantine double eagle as the symbol of Russia, introducing Byzantine ceremonies at court, and calling himself Autocrat and Tsar ("Caesar"). At Zoë's urging, Italian architects received commissions to design the Kremlin, a fortresslike palace befitting the tsar's pretensions to grandeur. Russian scholars contributed to the new image by asserting that Moscow was the third Rome (after Rome and Byzantium, each of which had fallen) and thus the center of Christianity. In the words of one Russian apologist, "The tsar is in nature like to all men, but in authority he is like to the highest God."

Ivan expanded the boundaries of his state, first by conquering the republic of Novgorod, a trading center with access to the Baltic Sea. Seizing approximately 80 percent of the former republic's land, he retained possession of more than half of it and used the rest to expand his serving aristocracy. In the process he exiled thousands of boyars, merchants, and smaller landowners. In 1500 he invaded Lithuania, hoping to conquer Smolensk; although he failed in this objective, by 1503 he had expanded his borders to the west. Above all, Ivan advanced his claim to be ruler "of all the Russias." Unlike his predecessors, who limited their claim of ownership to royal estates and their inhabitants, Ivan asserted an unprecedented right to all Russian lands. In this context he issued a new code of laws for the Russian people in 1497. Ivan can justly be regarded as the founder of the modern Russian state and the architect of an absolute tsardom.

The Spain of Isabella and Ferdinand

The unification of Spain was possible because of the marriage in 1469 of Isabella, the future queen of Castile (1474–1504), and Ferdinand, the future king of Aragon (1479–1516). This marriage, so crucial to the future history of Spain, took place only after Isabella rejected the plan of her brother, King Henry IV, for her to marry the King of Portugal. Of the two kingdoms of Castile and Aragon, the former was more populous and wealthier. It was, moreover, an expanding state as it continued the campaign to reconquer Granada from the Muslims, a goal achieved in 1492. That done, Spain could turn its attention to overseas exploration, a pursuit in which the Portuguese had already taken the lead.

The marriage of Isabella and Ferdinand did not effectively unite the two countries, each of which spoke a different language and retained its own laws, taxes, monetary system, military, and customs. The two sovereigns permitted Aragon to keep its provincial assemblies, the Cortes, although viceroys appointed by the crown exercised royal supervision. The monarchs concentrated on Castile, whose Cortes supported their quest for order and whose new council was the principal agency to implement royal policy. In the work of centralization the

MAP 15.2 THE EXPANSION OF RUSSIA

sovereigns had the support of the towns, which were liberally represented in the Cortes, and of the hidalgos—knights who did not enjoy the tax-exempt status of the nobles and therefore sought employment from the crown. A number of hidalgos served as *corregidors,* administering local districts, performing judicial functions, and supervising urban affairs. Although the role of the nobles in the government was somewhat reduced, they still exercised considerable influence through the powerful military brotherhoods established in the twelfth century, the Santiago, Calatrava, and Alcántara. To bring them under greater royal authority, Ferdinand became the head of each of these brotherhoods. The Mesta, the organization of large sheep farmers, also had to be controlled, for its payments were a primary source of royal revenue in the period before Spain began importing large quantities of American bullion.

The devout Isabella and the pragmatic Ferdinand made the Catholic church a key instrument in their centralizing work. Isabella's chief minister, Cardinal Francisco Ximenes (c. 1436–1517), restored church discipline, thus reinforcing central authority. In 1482 Pope Sixtus IV granted the sovereigns the *real patronato* ("Royal Patronage"), giving them the right to make the major ecclesiastical appointments in Granada; they later extended this to Spanish America and then to Spain as a whole. Even more striking as a demonstration of royal authority in religion was Isabella and Ferdinand's campaign to enforce religious orthodoxy. Although the Inquisition had been introduced into Spain by a papal bull in 1478, it soon became an instrument controlled by the crown and run by the queen's confessor, Tomás de Torquemada (died 1498). In 1492 the Jews received the option of being baptized as Christians or losing their

The marriage of Ferdinand of Aragon and Isabella of Castile made the unification of Spain possible.

property and going into exile; approximately 150,000 left. Ten years later Ximenes persuaded Isabella to expel professing Muslims. Jews and Muslims who converted—*Conversos* and *Moriscos,* respectively—were subject to the terrors of the Inquisition if their sincerity was in doubt. Spain achieved religious unity at the cost of expelling or alienating productive minorities, curtailing intellectual freedom, and destroying toleration.

England: The Struggle for the Throne

By the end of the Hundred Years' War in 1453, English royal authority, already checked by the growth of parliamentary power in the areas of legislation and taxation, had been undermined by bastard feudalism. By this practice a small group of powerful nobles who controlled much of the country's landed property used their wealth to employ private armies. The retainers in their hire, most of them veterans, wore distinctive clothing, served primarily for pay rather than for the use of land as in the traditional feudal arrangement, and could expect legal assistance—often involving intimidation or bribery—if they got in trouble while serving their lord. The magnates who hired these private armies exerted enormous influence on the monarchs through the royal Council and commanded support from their followers in Parliament. These circumstances made it possible for Henry of Bolingbroke, Edward III's grandson, to force the abdication of Richard II in 1399. Parliament dutifully confirmed Bolingbroke's assumption of the crown as Henry IV (1399–1413), the first ruler of the house of Lancaster.

During the reign of Henry IV's grandson, Henry VI (1422–1461), civil war erupted between the feuding factions, the houses of Lancaster and York. In the sixteenth century this came to be known as the Wars of the Roses when William Shakespeare, in *Henry VI,* assigned the symbol of the Tudor dynasty, a red rose, to the Lancastrians; the Yorkist symbol was a white rose. Henry's queen, Margaret of Anjou, was unwilling to see power pass to Richard, duke of York, great-grandson of Edward III and heir apparent before the birth of Henry's son. Richard's son, Edward IV (1461–1483), captured the throne in 1461 and forced Henry VI to abdicate. The house of Lancaster staged a brief comeback in 1470–1471, though Edward soon regained control, after which Henry VI mysteriously died in the Tower of London.

The Wars of the Roses were over, giving Edward the opportunity to improve his position by shepherding his finances, establishing firm control over the Council, and expanding royal authority in Wales and northern England. At his death in 1483 his brother Richard, regent for the young Edward V, imprisoned the new king and his brother. They died mysteriously, possibly at the instigation of their uncle, who assumed the throne as Richard III (1483–1485). In 1485 Henry Tudor, who was distantly related to the house of Lancaster, invaded England with French backing and defeated Richard in the battle of Bosworth Field. Once again Parliament recognized the victor's claim to the throne, and Henry's marriage to Edward IV's daughter, Elizabeth of York, helped to heal the wounds dividing the English ruling order.

Henry VII (1485–1509) resumed the task of strengthening royal authority that Edward IV had begun, notably by making the crown financially secure and building up a surplus in the treasury. Instead of increasing taxes, he relied heavily on income from crown lands, judicial fees and fines, and feudal dues such as wardship rights. He also avoided costly foreign adventures, with the exception of a brief invasion of France in 1492 in a failed attempt to keep Brittany independent. Apart from token forces, Henry had no standing army, but he made effective use of unpaid justices of the peace drawn from the ranks of the gentry to maintain order in the counties, thereby reducing the crown's dependence on the nobility. Henry also used his Council, which could sit as a court (called the Star Chamber), to maintain order and impose swift justice; people cited before this court had no right to legal counsel and could be compelled to testify against themselves. Like Edward IV, he selected men for the Council because of their loyalty to him rather than their status as magnates. He negotiated two strategic alliances, one of which involved the marriage of his daughter Margaret to James IV of Scotland. From that line came the Stuart dynasty, which would govern both countries in the seventeenth century and unify them in the kingdom of Great Britain in 1707. The second alliance led to the marriage of Henry VII's son, Prince Henry, to Catherine of Aragon, daughter of Ferdinand and Isabella. When Henry tired of Catherine in the late 1520s, he set in motion the events that led to England's break with the Catholic church. By the time of his death in 1509, Henry VII had imposed substantial order and unity on England and, in the Statutes of Drogheda (1495), had made the Parliament and laws of Ireland subject to English control as well.

Valois France

Charles VII (1422–1461) laid the foundation for the recovery of the French monarchy, not least by his victory over the English in the Hundred Years' War. Despite the large size of the kingdom, the continuation of feudal traditions and local privileges, and the existence of a representative assembly, the Estates General, the French kings were at last in a position to unify the country, aided by a new spirit of national feeling. During the war Charles had organized the first French standing army, supported with the *taille,* a direct tax for which he did not have to seek the approval of the Estates General after 1439. In fact, meetings of the Estates were rare between 1441 and 1614, after which no sessions convened until 1789. In 1438 Charles brought the French church under royal control in the Pragmatic Sanction of Bourges, which set forth "Gallican liberties" (similar to the *real patronato* later introduced in Spain) such as the right of the French church to choose its own bishops and an end to the payment of annates to Rome.

Once England had been defeated, the greatest threat to the French monarchy was the duchy of Burgundy, whose dukes, Philip the Good (1419–1467) and Charles the Bold (1467–1477), entertained thoughts of making their state a powerful middle kingdom between France and the Holy Roman Empire. Their lands included not only the duchy of Burgundy in eastern France but also the Franche-Comté, Flanders, and other areas of the Netherlands. To establish a viable middle kingdom, Charles the Bold attempted to conquer Alsace and Lorraine, thereby linking Burgundy with the Low Countries, the major source of his extensive wealth. The French king, Louis XI (1461–1483), responded to this threat by subsidizing the armies of the Swiss Confederation, which defeated the Burgundians in 1477, enabling him to annex Burgundy. The royal domains expanded again in 1480 and 1481, when Louis inherited the Angevin lands of Anjou, Maine, and Provence. Only Brittany remained beyond the pale of his authority, but his son and heir, Charles VIII (1483–1498), remedied that in 1491, when he married Anne, duchess of Brittany.

Charles VIII involved France in a disastrous attempt to dominate Italy. The stage had been set when Louis succeeded not only to the Angevin lands in France but also to the Angevin claim to the throne of Naples, now occupied by the Aragonese. Louis had done nothing about the claim, but Charles was determined to assert it. In 1494 he invaded Italy, precipitating a power struggle for control of the Italian peninsula that lasted 65 years. Although Charles failed to take Naples, his successor, Louis XII (1498–1515), determined to seize Milan, which he claimed as his own because his mother had been a member of the Visconti family, rulers of the duchy until 1447. Pope Julius II (1503–1513) enlisted Spain, Venice, the Swiss Confederation, and the Holy

The French king Louis XI was a homely man who enjoyed a game of chess. He significantly expanded the royal domain by acquiring the duchy of Burgundy.

Roman Empire in a Holy League to drive France out of Italy, an end they accomplished in 1513. Under Francis I (1515–1547) the French returned again in 1515, sparking a series of wars with the Habsburgs that drained France financially and damaged the prestige of the monarchy. Nevertheless, as in the case of the Hundred Years' War, military needs and financial demands led to the continued expansion and centralization of the royal administration, thus strengthening the king's hold on the realm and laying the foundation for the subsequent development of absolutism in France.

Italy: Papal States and City-States

While Russia and the western European states were developing stronger, more centralized governments in the fifteenth century, in Italy, Germany, Hungary, and Poland regional states and princes consolidated their power, effectively blocking the emergence of nations. The struggle in the High Middle Ages between the papacy and the Hohenstaufen emperors left the Italians without a strong government capable of extending its control throughout the peninsula. Nor did any state possess a theoretical claim to serve as the nucleus for a unified nation. From Rome the popes governed the Papal States, a band extending across central Italy, but their claims to authority were international in scope. The papacy's temporal authority in Italy declined during the Avignon period and suffered further damage during the great schism. Beginning with Martin V, the fifteenth- and early-sixteenth-century popes were preoccupied with reestablishing their temporal power. Popes such as Alexander VI and Julius II were less spiritual leaders than temporal princes willing to use any means to extend their rule. Alexander relied heavily on his son Cesare, who had few moral principles, and Julius personally led his forces into battle.

In the fourteenth and fifteenth centuries the communal governments of northern Italy experienced substantial internal tensions resulting from economic and social changes. Rapid urban growth, the development of textile industries, and the rise of a sizable proletariat excluded from the hope of prosperity by privilege-conscious guilds created such strife that Milan and Florence turned to virtual despots to preserve order. So too did some of the smaller cities. Often these men were *condottieri,* mercenary generals whose hired armies provided them with the force necessary to keep order.

In the south the kingdom of Naples and Sicily had problems of a different nature because of foreign domination. In 1282 the Sicilians revolted against their French Angevin rulers and turned for assistance to Aragon. Throughout the fourteenth century the Angevins and the Aragonese contested southern Italy until, in 1435, the Aragonese drove the Angevins out of Naples. As we have seen, Charles VIII's reassertion of the Angevin claim led to the French invasion of Italy in 1494.

The Duchy of Milan

From its strategic position in the Po valley and at the base of the trade routes leading across the Alps into northern Europe, Milan developed rapidly as an industrial center specializing in textiles and arms. The medieval commune suffered, however, from social tensions and a struggle for power between Guelph (propapal) and Ghibelline (proimperial) factions. Under the leadership of the Visconti family the Ghibellines triumphed in 1277, effectively ending communal government and establishing despotic rule. The Visconti—dukes of Milan beginning in 1395—employed *condottieri* to extend their control in the Po valley.

When the last Visconti duke died without a male heir in 1447, the Milanese revived republican government, but it was ineffective. Therefore in 1450 the *condottiere* Francesco Sforza reestablished ducal rule. Apart from extending Milan's control over Genoa, Francesco attempted to maintain a balance of power in Italy among the five principal states: Milan, Venice, Florence, Naples, and the Papal States. To this end he was an architect of the Italian League (1455), which was designed in part to prevent French aggression. However, Francesco's son Ludovico connived with Charles VIII of France to intervene in Italian affairs, thereby contributing not only to the devastating wars that ensued but to the demise of the Sforza dynasty. After the French retreated, the family briefly regained its power between 1512 and 1535, at which time the Holy Roman Emperor Charles V acquired Milan.

Caterina Sforza, the Despot of Forlì

The talented Caterina Sforza (c. 1463–1509) was the daughter of Francesco Sforza's son, the second duke of Milan. Although she received a humanist education (see Chapter 16), she displayed no interest in classical authors or philosophical issues, but history as well as riding and dancing intrigued her. For political reasons Cate-

MAP 15.3 ITALY, c. 1494

rina's father arranged her marriage to Pope Sixtus IV's nephew, Girolamo Riario. The pope subsequently gave them control of the towns of Forlì and Imola, northeast of Florence, but political rivals assassinated Caterina's husband in 1488. She retained power by ruling in her son's name, thanks to assistance from the armies of Milan and Bologna, and avenged her husband's murder by having the bodies of some of the conspirators dismembered and scattered in the piazza of Forlì. That done, she sought to restore unity to her possessions by launching a program of public building in Forlì, including a lavish park.

Although a campaign to extend her territory to the northeast failed because of opposition from Venice, all the major Italian states courted her as an ally. When the French invaded Italy in 1494, Caterina, fearful of Venice, refused to join the Holy League against France, opting for a neutrality that favored the French and their Florentine allies. The assassination of her lover in 1495 prompted her to instigate another bloody vendetta, but it also opened the way for her secret marriage in 1497 to Giovanni de' Medici, second cousin of the Florentine ruler Lorenzo the Magnificent. About this time she underwent a period of spiritual searching in which she wrote to the reformer Girolamo Savonarola, who urged her to seek redemption through pious works and just rule.

Caterina Sforza, countess of Forlì.

Caterina's final period of political crisis began in 1498, when the Venetians raided her lands, but military aid from Milan and the outbreak of fighting between the Venetians and the Florentines saved her. While Caterina was occupied with Venice, Pope Alexander VI and his son, Cesare Borgia, plotted to increase their control over the Papal States, particularly the region that included Caterina's lands. Her main ally, Milan, was preoccupied in 1499 with the threat of a new French invasion, thanks to a pact between France and Venice signed in February. A month later the pope, calling Caterina a "daughter of iniquity," claimed her lands. Negotiations with Niccolò Machiavelli, the Florentine envoy, failed to achieve an effective alliance, nor were the assassins she dispatched to kill Alexander VI successful. Cesare Borgia's army struck in the autumn, forcing Caterina to send her children and treasures to Florence for safety. She retreated to a fortress with her troops, destroying all buildings in the area that might shelter the enemy, cutting down the trees, and flooding the marshes. Italy watched as the papal army relentlessly attacked until she was finally captured—and raped by Cesare—in January 1500. For a year she was a prisoner in a Roman dungeon. Without support from any major Italian state, her efforts to regain her territories failed, forcing her to seek refuge in Florence. She spent her last years attending to her household, her garden, her horses, and her soul. Contemporaries called her the "Amazon of Forlì," a tribute to her ability to hold her own in a political world governed by the ethics of power.

Florence and the Medici

Bitter social conflict disrupted Florence throughout the fourteenth and early fifteenth centuries. Thanks to its banking houses and its textile industry the city was usually prosperous in this period, though it suffered severely when England's Edward III repudiated his debts and caused major banking houses to fail and again when 55,000 of its 95,000 inhabitants died in the plague. The periodic crises intensified social tensions. In part an unusual degree of social mobility in Florentine society caused the turmoil. The older nobles, the *grandi,* had been effectively excluded from power in 1293 through a constitution called the Ordinances of Justice, the work of the newly rich capitalists who dominated the seven greater guilds. In 1343 the artisans of the lesser guilds and their allies, the shopkeepers and small businessmen, successfully challenged the capitalists. The *ciompi* had their turn in 1378, when they revolted and won the right to organize their own guilds and have a say in political affairs. Feuding between the lesser guilds and the *ciompi* enabled various wealthy merchants to regain control in the early 1380s under the leadership of the Albizzi family. When the Albizzi blocked the rise of new capitalists to power but could not win a war against neighboring Lucca, partisans of the Medici family exiled them in 1434.

Cosimo de' Medici (1389–1464) and his successors, who dominated Florentine politics except for brief intervals until 1737, governed as despots by manipulating republican institutions, often from behind the scenes. In addition to working with Francesco Sforza to create a balance of power in Italy and prevent French aggression, Cosimo introduced a graduated income tax and curried favor among the lesser guilds and workers. His grandson, Lorenzo the Magnificent (1449–1492), was the target of an assassination plot by the Pazzi family that killed his brother while the two were worshiping in the cathedral at Florence in 1478. The plot had the support of Girolamo Riario, Caterina Sforza's husband, as well as Pope Sixtus IV. The pope resented the Medici's alliance with Venice and Milan, the intent of which was to block the extension of his authority in the northern Papal States. Like his grandfather, Lorenzo sought a balance of power in Italy and opposed French aggression. The Florentines ousted Lorenzo's son Piero when he made territorial concessions to the French in 1494. Florentines restored republican government and for four years religious frenzy prevailed under the sway of the fiery Dominican Girolamo Savonarola (see Chapter 16). The republic's alliance with France isolated Florence from other Italian states, but in 1512 Pope Julius II persuaded the Florentines to join the Holy League against Louis XII and allow the Medici to return.

Venice: The Republic of St. Mark

Unlike the Florentines and the Milanese, the Venetians enjoyed social and political stability. The merchant oligarchy that governed the republic was a closed group limited to families listed in the Golden Book, a register of more than 200 names that included only families represented in the Great Council prior to 1297. Venice had neither a landed nobility nor a large industrial proletariat to challenge the dominance of its wealthy merchants, and the republic, because of its relative isolation, had not become embroiled in the Guelph-Ghibelline feud that left cities such as Florence with a tradition of bitter factionalism. There was never a successful revolution in Venice.

The Venetian government was tight-knit. The 240 or so merchant oligarchs who sat in the Great Council elected the Senate, the principal legislative body, as well as the ceremonial head of state, called a *doge,* and other government officials. The most powerful body in the state was the annually elected Council of Ten, which met in secret, focused on security, and in an emergency could assume the powers of all other government officials. To the Venetians' credit, the merchant oligarchy disdained despotic rule, thereby maintaining the support of those excluded from the political process.

In the fourteenth and fifteenth centuries the Venetians became a commercial empire. This involved a bitter contest with Genoa for control of trade in the eastern Mediterranean, a struggle that ended with Genoa's defeat in 1380. In the meantime, the Venetians attempted to acquire territory in northern Italy to assure an adequate food supply and access to the Alpine trade routes. Conquering such neighboring states as Padua and Verona brought the Venetians face to face with Milan and the Papal States, both of which were also expanding, as well as with the Habsburgs and the Hungarians, who were unsettled by Venetian expansion around the head of the Adriatic. The struggle on the mainland diverted crucial resources from the eastern Mediterranean, where Turkish expansion threatened Venetian interests. More dangerous than the lengthy war with the Turks (1463–1479) was the threat posed to Venice by the League of Cambrai, formed in 1508 and 1509 by Pope Julius II to strip Venice of its territorial acquisitions. Members of the league included Emperor Maximilian, Louis XII, and Ferdinand of Aragon. Although the league seized some of Venice's Italian lands, a reprieve came when the pope, increasingly fearful of French ambitions, negotiated peace. Venice was still an important state, but Turkish expansion coupled with the discovery of new trade routes to Asia eroded its role as a Mediterranean power.

Built on an archipelago in a lagoon in the Adriatic Sea, Venice consisted of some 60 parishes in 1200, each typically on its own island. The heart of each parish was a square lined with a church, a wharf or a boatyard, and the

The square of St. Mark's Venice, as depicted by Canaletto.

houses of the wealthy. Each parish had its own saint, customs, and festivals. Wooden bridges and ferries linked the parishes. The heart of the city was the great piazza adjacent to the ducal palace, the church of St. Mark's, and a soaring campanile that served as a beacon for ships and whose bells marked the passage of time. The site of colorful festivities and pageantry on special religious and civic occasions, the piazza normally was filled with the booths of artisans and city officials. Much of Venice's trade moved on the canals, the greatest of which was the Grand Canal. Stoneyards and boatyards lined its banks until 1333, when the city ordered their removal to make room for the grand homes of the merchant elite.

At the peak of its influence in the fifteenth and early sixteenth centuries, Venice was a city of striking contrasts. The fabulous wealth of the merchant oligarchy was reflected in the new palatial houses along the Grand Canal, none more glittering than the Ca' d'Oro (1421–1440), with its polychrome marble and gilded paint. Living space in the city was at a premium, hence not even the wealthiest patricians could acquire spacious lots. Away from the Grand Canal there was no special residential district for the merchant oligarchy, whose homes were scattered throughout the city. Venice had its poor, some of whom lived in apartments squeezed between the floors or in the basements of the homes of the wealthy. Generally, there was employment for the indigent, particularly in the shipbuilding, textile, weapons, glass, and fishing industries. The city regulated food prices and periodically distributed free grain to the needy, but there was considerable reluctance to provide regular relief until 1528, when refugees inundated the city. The Venetians traded in slaves and kept some blacks as household servants, though the slave trade declined as the Turks pushed the Venetians out of the Mediterranean. The Venetians were mostly tolerant of the foreign minorities who settled in the city, but the attitude did not fully extend to the Jews. In the late fourteenth century the Jews of Venice had to wear yellow badges, and beginning in 1423 they could not own real estate. Finally, in 1516 the government forced the Jews to live in a special district, or ghetto. It was, however, unthinkable to exclude them from the republic, as they had been from Spain, for the community required their medical expertise and their ability to provide loans, particularly in time of war. Venice was more tolerant of the Jews than were other Italian states.

The Holy Roman Empire

The destruction of imperial power in the thirteenth century during the struggle between the Holy Roman Empire and the papacy left Germany badly divided. When the princes ended the Great Interregnum (1254–1273)

The Glories of Venice

The civic pride of the Venetians is manifest in the 1423 deathbed oration of the doge Tommaso Mocenigo, which he delivered to a group of senators.

This our city now sends out in the way of business to different parts of the world ten millions of ducats' worth yearly by ships and galleys, and the profit is not less than two million ducats a year. . . . Every year there go to sea forty-five galleys with eleven thousand sailors, and there are three thousand ship's carpenters and three thousand caulkers. . . . There are one thousand noblemen whose income is from seven hundred to four thousand ducats. If you go on in this manner you will increase from good to better, and you will be the masters of wealth and Christendom; everyone will fear you. But beware . . . of waging unjust war. . . . Everyone knows that the war with the Turks has made you brave and experienced of the sea; you have six generals to fight any great army, and for each of these you have . . . enough [men] to man one hundred galleys; and in these years you have shown distinctly that the world considers you the leaders of Christianity. You have many men experienced in embassies and in the government of cities, who are accomplished orators. You have many doctors of divers sciences, and especially many lawyers, wherefore numerous foreigners come here for judgment of their differences, and abide by your verdicts. You mint coins, every year a million ducats of gold and two hundred thousand of silver. . . . Therefore, be wise in governing such a State.

Source: P. Lauritzen, *Venice: A Thousand Years of Culture and Civilization* (London: Weidenfeld & Nicolson, 1978), p. 87.

by placing Rudolf of Habsburg (1273–1291) on the imperial throne, they were not interested in creating a strong centralized government. Although the Habsburgs dreamed of ruling a powerful dynastic state, their dominions were limited to Austria, giving them little control over the princes and towns in other regions. The virtual independence of the mightier princes was confirmed in 1356 when Emperor Charles IV issued the Golden Bull, affirming that the empire was an elective monarchy. Henceforth four hereditary princes, each of whom was virtually sovereign—the count palatine of the Rhine, the duke of Saxony, the margrave of Brandenburg, and the king of Bohemia—and three ecclesiastical princes—the archbishops of Cologne, Mainz, and Trier—chose the new emperors. In the century and a half that followed, lesser princes emulated the seven electors by establishing a strong degree of authority within their own states, a process that involved them in a struggle with the knights and administrative officials who wanted virtual independence for their fiefs. In Germany the territorial princes triumphed over both the emperor and the knights. Their power was reflected in the Imperial Diet, a representative assembly whose three estates comprised the electoral princes, the lesser princes, and the imperial free cities. Similar assemblies existed in the principalities. The Swiss took advantage of weak imperial authority to organize a confederation of essentially independent cantons or districts.

Although Habsburg power within the empire was weak, Maximilian negotiated strategic marriage alliances that vastly increased the family's power. His own marriage to Mary of Burgundy had led to the acquisition of the Low Countries, and the marriage of his son Philip to Ferdinand and Isabella's daughter Joanna made it possible for Maximilian's grandson Charles to inherit Spain and its possessions. Emperor Charles V (1519–1556) thus ruled the Habsburg lands in Germany, Austria, the Low Countries, Spain, Spanish territories in the New World, and the Aragonese kingdom of Naples and Sicily; no larger dominion had existed in Europe since the time of Charlemagne.

THE INHERITANCE OF CHARLES V

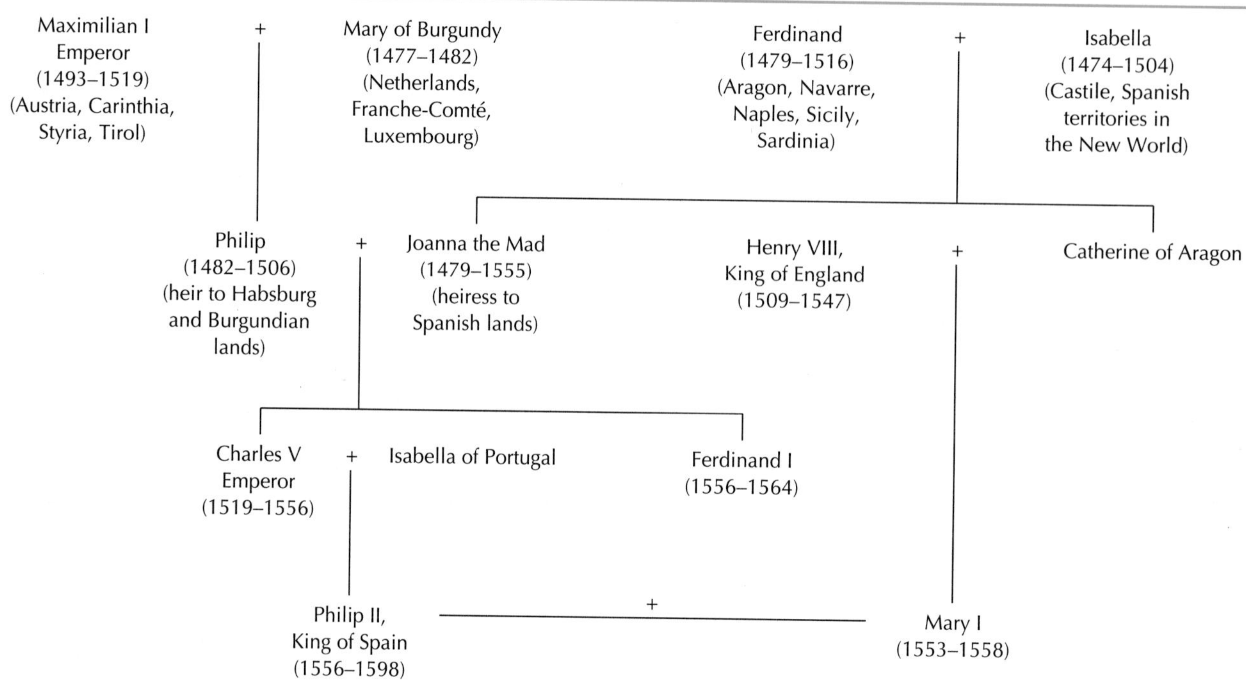

Spanish possessions in Italy brought Charles V into a bitter confrontation with the French king, Francis I, who was determined to press his own Italian claims. Although Charles was also concerned with the threat of advancing Turkish armies on the Danube, in 1525 he crushed the French at Pavia, near Milan, capturing Francis and forcing him to relinquish both his Italian claims and the duchy of Burgundy. Francis quickly reneged and allied with the Turks, who defeated the Hungarian army at Mohács in 1526. When the major Italian states (except Naples) allied with France in the League of Cognac, the imperial armies again invaded, this time sacking Rome in 1527 when their pay was late, an event widely regarded as the major atrocity of the sixteenth century. Louise of Savoy and Margaret of Austria negotiated a peace, the terms of which restored Burgundy to France. A year later, however, Pope Clement VII recognized Habsburg domination in Italy by crowning Charles both emperor and king of Italy, the last time the two crowns were bestowed on the same person. Although Francis renewed the war against Charles twice more (1536–1538, 1542–1544), not even an alliance with the Turks and German Protestant princes was sufficient to achieve a decisive military victory. When the Habsburg-Valois wars finally ended in 1559, Milan and Naples remained under Habsburg control. The Habsburgs, however, had failed to establish a unified state in Germany.

Eastern Europe

Although the Hungarians had developed a reasonably strong state in the 1200s, dynastic struggles during the following century weakened it. There were further problems due to the frequent absences of King Sigismund (1387–1437) from the country, partly because of his campaigns against the Turks and partly because of his responsibilities as Holy Roman Emperor (1433–1437). Matthias Corvinus (1458–1490), son of the great military leader János Hunyadi, who had successfully repulsed the Turks, increased royal authority through administrative and judicial reforms, higher taxes, and the creation of a standing army. Abroad he used Hungary's new power to conquer Bohemia, Moravia, and Austria. Following his death a disputed succession enabled Maximilian to regain Austria and bring Hungary into the imperial orbit by dynastic marriages involving his grandchildren. The nobles later took advantage of weak rulers to disband the standing army. As in Germany, the real struggle in Hungary then occurred between the magnates

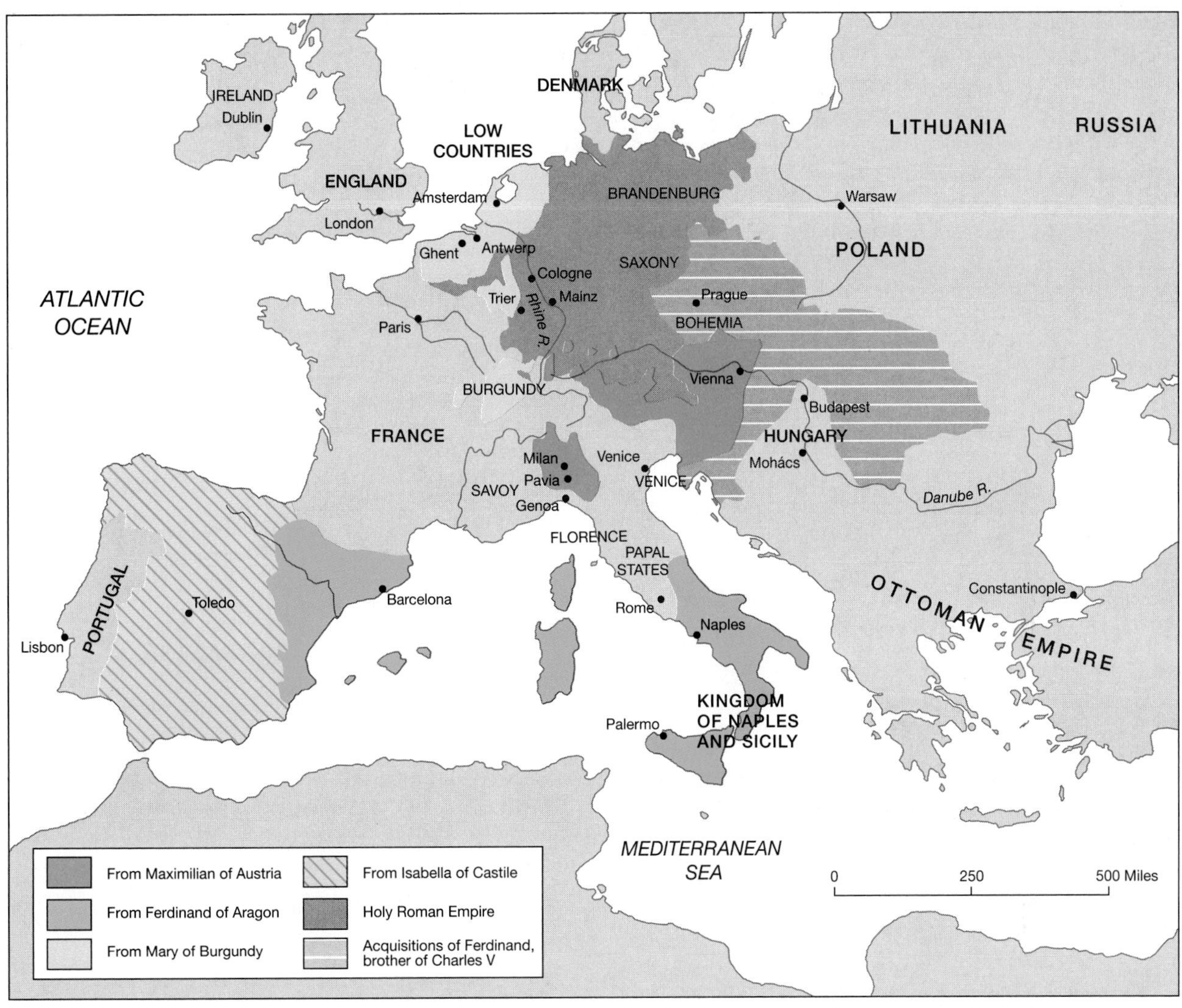

MAP 15.4 THE EMPIRE OF CHARLES I

and the lesser nobility. Although the latter won their claim to equality in the eyes of the law, in practice the magnates were dominant.

Poland was an immense state—the largest in Europe after its union with Lithuania in the late 1300s—but it too failed to establish a strong central government. The position of the nobles improved when King John Albert (1492–1501), in need of funds, allowed a national diet composed only of nobles to impose taxes on the towns and peasants. His successor accepted a statute requiring the diet's approval of all new legislation, further eroding royal authority. Although Sigismund II (1548–1572) allied with the lesser nobles to curtail the magnates' power, his death without an heir enabled the nobles to assert their right to elect a successor. Henceforth Poland was, in fact as well as in theory, an elective monarchy in which real power rested in the hands of the nobility.

SUMMARY

Politically, the fifteenth and early sixteenth centuries were a major watershed in European history. The failure of the Italians, Germans, Hungarians, and Poles to establish strong centralized states left them vulnerable to their neighbors and a perpetual source of temptation to expansionist-minded states. In contrast, the newly unified states of western Europe found themselves in an excellent position to take advantage of the economic possibilities opened up by the great voyages of discovery. It took the combined economic and military resources of these states to prosper in the expanding global trade. As the Black Death waned, Europe's population began growing again, prompting the expansion of commerce and manufacturing. Although the Italian states failed to unify, their impressive economic growth, historical tradition, and sense of civic independence enabled them to provide intellectual and cultural leadership for Europe in the Renaissance.

NOTES

1. R. S. Gottfried, *The Black Death: Natural and Human Disaster in Medieval Europe* (New York: Free Press, 1983), p. 36.
2. M. W. Dols, *The Black Death in the Middle East* (Princeton, N.J.: Princeton University Press, 1977), p. 113.

SUGGESTIONS FOR FURTHER READING

Bérenger, J. *The History of the Habsburg Empire, 1273–1700,* trans. C. A. Simpson. New York: Longman, 1994.

Bonfil, R. *Jewish Life in Renaissance Italy,* trans. A. Oldcorn. Berkeley: University of California Press, 1994.

Burns, J. H. *Lordship, Kingship, and Empire: The Idea of Monarchy, 1400–1525.* New York: Oxford University Press, 1992.

Contamine, P. *War in the Middle Ages,* trans. M. Jones. New York: Blackwell, 1984.

Crummey, R. O. *The Formation of Muscovy, 1304–1613.* New York: Longman, 1987.

Curry, A. *The Hundred Years' War.* New York: St. Martin's, 1993.

Goodman, A. *A History of England from Edward II to James I.* New York: Longman, 1977.

Gottfried, R. S. *The Black Death: Natural and Human Disaster in Medieval Europe.* New York: Free Press, 1983.

Guenee, B. *States and Rulers in Later Medieval Europe,* trans. J. Vale. Oxford: Blackwell, 1985.

Hay, D. *Europe in the Fourteenth and Fifteenth Centuries,* 2nd ed. New York: Longman, 1989.

Hook, J. *Lorenzo de' Medici.* London: Hamilton, 1984.

Kamen, H. *Spain, 1469–1714.* New York: Longman, 1991.

Kenny, A. J. P. *Wyclif.* New York: Oxford University Press, 1985.

Lane, F. C. *Venice: A Maritime Republic.* Baltimore: Johns Hopkins University Press, 1973.

Lambert, M. *Medieval Heresy: Popular Movements from the Gregorian Reform to the Reformation,* 2nd ed. Oxford: Blackwell, 1992.

Larner, J. *Italy in the Age of Dante and Petrarch, 1216–1380.* New York: Longman, 1980.

Leff, G. *The Dissolution of the Medieval Outlook.* New York: New York University Press, 1976.

Liss, P. K. *Isabel the Queen.* New York: Oxford University Press, 1992.

Nicol, D. M. *The Last Centuries of Byzantium, 1261–1453,* 2nd ed. Cambridge: Cambridge University Press, 1993.

Renouard, Y. *The Avignon Papacy, 1305–1403,* trans D. Bethell. London: Faber & Faber, 1970.

Sumption, J. *The Hundred Years' War.* Philadelphia: University of Pennsylvania Press, 1992.

Swanson, R. N. *Church and Society in Late Medieval Europe.* Oxford: Blackwell, 1989.

Vale, M. *The Angevin Legacy and the Hundred Years' War, 1250–1340.* Oxford: Blackwell, 1990.

Waley, D. *The Italian City-Republics,* 3rd ed. New York: Longman, 1988.

———. *Later Medieval Europe from Saint Louis to Luther,* 2nd ed. New York: Longman, 1985.

Wood, C. T. *Joan of Arc and Richard III: Sex, Saints, and Government in the Middle Ages.* New York: Oxford University Press, 1988.

Credits

*Positions of the photographs are indicated in abbreviated form as follows: top **T**, bottom **B**, center **C**, left **L**, right **R**. Unless otherwise acknowledged, all photographs are the property of Scott, Foresman and Company.*

Visual Experience

Color Insert 1 (following page 64): 1T Eisei-Bunko Foundation; **1B** SuperStock; **2T** Chinese Overseas Archaeological Exhibition Corporation; **2B** Courtesy of the Trustees of the British Museum; **3** Wim Swaan; **4T** SEF/Art Resource, New York; **4B** C. M. Dixon

Color Insert 2 (following page 224): 1T Scala/Art Resource, New York; **1B** Scala/Art Resource, NewYork; **2T** Scala/Art Resource, New York; **2B** Erich Lessing from Art Resource, New York; **3T** Edinburgh University Library; **3B** Edinburgh University Library; **4T** Francis Bartlett Donation of 1912 and Picture Fund. Courtesy, Museum of Fine Arts, Boston; **4B** Arxiu MAS, Barcelona

Color Insert 3 (following page 256): 1T The British Library; **1BR** Lee Boltin; **1BL** Kimbell Art Museum, Fort Worth, TX; **2T** Photograph by Hillel Burger. Peabody Museum, Harvard University; **2B** Library of Congress; **3T** Field Museum of Natural History, Chicago; **3B** Tony Linck; **4L** Photograph by Frank Khoury. Gift of Milton F. and Frieda Rosenthal, National Museum of African Art, Eliot Elisofon Photographic Archives, Smithsonian Institution; **4R** Phoebe Hearst Museum of Anthropology, University of California, Berkeley

Color Insert 4 (following page 416): 1T Art Resource, New York; **1B** Scala/Art Resource, New York; **2T** Scala/Art Resource, New York; **2B** Scala/Art Resource, New York; **3T** Scala/Art Resource, New York; **3B** National Museum, Poznan, Poland; **4R** Erich Lessing from Art Resource, New York

Color Insert 5 (following page 768): 1T The British Library; **1B** Spinks & Sons Ltd., London; **2T** John L. Severance Fund, 79.27b, the Cleveland Museum of Art; **2B** National Palace Museum, Taipei, Taiwan, Republic of China; **3T** The Metropolitan Museum of Art, Fletcher Fund, 1947 (47.18.116); **3B** Fujita Art Museum, Osaka; **4T** Fenollosa-Weld Collection. Courtesy, Museum of Fine Arts, Boston; **4B** Nezu Institute of Fine Arts, Tokyo

Color Insert 6 (following page 832): 1T Giraudon/Art Resource, New York; **1B** Erich Lessing from Art Resource, New York; **2T** Hamburg Kunsthalle; **2BL** Musée Carnavalet, Paris/Collection Viollet; **2BR** Erich Lessing from Art Resource, New York; **3** Bridgeman Art Library/Art Resource, New York; **4T** Cliché des Musées Nationaux, Paris; **4B** By permission of Birmingham Museums and Art Gallery

Color Insert 7 (following page 896): 1T Musée Royale de l'Afrique Centrale, Tervuren/Werner Forman Archive; **1B** Courtesy of the Freer Gallery of Art, Smithsonian Institution, Washington, DC; **1C** Asian Art Museum of San Francisco, the Avery Brundage Collection, Gift of Mr. Richard Gump (# B81 D6a,b,c); **2TL** Rijksmuseum, Amsterdam; **2BL** Van Gogh Museum, Amsterdam/Collection Vincent van Gogh Foundation; **2TR** Rijksmuseum, Amsterdam; **2BR** Van Gogh Museum, Amsterdam/Collection Vincent van Gogh Foundation; **3T** The Granger Collection, New York; **3BR** Courtesy of the Freer Gallery of Art, Smithsonian Institution, Washington, DC; **3BL** Gift of Mrs. Walter F. Dillingham in Memory of Alice Perry Grew, 1960, Honolulu Academy of Arts (2732.1); **4** The Metropolitan Museum of Art, Bequest of Sam A. Lewisohn, 1951 (51.112.2)

Color Insert 8 (following page 1152): 1T Erich Lessing from Art Resource, New York; **1B** Vincent van Gogh. *The Starry Night.* (1889.) Oil on canvas, 29 × 36¼″ (73.7 × 92.1 cm), The Museum of Modern Art, New York. Acquired through the Lillie P. Bliss Bequest. Photograph © 1995 The Museum of Modern Art, New York; **2T** Giraudon/Art Resource, New York; **2B** Pablo Picasso. *Les Demoiselles d'Avignon.* Paris (June–July 1907). Oil on canvas, 8′ × 7′ × 8″ (243.9 × 233.7 cm), The Museum of Modern Art, New York. Acquired through the Lillie P. Bliss Bequest. Photograph © 1995 The Museum of Modern Art, New York; **3T** George Roos/Art Resource, New York; **3B** Scala/Art Resource, New York; **4T** The Granger Collection, New York; **4B** Salvador Dali. *The Persistence of Memory (Persistance de la Mémoire).* 1931. Oil on canvas, 9½ × 13″ (24.1 × 33 cm). The Museum of Modern Art, New York. Given anonymously. Photograph © 1995 The Museum of Modern Art, New York

Title Pages

Single Volume Edition SuperStock; **Volumes I and A** Brown Brothers; **Volumes II and B** Sonia Halliday Photographs; **Volume C** Robert Frerck/Odyssey Productions

Prologue

1 Peter Kain, © Richard Leakey. From *The Making of Mankind* by Richard E. Leakey, E. P. Dutton, New York, 1981; **6L** From *The Story of Art,* 11th edition, by E. H. Gombrich, Phaidon Press Ltd., London, 1966; **6R** Neg. No. 329853. Courtesy Department of Library Services, American Museum of Natural History; **7L** Conservé au Museé d'Aquitaine, Bordeaux, France, tous droit réservés; **7R** Itar-Tass/Sovfoto; **10** Jane Taylor/Sonia Halliday Photographs; **11** Arxiu MAS, Barcelona; **12** From *The Gods and Goddesses of Old Europe* by Marija Gimbutas, University of California Press, 1974

Chapter 1

17 Harvard Museum of Fine Arts, Boston Expedition. Courtesy, Museum of Fine Arts, Boston; **19B** Hirmir Fotoarchiv, Munich; **19T** University of Pennsylvania Museum, Philadelphia; **23** Hirmir Fotoarchiv, Munich; **25** George Holton/Photo Researchers; **26** The Metropolitan Museum of Art, Rogers Fund, 1925 (25.3.182); **28** SuperStock; **31** Alinari/Art Resource, New York; **36** Drawing from *In the Shadow of the Temple* by Meir Ben-Dov, translation by Ina Friedman. Copyright © 1982 by Keter Publishing House Jerusalem Ltd.; English translation © 1985 by Keter Publishing House Jerusalem Ltd. Reprinted by permission of HarperCollins Publishers; **40** Courtesy of the Trustees of the British Museum; **42** Bildarchiv Preussischer Kulturbesitz; **44** Courtesy of The Oriental Institute of the University of Chicago

Chapter 2

46 Courtesy Indian Museum, Calcutta; **48** Borromeo/Art Resource, New York; **49** Archeological Museum, Mohenjo-Daro; **51L** Stella Snead/Archaeological Survey of India; **51R** National Museum of India, New Delhi/Art Resouce, New York; **55** Art Resource, New York; **60** Dinodia Picture Agency

Chapter 3

68 Ronald Sheridan/Ancient Art & Architecture Collection; **72** Courtesy of the Freer Gallery of Art, Smithsonian Institution, Washington, DC; **73** Courtesy of the Freer Gallery of Art, Smithsonian Institution, Washington, DC; **77** Neg. No. 219658/American Museum of Natural History; **83** Innervision/Overseas Archaeological Corporation; **84** The Granger Collection, New York; **86** Innervision/Sichaun Provincial Museum, China

Chapter 4

89 Ronald Sheridan/Ancient Art & Architecture Collection; **91** Hirmir Fotoarchiv, Munich; **92** Hirmir Fotoarchiv, Munich; **95** Scala/Art Resource, New York; **96L** Hirmir Fotoarchiv, Munich; **96R** Caroline Buckler; **98** *World Book* illustration by Richard Hook, Linden Artists Ltd., from *The World Encyclopedia.* Copyright ©1996, World Book, Inc. By permission of the publisher; **103** Alinari/Art Resource, New York; **104** American School of Classical Studies at Athens; Agora excavations; **106** Alinari/Art Resource, New York; **111** Deutsches Museen, Munich

Chapter 5

113 Marburg/Art Resource, New York; **114L** UPI/Corbis-Bettmann; **114R** Alinari/Art Resource, New York; **115** Ronald Sheridan/Ancient Art & Architecture; **116T** Hirmer Fotoarchiv, Munich; **116B** Ronald Sheridan/Ancient Art & Architecture; **117** Wim Swaan; **129L** Bildarchiv Preussischer Kulturbesitz; **129R** Victoria and Albert Museum, Scala/Art Resource, New York; **135** Bildarchiv Preussischer Kulturbesitz

Chapter 6

139 Giraudon/Art Resource, New York; **141** Alinari/Art Resource, New York; **145** Rheinischeslandesmuseen, Bonn/e.t. archive; **149** Bildarchiv Preussischer Kulturbesitz; **151** Steve Vidler/Leo de Wys Inc.; **154** Marburg/Art Resource, New York; **156** Alinari/Art Resource, New York; **164** Werner Forman Archive

Chapter 7

168 Cameramann International, Inc.; **172** Dinodia/N. G. Sharma from Dinodia Picture Agency; **174** Brown Brothers; **175** Neg. 35933/Field Museum of Natural History, Chicago; **181** Courtesy of the Union of American Hebrew Congregations; **184** Alinari/Art Resource, New York; **188** Alinari/Art Resource, New York; **191** Fitzwilliam Museum, Cambridge

Chapter 8

197 Museo Cristiano, Brescia; **198** Scala/Art Resource, New York; **200** Ronald Sheridan/Ancient Art & Architecture Collection; **206** G. E. Kidder Smith, New York; **207** Giraudon/Art Resource, New York; **209** Giraudon/Art Resource, New York; **210** Courtesy of the Freer Gallery of Art, Smithsonian Institution, Washington, DC; **212** Ronald Sheridan/Ancient Art & Architecture Collection; **218R** The Granger Collection, New York; **218L** The Metropolitan Museum of Art, Rogers Fund, 1913 (13.152.6); **222** University of Pennsylvania Museum, Philadelphia; **223** Fred J. Maroon/Photo Researchers; **225** Palestine Exploration Fund; **226** Ronald Sheridan/Ancient Art & Architecture Collection

Chapter 9

227 © 1995, The Detroit Institute of Arts. Founders Society Purchase, Eleanor Clay Ford Fund for African Art; **231** Courtesy Federal Department of Antiquities, Nigeria; **233** Sudan Museum, Khartoum/Werner Forman Archive; **234** Werner Forman Archive; **236** Victor Englebert/Photo Researchers; **241** Photograph by Franko Khoury, National Museum of African Art, Eliot Elisofon Photographic Archives, Smithsonian Institution; **243T** C./J. Lenars/Explorer/Photo Researchers; **243B** The British Library; **244L** Ife Museum, Nigeria; **244R** Photograph of Franko Khoury, National Museum of African Art, Eliot Elisofon Photographic Archives, Smithsonian Institution; **245** Photograph by Michael Cavanagh, Kevin Moniague, Indiana University Art Museum, Bloomington; **247** Jason Laure/Woodfin Camp & Associates

Chapter 10

249 North America, New Mexico, Cliff Valley Area, Mimbres Culture, Large Standing Figure, wood, stone, cotton, feathers, fiber, black, blue, yellow, red and white earth pigments, carbon black from vegetable source, c. 1150–1400, 63.5 × 17.1 cm, Major Acquisitions Centennial Fund, 1979.17.1 overall: front. Photograph © 1995, the Art Institute of Chicago. All Rights Reserved; **251L** Central America, Mexico, Teotihuacán Culture, Mask from incense burner depicting the old deity of fire, ceramic, 450–750 A.D., 36.8 × 33.5 cm, Gift of Joseph Antonow, 1962.1073 overall: front. Photograph by Robert Hashimoto. Photograph © 1995, the Art Institute of Chicago. All Rights Reserved; **251R** The Metropolitan Museum of Art, the Michael C. Rockefeller Memorial Collection, Bequest of Nelson A. Rockefeller, 1979; **252** Steve Vidler/Leo de Wys Inc.; **254** Doug Bryant/D. Donne Bryant Stock; **256T** The Metropolitan Museum of Art, the Michael C. Rockefeller Memorial Collection, Bequest of Nelson A. Rockefeller, 1979 (1979.206.1063); **256B** Photograph by Hillel Burger. Peabody Museum, Harvard University; **257** Werner Forman Archive/Art Resource, New York; **258** Werner Forman Archive/Art Resource, New York; **259L** Musée de l'Homme, Paris; **259R** Bodleian Library, University of Oxford; **260** Scala/Art Resource, New York; **263** The Metropolitan Museum of Art, Harris Brisbane Dick Fund and Fletcher Fund, 1967 (67.239.1); **265** George Holton/Photo Researchers; **267** Ohio Historical Society; **269** Werner Forman Archive/Art Resource, New York; **270** From the Smithsonian Institution Exhibition *Crossroads of Continents: Cultures of Siberia and Alaska.* From the collections of the Museum of Anthropology and Ethnography in St. Petersburg, FL

Chapter 11

273 Dinodia Picture Agency; **274** Roland Michaud/Woodfin Camp & Associates; **283** Dinodia Picture Agency; **284L** Jehangir Gazdar/Woodfin Camp & Associates; **284R** *Nataraja: Siva as King of Dance.* Bronze, h. 111.5 cm. South India, Chola Period, 11th c. © 1995, the Cleveland Museum of Art. Purchase from the J. H. Wade Fund, 30.331; **289** Wim Swaan; **291** Brian Brake/Photo Researchers

Chapter 12

295 The Granger Collection, New York; **300** Tokyo National Museum; **307** Courtesy of the Freer Gallery of Art, Smithsonian Institution, Washington, DC; **310L** Werner Forman Archive; **310R** Werner Forman Archive; **311** National Museum of Korea, Seoul; **314** Tony Stone Worldwide

Chapter 13

320 Mansell Collection; **331** Giraudon/Art Resource, New York; **332** The Walters Art Gallery, Baltimore; **337** Scala/Art Resouce, New York; **341** Bibliothèque Nationale, Paris; **344** Arxiu MAS, Barcelona

Chapter 14

348 Otto Müller Verlag; **350** Peter Paul Rubens, Flemish, 1577–1640. *Saint Francis,* oil on panel, c. 1615, 99.0 × 78.8 cm. George F. Harding Collection, 1983.372, the Art Institute of Chicago; **359** Scala/Art Resource, New York; **361** Marburg/Art Resource, New York; **362** Marburg/Art Resource, New York; **363** Marburg/Art Resource, New York; **364L** Marburg/Art Resource, New York; **364R** Bildarchiv Preussischer Kulturbesitz; **366** Marburg/Art Resource, New York; **372** Musée de l'Homme, Paris; **373** Deutsches Archäologisches

Institut/Kerameikos Museen, Athens; **374L** C. M. Dixon; **374R** Museen für Ostasiatische Kunst, Köln. Inv. – No. A.11.22. Photo: Rheinisches Bildarchiv, Köln; **376** Samuel H. Kress Collection, © Board of Trustees, National Gallery of Art, Washington, DC

Chapter 15

377 Bibliothèque Nationale, Paris; **380** Lauros-Giraudon/Art Resource, New York; **381** The British Library; **383** Giraudon/Art Resource, New York; **387** Giraudon/Art Resource, New York; **392** Arxiu MAS, Barcelona; **394** Ronald Sheridan/Ancient Art & Architecture Collection; **396** Alinari/Art Resource, New York; **398** Gift of Mrs. Barbara Hutton. © Board of Trustees, National Gallery of Art, Washington, DC

Chapter 16

403 Andrew W. Mellon Collection. © Board of Trustees, National Gallery of Art, Washington, DC; **412** Bayerische Staatbibliothek, Munich; **416** Corbis-Bettmann Archive; **417** Eric Lessing from Art Resource, New York; **420L** Marburg/Art Resource, New York; **420R** Alinari/Art Resource, New York; **422** Wim Swaan; **423T** Reproduced by courtesy of the Trustees, The National Gallery, London; **423B** © 1995, The Detroit Institute of Arts. City of Detroit Purchase; **427** Moravian Museum, Brno; **428L** Sopritendenza all'Antichita, Palermo; **428R** Eastfoto/Sovfoto; **429** Victoria and Albert Museum, London; **430** Alinari/Art Resource, New York; **431L** Marburg/Art Resource, New York; **431R** The Nelson-Atkins Museum of Art, Kansas City, MO (Gift of the Friends of Art) F75–13; **432TL** Museum of Antiquities, Ife, Nigeria; **432B** Doug Bryant/DDB Stock Photo; **432TR** D. Donne Bryant/Art Resource, New York

Chapter 17

437 Société de l'Histoire du Protestantisme Français, Paris; **438** Giraudon/Art Resource, New York; **440** The Metropolitan Museum of Art, Robert Lehman Collection, 1975 (1975.1.1138); **444** Zentralbibliothek, Zurich; **446** Staatliche Münzsammlung, Munich; **449** The British Library; **453** Reproduced by courtesy of the Trustees, National Portrait Gallery, London; **456** Verlag Herder, Freiburg; **458** Courtesy of the Trustees of the British Museum; **461** The Metropolitan Museum of Art, Harris Brisbane Dick Fund (43.106.2)

Chapter 18

464 British Museum, London/Werner Forman Archive; **467** National Maritime Museum Picture Library, London; **469** Grazia Neri Agency; **472** The Granger Collection, New York; **477** New York Public Library; **482** The Hispanic Society of America; **486** Ailsa Mellon Bruce Fund. © Board of Trustees, National Gallery of Art, Washington, DC; **488** Belgian Tourist Office, New York; **490** Courtesy of the Trustees of the British Museum; **491** Paolo Koch/Photo Researchers; **493L** Library of Congress; **493R** George Holton/Photo Researchers

Chapter 19

495 Duke of Portland, Welbeck Abbey; **496** Courtesy of the Trustees, National Portrait Gallery, London; **498** Giraudon/Art Resource, New York; **500** National Maritime Museum Picture Library, London; **505** Print Collection, Miriam and Ira D. Wallach. Division of Art, Prints and Photographs, the New York Public Library, Astor, Lenox and Tilden Foundations; **509** Rijksmuseum, Amsterdam; **511** Art Resource, New York; **515** Andrew W. Mellon Collection. © Board of Trustees, National Gallery of Art, Washington, DC; **517** National Museum, Copenhagen

Chapter 20

520 Courtesy of the Trustees of the British Museum; **521** Topkapi Palace Museum, Istanbul; **526** The British Library; **532** Pramod Mistry/Dinodia Picture Agency; **535** Four by Five/SuperStock; **543** National Palace Museum, Taipei, Taiwan, Republic of China

Chapter 21

545 Courtesy of the Trustees of the British Museum; **551** Angela Silvertop/Hutchison Library; **555** Photograph by Hillel Burger. Peabody Museum, Harvard University; **561** Jean-Claude Carton/Bruce Coleman Inc.

Chapter 22

569 National Palace Museum, Taipei, Taiwan, Republic of China; **571** The Metropolitan Museum of Art, Bequest of John M. Crawford, Jr., 1988 (1989.363.64); **579** National Palace Museum, Taipei, Republic of China; **585L** Paolo Koch/Photo Researchers; **585R** Marc F. Bernheim/Woodfin Camp & Associates; **589** *Beggars and Street Characters* (detail). Handscroll, ink and color on paper, 1516, overall 31.9 × 224.5 cm. Zhou Chen, Chinese, c. 1450–after 1536, Ming dynasty. © 1995, the Cleveland Museum of Art, John L. Severance Fund, 64.94

Chapter 23

592 The Metropolitan Museum of Art, Bequest of William K. Vanderbilt, 1920. (20.155.1); **595** Samuel H. Kress Collection. © Board of Trustees, National Gallery of Art, Washington, DC; **598** Reproduced by courtesy of the Trustees, The National Gallery, London; **602** Gift of Mr. and Mrs. Robert Woods Bliss. © Board of Trustees, National Gallery of Art, Washington, DC; **603** The Nelson-Atkins Museum of Art, Kansas City, MO (Purchase: Nelson Trust), 33–89/1; **605** Courtesy of the Trustees of the British Museum; **608** Courtesy of the National Gallery of Ireland; **611** Kupferstichkabinett, Staatliche Museen zu Berlin, Preussischer Kulturbesitz; **614** John Thomas/Harvard-Yenching Library, Harvard University

Chapter 24

616 Louvre, Réunion des Musées Nationaux; **619** Lauron-Giraudon/Art Resource, New York; **621** Corbis-Bettmann Archive; **622** Scala/Art Resource, New York; **623** Austrian National Library, Vienna, Picture Archives; **631** The Royal Collection. © Her Majesty Queen Elizabeth II; **636** Giraudon/Art Resource, New York

Chapter 25

638 Corbis-Bettmann Archive; **640** Alinari/Art Resource, New York; **641** Department of Special Collections, Stanford University Libraries; **643** Brown Brothers; **646** H. Josse/Art Resource, New York; **649** The Granger Collection, New York; **652** Collection: The Hague Historical Museum; **656** The Granger Collection, New York; **657** Wim Swaan

Chapter 26

661 The Granger Collection, New York; **663** Collection Viollet; **665** Corbis-Bettmann Archive; **669** Herdman Collection, Liverpool Public Library; **675** Yale University Art Gallery, John Trumbell Collection; **680** Mansell Collection; **681** The Granger Collection, New York

Chapter 27

685 Gift of Mrs. Mellon Bruce in memory of her father, Andrew W. Mellon. © Board of Trustees, National Gallery of Art, Washington, DC; **688** Bulloz/Musée Carnavalet; **690** Corbis-Bettmann Archive; **693L** Mansell Collection; **693R** Culver Pictures; **694** The Granger Collection, New York; **699** Historisches Museen der Stadt Wien; **700** Reproduced by courtesy of the Trustees, The National Gallery, London; **702** Culver Pictures; **704** Culver Pictures; **705** Reproduced by courtesy of the Trustees, The National Gallery, London

Chapter 28

710 Bibliothéque Nationale, Paris; **713** Bulloz; **716** Stock Montage; **720** Bulloz; **721** Bulloz; **722** Mansell Collection; **724** Bulloz; **729**

Chapter 28 continued
Samuel H. Kress Collection. © Board of Trustees, National Gallery of Art, Washington, DC; **734** The Metropolitan Museum of Art, Purchase, Rogers Fund and Jacob H. Schiff Bequest, 1922 (22.60.25–5); **737** Private Collection/Werner Forman Archive; **738** The Granger Collection, New York; **739** Courtesy of the Trustees of the British Museum; **740** Art Resource, New York; **741** Imperial War Museum, London

Chapter 29

743 Victoria and Albert Museum/e.t. archive; **752** Reproduced by courtesy of the Trustees, The National Gallery, London; **753** Victoria and Albert Museum, London; **759** The British Library; **760L** The British Library; **760R** The British Library; **762** The British Library

Chapter 30

765 Rhodes Murphey; **769** The Metropolitan Museum of Art, Rogers Fund, 1942 (42.141.2); **771** Marburg/Art Resource, New York; **777** Hulton Deutsch; **779** Wim Swaan; **781** Marburg/Art Resource, New York; **782** Anne Kirkup; **785** The Metropolitan Museum of Art, Henry L. Phillips Collection. Bequest of Henry L. Phillips, 1939 (JP 2972)

Chapter 31

788 The Granger Collection, New York; **791** The Science Museum/Science & Society Picture Library, London; **795** The Science Museum/Science & Society Picture Library, London; **797** Mansell Collection; **802** The Granger Collection, New York; **806** Mansell Collection; **808** Local Studies Unit, Manchester Center Library; **812** Hulton Deutsch

Chapter 32

814 Bulloz/Musée Carnavalet; **817** Bulloz; **820** Courtesy of The National Portait Gallery, London; **824** Bildarchiv Preussischer Kulturbesitz; **826** Mansell Collection; **827** Mansell Collection; **832** Camera Press/Globe Photos

Chapter 33

839 Culver Pictures; **842** Mansell Collection; **843** Culver Pictures; **846** Mansell Collection; **849** Mansell Collection; **857** Corbis-Bettmann Archive; **860** The Granger Collection, New York; **862** The Bancroft Library, University of California, Berkeley

Chapter 34

865 Museum of London; **867** Brown Brothers; **869T** Culver Pictures; **869B** Snark/Art Resource, New York; **874** Victoria and Albert Museum, London; **876T** Bulloz/Musée Carnavalet; **876B** Hulton Deutsch; **881** Culver Pictures; **887** UPI/Corbis-Bettmann; **891** The Granger Collection, New York; **893L** The Granger Collection, New York; **893R** Culver Pictures; **894** Culver Pictures; **895** Honeywell Ltd., Computer Operations, Northern Europe

Chapter 35

897 Courtesy of the Director, National Army Museum, London; **900** Brown Brothers; **905** Hulton Deutsch; **911** The British Library; **912** Rhodes Murphey; **913** Hulton Deutsch; **919** Courtesy of the Freer Gallery of Art, Smithsonian Institution, Washington, DC; **925** Courtesy, Peabody Essex Museum, Salem, MA

Chapter 36

929 Corbis-Bettmann Archive; **930** Corbis-Bettmann Archive; **933** Giraudon/Art Resource; **939** UPI/Corbis-Bettmann; **943** Corbis-Bettmann Archive; **944** Corbis-Bettmann Archive; **946** Brown Brothers; **951** The Granger Collection, New York; **953** Gropius, *Bauhaus.* Dessau, Germany, 1925–1926. Workshop Wing. Photograph courtesy The Museum of Modern Art, New York; **956** Bodleian Library, University of Oxford; **957** Ronald Sheridan/Ancient Art & Architecture Collection; **958L** Dumbarton Oaks, Washington, DC; **958R** The Metropolitan Museum of Art, Bequest of Mrs. H. O. Havemeyer, 1929. The H. O. Havemeyer Collection (29.100.16); **959T** William Sturgis Bigelow Collection, by exchange. Courtesy, Museum of Fine Arts, Boston; **959B** The Pierpont Morgan Library/Art Resource, New York; **960** The Louise and Walter Arenberg Collection, Philadelphia Museum of Art; **961** Bevan Davies/David McKee Inc.

Chapter 37

962 *L'Illustration*/Sygma; **964** Corbis-Bettmann Archive; **967** UPI/Corbis-Bettmann; **971** RIA-Novosti/Sovfoto; **979** Eastfoto/Sovfoto; **980** Noboru Komine/Photo Researchers; **981** *L'Illustration*/Sygma; **987** Culver Pictures

Chapter 38

990 Alfred Eisenstaedt/*Life* magazine, © Time Inc.; **991** Brown Brothers; **997** Ghitta Carell; **1001** The Granger Collection, New York; **1003** Formerly Collection Garvens, Hanover, Germany. From *History of Art,* 2nd edition, by H. W. Janson, Harry N. Abrams, Inc., Publishers, New York; **1005** Government Photo Archives, Berlin; **1006** UPI/Corbis-Bettmann; **1007** Ullstein Bilderdienst; **1011** AP/Wide World; **1012** Sovfoto; **1014** UPI/Corbis-Bettmann; **1017** UPI/Corbis-Bettmann

Chapter 39

1020 Stock Montage; **1022** Archive Photos; **1023T** Culver Pictures; **1023B** Corbis-Bettmann Archive; **1024** Arxiu MAS, Barcelona; **1029** Corbis-Bettmann Archive; **1032** Collection Viollet; **1033** AP/Wide World; **1035** UPI/Corbis-Bettmann; **1036** UPI/Corbis-Bettmann; **1041** Sergio Larrain/Magnum; **1043** Gamma-Liaison; **1044** Derek Hudson/Sygma; **1045** Imperial War Museum, London; **1049** Eve Arnold/Magnum; **1051** Bob Adelman/Magnum; **1052** Alex Webb/Magnum

Chapter 40

1055 Ira Kuschenbaum/Stock; **1058** UPI/Corbis-Bettmann; **1059** China Reconstructs; **1060** David Ball/Tony Stone Images; **1065** Eastfoto/Sovfoto; **1066** Rhodes Murphey; **1075** Henri Cartier-Bresson/Magnum; **1076** Phillip J. Griffiths/Magnum

Chapter 41

1081 UPI/Corbis-Bettmann; **1083L** UPI/Corbis-Bettmann; **1083** UPI/Corbis-Bettmann; **1089L** Corbis-Bettmann Archive; **1089R** UPI/Corbis-Bettmann; **1090** Dinodia Picture Agency; **1091** Marc and Evenlyne Bernhein/Woodfin Camp & Associates; **1097** UPI/Corbis-Bettmann; **1100** Keystone Paris/Sygma; **1105** Alain Dejean/Sygma

Chapter 42

1110 Carlos Carrion/Sygma; **1115** Jasun Laure/Woodfin Camp & Associates; **1117** David Brauchli/AP/Wide World; **1118** AP/Wide World; **1124** Bruno Barbey/Magnum; **1127** Corbis-Bettmann Archive; **1130** AP/Wide World; **1132** Sovfoto; **1134** AP/Wide World; **1142** The Granger Collection, New York; **1144** Yerkes Observatory Photograph; **1145** The Observatories of the Carnegie Institution of Washington, DC

Chapter 43

1147 National Aeronautics Space Administration; **1149** AP/Wide World; **1156T** Reuters/Corbis-Bettmann; **1156B** Reuters/Corbis-Bettmann; **1161T** AP/Wide World; **1161B** De Keerle/Grochowiak/Sygma; **1162** AP/Wide World; **1166** Cold Spring Harbor Laboratory Archives; **1169** AP/Wide World

Index